The Currency of Fame

PORTRAIT MEDALS OF THE RENAISSANCE

46 obv.

The Currency of Fame:

PORTRAIT MEDALS OF THE RENAISSANCE

CURATOR/EDITOR

STEPHEN K. SCHER

PHOTOGRAPHY

JOHN BIGELOW TAYLOR

HARRY N. ABRAMS, INC., PUBLISHERS, IN ASSOCIATION WITH

THE FRICK COLLECTION

Project Director: Adele Westbrook
Editor: Russell Stockman
Designer: Dirk Luykx

The contributions by Gay van der Meer have been adapted from articles previously published in the exhibition catalogue *Kunst voor de beeldenstorm. Noordnederlandse kunst 1525–1580*, Amsterdam, 1986; that of Anne Poulet from the article by Stephen K. Scher, Michele D. Marincola, and Anne Poulet, "Gothic, Renaissance, and Baroque Medals from the Museum of Fine Arts, Boston," in *The Medal* 9 (special issue 1986), pp. 79–105.

Additional Photography Credits:
Berlin, Staatliche Museen, Münzkabinett: 99a obv., 99a rev.; Bibliothèque Nationale, Paris, Service Photographique; 30 obv., 30 rev., 56a obv., 56a rev., 67 obv., 139 obv., 144 obv., 144 rev., 150 obv., 151 obv., 154 obv., 154 rev., 163 obv., 163 rev.; The British Museum, London: 76 obv., 167 obv.; J.P. Getty Museum, Malibu: 136 obv., 136 rev.; The Museum of Fine Arts, Boston: 27 obv., 27 rev., 59 obv., 59 rev., 80 obv., 149 obv.; Stephen K. Scher: 10 obv., 10 rev., 13 obv., 13 rev., 35 obv., 35 rev., 100 obv., 100 rev., 114 obv., 114 rev., 137 obv., 137 rev., 141 obv., 141 rev., 142 obv., 142 rev.

Library of Congress Cataloging-in-Publication Data
The Currency of fame : portrait medals of the Renaissance /
    curator/editor, Stephen K. Scher ; photography, John Bigelow Taylor.
        p.   cm.
    Catalog of an exhibition jointly sponsored by the Frick Collection
and the National Gallery of Art, and held in New York and
Washington, D.C.
    Includes bibliographical references and index.
    ISBN 0–8109–3191–5 (Abrams hard).—ISBN 0–8109–2572–9 (museum pbk.)
    1. Medals, Renaissance—Exhibitions.   2. Portraits, Renaissance—
Exhibitions.   I. Scher, Stephen K.   II. Frick Collection.
III. National Gallery of Art (U.S.)
CJ6094.C87   1994
737′.22′094074753—dc20   93–26690

Front cover: (Cat. no. 164 obv.). Nicholas Hilliard. *Elizabeth I* (born 1533, queen of England and Ireland 1558–1603). Gold, cast. London, The British Museum.

Back cover: CLOCKWISE FROM THE TOP: (Cat. no. 6 obv.). Pisanello. *Domenico Malatesta,* called Malatesta Novello (born 1418, lord of Cesena 1429–65). Bronze, cast. Washington, The National Gallery of Art, Samuel H. Kress Collection; (Cat. no. 7a rev.). Pisanello. *Cecilia Gonzaga* 1426–1451). Bronze, cast. New York, Michael Hall Collection; (Cat. no. 54 obv.). Jacopo da Trezzo. *Mary Tudor* (born 1516, queen of England and Ireland 1553–58). Gold, cast and chased. London, The British Museum; (Cat. no. 158 obv.). Jacques Jonghelinck. *Margaret of Austria,* duchess of Parma (1522–1586). Silver, cast. Brussels, Bibliothèque Royale; (Cat. no. 144 obv.). Germain Pilon. *René de Birague* (1507–1583). Bronze, cast and gilt. Paris, Bibliothèque Nationale, Cabinet des Médailles, formerly the Chevalier de Stuers Collection; (Cat. no. 129 obv.). Valentin Maler. *Wenzel Jamnitzer* (1508–1585). Lead, cast, uniface. Munich, Staatliche Munzsammlung.
CENTER: (Cat. no. 94 obv.). Friedrich Hagenauer. *Lukas (Laux) Furtenagel* (1505–after 1556). Wood model. Munich, Bayerisches Nationalmuseum.

Published in 1994 by Harry N. Abrams, Incorporated, New York
A Times Mirror Company

Printed and bound in Japan

CONTENTS

Foreword:

DIRECTORS OF THE NATIONAL GALLERY, WASHINGTON

AND

THE FRICK COLLECTION, NEW YORK

6

ACKNOWLEDGMENTS

7

EXHIBITION COMMITTEE

9

CONTRIBUTORS

10

LENDERS

11

Introduction:

STEPHEN K. SCHER

13

Prototypes: The Medals of the Duke of Berry, c. 1400

31

Italy, Fifteenth Century

39

Italy, Sixteenth Century

147

Germany, Sixteenth Century

201

France, Sixteenth and Early Seventeenth Centuries

305

England and the Low Countries, Sixteenth and Early Seventeenth Centuries

345

Documentation

375

Bibliography

400

Index

413

Foreword

IT IS ALTOGETHER appropriate that The Frick Collection and The National Gallery of Art should be the organizing institutions for *The Currency of Fame: Portrait Medals of the Renaissance*. The Frick Collection houses what has been called the finest group of Renaissance small bronzes in the United States, and The National Gallery possesses one of the leading collections of Renaissance medals in the world. This study of the early portrait medal in Europe is the first international effort of its kind.

Discussed and illustrated within this volume are more than 170 highly exceptional medals covering a 200-year period from about 1400 to 1600. Special attention is called both to the splendid artistry they exhibit in themselves and to the development of the medallic art wherever it flourished in Europe—Italy, France, Germany, England, and the Low Countries.

The Renaissance medal must be counted among the richest and most complex of art objects, both in intellectual concept and in terms of design. In its finest manifestation it combines portrait, narrative relief, text, iconographic puzzle, and historical reference in a compact, durable, and portable object. It is at once beautiful, stimulating, and of inestimable value as a document. For these reasons, the medal assumes a special place as a branch of portraiture, since it tells us much about the subject and is so effective a means of historical evocation.

Over the long history of its development from the scattered prototypes of the late fourteenth century to the present day, the medal has often been treated as a stepchild of numismatics, and consequently slighted as significant sculptural expression. It is one of the primary objectives of the present study to show this fascinating object as an important work of art in its own right, a frequently neglected example of the most subtle and delicate form of relief sculpture.

The Currency of Fame owes its being to Stephen K. Scher, art historian, author, noted scholar on medals, and onetime chairman of the Art Department at Brown University. It was he who conceived it, organized it, and wrote the far-reaching and perceptive introduction to this volume. It was also Dr. Scher who assembled the international team of thirty-one experts who contributed the individual entries. *The Currency of Fame* serves as both an introduction to the subject of Renaissance medals and a scholarly examination of the specimens included, in many cases providing a fresh look at objects whose attribution and meaning have not been reappraised for decades. We have taken special efforts to illustrate the medals as important works of art in their own right. We hope that this book will set a standard for the reproduction of medals.

We have also endeavored when exhibiting the medals in Washington and New York to create new ways of lighting and displaying them so that, at last, these works may be seen to the best possible advantage. We are particularly grateful to the design staff of The National Gallery of Art for working so hard and so long to help solve the very difficult problems of showing medals properly.

Finally, we wish to thank the Samuel H. Kress Foundation and the James M. Vaughn, Jr. Foundation Fund for their generous help in supporting this volume.

Charles Ryskamp, Director
The Frick Collection,
New York

Earl A. Powell III, Director
The National Gallery of Art,
Washington

Acknowledgments

THERE CAN BE few situations more satisfying than being given the opportunity to work on a project involving material for which one has a deep appreciation, and to be able to share this enthusiasm with others. Such satisfaction was mine in organizing this exhibition of Renaissance portrait medals. Because the subject is generally little known, it has been my intention to gather together some of the finest specimens of the greatest medals by the most celebrated artists and to demonstrate that these deserve to be considered as important works of Renaissance sculpture, not merely as a somewhat neglected branch of numismatics.

Of necessity, I had to make a strictly limited selection of objects to represent the subject. In doing so I had to exclude many artists and medals that deserved to be seen and will be missed by experts. It was my intention that the medals exhibited would inspire the viewer to seek out those that are missing.

The idea for this exhibition first surfaced during a luncheon with Harry Fowler, at that time president of the American Numismatic Society and member of the board of The Frick Collection. While exchanging comments about our respective interests as collectors, I mentioned that mine was Renaissance portrait medals. Harry remarked that the Frick's director, Charles Ryskamp, had expressed a desire to mount an exhibition of medals. I rashly volunteered to organize such an exhibition, then thought no more about it.

Subsequently, once again over a luncheon with the Frick's chief curator and longtime and valued friend, Edgar Munhall, I mentioned my conversation with Harry Fowler. Edgar presented the idea to Mr. Ryskamp, whose enthusiasm and energetic support proved to be a major factor in organizing a complicated exhibition. I wish to offer my deepest thanks to him and to all of his staff, especially Robert Goldsmith and William Stout.

Once the project had been set in motion, we felt it important to involve other museums and turned first to The National Gallery in Washington, since their Kress Collection of medals is one of the richest in the world. The former director, Carter Brown, reacted favorably to the idea and put at our disposal the considerable resources of his museum. His successor, Earl A. Powell III, has shared that interest and assured the museum's continued support. It is impossible to offer enough praise and thanks to his staff for all of their invaluable help, but I am particularly indebted to Patricia Waters and Diane Martini of the Exhibitions Department, to Douglas Lewis, Alison Luchs, and Donald Myers of the Sculpture Department, to Gill Ravenal, Mark Leithauser, and Gordon O. Anson of the Design Department, and to Elizabeth Perry and Sue Davis of the Corporate Relations Department.

As I traveled from collection to collection I was treated with great kindness, and I owe a debt of gratitude to many people, in particular those individuals, listed separately, who graciously consented to serve on the exhibition committee.

One cannot produce a book without a publisher, and being able to work with Abrams has been a delight. The unwavering support of Paul Gottlieb, the invaluable advice of Adele Westbrook, and the talents of Dirk Luykx have made it possible to overcome many obstacles.

It has also been a joy and honor to work with the photographer John Bigelow Taylor and his assistant, Diane Dubler. Faced with an extremely difficult task, they accomplished the superb results evident in this book.

Credit for the title of the exhibition goes to the fertile imagination and quick wit of Professor Kathleen Weil-Garris Brandt.

My secretary, Maureen Latham, acted as a vital liaison among the many parties involved and handled much of the paperwork with commendable efficiency.

The enormous load of work involved in translating the German texts and editing all of the manuscript as well as doing a considerable amount of rewriting was borne with incredible patience and skill by Russell Stockman. To him I offer special thanks.

My own involvement with medals and the slow process of learning the intricacies of the subject over a period of forty years has been enhanced by my association with Mark and Lottie Salton, themselves meticulous and extremely knowledgeable collectors. I owe them much, and hope that as their pupil I have given them satisfaction.

It is no merely conventional gesture to say that without the patient and wise support of my wife, Janie P. Woo, it would not have been possible to complete this project. She kept the path clear for me by accepting many difficult burdens over a period of several years. There is no way I can ever repay such a debt, nor are there words sufficient to convey my feelings of love and gratitude.

Stephen K. Scher

Exhibition Committee

Stephen K. Scher, guest curator

Kathleen Weil-Garris Brandt, Institute of Fine Arts,
New York University, New York

Jean-Baptiste Giard, Cabinet des Médailles,
Bibliothèque Nationale, Paris

Mark Jones, director, National Museums of Scotland,
Edinburgh

Douglas Lewis, Sculpture Department, The National Gallery
of Art, Washington

Hermann Maué, Münzkabinett, Germanisches
Nationalmuseum, Nuremberg

Graham Pollard, Cambridge, England

Mark Salton, private collector, Hartsdale, New York

Karl Schulz, Sammlung von Medaillen, Munzen und
Geldzeichen, Kunsthistorishes Museum, Vienna

Yevgenia Shchukina, Department of Numismatics,
State Hermitage Museum, St. Petersburg

Alan Stahl, American Numismatic Society, New York

Wolfgang Steguweit, Münzkabinett, Staatliche Museen,
Berlin

Richard Stone, Department of Object Conservation,
The Metropolitan Museum of Art, New York

Ingrid S. Weber, Staatliche Münzsammlung, Munich

Marjorie Trusted, Sculpture Collection, Victoria & Albert
Museum, London

Peter Volz, Heidelberg

Raymond Waddington, Department of English, University of
California, Davis

Contributing Authors

Phillip Attwood, Department of Coins and Medals,
The British Museum, London

Joseph Bliss, Cleveland

Lore Börner, Staatliche Münzsammlung, Berlin

James David Draper, Department of European Sculpture and
Decorative Arts, The Metropolitan Museum of Art,
New York

Thomas Eser, doctoral candidate, University of Augsburg

Peta Evelyn, Department of Sculpture, Victoria & Albert
Museum, London

Jean-Baptiste Giard, Cabinet des Médailles, Bibliothèque
Nationale, Paris

Mark Jones, director, National Museums of Scotland,
Edinburgh

Mary L. Levkoff, curator, Department of Painting and
Sculpture, Los Angeles County Museum of Art

Douglas Lewis, Department of Sculpture, The National
Gallery of Art, Washington

Alison Luchs, Department of Sculpture, The National
Gallery of Art, Washington

Hermann Maué, curator, Münzkabinett, Germanisches
Nationalmuseum, Nuremberg

Donald Myers, Department of Sculpture, The National
Gallery of Art, Washington

Graham Pollard, emeritus curator, Coin Cabinet, Fitzwilliam
Museum, Cambridge University

Anne Poulet, curator, Department of European Decorative
Arts and Sculpture, Museum of Fine Arts, Boston

Julian Raby, The Oriental Institute, Oxford University

Mark Salton, private collector and numismatic expert,
Hartsdale, New York

Marjan Scharloo, director, Rijksmuseum Het Koninklijk
Penningkabinet, Leiden

Stephen K. Scher, guest curator, The Frick Collection and
The National Gallery of Art, Washington

Karl Schulz, Münzkabinett, Kunsthistorisches Museum,
Vienna

Yevgenia Shchukina, Department of Numismatics,
State Hermitage Museum, St. Petersburg

Luc Smolderen, Société Royale Numismatique de Belgique,
Brussels

Alan Stahl, curator of medieval coins, American Numismatic
Society, New York

Wolfgang Steguweit, Münzkabinett, Staatliche Museen,
Berlin

Luke Syson, curator of medals, Department of Coins and
Medals, The British Museum, London

Ingrid S. Weber, Staatliche Münzsammlung, Munich

Marjorie Trusted, Department of Sculpture, Victoria &
Albert Museum, London

Gay van der Meer, Rijksmuseum Het Koninklijk
Penningkabinet (retired), Leiden

Peter Volz, private collector and numismatic expert,
Heidelberg

Susanne Wagini, Department of Sculpture, Bayerisches
Nationalmuseum, Munich

Louis Waldman, doctoral candidate, Institute of Fine Arts,
New York University, New York

Mark Wilchusky, doctoral candidate, Institute of Fine Arts,
New York University, New York

Lenders

Staatliche Museen, Münzkabinett, Berlin
Museum of Fine Arts, Boston
Fitzwilliam Museum, Cambridge
Kurpfälzisches Museum, Heidelberg
Rijksmuseum Het Koninklijk Penningkabinet, Leiden
The British Museum, London
Victoria & Albert Museum, London
Los Angeles County Museum of Art
The J. Paul Getty Museum, Malibu
Staatliche Münzsammlung, Munich
Bayerisches Nationalmuseum, Munich
American Numismatic Society, New York

The Metropolitan Museum of Art, New York
Michael Hall, New York
Germanisches Nationalmuseum, Nuremberg
Bibliothèque Nationale, Cabinet des Médailles, Paris
Nicolier Collection, Paris
State Hermitage Museum, St. Petersburg
University Art Museum, Sigmund Morgenroth Collection,
University of California at Santa Barbara
Institut für Numismatik, Vienna
Kunsthistorisches Museum, Münzkabinett, Vienna
The National Gallery of Art, Washington

A Note about Dimensions

In order to show exactly where a medal's diameter was
measured it is customary to include a diagram. We have not
done so in this catalogue, the overall diameter being of only
limited value. It can be assumed that the diameter given is
the largest for each medal. Wherever possible we have given
an internal measurement, which is far more useful. In
addition, it can be assumed that unless otherwise indicated
obverse and reverse are on the same axis rather than in
opposite directions.

7a rev.

12

Introduction

CONSCIOUSNESS of self has taken many forms throughout history, but at no time was it stronger than in the Italian Renaissance, giving rise to a whole body of literature, philosophy, and visual art devoted to the place of the human being in the universe and the distinct qualities and experiences of the individual. One of the most original and complete means of fulfilling the Renaissance desire for fame and immortality was the portrait medal, for within the confines of this small, durable, portable, and easily reproduced object was contained a wealth of information about the subject represented.[1]

Definition of a Medal

The portrait medal is usually circular, and normally has two sides: the obverse with a portrait and identifying inscription, and the reverse with a text or some sort of figure or scene associated with the sitter. There are, to be sure, many medals that are uniface and contain only a portrait, but compared to the ideal of the form these seem somehow incomplete.

Medals have usually been studied in a numismatic context because of their obvious similarity to coins and because they have often been issued by the same authorities, but there are certain fundamental differences. Coins are an official means of exchange, and are therefore controlled and issued by a central authority according to established weights, denominations, and materials. Medals need not be subject to such controls; they can be made at the request of private individuals, and are almost exclusively commemorative in nature. With very few exceptions, coins are struck at an official mint using special machinery. Medals can be either struck or cast, the latter method being most common in the Renaissance. Coins are issued in great numbers and circulate continuously; Renaissance medals were normally produced in only a very few examples for distribution among a select few, and were preserved carefully. Coins are struck from controlled metals having some intrinsic value related to their use as currency, while medals might be cast or struck in gold, silver, bronze, or lead, depending entirely on the whim of the artist or his patron.

There are many obvious ways in which coins and medals overlap, and sometimes it is difficult to distinguish between them (see cat. nos. 34, 137). Special coins have often been issued to commemorate a person or event, and it is not surprising that coins were among the main sources for the genesis of the medal. Yet because the medal was free of the restraints imposed on coinage, it could develop in ways that link it more closely with sculpture.

Materials and Techniques

With few exceptions, until the second half of the sixteenth century medals were produced by the casting method.[2] The artist might make a preparatory drawing, using this as the basis for a model.[3] In Italy it was most common to fashion on a disk of slate or wood a model from beeswax often mixed with other materials to make it easier to work and to give it color.[4] German medalists carved their models for the most part in wood or stone, and many more have therefore survived (see cat. nos. 80, 111, 123).[5] Having formed the images of obverse and reverse, whether in wax or some more durable material, the artist might then add the lettering and a pearled border or other decorative details to the model itself. If working in wax, he could shape the letters or ornamental elements separately, cutting out a ring of them and pressing them into place around the images, or create them by means of incuse punches leaving raised elements in the wax. One often encounters inscribed circles on medals; originally these served as guidelines for the lettering, but in some cases they become elements of the design itself. Working in stone or wood, the artist might simply carve the letters and borders as part of his design.

The completed model was then pressed into some soft material to create a negative mold. This might be a mixture of ashes, salt, and water; fine sand bound with some sort of glue; or a compound of gesso, pumice, water, and sizing. Lettering and ornamental features could also be added at this stage by means of punches impressed into the damp mold.

The obverse and reverse molds were then dried and fitted together with appropriate openings for the introduction of the molten metal and the escape of air and gases. Most scholars agree that the lost wax process, one in which the wax model is left in the mold and melted out either by direct heat or by the molten metal, was not employed in medalmaking. To produce a thin cast of a uniface medal in which the obverse image is seen in almost exact negative on the back, a positive image or mold might be made from the model and fitted above the negative mold.[6]

The molten metal, usually a copper alloy, a lead-tin alloy, gold, or silver, was then poured into the mold and allowed to cool. If possible, the mold, when opened, would be preserved, but a new mold could always be made, normally from a fine workshop trial cast, or from any example of the medal. Freshly cast bronze medals tended to be rather harsh and raw in color, requiring the addition of a lacquer or a chemical surface treatment to give them a more attractive tone.

In differentiating between coins and medals we have indicated that coins are almost always struck from dies. As the name implies, striking consists of the impression by force of images, letters, etc. cut into the faces of obverse and reverse dies onto a metal blank, called a planchet or flan. In antiquity and the Middle Ages this was done quite simply with a hammer, the lower die, or pile, being set into a block of wood or anvil, the upper die, or trussel, forming part of the end of a shaft held in the hand. The planchet, heated or not, was placed upon the pile, and the trussel centered over it. A few sharp blows of the hammer on the trussel forced the metal into the dies.

By the beginning of the sixteenth century, machinery from the printing trade and perhaps from wine production was being adapted for the striking of coins and medals in order to standardize coins and protect them from counterfeiting, to produce greater numbers with less effort, and to handle larger denominations of coins and the higher relief required, especially for medals. This was accomplished by means of the screw press, the invention of which for minting is generally ascribed to Donato Bramante (1444–1514, cat. no. 33) in around 1506 or 1507, but the early development and use of which is also associated with Benvenuto Cellini (1500–1571) and Baldassare Peruzzi (1481–1536).[7]

Here again the artist might prepare a drawing or even a wax model as a guide to the die-cutter. The image was either cut directly into the polished surface of the die or stamped into it after it had been softened by heating. Stamps, like the puncheons used to add letters to the casting mold, were carved in relief onto the face of a metal shaft, which was then hardened. In the press the trussel was fixed into the base of a descending screw topped by a long arm with heavy counterweights at each end. The planchet was placed upon the pile and the trussel driven down against it, impressing obverse and reverse images onto the blank simultaneously. Blanks were either cast in a mold or stamped from a rolled sheet of metal.

The complicated and expensive press was almost always in the possession of an official mint, thereby removing the production of medals from the hands of private patrons, who continued to commission cast medals. Issued by the State, the struck medal appeared in greater numbers for wider distribution and for propaganda purposes. (see cat. nos. 34, 66, 71, 72, 77, 137, 142) As the responsibility of mintmasters and die-cutters, the struck medal tends to be sharper and more brittle in its images, more monotonous and perfunctory in its style and design.

The Character and Purpose of the Medal

There are few objects as rich and complex in content or as fascinating as the Renaissance portrait medal, an intimate object meant to be held in the hand and studied at close range. The medal combines tactile and visual pleasure with mental exercise, as one traces the surface of the relief and appreciates the variations in tone of the metal and the patina, while absorbing the data provided by the images and texts and attempting to unravel the mysteries often contained in the emblems and devices displayed on the reverse.[8]

Above all, the medal is a very personal object. It informs us about the subject or subjects as they or others wished us to perceive them. It commemorates, memorializes, glorifies, criticizes, or even satirizes its subject. The message begins with the portrait, normally identified in an inscription providing the sitter's name and titles. In bearing and dress, whether in strictest realism or idealized, the portrait itself can convey the sitter's aspirations and accomplishments—or merely self-satisfaction. Lastly, the artist declares his presence, sometimes with his signature, always by means of style, and often by his handling of the portrait, revealing his attitude toward the subject.

The reverse adds to our knowledge of the subject. Text alone, in the form of mottoes, epigrams, or historical data, may be placed around the edge or even fill the field, but more commonly we encounter the subject engaged in some significant action, narrative scenes, heraldry, symbolic devices, allegories, or emblems that transmit in cryptic language a particular attribute of the subject, a favorite idea or ambition.

History of the Medal

The philosophical and spiritual foundations for the appearance of the portrait medal in Italy in the fourth decade of the fifteenth century are composed of two interconnecting factors: the Renaissance philosophy of man and the reevaluation of classical antiquity, or humanism.[9]

Individual achievement and prosperity within the structure of Italian urban society gave further impetus to the desire for personal recognition and the confirmation of one's unique identity. It was in Italy that one looked to the heritage of republican Rome, whose consuls and senators devoted themselves to public service and the good life described by Cicero. His picture of an ideal society whose leaders followed a life dignified by practical activity and rendered delightful by beauty and learning appealed strongly to the upper classes of the Italian city-state. The often glorious prospect of imperial Rome also offered a rich heritage from which to draw.

In the early fourteenth century one man in particular gave impetus to this development—Francesco Petrarch. It was he who embodied within himself and expressed with such clarity and vigor the individualist temper and the cult of fame. Petrarch assumed that human talent, if properly used, was certain of recognition. Therefore glory, or *fama,* was inevitably the result of excellence, or *virtus,* and this *virtus* was a function of a man's entire personality.

In its outward manifestation, *virtus* was most clearly seen in eloquence and purity of style no matter what the mode of expression. It was this excellence that raised a man above his fellows regardless of his material or social status. Increased consciousness of one's excellence resulted in an examination of one's own personality with the need to comment openly about such observations and do so in a way that would survive the erosion of time and fragility of men's memories. It was, in other words, important to establish a durable means of attaining earthly immortality.

The vulnerability of these means became a point of debate in the Renaissance, one camp supporting the written word, another relying upon more durable forms such as painted portraits and sculpture. The ideal fusion of the two, of course, was the portrait medal, combining text and image in an object that was produced in some numbers, could be distributed widely, and was made of lasting materials.

Origins

Although the point has often been debated, it is difficult to deny that the basic form of the Renaissance portrait medal was invented by Antonio Pisanello (cat. nos. 4–9) in 1438.[10] As a form of sculpture free of any connection with coinage, Pisanello's creation had no precedent, but several direct and indirect sources. With their wide circulation, coins have always been an ideal medium for the transmission of information, hence the early production of special commemorative issues. The Roman emperors utilized the potential of coinage for propaganda purposes extensively. In this sense all Roman coinage has a medallic quality, especially the large bronze sestertii so highly prized in the Renaissance. On the other hand, there are no Roman medals in the modern sense, that is objects independent of the state and divorced from specific denominations of weight and value. Nonetheless, at times limited numbers of a particular coin, often large in size as a multiple of an existing denomination, were issued for special distribution. These are now described as "medallions."[11]

A certain number of these ancient pieces survived, and were known to Renaissance artists and scholars, among them Pisanello himself. Collecting ancient Roman coins had already become popular in the fourteenth century. Petrarch was a collector, and he and his followers prized such coins not only for their aesthetic value, but even more for their evocation of a glorious past and the clear moral lessons they imparted. It was only a small step from such sentiments to the desire for a similar means of attaining immortality.

Not surprisingly, the first modern medal has a direct connection with Petrarch. For a time, one of the poet's patrons and closest friends was Francesco I da Carrara, master of Treviso and Padua, the latter a city noted for its university where classical literature was studied. Petrarch doubtless fostered an interest in antiquity on the part of both Francesco and his son, Francesco II, and may well have introduced them to the delights of antique coins and gems.

Petrarch's tutelage was to bear remarkable fruit, for when Francesco II recaptured Padua from Milan and freed his captured father in 1390 he commemorated the event by striking medals in imitation of Roman sestertii, with obverse portraits of both men in the guise of Roman emperors. These medals, along with certain imitations of Roman coins produced in Venice by the Sesto family and a peculiar coin of Brescia issued by Pandolfo Malatesta around 1400—again with a portrait in Roman dress—reflected a growing interest that would eventually lead to the more familiar form of the Renaissance medal, but they did not engender any immediate successors and seem to have had little influence.[12]

The Carrara medals, however, were widely known, one specimen finally coming to rest in the hands of one of the greatest patrons and collectors in the history of art, Jean de France, duke of Berry. An example in lead is listed in the 1413 inventory of his possessions.[13] The duke's collections also contained a group of objects much more important for an understanding of the origins of the Renaissance medal. Only two of them, or possibly two and a half, have survived in one form or another, namely the famous "medals" of Constantine and Heraclius (cat. nos. 1–2).

It is also probable that seals served as one of the sources for the distinctive size, type, and composition of the Renaissance medal.[14] Their extraordinary quality attests to their importance, and reflects the stature of the artists—goldsmiths and court painters—called upon to design and possibly even cut the dies for them. Seals manifest the large size, the extreme delicacy of work, the placement of the subject within a circular field, the use of inscriptions, the beauty of script, the frequent appearance of obverse and reverse, and the statement of social position that are all associated with the medal.

Italy, Fifteenth Century

Over a period of twenty-two years, the first true Renaissance medalist, Pisanello, fashioned over twenty-six medals in a number of locations, and it is apparent that almost immediately the new medium was received with great enthusiasm (cat. no. 4–9). His style is quite distinctive, and the quality of his work has never been equalled. Although we know from the large number of drawings that exist in, or close to, his style, that he did have an atelier and many followers, it is difficult to identify a specific school of medalists directly indebted to him.

When tracing the subsequent history of the medal it is perhaps somewhat misleading to attempt to group medals around the activities in a particular city, although the politics of Italy encourage such a method of categorization. Artists moved frequently from city to city, and were engaged in a variety of activites besides medalmaking. Among them we find sculptors, painters, die-engravers, mintmasters, jewelers, gem-carvers, goldsmiths, and architects. Such widespread activity is a clear indication of the passionate desire to

·MALATESTA·NOVELLVS·
·CESENAE·DO MINVS·

6 obv.

commission and collect these objects that developed so rapidly in the fifteenth and sixteenth centuries. Nonetheless, it is necessary to note that very rarely did a major artist engage in the making of medals, particularly in the fifteenth century. The painter Francesco Francia (born c. 1450–53, died 1517), also a goldsmith and die-engraver, did produce a number of good medals in Bologna,[15] and Gentile Bellini (1429–1507) made at least one—notably unsuccessful—attempt in the medium.[16] Francesco Laurana (born c. 1420–25, died c. 1502) demonstrated little mastery of the art, despite his skill at sculptured portraits.[17] A small group of medals has been attributed to the architect, sculptor, and painter Francesco di Giorgio (1439–1502), but these too are relatively undistinguished.[18] Nowhere does one encounter names such as Donatello, Michelangelo, or Leonardo, although Botticelli does reveal an interest in the form by his rather startling inclusion of a medal of Cosimo de' Medici in his well-known painted portrait of a young man.[19] It would appear that medals, although extremely popular, were considered peripheral to the major arts of painting and sculpture, and more often than not left to the practitioners of the so-called minor arts of gem-engraving, die-cutting, and goldsmithing, or to sculptors of small bronzes. One cannot draw strict lines, however, since any artist was usually proficient in several mediums, and was called upon to perform a wide variety of commissions.

It is also true that a number of medalists were amateurs, with no formal training as artists or craftsmen. One of these is the artist who went by the name of Lysippus the Younger (cat. no. 36). Another was Giovanni Candida (cat. nos. 37–38), who was himself clearly influenced by Lysippus. Born into an aristocratic Neapolitan family, Candida spent his entire life in the diplomatic service, working in turn for Charles the Bold, duke of Burgundy, Archduke Maximilian of Austria (cat. nos. 37, 79), and Charles VIII of France. Candida cannot be attached to any particular school, yet it is apparent that he was very talented and exerted considerable influence on the development of the medal in France at the end of the fifteenth century.

For a brief period under the rule of Sigismondo Malatesta (cat. no. 14), Rimini became a center of learning and the equal of any of the other northern Italian courts. As something of a parvenu, Sigismondo was not to be outdone by his fellow princes and engaged Pisanello to produce two medals of himself and one for his brother Domenico (cat. no. 6). He also attracted Leon Battista Alberti (cat. no. 3) to his court, to assist him in the construction of several buildings, most notably the church of San Francesco. The execution of Alberti's designs was entrusted to the painter and miniaturist Matteo de' Pasti (cat. nos. 11–14), who had also worked for Leonello d'Este (cat. no. 5) in Ferrara before moving to Rimini and undoubtedly came into close contact with Pisanello in both cities. It is therefore understandable that he would take up the new form and produce medals modeled on Pisanello's.

Matteo's style is nevertheless quite independent, and of a very high standard. His portraits, though lacking Pisanello's sophistication, are impressive in their veracity and power, and his reverses, such as the famous view of Sigismondo's castle and the charming Malatesta device of the elephant, are among the most successful of all medallic images.

Of the various courts in which Pisanello was engaged, Gonzagan Mantua would prove to be the richest and most productive in its patronage of all of the arts.[20] The influence of Andrea Mantegna (1431–1506) and a passion for the ancient past are both evident in the active production of small bronzes, plaquettes, and medals, and seen even in the names of two of the artists, Antico (cat. nos. 16–17) and Moderno (cat. no. 18). In all the medals of this school one finds precision and elegance of lettering, crisp details, finely drawn portraits, and an almost academic fixation with classical subjects.

The city produced or attracted a large number of artists, some of whom were natives but spent most of their careers elsewhere. Such a one is Cristoforo di Geremia (cat. no. 35), who worked in Rome, but whose work reflects the influence of Mantegna and in turn inspired the work of another important Mantuan medalist, Bartolommeo Melioli (1448–1514). Both combine fine portraits with beautiful Latin epigraphy and a graceful, yet forceful interpretation of classical forms. The medalist who called himself Lysippus the Younger (cat. no. 36), usually associated with the Roman school like his uncle Cristoforo di Geremia, might also be mentioned here, for the style and quality of his portraiture and the nobility of his lettering link him to a group that has its origins in Mantua.

Another medalist who worked for some time in Mantua as well as elsewhere was Giancristoforo Romano (active c. 1465–1512), a sculptor and architect who was one of the favorites of the court and particularly appreciated by Isabella d'Este (1474–1539), wife of Francesco Gonzaga. Documents relating to his medal of Isabella, showing her in all her beauty at the age of twenty-four, give us a rare insight into the role these objects played in Renaissance society. In 1495, Isabella wrote to Giancristoforo, then working for her sister Beatrice in Milan, asking him to make her "that engraved sculpture"—probably referring to the medal.[21] In early 1498 Isabella asked her kinsman, the brilliant courtier and poet Niccolò da Correggio, to compose an appropriate motto for the reverse. He complied with the phrase we now see on it, "benemerentium ergo" (for those who deserve well), a reference to her patronage of the arts and letters.[22]

Clearly the medal was then cast in a number of examples and distributed with some deliberation, since it was a mark of great favor to be given one. In one instance such a gift served as the occasion for a practical joke. Isabella had instructed Giancristoforo to give a copy of her medal to the famous poet Bernardo Accolti, but mindful of Accolti's legendary vanity, Elisabetta Gonzaga, duchess of Urbino and Isabella's sister-in-law (cat. no. 22), urged the artist merely to show the medal to the poet, telling him that he could not have one as there were no copies to spare. Once Accolti discovered that quantities of the medal had been distributed to Isabella's friends in Urbino and Rome, he was furious, and Isabella was obliged to go out of her way to placate him.[23] In a letter of September 1498, the Ferrarese poet Giacomo Faella tells Isabella that he has seen her medal and that it inspired him to write a sonnet.[24]

In the fall of 1507, Giancristoforo delivered still another specimen to Francesco Gonzaga's secretary in Naples. He wrote Isabella to tell her of the joy and enthusiasm with which the medal was received at the Neapolitan court, where the ladies had kissed her likeness and clamored for similar portraits of themselves by the same artist.[25]

Many examples of Isabella's medal survive today. In fact, a gold example now in Vienna, set in a frame of diamonds and enamels, is probably Isabella's own specimen, mentioned in the 1542 inventory of her possessions. Such specimens are extremely rare, for generally gold copies were only produced for the medal's subject, if he or she could afford it, and most were subsequently melted down.[26]

The last Mantuan deserving of special mention here is Sperandio (cat. nos. 23–26), one of the most famous and prolific medalists of the Renaissance. His style is derivative of that of Pisanello, though much heavier and more robust. He has little in common with the works of the other Mantuan medalists and worked chiefly in Ferrara, Bologna, and Venice. His portraits are hardly subtle, but powerful and expressive. He worked in a large scale and high relief, so that his pieces display a distinctly sculptural style as opposed to the more painterly approach of Pisanello, from whom he often, quite shamelessly and awkwardly, borrowed reverse compositions.

In the second half of the fifteenth century medallic activity could be found in all the major centers of artistic production. Among the medalists of Venice, working in a diversity of styles that cannot necessarily be characterized as Venetian, one encounters distinct artistic personalities such as Giovanni Boldù (cat. no. 27), with his taut portraiture and vigorous reverse compositions, and Vittore Gambello (cat. no. 28), a sculptor, jeweler, die-engraver, and armorer, the precision and delicacy of whose medals reflect these various professions. Also included in the Venetian school is Fra Antonio da Brescia (cat. no. 29), who recorded with simple fidelity and charming realism some of the prominent citizens of the Serenissima and their wives. By contrast, the medals attributed to Maffeo Olivieri (cat. nos. 30–31) show an elegance and refinement appropriate to his portraits of Venetian gentlemen. In neighboring Padua, the jurist and amateur medalist Giulio della Torre (born c. 1480, last mentioned c. 1530) is worthy of mention for the quality of his work and his obvious association with the style of Venetian medalists, particularly Olivieri.

Rome was one of the chief centers of artistic activity, attracting artists from all over Italy. The relative

54 rev.

stability of the papal court assured a continuing market for creative talent. In the quattrocento, most Roman medals were cast, and retained often admirable stylistic identities. Such were the often awkward but honest and effective portraits by the cleric Andrea Guazzalotti (or Guacialoti; born 1435, died 1494–95), who produced medals for Nicholas V, Calixtus III, Pius II, and Sixtus IV. We have already mentioned the Roman careers of the Mantuans Cristoforo di Geremia and his nephew Lysippus the Younger. Lysippus in particular produced a series of sharply modeled portraits of members of the papal Curia combined with beautiful Latin epigraphy.

It is surprising that Florence, the city most commonly associated with the Renaissance, with enlightened patrons and progressive artists, and with a devotion to the revival of classical philosophy, literature, and art, should have become interested in medals only in the last quarter of the fifteenth century. The first significant Florentine medalist, Bertoldo di Giovanni (cat. nos. 39–41), was a pupil of Donatello and the master of Michelangelo. Perhaps his most successful effort is his medal of Mehmed II (cat. no. 39), but it should be compared with the sculptural masterpiece on the same subject by Costanzo da Ferrara (cat. no. 21).

Bertoldo's efforts hardly prepare us for the greatest of all Florentine medalists, Niccolò di Forzore Spinelli, called Niccolò Fiorentino (cat. nos. 42–46). Niccolò's style would dominate the Florentine school of medalmaking throughout the remainder of the fifteenth century. His medals are for the most part large in scale, their portraits—including remarkably handsome portraits of women—bold and strong in their characterizations, with reverses that are, save for such triumphs as his depiction of the Three Graces (cat. no. 45), surprisingly indifferent in quality.

Italy, Sixteenth Century

The development of the medal in Italy in the sixteenth century was affected by the introduction of the screw press, by drastic changes in the political landscape, and by shifts in taste. With increasing frequency medals came to be the exclusive responsibility of die-engravers, being produced at official mints and struck in large quantities for use as propaganda. As a result, there is a noticeable decline in quality in this period, a dessication of style, regardless of the source of the design, owing to the new technology. This is not to say that all struck medals lack quality. Beginning in the sixteenth century there are many fine products from the hands of highly competent medalists, and a few of these are included in this exhibition, but it is still in the cast medal that one encounters the finest and most exciting work.

With the onset of the Italian Wars involving France, the Holy Roman Empire, and the local powers of Milan, Venice, Florence, Rome, and Naples, the centers of medallic production and patronage shift and expand. Nonetheless, among the many medalists active during this period there are only a few whose works rise above the ordinary. The papal mint, for example, attracted a steady stream of die-engravers who produced medals as well as coins, but few of them deserve much attention. The most famous of these—by his own report at least—was Benvenuto Cellini (1500–1571), but his struck pieces are by no means remarkable, and the attribution to him of the fine cast medal of Pietro Bembo (cat. no. 64) is open to serious doubt. A few other artists such as Alessandro Cesati (born c. 1500, last documented in 1564), Giovanni Bernardi da Castelbolognese (1496–1553), and Gianantonio Rossi (1517–c. 1575) rise above the common level at times, but cannot match the accomplishments of their contemporaries north of the Alps.

Even in cities like Florence and Venice, celebrated for their painting, sculpture, and architecture, it is difficult to find medals of any distinction. From Venice we have singled out only the work of the sculptor Alessandro Vittoria (cat. no. 70) as worthy of notice. Padua continued to be a major center of bronze casting, and produced several medalists whose attention seems to have been directed primarily to the imitation of Roman sestertii or the production of fantasy pieces in a classical style—understandable in a city that had given birth to the Carrara proto-medals over a hundred years earlier, and one in which the taste for the antique was so constantly nurtured. One may define these works as reproductions, imitations, or forgeries, depending on one's evaluation of the evidence. Among these artists, the most notorious and underrated is Giovanni Cavino (cat. nos. 71–72). All of his coinlike pieces and original medals were struck, and if we look only at his medals of contemporary subjects, we find an artist of some originality and precision, whose portraits on a small scale are quite attractive.

The grandducal Medici court in Florence provided another center of patronage and several of the more praiseworthy medalists of the period. A native of Siena, but resident in Florence most of his life and widely available as a medalist, Pastorino de' Pastorini (cat. nos. 67–69) was one of the most prolific and representative medalists of the sixteenth century. In over two hundred medals, most without reverses, he recorded in a coldly precise, detached manner the features of members of practically every prominent family in Italy, as well as many personalities from beyond the Alps. His portraits tell us nothing about the character and personality of his sitters, and the lack of reverses deprives us of any further insight into their natures, yet the virtuosity with which Pastorino describes the minutest details of dress and adornment is a dominant characteristic of the best of sixteenth-century Italian medals, and the one that would be of greatest influence in the development of the medal in other countries. A large number of his medals are devoted to female beauty, another preoccupation of the medalists of this century.[27] Pastorino was clearly extremely fashionable, and produced formula pieces of undeniable quality.

Among the many medalists engaged by the Medici court in Florence, several deserve mention. Pietro Paolo Galeotti (cat. no. 57) was a pupil of Cellini's who eventually settled in Florence around 1552. He produced roughly eighty cast medals bearing the sort of accomplished and courtly portraits we have already seen in the work of Pastorino. In contrast to the latter, however, Galeotti did not avoid the challenge of providing reverse compositions, which he handled with notable competence.

Cellini was also involved with two native Florentines whose careers began in that city but eventually diverged. Domenico Poggini (1520–1590) and his brother Gianpaolo (cat. no. 58) worked together at the Medici court as die-engravers, goldsmiths, and gem-carvers. Domenico stayed on in Florence until moving to Rome in the mid 1580s, when he achieved some renown as a sculptor, but Gianpaolo left Italy around 1540 for the Netherlands. There he became attached to the court of Philip II (cat. nos. 58, 156), and moving with the court in 1559 to Spain, remained there for the rest of his life. Both brothers produced cast and struck medals of some technical competence but lacking in vitality and imagination. Seen in conjunction with papal medals of the same period, their work is representative of the type of the often tedious official struck medal. The Pogginis in fact represent one of the more attractive moments in what is so often a rather dreary history.

From the fourteenth to the seventeenth century, Milan was the scene of a brilliant court and host to a succession of important artists, among them the most distinguished and influential medalist of the sixteenth century, Leone Leoni (cat. nos. 49–52). In Leoni we have the rare example of a major sculptor who is also active as a medalist, and in both areas—depending on attributions—we find the same fluctuations in quality. Trained as a goldsmith and medalist and active as a die-engraver, Leoni seems to have graduated to monumental sculpture only in the later 1540s. Hot-headed and unstable, Leoni was extremely ambitious, yet it is evident that his desire to produce complicated and grandiose sculptures to please his imperial patrons exerted constraints upon his abilities. Many of his most important monuments display a stiff and mannered awkwardness that belies the level of quality found in less inhibited works. These same contrasts are apparent in Leoni's medals. A portrait of Philip II is totally without character, coupled with a reverse showing muscular figures, both male and female, undoubtedly derived from Michelangelo, but often ill-proportioned and melodramatic. Yet portraits such as those of Michelangelo (cat. no. 52), Martin Hanna (cat. no. 49), and Andrea Doria (cat. no. 50) are eloquent, and reflect an obvious personal involvement of the artist when freed from the constraints of the courtier. His medal of Ippolita Gonzaga (cat. no. 51) establishes a vibrant style of mannerist female portrait that was imitated and carried to fantastic lengths by other medalists and is in contrast to the brittle and impersonal style of Pastorino.

Jacopo da Trezzo (cat. nos. 54–55), a native of Milan, can be called a follower, even an imitator, of

Leoni, yet his work has considerable merit. His portraits have great dignity, and he is capable of composing eloquent and legible reverses.

The refined court style as developed in Milan finds its fullest expression in the works of Antonio Abondio (cat. nos. 60–63). Clearly influenced in his early Italian period by Leoni, he later raised the fashioning of wax models to an extraordinary level of virtuosity, so that they ultimately came to be seen as ends in themselves. With a facility that stops just short of being monotonous, Abondio offers accurate and dignified portraits and highly detailed renderings of armor and clothing. Although a number of his medals are uniface, his reverses are relatively simple and restricted to emblems or heraldic achievements. The type of medal he established at the Habsburg court served as the pattern for endless imitations in German-speaking countries in the late sixteenth and entire seventeenth centuries.

Although formed in Milan, Leoni, da Trezzo, and Abondio traveled widely, largely in the employ of the Habsburg court. Leoni made at least two trips to Brussels and spent some time in Augsburg; da Trezzo settled in Spain; and Abondio was most active in Prague and Vienna. As a consequence, their highly sophisticated style was exported from Italy, and exerted great influence on the development of the medal in other countries.

In the later sixteenth century, the boundaries of stylistic restraint and propriety were shattered by a fascinating group of mannerist wax-modelers centered about Reggio Emilia. With an oblique reference to Leoni's earlier medal of Ippolita Gonzaga, these Emilian medalists, whose pieces are usually uniface and cast in a lead alloy, produced a series of bizarre and delightful portraits unforgettable in their originality. Both male and female subjects are dressed in agitated, filmy garments and richly coiffed. This school is composed of three artists in particular, Alfonso Ruspasgiari (cat. nos. 73–74), Gian Antonio Signoretti (active 1540–1602), and the artist called Bombarda (cat. no. 75), all of whom worked for the mint in Reggio, thus countering to some extent the theory that die-cutters only produce dry and uninteresting struck medals.

Germany, Sixteenth Century

If it is impossible to refer to Italy in the fifteenth and sixteenth centuries as a single country, the same may be said with even greater certainty of Germany. Yet in relation to the development of the medal in this period, one can speak confidently of a German Renaissance in learning, literature and the arts. The primary influence, of course, came from Italy as early as the fourteenth century in the person of Petrarch, and was fostered in the fifteenth century by Aeneas Sylvius Piccolomini (later Pope Pius II), who served for a time as secretary to Emperor Frederick III (cat. no. 40). Primary support for the spread of classical studies continued with Frederick's successor, Maximilian I (cat. nos. 37, 79), during whose reign German humanists who had traveled or studied in Italy, such as Konrad Celtis and Willibald Pirckheimer, argued passionately for the introduction of the *studia humanitatis* into German education and the enrichment of German culture by the teaching of classical languages and literature.

Yet the effect of such efforts on the visual arts varied greatly. With very few exceptions, the influence of the Italian Renaissance on architecture and sculpture was minimal, and did not displace the dominant Gothic style throughout the sixteenth—and perhaps not until the eighteenth—century. In painting and the graphic arts, on the other hand, Germany produced a spectacular group of artists who worked during the first three decades of the sixteenth century. The most prominent of these, Albrecht Dürer (cat. no. 84), had traveled in Italy and was a friend of humanists, a brilliant painter and printmaker, and a theoretician who strove to provide an intellectual foundation for German art. Yet not all of these artists drew upon classical or Italian models, and one must therefore use the term "German Renaissance" judiciously, recognizing the distinctly northern character of their art.

There is little question, however, that the medal was one form borrowed directly from Italy, but not before the first decade of the sixteenth century. Yet Italian medals were certainly known in Germany much earlier. In 1459 Ulrich Gossembrot, who was studying in Padua, wrote to his father, the burgomaster of

Augsburg, that he had sent home several portrait medals in lead. Apparently there was as yet little appreciation for this innovation, and it was not until humanism had taken firm root in German soil that a demand for medals arose. One notes the new thinking in the statement of Maximilian I, for example, that "the man who makes himself no memorial in life is forgotten with the tolling of his death bell."[28]

In most aspects German medals are distinctly different from their Italian counterparts. Although cast, they are generally made from stone and wood models carved by goldsmiths, die-engravers, and carvers in stone and wood whose techniques were often brilliant and tended toward fine detail. To some extent they were influenced by the equally young craft of printing: the meticulous linear style seen in woodcuts and the processes required in the casting of type.

Despite their foundation in humanism, German medals rarely display the complex imagery and intellectual sophistication of Italian medals. Only in rare cases does the reverse show anything other than a heraldic achievement, establishing the subject's place in society. Instead, all attention is focused on the portrait, which is usually uncompromisingly, even brutally, realistic.

It is apparent from the enormous number of medals produced in Germany beginning in the second decade of the century that they had become extremely popular. Given his connections with Italy and the intellectual foundations of his art, it is no surprise that medals were of great interest to Albrecht Dürer. We know that he made some attempt to design a medal for himself, but ultimately decided to turn the project over to Hans Schwarz (cat. no. 84). Until fairly recently a group of carvings in Solnhofen stone and medallic reliefs, some signed with his monogram, were assumed to be from the hand of Dürer himself, but this is now generally doubted. It is certain, however, that he designed the famous medal produced by the city of Nuremberg for Charles V in 1521 (cat. no. 77).

Nuremberg and Augsburg were the centers of medallic production in Germany through the whole of the sixteenth century, a lesser contribution coming from the mining regions of Saxony. The earliest Nuremberg practitioners of the art were members of the Fischer family, notably Peter Fischer the Younger (1487–1528), who traveled to Italy and whose few medals show Italian influence. The city's flourishing production of medals in the 1520s and 1530s was dominated by the work of Matthes Gebel (cat. nos. 109–13), but also included some fifty works created by several unidentified artists known simply by the dates of their pieces as the "Nuremberg 1525–1527" group. In the next two decades Nuremberg's prominent medalists included Joachim Deschler (cat. nos. 118–20) and Hans Bolsterer (cat. nos. 122–23).

Augsburg produced one of the most significant and powerful of the early German medalists in the person of Hans Schwarz (cat. nos. 81–84). Schwarz created his first portrait medals in his native city, but like many others he traveled constantly, working in Nuremberg in 1519–20 and also in Heidelberg. The Augsburg school was ultimately dominated by Christoph Weiditz (cat. nos. 87–91) and Friedrich Hagenauer (cat. nos. 92–100), although they too moved about with great regularity. They were both master wood-carvers, and their models and medals display an astonishing precision and refinement. Virtuosity in carving is also seen in the works of two other leading Augsburg medalists, Hans Daucher (cat. nos. 78–80) and Hans Kels (cat. nos. 102, 104).

In Saxony, Hans Reinhart (cat. nos. 125–27) produced several adequate portraits, but only displayed the full range of his craft in beautiful heraldic reverses and in a number of religious pieces dominated by his spectacular Trinity medal (cat. no. 127), a *tour de force* that betrays his training as a goldsmith. In the later sixteenth century, medals continued to be produced in great numbers, but with a certain monotony in style and presentation. The works of Valentin Maler (cat. nos. 129–31) and Ludwig Neufahrer (cat. nos. 115–16) display unquestioned virtuosity, but they scarcely manage to breathe new life into a form that had become repetitious.

France, Sixteenth Century

The medal's development in France was dependent almost entirely on the patronage of the crown. This is

95 obv.

ARMANDVS IOANNES CARDINALIS DE RICHELIEV

153 obv.

evident even in the earliest French medals, struck between 1451 and 1460, commemorating the expulsion of the English at the end of the Hundred Years War. These pieces resemble late medieval coinage, with no trace of Italian influence, and it is true that the Italian artists who worked in France in the later fifteenth century such as Pietro da Milano and Francesco Laurana produced medals of very questionable quality. A more important intermediary between Italy and France was the diplomat and distinguished amateur medalist Giovanni Candida (cat. nos. 37–38), whose work in France, especially for the court of Burgundy, found imitators who may have been French-born (cat. nos. 138–39).

At the very end of the fifteenth century, the wealthy commercial city of Lyon, with strong ties to Italy, commemorated on several occasions the visit of royalty with quite impressive medals characterized by a blend of late Gothic and Renaissance elements. The most spectacular of these is the large medal of Louis XII and Anne of Brittany from 1499 (cat. no. 140).

In the early sixteenth century, Francis I (cat. nos. 116, 139) made a point of importing Italian artists, most notably Benvenuto Cellini, and medallic production in France was certainly affected by that policy, but with results that are less than memorable. In the same period, however, Lyon continued to foster the creation of medals by native artists, some of whom, Jacques Gauvain for example (cat. no. 142), are certainly worthy of notice.

Royal involvement in coinage and medalmaking became firmly established with Henry II, who installed new machinery in the mint and expressed concern over the quality of its production. Charles IX, as committed to such matters as his father, created a new position at the mint and filled it with his court sculptor, Germain Pilon, charging him with the preparation of wax models for the mint's die-engravers. In 1577, Pilon produced a splendid large medallion with a portrait of chancellor René de Birague (cat. no. 144); related to that triumph is a series of dramatic uniface portrait medallions of members of the house of Valois (cat. no. 145) traditionally attributed to the same medalist, an attribution that has become controversial.

Little else attracts our attention until the very early seventeenth century, notable for the work of one of Pilon's successors at the mint and one of the greatest of all medalists, Guillaume Dupré (cat. nos. 146–50). Dupré drew on the accomplishments of the great sixteenth-century Italians such as Leoni, da Trezzo, and Pastorino to reach new heights of technical brilliance, bringing to a close the tradition of the cast medal until its revival in the nineteenth century. His portraiture, though not altogether lifeless, is detached, and his reverses are often mechanical, but his virtuosity is unparalleled.

The flowering of the cast medal in France actually ends with Jean Warin (cat. nos. 152–54), who was also responsible for launching the often tedious series of struck medals institutionalized by Louis XIV. Warin's cast pieces include a number of very impressive compositions, all in the tradition of Dupré but by no means of inferior quality. He may even surpass Dupré with his sympathetic portraiture and richly sculptural reverses.

England and the Low Countries, Sixteenth Century

In part owing to the Hundred Years War, England, like France, developed a distinct sense of nationality over the course of the fifteenth and sixteenth centuries. Yet England's geographical isolation did not at all remove it from the flow of Italian influence. As early as the late fourteenth century, Chaucer (c. 1340–1400) had visited Italy and come under the spell of the great proto-humanist Petrarch. During the fifteenth century Italian and other European humanists had come to England in increasing numbers, and Humphrey, duke of Gloucester (1391–1447), saw himself as a Renaissance prince whose patronage was important to the establishment of Italian humanism in his own country. By 1500 such a tradition was firmly established, especially at Oxford, nurtured by such luminaries as John Colet (1466–1519), Sir Thomas More (1477–1535), and, on his visits to England, Desiderius Erasmus (cat. no. 157).

After 1531, and the recognition of Henry VIII as head of the Church of England, most of the traditional subject matter of painting and sculpture was proscribed. Portraiture alone continued to be acceptable. Although there are certainly elements of the Renaissance in England, it is almost impossible to identify an English Renaissance art. Certainly this is true of medals, which are relatively few in number and often produced by non-English artists. A number of medals of Henry VIII come from German sources, while others appear to be later restitutions. As an exception, Mary Tudor is admirably represented in a medal by Jacopo da Trezzo (cat. no. 54), probably based on a painting by Anthonis Mor. The reign of Elizabeth I saw little improvement. Only rarely does one find a work of the quality of the pieces produced by Stefan van Herwijck during his visit to England in 1562 (cat. no. 169). The dominance of painting is evident in the best of Elizabeth's medals, either based on the work of the greatest miniaturist of the period, Nicolas Hilliard, or actually designed by him (cat. no. 164). In fact, the strong influence of painting on medallic portraiture is evident from the frequent use of the three-quarter pose.

One does find occasional medallic portraits commissioned by Englishmen abroad, but native production of medals was minimal up until the end of the first quarter of the seventeenth century.

The situation in the Netherlands is similar. The Burgundian dukes had commissioned medals of themselves, their families, and their courtiers from Italian artists, notably Giovanni Candida (cat. nos. 37–38) and Niccolò Fiorentino (cat. nos. 42–46). The Habsburgs also favored Italian masters, and as we have seen imported medalists such as Leone Leoni (cat. nos. 49–52), his son Pompeo, Jacopo da Trezzo (cat. nos. 54–55), and Gianpaolo Poggini (cat. no. 58). It was they who set the style for the few native medalists active in the second half of the sixteenth century.

As an isolated instance without much influence on subsequent medalists, the renowned Flemish painter Quentin Matsys produced at least one medal that deserves to be numbered among the greatest examples of the art, his portrait of Erasmus (cat. no. 157).

The work of the Italians in Ghent and Antwerp helped to create an enthusiastic demand for medals, not only among princes and their followers, but also on the part of private individuals imbued with a humanist sensibility. The sculptor Jacques Jonghelinck (cat. nos. 158–163) was one of the most prominent artists active in satisfying that demand. His work is always extremely proficient technically, but his inspiration seems to have varied, resulting in portraits that are often lifeless and reverse compositions only occasionally reaching a superior level of design (cat. no. 161).

Of a more sympathetic character are the medals of Steven van Herwijck (cat. nos. 166–69), who was widely traveled and thus seems to have been exposed to a greater range of outside influences. Van Herwijck combined excellent technique with accomplished design and sensitive portraiture.

We must be content to let these few artists represent the medallic art of the Renaissance in the Low Countries. It was only in the mid seventeenth century that the art was revived, with the introduction of a very particular technique and dramatic style of portraiture that was uniquely Dutch and appropriate for Holland's Golden Age.

Connoisseurship

The confident acquisition of any work of art of fine quality requires both a considerable fund of knowledge gained through study and experience and an instinct for quality and authenticity—sometimes defined as "having an eye"—something with which the consistently successful collector is naturally endowed. One of the most effective means of learning the characteristics of a superior work of art is the study of those examples generally accepted as being not only authentic, but of the highest quality in design, workmanship, and content. It has been the purpose of this exhibition to provide such examples in the field of Renaissance medals for the collector and student who may thus achieve a heightened awareness of some of the most important aspects of medallic connoisseurship, about which much more will be published in the near future.[29]

Stephen K. Scher

157 obv.

29

la rev.

Prototypes:

THE MEDALS OF THE

Duke of Berry

Among the most important sources of the portrait medal are certain objects recorded as being in the collection of Jean de France, duke of Berry (1340–1416), the Valois prince whose activities as a patron of the arts were to leave such a rich heritage. Among these medals, eight in all, the two that were to exert the most influence and fascination were those depicting the emperors Constantine the Great (cat. no. 1) and Heraclius (cat. no. 2).

The story of the Constantine and Heraclius medals is extremely complex. There is much having to do with both their authorship and their iconography that is obscure.

Among the many pieces described as part of the personal jewelry of the duke of Berry, there is a curious series that has interested and puzzled scholars ever since the publication of the duke's inventories in 1896.[1] The objects in this series were all round and made of gold, with persons or scenes in relief, usually on both sides and usually mounted in rich jeweled frames to be worn around the neck at the end of a chain. The subjects included Julius Caesar, Octavian, Tiberius, and the two emperors represented here. The Octavian and Tiberius pieces were purchased in March of 1401 from a merchant named Michiel de Paxi, presumed to have been Italian. From the description of these pieces and from their types and legends it seems clear that what the duke purchased were pastiches, or, to put it bluntly, forgeries, for at the time, in fact until the seventeenth century, they, and the Constantine and Heraclius medals as well, were taken to be genuine objects from Roman and Byzantine antiquity.

The inventories of the duke of Berry state that the Constantine medal, in gold and garnished with jewels, was bought at Bourges on November 2, 1402, from the Florentine merchant Antonio Mancini, who was then living in Paris.[2] There is no indication of where the Heraclius medal came from, but it has generally been assumed—though it is not necessarily the case—that the two, being very much alike, were purchased together.

In fact, many of the assumptions made about these medals heretofore have failed to pay sufficient attention to the two entries in the inventories that follow the primary description of the Constantine and Heraclius pendants. They inform us that the duke caused to be made in gold, but not mounted or garnished with jewels, one copy each of the Constantine and Heraclius pieces. These copies, but not necessarily—in fact not even probably—the originals, were unquestionably made by one of the duke's own court artists, presumably, as we shall see, a painter-illuminator-goldsmith. Strictly speaking, we know nothing of the style of the original pieces, now lost, that he bought from the Italian merchant. We can only speak of the copies.[3] The originals could have come from anywhere, even Italy, and could have been in a quite different style, whereas the style of the copies, repeatedly reproduced in succeeding centuries, is Franco-Flemish, as has always been recognized, and is the same in both medals.

If the original Constantine "medal" was purchased at the end of 1402, but first appears, along with the Heraclius medal and

the copies, in the duke's second inventory, dated 1413, then the copies, from which we presume all later examples are derived, would have been made in the intervening period, between 1402 and 1413.[4] It is also important to note that the best surviving examples of the Constantine medal, the one from Paris exhibited here and a counterpart in the British Museum, are made of two repoussé silver shells soldered together, whereas most other examples are solid casts in silver or bronze. Repoussé is a goldsmith's technique, whereas solid casting is one more commonly employed by sculptors and medalists. We have no way of knowing what technique was employed in either the original "jewelry" or the copies the duke had made.

Because of their Franco-Flemish style, the Constantine and Heraclius medals have frequently been attributed collectively to the Limbourg brothers, Paul, Herman, and Jean, who were among the most important of the artists employed by the duke of Berry and who painted, among other masterpieces, the incomparable Très Riches Heures (Chantilly, Musée Condé; c. 1413–16). The Limbourgs incorporated figures from the two medals in a number of the illuminations in both this manuscript and the Belles Heures (New York, The Metropolitan Museum of Art, Cloisters Collection; c. 1408).[5] This borrowing, and a general correspondence in style, would tend to confirm the attribution, although close comparison of the medals and illuminations reveals certain stylistic variations that could be the result of translation from one medium to another or the collaboration of several different hands.

There is another painter, however, whose name has also been associated with the medals at times and whose authorship is just as likely. The duke's 1416 inventory includes the description of an extremely significant object: "A round gold piece of jewelry, not garnished, on which there is, on one side, an image of Our Lady holding her child and four small angels bearing a canopy, and on the other side a half-length image with the features of Monseigneur [the duke of Berry], holding a golden tablet in his hand . . . which jewel Monseigneur purchased from Michelet Saulmon, his painter."[6] Unfortunately, the reverse, or portrait, side of this object is lost, though we may have some indication of what it looked like from the duke's seals.[7] We do possess what is probably its obverse, however, in a circular plaquette in Berlin, a work that matches the inventory description exactly.[8] Since the style of this work is very close to that of the reverse of the Constantine medal, particularly in the treatment of the figures of the Virgin and the two women, we are more inclined to attribute the medals to Saulmon than to the Limbourgs, if the former not only sold the piece to the duke but also made it.

Stephen K. Scher

Artist Unknown
Constantine the Great (born 285, emperor 307–37)
1
Silver, two repoussé plates soldered together
Diameter 88 mm

Paris, Bibliothèque Nationale, Cabinet des Médailles, Frignon de Montagny Collection

Obverse: The emperor rides to the right on a stallion with a long flowing tail, the harness made up of wide, decorated bands, the saddle blanket having scalloped edges and a pebble design. Constantine holds the reins in his left hand, while with his right he gathers up the folds of his robe. He is bearded and wears a large crown made up of a coronet, within which stands a group of leaflike shapes, and strips of cloth hanging down the back. His long outer robe hangs in many folds, has a decorated border along its vertical front edges and its V-shaped collar, and half-length sleeves with long hanging ends in the back. Around the emperor's neck hangs a large cross that rests on a pleated undergarment or shirt. Legend: + CONSTANTINVS • INXRO • DEO • FIDELIS • IMPERATOR • ET • MODERATOR RO-MANORVM • ET • SEMPER • AVGVSTVS (Constantine, faithful in Christ our God, emperor and ruler of the Romans and forever exalted). In the field beneath the horse: 234.

Reverse: The center is occupied by a large fountain composed of a high, round outer basin filled with water. Within this stands a second circular enclosure upon which is carved a small, naked child, seated and facing forward, his head turned to the left. In each hand he holds by the tail a serpent which coils away from him, their mouths spouting jets of water into the outer basin. The inner enclosure contains a tall plant with long, flat leaves, from the midst of which appear stalks with flowered ends. Out

of the center of the plant rises a large cross topped by a circular finial surrounded by four bird's heads, from which water gushes down over the cross and the plant into the inner basin. A short tubular projection with a T-shaped head bent out at an angle rises up on either side of the foot of the plant. On the front of the outer basin there is an arched opening, above which a lion strides to the left. At the springing of the arch on either side is what appears to be a bird's head. Through the opening we see the columnar base of the cross with a single serpent twining around it, the head of which is visible just below the center of the arch and to the right of the column.

The fountain rests upon a platform with flat projections running out at an angle on either side. Each of these supports a bench on which is seated a female figure, one old, one young. The young woman's right leg is bent back, but her left one extends forward, long and elegant, beneath its drapery. Her foot rests on a small animal of some kind. Legend: • MIHI • ABSIT • GLORIARI • NISI • IN • CRVCE • DOMINI • NOSTRI • IHV • XRI • ("God forbid that I should glory in anything save in the Cross of our Lord Jesus Christ"). The text is from Galatians 6:14.

1a
Bronze, cast
Diameter 95 mm
New York, The Metropolitan Museum of Art, the Cloisters Collection
1988.133

1a obv.

1a rev.

Obverse and reverse as above.

The medal's obverse is quite straightforward. Constantine appears in triumph, in beautiful robes, upon his high-stepping mount, the cross prominent upon his breast. Except for his shorter beard, his appearance is much like that of Heraclius, and the inscription is an almost exact Latin counterpart to the list of titles in Greek on the latter's medal.

The number 234 appearing on the obverse of the Constantine medal, like the 235 on the reverse of some specimens, does not seem to have any iconographic significance, and has never been explained satisfactorily. To judge from their style, it would appear that these numbers were not part of the original design. None of the examples of the Heraclius medal have similar numbers.

Most puzzling in the Constantine medal is its reverse. In the center is the True Cross as part of the Fountain of Life (*fons vitae*) rising from the Tree of Life (*lignum vitae*). The major theme of the *Adoratio Crucis* of Good Friday is the celebration of the Cross as the tree of everlasting life and salvation, and the climax of that short service is the great double hymn *Crux fidelis/Pange lingua*, which virtually describes the form of the cross on the medal. While these texts represent some of the literary tradition behind the medal's imagery, artistic precedent can be seen in early Christian and medieval mosaics, in particular the great apse mosaics of the Roman basilicas San Clemente (c. 1120–25) and San Giovanni Laterano (originally created c. 234, restored 1291). Many of the elements found in these mosaics are repeated in the medal so closely that a direct influence could be postulated.[1]

As we see through the arched opening in the basin of the fountain, the Cross triumphs over the serpent entwined around its base. This victory is underscored by the appearance of a lion, the lion of Judah, a symbol of Christ, above both the arch and the serpent.

The scene on the rim of the inner basin must represent the infant Hercules killing the serpents. Hercules is another Christ symbol, and his precocious strangling of the two snakes suggests Christ's triumph over evil. It is somewhat puzzling that water pours from the mouths of these serpents into the Fountain of Life, but perhaps this is merely a practical device with no particular meaning.

The interpretation of the figures flanking the fountain has always been difficult. They clearly present an opposing duality, and have been identified variously as Sacred and Profane Love, Human and Celestial Love, the Old and New Testaments, Church and Synagogue, Nature and Grace, Sarah and Hagar (the wives of Abraham, representing the Christian and Judaic covenants), or St. Helena and Venus.[2] None of these explanations is entirely adequate. It would help if we could identify the

2 obv.

2 rev.

animal the younger woman employs as a footrest. It may be a dog, a symbol of either fidelity (perhaps a contradiction in this case) or worldly pleasure, or possibly it is a weasel, a definite symbol of worldly pleasure in medieval bestiaries.

The birds beside each of the women have often been referred to as eagles, and to be sure they are birds of prey, for they are clearly represented in the context of falconry. Each stands upon a block or cage next to a perch. A leash hangs from the legs of the bird to the left, and though it is difficult to decipher in the best examples, it is possible that it is holding its prey or a lure beneath its right foot. It is also clear that the old woman ignores it.

On the right side, however, the jesses and swivel are quite visible in addition to the leash. The woman is holding in her right hand a very common accessory in falconry, the lure made from the parts of a bird, in this case the head and wings, used to attract and call in the bird of prey. The young woman appears to be thoroughly engaged by both the bird and the activity of falconry, which would suggest that we are to think of the two figures as Christian piety on the one hand and worldly pleasure on the other. The old woman, possibly St. Helena, the discoverer of the True Cross, would thus represent virtue, while the younger one symbolizes vain and sinful pursuits.

Stephen K. Scher

Artist Unknown
Heraclius (born c. 575, emperor of Byzantium 610–41)
2
Bronze, cast
Diameter 100 mm (95 mm excluding the rim)
Paris, Bibliothèque Nationale, Cabinet des Médailles

Obverse: Bust of the emperor facing three-quarters to the right, the face in profile. On his head is an elaborate crown composed of a circlet with points resembling fleurs-de-lis, two rows of leaflike projections with knobbed tips, and a conical center which appears to be made of cloth, like a turban. A line is visible over the brow and across the temple, and is perhaps part of the ribbon tied in a bow at the back of the crown. The emperor has long hair reaching to his shoulders, long moustaches, and a very full, luxuriant beard. He has grasped his beard with his left hand. The ends of it weave through the finely modeled fingers of his right hand, which emerges from a slit in what appears to be an outer cloak that falls in deeply-pleated folds. The sleeve of an undergarment is visible on his right wrist. Heraclius's thin and anxious face is tilted back as he gazes up at a burst of light rays extending downward from the medal's upper edge. To the left, behind his head, is the word: •ΑΠΟΛΙΝΙC • (see explanation below), and in front of him, at

35

the level of his mouth, is the legend: • ILLVMINA • VVL • TVM • TVVM • DEV[s] • (Cause thy face to shine, O Lord . . .). His bust rests upon the sickle of a waning moon, the upper and lower bevels of which continue this inscription: • SVPER • TENEB[r]AS • NOSTRAS • MILLITABOR • IN • GENTIBVS • (. . . upon our darkness; I will make war upon the heathen). The legend around the edge reads: + ΗΡΑΚΛΕΙΟC + ΕΝ + ΧΨ + ΤΨΘW + ΠΙCΤΟC + ΒΑCΙ + ΚΑΙ + ΑVΤΟ + Pω + ΝΙΚΙΤΗC + ΚΑΙ + ΑΘΛΟΘΕΤΗC + ΑΕΙ + ΑVΓVCΤΟC + (Heraclius, faithful in Christ our Lord, king and emperor of the Romans, victorious and triumphant, forever exalted).

Reverse: An elaborate four-wheeled cart moves into the field from the left, with only one full wheel and a portion of a second visible. It is drawn by three horses, their harness consisting of wide bands decorated with high raised knobs. A small bell can be seen between the front legs of the lead horse. A groom, visible to the waist and dressed in a cap and short-sleeved blouse, stands beside them, holding their reins in his left hand. We see his feet and the hem of his robe through the legs of the horse in the foreground. In his right hand he brandishes a forked whip, and his ugly, menacing face is turned toward the rear. The cart is covered with heavy drapery, which hangs from its roof and has a double window opening on the side. The emperor Heraclius, dressed as on the obverse, sits in the front of the cart on a draped bench or throne. With his right hand he gathers up his cloak, and with his left holds a small cross. Above his head is a conical canopy, from which hang curtains decorated with tiny stars. The curtains are further supported by two posts topped with finials. Above the procession four lamps hang from a pole stretched across the top of the field. Legend: + SUPER + ASPIdEM + ET + BAXILISCVM + AM-BVLAVIT + ET + CONCVLCAVIT + LEONEM + ET + dRACONEM + (He has trodden on the asp and the basilisk and trampled on the lion and the dragon). In the field: ΔΟ϶Α • ΕΝ • VΨICTIC • ΧΨ • ΤΟ ΘΨ • ΟΤΙ • ΔΙΕΡΡΙΖΕ • CΙΔΙΡΑC • ΠΙΛΑC • ΚΑΙ • ΕΛΕVΘΕ + PΨCΕ + ΑΓΙΑΝ • ΒΑCΙ • ΗΡ ΑΚΛΕ (Glory in the heavens to Christ the Lord, for Emperor Heraclius has broken through [the] iron gates and set free [the] Holy Cross).

2a
Bronze, cast
Diameter 98 mm (95 mm excluding the rim)
London, The British Museum
MO 268

Obverse and reverse as above.

Whether originally intended to be part of a set or not, there is no question that the Constantine and Heraclius medals are closely linked, both iconographically and—in their present form—stylistically.[1] If the Constantine medal represents the establishment of Christianity by the triumph of the Cross and its eventual discovery by Constantine's mother, St. Helena, the Heraclius medal recalls the recovery of that same Cross from the hands of unbelievers.

Heraclius was unquestionably one of the greatest of the Byzantine emperors, an outstanding figure in military and political history and a shining hero to medieval Christianity. In the year 614, the Persians sacked Jerusalem and carried away to Ctesiphon the most holy of relics, the True Cross. Through military and governmental reforms, Heraclius was able to place himself at the head of a large army and begin a successful campaign against the Persians. At the beginning of December 627, his forces drew up before ancient Nineveh and there delivered a blow that brought the enemy to its knees. Heraclius continued to advance during 628, but in the spring of that year the Persian king, Chosroës II, was deposed and murdered. He was succeeded by his son, Kavadh-Siroe, who quickly came to terms with Heraclius, restored to Byzantium all of its former territories, and delivered the Holy Cross into the emperor's hands. Heraclius, the savior of his faith, returned with the sacred wood to Constantinople, where he was received with wild fervor. In 630 he journeyed to Jerusalem, and on March 21 restored the Holy Cross to its rightful place.

A number of legends grew up around the heroic exploits of Heraclius. Some of these are reflected in Jacobus de Voragine's *Golden Legend*, in the text associated with the September 14 Feast of the Exaltation of the Holy Cross.[2] It is the account of Heraclius's entry into Jerusalem that concerns us here: "When he [the emperor] descended the Mount of Olives, riding upon his royal charger and arrayed in imperial splendor, and was about to enter by the gate through which Christ had gone to His Passion, suddenly the stones of the gate fell down and formed an unbroken wall against him. Then to the astonishment of all, an angel of the Lord appeared over the gate, holding a cross in his hands, and said, 'When the King of Heaven, coming up to His Passion, entered in by this gate, He came not in royal state, but riding upon a lowly ass; and thus He left an ensample of humility to his worshippers!' With these words the angel departed. Then the king burst into tears, took off his shoes, and stripped himself to his shirt, took up the Cross of the Lord and humbly carried it to the gate. Instantly the hardness of the stones felt the power of God go through them, and the gate lifted itself aloft, and left free passage to those who sought to enter."

The iconography of the Heraclius medal has been drawn from these legends and the liturgy based upon them. The obverse is ringed by the emperor's formal titles. As in the Constantine medal, they follow the formula in use in the fourteenth century. The wording of the legend, with the emperor's titles listed in the form established by the Byzantine chancellery, may reflect the visit to Paris from 1400 to 1402 of Emperor Manuel II Paleologus.

Heraclius raises his eyes imploringly to heaven, while from his lips come the words: "Illumina vultum tuum Deus." This is a modification of a line from the Introit of the September 14 liturgy, which is in turn taken from Psalm 66:2, King James version (Vulgate; 67:1). His prayer is continued on the crescent moon beneath him, which may represent either the city of Byzantium, for which it was an ancient symbol, or the unbelieving Persians, upon whom Heraclius will wage war. In either case it is darkness illuminated by the divine light.

As it stands, the word ΑΠΟΛΙΝΙϹ behind Heraclius's head is meaningless, and probably reflects an ignorance of Greek on the part of either the author of the iconography or the medalist. G. F. Hill proposed that it be read as ΑΠΟΛΕΙ ΠΕΙϹ, or "thou art waning," which would fit the context nicely.[3]

The reverse obviously illustrates the scene related above from the *Golden Legend*, or a variant of it, in which Heraclius was suddenly rendered powerless to move. Here is the rich cart (rather than a royal charger), the jeweled crown, the emperor resplendent in his robes. The horses strain forward, but are held in check by some mysterious force. The groom, whip in hand, turns back in consternation at this strange phenomenon, seeking orders from his master. The entire sequence of events, including this scene from the medal, was illustrated by the Limbourg brothers in the *Belles Heures*, created for the duke of Berry in about 1408.[4]

The legend around the border of the reverse is taken from Psalm 90:13, King James Version (Vulgate; 91:13), only the person and tense of the verbs has been changed. It is Heraclius in his triumph who has trodden upon the adder and the basil-isk, and trampled underfoot the lion and the dragon, all, in this case, symbols of evil and unbelief.

The Greek legend in the field cannot be traced to any liturgical or Biblical source, nor is it entirely clear how it should be translated, for once again it is faulty. Assuming the translation given above, the only point in need of explanation is the reference to the "iron gates." In his advance against the Persians, Heraclius was required to break through one of the several important mountain passes, called gates, leading from the coastal plains of Asia Minor to the interior. Yet the real Iron Gate was over 800 miles away, a spot of considerable strategic importance on the Danube between Belgrade and Vidin. To be sure there was a strong fortress there, but it had nothing to do with Heraclius's Persian campaigns. How could the author of the medal inscription have confused two locations so far apart? Again, the answer is provided by the *Golden Legend*: "Thereupon the emperor Heraclius gathered a mighty host, and advanced to the banks of the Danube to meet the son of Chosroës."[5] One version of the Heraclius legend apparently had it that the Persian defeat occurred on the Danube, and the author of the medal's inscription took this to mean that the emperor met the Persians at the Danubian fortress known as the Iron Gate.

Stephen K. Scher

ISOTE ARIMINENSI FORMA ET VIRTVTE ITALIE DECORI

12 obv.

Italy

FIFTEENTH CENTURY

For the convenience of the reader, the dates of religious and political leaders most frequently encountered are provided below. All other life dates appear in the text.

The Papacy

Alexander V (Pietro di Candia; born c. 1340, pontiff 1409–10)

Martin V (Oddo Colonna; born 1368, pontiff 1417–31)

Eugenius IV (Gabriele Condulmaro; born 1383, pontiff 1431–47)

Nicholas V (Tommaso Parentucelli; born 1397, pontiff 1447–55)

Calixtus III (Alfonso Borgia; born 1378, pontiff 1455–58)

Pius II (Aeneas Silvius Piccolomini; born 1405, pontiff 1458–64)

Paul II (Pietro Barbo; born 1417, pontiff 1464–71)

Sixtus IV (Francesco della Rovere; born 1414, pontiff 1471–84)

Innocent VIII (Giambattista Cibo; born 1432, pontiff 1484–92)

Alexander VI (Rodrigo Borgia, born c. 1431, pontiff 1492–1503)

Pius III (Francesco Nanni-Todeschini-Piccolomini, born 1439, pontiff 1503)

Julius II (Giuliano della Rovere, born 1443, pontiff 1503–13)

Leo X (Giovanni de' Medici; born 1475, pontiff 1513–21)

The Holy Roman Empire

Sigismund (born 1368, emperor 1411–37)

Frederick III (born 1415, emperor 1440–93)

Maximilian I (born 1459, emperor 1493–1519)

Byzantium

Manuel II Paleologus (born 1350, emperor 1391–1425)

John VIII Paleologus (born 1391, emperor 1425–48)

Constantine XI (born 1404, emperor 1448–53)

Mehmed II, "the Conqueror" (born 1430, sultan 1453–81)

France

Charles VI (born 1368, king 1380–1422)

Charles VII (born 1403, king 1422–1461)

Louis XI (born 1423, king 1461–83)

Charles VIII (born 1470, king 1483–98)

Louis XII (born 1462, king 1498–1515)

Naples

Joanna II (born 1371, queen 1414–35)

Alfonso of Aragon, "the Magnanimous" (born 1385, king 1443–58)

Ferrante I (born 1423, king 1458–94)

Ferrante II (born 1469, king 1495–96)

Ferrara

Niccolò III d'Este (born 1383, lord 1393–1441)

Leonello d'Este (born 1407, marquess 1441–50)

Borso d'Este (born 1413, marquess 1450–71, duke 1471)

Ercole I d'Este (born 1431, duke 1471–1505)

Alfonso I d'Este (born 1486, duke 1505–1534)

Florence

Cosimo de' Medici, "the Elder" (born 1389, ruled 1434–64)

Piero de' Medici (born 1416, ruled 1464–69)

Lorenzo de' Medici, "the Magnificent" (born 1449, ruled 1469–92)

Mantua

Gianfrancesco Gonzaga (born 1395, marquess 1432–44)

Lodovico Gonzaga (born 1414, marquess 1444–78)

Federigo I Gonzaga (born 1440, marquess 1478–84)

Francesco II Gonzaga (born 1466, marquess 1484–1519)

Federigo II Gonzaga (born 1500, marquess 1519–30, first duke 1530–40)

Milan

Filippo Maria Visconti (born 1392, duke 1412–47)

Francesco Sforza (born 1401, duke 1450–66)

Galeazzo Maria Sforza (born 1444, duke 1466–76)

Giangaleazzo Maria Sforza (born 1469, duke 1476–81, died 1494)

Lodovico Sforza, "il Moro" (born 1451, duke 1481–99)

Rimini, Cesena, and Fano

Carlo Malatesta (born 1368, lord of Rimini 1385–1429)

Pandolfo III Malatesta (born 1370, lord of Fano 1386–1427)

Galeotto Roberto Malatesta, "il Beato" (born 1411, lord of Rimini 1429–32)

Sigismondo Pandolfo Malatesta (born 1417, lord of Rimini and Fano 1432–68)

Domenico, "Malatesta Novello" (born 1418, lord of Cesena 1429–65)

Urbino

Guid'Antonio da Montefeltro (count 1404–43)

Oddantonio da Montefeltro (count 1443–44)

Federigo da Montefeltro (born 1422, count 1444–72, duke 1472–82)

Guidobaldo da Montefeltro (born 1472, duke 1482–97, 1503–8)

Francesco Maria della Rovere (born 1490, duke 1508–38)

Leon Battista Alberti
(1404–1472)

Widely traveled, and versed in philosophy, law, music, and mathematics, Alberti practiced as an artist, cartographer, cryptographer, and architect. No one better personifies the ideal of the Renaissance man. He designed imposing edifices for three important churches: in Rimini the Tempio Malatestiano (San Francesco; 1450), and in Mantua San Sebastiano (1460) and Sant'Andrea (1470). He also functioned as both a painter and a sculptor, but only a few pieces of his sculpture survive, so that it is difficult to evaluate his accomplishments.

Born in Genoa on Feburary 14, 1404, Leon Battista was the second illegitimate child of a banker exiled from his native Florence. He was first schooled at Padua and later attended the University of Bologna. In 1432 he secured a secretarial post with the papal Curia in Rome. This led to a generous benefice from Pope Eugenius IV, affording him the luxury of financial independence and allowing him to pursue his writing. Two years later, Alberti accompanied the pope to Florence, where he admired the city's artistic achievements and cultural ferment and befriended several of its foremost artists. As a member of the papal entourage, Alberti attended the ecumenical council of the Greek and Roman Churches in Ferrara in 1438. Pope-Hennessy has offered the suggestion that it may well have been during this visit to Ferrara that Alberti produced his relief self-portrait (cat. no. 3). If he is correct, that work may have served as a direct inspiration to Pisanello (cat. nos. 4–9). Alberti subsequently maintained a professional relationship with yet another medalist, Pisanello's successor Matteo de' Pasti (cat. nos. 11–14), collaborating with him on the execution of the Tempio Malatestiano.

Alberti's critical treatises on painting, sculpture, and architecture expressed for generations of Renaissance artists the innovative artistic principles of Filippo Brunelleschi (1377–1446), Donatello (1386–1466), Masaccio (1401–c. 1428), and their Florentine compatriots. He was the first to develop a sound critical apparatus that included a recognition of the artist's creative faculties. His *Della pittura* codified the rules for producing geometrically perceived, rational space, and using light and shade to achieve actual physical appearances. His famous *De re aedificatoria*, an architectural treatise in ten books, was completed in 1452, but the first edition of the work was only produced in 1485, long after his death. Alberti died in Rome in 1472.

Joseph R. Bliss

Leon Battista Alberti
Self-Portrait in the Roman Style
3
Bronze, cast, uniface
Oval, 201 × 135.5 mm
Washington, The National Gallery of Art, Samuel H. Kress Collection
1957.14.125

Obverse: Head of a young man, clean-shaven and with close-cropped hair, facing to the left. A loose garment encircles his neck and is knotted above his left shoulder. In the left field, at the level of the neck, is a winged eye. Along the right edge is the legend: • L[eo] • BAP[tista] • (Leon Battista). The terminal stops are in the form of eyes, while the intermediate one represents a pair of open wings(?).
Reverse: Plain.

This great work is one of the true milestones in Western art. It is the first major Renaissance revival of a Roman imperial cameo, as well as the first monumental post-classical profile portrait and the first labeled self-portrait of an artist. These latter priorities, together with its execution in bronze, make it the effective progenitor of Renaissance profile portrait medals.[1] As a uniface, portable relief, it is also the first Renaissance bronze plaquette. With its self-consciously classicizing epigraphy, costume, and meaning, it is a crucial harbinger of the antique-inspired humanism of the early Renaissance.

Following his schooling in Padua and Bologna in the 1420s, a papal appointment had enabled Alberti to spend the years 1432–34 in Rome, where he was an intimate at the court of the newly elected Pope Eugenius IV. During this period he was able to study classical antiquities at first hand, probably even in the company of Donatello (1386–1466), who also worked for the Curia in Rome in 1432–33.[2] To judge from this relief, it appears that he—or they—had access to the collections of antique coins and gems being formed by Eugenius's courtiers, above all Lodovico Scarampi, soon to become a cardinal and appointed patriarch of Aquileia in the later 1430s, and his colleague Pietro Barbo, the future Pope Paul II.

Donatello returned to Tuscany in 1433, Alberti in 1434. The former promptly distilled his Roman experience in the classicizing friezes of the Prato Pulpit and the Cantoria in Florence. Apropos the present bronze, it is especially significant that Donatello added to the marble and mosaic ensemble of the latter work two frontal, high-relief bronze heads of antique sages, presumably representing the humanist ratiocinations of ancient philosophers, their reveries interrupted by the joyful noise of the coming of the Lord.[3]

In precisely analogous fashion, Alberti's relief self-portrait—conventionally dated to 1434–36, as he appears to be at most in his early thirties and was at that time back in Florence, again alongside Donatello—transforms a classical prototype into the proudly confident image of an individual Renaissance man as master of the perceptible universe. The closest antique parallel for it is the British Museum's noble cameo portrait of Augustus, appropriated with a "rebaptism" and the addition of a new diadem by Constantine the Great.[4] That work—or others like it—provided a precedent for the size, shape, relief handling, costume, and iconography of Alberti's creation. The key to Alberti's extraordinary appropriation of imperial preeminence in this deliberate revival of the character of Augustan cameo reliefs is his invented hieroglyph of the "winged eye," repeated three times on the plaque itself and also used, enlarged, as the

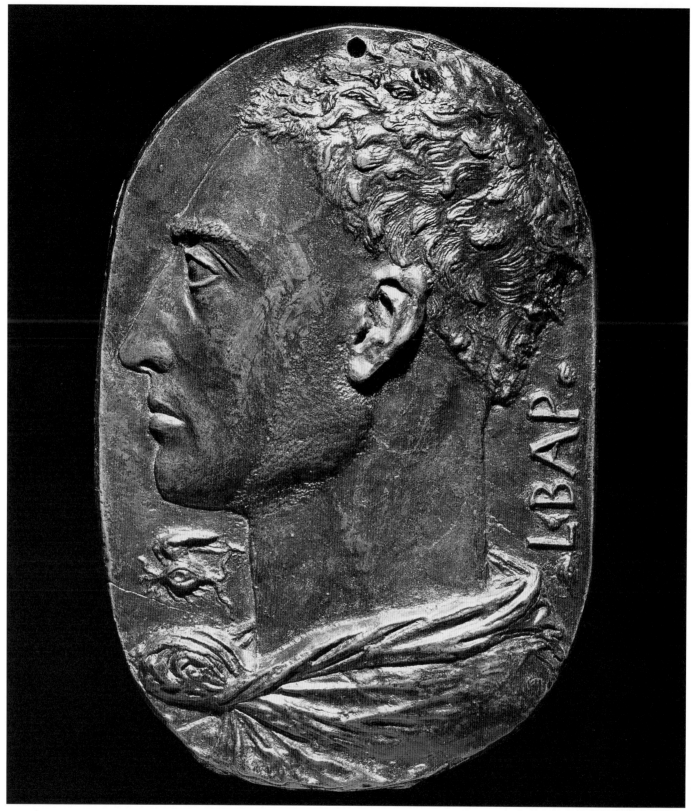

3 obv.

reverse *impresa* on the medal his fellow sculptor Matteo de' Pasti created of him.[5]

In this emblem a human eye—understood by association to be the artist's own—is borne aloft by the wings of a raptor, a falcon or an eagle, to a height from which the entire universe is visible. The eye not only sees all, it is also all-powerful, for the thunderbolts of Jupiter are grafted onto its ends. Through his art, the new, all-seeing, humanist artist wields a potentially godlike power. That such lofty ambition may indeed be accomplished in the revived classical culture of the modern world is

42

attested by the laurel wreath of achievement surrounding the hieroglyph on Matteo's medal of Alberti.[6] Metaphorically, at least, the inspired Renaissance artist can rival even an Augustus in his dominion over all the known world, and still ask, like Alexander, for new worlds to conquer. Linked to the emblem on the medallic reverse is the motto QUID TUM—what then, or what next?—implying that there is nothing that cannot be imagined or attempted.

It is difficult to identify any other object that encapsulates as perfectly as this one the full meaning of the classical *rinovatio* of the Florentine fifteenth century. That a young artist should have appropriated the style of Roman imperial portraits for a naturalistic portrait of himself is extraordinary enough. For him to have claimed, moreover, that as a creative artist he wielded a power comparable to that of the greatest of the emperors is virtually miraculous. This icon from the dawn of the Renaissance has lost none of its radiance through the intervening centuries, rooted as they are in that pioneering moment and deriving as they do so much of their vitality from its confident exaltation of human genius.

Douglas Lewis

Antonio di Puccio (Pisano) called Pisanello
(c. 1395–1455)

Pisanello was probably born in Pisa around 1385, the son of a native of that city, Puccio di Giovanni di Cereto, and his wife Isabetta di Nicolo, from Verona. It appears that the artist's father died when he was still an infant, for in 1404 his mother married another Pisan, Bartolommeo da Pisa, and moved to Verona, which would become Pisanello's official residence and that of his family for the rest of his life, despite his constant movement from one court or city to another.[1] He was trained within the North Italian schools of painting, blending Tuscan elements with local variations of the International Gothic style. Pisanello was also exposed to the newer art and ideas eagerly nurtured within the courts where he worked.

Some hint of the possibility that he was given a humanist education is contained in a reference from 1416 to the effect that the young Pisanello carried from Padua to Venice a manuscript belonging to the great humanist Guarino da Verona (cat. no. 11).[2] Around the same time he was possibly engaged in the painted decoration of the Sala del Gran Consiglio of the Doge's Palace in Venice.[3] In 1422, Pisanello purchased a house in Verona, but also established residence in Mantua, where he was employed in 1425 and 1426 by the youthful Lodovico Gonzaga and in the latter part of the decade by the duke of Milan, Filippo Maria Visconti.[4]

By this time there is no doubt that the painter was fully matured and had gained a considerable reputation. In a document dated 1424, he is referred to as "pictor egregius" (distinguished painter).[5] Unfortunately little remains to us that is generally accepted as being from his hand. The signed *Annunciation* fresco above the tomb monument of Niccolò Brenzoni in

the church of San Fermo Maggiore, Verona, dated around 1426, is the earliest surviving work documented as his.

Pisanello's movements during the 1430s are extremely difficult to trace. In 1431 he was in Rome, having been engaged by the Venetian Pope Eugenius IV to complete the fresco cycle on the life of St. John the Baptist in St. John Lateran begun by Gentile da Fabriano, but left unfinished on his death in 1427. Like his earlier frescoes in Venice, these too were later destroyed. While in Rome, Pisanello inevitably studied the remains of ancient sculpture, although most of the drawings of these subjects once attributed to him have now been assigned to his followers.

Though he is difficult to trace in this decade, we know that this was an extremely important period in his career, and that he divided most of his time between the courts of the Gonzaga in Mantua and the Este in Ferrara, at the latter establishing a close relationship not only with Leonello d'Este (cat. no. 5) but also with the brilliant group of humanists gathered at his court. He also continued to be active in Verona, where he produced perhaps his most famous surviving work, outside of his medals, the fresco *St. George and the Princess of Trebizond* in the church of Sant' Anastasia, dated to the mid or late 1430s.

From this period we also encounter an example of Pisanello's celebrated skill as a portrait painter in the panel, now in the Louvre, depicting Ginevra d'Este (1419–1440) and dated to c. 1433–34.[6] Several years later, in 1441, Pisanello was to enter into a competition with Jacopo Bellini (1400–1471) for a portrait of Ginevra's brother, Leonello d'Este. Bellini was victorious, but only Pisanello's contribution appears to have survived, if indeed it is the picture that now hangs in the Accademia Carrara in Bergamo.

Pisanello was in Ferrara in 1438, where he witnessed the arrival of the Byzantine emperor John VIII Paleologus and his large retinue. Fascinated by the costumes and accoutrements of the visitors, he made several sketches.[7] From these, and for reasons that can only be conjectured, the artist then created a circular, cast commemorative relief with a portrait of the emperor on one side and a narrative scene on the reverse. Thus was born the first true Renaissance portrait medal (cat. no. 4).

From the same period, that is c. 1436–38, there survives another of the paintings generally attributed to Pisanello, the *Vision of St. Eustace* in the National Gallery, London. In Pisanello's only signed panel painting, the *Apparition of the Virgin with Saints Anthony and George*, also in the National Gallery, London, and dated c. 1445, the artist appears to have reached a new level of accomplishment.

During the 1440s, Pisanello continued to work mainly in Ferrara and Mantua. In the latter city, probably around 1447–48, he began, but never finished, the decoration of a room in the ducal palace with frescoes depicting scenes from an Arthurian romance.[8] These paintings were rediscovered in the 1960s and have added much valuable material to our meager knowledge of Pisanello's development as a painter.

The great success of the painter's first medal is clear from the steady flow of commissions that followed. Around 1441 he produced medals for Filippo Maria Visconti; one of Filippo's *condottieri*, Niccolò Piccinino (c. 1386–1444); and his adversary and eventual successor, Francesco Sforza.[9] These three names, and that of another of the sometime Visconti generals, Gianfrancesco Gonzaga, marquess of Mantua, have a special significance for the artist at this moment.[10]

Apparently, despite his wanderings, Pisanello preserved a constant loyalty to Verona, which in 1405 had passed from Milanese to Venetian overlordship—to the evident dismay of many of its citizens. In mid November 1439, during the course of hostilities between Milan and Venice in which Sforza captained the armies of the Maritime Republic while Piccinino and Gonzaga headed the Milanese troops, the latter captured and sacked Verona. Three days later the Venetian forces reoccupied the town, and their investigation of the incident determined that Pisanello had sided with the Gonzaga faction of the Milanese army. Since Pisanello was in Mantua during this period, but continued to visit Verona, he found himself in serious trouble with the Venetian authorities, who considered all Veronese in Mantua disloyal and referred to him as "Pisan the painter, a rebel." In 1441 and 1442, Pisanello was threatened with confiscation of his property in Verona, and at one point, for alleged slanders against Venice, was condemned to have his tongue ceremonially cut out in the Piazza San Marco, a sentence that was immediately reversed in favor of simple confinement to that city.[11]

It is a measure of Pisanello's importance and influence that he was ultimately released from all punishment and allowed to continue his work in Ferrara, where he stayed until 1448. At this time (c. 1443) he made roughly eight small (69 mm) medals for Leonello d'Este, with abstruse allegorical reverses reflecting the intellectual sophistication of Leonello's court.[12] The following year, in celebration of the marquess's second marriage, to Maria of Aragon, the artist produced a large medal (103 mm) with the famous reverse of Amor teaching a lion to sing (cat. no. 5).

The popularity of this new form continued to grow, as evidenced by the series of medals commissioned from Pisanello between 1445 and 1448. In 1444 and 1445 the Malatesta brothers, Sigismondo and Domenico, sought this particular form of immortality in three medals. One of the Sigismondo portraits is dated 1445; that of Domenico is one of the most sensitive and attractive of all Pisanello's creations (cat. no. 6). The Gonzagas, longtime patrons of the artist, were not to be left behind. Around 1446–48 the artist produced medals of Gianfrancesco, his son Lodovico, and his daughter Cecilia (cat. no. 7).[13] Prominent humanists, scholars, and educators attached to the two courts, such as Vittorino da Feltre (cat. no. 8), Belloto Cumano, and Pier Candida Decembrio (1392–1477), were also similarly honored.[14]

At the end of 1448, possibly thanks to his contact with the Aragonese entourage of Leonello d'Este's new wife, Pisanello received a summons from Alfonso of Aragon, the king of Naples (cat. no. 35).[15] Nothing remains of Pisanello's activities during this period except for three medals of Alfonso, one of them dated 1449, and the incomparable medal of Alfonso's grand chamberlain, Don Iñigo de Avalos (cat. no. 9).

After 1450 there is no further documentary mention of Pisanello, but he must have died between July 14 and October 31, 1455, possibly in Rome.[16] During his lifetime, and immediately after his death, he was often singled out for lavish praise by many of the leading humanists of the fifteenth century.[17] For contemporaries, obsessed with the concept of fame and the immortality it brought, he had invented an indestructible form that guaranteed both. Yet he was primarily lauded as a painter, and it was as such that he modeled his medals and signed them: OPVS PISANI PICTORIS.

Few would deny that in addition to achieving fame as the virtual creator of the portrait medal, Pisanello has never been displaced as the greatest of all medalists in any period. He produced some twenty-six medals over a period of ten years. Only the very best surviving specimens of them preserve the extraordinary subtlety of modeling, the remarkable sensitivity of the portrait, and the fineness of line in the profile. Working within the demanding confines of a small circle, Pisanello maintained a careful balance between the portrait, the field, and the lettering, which is clearly modeled on classical forms, adding greatly to the confident dignity of the portrait.

In his reverses, he uses in some cases the vocabulary we can see in his paintings and drawings: knights in armor, horses turned at various angles to define a shallow and ambiguous space, and birds and other animals that now have a specific, symbolic meaning. But he also introduces a new and extremely important element. From his contacts with the exciting revival of classical art and literature in various humanist courts and from his sojourns in Rome, Pisanello has recognized his role as heir to the forms and implications of ancient coinage, in which he seems to have had a personal interest as a collector.[18] This is particularly evident in the medals produced for Leonello d'Este and in the remarkable medal of Cecilia Gonzaga, where the artist has introduced naked or near-naked human figures *all'antica*. We see the sources of these figures in his drawings, but it was for a particular patron and for a special type of object that he used them, and it was in this mode of expression that he had himself invented that Pisanello truly became a Renaissance artist.[19]

Stephen K. Scher

Pisanello
John VIII Paleologus (born 1392, emperor of Byzantium 1423–48)
4
Bronze, cast
Diameter 103.6 mm
Berlin, Staatliche Museen, Münzkabinett, formerly Benoni Friedlaender Collection, 1868

Obverse: Bust to right with moustache, sharply pointed beard, and long spiral curls emerging from beneath a hat with a tall, conical crown and high, upturned brim, pointed at the front.

4 obv.

4 rev.

The emperor wears a light jacket open in front over a high-collared shirt. Legend: + IωANNHC • BACIΛEVC • KAI • AVTO • KPATωP • PωMAIωN • Ο • ΠΑΛΑΙΟΛΟΓΟC • (John, king and emperor of the Romans, the Paleologus).

Reverse: In the foreground of a rocky landscape, the emperor on horseback and in hunting garb, with a bow and quiver of arrows. He has halted to pray, facing right in profile, before a wayside cross. On the left, seen from the rear, is a page, also on horseback. At the top, the inscription: • OPVS • PISANI • PICTORIS • (The work of Pisano the painter). At the bottom, the same inscription in Greek: EPΓON • TOV • ΠICANOV • ZωΓPAΦON.

4a
Lead, cast
Diameter 101.4 mm; diameter of the outer perimeter of the inscription from the C in IωANNHC to the first ω in PωMAIωN, 95.5 mm
New York, Michael Hall Collection

Obverse and reverse as above.

Pisanello's medal of John VIII Paleologus may be considered the first true portrait medal of the Renaissance, the progenitor of all subsequent medals and therefore of immense importance. Although a number of Pisanello's medals are lost, including,

perhaps, one that may have predated the Paleologus, it is fitting that this medal should be the point of departure.[1] It is an extraordinary synthesis of a number of diverse elements, yet an entirely new concept in the hands of an artist who, though essentially old-fashioned, found himself working in the midst of an intellectual, artistic, and cultural revolution.

It is ironic that this medal, which represents so significant a beginning, commemorates an individual who signifies a conclusion. John VIII Paleologus was the penultimate Byzantine emperor, and was thus in a sense the last ruler, but one, of the old Roman empire. By John's time, what had once been a mighty power, controlling a large portion of the known world, had shrunk to a small and fragile entity comprising little more than the city of Constantinople and several outlying territories in the hands of petty princes who constantly challenged imperial authority.

His major adversary, however, was the Turk, who had effectively conquered most of what had been the Byzantine empire and who, in 1453, would finally end its history by taking Constantinople from John's successor, Constantine XI.

John had received the imperial crown from his father, Manuel II. After having ruled successfully for thirty-two years, Manuel suffered a stroke and retired to a monastery, where he died on July 21, 1425. The new emperor was an experienced soldier, and a man dedicated to the outdoor life. His primary passions were riding and hunting, although he is reported to have been very fond of music as well.[2] To preserve his house and the lands it ruled, John had to find some way to meet the menace of the Turks, and this could be done only with help from the West. Such help had been sought in vain for almost four hundred years, and when John himself journeyed to Venice, Milan, Mantua, and the court of the Holy Roman Emperor Sigismund in 1423, he encountered consistent refusal of his appeals.

One of the key issues in the repeated attempts to effect a reconciliation between the Eastern and Western empires and construct a bastion against Islam was the possibility of a union between the Roman Catholic and Greek Orthodox churches. Perhaps John was encouraged by developments in the Roman Church. Pope Eugenius IV was having problems with the churchmen who had convened the Council of Basel (1431–49) with a desire to democratize the Church. If Eugenius could bring about a successful union with the Eastern church, it would enhance his prestige greatly and counter the activities of the insubordinate fathers attending the council. They, in turn, were also courting the emperor for the same reasons.

Having convened a council in Ferrara to deal with other problems of the Church as well as the question of union, Eugenius invited the Byzantine emperor to attend, foolishly offering to pay the expenses of his delegation, which eventually numbered 700. John accepted and left Constantinople in November 1437. After repeated delays caused by poor weather, seasickness, and the emperor's crippling arthritis, the delegation arrived in Venice in February 1438.

The council finally convened in Ferrara on October 8, 1438.[3] Its opening had been repeatedly postponed in order to allow time for representatives from the major European powers to make their appearance. There was, in fact, little interest in the rest of Europe in supporting what was clearly perceived as a lost cause. As it happened, Ferrara soon experienced an outbreak of the plague, and on receiving an invitation from Florence, the council chose to remove to that city in February of 1439. There the various points of theology that had been in contention were resolved. Unification seemed possible, and John could feel some confidence that help would be offered to him against the Turks. Returning to Constantinople early in February 1440, however, he found that, as he had been warned, his own subjects considered the notion of a reconciliation between the two churches unacceptable and proceeded to riot.

By the end of his long reign, John VIII Paleologus was a broken man. He died on October 31, 1448, and because of his perceived betrayal of his religion, was refused the funeral rites of the Orthodox church.

If John gained little of value from his trip to Italy, that country benefited greatly. Among his delegation were scholars and men of letters delighted to find themselves in an environment conducive to new ideas and reverent of the ancient past. The Greeks were welcomed enthusiastically and encouraged to stay, thus accelerating the revival of Greek studies in Renaissance Europe.

Pisanello, working in Ferrara for Leonello d'Este (cat. no. 5), watched the arrival of the Byzantine emperor and his entourage, and was clearly fascinated by the exotic appearance of many of the visitors, as we learn from several of his drawings and details of his paintings. Among his drawings we find material from which he drew for his reverse of the present medal and perhaps even for the portrait,[4] yet just how he conceived the idea of producing the work is a puzzle.

There is the tantalizing possibility that others may have participated in his design of the new form. Leonello d'Este was dedicated to humanist studies and the revival of antiquity, and made of his court a center of such activities. Although in 1438 he was only heir apparent to the marquisate, he and his family would have joined the pope in hosting the visiting Byzantine delegation, and he would have had an interest in commemorating the emperor's visit in a fashion similar to that chosen by the ancient Romans in their coinage.

Even more important, Leon Battista Alberti also happened to be in Ferrara as a member of the papal Curia. Highly significant here is the survival of his self-portrait *all'antica*, in a bronze relief (cat. no. 3). It is tempting to think that the spiritual father of the medallic form as it came to life in the hands of Pisanello was actually Alberti, who may have recognized the opportunity presented by the presence of the Byzantine emperor in Ferrara to continue the tradition of representing a Roman emperor on an imperishable, coinlike object. It would have been natural for him to consult with one of the most famous portraitists in Italy, also present in Ferrara, to realize his idea in tangible form, perhaps under the patronage of Leonello d'Este, the result being the first medal.[5]

The extent of Pisanello's talent is clearly evident in this medal. His first known effort in the form, it achieves a measured nobility in the lettering, a balance of proportions in the obverse composition, sensitivity and character in the portrait, subtle delicacy in the modeling of drapery, and control of the relief. On the reverse, the artist has with some difficulty attempted to include several large elements in a very small space, yet his suggestion of depth through the device of the foreshortened page on horseback perpendicular to the full figure of the emperor in profile, though somewhat awkward, is nonetheless successful. Of particular note is the intrusion of the ear of the page's horse across the border of the medal, creating a strange ambiguity that at the same time diminishes the assertion of the two-dimensional surface. This detail and the entire handling of the reverse indicate undeniably the hand of a painter, which is left in no doubt by the signature.[6]

The medal presents no iconographic mysteries, but associates with the portrait some of John's salient interests, riding and hunting, and by showing him at prayer suggests the purpose of his visit to Ferrara.

One cannot overestimate the influence exercised by this medal, not only on the proliferation of the form itself, but on other mediums. The portrait of the emperor was used frequently in sculpture, painting, and engraving, and adapted to many purposes—in one instance, ironically enough, serving as the likeness of a Turkish sultan.[7]

Stephen K. Scher

Pisanello
Leonello d'Este (born 1407, marquess of Ferrara 1441–50)
5
Lead, cast
Diameter 103 mm; height of bust through center line, 70.7 mm
Berlin, Staatliche Museen, Münzkabinett, formerly Benoni Friedlaender Collection, 1868

Obverse: Bust of Leonello to the left wearing a richly embroidered *giornea*. Legend: (top) • GE[ner] • R[egis] • AR[agonum] • (Son-in-law of the king of Aragon); (two lines flanking the bust)· • LEONELLVS • MARCHIO • ESTENSIS • (Leonello Marquess d'Este); (bottom) • D[ominus] • FERRARIE • REGII • ET • MVTINE • (Lord of Ferrara, Reggio, and Modena).
Reverse: In a rocky landscape a lion stands facing right before a winged genius of Love (Amor), who is holding a scroll of music. Behind the lion's head is a stele with one of Leonello's devices, a mast with billowing sail set into a piece of earth. Beneath the device is the date • M • CCCC XLIIII. In the left background is a rocky hill from which protrudes a bare tree branch. An eagle is perched on the branch, its back to the viewer. To the right of the stele is the legend: • OPVS • PISANI • PICTORIS • (The work of Pisano the painter).

5a
Bronze, cast
Diameter 100.5 mm; height of bust through center line, 69.5 mm

Washington, The National Gallery of Art, Samuel H. Kress Collection
1957.14.602

Obverse and reverse as above.

Leonello d'Este probably provided Pisanello with his most stimulating and intellectually challenging environment. All contemporary accounts agree that he was an ideal ruler, a perfect prince: wise, gentle, learned, just, pious, unpretentious.[1] Leonello was given a careful training in both the traditional disciplines and military skills, but his education took an important turn when the great humanist Guarino da Verona (cat. no. 11) arrived in Ferrara in 1429 to create, with the humanists already in residence, a school on the order of the one established in Mantua in 1423 by Vittorino da Feltre (cat. no. 8).

With this background and his own intense interest in the new learning, Leonello came the closest of any Renaissance prince to Plato's vision of the philosopher king. He was not merely a fashionable humanist, but a true intellectual; not a self-indulgent dilettante, but a passionate lover of literature and, secondarily, the visual arts. It is tragic that so gifted and effective a ruler should have died so young.

As a scion of the ancient house of Este with an hereditary title, Leonello had none of the concerns and desires of Sigismondo Malatesta (cat. no. 14), who so desperately tried to acquire the security and status of his brother-in-law in Ferrara,

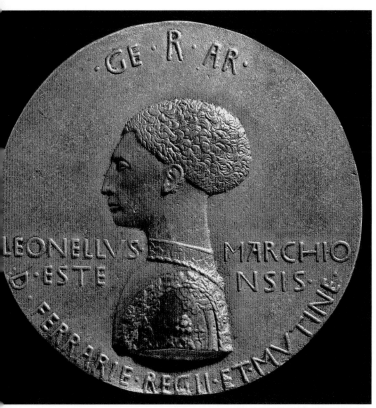

5a obv.

5a rev.

5a rev.

6 rev.

and this is evident in the medals produced for them. Leonello delighted in pairing with his portraits obscure and complicated images, rich in symbolism and in allusions to classical art and learning. His intent was to distribute such medals to those who would understand them, a cultural elite proud of its learning and insulated from the outside world. Leonello's medals were part of a sophisticated dialogue; Sigismondo's a kind of public relations campaign.

Leonello was the embodiment of *virtù* and *grazia*, qualities highly valued in the Renaissance. The bastard son of Niccolò III and a Sienese lady, Stella dell'Assassino, he was legitimated in 1429 by Pope Martin V, and when his notoriously promiscuous father married for the third time, in 1431, part of the marriage contract stipulated that Leonello would inherit the title even if the marriage produced sons. In 1435, Leonello had taken as his first wife the seventeen-year-old Margherita Gonzaga, a learned princess trained in the Mantuan school of Vittorino da Feltre. Though Margherita died in 1439, he did not marry again until 1444; this time his bride was Maria of Aragon, a natural daughter of King Alfonso of Naples (cat. no. 35). It was for this occasion that Pisanello was called upon to fashion the medal under discussion here.

If the artist responded in his other medals of Leonello to his patron's taste in abstruse images,[2] in this case both seem to have decided to introduce a certain amount of whimsy, making this medal one of the most charming and delightful of any produced in the Renaissance. The symbolism is quite straightforward. Love, in the form of Cupid, is teaching the lion (Leonello) to sing. The lion's actual family ties seem to be indicated by the eagle, the heraldic charge of the Este, perched upon a bare branch.

The inclusion of the emblem of the billowing sail attached to a mast or column adds further depth to our understanding of the character and intentions of the medal's patron. The image appears to allude to Leonello's steadfastness in the face of the buffeting winds of life, but Edgar Wind has suggested that it was also one among the many ways chosen to represent a favorite Renaissance concept drawn from antiquity, namely *festina lente*, or "make haste slowly." It was held that one ought to proceed through life with determination and energy tempered with caution and prudence.[3]

In this, as in almost all of his medals, Pisanello reveals his genius in both his composition and in the subtle variations of the planes and surfaces of his delicate reliefs. By putting the lion's tail between his legs, for example, the artist is able to solve a difficult compositional problem within the restrictions of his space, and at the same time convey the lion's total and altogether willing subjugation to the power of love.

It is apt that music was chosen to illustrate such surrender, for Leonello was an accomplished and enthusiastic musician. This would suggest that the prince himself devised the imagery for the medal and for his other commissions to the artist.

Stephen K. Scher

Pisanello
Domenico Malatesta, called Malatesta Novello (born 1418, lord of Cesena 1429–65)
6
Bronze, cast
Diameter 85.7 mm; height of bust on center line, 67.8 mm
Washington, The National Gallery of Art, Samuel H. Kress Collection
1957.14.607

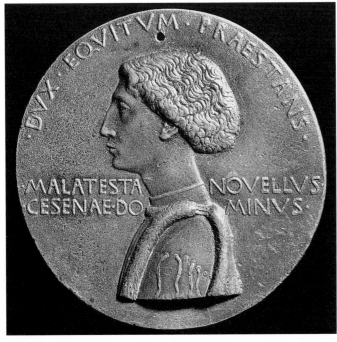

6 obv.

6 rev.

Obverse: Bust of Domenico to the left, wearing a fur-edged tunic or *giornea* over a high-necked shirt (*camicia*). Legend: (across the field on either side of the bust) • MALATESTA NOVELLVS • • CESENA • DOMINVS • (Malatesta Novello, lord of Cesena); (above this) • DVX • EQUITVM • PRAESTANS • (Superior leader of knights).

Reverse: In a rocky landscape, a figure in full armor is kneeling and embracing the foot of a crucifix. To the left, a horse seen from the rear in foreshortened perspective is tied to a barren tree. To the right, a small leafless tree grows from rocks. Legend: • OPVS • PISANI • PICTORIS • (The work of Pisano the painter).

6a
Lead, cast
Diameter 85.3 mm; height of bust on center line 67.5 mm
New York, private collection

Obverse and reverse as above.

Historically, Domenico Malatesta has lived in the shadow of his older brother Sigismondo (cat. no. 14), and it is true that in contrast to his brother, Domenico appears to have been a quiet, prudent, retiring person, studious and given to sedentary pursuits.[1]

Domenico, born in Brescia in 1418, was the third illegitimate son of Pandolfo III Malatesta, who had no surviving legitimate children. Domenico and Sigismondo were raised in the household of Pandolfo's brother Carlo and his wife, Elisabetta Gonzaga (m. 1389), who were also without legitimate heirs. Pandolfo had been a brilliant *condottiere*, while Carlo had ruled the city of Rimini as papal vicar with great success. Between them they had established the Malatesta name as a force to be reckoned with not only in Italy, but internationally. In 1428, Sigismondo, Domenico, and their eldest brother Galeotto Roberto were legitimated by Pope Martin V, which made them eligible to succeed to the Malatesta lands upon Carlo's death in 1429. Despite attempts to deprive the brothers of their inheritance, they managed to remain in power with the support of their subjects. Galeotto Roberto, an extremely pious man who was eventually beatified, became ruler of Rimini until his death three years later, at which time he was succeeded by Sigismondo. The latter, originally given the territory of Fano, was now ruler not only of Rimini, but also of the lands south of the Marecchia. Domenico, who had received Cesena, Bertinoro, Meldola, and Sarsina, was made lord of the lands north of the Marecchia, and was also entrusted by Sigismondo with the governance of Fano in the 1430s.[2]

In 1435, Pope Eugenius IV arranged a marriage between Domenico and Violante da Montefeltro, daughter of Guid'Antonio, count of Urbino, in order to ensure peace between that city and Rimini. Violante was only a child at the time; the actual wedding took place much later. She had taken a vow of chastity with the intention of entering orders, and although she was relieved of her vow by the pope, she remained chaste even after marriage and lived a saintly life. After Domenico's death she entered a convent in Ferrara, where she died as a result of the extremes of religious mortification she imposed upon herself.

In September 1433, on his return to Hungary after his coronation in Rome, the emperor Sigismond visited Rimini and knighted Sigismondo and Domenico. Since the ceremony of knighthood allowed a change of name, Domenico chose to be called henceforth Malatesta Novello, or Malatesta the Younger.

As a humanist prince, Malatesta Novello focused his attention on literary studies, in particular poetry. One of his most important activities was his support of the Biblioteca Malatestiana in Cesena, which included an important scriptorium in which many fine illuminated manuscripts were produced.

Though of a pacific nature, Domenico could not avoid becoming embroiled in the endless military activities that plagued Italy at this time. He was appointed a captain of papal troops and at the age of seventeen fought under the command of the illustrious general Francesco Sforza. The incident that appears to be the basis for Pisanello's medal occurred in the course of his military career. At the battle of Montolmo in 1444, Malatesta, now in opposition to Sforza, found himself in danger of being captured. He is said to have vowed that if he escaped he would build a hospital dedicated to the Holy Crucifix, an oath he finally fulfilled in 1452.

Pisanello's moving reverse, probably done around 1444–45, at the same time as his medals of Sigismondo,[3] shows Domenico in full armor on his knees, grasping the base of a crucifix and presumably making his vow. As in many of his other medals,[4] the artist defines a sort of L-shaped space of foreground and recession with the device of the foreshortened horse, in this case seen from the rear and tied to a tree set back in a somewhat ambiguous middle ground. Further articulation of space is achieved by turning the horse's head slightly, so that one sees a portion of his left eye beyond the edge of the saddle. Pisanello's genius in manipulating space through shallow relief and foreshortening is best seen here in the transition from the highest surfaces of the armor and the rump of the horse, which connect the viewer's space with that of the medal, to the angled crucifix and receding ground and rocks, and finally back to the empty field.

Although there appear to be no drawings from the hand of Pisanello that can be considered direct precursors of the Malatesta Novello medal, there are two of his numerous studies of horses that are closely related. There is also a sheet of sketches of the Crucifixion, several portions of which bear a definite resemblance to the one on the medal.[5]

As a result of bungled surgery on varicose veins combined with old battle wounds, Malatesta Novello became lame after 1447. From this time on he devoted himself to his beloved studies, to collecting books, and to constant communication with writers, humanists, historians, scholars, and other princely collectors. He was honored among this distinguished company and maintained with them a steady correspondence. In some ways he resembles Leonello d'Este of Ferrara, who had a similar character and interests.

In the end, however, he could not escape the consequences of his brother's unsuccessful struggle against the Holy See. By the time he died he had lost most of his territories and been forced into total submission to Pope Pius II, who had so bitterly castigated Sigismondo and darkened the Malatesta name for centuries to come.

Stephen K. Scher

Pisanello
Cecilia Gonzaga (1426–1451)
7
Bronze, cast
Diameter 87 mm; height of bust at center line, 72.0 mm
Paris, Bibliothèque Nationale, Cabinet des Médailles
Ital. 572.15

Obverse: Half-length bust of Cecilia, her hair tightly bound with a ribbon, wearing an embroidered gown with a tight bodice, pleated skirt, and full sleeves. Legend: CICILIA • VIRGO • FILIA • IOHANNIS • FRANCISCI • PRIMI • MARCHIONIS • MANTVE (Maiden Cecilia, daughter of Gianfrancesco first marquess of Mantua).
Reverse: In a rocky landscape, a half-naked young woman sits facing left, her left hand placed on the head of a reclining goatlike unicorn, whose head rests in her lap. Behind, to the right, a stele with a floral ornament fixed to the top and bearing the inscription: OPVS PISANI • PICTORIS • M CCCC XLVII • (The work of Pisano the painter. 1447). In the sky a crescent moon.

7a
Bronze, cast
Diameter 85.78 mm; height of bust at center line, 72.5 mm
New York, Michael Hall Collection

Obverse and reverse as above.

Born in 1426 to Gianfrancesco Gonzaga and Paola Malatesta (1393–1453), Cecilia Gonzaga became, in her short life, an accomplished classical scholar and one of the most learned young persons in Italy, although she left behind no published work. She had mastered Greek by the age of seven and was a star pupil in the famous school founded in Mantua in 1423 by Vittorino da Feltre (cat. no. 8).

The young Gonzaga princess had resolved to retire to a convent in order to pursue her studies without the interference of marriage, but met with the angry opposition of her father, who had contracted a match for her with Oddantonio da Montefeltro of Urbino, a depraved monster whose excesses eventually led to his assassination in 1444.

Cecilia's obstinate refusal to deviate from her chosen path was aided by the persuasive arguments of Vittorino, who pointed out that "perserverance and strength in a girl [is] not without the special disposition of heaven; to counter it would be prideful and impious."[1] In the end, Gianfrancesco relented

7a obv.

7a rev.

and cancelled the marriage contract. After her father's death in February 1445, Cecilia became a Clarissan nun at Santa Paola, the convent attached to the church of Corpus Domini in Mantua, and was joined there by her mother.[2]

Her medallic portrait seems to confirm a contemporary report that she was tall and beautiful.[3] By the date on the reverse, she would already have been a nun for two years, yet Pisanello chose to represent her in secular court dress, suggesting that he was working from an earlier portrait or study from life, merely indicating in the inscription her status as a *virgo*.

What is stated verbally on the obverse is indicated in a far more poetic and meaningful way on the reverse. The half-naked maiden represents innocence and chastity, and according to medieval lore it is only a woman with such virtues who can subdue the fierce and immortal unicorn—in such a context, a symbol of Christ. On a further level of meaning Pisanello has chosen to present the unicorn in the form of a goat, a symbol of knowledge, thus alluding to still another of Cecilia's qualities. This tranquil, haunting scene is set in the barren and rocky landscape so common to Pisanello's medals, and its mystery is enhanced by the appearance of a crescent moon, also a symbol of chastity.

We have described the most immediate content, but is it possible that the medieval sources for much of the imagery may also be amplified by classical allusions to the purity of the goddess Diana through the half-naked female figure and the crescent moon? Or did Pisanello have some contact with a copy of the Constantine medal from the collections of the duke of Berry (cat. no. 1), appropriating the half-clad figure of a young woman seated beside the Fountain of Life on its reverse?

There is only one drawing related to this medal that is securely attributed to Pisanello. It is a study of a goat, probably drawn from life, in the *Codex Vallardi*. Fossi Todorow and others believe that it was made around the time of the Sant' Anastasia frescoes (mid to late 1430s) and used as the basis for the reclining goat in the right foreground of the scene with St. George and the princess.[4] If this theory is acceptable, Pisanello would have returned to the drawing a decade later as a source for the unicorn-goat on the medal of Cecilia Gonzaga.

Among the drawings sometimes attributed to Pisanello or his circle are several that show figures obviously based on Roman sarcophagi, including lightly draped females that could have been a source for the personification of Innocence on the reverse of this medal. If by Pisanello or copied after him, the drawings would have been done during his early sojourn in Rome, c. 1431–32, but the connections are very tenuous.[5] At best they indicate an interest in collecting a vocabulary of ancient forms to be used in medals such as this one and the series made for Leonello d'Este.

Stephen K. Scher

Pisanello
Vittorino Rambaldoni da Feltre (1378–1446)
8
Bronze, cast
Diameter 67.3 mm; diameter of the outer perimeter of the inscription from the I in VICTORINVS to the first S in SVMMVS, 63.5 mm
University of California at Santa Barbara, University Art Museum, Sigmund Morgenroth Collection
1964.203

Obverse: Bust of Vittorino facing left, wearing a *berretto* and a high-necked tunic, with an undergarment showing at the back of the neck. In the best specimens a stubble of beard and moustache is visible. Legend: • VICTORINVS • FELT RENSIS • SVMMVS (Vittorino of Feltre, most distinguished . . . [inscription continues on reverse]).
Reverse: A pelican with wings half extended stands upon her nest with her head bent to her breast. Three young birds stand before her, their heads raised toward her bill. Legend: (outer circle) [flower on stalk] MATHEMATICVS • ET • OMNIS • HVMANITATIS • PATER (. . . mathematician and father of all the humanities); (inner circle) • OPVS • PISANI • [rosette] PICTO RIS • (The work of Pisano the painter).

8 obv.

8 rev.

8a

Bronze, cast

Diameter 66.4 mm; diameter of outer perimeter of the inscription from the first S in SVMMVS to the R of VICTORINVS, 63.0 mm

Paris, Nicolier Collection

Obverse and reverse as above.

Vittorino Rambaldoni was born into a poor family in the town of Feltre, north of Venice. We know that he studied in Padua under Giovanni Malpaghino da Ravenna, one of the most prominent disciples of Francesco Petrarch (1304–1374) and a teacher of Guarino da Verona (cat. no. 11). It was apparently Guarino, himself the founder of a school in Ferrara for the Este family, who recommended Vittorino to the Gonzagas. They had probably met in Venice, to which Vittorino had moved in 1417. Both were bringing to fruition theories of learning and education that began with Petrarch, were based ultimately on the values of Cicero, and were calculated to develop worthy citizens and wise and moderate rulers from the sons of merchants and princes.

In 1421, Vittorino was appointed to the chair of rhetoric at the university of Padua, where he had studied and taught intermittently since 1396. Besides being a distinguished literary humanist, he was also an accomplished and celebrated mathematician, as we learn from many sources, among them the inscription on Pisanello's medal.

While in Padua, Vittorino had opened a private school for young men, both rich and poor, which he maintained until 1423, when he returned to Venice to continue his work as a private tutor.

When Vittorino arrived in Mantua in 1425 he was given a building in the gardens of the Castello for his school, a former pleasure-house that he promptly named "La Casa Giocosa." In some of its rooms he had frescoes painted showing children at play, and soon introduced severe discipline, simple habits, plain clothing, and modest dining to this structure that had formerly seen only indolent and pleasure-loving young nobles, attended by their servants, gathered around tables laden with gold and silver plate filled with rich foods, and soothed by courtly music.

The Gonzaga children were sent to this school when they reached the proper age: the fat and clumsy Lodovico, together with his plain and lonely little fiancée Barbara of Brandenburg (1422–1481), the precocious Gianlucido (1423–1448), the brilliant and dedicated Cecilia (cat. no. 7), as well as Carlo (1417–1456), Margherita (1418–1439), and Alessandro (1427–1466). The school was soon famous, and attracted children from Venice, Padua, Faenza, Florence, and other cities. Many of these went on to become leading figures in the Church and in government, perhaps the most famous of them being Federigo da Montefeltro of Urbino (cat. no. 25), the very model of a humanist prince and *condottiere*.

Vittorino had contemplated entering the Church before Gianfrancesco proposed that he start the school. Apprehensive about the luxuries and ostentation of a court, he demanded that he have absolute control over the school and its pupils, especially young Lodovico, whom he forced to diet and take rigorous exercise in order to control his obesity.

Vittorino developed a fully-rounded curriculum combined with a strict daily regimen and a schedule of physical activities. Greek and Latin literature and grammar, music, moral philosophy, mathematics, dancing, astrology, history, and drawing alternated with exercise and games in an environment offering no frivolous distractions. To assist him, he engaged a subordinate staff of grammarians, logicians, mathematicians, painters, and masters of riding, dancing, singing, swimming, and fencing. He did not believe in corporal punishment, and seems to have treated his charges with a combination of harshness and benevolent understanding for which he earned their lasting gratitude and affection.[1]

Having been provided with the means to maintain the school and a salary of three hundred ducats a year, Vittorino felt an obligation to offer an education as well to those who could not afford to enter the Casa Giocosa. These he paid for out of his own pocket, often exceeding his salary. As a result, he was obliged to approach his patron for further funds, which were immediately forthcoming.[2]

He was primarily a learned pedagogue, not a scholar, since he seems not to have published. Yet among other humanists, who often regarded each other with jealousy and spite, he was universally respected.[3] His life was entirely devoted to his students, and it is this outstanding characteristic that Pisanello has chosen to highlight in his medal. It is probable that Lodovico Gonzaga commissioned the piece to commemorate the career of his great teacher around the time of Vittorino's death.

Pisanello depicts the educator with a lean, grizzled face, an intense gaze, a faintly bemused smile, an undecorated robe, and a plain hat. On the reverse, Pisanello has characterized his subject in his usual succinct manner with an image rich in implications. Although the precise identity of the birds is somewhat ambiguous, there seems little doubt from the overall composition that it is the image of the "Pelican in her Piety," drawing upon medieval bestiaries and texts such as the twelfth-century *Speculum ecclesiae* of Honorius of Autun.[4] According to legend, the pelican kills its young, then brings them back to life again after three days by opening its breast and sprinkling them with its own blood. In another version, the bird feeds its young by opening its breast and allowing the chicks to drink its blood. In both cases the pelican is a symbol of the Passion of Christ, in which God the Father resurrects His Son after three days. Pisanello has adapted this appropriate Christian symbol to represent the great educator whose life was devoted entirely to his students. Perhaps to identify more precisely the family whose fledglings Vittorino nourished, the artist has included what is certainly a sunflower, one of the Gonzaga emblems, at the beginning of the reverse inscription.

Stephen K. Scher

9 obv.

9 rev.

Pisanello
Don Iñigo de Avalos, master chamberlain of the kingdom of
   Naples (documented between 1435 and 1471)
9
Bronze, cast
Diameter 78.5 mm; height of bust on center line, 66.8 mm
Washington, The National Gallery of Art, Samuel H. Kress
   Collection
1957.14.614

Obverse: Bust of Don Iñigo facing right, wearing a fur-trimmed
outer cloak over a shirt with a high collar. On his head, the
particular form of mid-fifteenth-century *chaperon*, or hood,
permanently fixed on a *bourrelet*, or padded ring, with a long
strip of cloth (*patte, cornette, lambeau*) falling over the rim and
onto the right shoulder. Legend: • DON • INIGO • DE •
DAVALOS • (olive branch).
Reverse: In the center of the field, a globe with the sea at the
bottom, a mountainous landscape with buildings in the center,
and a starry sky above. Over the globe, the Avalos arms[1] flanked
by two rose stalks. Legend: (beneath the globe) • PER VVI SE
FA • (For you it is made); (around the edge) • OPVS • PISANI •
PICTORIS • (olive branch) (The work of Pisano the painter).

9a
Bronze, cast
Diameter 77.5 mm; height of bust on center line, 65.8 mm
Berlin, Staatliche Museen, Münzkabinett, formerly Benoni
   Friedlaender Collection, 1868

Obverse and reverse as above.

Despite questions that could be raised regarding the apparent
age of the sitter, there has never been any hesitation among past

scholars in assuming that the Don Iñigo—in Italian, Indico or
Innico—de Avalos represented on the medal was that Don Iñigo
who accompanied Alfonso of Aragon (cat. no. 35) on his conquest of Naples in 1442. His birth and death dates are unknown, but it is certain that he was the eldest son from the third
marriage of Ruy Lopez de Avalos, constable of Castile and
count of Ribadeo.[2] The Avalos family claimed ancient roots in
Aragon, tracing its heritage back to the Roman conquest, when
Attilius Regulus was proconsul in Spain with the Second
Legion.[3]

Iñigo appears to have been a close companion of King Alfonso from an early date, and to have participated in most of the
monarch's eventually successful attempts to build a powerful
Mediterranean kingdom. During the course of his conflicts
with Genoa and Milan, Alfonso was defeated at sea by the
Genoese in 1435, at the battle of Ponza. He was taken prisoner,
and brought to Milan. Avalos was present at the battle and also
taken prisoner. This appears to be the earliest mention of his
name.[4]

When Alfonso established his authority in Naples in 1442,
he rewarded many of his Spanish followers with important
positions in his government and with titles and lands. Apparently a great favorite, Don Iñigo received a number of benefits.[5]
In 1444, he was given the very lucrative grant for life of the
gabella, the duties on exported foodstuffs.[6] We know that he
was *locum tenens* to the king's chamberlain, Francesco d'Aquino, until the latter's death in about 1449, when he himself
became master chamberlain, or director of all finances, a position that remained in the Avalos family for 195 years.[7] Iñigo
was married to d'Aquino's sister, Antonella, and by her had
three daughters and three sons, the youngest of whom was also
named Iñigo.

Pisanello's medal can only be dated to 1449–50, at which
time Don Iñigo would have been at least in his early thirties.[8] In

9 obv.

CICILIA·VIRGO·FILIA·IOHANNIS·FRANCISCI·PRIMI·MARCHIONIS·MANTVE

7a obv.

the portrait of Don Iñigo, Pisanello reaches his highest level of accomplishment. All elements are in harmony: the simple inscription acts as parentheses to the delicate variations in the low relief of the portrait, which is not overpowered by the strong horizontal volume of the *bourrelet* or the long rhythms in higher relief of the fabric flowing down behind the head and across the shoulder. If any medal has captured the mixture of *gravitas* and youthful self-confidence of the quattrocento, it is this one.

In combination with such an obverse, we would expect from Pisanello a reverse of equal quality, but such is not the case. The artist has compressed a complex landscape into a small circle within the disc of the medal itself, leaving an excessive portion of the field for the inscriptions and heraldry. The contents of the globe, though ambitious, are difficult to read, and are out of proportion with the rest of the reverse.

A drawing in the Louvre, the attribution of which to Pisanello is disputed, appears to be related to this reverse, and is indeed quite similar in its disposition of mountains and Gothic buildings, but otherwise varies in the placement of the sea and in the absence of stars in the sky.[9]

The precise meaning of the reverse is something of a puzzle, as so many Renaissance medallic reverses were meant to be. In the sixteenth century, Giuseppe Castaglione da Ancona (died c. 1616) addressed a poem in honor of Pisanello to his pupil, Tommaso d'Avalos, a descendent of Don Iñigo, in which he described the reverse and related its form to the shield of Achilles, as described in detail in the eighteenth book of the *Iliad*.[10] Castaglione says that the artist "has represented by mystic signs the excellence of the man [Don Iñigo] in the arts of peace and war; for he has wrought cunningly Olympus, and the constellations, and in the midst the Earth with woodlands and wild creatures, and cities, and castles twain on the mountaintops, and below the coast where the breakers roar, and the watery plains of Ocean, and has fashioned the whole world for his hero. Such was the shield which Mulciber is said to have shaped for Achilles; such does Martian Rome devise, stamped on the yellow brass, for its Caesars, under whose laws the whole world is set."[11]

It is possible that, as Castaglione maintains, the image on the reverse could refer, indirectly and in greatly abbreviated form, to the shield of Achilles, and that in conjunction with the inscription "For you it is made," the medal thereby honors Don Iñigo's role as King Alfonso's most important military commander. In the end, however, the link is tenuous, leaving open a final interpretation of the medal.

Stephen K. Scher

Unknown Ferrarese Master
Antonio di Puccio, called Pisanello (c. 1395–1455)
10
Bronze, cast
Diameter 58.5 mm
St. Petersburg, State Hermitage Museum
5175

10 obv.

10 rev.

Obverse: Bust to left in tall cap and brocaded cloak. Legend: PISANVS PICTOR (Pisano the painter).
Reverse: In two lines within a wreath of foliage, the initials of the seven Virtues: F[ides] S[pes] K[aritas; *sic*] J[ustitia] P[rudentia] F[ortitudo] T[emperantia] (Faith, Hope, Charity, Justice, Prudence, Fortitude, Temperance).

In this medal Pisanello is portrayed at the height of his career. Its expressive and elegant portrait was copied by Giovanni Badile in his fresco in Verona's Santa Maria della Scala in 1443,[1] indicating that the medal was created before that date. Pisanello's contemporaries and his own drawings reveal that the master had a taste for fine clothes.[2]

The medal's reverse is one of the first examples to present nothing but an inscription. Symbols and emblems were essential to the idiom of the medal from the beginning. Repeatedly in Pisanello's own emblematic reverses one encounters a reflection of the courtly, chivalric tradition combined with the new humanism. The sword and books on his medal of Francesco Sforza, the sheet of music in front of the lion on that of Leonello d'Este (cat. no. 5), and the hunting scene on his medal of

Alfonso are all symbolic of the *uomo universale*, the Renaissance ideal. Abbreviating words to only their initial letters was common in classical inscriptions. The appearance of the initials of the Virtues can be taken as a highly generalized sign within the system of symbolism; they honor the master as a representative of the humanistic elite of his time.[3]

The Pisanello medal was originally thought to be a self-portrait, then later as the work of Antonio Marescotti.[4] Scholars now connect it to the works of the Ferrarese medalists, without attributing it to a specific master. A number of gifted medalists were present in Ferrara by the mid fifteenth century, among them Lixignolo, Coradino, Marescotti, and Baldassare d'Este. The most notable characteristic of these medalists is the high bust truncations of their portraits, which serve to focus our attention on the facial features themselves. Ferrarese medals are noted for their restraint and nobility.

It is impossible to attribute the Pisanello medal with any assurance to one of these contemporary masters. If one compares it to medals by Marescotti, for example, specifically his St. Bernard or his Ginevra Sforza, one notes that its modeling is sharper and less fluid. Pisanello's own works had a great influence on his contemporaries, and whoever the author of this medal may have been, he has created a worthy monument to the master, the true founder of this noble branch of smaller sculpture.

It is highly instructive to compare this portrait with the other medallic portrait of Pisanello from roughly 1455–60 by the Ferrarese master Nicolaus.[5] There one sees the image of a tired old man nearing his death. Even so, his facial features are easily recognizable, and the entire likeness is infused with sympathy and warmth.

Yevgenia Shchukina

Matteo di Maestro Andrea de' Pasti
(active 1441–1467/68)

While Matteo de' Pasti is also documented as a manuscript illuminator, painter, and architect, his only secure surviving figural works are portrait medals. Probably produced in the 1440s and 50s, these suggest admiration for Pisanello's medals, but emphasize "simple forms, precise modeling, and clear and harmonious compositions"[1] that place them among the finest early medals. Most relate to Matteo's role as artist and counselor to the Malatesta court at Rimini.

The son of a physician, Matteo came of a propertied Veronese family. His grandmother was a Bardi of Florence, and his first recorded activity involves a painting commission for Piero de' Medici of that city. He wrote to Piero from Venice in 1441, promising splendors of powdered gold in the Petrarchan *Triumph of Fame*—probably an illuminated manuscript—that he was painting, and requesting Piero's instructions on details. It would appear that he was thus an established illuminator and experienced courtier by that time.[2]

Between 1444 and 1446 he was illuminating books for Leonello d'Este of Ferrara (cat. no. 5), although apparently working in Verona. Surviving manuscripts have occasionally been attributed to him.[3]

When he took up medallic sculpture is not known. The earliest date to appear on medals of his, 1446 (on several of Sigismondo Malatesta and Isotta da Rimini; see cat. nos. 12–14), may actually record events commemorated rather than the date of production. He was in Verona in 1446 and is first documented in Rimini only in 1449, when he had sold his house in Verona and taken a Riminese bride. He became a valued friend and counselor to Sigismondo Malatesta and supervised architectural works in the Malatesta lands. This probably included the interior renovation of San Francesco in Rimini, under way in the late 1440s. When Leon Battista Alberti (cat. no. 3) took over the remodeling in about 1450 (or later), designing the Romanizing exterior shell and façade for the building, Matteo acted as superintendent. The extent of Matteo's share in the design or execution of the interior sculpture is debated.[4] His name as architect appears carved high up on the interior frieze of the church, opposite that of Agostino di Duccio as sculptor.[5]

A colleague of humanists such as Alberti and Guarino (cat. no. 11), Matteo is praised in contemporary accounts for his nobility and intellect. Sultan Mehmed (cat. nos. 21, 39) in Constantinople requested his services from Sigismondo Malatesta in 1461, to paint and sculpt his portrait. Sigismondo dispatched the artist as a special favor, with gifts including maps and a manuscript of *De Re Militari* by Sigismondo's secretary Roberto Valturio. These led to Matteo's arrest and imprisonment as a spy by Venetian officials on Crete. He was sent from there back to Rimini by 1462.[6] The last record of him is from May 15, 1467; another document indicates that he had died by mid 1468.[7]

As a medalist, Matteo is considered a follower of Pisanello, but the degree of direct contact between the two is uncertain. His portraits show powerful observation, a feeling for strong contours and subtle textures, and an ability to marshal details to enhance characterization. Although his medals are all of friends, relations, and patrons, it is difficult to accept Middeldorf's proposal that he produced them as a dilettante and "certainly not . . . for gain."[8]

Alison Luchs

Matteo de' Pasti
Guarino da Verona (1374–1460)
11
Copper alloy, cast
Diameter 93.5 mm; diameter of the outer perimeter of the
    obverse inscription from the first V in GVARINVS through
    the first E in VERONENSIS, 91.9 mm
Washington, The National Gallery of Art, Samuel H. Kress
    Collection
1957.14.647

Obverse: Guarino facing left, wearing a classicizing mantle pinned with a round clasp at the shoulder. Legend: GVARINVS VERONENSIS (Guarino of Verona), the G and first E in VERONENSIS in Gothic majuscules.[1]

11 obv.

11 rev.

Reverse: Nude youth with a shield and mace (?), standing on a globe atop a two-tiered fountain in a flowering meadow, surrounded by a laurel wreath. Legend: • MATTHEVS • DEPASTIS • F[ecit] (Matteo de' Pasti made it), the E in MATTHEUS in Gothic majuscule.

11a
Bronze, cast
Diameter 95.0 mm
London, The British Museum

An avid scholar and tireless teacher, Guarino Guarini was a uniquely influential figure in the early Italian Renaissance. Like his friend and pupil Vittorino da Feltre (cat. no. 8), Guarino played an incalculable role in spreading the *studia humanitatis*, an education based on the orators, poets, and historians of antiquity, through northern and north-central Italy in the period from 1430 to 1460.[2]

Energetically promoting classical learning as relevant to the humane exercise of power, Guarino spent his long career educating and counseling future princes, civil servants, and teachers. After five years in Constantinople mastering Greek (1403–8), he taught the language in Florence and Venice. From 1420 to 1430 he lectured in rhetoric in his native Verona, and from 1430 until his death taught in Ferrara, having been engaged there as tutor to the young Leonello d'Este (cat. no. 5). At his funeral, Guarino was praised for single-handedly turning Ferrara into a center of the new humanistic culture.

Besides his writings, including a Latin grammar manual that enjoyed wide use for three centuries, Guarino left a body of letters commenting on subjects that include the visual arts.[3] His letter of November 5, 1447, to his pupil Leonello d'Este (cat. no. 5), explaining how the nine Muses should be depicted, has been termed "the one best text of the [fifteenth] century for a 'program' of paintings."[4] Baxandall suggests that Guarino may have played a catalytic role in the invention of the portrait medal through his claim that paintings and statues, unlike literature, are poor vehicles for transmitting personal fame in that they are not portable and lack labels.[5] While this complaint appears in a Guarino letter from 1447, if he had expressed the same sentiments to his friend Pisanello, it might have constituted a challenge that the portrait medal could answer.

In a medal that has been called his most powerful,[6] Matteo depicted Guarino with unsparing naturalism. For an aged intellectual he exudes remarkable physical vigor and determination, reminding us that Guarino was the son of a blacksmith.[7] Yet this is also one of the earliest medals to idealize a Renaissance personality by draping him *all'antica*,[8] something this medalist did for no other sitter. Matteo may have got this idea—and his close-up focus on the scholar's head—from the self-portrait by his learned colleague Alberti (cat. no. 3).[9] The costume in any case suits a subject with Guarino's dedication to knowledge of the ancient world.

The meaning of the reverse seems clear in general, but mysterious in certain details. Chief among these are the attributes held by the nude youth standing, in classical contrapposto, atop the fountain. Hill identified them as a shield (which in the best examples bears a tiny face in profile) and a mace. The meaning

12 rev.

of this combination is not clear. The shield with a Medusa head is a frequent attribute of Minerva, the Roman goddess of wisdom,[10] but the figure is obviously not she.

The youth (or statue of one) slightly resembles Donatello's slender bronze *David*, sword in hand, in the Bargello in Florence,[11] but recalls even more a small-scale relief prototype, the Apollo carved on a famous ancient gem of Apollo and Marsyas, for which the great sculptor Ghiberti made a gold setting in the late 1420s.[12] That gem, whose whereabouts before it entered the collection of Lorenzo de' Medici (cat. no. 42) are controversial,[13] was copied in numerous bronze plaquettes, and Matteo could have known either the original or an early cast. Whether he recognized the graceful standing figure—Ghiberti apparently did not—as Apollo, the Greco-Roman sun-god who leads the Muses and fosters the arts and literature, would be a question. In any case, the elegant young nude surely evokes the living glory of the ancient world, with benevolent waters flowing down from tier to tier and ultimately making the meadow verdant, just as the ancient knowledge taught by Guarino flowed from generation to generation and benefited all Italy. In the 1420s the blessed Alberto da Sarziano even referred to Guarino as "the font of Greek and Latin learning."[14]

The laurel wreath surrounding the fountain is a traditional crown honoring literary achievement.[15] The laurel's sanctity to Apollo may confirm the identity of the figure atop the fountain. Matteo playfully devised a wreath with projecting berries that are difficult to distinguish from the round, free-floating stops between the words.

The date and commission of this medal are unknown; the repeated use of Gothic letters and the form of the laurel wreath, quite simple when compared with the richer and more complex wreath on Matteo's Alberti medal,[16] might support the relatively early date of c. 1446 proposed for it by Hill.[17] Both lead and bronze examples soon became available. A German student in Padua, Ulrich Gossembrot, sent a lead one home with other medals to his father in Augsburg in November 1459.[18]

Alison Luchs

Matteo de' Pasti
Isotta degli Atti of Rimini (born 1432/33, died 1474)
12
Bronze alloy, cast
Diameter 84.8 mm; diameter of outer perimeter of obverse inscription from the T in ITALIE through the second I in ARIMINENSI, 81.6 mm
Washington, The National Gallery of Art, Samuel H. Kress Collection 1957.14.651

Obverse: Bust-length figure of Isotta facing right, wearing a pleated *giornea* over a high-necked *gamurra* or *cotta*. Her hair, piled high in late-Gothic French or Flemish style (enhanced by padding, a frame, or a hairpiece), is covered by a fine veil that is fastened with a jewel at the center of her plucked forehead.[1] Legend (with floral stops): • ISOTE • ARIMINENSI • FORMA • ET • VIRTUTE • ITALIE • DECORI • (To Isotta of Rimini, the ornament of Italy for beauty and virtue).
Reverse: An elephant in a flowery meadow. Legend: OPVS • MATHEI • DE • PASTIS • V[eronensis] • M·CCCC·XLVI • (The work of Matteo de' Pasti of Verona. 1446).

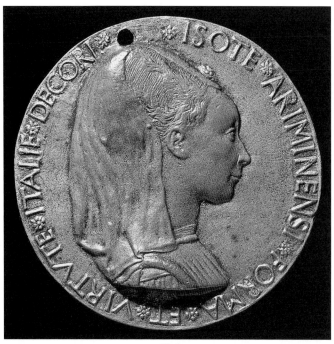

12 obv.

12 rev.

12a
Bronze, cast
Diameter 83.0 mm
University of California at Santa Barbara, University Art Museum, Sigmund Morgenroth Collection

Obverse and reverse as above

13
Bronze, cast
Diameter 83.3 mm; height of bust, 57.5 mm
St. Petersburg, State Hermitage Museum
5178

Obverse: Bust to right, hair over high frame, confined by crossing bands, fastened with jewel on top and falling in two pointed masses behind. Legend: • D[ominae] • ISOTTAE •• ARIMINEN-SI • ([Likeness of] the lady Isotta of Rimini).
Reverse: As above, but lacking signature and two rose bushes.

The portrait medal was still a novel art form when Sigismondo Malatesta (cat. no. 14) adopted it to celebrate himself and his beloved, Isotta degli Atti.[2] The beautiful daughter of a Riminese merchant had inspired his passion when she was barely thirteen years old. The date 1446 appears on three of four dated medals of her[3] and marks the tomb monument installed around 1449 in her chapel in San Francesco in Rimini, bearing an inscription virtually identical to the one on this medal. The date 1446 recurs on medals of Sigismondo himself; to all evidence this date commemorates not the production of the works of art, but the triumphal year when Sigismondo consolidated his political power, dedicated his new castle, and won Isotta as his mistress.[4]

Sigismondo evidently began to commission medals of Isotta only after the death of his second wife, Polissena Sforza, in 1449.[5] He married Isotta at an uncertain date, but probably in 1456, finally choosing a love match over the political and military advantages he might have gained from yet another dynastic marriage. She went on to become his heir, and along with his son Sallustio she ruled Rimini briefly after Sigismondo's death.

The numerous surviving medals of Isotta testify to the wide distribution Sigismondo gave them. Besides proclaiming his love, they served a conscious policy of exalting the cultural glamor of his court at Rimini through commissions of the most modern art forms, as well as through the celebration of his lady's beauty, brilliance, and virtue.[6] As with medals of himself, Sigismondo heaped medals of Isotta for posterity to discover in the walls of buildings he founded. The tower of San Giovanni in Senigallia, for instance, built in 1455, was called the Isotto or Isotteo, because its foundations contained "a potful of medals of Madonna Isotta," and many came into the hands of private Riminese citizens like Lodovico Mengozzi, who at his death in 1457 owned eleven medals of Sigismondo and Isotta.[7]

Isotta is presented in the signed Pasti medals (cat. nos. 12, 12a) with sensitivity and tenderness. In a high-necked dress, with her gaze slightly lifted, her lips closed in a calm smile and her chin a little withdrawn, the teenage girl projects a wide-eyed charm not devoid of calculation. The filmy veil and delicately waving strands of hair enhance the effect of softness. This

13 obv.

13 rev.

image contrasts with the one on unsigned pieces (cat. no. 13), where she appears quite formidable in a richly woven garment and horned, beribboned hairstyle with tresses hanging down the back. This second image is easy to conceive as a later portrayal of the assured court lady she became.

The elephant on the reverse has been aptly described as "one of the most impressive representations of animals on a Renaissance medal, with its bold and fluid design, massive in its modeling yet sensitive to the subtle details of the skin; a natural and heraldic figure. . . . "[8] Many meanings, several potentially relevant, have been assigned to this animal. As a favorite Malatesta device, sculptured elephants abound in San Francesco in Rimini, the family church renovated for Sigismondo to designs by Leon Battista Alberti (cat. no. 3) and filled with family and court tomb monuments. The motto "Elephas Indus culices non timet" (the Indian elephant fears no mosquitoes) accompanies elephant images used by Sigismondo's brother and nephew.[9] In Malatesta contexts, the elephant evidently stands for regal strength and for the fame that confers immortality. Matteo de' Pasti himself had shown elephants pulling the chariot in a Petrarchan *Triumph of Fame* he painted for Piero de' Medici in 1441, and elephants support the throne of Fortitude in one of his medals of Sigismondo.[10]

As if to stress the link between elephants as symbols of fame and medals as a means to realize it, Sigismondo placed twenty-two medals of himself on the backs of the elephants in the St. Sigismund Chapel in San Francesco in Rimini in October 1450.[11]

A more personal (though conventional) compliment to Isotta would lie in the elephant's ancient associations with piety and chastity.[12] Pasini argues persuasively that on medals of her it symbolized above all her share, through her connection with Sigismondo, in Malatesta fame and power.

Matteo indulged in some appealing visual puns on this medal. The floral stops on the obverse, in the form of heraldic four-petaled Malatesta roses,[13] also seem to echo the jewel on Isotta's forehead. On the reverse, heraldic roses sprout from the meadow behind the elephant to form stops framing Matteo's signature.

Alison Luchs

14 obv.

14 rev.

Matteo de' Pasti
Sigismondo Pandolfo Malatesta (born 1417, lord of Rimini and
  Fano 1432–68)
14
Bronze, cast
Diameter: 79.1 mm; height of bust through center line,
  64.7 mm
New York, private collection

Obverse: Bust of Sigismondo to the left wearing plate armor over mail. Legend: • SIGISMVNDVS PANDVLFVS • MALATESTA • PAN[dulfi] • F[ilius] • (Sigismondo Pandolfo Malatesta, son of Pandolfo).

Reverse: The castle of Rimini. Legend: • CASTELLVM • SISMVNDVM • ARIMINENSE • M•CCCC•XLVI • (Castle Sigismondo at Rimini. 1446).

14a
Bronze, cast
Diameter: 82.4 mm; height of bust through center line,
  62.0 mm
Washington, The National Gallery of Art, Samuel H. Kress
  Collection
1957.14.652

2 obv.

2 rev.

65

3 obv.

5a obv.

5a rev.

6 obv.

6a rev.

7a rev.

7 obv.

8 obv.

69

9 obv.

14 rev.

12 obv.

12 rev.

18a rev.

19 obv.

20 obv.

20 rev.

Obverse: Bust of Sigismondo to the left, wearing a *giornea* over a high-necked shirt (*camicia*). Legend: (rose) SIGISMONDVS • PANDVLFVS • DE • MALATESTIS • S[anctae] • RO[manae] • ECLESIE • C[apitaneus] • GENERALIS (Sigismondo Pandolfo Malatesta, captain general of the Holy Roman Church).
Reverse: The castle of Rimini. Legend: (rose) CASTELLVM • SISMONDVM • ARIMINENSE • M•CCCC•XLVI (Castle Sigismondo at Rimini. 1446).

Sigismondo Pandolfo Malatesta, like Richard III of England or the Borgias, is a perfect example of an historical figure whose evil reputation was firmly lodged in the minds of all succeeding generations by deliberate propaganda. In the case of Sigismondo this occurred through the severely biased opinion of one man, Pope Pius II, who in his memoirs thoroughly castigated Sigismondo as the worst ogre that ever walked the face of the earth. His hatred was so intense, in fact, that in 1462 he caused Sigismondo to be canonized in Hell and burned in effigy on the steps of St. Peter's.[1] The reasons for such animosity, it must be admitted, lay partially in the particular composition of Sigismondo's character, making him, from our point of view, more of a figure of minor tragedy rather than a totally malevolent villain.

Born in 1417, Sigismondo was the second illegitimate son of Pandolfo Malatesta, lord of Fano and brother of Carlo Malatesta, lord and papal vicar of Rimini and the surrounding territories.[2] Upon his father's death in 1427, Sigismondo, with his elder half-brother Galeotto Roberto ("il Beato") and younger brother Domenico ("Malatesta Novello"; cat. no. 6)—they too illegitimate—was adopted by Carlo. With his wife Elisabetta Gonzaga, Carlo had established a stable and prosperous court in Rimini that was respected throughout Europe and played an important role in the politics of the period.

In 1428, Pope Martin V took the important step of legitimating Pandolfo's three sons, thus making them eligible to succeed as vicars of the papal territories already ruled by the Malatesta, since neither Carlo nor Pandolfo had produced a legitimate heir. The succession was thus dependent entirely upon the will of the pope, who, upon Carlo's death, attempted to deprive Sigismondo and his brothers of their inheritance. Sigismondo never forgot the pope's treachery, and was driven throughout his life to seek an hereditary title removed from the uncertainties of papal politics. It was this determination that formed the core of his conflict with Pius II.

In 1429, Galeotto Roberto unwillingly became lord of Rimini, but devoted himself to an austere religious life that led to his death three years later in an odor of sanctity. The Malatesta patrimony was then divided between Sigismondo and Domenico, each of whom established important courts, the one in Rimini, the other in Cesena. Their own relationship was not a happy one and was punctuated with frequent quarrels.

In 1433, two important events occurred in the life of the sixteen-year-old Sigismondo: He took as his first wife Ginevra d'Este, thus establishing a life-long bond with one of the oldest and most respected families in Italy, and he was knighted by Sigismund, the Holy Roman Emperor. In response to the latter distinction, he changed his name from the Italian Gismondo to Sigismondo, and in various ways, especially in the naming of his castle, Castel Sismondo, made reference to an honor that was particularly precious to him as he strove to realize his ambition to establish a secure position among the hereditary princes of the other Italian states.[3]

One way of doing so was through military prowess, which Sigismondo possessed to a high degree. The practice of hiring mercenaries under the command of a *condottiere* through a contract, or *condotta*, was widespread, and in an Italy torn by conflicts among many constantly shifting factions, both foreign and domestic, the opportunities to acquire wealth, territories, and a title were frequent. Sigismondo was among the cleverest and most skilled of these militray leaders. He was fierce, even impetuous, in battle and was one of the first to exploit the advantages of artillery. A minor accomplishment was his invention of the hand grenade, and, as we shall see, he was ahead of his time in the design of fortifications.

Between 1433 and 1454, Sigismondo came closest to realizing his aspirations. On March 18, 1435, he was named captain general of the Church, now headed by Eugenius IV, a pope with whom he had good relations. During this time he established close ties with the Medici in Florence, and became familiar with the work of the great architect Filippo Brunelleschi (1377–1446) and the humanist-architect-artist Leon Battista Alberti (cat. no. 3), both of whom were to participate in Sigismondo's considerable building activities in Rimini.

Active as a *condottiere* during these chaotic years, Sigismondo forged further links with other important families, taking as a second wife in 1441 an illegitimate daughter of Francesco Sforza, Polissena, who died of the plague eight years later, but became a part of the Malatesta legend with the report that she had been murdered by her husband so that he could marry his famous mistress Isotta degli Atti (cat. nos. 12–13). Shortly thereafter, in 1444, Federigo da Montefeltro (cat. no. 25) became count of Urbino. He inherited disputes over what had once been Malatesta land and began a conflict with Sigismondo that raged for twenty years, becoming part of the legend, with Federigo representing the pious, learned, skilled, and just ruler in contrast to the cruel pagan monster Sigismondo.

Sigismondo's constant purpose, as a prince who espoused enthusiastically the new values of the quattrocento, was the perpetuation of his fame, the continuation of his name and family, the display of his power, his military ability, his skills as a ruler, his piety and justice, and his links with the ancient past. This led to the construction of a string of castles throughout his territories, most notably the great castle of Rimini, the so-called Rocca Malatestiana, which appears on the reverse of several of his medals. Years later it also inspired his rebuilding of San Francesco in Rimini as an official church and mausoleum for both his family and the more illustrious members of his court.

To be doubly certain of the perpetuation of his name in conjunction with his most important projects, Sigismondo con-

SIGISMVNDVS PANDVLFVS MALATESTA PAN F

14 obv.

14 rev.

cealed within the fabric of his buildings—the castle of Rimini, other castles in his territory, and the church of San Francesco—a large quantity of medals, almost all of which were discovered after World War II.[4] Although many of these bear the date 1446, including those with the portrait of Isotta (cat. nos. 12–13), it is now generally agreed that this is a commemorative date representing a very important year in Sigismondo's life, but that the medals themselves probably date from c. 1448–50 or 1452.

Although there are a number of types among the medals of Sigismondo, both large and small, the portrait remains more or less the same, the only changes being in the inscriptions and the dress, these reflecting, however, important points that the patron wished to communicate.[5] In the earlier of the two examples shown here (cat. no. 14a), Sigismondo is in court dress, but identified as a captain of the papal forces. In the second type (cat. no. 14), he is in armor, emphasizing his importance as a military leader, but is no longer referred to as a soldier of the pope.

Constant to these medals is the reverse with its famous view of the castle of Rimini, the first architectural reverse on a medal, picking up a tradition common to Roman coins. This structure can be read on many levels of meaning. As a castle, of course, it demonstrates once again Sigismondo's skill as a soldier and as a military engineer. It also stands for the city of Rimini and the ruler's control of his domain, his ability to maintain peace and good government, to exercise justice, and to protect his subjects against any enemy. Finally, in the broadest sense, it is the ruler's palace, the center of his universe, and reflects the power of the cosmic ruler, the supreme dispenser of justice, God, or the sun.[6]

Stephen K. Scher

Bartolo Talpa
(active as medalist c. 1495)

Little is known of Talpa's career except that he worked for the Mantuan court of Francesco II Gonzaga, fourth marquess of Mantua, and that his master was Andrea Mantegna (1431–1506). He is probably identical with the artist referred to as Bartolino Topino (*talpa* = mole or gopher; *topino* = little mole or mouse), nicknamed "the Philosopher." In a letter dated October 21, 1495, Bernardo Ghisulfo writes to Francesco II of two ground-floor walls at the Palazzo Marmirolo decorated by one "Bertolino called the Philosopher." Another letter between the same correspondents, dated July 28, 1496, discusses paintings delivered by "Bartolino Topina [Topino?]."[1] Both may relate to Bartolo Talpa.

Talpa's style was decisively influenced by that of Mantegna. From him he adopted the severe classicism, the sharp linear contours, and a two-dimensional concept. His lettering is modeled with a secure hand, well proportioned, and carefully placed in relation to the composition. He produced only two medals, both signed and executed for the Gonzaga, one of Federigo I (cat. no. 15), the other of his son Francesco II.[2] The reverse of Francesco's medal celebrates him, somewhat hyper-

bolically, as LIBERATORI VNIVERSAE ITALIAE (liberator of all Italy), an allusion to Francesco's role in the struggle against the French invasion. He is compared to Marcus Curtius riding into the flaming abyss to save Rome in 362 B.C. The representation manifests Talpa's close connection with the humanist atmosphere of the Gonzaga court, a center of arts and letters, and the quattrocento predilection for paralleling contemporary events with subjects derived from classical sources.

Mark M. Salton

Bartolo Talpa
Federigo I Gonzaga (born 1440, third marquess of Mantua 1478–84)
15
Bronze, cast
Diameter 82 mm; internal measurement from the upper crossing of branches to the lower point of the second V in BARTVLVS, 61 mm
Berlin, Staatliche Museen, Münzkabinett

Obverse: Bust of Federigo facing left, with medium-long hair, the ends turned inward at the nape of the neck. He wears a soft cap with a broad turned-up brim and a tight-fitting robe circled at the neck by two thin bands. Arched truncation. Legend: FREDERICVS GON[zagus] MAN[tuae] MAR[chio] III [= tertius] (triangular stop) (Federigo Gonzaga, third marquess of Mantua).
Reverse: Two crossed laurel branches, each carrying four twigs with leaves and berries, passing through the triangular ansae of a rectangular, double-outlined tablet inscribed: E[picorum] P[hilosophorum] O[ptimus] (foremost of epic philosophers). Below, in a semicircle, the signature: BARTVLVS TALPA.

Federigo's portrait derives from Mantegna's design for the *Meeting Scene*, one of the frescoes in the Camera degli Sposi[1] at the Castello di Corte (the Gonzaga castle) in Mantua.[2] That painting shows the arrival of Cardinal Francesco Gonzaga (born 1444, cardinal 1461–83), Federigo's brother.[3] On the right it depicts a man with similar facial features, cap, and hairstyle, who can be identified with the help of this medal as Federigo.[4] The marquess is also shown on an undated ducato,[5] probably struck shortly after his accession in 1478. To judge by its veristic portrait, Federigo's character, about which we know little, may have been less than pleasant. He is there portrayed with an obese face, bloated lips, heavy bags under his eyes, and a chin that merges with his neck. His medallic portrait, on the other hand, is not modeled *ad vivam*, since it originated c. 1495, some eleven years after his death. It depends upon the fresco, which was done no later than 1474, thus about five years earlier than the ducato, and presents him idealized and at a younger age, with less pronounced, unprepossessing features.

The reverse inscription E P O has been conjectured to represent a specific Mantuan device. It occurs again on an anonymous Mantuan quattrino[6] struck under Federigo II, with a portrait of Virgil (70–19 B.C.), the city's favorite son, and also

76

on a medal of the youthful Francesco II by Gianfrancesco Roberti della Grana (active in Mantua 1483–c. 1523), where the letters are engraved on a shield.[7] On the Virgil coin they have been interpreted as an abbreviation of "epicorum poetarum optimus" (foremost of the epic poets), an unlikely reading in connection with either Federigo I or Francesco II. If on Federigo's medal the P were to be understood as "philosophorum," however, it could refer to Talpa himself, apparently nicknamed "the Philosopher." It could also stand for "pictorum" (of painters), alluding to Talpa's primary activity as a painter. By placing his signature assertively below the E P O, the artist may have wanted to adapt Virgil's epithet to himself, indicating what he thought of his own literary and pictorial dexterity. This would exemplify a facet of the Renaissance mind, with its penchant for veiled allusion, for riddles to be solved only by those who know — or can guess at — their hidden meaning.

Federigo's medal forms a pair with that of his son Francesco II.[8] The two pieces date from shortly after the battle of Fornovo on the Taro River, in July 1495, in which both Charles VIII of France and Francesco, who led the allied troops, claimed victory. A painting by Mantegna, executed in 1495 for the church of Santa Maria della Vittoria at Mantua, celebrates the "victory." The pair of medals would be another manifestation of Francesco's pretense, and, beyond that, a hint at the military prowess of both father and son. Armand did not consider the two pieces to form a pair, and placed Federigo's medal prior to the year of his demise.[9]

Federigo was born in 1440, the eldest of five sons of Lodovico III and his wife, Barbara of Brandenburg (d. 1484).[10] Fond of luxurious living, the young prince liked theatrical performances and music and could hold his own at any banquet. In 1463 he married Margaret of Bavaria (d. 1519), a lady of plain appearance, but of wealthy Wittelsbach pedigree.[11] As a *condottiere*, Federigo served under various foreign sovereigns. In 1470 he was offered the command of the troops of Galeazzo Maria Sforza, fifth duke of Milan, and successfully repulsed the Swiss, who at the instigation of Pope Sixtus IV had tried to invade Lombardy. After Galeazzo's death, Federigo continued in the service of his widow, Bona of Savoy (d. 1494), mother and guardian of the young successor, Giangaleazzo Maria Sforza. When Lodovico III died of the plague, on June 4, 1478, Federigo acceded to the marquisate of Mantua, while his four brothers shared in a number of smaller Gonzaga territories.[12] The brothers conspired to poison him, but a timely warning by an informer saved his life, and Federigo continued his career as a *condottiere*, leaving Mantua in the care of administrators during his absences.[13] One of his exploits was the defense of the house of Este against the territorial designs of the pope and the Venetians, whose claims menaced the Gonzaga dominions as well. In 1490, after Federigo's death, Francesco II married the famed Isabella d'Este (1474–1539),[14] daughter of Ercole, further strengthening the ties between two great princely families.

Mark M. Salton

Pier Jacopo di Antonio Alari Bonacolsi, called Antico
(c. 1460–1528)

In the inaugural issue of the *Rivista italiana di Numismatica* of 1888, Umberto Rossi laid the foundation for all subsequent studies of medals by Antico. Dating them to the early 1480s, Rossi deduced that the artist would have been born in about 1460 in Mantua, where his father, Antonio Alari Bonacolsi, owned a house.[1] To judge from the remarkable delicacy, brilliant execution, and sumptuous finish of his surviving bronze statuettes and life-size busts, it is assumed that he was trained initially as a goldsmith. Furthermore, we know that in 1487 he fashioned a "golden" girdle for Antonia del Balzo (1441–1538), wife of Gianfrancesco Gonzaga (cat. no. 16), the patron for whom he made most of his medals. Antico's later benefactors and the known recipients of his austerely classicizing bronze statuettes—Bishop Lodovico Gonzaga (1459) and the incomparable Isabella d'Este (1474–1539)—were both members of the powerful and artistically sensitive Gonzaga dynasty centered at Mantua.

As a Gonzaga court sculptor, Antico was naturally influenced by the archeological exactitude that permeates the works of the older Mantuan court artist Andrea Mantegna (1431–1506), and was also exposed in some way to the style of the Florentine sculptor Donatello (1386–1466). His steadfast devotion to and direct familiarity with classical art manifests itself from the earliest decades of his career, not only in his incisive yet subtle medallic portraiture, but also in his documented activity as a restorer of classical sculptures. He is first recorded in Rome in early 1497, as an advisor on the acquisition of antiquities, but it is safely supposed that this was not his first visit there. After 1501, Antico settled permanently at the Gonzaga court at Gazzuolo, where he died in mid July 1528.

It was certainly this sculptor's unswerving commitment to the revival of antiquity with the greatest possible accuracy, yet with fresh vitality and grace, that earned him the sobriquet Antico in his own time and his continuing renown in our own. While his work as a medalist is an important element in his overall stylistic evolution, it must be viewed as but one expressive outlet for a highly complex and multi-faceted artistic personality.

Joseph R. Bliss

Antico
Gianfrancesco Gonzaga di Rodigo (born 1443, lord of Sabbioneta 1479–96)
16
Bronze, cast
Diameter 40.7 mm
Washington, The National Gallery of Art, Samuel H. Kress Collection
1957.14.664

Obverse: Diagonally truncated profile bust facing to the left, wearing a classical cloak fastened at the shoulder. The subject's strong features and fleshy face are framed by long, flowing hair terminating in a mass of curls at the nape of the neck. Legend: (triangular stops) IOHANNES FRANCISCVS • GONZ[aga] • (Gianfrancesco Gonzaga). Pearled border.
Reverse: In the center, the figure of Fortune standing on a starry orb, flanked by a nude male tied to a tree and a female figure carrying a spear. On either side are trophies symbolizing the spoils of war. The shield next to the youth is charged with the

16 obv.   16 rev.

Gonzaga device of the thunderbolt. All three stand on a ground line above the exergue. Legend: FOR[tunae] • VICTRICI (To Fortune the victress—or: To Fortune, Victory). The T and R are conflated, and the second I is smaller and placed inside the C. In the exergue, the signature: ANTI[co]. Pearled border.

16a
Bronze, cast
Diameter 40 mm
Paris, Bibliothèque Nationale, Cabinet des Médailles
Ital. 222

Obverse and reverse as above.

Only a decade before the birth of this Gianfrancesco Gonzaga, his grandfather—also Gianfrancesco—had been named marquess of Mantua by Emperor Sigismund. That event was of paramount importance for the subsequent history of the family, as it marked the beginning of two centuries of fully sanctioned Gonzaga rule over Mantua and its surrounding territories. It also signaled their emergence as a true princely family of the Renaissance, one that henceforth patronized the arts with new vigor and seriousness of purpose.[1]

On the death of his father, Lodovico II, in 1478, the younger Gianfrancesco and his four brothers divided up the Gonzaga holdings, creating principalities with distinct ancestral lineages separate from the parent court in Mantua, but under its control both politically and artistically.[2] Gianfrancesco received properties to the west of Mantua, including Bozzolo, Sabbioneta, and Gazzuolo, and in the following year Emperor Frederick III (cat. no. 40) named him count of Rodigo as well. In the same year, while serving as a *condottiere* in the army of Ferrante I of Naples, he met and married Antonia del Balzo (1441–1538), daughter of the prince of Altamura. They made their residence at Bozzolo, and reigned there over a highly cultivated court until Gianfrancesco's death in 1496.

Antico produced a number of medals of this couple shortly after their marriage, and ever since these were first studied they have been regarded as Antico's earliest surviving works, created shortly after their marriage in 1479.[3] Recently, however, a more precise chronology for these medals has been established, based on a thorough examination of their style and iconography.[4] There is throughout the series a definite change in the treatment of the portrait bust from a more naturalistic style to increasing classicism. The handling of the lettering also becomes more assured. It therefore appears that the pieces range in date from about 1478–79 to 1486–90.

The present medal would thus be the last of Antico's portraits of Gianfrancesco.[5] Here the corpulent, middle-aged ruler is depicted in classical dress, while earlier medals show him to be younger and wearing contemporary court attire. The iconography and style of its reverse would also suggest that this medal was the last of the series. With the exception of the very earliest of them, all of the other reverses are devoted to Gianfrancesco and Antonia's *imprese*, or personal devices.[6] This three-figure image is less dynastic in intent, and certainly alludes to Gianfrancesco's numerous accomplishments. It is generally believed that the two figures flanking the central figure of Fortune are Mars and Minerva, but this should be seriously questioned.[7] It is more plausible that the nude youth tied to a tree is a bound captive symbolizing military defeat, and that the female figure is Victory.[8]

Joseph R. Bliss

17 obv.   17 rev.

Antico
Diva Giulia
17
Bronze, cast
Diameter 34.9 mm
Washington, The National Gallery of Art, Samuel H. Kress
   Collection
1957.14. 666

Obverse: Portrait bust of a woman to the right. Her wavy hair is brushed back at the sides and bound up at the back with a pearl-studded headdress and a wide laurel wreath. She is fashionably attired in a pleated over-dress fastened with a satyr-head brooch over a rumpled blouse. Legend: (triangular stops) • DIVA IVLIA • PRIMVM • FELIX • (The divine Giulia, happy—or lucky—for the first time). Pearled border.
Reverse: A highly charged and tightly compacted battle scene between soldiers and Amazons. In the center, a nude warrior prepares to slay a kneeling Amazon, who rests her left leg on the body of a slain foe or comrade. This group is encircled by the figures of another warrior attempting to unhorse another Amazon and a mounted soldier attacking an Amazon standing

next to her fallen mount. The exergue is filled with military and naval trophies and devices, including a cuirass, helmet, shield, cornucopia, trident, ship's prow, anchor, and small dolphin. Legend: (triangular stops) DVBIA • FORTV[n] • A (Uncertain—or doubtful—fortune). Engraved on the lower ridge of the exergue line, the signature: ANTICVS. Pearled border.

17a
Bronze, cast
Diameter 35 mm
London, Victoria & Albert Museum, Salting Collection
A210–1910

Obverse and reverse as above.

Masterful as it is in terms of its delicacy and technical refinement, this medal is nonetheless a mystery, for scholars have yet to identify its subject. On two occasions Hill advanced the theory of Mrs. Ady that the sitter might be Giulia Gonzaga Colonna (1513–1566), but in his *Corpus* he retracted that identification.[1] More recently it has been revived, with the suggestion that the medal was made to commemorate her wedding to Vespasiano Colonna in 1528. Because Giulia was only thirteen when she married and only fifteen when Antico died, the identification is still unlikely inasmuch as the woman on the medal is far from being a nubile young girl.[2] In fact she appears somewhat matronly, and the violent battle scene replete with an ominous legend on the reverse would be inappropriate for a marriage medal. As is often pointed out, too, the Gonzaga device of a thunderbolt is found on the shield held by one of the Amazons. It does not necessarily follow, however, that the female depicted was a Gonzaga by birth. Perhaps she was one of the many female members of the Gonzaga court, and as such was entitled to use the thunderbolt device. Finally, it seems to have escaped attention that she wears a laurel wreath. This may be funerary in nature, indicating that she had died before the medal was cast, which would help explain both the scene of mortal combat on the reverse and the inscription on the front. In imperial Rome, the appellation "divine" was only accorded to the emperor and members of his family posthumously.

In any event, the superb design and meticulous execution of the reverse Amazonomachy vibrantly attest to Antico's virtuosity and place him among the leading Renaissance medalists. Within the restricted space available to him, he has compressed a dynamic and tightly interwoven composition of tiny but highly energized combatants and agitated steeds. Effortlessly assuming a rich variety of poses, the figures thrust emphatically to the right. No less impressive are the expansive spatial recession, conveyed in relatively shallow relief on such a diminutive scale, and such intricate details as the fluent anatomy of the central warrior or the diaphanous drapery of the Amazon fallen to his mercy.

To judge from this sculptor's bronze statuettes, he did not slavishly copy classical antiquities, but rather used them as points of departure, transcribing them into his own stylistic idiom. The same seems true of his medals. Although he would have been familiar with antique coins and gems, Antico obviously based this particular reverse composition on the narrative reliefs found on classical sarcophagi. As Ann Hersey Allison has postulated, its two central figures may have been taken from a fragmentary Amazon sarcophagus in Rome.[3] The mounted soldiers populating the remainder of the scene were no doubt inspired by those often encountered on a different type of battle sarcophagus such as the one brought to Mantua in 1524 or 1526 by the Italian painter Giulio Romano (c. 1499–1546).[4]

Various features make this the master's choicest medal and indicate that it was his last. Of all his medallic portrait busts, this one is the most overtly classical in mood, not because of the externals of the sitter's dress or hair style, but rather her stoic demeanor and sullen aloofness, reminiscent of many ancient Roman portrait coins. The sublime reverse is relentless in its classical detail and character.

With this medal he reached a true maturity, resolving many of the problems evident in his earlier designs and attaining an epigrammatic lucidity and balance. In his exploration of the emergence of the Mantuan medalist and plaquette artist Moderno, Douglas Lewis has initiated the task of investigating the mutual influences among the many medalists who flourished within the milieu of the Gonzaga court.[5] For sound reasons, he dates the present medal to c. 1500–1502.[6]

Joseph R. Bliss

Galeazzo Mondella, called Moderno
(1467–1528)

A coherent group of twelve plaquette designs (from some forty-five related inventions currently credited to this master) is signed with either the initials or contractions of "Modernus Fecit" or "Opus Moderni." Both the signed and attributed groups establish an insistent claim for the recognition of their author as the most accomplished artist of Italian Renaissance plaquettes. A constantly recurring focus on the art of the western Veneto in his early work, as well as his gravitation to Venice in the latter stages of his career, make it virtually certain that Moderno was Galeazzo Mondella of Verona. His plaquettes display an intimate awareness of preceding and contemporary Veronese art. Galeazzo Mondella's brother Girolamo was a celebrated painter and an intimate of the Este court in Ferrara, and Moderno's earliest works, from about 1485, show a lively interest in Ferrarese painting as well as a disposition toward humanist themes. His main inspiration came from Mantegna (1431–1506), above all during the principal period of the latter's life in Mantua, where Moderno may have had access to the master's studio. It is striking that Moderno's work has virtually no parallels at all with the art of Padua.

As early as 1487, Antico (cat. nos. 16–17) and Moderno appear to have chosen their pseudonyms simultaneously at Mantua, where Moderno evidently worked as a medalist. Thereafter he must regularly have frequented the city and its court. Within this narrow range bounded by Verona, Ferrara, and Mantua, he seems to have been almost as peripatetic as a contemporary engraver, Nicoletto da Modena, whom he may well have known: Nicoletto's prints very frequently reflect Moderno's plaquettes and are themselves often the sources of later copies by Giovanni Antonio da Brescia. By about the turn of the sixteenth century, Moderno seems to have had first-hand experience of the emotionally expressive terracotta sculpture groups then characteristic of Modena and Bologna. Humanist, ecclesiastical, or even ducal contacts at Mantua may have introduced Moderno to the greatest patron of his late years, Cardinal Domenico Grimani of Venice. Through this connection, he seems to have developed a considerable Venetian clientele, and perhaps to have turned more exclusively to gem engraving.

His work moves from a tentative provincial eclecticism to a confident and authoritative Roman Renaissance classicism influenced by Raphael and the antique. He may never have traveled at any distance beyond the Veneto during the discernible thirty years of his working life (1485–1515), although Cardinal Grimani's support is likely to have helped him to visit Rome in the latter years of that span—perhaps particularly during the imperial invasions of the Veneto (1509–1516). After the restoration of his family to the noble council in Verona in 1517, Moderno may have turned from art to civic affairs, or possibly even traveled to France, as Vasari supposed. At the end of the decade 1517–27, one in which there are no records of his whereabouts, he is once more documented in Verona, where he died in the following year.

The family shop, of which Moderno had become the head in 1512, was inherited by his son Giambattista Mondella (1506–c. 1572), whose profession was also fine metalworking. For some time Moderno's designs continued to be reissued, also augmented, adapted, and further developed. There is some evidence that a few of his most popular matrices may have been transferred to Padua after his death. His plaquettes were widely admired and conspicuously influential in the Veneto, Emilia, and Lombardy. Farther afield, his designs were sketched by Dürer and Holbein, and incorporated into French Renaissance sculpture. One of the best of them, *David and a Companion with the Slain Goliath*, provided Michelangelo with the model for a figure in his *Last Judgment* in the Sistine Chapel.

Douglas Lewis

Attributed to Moderno
Magdalena Mantuana
18
Bronze, cast
Diameter 46.8 mm
Washington, The National Gallery of Art, Samuel H. Kress Collection
1957.14.1321

Obverse: Bust with double-curved truncation to right. The sitter's hair is parted in the center of her forehead and combed into a straight long fall over the cheeks, the rest gathered in a coif behind. She wears a brocade or embroidered dress with a low, square-cut neckline and separate sleeves, of which one attachment bow is visible on the shoulder. A chain of heavy links falls from the nape of her neck over her bodice. Legend: MAGDALENA MANTVANA DIE XX NO[vembris] MCCCCCIIII (Magdalena Mantovana [i.e. of Mantua] on the 20th day of November, 1504). Pearled border.

Reverse: Opportunity, represented with the forelock of Fortune, seizing Time. The latter, in flight, looks back over her shoulder. She holds an hourglass in her left hand and the bar of a scale in her right.[1] Both allegorical female figures wear loose, fluttering drapery, their hair streaming in the wind behind them. Legend: BENE HANC CAPIAS ET CAPTAN [for CAPTAM] TENETO (leaf stop) X (leaf stop) (Seize her well, and once she is caught, hold on to her; X). Pearled border.

18a obv.   18a rev.

18a
Bronze, cast
Diameter 46.5 mm
London, The British Museum

Obverse and reverse as above.

In terms of its handsomely resolved unity of sensitive portraiture, classically balanced epigraphy, and a reverse as creatively composed as the best Renaissance plaquettes, this grandly conceived and delicately wrought masterwork, hitherto (quite correctly) attributed to an artist working at Mantua "in the manner of Antico,"[2] is the finest of the half-dozen medals recently attributed to Galeazzo Mondella, called Moderno.[3] It is most immediately notable in devoting a full half of its monumental obverse inscription, directly opposite the two elements of the lady's name, to an invocation of a specific day—perhaps the only such dedication among Italian medals. The *impresa* on its reverse reinforces this temporal specificity, with a magnificently elaborated image of Opportunity seizing Time.[4]

The figure of Time is an almost exact reversal, with slightly modified gestures of the arms and somewhat more simply rendered draperies, of the right-hand Maenad in Moderno's nearly contemporaneous plaquette of *The Death of Orpheus*, which probably shortly predates the spring of 1503.[5] An earlier stage in his development of these related figures is evident in the Deianira from his splendid *Nessus* plaquette,[6] where almost every detail of attitude and gesture is closely related to those of the present Time, even to waving tresses flowing horizontally rather than diagonally from the back-turned head, in a movement directly opposing the outstretched arms. Moderno's *Entombment* plaquette with a figured sarcophagus[7] has the distinction of reusing both of the figures from the present reverse: the Time is reversed—and her draperies once more elaborated—to become the wailing Magdalene, while the Opportunity is directly transposed, now as a male nude, into the central relief group on the sarcophagus. The Opportunity figure, with only a turn of her head and the slipping off of her draperies, becomes the identically posed Nike on Moderno's *Mars and Victory* plaquette.[8]

Moderno's obverse portrait of Magdalena Mantuana[9] has a more interesting progeny than it does a parentage: it allows us to see Moderno as a distinctly innovative medalist whose designs deeply interested his Mantuan colleagues. Magdalena's portrait has consorted most oddly with Antico's likenesses of Antonia del Balzo and Diva Giulia (cat. no. 17), on the plate in Hill's *Corpus* where it was placed among works of "Antico and his school"—accurate though that designation may have been with regard to its reverse.[10] Magdalena's calm, full, and gentle image, informally coiffed and attired in a simple dress with only one plain necklace, contrasts sharply with the taut, wiry profiles of Antico's ladies, elaborately draped, coiffed, and jeweled. Its intimate realism finds its closest parallel—apart from the somewhat coarsened Modernesque medal of Luca de' Zuhari, with which Hill had already connected it—among the portraits of the courtier-medalist Giancristoforo Romano (1470–1512).

Closer to home, an associated Mantuan medalist made an exact reproduction of Moderno's Magdalena portrait, with strangely debased lettering repeating the sitter's name and year date.[11] Two earlier and somewhat related medals by another hand, one of them perhaps representing our original lady, somewhat younger, are the ones of Madalene Mantuana, with a reverse emblem of Chastity assaulted by Love,[12] and F. Francinae, with a twin device of the phoenix on a burning pyre.[13] Hill was close to the mark in assigning them to a medalist "in the neighborhood of Giancristoforo Romano," though I would prefer "close to Moderno." I do not accept Hill's theory that the letters PM immediately following the earlier Madalene's name may constitute the initials of an unknown master signing himself "P . . . Mantuanus."[14] The same enigmatic letters in fact occur in quite a different way on two other contemporary Mantuan medals discussed below (cat. no. 20), together with the small, twin designs of the Madalene and Francinae pieces just mentioned.

Douglas Lewis

18a obv.

19 obv.

19 obv.

19 rev.

Mantuan School ("manner of Antico")
Giulia Astallia
19
Bronze, cast
Diameter 61.8 mm; diameter of the outer perimeter of the
  obverse inscription from the A in DIVA through the T in
  ASTALLIA, 59.2 mm
Washington, The National Gallery of Art, Samuel H. Kress
  Collection
1957.14.668

Obverse: Half-length figure of a young girl, facing left, with an
elaborate coiffure. She wears a close-fitting *gamurra*, split and
laced aross the chest, with an apronlike overskirt tied around
her waist.[1] The neckline has a border of vine-scroll ornament.
Legend: • DIVA • IVLIA • ASTALLIA • (The divine Giulia
Astallia).
Reverse: A phoenix on a flaming pyre looking up at light rays
streaming forth from a cloud. Legend: • EXEMPLVM VNICVM •
FOR[mae, or -titudinis] • ET • PVD[icitiae] • (A unique example of beauty [or fortitude] and modesty).

19a
Bronze, cast
Diameter 64.0 mm
London, The British Museum

Obverse and reverse as above.

Justly praised as "one of the most fresh and charming medals in
the whole Italian series,"[2] this is also one of the most mysterious. It has been assigned to Mantua since Friedländer first
catalogued it following medals by the Mantuan Bartolo Talpa
(cat. no. 15), though he was, quite rightly, unable to attribute it
directly to that artist.[3] Subsequent scholars continued to debate
the attribution.[4] In 1930, Hill finally offered the designation it
has usually borne ever since: "manner of Antico."[5] Several
factors suggest that the Giulia Astallia was created in the 1480s,

about a generation earlier than the more delicately modeled
Magdalena (cat. no. 18), by an artist formed in the tradition of
Pisanello, but also aware of recent Florentine innovations.

Yet one must wonder if the often-noted similarity to Florentine late quattrocento painted profile portraits[6] is purely coincidental. In particular, the crisp profile, the turned torso, the
elegant curving contour down the long neck and slightly sloped
shoulder, and the fantastically woven hairstyle recall Piero di
Cosimo's so-called Simonetta Vespucci at Chantilly, most convincingly dated to the 1480s.[7] The spatially involved pose, with
the chest turned in three-quarter view leading the eye into
depth and showing both arms, is apparently unprecedented in a
medallic portrait.

This peculiar convergence of northern and central Italian
features may perhaps be explained by the identity of the sitter.[8]
Friedländer proposed that she was from the Mantuan region, a
peasant girl known as Giulia of Gazzuolo, whose tragic story
Bandello tells in his *Novelle*.[9] Raped at age seventeen by a
servant of the bishop of Ferrara, she chose to drown herself
rather than outlive her honor. Her courage prompted Bishop
Lodovico Gonzaga (in office 1483–1511) to propose a monument to her in Gazzuolo's central piazza. The presence on the
medal of the self-immolating phoenix and the high praise of the
subject's unparalleled modesty and fortitude (according to one
reading of the inscription) nicely supported this identification,
which quickly won general acceptance. But Friedländer himself
admitted that research in Mantua did not confirm the surname
Astallia for Bandello's unhappy Giulia. And in fact the name
Astallia (also Astalli, Astaglia) is associated with an old Roman
family, among whose members several variants of the name
Giulio or Giulia occur.[10]

How might a Mantuan medalist have produced a portrait
medal of a Roman girl? And why? If she had been betrothed to a
Mantuan, a portrait drawing or painting could have been sent
north to her fiancé. Such a portrait might have been commissioned in Rome from one of the Florentine artists who arrived in
1481–82 to work on the wall frescoes of the Sistine chapel,
perhaps in the entourage of Botticelli, Ghirlandaio, or Cosimo

Rosselli.[11] Yet essential aspects of the medal taken together—the sorrowfully downcast gaze, the fantastic coiffure contrasting with the simple dress, the appellation "divine" (see cat. no. 17), and the phoenix on the reverse—suggest a commemorative purpose. The legendary phoenix was quite literally unique, for only a single specimen lived at any time. It ended its life by building a pyre of aromatic woods and spices and immolating itself in the flames. Its next incarnation then arose from the ashes. The bird is thus an appropriate symbol for any unique being, for immortal Virtue, or for resurrection.[12]

If the girl died betrothed, the hypothetical portrait sent from Rome might have served as a model for a medal.[13] Or perhaps there was no betrothal, and some astute Astalli patron simply chose to bypass the available Roman medalists and the robust naturalism of Niccolò Fiorentino, and turn instead to the region where Pisanello's influence lived on, to commission a delicate and poignant memorial to a girl who, like Cecilia Gonzaga (cat. no. 7), had died young.

Documents yet to be discovered in the Vatican or Astalli archives in Rome may illuminate the origins of this lovely and popular medal, as unique as the proclaimed virtues of the subject.

Alison Luchs

Mantuan School
Jacoba Correggia
20
Bronze, cast
Diameter 54 mm
London, The British Museum, George III Collection

Obverse: Bust with a triple-curved truncation to right. The sitter wears loosely dressed long hair in a netted coif held by a jeweled fillet, a brocade or embroidered heavy gown with a deeply cut bodice laced over a sheer blouse with gathered sleeves, and two chains with pendant jewels. In the field, a day lily, a branch of laurel, and an oak twig, all bound together with a buckled leather strap. Legend with triskele stops: (leaf) IACOBA • CORRIGIA • FORME • AC MORVM • DOMINᴬ (Jacoba Correggia, mistress of beauty and manners). Pearled border.

Reverse: Nude, winged Love, blindfolded, seated on a tree stump sprouting a single, leafless branch to which the figure is bound by a buckled leather strap. Another such strap is tied to an upper limb. Beside the stump on the left, a broken quiver with arrows, and on the right, a bow with a broken string. Legend, with hollow cinquefoil stops: CESSI • DEA MILITAT ISTAT • (In such wise does the goddess wage war [that] I have surrendered). In the field, flanking the figure of Love, the larger letters P M. Plain rim fillet.

This unusual and impressive medal has several idiosyncratic features, of which the most striking is its shift of the portrait forward and downward in the field so as to make room for an *impresa*, normally to be expected on the reverse. This device consists of a day lily, a sprig of laurel, and an oak twig tied together with a leather strap, or *correggia*. The strap is a visual pun on the sitter's family name, and indeed this connection is emphasized in that the end of the strap, rebuslike, virtually underlines her given name in the inscription. All three plants reinforce much the same meaning: the lily (in one form or another) is usually a symbol of purity, the laurel of chastity, and the oak of faith. All are here bound together by the reference to the sitter, who exemplifies these virtues.

The two classic components of the medal, a portrait and a personal emblem, are here conjoined on a single surface, which is nonetheless surprisingly uncrowded, and indeed very appealingly balanced.[1] The large and comparatively massive portrait is tellingly offset by the calligraphic elegance of the belted bouquet, and the two are beautifully unified by the festive form of the inscription with its dynamic, wavy stops.

The reason for such an unaccustomed concentration of all the sitter's personal references on this obverse is the more impersonal, even public character of its reverse. As Hill remarked, the articulation of the two sides is very different.[2] In fact, we know

20 obv.

20 rev.

20 obv.

that this reverse was adapted—with the addition of two buck-led straps as a link to the lady of the obverse—from a preexist-ing design with a much more generic provenance and meaning.

The original pattern for the design was a reverse from the early 1490s by Niccolò Fiorentino (cat. nos. 42–46), showing Virginity tying Love to a tree.[3] That composition was bor-rowed—reversed, but otherwise quite exactly—by Moderno (cat. no. 18) for his *Death of Orpheus* plaquette (c. 1500–1502), in which the hero is tied to a dead tree and beaten by Maenads,[4] proof that the Mantuan masters were fully familiar with the medallic designs of central Italy. An accomplished Mantuan medalist (possibly Melioli?) subsequently combined Niccolò Fiorentino's original iconography and Moderno's more classical image to form the beautiful reverse of Love tied to a laurel tree for the 1505 medal commemorating the accession of Lucrezia Borgia (1480–1519) as duchess of Ferrara.[5]

The image of Love restrained by circumstance was bound to intrigue the amorous court of Mantua, and our unknown medalist devised this reverse as a simplified copy after Lu-crezia's. In it, he restores the bare tree from Moderno's pla-quette. Confusingly, the identical reverse—complete with the *correggie* and the letters P M—appears on the medal of a Maddalena Rossi, another otherwise unrecorded lady of the Gonzaga or Este courts.[6]

The portrait on the present medal is treated very appealingly as an early sixteenth-century development directly out of Antico (cat. nos. 16–17),[7] while the one of Maddalena Rossi is an even more specific (though less talented) parallel to Mod-erno's portrait of Magdalena Mantuana (cat. no. 18).

G. F. Hill wondered whether the letters P M, found on this reverse and on the obverse of the Madalene Mantuana medal, might constitute an artist's signature, possibly a "P . . . Man-tuanus."[8] This is manifestly impossible, for in the latter in-stance they appear as a qualification to the lady's name. They are much more likely to abbreviate one of the Gonzaga court's stock descriptive epithets such as "pulchra(e) Mantuana(e)" (pretty Mantuan[s]) or, more plausibly yet, to stand for a still more generalized formula such as "pro merenti" (for the one who is deserving)[9] or "pro meritis" (as [she] deserves, or in accordance with [her] deserts).[10]

Douglas Lewis

Costanzo da Ferrara
(c. 1450–c. 1525)

Costanzo's portrait medal of Sultan Mehmed II is his only known signed work, but its trenchant characterization and technical mastery are ample proof of his talents. It should caution us that fame has not dealt evenly with artists of skill. Costanzo deserves greater recognition, but he is little known for several reasons. In the first place, he led a peripatetic exis-tence in the early part of his life, and records of his activity are scant. When he did settle, it was in Naples, which did not develop a critical record of its artists in the late fifteenth and early sixteenth centuries as did Venice or Florence. Until re-

cently, no serious attempt has been made to establish a corpus of his surviving works, and attributions to Costanzo have been complicated by the fact that almost any Italian depiction of a Turk from the late fifteenth century has been ascribed to an-other artist who visited Constantinople during the reign of Mehmed the Conqueror, Gentile Bellini.[1] The result has been to obscure our understanding of Bellini's work and to diminish the contribution of Costanzo.

A letter sent in 1485 to the duke of Ferrara by the Este ambassador in Naples, Battista Bendidio, states that Costanzo had been sent to Turkey by Ferrante I of Naples, following a request by Mehmed II. The sultan did not apparently ask for Costanzo by name, but merely requested a painter with a high reputation.[2] The date of his visit is not given, but Costanzo is said to have lived in Turkey "many" years, and to have so pleased the sultan that he was made a *cavaliere*. Bendidio adds that he was known as Costanzo da Ferrara, as he had lived in Ferrara for a long period, and his wife was Ferrarese.[3] Archival records document the presence of a Costanzo Lombardo and a Costanzo de Moysis in Naples in the 1480s and 1490s, and it is generally agreed that the three Costanzos are one and the same person. Costanzo de Moysis is further identified in a document of 1488 as a "Venetian painter."[4]

Costanzo's career, then, seems to have taken him from his native city of Venice to Lombardy, Ferrara, and ultimately Naples. The only known records of his work are from Naples, and it was there that he achieved considerable success, perhaps beginning his career in the workshop of another Venetian painter, Antonio Solario, "lo Zingaro." Following his successful visit to Turkey, Costanzo continued to receive princely com-missions. In 1485 he painted a portrait, on the orders of Battista Bendidio, of Ferrante d'Este, who was staying in Naples at the time. In 1488, Costanzo painted a historical picture of the rebel leader Marino Marzano for Alfonso of Aragon's villa, "La Duch-esca." Other paintings in the villa depicted the Turkish siege of Otranto. Given his experience of Turkey, Costanzo may have been involved as an adviser, if nothing else, in these other works. In 1491 he agreed to collaborate with the Sicilian artist Riccardo Quartararo, and in 1492 he was working with yet another painter, Carluccio da Padova.[5]

There is as yet no agreement on which paintings, if any, should be attributed to Costanzo.[6] A miniature in the Topkapi Sarayi Museum in Istanbul is closely related to his medal of Mehmed II. It has been uncritically ascribed to Costanzo since its first publication in 1932, but it is difficult to reconcile the anodyne appearance of the miniature with the incisive and animate rendering of the medal, which though half the size is more lively in detail and more thoughtful in expression. As I have argued elsewhere, the miniature should be attributed instead to an Ottoman follower of Costanzo, one trained in the Western manner.[7]

The lack of signed or securely attributable works makes it difficult to reconstruct Costanzo's artistic career. He is said, however, to have been particularly gifted as a draftsman, for Summonte, writing to his fellow critic the Venetian Marcan-

21 obv.

tonio Michiel in 1524, describes him as "pictor di bon disegno più che di altra cosa."[8] Summonte's claim is fully borne out if we attribute to Costanzo a series of drawings of Turks that have long been assumed to be the work of Gentile Bellini.[9] These include the gouache *Seated Scribe* in the Isabella Stewart Gardner Museum in Boston, and a pair of pen-and-ink drawings in the British Museum of a seated Turkish archer and a seated Turkish lady. The Boston drawing is of especial importance for two reasons. First, it bears a Persian inscription of the sixteenth century that ascribes the work to Costanzo rather than to Bellini, as Sarre attempted to argue.[10] Secondly, it was a painting of considerable influence in the East. There is a close copy of it in the Freer Gallery of Art, and there are several other derivatives by Turkish, Persian, and possibly also Deccani painters.[11]

The pair in the British Museum are the key drawings of a group of seven single-figure studies of orientals. Not all seven are originals, but they reflect a common source. This is not the context in which to discuss the drawings fully, but if Costanzo is accepted as that source, it is clear that his influence extended to the West as well as the East. Several of the figures were copied by Pinturicchio (1454–1513) for his frescoes in the Borgia apartments in Rome, begun in 1492, and later in the Piccolomini Library in Siena. The reattribution of these draw-

ings to Costanzo would establish him as an artist of considerable talent and influence, and confirm the impression conveyed by his medal of Mehmed the Conqueror, justly described as one of the "finest portrait medals of the Renaissance."

Julian Raby

Costanzo da Ferrara
Mehmed II (1432–1481)
21
Copper alloy, cast
Diameter 123 mm
Washington, The National Gallery of Art, Samuel H. Kress Collection
1957.14.695

Obverse: Bust facing to the left, wearing a turban and broad-collared outer garment over a loose-fitting robe. Legend: SVITANUS [*sic*] • MOHAMETH • OTHOMANVS • TVR-CORVM • IMPERATOR (Sultan Mehmed of the house of Osman, emperor of the Turks).
Reverse: HIC • BELLI • FVLMEN • POPVLOS • PROSTRAVIT • ET • VRBES (This man, the thunderbolt of war, has laid low peoples and cities). In a *tabula ansata* in the exergue, the signature: CONSTANTIVS F[ecit].

21 rev.

The medal depicts the Ottoman sultan on both the obverse and reverse. The bust portrait on the obverse reveals a ruler whose power and determination were as yet undiminished by advancing years. It thus contrasts with the portrait by Gentile Bellini in the National Gallery in London, which was painted in the last year of Mehmed's life and shows him etiolated and unwell.[1] Costanzo's image depicts a man of powerful physique, and conveys a sense of the ruler who seized Constantinople for the Ottomans in 1453 and whose subsequent expansion of the empire through victories in the Balkans and Anatolia are alluded to in the stern inscription on the reverse.

Costanzo has emphasized the sultan's physical presence by exposing part of his bull neck and by concentrating the weight of the image to the rear of the neck and into the shoulders. To do so, he has extended the back of the turban, which he has angled to meet the broad revers of the sultan's outer garment. There is a deliberate contrast between the texture of the pleated folds of the turban and the smooth collar, but together they form a solid frame for the sultan's features. By sharply delineating Mehmed's aquiline nose, pointed chin, and high cheekbone, Costanzo conveys a definite alertness to balance the impression of stolid power. The emphasis on Mehmed's eye and raised eyebrow suggests a watchful and questioning nature.

The equestrian image on the reverse shows the sultan against a rocky landscape with leafless trees. This follows medallic conventions of the period, based on the compositions of Pisanello (cat. nos. 4–9). The date of the medal is unknown, as are the dates of Costanzo's visit to Constantinople.

Another version of the medal bears the date 1481. It is less finely modeled than the unicum in the National Gallery of Art, and carries an obtrusive double circular border and a remodeled inscription. It was perhaps issued on the news of Mehmed's death in that year.[2] Costanzo's medal is possibly the one referred to by the Mantuan ambassador in 1489, and it is certain that both Paolo Giovio, bishop of Como, and Giorgio Vasari owned copies of the 1481 version.[3] The medal—most probably in this later edition—appears to have been the basis for a somewhat fanciful sixteenth-century engraving of Mehmed II, while Giovio's specimen served as the basis for a painted portrait of which copies exist in both the Uffizi and Vienna.[4] Costanzo's medal thus did much to disseminate Mehmed's likeness in Europe.

Giovio and Vasari both attributed the medal to Pisanello, despite the signature in the exergue, in their copies: OPUS COSTANTII. The mistake nevertheless reflects the ultimate inspiration behind Costanzo's work as a medalist and draftsman.

Julian Raby

22 obv.

22 rev.

Adriano Fiorentino (Adriano di Giovanni de' Maestri)
(born c. 1450–60, died 1499)

The first document we have for Adriano is apparently the signature on the bronze group *Bellerophon Taming Pegasus* in the Kunsthistorisches Museum, Vienna. It is undated, but co-signed by Bertoldo di Giovanni (cat. nos. 39, 40) as modeler and Adriano as founder. Given Bertoldo's position in the Medici household and Adriano's later proven skills as a courtier, there is a strong possibility that the latter started as a member of the Medici palace staff. He left Florence around 1488 to work with Buonaccorso Ghiberti, who was employed as sculptor as well as artillery worker by Virginio Orsini, a *condottiere* in the service of the house of Aragon. In Naples he made medals of King Ferrante II and the writers Pietro Compatre, Jacopo Sannazaro, and Giovanni Gioviano Pontano, as well as a bronze bust and a marble relief portrait of the latter. By 1495, when he made two medals, he was working for the court of Urbino. A bronze bust of Frederick the Wise of Saxony, in Dresden, is signed and dated 1498, and two medals with German subjects must date from about the same time. Adriano's burial in Santa Maria Novella, Florence, is recorded on June 12, 1499.

James David Draper

Adriano Fiorentino
Elisabetta Gonzaga, duchess of Urbino (1471–1526)
22
Bronze, cast
Diameter 83.0 mm
London, Victoria & Albert Museum, Salting Collection
A204–1910

Obverse: Bust facing right, wearing a necklace, her hair netted and tied into a long braid. Legend: ELISABET[ta] • GONZAGA • FELTRIA • DVCISS[a] • VRBINI • (Elisabetta Gonzaga of Montefeltro, duchess of Urbino).
Reverse: A woman naked above the waist, reclining with her head supported against a boxy enframement, raising the ends of her girdle with both hands. In the air, a rain cloud approaches. Legend: HOC FVGIENTI FORTVNAE DICATIS (This you dedicate to fleeting fortune).

22a
Bronze, cast
Diameter 85.80 mm; diameter of the outer perimeter of the inscription from the V in VRBINI to the first A in GONZAGA, 67.43 mm
Washington, The National Gallery of Art, Samuel H. Kress Collection
1957.14.700

Obverse and reverse as above.

Elisabetta Gonzaga, born into the ruling house of Mantua, was the wife of Guidobaldo da Montefeltro, the only son of the illustrious *condottiere* and lord of Urbino, Federigo da Montefeltro (cat. no. 25). Guidobaldo succeeded his father in 1482 and wed Elisabetta in 1489.

She was the sister-in-law and a close companion of Isabella d'Este, and with her husband a victim of the territorial ambitions of Cesare Borgia (born 1475–76, died 1507). The couple had no children, and Guidobaldo's heir was his nephew Francesco Maria della Rovere, whom he adopted in the year of his death.

A letter survives that Elisabetta wrote in May 1495 to her older brother Francesco II Gonzaga, fourth marquess of Mantua. It is a document precious for the light it sheds on the courtly milieu of the medalist. Noting that Adriano, "servant and familiar" of the late king of Aragon, had recently arrived in Urbino altogether destitute, she recommends him to the marquess's service as a "good sculptor" who has "made here some very beautiful medals," and as a "good composer of sonnets, a good player of the lyre, and he also improvises rather outstandingly."[1]

Adriano seems to have produced only two medals in Urbino, this one and one of Emilia Pia Montefeltro, wife of Federigo's natural son Antonio and Elisabetta's boon companion.[2] With identically pearled borders, each portrays a long-necked beauty with a stiff braid down her back, the *tranche* of each bust shaped much like the profile of an actual statuary bust. In the best specimens of the Elisabetta Gonzaga, a living quality is induced by the truant curls at the sitter's temple, recalling those of Adriano's best-known independent bronze statuette, the *Venus Marina* in the Philadelphia Museum of Art.

Hill mistook the reverse of the present medal for an image of ill fortune, supposing that it referred to the woes that befell the duchy after it was seized by Cesare Borgia in 1502, thus casting doubt on its dating within Adriano's lifetime. However, Settis has demonstrated beyond question that it is compatible with a date of 1495, that the figure represented is Danae, and that the object against which she reclines is a window grate. Danae's father Acrisius imprisoned her to prevent her conceiving the child who would cause his destruction. His exertions were in vain, however, for Jupiter penetrated Danae's cell in the form of the golden shower by which she conceived Perseus. Medieval writers imputed virtue to Danae because she unquestioningly received the god's favor. The *Ovide moralisé* characterizes her as the recipient of the Holy Spirit, and she was even considered a forerunner of the Virgin Mary. Before the sixteenth century investigated the subject for its erotic value, Danae was considered an embodiment of modesty. Medieval convention showed the "Christian Danae" fully clothed, gathering the sacred shower into her skirts. Adriano's midway approach shows her bare above the waist. The fleeting fortune of the legend is to be interpreted in some sense as a passage from imprisonment and misfortune to fecundity and heavenly grace. It is not known precisely how this applied to Elisabetta's fortunes, but it is surely of relevance that contemporary writers refer to her as "the most modest lady on earth."[3]

James David Draper

Sperandio of Mantua
(born 1425–28, died after 1504)

For many years Sperandio's only identifiable works were medals, and although other works of sculpture have been attrib-

uted to him on the basis of documentary evidence, he continues to be known primarily as a medalist.

In fact his activities were more varied. In letters and payments from 1445 and 1447 for unspecified works from Leonello d'Este (cat. no. 5) he is generally described as a goldsmith,[1] and Leonello's brother Ercole paid him in 1476 for work as a painter.[2] During his brief sojourn in Faenza in 1477, he was contracted by the Manfredi family to work in bronze, marble, terra-cotta, and lead, and to produce works in gold, drawings (or designs), and paintings.[3] Lodovico Gonzaga, the bishop of Mantua, recommended him to his brother Gianfrancesco in 1495 as a cannon-founder and architect,[4] and it is as a cannon-founder, or *bombardierus*, that he spent his last working years in Venice.[5]

Sperandio was born in Mantua at an unknown date, but probably between 1425 and 1428. He almost certainly received his earliest training at the hands of his father, Bartolommeo di Sperandio Savelli, an artist of Roman extraction whose name is found in the register of the guild of Mantua's goldsmiths in 1433.[6]

Sperandio grew up in Ferrara, where Pisanello had produced a number of medals. His father's expertise in the manufacture of seal dies would also have been helpful to him as an aspiring medalist. It is unclear when exactly he began his medallic career; no works earlier than 1460 have been attributed to him. The dating of his earliest Ferrarese pieces is highly speculative, and there seems to be no particularly good reason for placing his medal of Bartolommeo Pendaglia (cat. no. 23), for example, or that of the jurisconsult Giustiniano Cavitelli so firmly in the early 1460s.

In 1451, Borso d'Este, only newly succeeded to the dukedom, wrote to the marchioness of Mantua, Barbara of Brandenburg, wishing to know Sperandio's whereabouts. She reported back that he had just left Mantua for parts unknown.[7] By the early 1460s, Sperandio seems to have been in Borso's continual employ; he was salaried in 1463 and 1464, his rent was paid for six months in 1467, and he again received wages in 1468.[8] The account books of Francesco Sforza, the duke of Milan, settled after his death in 1466, show a payment of 31 lire, 6 soldi to Sperandio for an unidentified work. The sum is quite substantial, and the object was probably the portrait medal of the duke—or rather, given the amount, a group of medals.[9] The unusual three-quarter view suggests that the portrait was taken from a drawing or painting, there being no need to suppose that Sperandio ever visited Milan himself.

Borso d'Este's death in 1469 caused a small crisis in the artistic community of Ferrara. Artists and craftsmen could not guarantee the continued patronage of his successor, Niccolò d'Este's legitimate son Ercole. Sperandio wrote to the duke, begging assistance for his impoverished family and sending him, unsolicited, "La Imagine de v[ost]ra Ex[cellen]cia"—probably a medal.[10] He signed himself a goldsmith. His appeal to the new duke of Ferrara appears to have borne fruit, for he continued to work for the Este court.

In May 1476, Carlo Manfredi, the lord of Faenza, requested

22 obv.

23 obv.

Ercole's permission for the artist to visit his city for a few days. He was maneuvering to get Sperandio into his own service, and the next year he wrote again asking the duke to let Sperandio go, specifying that he wanted him to make "many sculptures and other figures carved in stone" for Faenza's cathedral. There is a contract between Carlo Manfredi and the sculptor-medalist from July 1, 1477, and a relief of the Annunciation, still *in situ*, seems likely to be a product of it.[11]

When Carlo was overthrown in a *coup d'etat* by Galeotto Manfredi, Sperandio appears to have survived long enough to produce a medal of the new ruler, but by mid 1478 he had removed with his family and assistants to Bologna.

We are fortunate in having documentation of a dispute in 1479 between the artist and the Bolognese cloth merchant Giacomo del Gilio, who had complained about the price of a Sperandio medal or medals.[12] The piece in question does not survive, but the record reveals something about how medals were thought of and interesting details regarding their manufacture. The work being assessed was in lead, ordinarily a cheap material used either for making workshop models or for copying pre-existing works, but here used for a proof. It showed Gilio on the obverse, together with an inscription identifying him as a Bolognese and asserting that this was a likeness "cum naturalj figura dicti Jacobi" (with the face of the natural Giacomo de Gilio—i.e. with his natural features). It may have been struck ("impresa"), not cast. The goldsmith Francesco Raiboldini (known as Francia; c. 1450–1517), later a noted painter, was called upon for an opinion, and he insisted that given their "mastery" and "manufacture," the works in question were worth not less than thirty gold ducats. This document reveals that medals were sometimes made in editions, the whole of which were the property of the medal's subject.

Despite the large number of medals he made during this period, his career in Bologna, so auspiciously begun, appears to have foundered. His name appears on the list of the poor to whom the commune gave alms at Christmas in the years 1486, 1487, and 1488.[13]

By the late 1480s, Sperandio was back in touch with the Gonzaga of Mantua. A letter of 1488 from Lodovico to his brother Gianfrancesco reveals that the artist was then making a medal or copies of an earlier medal of their late uncle, Cardinal Francesco Gonzaga.

At the beginning of the following decade he had returned to Ferrara; however in early 1494 he left for Padua. The reasons for this journey are unclear, and he left behind no evidence of his stay there.[14]

The recommendation from Bishop Lodovico Gonzaga to his brother the marquess from 1495, mentioned above, appears to have met with some measure of success, for Sperandio soon fashioned medals of both Gianfrancesco and his military employer, Doge Agostino Barbarigo.[15] It was perhaps in response to the opening offered by the Barbarigo medal that he then moved—for the last time—to Venice, where he worked for the arsenal as a cannon-founder. Although no medals can be ascribed to his last years with certainty, he continued to be active

23 obv.

as a sculptor. By 1504 he was too old to work, and though his rent was still covered, his arsenal salary was discontinued. He probably died shortly afterward.

Luke Syson

Sperandio
Bartolommeo Pendaglia (died 1462)
23
Bronze, cast
Diameter 84 mm; diameter of the outer perimeter of the reverse inscription from the N of CAESARIANA to the opposite R, 82 mm
Washington, The National Gallery of Art, Samuel H. Kress Collection
1957.14.705

Obverse: Bust in profile to the left. The sitter's hair is cropped, and he wears a flat-topped hat or mortier. His pleated robe has a stiff, expanding collar. Incised lines on the robe suggest a brocade pattern. Legend: BARTHOLOMAEVS • PENDALIA • INSIGNE • LIBERALITATIS • ET • MUNIFICENTIAE • EXEMPLV[m] (Bartolommeo Pendaglia, the emblem of liberality and model of munificence).
Reverse: A nude male figure is seated on the spoils of war, a cuirass and two shields. He holds a spear in his left hand and a round object (a pearl?) in his right. A thin scarf is draped over his shoulders and flutters down his arms. His left foot rests on a small sack, from which innumerable coins are escaping. Legend: (rose stop) CAESARIANA LIBERALITAS (The liberality of Caesar). Below, the signature: OPVS SPERANDEI (The work of Sperandio).

23 rev.

23a
Bronze, cast
Diameter 88.0 mm; height of bust, 70.4 mm
New York, Michael Hall Collection

Obverse and reverse as above.

The second part of the obverse inscription makes much of the subject's generosity, but Pendaglia could well afford it, for he was perhaps the wealthiest man in Ferrara in the mid fifteenth century. In practice, wealth alone was enough to give a man status, but in fact the Pendaglia claimed noble descent from one of the retinue of Emperor Frederick Barbarossa (born 1123?, reigned 1152–90).[1] Whether or not tradition accorded with fact, Bartolommeo's father, Gabriele Pendaglia, had worked his way up in the court of the Este in Ferrara from cameral notary to the key post of *fattore generale*, administrator of the Este estates, a position he held for nineteen years until his death in 1429.[2] A poem dated 1563 credits Gabriele with laying the foundations of the family's enormous wealth.[3] Certainly Bartolommeo did not have to wait very long to be appointed *fattore generale* himself in 1434, and he was reconfirmed in the post in 1439 and 1452.[4] As a reward for his services, he received considerable benefits from successive Este rulers. In 1435 he added to his agricultural holdings in the Valli with the gift of the stewardship of Consandolo, a piece of land consisting of 4,500 *storii* (about 1,200 acres), two *palatia* (villas), one called "the castle," numerous vineyards, an inn, and livestock. On all of this Bartolommeo and his workers were given tax immunities.[5] More exemptions were granted in 1448 by Leonello d'Este (cat. no. 5), when Pendaglia was allowed to import goods of all kinds

into Ferrara without paying duties.[6] Still another tax exemption extended to him and his cousin Giovanni Romei in 1457 was the excuse for a holiday and grandiose feast in Ferrara's main square. A contemporary chronicle informs us that it was the delight of the people of Ferrara that occasioned the festivities, but one suspects that they were an instance of self-aggrandizing generosity on the part of the two exemptees.[7]

Bartolommeo Pendaglia had reached his apogee in 1452, the year in which Emperor Frederick III (cat. no. 40) made a pilgrimage to Rome. On his return journey, the emperor stopped in Ferrara, where he named Borso d'Este first duke of Modena. Gundersheimer finds proof of Borso's influence with the emperor in the fact that he induced his visitor to take an important role in the wedding ceremonies of his *fattore generale*, Bartolommeo.[8] The bride was Margherita Costabili, who, as she came from one of Ferrara's most ancient and noble families, added considerably to Bartolommeo's social position. She was accompanied to her husband's house by Emperor Frederick and King Ladislav of Hungary (1440–1457). Duke Borso himself attended the celebrations, along with a papal ambassador and sundry other princes. The emperor presented Margherita with a jewel that included a very valuable and beautiful pearl. His gift to Bartolommeo was a knighthood.

As Bartolommeo's wealth and status increased, so did his artistic and cultural patronage. His house, with much use of pure gold, was reckoned the most beautiful in Ferrara, and was considered worthy to receive the connoisseur Pietro Barbo, cardinal of S. Marco and later Pope Paul II, during his sojourn in the city in 1459.[9] Like so many other Ferrarese courtiers, Bartolommeo had the poet Ludovico Carbone write an oration in his honor,[10] and commissioned a medal from Sperandio.

The reverse inscription makes clear reference to Bartolommeo's knighthood. It has been pointed out that the reverse image resembles the famous Felix gem in Oxford, an antique piece with a depiction of the Greek hero Diomedes and the Palladium, the small statue of Pallas that represented the security of Troy.[11] Such a borrowing, however, merely shows that the medalist was familiar with antique prototypes; it has no bearing on the message of his medal.

The nude figure can only symbolize the emperor, his authority represented by the spoils of victory on which he sits and the spear he holds. His liberality is indicated by the gold spilling from the bag beneath his foot. Some have read the sphere he holds in his right hand as an orb, another part of the regalia of authority, but it seems clear that the sphere is being extended as a gift. It is likely that this is the pearl attached to the emperor's wedding gift to Margherita. The combination of the symbolic and the narrative lends the reverse a nice double edge.

The vigorous modeling of the portrait is extended to the reverse, where a slight exaggeration of the musculature and ligaments of the legs and arms gives the figure considerable energy. That energy is underscored by the fact of the spear's breaking through into the inscription. This is evidently one of Sperandio's first surviving medals, and it must be considered early whether it retains its current dating to the early 1460s or is

24 obv.

24 rev.

held to be more or less contemporary with Pendaglia's knighthood.

Luke Syson

Sperandio
Giovanni Bentivoglio (1443–1508)
24
Lead, cast
Diameter 97 mm
University of California at Santa Barbara, University Art Museum, Sigmund Morgenroth Collection

Obverse: Bust-length portrait wearing a soft round cap with an upturned brim and plate armor over chain mail. Legend, with rose stops: IO[hannes] • BENT[ivolius] • II • HANIB[ali] • FILIVS • EQVES • AC • COMES • PATRIAE • PRINCEPS • AC LIBERTATIS • COLUMEN (Giovanni II Bentivoglio, son of Annibale, knight and count, first of his country and supporter of liberty).
Reverse: Giovanni Bentivoglio on horseback, in armor, with a sword at his side and carrying the baton of command. The barding of the horse is decorated in three places with what is probably the Bentivoglio arms.[1] Behind him rides a squire with an elaborate crest on his helmet and carrying a lance. Inscription, with leaf stops: OPVS • S P ERANDEI (The work of Sperandio).

24a
Bronze, cast
Diameter 96.6 mm; diameter of the outer perimeter of the

inscription from the O of IO to the T of PATRIAE, 90.5 mm
London, Victoria & Albert Museum, Salting Collection
A196–1910

The iconography of Sperandio's medal of Giovanni II Bentivoglio is not, apparently, very complicated. It has often been remarked that the reverse is a reworking of Pisanello's medals of Gianfrancesco Gonzaga and Filippo Maria Visconti,[2] a fact sometimes interpreted as demonstrating Sperandio's lack of originality. This choice of models, however, is probably more revealing when seen in the context of Bentivoglio's personal and political ambitions. The rationale behind the medal's production becomes apparent when something of Bentivoglio's biography and the complicated political history of Bologna, his native city, is known.[3]

Bologna was a papal possession, and thus not subject to dynastic rule like that of the Este in Ferrara or the Gonzaga in Mantua. It did, however, have considerable autonomy, maintained in part through the efforts of Annibale Bentivoglio, Giovanni's father. While its laws were subject to the approval of the papal legate, the city was effectively governed by councils drawn from the Bolognese aristocracy, the Riformatori and the Sei di Balia. The ruling class was keen to maintain its autonomy, and part of its strategy was to identify this quasi-independence with the Bentivoglio family. The position of "first citizen" was established, identical with that of *gonfaloniere* of justice, to be held by a member of that family. In addition, the Bentivoglio accumulated great wealth. Annibale was rewarded for his military skills by a five percent levy on every sales contract and every dowry portion made in the city. After Annibale's death in

1445, he was succeeded by his cousin Sante, who was meant to keep the position warm for the two-year-old Giovanni. During Sante's period of office, the young Giovanni Bentivoglio accumulated various honors, including a knighthood from Frederick III (cat. no. 40) in 1452, senatorial rank, and the priorship of the Riformatori in 1459. Immediately after Sante's somewhat suspicious death in October 1463, Giovanni was elected *gonfaloniere* of justice, inheriting not only his cousin's position, but also his wife, Ginevra Sforza, whom he married the following year.

During the first years of his rule, he depended on the consensus of the leading families in Bologna. Giovanni had larger ambitions, however; he wished to be not simply Bologna's first citizen, but its *signore*, and it was to that end that he directed both his domestic and his foreign policy. The political balance of Italy was always precarious, and Bologna's topographical position at the crossroads of the peninsula gave Bentivoglio a power base out of proportion to the size of the city itself. He was able to buttress this by his military skills, entering the service of Milan in 1471 and of Florence in 1479. The peace signed in 1480 added Naples to his list of allies. The rewards of these alliances were immense. His own reputation in Italy grew steadily, as did his fortune, for he was paid extremely well by the two great city-states. Not least important, however, in the light of his domestic policies, was his accumulation of titles, beginning in 1480 when the Sforza duke of Milan, Giangaleazzo, granted him in perpetuity the lordships of Covo, Antignano, and Pizzighettone in Lombardy. On the very day he returned to Bologna after accepting these honors in Milan, he began to be called *signore*. In 1482 he was adopted by the rulers of Naples into the house of Aragon.

Having established himself as virtual dictator, Bentivoglio wisely realized that he needed wider support among the city's ordinary citizenry. He therefore wooed the populace by staging tournaments and elaborate games combining personal display with popular entertainment.[4] He also sought to impress by his increasing artistic patronage, speeding up the building of his palace and decorating the family chapel at San Giacomo Maggiore with a series of magnificent canvases by Lorenzo Costa. The inclusion of his own portrait in this display was a primary consideration.

The following years of peace served to bolster Bentivoglio's authority, which was triumphantly acknowledged when Emperor Maximilian I (cat. nos. 37, 79) granted him the right to strike coins with his own image. Bentivoglio's right to rule depended to a large extent, however, on his successful balancing act between the various powers in Italy, and when the French king Charles VIII invaded the peninsula with his armies, the political balance of Italy itself was so altered that Bentivoglio's and Bologna's strategic importance was undermined. The continuing claim to Bologna by Cesare Borgia (born 1475–76, died 1507), son of Pope Alexander VI, in the last years of the century and first years of the next was a further factor in Bentivoglio's decline. The papal threat reasserted itself in the form of Pope Julius II, and with the fall of his old supporters, the Sforza in Milan, Giovanni Bentivoglio found himself unable to resist. The despotic activities of his large brood of sons had destroyed the last vestiges of the old domestic consensus, and Bentivoglio went into exile in November 1506. Old and disheartened, he died less than two years later.

The present medal reflects the period of Giovanni Bentivoglio's greatest authority. Though variously dated, it has always been held to be the last of Sperandio's three medals of him. Fabriczy's suggestion of a date of 1495 has rightly been rejected.[5] Foville considered the work stylistically most compatible with a date in the mid 1480s.[6] Hill, however, pointed out that the absence of the title "Ragonensis," referring to Giovanni's adoption by the king of Naples, dated the piece to before March 1482[7]—though later images of Bentivoglio also fail to include it.[8] However, since the style of the piece suggests a date in the early 1480s, it might be expected that a newly acquired title would indeed have been added. Hill's dating is confirmed by the probable connection of the piece with Sperandio's medal of Federigo da Montefeltro (cat. no. 25).

Sperandio's reuse of imagery applied earlier to genuine *signori* thus takes on political weight. Giovanni Bentivoglio was asserting his right to absolute rule by the visual association with two prominent rulers of the previous generation. The baton he holds is a baton of rule. Referring in addition to his successful military career and to the tournaments he organized, the medal further asserts his right to rule by virtue of his personal abilities. Thus a full appreciation of this work required a knowledge of other medals. In the context of a quattrocentro collection its meaning would have been abundantly clear.

Luke Syson

Sperandio
Federigo da Montefeltro (1422–1482)
25
Bronze, cast
Diameter 89.5 mm
London, The British Museum, George III Collection

Obverse: Bust-length portrait turned to the left. Federigo wears a mortier and is armored. Legend: DIVI • FE[derici] • VRB[ini] • DVCIS • MO[n]TE[feltri] • AC • DVR[antis] • COM[itis] • REG[ii] • CAP[itanei] • GE[neralis] • AC • S[anctae] • RO[manae] • ECCL[esiae] • CON[falonerii] • INVICTI ([Image] of the divine Federigo, duke of Urbino, count of Montefeltro and Durante, royal captain-general and unconquered *gonfaloniere* of the Holy Roman Church).
Reverse: Federigo mounted on a horse decorated with one of his devices, quartered on the trapper of the horse (four flames issuant from the chief, the letter D containing VX and the letters FE for Federigo). He leans forward over the head of the horse, brandishing a baton or scepter. He wears a sword at his side, a mortier on his head, and armor. Inscription: • OPVS • (spray of oak leaves) SPERANDEI (The work of Sperandio).

24 obv.

26 obv.

25a
Bronze, cast
Diameter 91.0 mm
London, Victoria & Albert Museum, Salting Collection
A210–1910

Obverse and reverse as above.

A *condottiere* of remarkable ability, Federigo da Montefeltro enjoyed an extraordinary reputation, both during his lifetime and after his death, for his military sagacity, his scholarly devotion, and his just rule of Urbino.[1] The illegitimate son of Guid'Antonio, count of Montefeltro and Urbino, he received a humanist training under Vittorino da Feltre (cat. no. 8) in Mantua. He then took up a military career in the year 1437, when he served under a skillful mercenary of the previous generation, Niccolò Piccinino. In the same year he married his first wife, Gentile Brancaleoni. When his brother Oddantonio was murdered, Federigo was called to succeed him as *signore* of Urbino. His marriage and his activities as a *condottiere*—by then in the service of Francesco Sforza, the mercenary who was to become duke of Milan—accrued land for the *signoria* of Urbino. He continued to fight for Sforza and the Florentines until 1451, when Ferrante of Aragon, the future king of Naples, became his employer. His skills became widely celebrated after the inconclusive battle of San Fabiano d'Ascoli on July 22, 1460. His battles against the Malatesta in the Romagna gained him a large part of the Malatesta territory in that region, the Marche.

In 1466 he was appointed captain general of the newly formed Italian League, consisting of Naples, Florence, and Milan. Wary of papal power, he fought as the league's captain to secure Rimini for the Malatesta, despite the longstanding enmity between Urbino and its near neighbors. 1472 found him employed by the Florentines to put down the rebellion in Volterra. On August 21, 1474, Pope Sixtus IV, who had need of him to fight Niccolo Vitelli, *signore* of Città di Castello, made him duke of Urbino. Federigo's ties with the papacy in the person of Sixtus, the della Rovere pope, remained strong—his daughter Giovanna was married to Giovanni della Rovere—and in 1479 he led the papal troops against his old employer Florence.

By 1482 he was prey to the usual afflictions of old age, but his reputation and judgment were undimmed. Once again he was considered the only possible choice for the position of captain general of the Italian League, then fighting against the pope and Venice to preserve the Este regime in Ferrara. Federigo accepted the post, but only after he had negotiated terms by which he would not be brought into direct conflict with his old ally and relation by marriage, Sixtus IV. Attacks of fever had laid him low from the middle of that year, and on September 10 he finally succumbed to them in the ducal palace in Ferrara.

This bare account of Federigo's life takes little account of the esteem in which he was held by his contemporaries, both at home and abroad. He was awarded the Order of the Garter by

25 obv.

25 rev.

King Edward IV of England in August 1474, and the Collar of Ermine by King Ferrante I of Naples in September of that same year. His abilities were recognized even by the shah of Persia.

Sperandio's portrait shows the duke in old age, in an image containing the weight of his experience and reputation. The fact that this image is almost certainly posthumous is implied by the inclusion of the word DIVI in the inscription, a deliberate imitation of the posthumous deification of Roman emperors. If posthumous, Sperandio's depiction might be supposed to be based on a model created by another artist. Sperandio's armored portrait often seems to combine the variety of portraits of Federigo that remain. Apparently he did not base his work on any single pre-existing image by another artist conveyed by drawing—unless this unknown artist's work is now lost.

The reverse, with its equestrian portrait of the duke, is very close to Sperandio's equestrian portrait of Giovanni II Bentivoglio (cat. no. 24). Close examination of the two reverses reveals that Sperandio actually reworked his model for the Bentivoglio medal—or took an impression of the earlier piece as the starting point—for his mounted Federigo. Military events in the year 1482 suggest that a pairing of the two medals would have been appropriate. On April 12, 1482, Federigo was officially confirmed captain general of the Italian League. Giovanni Bentivoglio, similarly caught between his allegiance to the pope and his salaried military position with Giangaleazzo Sforza, duke of Milan, served under Federigo, taking orders from him during the failed defense of Ficarolo in June 1482.

Luke Syson

26 obv.

Sperandio
Carlo Grati (died 1519)
26
Lead, cast
Diameter 112 mm; diameter of the outer perimeter of the
 inscription from the G in GRATI to the first N in BONO-
 NIENSIS, 98 mm
University of California at Santa Barbara, University Art Mu-
 seum, Sigmund Morgenroth Collection
1964.242

Obverse: Profile portrait to the left. The sitter is portrayed in late middle age, wearing armor and a round cap with the back flap turned up. Legend: • CAROLVS • GRATVS • MILES • ET • COMES • BONONIENSIS (Carlo Grati, knight and count of Bologna). Linear border.
Reverse: Grati is shown kneeling before a roadside crucifix, his cap and sword on the ground beside him. Behind him is a horse, viewed from the back. A mounted squire rides on with a lance in his right hand and a small forked pennon as the helmet crest. Legend: • REC ORDATVS • [est] MISERI CORDI[a]E • SV[a]E ("He hath remembered his mercy"). The text is from Psalm 98:3 (King James Version; Vulgate 97:3). Below, the signature: • OPVS • SPERANDEI • (The work of Sperandio). Issuing from Grati's mouth, the word: SALVE (Hail). Linear border.

In 1459, Pope Pius II granted a knighthood to Giacomo di Peregrino d'Antonio Ingrati, of Bologna. On that occasion, he

26 rev.

appears to have instructed Giacomo to drop the first syllable of his surname, changing it from Ingrati (= ungrateful) to Grati (= grateful).[1] The Ingrati, whose origins are unknown, had risen to prominence in Bologna in the 1450s. Much of their status they owed to the political patronage of the Bentivoglio, the first citizens of the city. Tradition has it that they were the *padroni* of the Castel de' Britti,[2] but theirs was more likely a bourgeois success story. As furriers they had acquired considerable wealth and the status that came with it.

Giacomo had two sons, neither of whose birth dates are known. Andrea's career was not dissimilar to his father's. He too became a senator, in 1488, and he too was knighted.[3] The subject of the present medal, Carlo di Giacomo Grati, doubtless the younger of the two, led a somewhat different life—at least initially. He only became a senator after the death of Andrea in 1502.[4] Up to that point he had served primarily as a military man. In 1486 he was knighted by Giovanni II Bentivoglio (cat. no. 24) and appointed commander of Bentivoglio's personal army.[5] In that capacity, he was sent on an embassy to the duke of Milan in 1488,[6] and subsequently accompanied Giovanni Bentivoglio to Ferrara in 1493[7] and the young Alessandro Bentivoglio on his visit to Emperor Maximilian in 1496. In 1501 he was named ambassador to the pope, and from that time on functioned primarily as a diplomat. In his remaining years he traveled between Rome and Bologna, passing in and out of the Bentivoglios's favor.

Judging from its style, it is possible to date Sperandio's medal of him to the mid 1480s. The reverse appears to have been influenced by Pisanello's reverse for his medal of the very civilized *condottiere* Domenico Malatesta (cat. no. 6), created over forty years earlier. It has been pointed out that Sperandio seems to have borrowed Pisanello's designs repeatedly during his Bolognese period—something that could have had as much to do with the desire of his patrons to be associated with the famous subjects of Pisanello's medals as to a lack of inventiveness on the medalist's part.

The stylistic dating is confirmed by the probable reason behind the commissioning of the piece. Grati's identification in the obverse inscription as MILES ET COMES would suggest that the work was meant to commemorate his knighthood and appointment as army commander in 1486, and it is most likely that it was cast in that year.

The reverse demonstrates the devotion to God that Grati held to be the key to his power and position. In this context, even the medalist's signature takes on a secondary meaning, for OPVS SPERANDEI might be literally translated as "the work of hope in God."

Both the obverse and reverse of the medal are rapidly modeled, the detail rendered by scratching the surface with a sharp point. In the past, this dynamism has been misinterpreted as mere shoddiness. It is true that Sperandio's modeling of larger works in terra-cotta was bold and broad, rather than finicky and detailed, and he certainly transferred some of that same technique to the wax in which he must have modeled this piece.

Luke Syson

Giovanni (Zuan) di Pasqualino Boldù
(active 1454–75, died before 1477)

Although Giovanni Boldù describes himself on the five medals he signs as a painter, a designation also found in documents, there are no extant paintings to support this claim. A member of a Venetian family, he is mentioned in documents between 1454 and 1475, and his will is dated May 4, 1473. In the will of his widow, dated October 11, 1477, he is spoken of as already deceased.[1]

Whatever else we know of him is based on his signed medals. They include portraits of Pietro Bono, a Belgian musician active at the Ferrarese court, dated 1457; Filippo Maserano, a Venetian poet, dated 1457; Nicolaus Schlifer, a German musician, dated 1457; Filippo de' Vadi, a Pisan physician, dated 1457; and two self-portraits, both dated 1458.[2] It is evident from the manner of his signature, his approach to composition and lettering, and his refined, though sharper and more linear style, that he was strongly influenced by Pisanello. Except for those of his more complicated self-portrait medals, his reverses combine simplicity and grace with the forceful presence of a single figure that dominates and even overpowers both the field and its circular limit.

It is in these reverses and the form of his inscriptions that we discover Boldù's deep involvement with humanist interests and his probable contact with learned circles in Padua. A naked, winged youth plucking a lute accompanies the portrait of Pietro Bono, while an elegant, standing figure of Apollo holding a lyre—copied from an ancient engraved gem—alludes to the profession of the musician Nicolaus Schlifer. The standing figure in classical armor accompanying the medal of Filippo de' Vadi is particularly complicated in its attributes and obscure in its symbolism, yet it is beautifully executed.

Stephen K. Scher

Boldù
Self-Portrait *all'antica*
27
Bronze, cast
Diameter 85 mm
Boston, Museum of Fine Arts, Theodora Wilbour Fund in
  memory of Zoë Wilbour, September 12, 1957
57.603

Obverse: Bust to left, unclothed, wearing an ivy wreath. Pearled border. Legend: IѠANEΣ MΠѠΛNTOY ZѠΓΡAΦOY BEN-AITIA (in faulty Greek: Ioannis Boldù, painter of Venice).
Reverse: At the left, a naked youth sits upon a flat rock holding his head in his hands. Opposite, a winged genius of Death or funerary Eros sits in a rocky landscape, eyes downcast, his left hand holding a bundle of flames, his right arm resting on an outsized human skull, before which lies a bone. Partially pearled border around the top. Legend: • OPVS • IOANIS • BOLDV • PICTORIS • VENETVS • XOGRAFI • (The work of

27 obv.

27 rev.

Giovanni Boldù, painter of Venice, painter). At the base, in a sunken band, the date: • M • CCCC • LVIII (1458).

Boldù's strong interest in classical antiquity is nowhere more evident than in this self-portrait *all'antica*, where his meditation on death is expressed in humanist-classical terms.[1] In the same year, however, and as a pendant to this medal, Boldù produced another self-portrait, this time in contemporary garb.[2] In this second one, the reverse shows Death in the context of Christian allegory, as the artist, once again naked, sits not in the despairing attitude seen here, but in a meditative position between the figures of Faith, raising a chalice, and Penitence, who scourges him.

Although both the seated youth and the genius of Death (Thanatos or the funerary Eros) are clearly derived from classical sources, the former having its ancestry in seated mourning figures on Greek grave *stelae*, the latter often found on Roman sarcophagi, this is the first appearance in Renaissance art of the putto with the skull, a theme that was frequently repeated.[3] According to Hill, the actual form of the putto may have been inspired by a similar figure on an earlier (1450–57) medal by Pietro da Fano (active 1452–1464) of Lodovico Gonzaga.[4]

In such a meditation on death, the skull refers to the human body in a state of transition between death and resurrection, as the skull and sometimes the bones of Adam are shown at the base of the Cross in scenes of the Crucifixion.[5] The flames refer both to the all-consuming nature of death and, paradoxically, to the immortal soul.[6]

With one slight but very important modification, the *me-mento mori* reverse reappears on a medal once attributed to Boldù, but now accepted as being by another artist who borrowed and adapted his design. This is the medal of Caracalla on which Boldù's reverse legend is replaced by the phrase IO SON FINE (I am finished), further reinforcing the allegory of death.[7] Boldù's reverse must have been much admired, for it was included among the marble medallions ornamenting the north face of the socle of the Certosa da Pavia, carved between c. 1494 and 1497 and attributed to Cristoforo Solari (active c. 1480–c. 1525, died 1527).[8] It is also found in a decorative roundel from the tomb of Marc Antonio Martinengo by Maffeo Olivieri (see cat. nos. 30–31), now in the Museo Cristiano, Brescia. Of particular interest is its adaptation by the great Nuremberg medalist Matthes Gebel on the reverse of his medal of Georg Ploed (cat. no. 112), dated 1532. Boldù's two self-portrait medals are a perfect reflection of essential Renaissance interests. They present the artist's self-absorption in two vigorous and youthful portraits, one in the classical mode, the other in contemporary dress, the one combined with a despairing meditation on the inevitability of death using symbols from antiquity, the other with a melancholy representation of the same subject mitigated by the hope offered by the Christian faith.

Stephen K. Scher

Vettor di Antonio Gambello (Camelio)
(active from 1484, died 1537)

Gambello was probably born in Venice between 1455 and 1460. He is first documented in 1484 as master of dies in the Venetian mint.[1] He was the son of the architect Antonio Gambello, who oversaw the building of the church of San Zaccaria in Venice. His training almost certainly took place in the sculpture workshop attached to that church, and his ability as a sculptor is evident from two signed bronze reliefs in the Ca d'Oro.[2]

The artist was chiefly employed, however, as a die-engraver and medalist. He was mintmaster in Venice from 1484 to 1510 and from 1516 until his death, and in the interim served as engraver to the papal mint in Rome. With cold precision, he portrayed a number of high dignitaries of the time, among them Pope Sixtus IV, Pope Julius II, and the doge Agostino Barbarigo (1486–1501).[3] More intimate are his medals of the painters Giovanni Bellini (cat. no. 28) and his brother Gentile.[4] Gambello was especially proud of his portrait of the latter, for he states on the reverse that he had equalled and surpassed nature itself.

Gambello signed twelve medals—seven cast, five struck—with variations of the name Camelius.[5] Critics insist that his cast pieces have greater artistic merit, though these too are faulted for a lack of imagination in their reverses. The first to belittle Gambello was the Venetian Enea Vico, who in his 1555 *Discorso sopra le medaglie de gli antichi* grouped the artist among those medalists dismissed as "imitatori" of ancient coins.[6] Recent writers have tended to defend Gambello's intense enthusiasm for the ancients, and one insists that his medals are "creations inspired by antique prototypes or inventions of classical portraits, but were never made to deceive."[7] That his reverence for antiquity was tinged with an imaginative sense of humor is best seen in his lovely self-portrait as Augustus.[8]

Gambello is especially important for his technical innovations in the art of die-engraving. In 1509 he patented a type of steel he had discovered, and he was among the first to cut dies in this harder metal rather than iron.[9] He is further credited with having improved the striking process. His work thus ushered in a new era in the creation of struck medals, for it was now possible to achieve finer detail and higher relief than before.

Mark Wilchusky

Vettor Gambello
Giovanni Bellini (c. 1430–1516)
28
Bronze, cast
Diameter 58 mm
New York, The Metropolitan Museum of Art, Bequest of Anne D. Thompson, 1923
23.280.32

Obverse: Bust to left, wearing a plain cap over long hair and a high-collared Venetian toga, with shirt visible at the neck. A stole across the right shoulder. Legend: • IOANNES BELLINVS • VENET[us] • PICTOR[um] • OP[timus] • (Giovanni Bellini the Venetian, greatest of painters). Pearled border.
Reverse: An owl perched on a branch. Above the owl, the

28 obv.

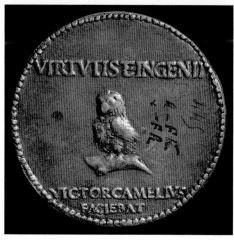

28 rev.

inscription: VIRTVTIS E[t] INGENII (Of merit and inventiveness). Below it: VICTOR CAMELIVS FACIEBAT (Victor Camelius made [this]). Pearled border.

One of Gambello's most beautiful creations, the medal of Giovanni Bellini is an example of the vigorous realism of the early Renaissance. Gambello has recorded the painter's long nose and thin lips without idealization and suggested his advanced age with hints of a narrow gaze and double chin. Hill thought that Gambello's medal of the painter's brother Gentile (1429–1517) was somewhat finer, perhaps because the bust is larger relative to the size of the field. The bolder impression of personality in the Gentile medal suggests that it was created after the present one; there is, however, no evidence for dating either piece.

Despite their slightly different diameters (58 and 63 mm), the two medals constitute a pair. The stole on the present one shows Giovanni as belonging to Venetian high society, and its inscription refers to his primacy among painters. The one of Gentile displays the decoration and titles bestowed on him in 1469 by Emperor Frederick III (cat. no. 40). They thus convey the prominence of these two successive official painters to the Venetian Republic.

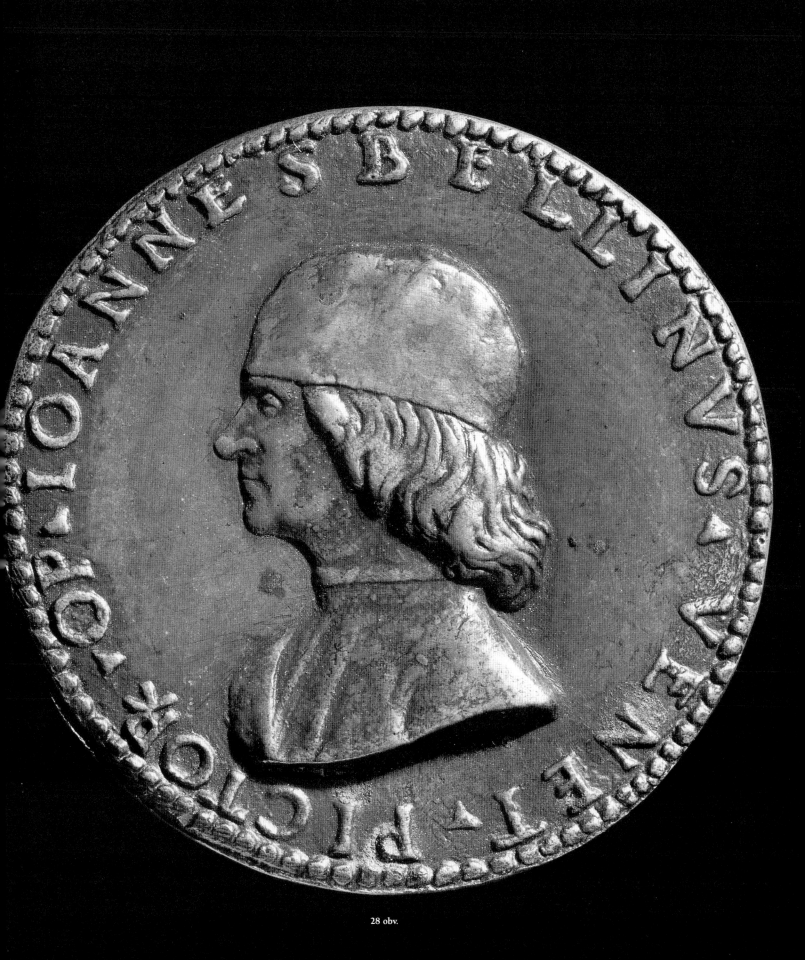

28 obv.

Giovanni's birth date is unknown, but he is on record as a painter before 1460. One of the most prolific, innovative, and long-lived of Renaissance artists, he enriched the genres of the Madonna, the altarpiece, and the portrait immeasurably. His numerous paintings are revered for their emotional intensity and quiet grandeur no less than for the virtuosity with which they mirror the light of the natural and supernatural worlds.

The medal is of great interest because it is one of three certain portraits of the painter. The others are Vittore Belliniano's profile drawing dated 1505 in the Musée Condé, Château de Chantilly, and an anonymous deathbed sketch in an English private collection.[1] The medal portrait is similar to the former, though not so close as to suggest that it was based on it.

The dates proposed for the work range from 1485 to 1505. Judging from Bellini's apparent age in the portrait, Hill ascribed it to about 1490,[2] while Habich suggested that it was made in the same year as the 1505 drawing mentioned above.[3] Rapp argues that the painter is here some five years younger than he is in the drawing, and dates the piece to about 1500.[4] The impossibility of guessing the subject's age with any degree of precision renders all of these proposals invalid. Yet the question of the date remains intriguing. Were it known, we might better understand the piece's intended function. The encomium on the obverse is echoed in Albrecht Dürer's (cat. no. 84) observation from 1506 that "though [Bellini] is old, he is still the best in painting."[5] On the morning of the painter's death, the chronicler of all things Venetian, Marino Sanuto (1466–1535), again describes him in the exact words of the medal: "se intese esser morto Zuan Bellin optimo pitor."[6] Clearly it was common to refer to Bellini as supreme among painters, and it is tempting to think that Gambello's having literally cast such a judgment in bronze helped to spread the idea.

The owl on the reverse, haunting in its simplicity, is the bird sacred to Minerva, goddess of wisdom. It effectively symbolizes Bellini's moral and intellectual qualities, but one wonders how this fitting symbol came to be selected. Gambello's knowledge of ancient coinage is well attested, for his works rely heavily on Roman examples. Venice's dominance in the Aegean also insured that Greek coins found their way to the city. Bellini's father, for example, either owned or had access to such pieces, for several are recorded in his drawings.[7] It is just possible that an Athenian silver tetradrachm with its famous owl reverse served as the pattern for Gambello's homage to the prince of painters.

Mark Wilchusky

Fra Antonio da Brescia
(active 1487–1514)

This name has been assigned to the maker of a stylistically coherent group of eight medals signed with either a simple A, the monogram F • A • B, or FRA • AN • BRIX.[1] Nothing is known of the artist's life, but the signed medal of Albertino Papafava and the attributed medal of Girolamo Savorgnan show him to have been active between the years 1487 and 1514.[2]

In his finest medals he reveals himself to be among the most gifted practitioners of realistic portraiture. To judge from his subjects, he must have worked in Padua, Treviso, Verona, and Venice. It seems likely that he was an itinerant friar-medalist, for most of these towns had bronze founders who could have cast his models. His habit of emphasizing his Brescian roots in his signatures also supports the conjecture that he did not work in his native city.

In a sense he was the Michiel portraitist, since four of his eight signed medals honor members of that patrician Venetian family. One of these presents Niccolò Michiel and his wife (cat. no. 29), the other three their son Simone.[3] The latter served as a canon, first in Verona and later in Treviso.[4] Among the medalist's other subjects were Niccolò Vonica, a citizen of Treviso, and Fra Antonio Marcello, who was probably deacon at Padua.

It would be helpful to know the nature of the artist's training[5] and just how he relates to other medalists of the Venetian school with whom he is often compared, for example Giovanni Boldù (cat. no. 27), Vettor Gambello (cat. no. 28), or the "Medalist of 1523." His works are undated, and can only be arranged chronologically on the basis of our knowledge of the sitters. His style, distinguished by sober, precise portraits in spacious fields, seems to have changed little over the twenty-five or so years of his career. His was an age in which friars tended to be schooled in manuscript illumination rather than medalmaking, and it is remarkable both that he found employment in the Veneto as a medalist and that he managed to make a distinguished contribution to the genre.

Mark Wilchusky

Fra Antonio da Brescia
Niccolò Michiel (1440–1518) and his wife Dea Contarini
29
Bronze, cast
Diameter 72 mm
London, The British Museum

Obverse: Bust to left, wearing the *tocco* (a round *berretto* worn by Venetian magistrates), and a robe pleated in the front. The hair quite full at the back of the neck. Legend: NICOL[aus] MICHAEL DOC[tor] ET EQ[ues] AC • S[ancti] M[arci] PRocv[rator] • OP[us] F • A • B (Niccolò Michiel, doctor and knight, also procurator of San Marco. The work of F. A. B.). *Reverse*: Bust to left in a plain dress, the hair worn in a knot at the back of the neck and caught in a cap or net. Legend: VXOR EIVS DEA CONTARENA (His wife Dea Contarini).

This medal is widely regarded as Fra Antonio's masterpiece, a striking example of what Fabriczy referred to as the artist's "absolute photographic truth."[1] To achieve such faithful likenesses the medalist apparently developed a kind of shorthand, concentrating on only a few telling details in his rendering of a profile.[2] He has conveyed the sitter's advanced age and grave demeanor with great economy; the hollow cheeks and tight lips

29 obv.

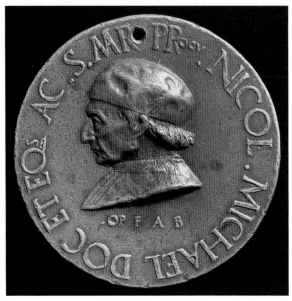

29 obv.

29 rev.

are passages of descriptive genius, yet no part distracts from the dignified whole.

The artist portrays Niccolò's wife with similar efficiency. Dea Contarini's cheeks blend into her jowls as one broad plane. Her fleshy eye sockets and thick neck are so vividly described that one can imagine her having just stepped out of a back-street Venetian kitchen. She may not have her eminent husband's titles, but her portrait carries equal weight. This balance goes a long way toward explaining the success of the medal and the particular appeal of this frankly homely couple.[3]

We know Niccolò's birth date from the diaries of Sanuto, who records his death in 1518 at the age of seventy-eight.[4] Born into an established patrician family, he married in 1466 a Venetian noblewoman, Alidea Contarini, by whom he had six sons.[5] A hardworking servant of the state, Michiel was, in addition, a humanist scholar who found time to publish a commentary on Demosthenes. At the age of sixty, in 1500, he summed up his career in a speech to the council, reminding his supporters that he had already served Venice as mayor and as both civil governor and military governor, been an ambassador in Spain, Naples, Rome, and France, and for a number of terms functioned as "avogador di comun," or state's attorney.[6] He concluded by saying that he felt bound to give his life and the lives of his sons for the Republic.[7]

The high point of his career was his prosecution of Antonio Grimani (1436–1523), the general of the Venetian armada, who had failed to engage the Turkish fleet in battle near Lepanto in 1499. Michiel delivered a caustic and lengthy condemnation of Grimani patterned after the invective of Cicero.[8] As a result, Grimani was exiled, and Michiel was rewarded with the post of procurator.

Clearly the medal was cast after that dignity had been bestowed on him. It probably dates from the same year, 1500, but to judge from his wife's hair style is in any case no later than

about 1510.[9] His *tocco* identifies him as a magistrate. Dea Contarini's plain appearance is explained somewhat by the fact that in 1511 her husband was appointed to a two-man commission charged with enforcing Venice's laws against lavish dress.[10]

Mark Wilchusky

Maffeo Olivieri
(born 1484, died 1543–44)

Four documents are all we have relating to the work of the Brescian sculptor Maffeo Olivieri. His first known commission is for a wooden altarpiece, now lost, for the town of Tione, north of Brescia, in 1515.[1] In 1527, Sanuto recorded in his diary that the papal legate and bishop of Pola, Altobello Averoldo (cat. no. 30), gave the church of San Marco a pair of beautiful bronze candlesticks bearing his name.[2] These are inscribed MAPHEVS OLIVERIVS BRIXIANVS FACIEBAT, and Sanuto noted that the legate's candlesticks were much more beautiful and elegantly cast than the two larger ones already owned by the church. Finally there are two contracts from 1538, one for a life-size wooden crucifix for the parochial church of Sarezzo,[3] and one for the high altar of S. Maria in Condino, another town north of Brescia.[4]

Despite this meager documentation, a large number of works in bronze, marble, and wood have been attributed to the artist. Olivieri's reputation reached a high point early in this century, when Bode and Planiscig ascribed eleven bronze statuettes to his hand, praising him as the harbinger of the High Renaissance in Venetian sculpture.[5]

His degree of responsibility for the masterpiece of Brescian Renaissance sculpture, the Martinengo monument, is the subject of ongoing debate.[6] There is also disagreement about the attribution to Olivieri of a series of twelve medals, two of which bear the date 1523.[7] Only recently an inventory of his studio taken shortly after his death in 1544 was discovered in the Brescia archives. Its mention of "60 medals, large and small" strengthens the argument of those who equate him with the "Medalist of 1523."[8] The medals in his studio may have been ancient coins, works by his contemporaries, or Olivieri's own casts; what is important is their number, which attests to his considerable interest in medallic art. In some of their details the San Marco candlesticks also evince the sensibility of a sculptor capable of making medals. The Averoldo coat of arms on the candlesticks has the same delicacy of design and facture as the brazier on the reverse of the Jacopo Loredano medal (cat. no. 31).

Questions of attribution aside, this series of twelve medals is prized for the vibrancy of the portraits and the architectonic beauty of their reverses.

Mark Wilchusky

Maffeo Olivieri
Altobello Averoldo, bishop of Pola (c. 1465–1531)
30
Bronze, cast
Diameter 94.3 mm; diameter of the outer perimeter of the inscription from the O in ALTOBELLVS to the E of POLEN, 82.7 mm
Paris, Bibliothèque Nationale, Cabinet des Médailles
AV 1906

Obverse: Bust to the right, wearing a lobed *berretto* and a rochet. Legend: • ALTOBELLVS • AVEROLDVS • BRIXIEN[sis] • POLEN[sis] • EP[iscopu]S • VEN[etiae] • LEG[a]T[u]S • APOST[olicus] • (Altobello Averoldo of Brescia, bishop of Pola, apostolic legate at Venice).
Reverse: Two nude men struggling with a nude female figure and seemingly attempting to tear away her veil. Her head is thrown back. With her right hand she clutches the veil, while grasping the right arm of the man in the foreground with her left. Legend: • VERITATI • D[icatum] • (Dedicated to truth).

The authorship of this medal is of consequence, for the reverse is held to be the finest in the Venetian series. Bode attributed it to the "Medalist of 1523."[1] Rosenheim, followed by Hill, argued three points in favor of ascribing it to Olivieri: (1) Averoldo was Olivieri's patron; (2) the legend on the medal is almost identical to the inscriptions on Olivieri's San Marco candlesticks; and (3) the reverse design has much in common with compositions on those works.[2] It is possible to make a valid comparison between the nude males striding around one of the upper registers of the candlesticks and the man seen from the rear on the medal. They share the same mastery of the human figure in motion and a similar treatment of the muscles of the back and legs. For this reason it seems legitimate to continue to attribute the medal to Olivieri.

That Olivieri executed portraits is assured by the mention in

30 obv.

30 rev.

the inventory of his studio from 1544 of a wax head of a man wearing a *berretto*. One may judge his skill by comparing the medallic likeness with the bishop's appearance in Titian's dated Resurrection polyptych in Brescia's SS Nazaro e Celso. Titian portrays him as he looked in around 1522, comparing quite favorably with the medallic portrait. Hill noted that the latter has a sense of "swagger," a quality understandably absent from Titian's portrayal of a reverent donor. The medalist achieved a bolder impression in part by increasing the size of the portrait relative to the field.

A bastard son from a prominent Brescian family, Averoldo took a doctorate in law at Padua. Pope Alexander VI named him bishop of Pola in 1497, under circumstances that prompted censure. We read in Sanuto's diaries that Niccolò Michiel (cat. no. 29) had given the pope 800 ducats in an attempt to obtain the bishopric for his son Simone, but the pope selected Averoldo, who had paid nearly twice as much.[3] Averoldo was further reputed to have purchased his initial tenure as apostolic legate—he served twice, from 1517 to 1521 and again from 1526 to 1530—for 6,000 ducats, and detractors after his death alluded to the corrupt nature of his administration.[4]

The present medal would appear to date from 1517–21, for another one commissioned by the bishop explicitly states that he was then in his second tenure as papal legate.[5] Two events in 1518 might shed light on this puzzling reverse. First, he served as the head of a commission charged with finding out the truth behind the witch burnings in Valcamonica, a valley north of Brescia.[6] Second, and more intriguing still, he single-handedly obtained the banishment of a Count Camillo Martinengo, who together with four armed men of the Martinengo da Barco family had raped a ten-year-old girl in Brescia.[7] The girl was the stepdaughter of a close relative of Averoldo's, and the bishop agitated in the Venetian *signoria* with furor. The Council of Ten decreed that all five of the assailants be banished from Verona for periods ranging from three to ten years, and that if the principal villain ever showed himself in Brescia, his right hand be cut off in front of the house of the raped girl. The council ordered the condemnation published above the steps of the Rialto Bridge. On this announcement, a crowd accompanied by trumpets followed the girl's stepfather from the ducal palace to Averoldo's house on the Grand Canal, where a day-long ball was held to celebrate the vindication of the family honor.

Mark Wilchusky

Maffeo Olivieri
Jacopo Loredano (died 1535)[1]
31
Bronze, cast
Diameter 62.5 mm; height of bust, 46.0 mm
Berlin, Staatliche Museen, Münzkabinett

Obverse: Bust to right with long, wavy hair, wearing a coat-like outer garment opened at the neck to reveal a finely pleated, collarless shirt and a sash cutting across the subject's chest.

Legend: IACOBVS LAVREDANVS IO[hannis] F[ilius] (Jacopo Loredano, son of Giovanni).
Reverse: The Roman hero Caius Mucius Scaevola, wearing a molded cuirass over a pleated leather doublet, his left hand resting on his breast while with his right he holds a dagger into the flame of an altar. The altar consists of a vase-shaped brazier supported by a tripod resting on a base ornamented with griffins or lions flanking a putto (?). At the right, behind Scaevola, are the arch and pilasters of a classical structure. Legend: • MANVV[m] • P[ro] • PATR[ia] • VSTIONE • GENTIS • AVTOREM • IMITAT[ur] • APVD • BRASEGELI • (By burning his hands in the service of his country at Brisighella, [Jacopo Loredano] imitated the founder of his race).

31a
Bronze, cast
Diameter 63 mm
London, The British Museum

Obverse and reverse as above.

Jacopo Loredano's medal shows a slight refinement over that of Altobello Averoldo (cat. no. 30). The illusionism of the foreshortened bust is more assured, and the handling of the lettering more delicate. It belongs to a group of medals of smaller size that also includes portraits of Francesco and Vincenzo Malipieri.[2] As the Malipieri medals are both dated 1523, we may assume that the Loredano was executed in the same year or shortly thereafter. Loredano's collarless shirt would tend to confirm this, for standing collars were the fashion in Italy by 1525.[3] The fact that Loredano married in 1523 might also be considered,[4] for in the Renaissance medals were often commissioned in celebration of marriages.[5]

Whatever the occasion for the medal, its reverse image and inscription refer to an event that occurred in 1509, some fourteen years before. As a member of a noble Venetian family, it was only natural that Jacopo should serve the Republic in various official capacities.[6] His first position of importance was as *podestà* at Portogruaro, a town north of Venice.[7] In 1508 he was appointed *castellano*, or lord of the fortress at Brisighella, a town in the Romagna.[8] In that year Pope Julius II quarreled with Venice and formed with the major European powers the League of Cambrai, determined to thwart Venetian incursions onto the mainland. Four thousand papal troops swarmed into the Romagna under the command of the young duke of Urbino, Francesco Maria della Rovere, the pope's nephew. They bombarded Brisighella through the night of May 1, 1509, and Loredano was taken prisoner and held for six weeks.[9] In his recollections of illustrious men published in 1541, Pietro Contarini writes: "And there sat Jacopo Loredano, who, being castellan at Brisighella, burned a hand in battle and the scar improbably remained, testifying to his love for his country."[10] Contarini's comment reads like a gloss of the legend on the medal's reverse.

Caius Mucius Scaevola was a young Roman noble of legend

31a obv.'

31a rev.

who was captured in his attempt to kill Lars Porsena, an enemy king besieging Rome in 509 B.C. As punishment, Porsena ordered Mucius to be flung into the flames of an altar. According to Livy, the youth replied, "Look, that you may see how cheap they hold their bodies whose eyes are fixed upon renown!" With that he thrust his right hand into the fire and held it there until it was wholly consumed. Porsena was so impressed by the Roman's valor that he commanded his release. The hero was henceforth known by the epithet Scaevola, or "left-handed."

It was altogether appropriate, then, for Loredano to request such a reverse on a medal to be circulated among his friends. Its evocation of the Roman patriot would serve as a reminder of his own heroism. The somewhat puzzling inscription was only explained in 1834, when Cicogna discovered in books dealing with the genealogy of Venetian nobles that the Loredano family in fact claimed descent from Caius Mucius.[11] Having burned a hand in the service of his country, the subject of the medal truly had "imitated the founder of his race."

Mark Wilchusky

Venetian School
Eustachio di Francesco Boiano (born 1463)
32
Bronze
Diameter 69.5 mm
London, The British Museum

Obverse: Bust to right with short hair and beard, wearing a pleated shirt with a drawstring below its frilled collar and a coat or gown with broad lapels, its edges trimmed in a criss-cross pattern. Between inscribed double circles, the legend: EVSTA-CHIVS BOIANVS FRANC[esci] • EQVIT[is] • FIL[ius] • FABRICAR[e] • CÆPIT • AN[no] • SVO • LXII • (Eustachio Boiano, son of the knight Francesco, began to build in his sixty-second year).

Reverse: A greyhound with a leash looped through its collar lies to the right in a flowery field at the foot of a fruit tree. A vine has been trained through the tree, and a bird is perched on its top. Between inscribed double circles, the legend: SIC VIVENDO DIV VIVITVR AN[no] • M • D • XXV • CVR[am] • CV[m] •

32 obv.

32 rev.

111

ÆTATE SVA AGRICVL[turae] • CÆPIT (vine-leaf stop) (Living thus as a means to long life, he began the study of agriculture at his [advanced] age in 1525).

The provenance and style of this medal place it firmly within the Venetian school. The Boiani were a distinguished family in Cividale del Friuli—a possession of the Venetian Republic since 1419—and the specimen of the medal in the Museo Friulano at Udine was discovered during the demolition of a wall of the Boiano family villa at Ipplis, a small village south of the Cividale city limits.[1]

The style of the obverse is reminiscent of works by the "Medalist of 1523." The reverse inscription refers to the date 1525, and if the piece was made in that year, as seems likely, its similarity to the work of that unidentified medalist is understandable. The portrait is more natural, however, and Boiano's clothing and hair are free of the crisp stylization and love of linear patterns apparent in the work of the "Medalist of 1523." The skillful handling of the texture of the hair and beard calls to mind another rare unattributed Venetian medal of about the same period, that of Giovanni de Nores, count of Tripoli, from c. 1530–40.[2]

Nothing is known about Eustachio Boiano beyond what the medal tells us.[3] The building referred to on the obverse was probably the villa where the Udine medal was found, for medals were sometimes placed in the fabric of buildings in the Renaissance.[4]

The magnificent reverse is the finest of three on which we find the motif of a hound at the foot of a tree. The earliest is Gianfrancesco Enzola's 1456 medal of Francesco Sforza, duke of Milan.[5] There the tree bears fruit like this one. On the ground below the greyhound is a bridle attached to the tree. The principal difference is that the dog is touched by a hand issuing from a radiant cloud. Hill thought the reverse represented the duke's device. The second is an unattributed medal of Pierantonio di Castello, cast in 1515, perhaps in Rome.[6] It shows a hound clearly tethered to a laurel tree by a leash.[7] Hill interpreted this hound as symbolic of fidelity, with the further suggestion that the sitter was an adherent of the Medici, whose shield leans against the trunk of the tree.

These earlier reverses seem simple and heraldic compared to the pictorial vision on the Boiano medal. Subtle modeling has created the illusion of light playing on the leaves of the tree and the greyhound's coat. The large bunches of fruit must allude to the abundant harvests—expected or actual—resulting from Boiano's agricultural studies, as do the vine in the tree and the vine-leaf in the inscription. The bird and greyhound are predictable inhabitants of this pastoral world, of course, but beyond that the greyhound was often equated in this period with the virtuous ruler.[8] Boiano was no prince, to be sure, but in a sense he was the ruler of the small realm of his country villa.

As the three medals attest, the motif of the greyhound beneath a tree had a specific meaning in the Renaissance. The dog itself automatically suggests fidelity, while the notion of tethering the greyhound, the fastest of dogs, adds a further note of patience, constancy, and permanence. The greyhound on the Boiano medal wears a leash, but is not clearly tied to the tree as is the one on the medal of Pierantonio di Castello. Perhaps he is free to run, like the one that has slipped out of its bridle on the medal of Francesco Sforza. Small variations like these are crucial in Renaissance symbolism, that enigmatic language so richly preserved in the art of the medal.

Mark Wilchusky

Donato Bramante
(1444–1514)

This catalogue is the first to propose Donato Bramante as a medalist or designer of medals. The argument behind this proposal follows in the discussion of his self-portrait medal, formerly attributed to Cristoforo Caradosso Foppa. The customary view of Bramante is dominated by his huge achievements in the field of architecture. It appears that he was trained primarily as a painter, however, and various convincing but unprovable attributions of works in different mediums indicate that in his earliest years he worked as a *progettista*, or designer, for other artists and as a painter of perspective scenes.

It is known that Bramante was born in Monte Asdrualdo (Fermignano), but his career is wholly undocumented until the year 1477, when he was to be found painting philosopher figures in fresco on the façade of the palace of the *podestà* in Bergamo.[1] Bramante is first documented as practising as an architect only in 1482, by which time he was already thirty-eight years old. This was in Milan, where he remained until the turn of the century. The paintings ascribed to him are not documented, and their attribution is based in large part on the well-informed writings of Lomazzo, specifically his *Trattato dell'Arte* of 1585 and his 1590 *Idea del Tempio della Pittura*. It is due to Lomazzo that Bramante is credited with the frescoed room from the Casa dei Panigarola in Milan, which survives in fragments in the Brera and can be dated to the 1480s. The same author is responsible for the attribution of Bramante's only panel painting, *Christ at the Column*, also in the Brera, and generally dated to the early 1490s.

Bramante moved to Rome in 1500, where his first commission for Alexander VI was a fresco of the papal arms supported by figures and angels at the Lateran. For Spanish patrons, he designed the cloister and convent of Sta. Maria della Pace, where in 1500 Bartolommeo di Francesca carved columns and capitals "according to the design" of Bramante, and the Tempietto at S. Pietro in Montorio, the dating of which is controversial, but where work seems to have begun in 1502. During this period he also consolidated his knowledge of antiquity by making careful observations and measurements of many of Rome's ancient monuments.

Bramante was immediately employed on the renovation of the Vatican complex on the election of Julius II in 1503, and before 1505 he had designed the Cortile del Belvedere and the Cortile delle Statue. In 1505, Bramante appears to have been working, again in collaboration, this time with Giuliano da

33 obv.

Sangallo and Fra Giacondo, on the new St. Peter's basilica, the ground plan of which is partially preserved in the Uffizi.

At about this time, Julius II appointed Bramante superintendant of all papal building, including military construction. Bramante was also given the post of *piombatore*, or papal sealer, ordinarily a job with little more than a title and salary, but one that the artist took seriously enough to devise, according to Vasari, "a machine for stamping the bulls, with a fine winch." He died in April 1514 and was buried in St. Peter's.

An architect is of necessity a collaborator. It is not surprising to find Bramante providing plans for others to realize. His great achievement was to promote stylistic change within such a system through his profound understanding of antiquity.

Luke Syson

33 obv. 33 rev.

Attributed to Donato Bramante
Self-Portrait *all'antica*
33
Gilt bronze, cast
Diameter 44.0 mm
London, The British Museum

Obverse: Nude bust in profile to the left. The arm truncation suggests a break appropriate to an antique statue, and the modeling of the torso accords with such an association. The inscription is unusual in that it is designed to be read outwardly. Legend: BRAMANTESASDRVVALDINVS (Bramante of Monte Asdrualdo). Pearled border.
Reverse: A seated allegory of Architecture, wearing a Roman tunic and diadem from which flutters a long tie. She holds in her left hand a pair of compasses and in her right an architectural measuring rod or rule. She rests her foot on a weight. In the background is the façade of St. Peter's according to Bramante's own proposed reconstruction. Legend: FIDELITAS LABOR (Fidelity and toil). Pearled border.

33a
Bronze, cast
Diameter 43.0 mm
Washington, The National Gallery of Art, Samuel H. Kress Collection
1957.14.786

Obverse and reverse as above.

Bramante's portrait medal is generally, and probably correctly, dated to 1505, the year in which the architect began work on his designs for the new St. Peter's.[1] Unusual in several ways for its date, it has traditionally been attributed to Cristoforo Caradosso Foppa (c. 1452–1527) of Lombardy, the most celebrated goldsmith and gem-cutter of his day. Caradosso is first recorded in Milan in 1475, employed by the Sforza court as a jeweler and for the valuation of gems and precious stones, in which capacity he traveled throughout Italy.[2] Milan remained his base until, at the earliest, October 1505. In that year he traveled to Mantua with a crystal vase that Giancristoforo Romano had recommended to Isabella d'Este, the marchioness, for her *studiolo*.[3] Giancristoforo also suggested she buy, for the high price of 1,000 ducats, an inkstand Caradosso had made.[4] It is only around this inkstand that primary documentation and later descriptions by Ambrogio Leone and Saba da Castiglione coincide, permitting the identification of works by Caradosso. These pieces were probably executed in Milan, and certainly before Caradosso's removal to Rome, where he is first recorded in 1508.[5] In Rome he specialized in making paxes and crucifixes from precious metals as well as hat-badges (confusingly called "medaglie" in the documents),[6] and was a founding member of the goldsmiths' guild in 1509. His most important commissions during his Roman years were Julius II's papal tiara and morse.[7]

Caradosso is always called a medalist. However, art historians have relied on sources significantly postdating Caradosso's death in 1527, namely Lomazzo's 1585 *Trattato* and Vasari's 1568 *Vite*. Lomazzo's knowledge of things Milanese was unparalleled at the end of the sixteenth century, and his information is generally reliable. He gave a "medaglia" of Giangiacomo Trivulzio to Caradosso.[8] He also mentions struck medals of the Milanese dukes Giangaleazzo Sforza, his father Galeazzo Maria, and his uncle, Lodovico.[9]

The attribution to Caradosso of the Bramante medal rests on Vasari, who mentions the work in the context of Bramante's designs for St. Peter's: . . . "that hearing that he had the wish to pull to the ground the church of St. Peter to make it anew, he made numerous designs; but among the others he made one which was most admirable, where he showed that great intelligence of which he was capable, with two bell-towers that had between them the façade, as one sees in the coins that first Julius II, then Leo X struck, made by the most excellent goldsmith Caradosso, who in the making of dies had no compare, as one also sees [in] the medal of Bramante made most beautifully by him."[10]

This passage, generally quoted only in part, tells us that Caradosso made dies for papal coinage. Although there is no documentary evidence of Caradosso's having worked at the mint, a coin of Leo X with a representation of Bramante's design for St. Peter's survives.[11] Vasari lays such stress on his ability as a die-engraver, both here and in his life of Francia, that this work may reasonably be considered his. Its depiction of St.

Peter's differs significantly, both in detail and in its overall proportions, from that of the present reverse. Those who have used the passage to show Caradosso's responsibility for the medal have not read it carefully enough. The focus here is on Bramante's designs for the new basilica, not Caradosso's skill as a die-engraver. In any case, the medal is cast, not struck, and while this has been explained away as numismatic incompetence on Vasari's part, it is not necessary to do so. Caradosso is thought to have made medals; Bramante is not. Alternative readings of the passage have therefore been glossed over or rejected. The "by him" is ambiguous, but given the fact that Bramante is the subject of the sentence, and also the last name mentioned, it is highly probable that Vasari was referring to a work by Bramante himself. There is in any case nothing to show that Caradosso was even in Rome when the medal was cast.

Is there other evidence, internal or documentary, to support an attribution to Bramante? It seems clear that the architect provided designs for other medals relating to his work. While this is only probable in the case of the 1504–8 "Belvedere" medal of Julius II,[12] it is virtually certain in the case of the struck piece showing the façade of Sta. Maria di Loreto, convincingly attributed to Giancristoforo Romano.[13] The authors of these medals could scarcely have known the details of Bramante's plans unless he had given them the designs. Another struck Julius medal with Bramante's façade of St. Peter's filling the reverse was probably issued in conjunction with two cast medals of the same subject.[14] All three must have been based on drawings by Bramante, according as they do with the surviving autograph ground plan, although the cast pieces are, almost certainly erroneously, always given to Caradosso.

The present piece is not an architectural medal as such, but there appears to be enough evidence to suggest that the design, at least, was Bramante's. The portrait is close in style to his painted works. The reverse figure of Architecture compares favorably with the figures in the famous architectural print by the Milanese engraver Bernardo Prevedari after Bramante's design.[15]

It is impossible to know whether Bramante possessed the requisite skills to sculpt the medal himself, but if authorship is to be measured, then it is perhaps the design that most affects a medal's appearance, and the design, it seems clear, should be given to Bramante. Iconographically as well, the medal reveals a sophistication uncharacteristic of most contemporary pieces, since Bramante is presented nude. The only medallic precedent for this is the self-portrait of Giovanni Boldù (cat. no. 27).[16] The medal evokes ancient Roman statuary and coinage. The unusual placement of its inscription, for example, requiring that it be read from the outside, links it to coins of Tiberius.

From the twelfth century on, the geometrician Euclid was depicted in different guises, either alone, as a representation of Geometry, or together with a personification of that art.[17] In Rome, however, there was an obvious and recent pattern for Euclid in the painting by Pinturicchio (1454–1513) in the Borgia Apartments in the Vatican,[18] where he is again an adjunct of Geometry. The close resemblance between that portrayal and the portrait of Bramante on the medal may suggest, as has been supposed, that Pinturicchio's Euclid is a disguised—though more accurately balding—portrait of Bramante, and that thus from the early 1490s, when Bramante may be suspected of having made his first visit to Rome, an iconographic connection was being established. Alternatively, it may be that Bramante fashioned himself as Euclid on the medal in imitation of Pinturicchio's painting.

There was also no established iconography for the personification of Architecture. In Bramante's medal she has been given the attributes of Geometry, the compass and rule—though these do not appear in Pinturicchio's painting. Thus it may be argued that Bramante himself, perhaps Pinturicchio, and certainly Raphael in his later *School of Athens*, where Euclid has the features of Bramante, deliberately created visual parallels between the architect of St. Peter's and Euclid, Geometry, and the art of architecture *per se*.

The attribution of this medal to Bramante has important implications. It reveals him to be a skilled portraitist, and must also give reason to doubt the attribution of some other medals currently given to Caradosso on the basis of their similarity to the Bramante. It seems very likely that Bramante was also responsible for the design, and conceivably the execution, of a group of three medals of Julius II (including the 1506 St. Peter's foundation medals)[19] and another piece of Enrico Bruni, bishop of Tarentum, who laid the foundation stones for three of the four great piers of St. Peter's in 1507.[20] All of these medals were connected with the building history of St. Peter's, and Bramante's involvement in the production of them is therefore unsurprising. That the attribution also reveals Bramante's own design for the St. Peter's façade is an additional bonus.

Luke Syson

Artist Unknown
Marguerite de Foix, marchioness of Saluzzo (1473–1536)
34
Silver, struck
Diameter 43.7 mm; internal measurement from top of head to bottom of bust, 31 mm; weight 39.17 g
New York, private collection

Obverse: Bust facing to the left, wearing a widow's veil. Inscription framed, on the outside by a pearled border around a single ridge, on the inside by a pearled border flanked on the outside by a single ridge and on the inside by a double ridge. Legend: + MARGARITA • DE • FVXO • MARCHIONISA • SALVCAR[um] T[utrix et] • C[uratrix] • 1516 (Marguerite de Foix, marchioness of Saluzzo, protector [and] guardian. 1516).
Reverse: On a barren tree eradicated on which perches a dove, hangs a jousting shield with the arms of Saluzzo impaled by Foix and Béarn.[1] The inscription framed on the outside by a pearled border outside a double ridge, on the inside by a pearled border between double ridges. Legend: (cross patonce) DEVS • PROTECTOR • ET • REFVGIVM • MEVM • I IC • (God is my protector and my refuge. The I IC is discussed below).

34 obv.   34 rev.

34a
Silver, struck
Diameter 45.0 mm; weight 38.941 g
New York, American Numismatic Society

Obverse and reverse as above.

During the long series of destructive wars fought on Italian soil roughly between the invasion of Charles VIII of France in 1494 and the Treaty of Cateau-Cambrésis in 1559, involving England, France, the Italian city-states, the papacy, Spain, and the Holy Roman Empire, the small marquisate of Saluzzo remained fiercely independent and loyal to France. Located in the present-day Piedmont to the southwest of Turin, Saluzzo was in a vulnerable position, and it was only with difficulty that its rulers, especially Lodovico II (born 1438, ruled 1475–1504), were able to maintain both their political identity and a humanist court noted for its brilliance and culture.

In 1492, Lodovico II took as his second wife Marguerite de Foix, by whom he had four sons: Michelantonio (1495–1528), Gianlodovico (1496–1563), Francesco (1498–1537), and Gabriele (1501–1548). He served both Charles VIII and Louis XII (cat. no. 140), joining the latter in his war with Spain (1502–4) over control of Naples. First at the battle of Cerignola (April 26, 1503) and later at the battle of the Garigliano (December 29, 1503), where the Franco-Italian army was under Lodovico's command, the French were soundly defeated by "el Gran Capitan," Gonzalo de Córdoba. Making his way home on foot from Naples, Lodovico became ill and died in Genoa on January 27, 1504.

Since his eldest son and heir was only nine years old, Marguerite became regent, a position she would hold until 1521. She is described as a very spirited woman and a lover of literature who brought an atmosphere of refinement and culture to the court of Saluzzo.[2] Though she served as regent for seventeen years, she did not enjoy governing, and placed the administration of the state in the hands of subordinates. Apparently she was in constant conflict with her sons and sowed discord among them, going so far as to accuse her second son, Gianlodovico, of madness, and having him thrown into prison in the castle of Verzuolo. The rightful heir, Michelantonio, was sent to France, and it was only her third son, Francesco, who finally succeeded in taking power in 1528. Marguerite was exiled to the county of Castres, and she died there in 1536, completely abandoned and alone, having no desire to see her sons again.

The piece made for Marguerite de Foix falls into the very special category of the medallic coin. Though perhaps never meant for actual circulation, Marguerite's medal is struck, not cast, and is a multiple of a particular denomination of active currency. It represents forty grossi, the grosso being a coin that had first appeared in Venice early in the thirteenth century and was current in Milan at the time when Lodovico II of Saluzzo was striking his coins.

Hill includes this piece in his *Corpus* as a medal, while in the *Corpus Nummorum Italicorum* and other sources it is considered a medallic coin and given the name tallero.[3] If a medal is often meant to commemorate a specific event, it is difficult to associate the date given on this one, 1516, with any particular occurence in Marguerite's life. In 1503 Lodovico had struck large gold coins and talleri with his portrait facing that of Marguerite on the obverse, and this must have been the most immediate precedent for Marguerite's tallero of 1516. She had already assumed the regency in 1504, and refers specifically to that role in the inscription on the obverse: T[utrix et] • C[uratrix].

The reverse certainly contains direct references to her widowhood and the regency. The coat of arms Saluzzo/Foix hangs from a tree denuded of all foliage, signifying Lodovico's death. Yet the tree itself stands for the ruling house and the continuation of the dynasty.[4] One interpretation sees the bird as a dove, representing the soul surviving the sorrows of death and referring to the hope expressed in the inscription.[5]

Some differences of opinion have been expressed over the peculiar letters I IC, which appear at the end of the reverse inscription as well as on Lodovico's coins from 1503. Hill had no doubt that they stood for ETC, but this makes little sense, for the inscription is complete in itself, and there is no need to continue it.[6] Both Armand and Forrer thought the initials referred to Ianuae Iohannes Clot, a German engraver who worked at the Genoese mint in the early sixteenth century, but there seems to be no other basis for connecting the medal with this gentleman.[7] Another theory, finally, one in favor with contemporary numismatists, links the letters to a Milanese family of mintmasters and engravers, the da Clivates, Francesco, Maffeo, and Gianluca, who were contracted to the mint in Carmagnola that served Saluzzo. The design of the medal, with its sensitive and delicate portrait of Marguerite, has been further associated with the Milanese sculptor Benedetto da Briosco, who was a friend of the da Clivates and whom Marguerite also summoned to Saluzzo to work on the ancestral chapel in the church of San Giovanni.[8]

All of these theories have varying merits, but none is entirely convincing. The mystery of I IC must remain unsolved for the moment, but such irresolution cannot diminish the beauty of Marguerite's medal.

Stephen K. Scher

34 obv.

35 obv.

Cristoforo di Geremia
(c. 1430–1476)

The sculptor, goldsmith, and medalist Cristoforo di Geremia was born in Mantua, the son of a goldsmith. Almost nothing is known of his early career.[1] By 1456 he was in Rome, where beginning in 1461 he worked in the service of Cardinal Lodovico Scarampi. The commander of the papal troops, Scarampi was also a well-known admirer and collector of ancient art. Geremia accompanied his patron to Perugia in 1461, and to Florence in 1462.[2] The artist had meanwhile received a number of commissions from the Gonzaga family, including a rock crystal salt cellar for Marquess Lodovico III.[3] He stayed for a month at the Gonzaga court as the guest of Lodovico and his wife, Barbara of Brandenburg (died 1484), and he presented his host with four antique busts.[4]

After the death of Scarampi in 1465, Geremia attached himself to the papal court. Among his various projects for Pope Paul II, and the one that brought him fame and honor, was his restoration of the statue of Marcus Aurelius in 1468.[5] We know of only a few medals by his hand, despite the fact that Geremia was one of the most gifted masters of this branch of smaller sculpture.[6]

Geremia was greatly influenced by the art of antiquity. The sharp profile of his Scarampia medal reminds one of busts of late Roman emperors, and the triumphal scene on its reverse has much in common with coins of that period. The reverse of his famous Constantine medal, with its two figures and the inscription S[enatus] C[onsulto] is a deliberate imitation of the type of the Roman coin.[7]

Geremia spent almost the whole of his life in Rome, yet the artistic traditions of the Mantuan school remained a vital force in his work. He was indebted most of all to Mantegna (1431–1506), an influence easily seen in his medals. He died at the age of forty-six, at the height of his powers. It is generally considered that his medal of King Alfonso (cat. no. 35) is his masterpiece.

Yevgenia Shchukina

Cristoforo di Geremia
Alfonso of Aragon, king of Naples and Sicily (1396–1458)
35
Bronze, cast
Diameter 77.1 mm
St. Petersburg, State Hermitage Museum
5203

Obverse: Bust to right in armor and cloak on a pedestal. The armor is splendidly ornamented with relief designs. In the field, Nereids riding on sea-centaurs, and below, a Medusa mask. Legend: ALFONSVS REX REGIBVS IMPERANS ET BELLORVM VICTOR (King Alfonso, commander of kings and victor in wars).
Reverse: A winged Bellona and a nude Mars crowning Alfonso, who is seated on a throne in the costume of a Roman emperor,

35 obv.

holding a sword in his right hand and the imperial orb in his left. Bellona carries a palm branch, Mars a trophy. Legend: VICTOREM REGNI MARS ET BELLONA CORONA[n]T (Mars and Bellona crown the victor of the realm). In the exergue, the signature: CRISTOPHORVS HIERIMIA.

Alfonso was born in Medina del Campo, in Castile, the son of Ferdinand I of Aragon (1379?–1416) and Eleonore Albuquerque. In 1421 the queen of Naples, Joanna II, adopted him as her

35 rev.

heir, but in 1423 she decided instead to leave her throne to Louis III of Anjou (1403–1434). Alfonso captured Naples on June 15, 1423, but immediately left for Spain to help his brother, Juan II of Navarre (1397–1479), in his war against the king of Castile. In his absence, Louis of Anjou recaptured Gaeta and Naples.

Alfonso left Spain for good on May 23, 1432. After a campaign in Tunis, he returned to Sicily in the fall of 1434. New negotiations with Joanna resulted in a second adoption, yet before her death, on February 4, 1435, the queen willed Naples to the cousin of the deceased Louis III, Duke René of Anjou (1409–1480).

Alfonso fought the Angevins until the summer of 1442, when he was finally proclaimed king of Naples. He ruled for fifteen years before dying in his Neapolitan palace on June 27, 1458. His wife, Marie of Castile, failed to produce an heir. He willed the kingdom of Naples to his illegitimate son Ferrante I, the crown of Aragon and Sicily to his brother Juan II, king of Navarre.[1]

The preeminent ruler of his time, Alfonso was also highly cultivated, and a devoted student of the classics. His art collection included numerous ancient coins. He was a generous patron, and did much for the development of the art of the medal, especially for Pisanello. His proud features are preserved on Pisanello's medals of him and in his numerous sketches in the *Codex Vallardi*.[2] Geremia's medal gives us a somewhat different view of him.

Scholars have offered various dates for the medal, even suggesting that it was produced after Alfonso's death.[3] When fashioning his own medal, Geremia doubtless consulted those of Pisanello and Paolo di Ragusa.[4] It is worth noting that, like Pisanello, he placed the bust of the king above a crown, emphasizing his rank.

Habich noted how uncommonly lifelike Alfonso appears on the Geremia medal. He was convinced that the portrait was done *ad vivam*, or before 1458, and that the depiction of the king on the reverse was that of a living ruler.[5] Panvini Rosati suggested that the medal was made to celebrate Alfonso's victory over the Angevins.[6]

The medallion on Alfonso's cuirass is an obvious sign of Mantegna's influence, for that master had used such medallions as ornaments on a decorative pilaster in his altarpiece in San Zeno in Verona.[7] Clemente da Urbino later copied the shape of the truncation on the Alfonso medal for his portrait of Federigo da Montefeltro from 1468.[8]

The scene on the reverse resembles a classical relief, and follows the ancient principle of isocephaly: the heads of the three figures, even though the king is seated, appear at the same level. The group is tightly compressed into the round of the medal, serving to heighten the effect of monumentality. Mantegna often employed such a technique, and we have already noted how strongly Geremia was influenced by his fellow Mantuan.

Certain features of the relief on the Alfonso medal reflect both the period and the personal taste of its creator. As a master

of the late quattrocento, Geremia sought new sculptural effects, and as a goldsmith strove for a maximum amount of detail in the medallic surface. Many of the decorative elements—the decoration of the armor, the flowing folds of Bellona's drapery, even the sphinx figures on the legs of the throne—are executed with masterful brilliance. Most impressive, however, is the painterly modeling of Alfonso's face, which is full of strength and intelligence.

Yevgenia Shchukina

Lysippus the Younger
(flourished c. 1471–1484)

There are no surviving payment records or other documents relating to the career of the self-styled Lysippus the Younger, and his real name is unknown. His pseudonym alludes to the famous sculptor Lysippus of ancient Greece. Our only biographical information comes from the historian Raphael Maffei da Volterra's *Commentarii Urbani* of 1506, which relates that "Cristoforo of Mantua modeled Paul II numismatically, copied from life, while Lysippus his young grandson [or nephew: nepos] modeled Sixtus IV numismatically."[1] It would thus appear that Lysippus' background was Roman.

Any reconstruction of his oeuvre must therefore rest on his two signed medals, one in Turin of Giulio Marasca—once assumed lost—with the reverse signature LYSIPPVS AMICO OPTIMO, implying that the piece was a personal gift,[2] the other, of which there are two examples, portraying Martinus Philethicus, a Roman professor of Greek.[3] The reverse of the latter, featuring a pelican in imitation of Pisanello's medal of Vittorino da Feltre (cat. no. 8), has the inscription: ΕΡΓΟΝ ΛΥΣΙΠΠΟΥ ΝΕΟ ΤΕΡΟΥ (The work of Lysippus the younger). All further attributions to the artist, including that of the medal of Sixtus IV, assumed to be the foundation medal for the Ponte Sisto,[4] have been based on stylistic grounds. Collected together, they reveal a clientele drawn from the university in Rome and the papal Curia, and it seems likely that the medalist's main period of activity coincided with the pontificate of Sixtus IV. He appears to have absorbed some of the humanist atmosphere of Rome and was one of the earliest artists to employ Roman lapidary capitals.[5]

Given the lack of documentary evidence, one might suppose that the artist may also have worked under another name. It may be that he did not even work as an artist, but was a scholar, his adoption of the ancient sculptor's name being a scholarly conceit. His stylistic similarity with the gifted gentleman-amateur Giovanni Candida (cat. nos. 37–38), thought by some to have been his pupil, could indicate that he was a man of the same ilk.[6]

The signed works reveal certain consistent stylistic and epigraphic practices. Both have a strongly curved bust truncation running to an especially sharp point in the front. They are confidently, if somewhat broadly, modeled with the separate features generally large in the space of the profile and the hair simplified into rather generalized locks. The pointed truncations seem intended to provide a visual link between the heads and the inscriptions, which are notable for their large, fine, crisp lettering and triangular stops.

The medal of Marasca, evidently a friend of the artist, has ivy leaves on the reverse. Inasmuch as they appear in conjunction with the signature, they may have been meant to be a part of it, although their meaning is obscure. Some writers have held the appearance of such leaves to be a Lysippus cipher,[7] but they also appear on works that are clearly by another hand.

Luke Syson

Lysippus the Younger
Self-Portrait (?)
36
Bronze, cast, uniface
Diameter 82.5 mm
London, The British Museum

Obverse: Bust of a young man facing to the left. He wears a gown over a vest buttoned down the front. Below the portrait are two leaves on a stalk. Legend: DI LA IL BEL VISO · E QVI IL TVO SERVO MIRA (Admire on one side your own beautiful face, and on the other that of your servant[1]). Triangular stop and broad molding as the border.
Reverse: Plain.

The shallow curve of the bust truncation as well as the strong but subtle modeling of the cheek and eye-socket — the bridge of the nose in very shallow relief — closely link this piece to Lysippus's signed works. It is larger than they, however, so there is room for a more naturalistic rendering of the facial features. The bold profile, again characteristic of Lysippus the Younger, has here been emphasized by chasing of the field. The attribution cannot be absolutely certain, but the style of this medal is closer to that of Lysippus than anyone else's.

The inscription provides a clue to the medal's function. It can be assumed that the plain reverse was to have been polished as a mirror in which the object of the young man's devotion could look at herself. Other examples of mirror-medals are known. Two octagonal medals of the Ferrarese poet and philosopher Tito Strozzi were cast from speculum metal,[2] and Hill has suggested that the Lysippus piece may have been first made of silver.[3] The present specimen certainly shows no sign of ever having been polished, but the inscription cannot be explained in any other way.

As a love-token, the mirror-medal has been called "cheerfully unscrupulous," for different copies might mirror the faces of different women.[4] Only three examples of the present piece survive. All of them are in bronze, and cast, if the theory of a silver original is true, from an earlier example.

The mirror has a long tradition as a token of love. Anecdotes published in the sixteenth century by Saba da Castiglione and Brantôme tell of mirrors used as cases for portraits of themselves that lovers gave to their mistresses.[5] Such gifts appear to have had a symbolic meaning, since the mirror was one of the

36 obv.

attributes of Venus. The Venus of Arles, a bronze statue in which the goddess holds a mirror, was greatly admired in the fifteenth and sixteenth centuries. Thus apart from its value as a functional object, the mirror represents love itself.

In the *Iconologia* of Cesare Ripa, from 1593, the mirror is connected with feminine beauty, and by way of a Neoplatonic extension to a perfection even more profound: "The mirror shows that female beauty is . . . in itself a mirror in which everyone, seeing himself in a more perfect way, for love of his image, is stimulated to love those aspects of himself where he has perceived the greatest perfection, and then is initiated to love himself [i.e. aspires to a profound self-love or love of his soul]."[6]

It has long been assumed that this is a self-portrait medal. The artist's choice of a pseudonym may help to identify the portrait with Lysippus the Younger, and certainly confirm his authorship. In his *Natural History*, Pliny relates that the original Lysippus was self-taught, and that he boasted of making images of men as they really looked.[7] One might thus interpret the medal as a kind of dialogue between the perfect reflection of nature provided by its reverse and the necessarily less faithful copy on the obverse. Its inscription might then be addressed to Nature herself, rather than some specific object of the medalist's adoration.

Luke Syson

Giovanni Filangieri Candida
(born c. 1445–50, died c. 1498–99?)

The authors of most early medals were, in a certain sense at least, amateurs. They tended to be painters, sculptors, die-engravers, or goldsmiths who turned to the medal as occasion demanded. Other medalists, even more justly to be called amateurs, assume a certain prominence in the art of the medal from the late quattrocento onward. These were humanists—men with little or no formal training as artists—whose real occupations were in the world of affairs and of letters.[1] A few of them—like Andrea Guacialoti, a papal scriptor and canon of Prato, or the Paduan law professor Giulio della Torre—made major contributions to the art, but none produced a body of work as significant or as problematic as Giovanni Candida's.

Giovanni Filangieri was born into the Candida branch of a noble family of the kingdom of Naples, probably around 1445–50, and received a solid humanist education.[2] He joined the retinue of John, duke of Calabria, during the latter's unsuccessful campaign for the Neapolitan crown. In November 1467, Candida was in the service of the duke of Burgundy, Charles the Bold (born 1433, ruled 1467–77), and in 1472 the documents refer to him as the duke's secretary.[3]

When in Flanders, Candida corresponded extensively with foreign powers on his employer's behalf, but he spent much of his time abroad on diplomatic missions—many of them secretive—to Italy and Germany.[4] He was off on one of these when his patron, Charles the Bold, was killed at the battle of Nancy on January 5, 1477.

Candida arrived back in Ghent in August, two days before the wedding of Charles's daughter Mary of Burgundy to Maximilian of Austria (see cat. no. 37), where he became secretary to the ducal couple. In March 1478 he resumed his diplomatic travels.[5] At Rome, Candida was accused of slandering Pope Sixtus IV and stripped of certain ecclesiastical benefices.[6] Worse, a letter of his critical of Archduke Maximilian or his father Emperor Frederick III (cat. no. 40) fell into the wrong hands, and he was arrested and briefly imprisoned while passing through Germany on his way back to Burgundy.[7] On his return to Bruges in September 1478, however, he was reinstated as Maximilian's secretary. Soon afterward, Candida was imprisoned a second time—perhaps for his papal *lèse majesté*—in the château at Lille. Most of what we know of this incident comes from the medal, dated 1479, that he made of his jailors, Jean de la Gruthuse and Jean Miette, seemingly the artist's thank-offering for their role in his release.[8] Candida was back at his post by March 1479, but in the meantime the atmosphere at Maximilian's court had chilled. In the summer of 1480 he was granted permission to return to Naples, but apparently once out of Burgundy he set his sails for France.[9]

While serving as *conseiller du roy* to Charles VIII and ambassador to the the Holy See, Candida was naturalized a French citizen, and in April 1488, at the king's request, the pope named him protonotary apostolic and supplied him with benefices in Provence and Burgundy.[10] He had propounded the French crown's claim to the kingdom of Naples in his writings, and, may have been with Charles when the king entered Naples on February 22, 1495; documents definitely confirm that he was there in April and June.[11] The last record of him is his brief *Chronicle of the Kings of Sicily*, which internal evidence dates between April 1498 and August 1499.[12] He may have died shortly afterward, but it is equally possible that the silence of the documents merely indicates that he had fallen out of favor at court or chosen to retire in Naples.

Candida worked as a medalist only on rare occasions, but an undated letter reveals how highly his efforts in this direction were regarded. It was written by Guillaume de la Mare, secretary to Robert Briçonnet, a high-ranking figure in the French government who later became archbishop of Reims. It reveals that Candida had made a medal of Briçonnet as well as a seal matrix.[13] Two nearly identical medals of Robert Briçonnet survive.[14] There are also three signed medals, all dating from the late 1470s, one of Charles the Bold and Maximilian of Austria, one of Antonio Gratiadei, and the piece commemorating Candida's release from the château at Lille.[15] The early works are notable for their straightforward portraiture, more factual than expressive, with great emphasis on the profile and slight relief; their lettering is midway between true Roman and sans-serif, with circular stops sometimes arranged in clusters. At the other end of Candida's career the documented medals of Robert Briçonnet are larger, in extremely low relief, with subtle surface modeling; the lettering is more classical, with much use of triangular stops. Without signatures or documentation, one would hardly dare attribute the Briçonnet medals to the same hand that made the early Burgundian pieces.

More convincing is the attribution of two medals representing Maximilian of Austria and Mary of Burgundy (see cat. no. 37). The Briçonnet medals leave little doubt that Candida is the author of the medal depicting Giuliano and Clemente della Rovere (cat. no. 38). The latest works to have been assigned to Candida are a small group of medals made at the French court in the first decade of the sixteenth century (see cat. nos. 138, 139), but there is no evidence that he was active after the 1490s.[16] While several of the latter clearly belong to a single hand, their resemblance to Candida's authenticated work is rather superficial; the incisiveness of his modeling is exchanged in them for a decorative smoothness. Yet they do attest to Candida's influence on the art of the medal in France.

Candida's travels and his diplomatic functions at court would have given him the opportunity to see a wide spectrum of Italian medals. His work is often compared to that of Lysippus the Younger (cat. no. 36), but it is possible that too much is made of the perceived similarities between their styles. The Roman medalist was certainly responsible for one of the two surviving medals depicting Candida himself, a unique oblong lead in the Kress Collection.[17] From his early days at the Angevin court, Candida surely knew the works King René was then commissioning from Laurana and Pietro da Milano, two medalists who, like Candida, had recently come from Naples.[18] Drawing upon his continually renewed contact with Italian art, Candida slowly but consistently developed a manner that reflected Italian technique but remained highly original nonetheless. His late work—as distinguished as anything made in France before his time—provided a model that later, native French medalists found worthy of imitation.

Louis Waldman

Candida

Maximilian I of Austria (born 1459, emperor 1493–1519), and
  Mary of Burgundy (1457–1482)

37

Bronze, cast

Diameter 48.8 mm

New York, The Metropolitan Museum of Art, Gift of Ogden
  Mills, 1925

50.58.16

37a obv.   37a rev.

Obverse: Bust of Maximilian to the right, with shoulder-length
wavy hair secured by a twisted fillet and myrtle (?) wreath,
wearing a coat with lapels over a laced doublet with a high,
banded collar. Legend: MAXIMILIANVS • FR[ederici] •
CAES[aris] • F[ilius] • DVX • AVSTR[iae] • BVRGVND[iae] •
(Maximilian, son of the emperor Frederick, duke of Austria
[and] Burgundy). Pearled border.

Reverse: Bust of Mary of Burgundy to the right, her hair plaited
(?) and decoratively knotted on the back of her head. She wears
a plain dress with gossamer material from the neck to its
V-shaped front. Behind her, two M's interlaced and surmounted
by a crown. Legend: MARIA • KAROLI • F[ilia] • DVX •
BVRGVNDIÆ • AVSTRIÆ • BRAB[antiae] • C[omitissa] •
FLAN[driae] • (Maria, daughter of Charles, duchess of Burgundy, Austria, [and] Brabant, countess of Flanders). Pearled
border.

37a

Bronze, cast

Diameter 48.0

Washington, The National Gallery of Art, Samuel H. Kress
  Collection

1957.14.819

Obverse and reverse as above.

Though undated, this medal clearly dates from the five-year
period of Maximilian's first marriage to Mary of Burgundy, and
thus depicts him somewhere between the ages of eighteen and
twenty-three. The medal is attributed to Candida on the basis of
two facts: Candida had portrayed Maximilian on the reverse of
his signed medal of Charles the Bold, duke of Burgundy, most
likely created between 1475 and 1477,[1] and he served the
young couple as secretary from August 16, 1477, to July 12,
1480. The attribution has never been seriously questioned. In
fact, the placement of the crowned and interlaced M's to the left
of the bust of Mary on the reverse is a stylistic peculiarity of
Candida's; his signed medal commemorating his release from
the château at Lille displays the same device on both obverse
and reverse.[2]

   This medal is the most beautiful double portrait of Maximilian and Mary to survive. It functioned as the only official
portrait of Maximilian for twenty-five years, and he revealed his
fondness for it in 1517, when he commissioned the mint at Hall,

in the Tyrol, to strike a *Schautaler* based on these charming
early renditions.[3]

   The union of Maximilian and Mary has been called the most
important marriage in history, for it united the son of the Holy
Roman emperor Frederick III (cat. no. 40) with the richest
heiress in the world. Born in Brussels in 1457 to Charles the
Bold and Isabelle de Bourbon (died 1465), Mary represented to
the eager princes who sought her hand an inheritance of stag-
gering proportions: the duchy of Burgundy, stretching from
present-day Switzerland to the North Sea and including the
Franche-Comté, Flanders, Brabant, Zeeland, Holland, Fries-
land, and Luxemburg. Charles the Bold promised her to the
seventeen-year-old Maximilian, archduke of Austria, in 1476,
even though he had sent his secretary, the medalist Candida, to
negotiate with the king of Naples the previous year.[4] Candida's
signed medal pairing the duke of Burgundy with his chosen
son-in-law logically appeared between 1476 and 1477, a proc-
lamation in bronze of the hoped-for alliance with the house of
Habsburg.

   When Charles died in battle near Nancy on January 5, 1477,
Mary began to take control of her own destiny. Having seen a
portrait of Maximilian and been pleased by it, she wrote him a
secret letter on March 26,[5] thus managing to resist pressure
from her father's enemy, Louis XI of France, who had demanded
that she marry his son, the future Charles VIII. Maximilian
quickly sent his proxy to wed her at Bruges on April 21, buying
time until he could come to her in person at Ghent on August 18.

   On that later occasion, thanks to funds sent to him by Mary,
the insolvent Maximilian made a splendid entry into the Low
Countries.[6] He rode into Ghent at sunset, looking, it was said,
"like an archangel," dressed in silver armor, wearing a garland of
pearls and precious stones on his head, and followed by a
thousand retainers. The Burgundian court chronicler Jean Molinet praised the groom's noble deportment and manly beauty,
comparing him in the literary fashion of the time to Narcissus,
and likening his long blond hair to that of Absalom. Maximilian
was somewhat less flowery in the description of Mary he included in a letter to his friend Prüschenk, gauging her against
his previous Austrian mistresses: "I have a fair, devout, and
virtuous wife . . . the same size as the Leyenbergerin, much

37a obv.

smaller than Rosina. She has skin white as snow, brown hair, a small nose, a small head and face, eyes a mix of brown and gray, lovely and clear. Her mouth is a bit high, but pure and red. She is the most beautiful woman I have ever seen." An avid hunter, Maximilian went on to stress one of the qualities that doubtless accounted in no small part for their compatibility: "My wife is a superb huntress with falcon and hound. She has a white greyhound that is very swift. It sleeps almost every night by our bed."[7]

Mary's passion for hunting was the cause of her tragic death a mere five years later. While living at Bruges, she rode out with her falcons. Her horse stumbled, and she was thrown into the bole of a tree. She died of internal injuries on March 27, 1482, at the age of twenty-five.

This medal is usually said to have been made on the occasion of the couple's wedding in August 1477. Yet this cannot be, for the other medal of the pair that is also attributed to Candida indisputably shows them to be younger.[8] There Mary is portrayed on the reverse with her hair cascading down her back, in the way all the sources relate that she wore it on her wedding day.[9]

The ducal crown appears on the present medal above the intertwined initials of Maximilian and Mary, and hints at the reason behind the commissioning of the piece. Wearing the crown at her marriage, Mary had promised her Austrian husband "fidelity and love, and to hold to that which was agreed between your father and mine concerning my lands and provinces."[10] The eighteen-year-old Maximilian had thus become the ruling duke of Burgundy. Barely three months after his wedding, he found himself locked in a power struggle with Louis XI of France. He defeated his adversary's troops at Guinegatte in 1479, dismounting and fighting alongside his German and Flemish foot-soldiers.

The medal cannot be linked directly to either Maximilian's victory in 1479 or Mary's death in 1482. Maximilian's headdress might provide some clue to its date, but there is little agreement about whether the wreath is of myrtle, signifying conjugal happiness, or laurel, the symbol of victory.[11] Here the couple appears older and more dignified. Mary's chignon, especially, lends her an air of the mature woman and ruler, rather than the maiden heiress and bride of the earlier medal. While we cannot establish the exact reason behind the issuing of the piece, its message is clear.

Mark Wilchusky

Candida
Giuliano della Rovere, later Pope Julius II (born 1443, pontiff 1503–13), and Clemente della Rovere (birth date unknown, bishop of Mende 1483–1504)
38
Bronze, cast
Diameter 61.3 mm
New York, The Metropolitan Museum of Art, Ann and George Blumenthal Fund, 1950 (ex collection J. Pierpont Morgan)

Obverse: Bust of Giuliano to the right, tonsured, wearing collarless shirt and rochet. Legend: IVLIANVS • EP[iscopu]S • OSTIEN[sis] • CAR[dinalis] • S[ancti] • P[etri] • AD • VINCVLA • (Giuliano, bishop of Ostia [and] cardinal of San Pietro in Vincoli).
Reverse: Bust of Clemente to the right, tonsured, wearing collarless shirt and rochet. Legend: CLEMENS • DE • RVVERE • EP[iscopu]S • MIMATEN[sis] • (Clemente della Rovere, bishop of Mende).

38a
Bronze, cast
Diameter 62.0 mm
London, The British Museum

Obverse and reverse as above.

Julius II is best known as the warrior pope who restored authority over the estates of the Church and the patron who

38a obv.

38a rev.

exhorted Michelangelo to finish the frescoes on the Sistine Chapel ceiling. Less familiar is his earlier career as "the rebel cardinal." For thirty-three years before becoming pope, Giuliano ranked as one of the most powerful and ambitious churchmen in Europe.

The medal is attributed to Candida because it is extremely close in size and style to one of the artist's medals of Robert Briçonnet,[1] which can be dated with precision to the end of 1493, when he was staying in Rome at the expense of Briçonnet, then vying for a cardinal's hat.[2]

Stylistically, the medal of Giuliano della Rovere appears to date from the year 1494 or shortly after. A review of the cardinal's prior history helps to explain just why the work was issued and the presence of Clemente on its reverse.

Born in 1445 in the region of Liguria near the town of Savona, Giuliano studied law in Perugia and joined the Franciscan Order in emulation of his paternal uncle, Francesco della Rovere. The latter became Pope Sixtus IV in 1471, and within months of his election he instituted a program of nepotism whereby the twenty-six-year-old Giuliano became cardinal of San Pietro in Vincoli. Over the next eight years the ambitious nephew received one new bishopric a year—Lausanne, Catana, Messina, Avignon, Coutances, Viviers, Mende, and Sabina—garnering much wealth and influence in the process.

The year 1483 saw his preferment to the strategically important bishopric of Ostia, the port of Rome at the mouth of the Tiber. His first act in Ostia was to build a fortress, ostensibly to protect the port, but in reality for his eventual use as a private base of operations against Rome.[3] During the pontificate of Innocent VIII, Cardinal della Rovere was perhaps the most important member of the Sacred College, effectively controlling the Vatican to the dismay of the quiet pope. He made a bid for the papal throne himself on Innocent's death, but lost out to his bitter enemy Rodrigo Borgia, who became Pope Alexander VI. Once the latter was formally installed, Giuliano retreated to Ostia and shut himself up in his fortress, thereby threatening Rome's maritime communications. A brief reconciliation was effected in July of 1493, when he became "quasi secondo papa," but second pope was not the office to which he aspired.

On the night of April 23, 1494, Giuliano quietly slipped away from Ostia by ship. Having served as papal legate to France since 1476, he had become known to that country as "a great and faithful friend," and he was warmly received when he arrived at the court of Charles VIII in Lyon on June 1, 1494. Since February, the king and the cardinal had been plotting an invasion of Italy with the aim of deposing Alexander VI. Before the end of June there were forty thousand French troops on the march toward Italy. The French flag was hoisted above the fortress of Ostia in September, and on December 31 Giuliano and the king entered Rome in triumph.

One can therefore imagine the cardinal's frustration when, on January 19, 1495, he was forced to watch Charles VIII, the would-be deposer, bend in all obedience to kiss the papal foot. He nevertheless chose to continue with his French ally, who went on to claim the Angevin rights to the kingdom of Naples in

May. Meanwhile, the pope had had time to ally himself with Venice, Milan, and Austria, so that Charles was faced with the problem of getting out of Italy. He barely escaped at the battle of Fornovo in July, as Giuliano was attempting to secure French control of Genoa.

Thus ended the first phase in the conspirators' grand design. Having lost nothing, Charles VIII regrouped at his court in Lyon. Giuliano returned to Avignon on October 21, 1495, where he was given a hero's welcome by the town and by Clemente della Rovere, whom he had left in charge of his affairs in his absence.[4]

This would appear to be the logical moment for the creation of the present medal. October 1495 seems to be the only time that Giuliano and Clemente are documented as being in the same place, and more important, the only time that Clemente had done something worthy of praise in the form of a medal; he had successfully guarded Giuliano's interests while the cardinal was away.

Called "Le Gros" (the Fat), Clemente appears to have been Giuliano's brother, though some scholars refer to him as a nephew or other close relative. Also a member of the Franciscan Order, Clemente benefited handsomely from Giuliano's powerful position in the Church. In 1483, Giuliano gave him the bishopric of Mende, which he had held for five years. To Giuliano, Clemente represented a trusted ally who had helped to protect the family interests in France.

There remains one obstacle to the theory about the genesis of the medal presented here, namely our lack of knowledge regarding Candida's whereabouts in October 1495. There is no record of him after June 17, 1495, when he was acting as secretary to Charles VIII in Naples. We know that he was still alive in 1498–99, and it takes but a small leap of faith to imagine him stopping long enough in Avignon on his flight from Italy to model the portraits of Giuliano and Clemente della Rovere.

Mark Wilchusky

Bertoldo di Giovanni
(d. 1491)

Bertoldo was a member of Lorenzo de' Medici's (cat. no. 42) entourage, as servant and familiar, artist and advisor. In a comic letter of 1479 to Lorenzo, he claims to have been a disciple of Donatello, a claim seconded by Vasari, who in his life of Donatello says that Bertoldo was chiefly responsible for the completion of Donatello's late works. Vasari also has Bertoldo serving as mentor to the budding genius Michelangelo (cat. no. 52) and other young Florentines who studied ancient and modern masters in the Medici garden near the church of San Marco. Bertoldo's output of statuettes, reliefs, and medals was initially established by Bode.[1] Bertoldo was responsible additionally for a wood statue of St. Jerome in Faenza, the glazed terracotta frieze on the façade of the Medici villa Poggio a Caiano, and twelve stucco reliefs in the Palazzo Scaladella Gherardesca in Florence. In a letter announcing Bertoldo's death, Bartolommeo Dei stresses the Medicean nature

39 obv.   39 rev.

of his creations, for he "always did worthy things with the magnificent Lorenzo," and praises him as a "capital manufacturer of medals." He produced only six medals over a period of about fifteen years, the present three and those of Filippo de' Medici, archbishop of Pisa; Antonio Gratiadei, emissary of the archduke Maximilian; and Leticia Sanuto, a lady of Venice.[2]

James David Draper

Bertoldo di Giovanni
Mehmed II (1430–1481)
39
Bronze, cast
Diameter 94.2 mm; diameter of the outer perimeter of the inscription from the E of ASIE to the G of GRETIE, 88.6 mm
University of California at Santa Barbara, University Art Museum, Sigmund Morgenroth Collection
1964.287

Obverse: Bust facing left, bearded, wearing a turban and a cord suspending a medallion with a crescent moon. Legend: MAVMhET ASIE AC TRAPESVNZIS MAGNE QVE GRETIE IMPERAT[or] (Mehmed, emperor of Asia and also Trebizond and Magna Graecia).
Reverse: A triumphal chariot drawn to the right by two prancing horses, led by a helmeted male who is nude but for a band around his waist, and who shoulders a trophy while looking backward. The side of the chariot is decorated with a garland suspended from two lion masks framing the image of a throne

with flames issuing from its seat. On a pedestal rising from the car stands a young nude male wearing boots, a hat that may be supposed to be a turban, a band around his waist, and a cloak flying out behind. He displays a statuette of a nude male and holds a rope that encircles three nude, crowned women standing in the rear of the car. These are identified by inscription as GRETIE (Greece), TRAPESVNTI (Trebizond), and ASIE (Asia). The designations for Greece and Asia are placed vertically. The exergue is inscribed: OPUS / BERTOLDI / FLORENTIN[vs] / SCVLTOR / IS (The work of Bertoldo, Florentine sculptor). Flanking the inscription are a reclining nude male with trident and a reclining nude female with cornucopia, their feet touching.

39a
Bronze, cast
Diameter 93.0 mm; diameter of the outer perimeter of the inscription from the E in IMPERAT to the V in TRAPESVNZIS, 89.2 mm
Berlin, Staatliche Museen, Münzkabinett

Obverse and reverse as above.

This is Bertoldo's largest and only signed medal. Unlike Costanzo da Ferrara (cat. no. 21), Gentile Bellini, and Bartolommeo Bellano, Bertoldo never visited Constantinople, and for his obverse used Bellini's medal of the sultan.[1] His rendition is more convincingly fleshy, however, and he added the medallion around the neck.

Relations between Florence and the sultan were especially close in these last two years of the Turk's life. He did Lorenzo de' Medici a signal favor by returning to him Bernardo Bandini de' Baroncelli, who had fled to Constantinople after the Pazzi Conspiracy (cat. no. 41). Bandini, last of the Pazzi conspirators to be punished, was hanged on December 29, 1479. Lorenzo's notes indicate that on May 11, 1480, he sent the sultan a letter thanking him for the gift of a saddle.[2] According to the elaborate thesis of Emil Jacobs,[3] this message would have been accompanied by Bertoldo's medal.

Jacobs's ideas, which on first reading may seem almost too far-fetched to be true, are basically reliable, rooted as they are in a keen understanding of the medal's diplomatic background. The reverse reflects Lorenzo's desire to flatter the Turk, who had known decades of military glory. Mars leads the triumph, while Mehmed is represented by the victorious central figure in the chariot. Though turbaned, he is youthful and unbearded, and so personifies the sultan's genius. The image he displays, according to Jacobs, is the Roman agricultural diety Bonus Eventus, but that divinity's usual attributes are lacking, and the statuette could as easily be a Victory. The triumph occurs before Sea and Air, the exergue figures. Mehmed's captives, secured by a rope, are identified as Asia, Greece, and Trebizond, the last of which had been conquered in 1461. The obverse spells out Greece as "Magna Gretia," or Magna Graecia, an ancient name for the Greek cities of the South Italian coasts. The reason for this emphasis is that Mehmed had designs on the Aragonese kingdom of Naples, and Lorenzo was fanning his hopes because of his own embarrassments in Italy. In the wake of the Pazzi Conspiracy, Florence was at war with the Holy See. The duke of Calabria still occupied much of Tuscany in the spring of 1480. When in July of that year the Turks besieged Otranto, the Neapolitan armies left Tuscany to defend the South. It was widely suspected that the Florentines had foreknowledge of the Turk's bellicose preparations and had abetted them, and in fact the medal, in which Mehmed seems to be invited to help himself to Magna Graecia, suggests as much. The flaming throne on the chariot's side is the Siege Perilous, a device of Alfonso V of Aragon, king of Naples, also used by his successors. Here Lorenzo appropriated it as a gratuitous sign that he approved of the enterprise.

Ancient glyptic and numismatic influences on the medal include the famous *Tazza Farnese*,[4] whose pleasing rhythms and lithe figures inform the design, and Hadrianic coins with reclining river gods, echoed here in the exergue. Vermeule traces some elements of the reverse to a coin from Maconia in Lydia, in which Septimius Severus, Caracalla, and Geta are borne in a quadriga. That he is correct in doing so is proved by the fact that Bertoldo borrowed the overhead Victory from that design for the reverse of his last medal, the Leticia Sanuto.[5]

James David Draper

Bertoldo di Giovanni
Frederick III (born 1415, emperor 1452–93)
40

40 obv.

40 rev.

Bronze, cast
Diameter 56.3 mm; diameter of the outer perimeter of the inscription from the T in IMPERATOR to the S in FEdERIGUS, 53.7 mm
American private collection

Obverse: Bust facing left, with long hair, wearing a fur hat with rolled brim and fur-collared robe. Inscribed at outer edge: FREdERIGVS TERCIVS ROMANORVM IMPERATOR SENPER [*sic*] . . . , and on an inner arc: AVGVSTVS (Frederick III, emperor of the Romans, forever . . . exalted).
Reverse: Within a molded rim, a scene on the Ponte Sant'Angelo in Rome. The emperor is creating knights in the presence of the pope, cardinals, and foot soldiers. A boat is visible under the bridge, from which hangs a garland supported by two putti. The parapet bears the imperial two-headed eagle separating the inscription: CXXII EqVITES • CREA[vi]T KALEN[dis] • IANVARI[is] • MCCCCLXIX ([He] created 122 knights on the first of January, 1469).

The fur hat and coat trim pertain to the imperial office, not to the wintry weather, as implied by Meiss.[1] Frederick arrived in Rome on Christmas Eve, 1468, seeking military aid against the Turk. On New Year's Day, 1469, he attended a dawn Mass in San Giovanni in Laterano, then proceeded on a white horse, the gift of Pope Paul II, to the Ponte Sant'Angelo, where he bestowed knighthoods and other honors in the papal presence. In the crowded scene on the reverse, the emperor is distinguishable at the center in his heavily trimmed mantle, while the pope, at the left, wearing tiara and pluvial, lends his blessing.

This is Bertoldo's only dated medal. There are not many examples with the original (and quite Medicean) misspelling of SENPER for SEMPER in the reverse inscription; later casts corrected this. Also a sizable number of specimens in German collections are extensively retouched with strokes of tooling. Fine early casts like the present one are rare, but they show an overwhelming number of traits in common with the core of Bertoldo's medallic oeuvre, such as the small, fat letters, which occasionally include a lower-case letter among the capitals, and the densely packed scenes themselves.

The design is particularly intimately bound up with the style and circumstances of the Filippo de' Medici reverse, made during precisely this period as part of the effort to win a cardinal's hat for Archbishop Filippo (1426–1474), a distant cousin of Lorenzo de' Medici.[2] Many Florentines viewed the imperial creation of knights as a money making sham, but Filippo would have countenanced it gladly. Part of his mission to Rome was to press the emperor to use his influence with the pope in designating a Florentine cardinal—namely himself. The Frederick III medal was probably the archbishop's gift to the emperor on this occasion. Not least because of the fresh, eyewitness character of the Frederick III reverse, there is reason to believe Bertoldo was also in Rome, probably as a member of the archbishop's retinue, when he made the medals.

Bertoldo's literal account is without precedent. He arrived at it not only through his own observation of the scene, but through a judicious consultation of sources and options. A coin of Septimius Severus, showing a bridge decked for a triumph, probably gave him the sense of how to frame his vignette.[3] He was also the first to show such an Albertian variety of poses in

medals. The head-on foreshortening of the horses may derive from knowledge of *cassone* painting, and the knights seen from behind could stem both from Bertoldo's study of the columns of Marcus Aurelius and Trajan and his experience of Masolino's great Crucifixion fresco in San Clemente, Rome, now sadly diminished, but at the time an unrivaled repository of varied stances in a successfully captured atmosphere.

The obverse profile was authoritative enough to have furnished the basis for most later portraits of Frederick.[4]

James David Draper

Bertoldo di Giovanni
The Pazzi Conspiracy, 1478
41
Bronze, cast
Oval, 63.9–66.7 mm; internal measurement from the outside left of choir screen to the S in MEDICES, 53.4 mm
New York, The Metropolitan Museum of Art, Bequest of Anne D. Thomson, 1923
23.280.44

Obverse: LAVRENTIVS and MEDICES (Lorenzo de' Medici) inscribed on either side of a colossal head of Lorenzo in three-quarter right profile, base of neck draped, resting above an open octagonal structure (the choir screen of Florence Cathedral) with low walls and eight columns supporting an octagonal cornice, each surmounted by a flaming torch (?). In the central space: SALVS • PVBLICA (the public health). At left, an animal lying under a tree; at right, a gowned figure holding a wreath. Within the choir, left to right: four churchgoers making gestures of surprise; the lectern (triangular, as it is seen from the side); the torso of a man in a hat with a cloak over his arm; two ecclesiastics approaching the raised altar, on which are a crucifix and candles; a priest at the altar who appears to place his right hand on the missal and raise his left over a chalice; a

41 obv.

41 rev.

cardinal in his *biretta* looking on from the rear of this group. In front of the choir screen, left to right: four men, two running to the left, the other two falling back with startled gestures; a man in cloak and hat with sword raised in his right hand, set upon by two men with swords; slightly behind these a man with a sword, seen from behind, attacking a man in a cloak and hat. *Reverse*: IVLIANVS and MEDICES (Giuliano de' Medici) inscribed on either side of a colossal head of Giuliano in three-quarter left profile, base of the neck draped, resting above the same structure, now reversed. Below the rail: LVCTVS • PVBLICVS (public mourning). At left, a draped figure with a staff; at right, a figure in a tunic with his right arm raised to his head. Within the choir is a mirror image of the corresponding group on the obverse, so that the altar is now at the left and the cardinal is the nearest inner figure. In front of the choir screen, left to right: two males with daggers attack from behind a man clad in a large mantle, who raises his arms; a man with raised arms steps right; a cloaked figure lies on the floor; above him, a man stabs downward with his dagger; three men circle behind them, brandishing swords.

On Sunday, April 26, 1478, a faction led by members of the Pazzi family assaulted Lorenzo de' Medici (cat. no. 42) and his brother Giuliano (1453–1478) as they attended Mass in Florence Cathedral. Giuliano was slain, while Lorenzo escaped with a light neck wound. This plot and its aftermath were commemorated in a number of works of art that include, in addition to Bertoldo's painstaking reconstruction of the fell deed itself, representations by Botticelli and Leonardo da Vinci of the perpetrators' punishment.

Vasari described this reverse, believing it to be by Pollaiuolo, associating type with style and the maker of the engraving *The Battle of Nude Men*. It was Bode who established that the medal is the one referred to by Andrea Guacialoti on September 11, 1478, four and a half months after the attack, in a letter to Lorenzo de' Medici.[1] The letter accompanied four examples of a medal cast by Guacialoti after Bertoldo's proof-cast or model, which he praised enthusiastically.[2] Orders no doubt soon multiplied, as reflected by fairly numerous early examples, due to Lorenzo's evident desire to spread the message of *salus publica / luctus publicus*, or civic health versus sorrow. The basic concept in fact occurred to him within hours of the attack. He wrote the same day to his allies the duke and duchess of Milan, informing them that Giuliano was slain, and equating his own defense with the city's well-being and salvation.[3] The medal's design subsequently crystallized probably through consultation with Angelo Poliziano (1454–1494), the great humanist who wrote an account of the Pazzi Conspiracy in Latin,[4] as well as with Bertoldo. In fact, the design tallies most closely with the official account drawn up by the Synodus Florentinus, a cathedral council that gave its own version of the event. Many versions survive, offering conflicting details as to the moment chosen by the conspirators, but it was the synod that reported that their first choice for a signal had been the elevation of the host, but that they later switched to the priest's communion;[5] a bell is rung at both points in the Mass. Bertoldo's celebrant on both sides of the medal faces the altar, as yet unaware of the turmoil outside the choir screen, and the graduated alignment of the clergy resembles that in manuscript illuminations of the *Te igitur*. The cardinal within the choir is Raffaello Sansoni, whose visit prompted the Medici brothers' attendance at Mass, and who was suspected of being a co-conspirator.

Lorenzo and Giuliano were assaulted on opposite sides of the choir, and that is what prompted the altogether extraordinary solution of reverse mirroring obverse. The degree of hyperactivity is equally without numismatic precedent. To give his medal maximum legibility, and also perhaps to stress the sacrilege of the event, Bertoldo chose to show the attackers nude, or at least with no visible signs of clothing. Only the Medici brothers are attired, so as to distinguish them from the rest. It is thus that Bertoldo can be detected resorting to the typical quattrocento strategem of continuous narrative, by which figures can be repeated to suggest succeeding stages of an episode. On the reverse, Giuliano appears twice. He is the cloaked man with upraised arms at the lower left, being stabbed in the back and side by two figures representing Francesco de' Pazzi and Bernardo Bandini de' Baroncelli. At the right he is the fallen cloaked figure being stabbed repeatedly by Pazzi (Poliziano mentions nineteen wounds counted on Giuliano's body).

On the obverse, Lorenzo occurs no fewer than three times. While nearby figures express shocked surprise, the cloaked Lorenzo at right of center is set upon by two figures—priests, in fact, who botched the job. At far right, pursued by a swordsman, Lorenzo is the hatted figure parrying blows with his cloak and about to enter the choir. In the center, just over the edge of the choir screen, is the torso of the cloaked and hatted Lorenzo once more, looking over his shoulder as he rushes through the choir to safety. Once his partisans swung the bronze door of the New Sacristy behind him, the danger was over. The plot immediately disintegrated, and those responsible were savagely punished as public support rallied behind Lorenzo.

Draper identifies several sources that influenced the design, first and foremost Donatello's *Raising of Drusiana*, one of the monumental stucco perspectival reliefs in the Old Sacristy of San Lorenzo, all remarkable as exhaustive penetrations of space, creating layers of depth that encourage freedom and clarity of movement.[6] Bertoldo's yet more radical semi-bird's-eye view, one that allowed him to trace the action to the choir screen's opposite wall, is also encountered in *cassone* paintings. The assassination of Julius Caesar, a popular subject in such works, would have sprung to mind readily enough for its topical relevancy. Roman coins also employ the semi-bird's-eye vantage point, opening the interior of buildings up to view, as in one of Alexander Severus, showing the Temple of Jupiter.[7] Ancient coins apparently prompted the flanking allegorical figures as well, which have not found a satisfactory interpretation. As for the three-quarter-profile heads, looming so incongruously above the scenes, that of Giuliano certainly derives from portraits by Sandro Botticelli,[8] and that of Lorenzo may also, although Bertoldo had plenty of access to his master's features—increasingly so, for his fortunes became inseparably bound up with those of Lorenzo, and references to him in the Magnifico's service multiplied dramatically in the wake of the Pazzi Conspiracy.

James David Draper

Niccolò di Forzore Spinelli, called Niccolò Fiorentino
(1430–1514)

Niccolò's family were goldsmiths in Florence, and he was a grand-nephew of the painter Spinello Aretino (c. 1346–1410). He is believed to have worked for the dukes of Burgundy, for a "Nicolas de Spinel" is mentioned in the ducal accounts in 1468 as having engraved seals for Charles the Bold. He married Alessandra di Lionardo de' Paolo in 1471. In 1484 he repaired the great silver guild seal of Florence's Arte de' Giudici e Notai.[1] He is known to have been in Flanders, thanks to a casual remark by Leonardo da Vinci (1452–1519) to the effect that something might be done "as was done in Flanders, according to what Niccolò di Forzore told me."[2] Apart from these sparse facts and the existence of five signed medals, Niccolò's career is a mystery. The signed medals include two dated pieces from 1485 and 1492. One medal, of Alfonso I d'Este, is documented by a payment recorded in the Este archives: Alfonso visited Florence on April 2, 1492, during a pilgrimage to Rome, and on that occasion Niccolò made a silver portrait medal of him.[3] A total of 148 medals have been either attributed to him or identified as related to his style. They represent a wide range of sitters drawn from the ruling and patrician families in Florence, the papal court in Rome—there is even one of Innocent VIII—and French court circles at the time of the French invasion of Italy in 1494–95. For an Italian medalist of the fifteenth century this is an absurdly large group, but a core of medals could be represented as the work of one master or his carefully controlled studio. Niccolò is the most powerful portrait maker

of the Italian Renaissance medalists. His effigies are bolder in scale, more varied, more bluntly realistic, and more personal than anything produced earlier. Heretofore, only one artist, Enzola of Parma (active 1465–78), had modeled portraits on a similarly bold scale, but he left only three likenesses. The Florentine conventions of the sculpted portrait bust in the hands of artists like Mino da Fiesole (c. 1430–1484) and his successors appear to have had no effect on Niccolò, but his extensive series of portrait medals supplied the same family market.

The earliest of Niccolò's medals appear to date from about 1480, when he was already in his fifties. Their reverses are generally awkward and ill-conceived, the medalist being content to quote motifs from antique gems or sculptures. They have no reference to contemporary Florentine art and are informed with a merely superficial humanist culture.

Two painted portraits have been mistakenly identified as likenesses of the medalist.[4]

Graham Pollard

Niccolò Fiorentino
Lorenzo de' Medici, "il Magnifico" (1449–1492)
42
Bronze, cast
Diameter 91.6 mm; diameter of the outer perimeter of the inscription, 70.9 mm
New York, The Metropolitan Museum of Art, Ann and George Blumenthal Fund, 1950
50.58.4

Obverse: Bust to the left, wearing a simple gown. Legend: MAGNVS LAVRENTIVS MEDICES (Lorenzo de' Medici, the Great).
Reverse: A female personification of Florence, wearing tunic and mantle, seated to the right under a laurel tree. In her out-

42 obv.   42 rev.

42 obv.

stretched right hand she holds a stalk of three lilies. Legend: TVTELA PATRI[a]E (Guardian of the homeland). Below the figure, her name: FLORENTIA[e] (Florence).

Lorenzo became Florence's leading citizen on the death of his father, Piero, in 1469. He was then only twenty years old. Under his father and his grandfather, Cosimo the Elder, the dynasty had taken the leading role in the public affairs of the city, although there was no formal civic commission for such responsibilities. Lorenzo had been thoroughly groomed for his duties as a politician and diplomat, but was unprepared to take control of the vast international banking business that was the source of the family's power. During his lifetime, the traditional Florentine alliances with Milan and Naples were upset by the ambitions of Pope Sixtus IV, involving Florence in a costly war between 1478 and 1480. The pope's personal enmity fomented the Pazzi Conspiracy against the Medici, and led to its attack on Lorenzo and his brother Giuliano in 1478 (see cat. no. 41). The Italian wars eventually led to the invasion of Italy by the king of France, Charles VIII, in 1494. The declining fortunes of the Medici bank and Florence itself occasioned such disaffection that two years after Lorenzo's death the family was expelled from the city. Nevertheless, his remarkable humanist learning, his skill as a poet, his intelligent patronage of scholars, and his passionate interest in civic architecture had helped to shape a period of uncommon cultural brilliance.[1]

The medal is one of five pieces that the artist signed. Among the rocks on the reverse of the specimen in the Bargello in Florence is the signature: OP[us]. NI[ccole]. F[iorentinu]s (sic: the work of Niccolò the Florentine). Niccolò's portrait presents Lorenzo as a simple citizen of Florence, and is one of the last likenesses made of him. An anonymous terra-cotta bust in Prague, shows him with the same little lock of hair over the left eye.[2]

The medal's reverse, while very clumsy, is the only one of Niccolò's reverse types that was not copied from some misunderstood gem or coin. It was not originally prepared for this medal, but was adapted from some other piece projected by the artist, as it does not correctly fit with the roundel of the effigy and has been cut down, the lettering having been cropped in the process. Such carelessness would suggest that the medal was not commissioned by its subject, but rather made as an act of homage on the part of the artist. One cannot believe that so discriminating a patron would have tolerated such an effect.

Graham Pollard

Niccolò Fiorentino (?)
Girolamo Ridolfi (1465–1526)
43
Bronze, cast
Diameter 49.0 mm
Washington, The National Gallery of Art, gift of Elaine Rosenberg in Honor of Alexandre P. Rosenberg and the 50th anniversary of the National Gallery of Art
1991.198.1

43 obv.   43 rev.

Obverse: Bust to the left, wearing a simple cap and plain gown. Legend: HIE[ronymus] DE SANCTO GEMINIANO S[ecretarius] AP[ostolicu]S (Girolamo of San Gimignano, apostolic secretary).
Reverse: Pegasus springing to the right. Legend: GEMINIO DICATVM (Dedicated to Geminio).

Girolamo was a son of Lodovico Ridolfi of San Gimignano, in Tuscany. In 1477 he was living in Rome, presumably at school. He was such a distinguished scholar that by the mid 1480s he had been appointed apostolic secretary. Pope Julius II later named him consistorial advocate.

The medal is one of a group of nineteen, consistent in style and attributed to Niccolò, portraying sitters connected with Rome. They date between roughly 1480 and 1486, and among them is a portrait of Pope Innocent VIII. In the 1480s, the papal court attracted numerous brilliant young humanists seeking patronage, and there are portrait medals of such people by Lysippus (cat. no. 36) and Candida (cat. nos. 37–38).

This medal's reverse, showing Pegasus, the mount of the Muses, must refer to Ridolfi's reputation as a writer. Its inscription suggests that he wrote in honor of the patron saint of his native city.[1]

Graham Pollard

Niccolò Fiorentino (?)
Filippo Strozzi (1428–1491)
44
Bronze, cast
Diameter 88.8 mm
Washington, The National Gallery of Art, Samuel H. Kress Collection
1957.14.880

Obverse: Bust to the left, wearing a simple gown. Legend: PHILIPPVS STROZA (Filippo Strozzi).
Reverse: An eagle with spread wings standing on a sprouting oak stump, to which is tied a shield charged with the Strozzi arms,[1] in a landscape of pine trees, the field semé of plumes. No inscription.

Filippo Strozzi was a Florentine merchant-prince from a family second only to the Medici. Like the Medici, his had suffered

44 obv.

44 rev.

political banishment. Filippo returned to the city in 1466, and became an invaluable financial supporter of the young Lorenzo the Magnificent (cat. no. 42). In 1489, at the age of sixty-one, Filippo began building the gigantic family palace that still stands. A contemporary diarist records that medals were placed in the palace's foundations on August 6, 1489, and this medal was doubtless made for that occasion. One of the designers of the palace was Benedetto da Maiano (1442–1497), who also produced, probably in about 1491, a marble bust of Filippo, now in the Louvre. Because the likenesses are similar, the medal has also been ascribed to Benedetto, but it is not his work.[2] The medal is consonant in style with other medals that use the eagle reverse type, so that they form a group that fits into the rag-bag designation of medals more or less in the style of Niccolò.[3] A wax model of the portrait has survived, now in Paris, but it is probably an independent work rather than a preparatory model for the medal.[4]

The eagle was the Strozzi family emblem, and the reverse motif appears on two chairs from among the furnishings of the Palazzo Strozzi, one in the Museo Horne, Florence, and one in The Metropolitan Museum of Art, New York.[5] The sprouting oak tree is probably intended as a symbol of the family's changing fortunes.

Graham Pollard

Niccolò Fiorentino (?)
Giovanna Albizzi Tornabuoni (died 1488)
45
Bronze, cast
Diameter 76 mm
London, The British Museum

Obverse: Bust to the right, wearing a plain dress with square-cut bodice and a massive pendant jewel on a necklace. The hair

forms a thick tress over the back of the head. Legend: UXOR LAVRENTII DE TORNABONIS IOANNA ALBIZA (The wife of Lorenzo Tornabuoni, Giovanna Albizzi)
Reverse: The Three Graces. Legend: CASTITAS PVLCHRITV-DO AMOR (Chastity, Beauty, Love).

46
Bronze, cast
Diameter 78 mm
Los Angeles County Museum of Art
79.4.362

Obverse: As above.
Reverse: The martial Venus, a Spartan deity. The legend is taken from Virgil's *Aeneid*, Book 1, line 315: VIRGINIS OS HAB-ITVM QVE GERENS ET VIRGINIS ARMA ("With a maiden's face and mien, and a maiden's weapons").

Giovanna Albizzi married Lorenzo Tornabuoni in 1486, and these medals were probably made for that occasion or very shortly afterward. They are certainly among the most charming of all marriage medals. The necklace of pearls confirms that the sitter is a bride, for pearls, symbols of the immaculate Virgin, were traditional elements of wedding costume. To commemorate the union, the Tornabuoni family also commissioned Botticelli to paint fresco decorations of Lorenzo with the Liberal Arts and Venus offering gifts to Giovanna in the Villa Lemmi, near Florence, then belonging to Lorenzo's uncle. The obverse is one of a group of seventeen similar portraits of young patrician women of Florence produced by or under the influence of Niccolò Fiorentino. In one of them, of Costanza Rucellai, the hair is dressed in a very similar way.[1] Giovanna Albizzi died in childbirth in 1488. She was immortalized in Ghirlandaio's *Visitation*, part of a series of frescoes on the life of the Virgin

46 obv.

46 rev.

commissioned by the Tornabuoni family in the Cappella Maggiore in Santa Maria Novella, Florence. There Giovanna's features are given to the Virgin, the portrait head taken from this medal.[2] A panel painting of her by Ghirlandaio also survives.[3]

The reverse of the Three Graces (cat. no. 45) is a charming compliment to Giovanna's beauty and virtues. Niccolò had also used it shortly before this on medals of Pico della Mirandola.[4] In the present version, the center figure has been read as Giovanna herself.[5] The Three Graces always symbolized what was good and most civilized in life, and the interlacing of the figures was associated with the acts of giving, accepting, and returning.[6] The medalist's source for the motif was most probably a lost figural grouping from antiquity[7] or even an ancient painting, but the only precise parallel that has been found is a Roman terra-cotta lamp.[8]

The martial Venus of the alternate reverse (cat. no. 46) personifies both carnal love and chastity, and was a recurrent image in the art and writing of Florence in the late fifteenth century. Equally appropriate to a marriage medal, she combines the qualities exemplified by the Three Graces on the other version.[9]

Graham Pollard

Florentine School
Girolamo Savonarola (1452–1498)
47
Bronze, cast
Diameter 86.5 mm
New York, The Metropolitan Museum of Art, Ann and George
    Blumenthal Fund, 1950 (ex collection J. Pierpont Morgan)
50.58.5

Obverse: Half-figure facing left, in habit with hood raised, but with tonsured hair showing at forehead. Savonarola holds a crucifix (inscribed INRI) with both hands, and gazes at the face of Christ in an attitude of meditation. Legend: HIERONYMVS •

SAV^O[narola] • FER[rariensis] • ORD[inis] • PRE[dicatorum] • VIR • DOCTISSIMVS • (Girolamo Savonarola of Ferrara, of the Order of Preachers, a most learned man). Traces of a plain raised border.

Reverse: The field is divided by a vertical raised line. On the right, a right hand issuing from a cloud and wielding a dagger over a fortress, with the legend: GLADIVS • DOMINI • SVP[er] • TER[r]A[m] • CITO • ET • VELOCITER • (The sword of the Lord over the earth quickly and swiftly). On the left, the dove of the Holy Spirit on a cloud above a fortified city, inside of which there appears to be a cupola topped by a cross. Legend: SPIR-ITVS • D[omi]NI • SVP[er] • TERRA[m] • COPIOSE • [e]T • HABV[n]DA[n]T[er] • (The spirit of the Lord over the earth copiously and abundantly).

Girolamo Savonarola, executed in the Piazza della Signoria in Florence in 1498, is sometimes said to have been burned alive. In truth, he was hanged first, then burned. His executioners hired a mob of boys to throw stones at his half-consumed body, so that from time to time fragments of his corpse fell down into the fire, and an eyewitness was moved to write that "it rained blood and entrails."[1]

The medals of Savonarola likely to have been executed in the last decade of the fifteenth century comprise ten distinct types and fall into two groups. Group I portrays the monk with his head completely covered by his hood. In Group II, Savonarola's hood reveals a tuft of his tonsured hair at the forehead. On the basis of a passage in Vasari, the latter group has been attributed to two sons of Andrea della Robbia (1437–1528), a master of glazed terra-cotta sculpture. Vasari wrote: "Andrea . . . left two of his sons as *frati* in San Marco [where they] were given the cloth by the reverend Fra Girolamo Savonarola, to whom these della Robbia were always very devoted, and they portrayed him in that manner which is still seen today in the medals."[2] Sir George Hill interpreted this as meaning that they did not make actual medals, but rather glazed terra-cotta medallions, and that

136

21 obv.

22 obv.

23 obv.

26 obv.

33 obv.

33 rev.

37 obv.

37 rev.

45 obv.

45 rev.

42 obv.

47 obv.

48 obv.

48 rev.

51a obv.

51a rev.

53 rev.

54 obv.

54 rev.

47 obv.

47 rev.

others then reproduced the portrait type in bronze. Hill's sure instincts were confirmed when Ulrich Middeldorf identified Savonarola's portrait on a majolica tondo in Lille, from the workshop of Andrea della Robbia's sons.[3] The tondo seems to be the work of Francesco Iacopo della Robbia, who was given the Dominican habit by Savonarola in San Marco on December 8, 1495, along with the name Fra Ambrogio.[4]

Adding the evidence of Vasari and the Lille tondo to Hill's stylistic classification of the Group II medals in the vicinity of Niccolò Fiorentino, we are still no closer to knowing who made the medals. We only assume that it was some anonymous Florentine inspired by a portrait in della Robbia ware.

The meaning of the obverse of our medal has received scant attention. It is exceptional in that the other nine obverses simply show a portrait bust of the monk. This obverse, with Savonarola staring in trancelike meditation at the face of Christ, bears comparison with a woodcut of a monk in his cell, kneeling and gesticulating at the foot of a crucifix,[5] used to illustrate a 1501 German edition of one of Savonarola's tracts.

The reverse has been criticized for its awkward composition, and indeed the vertical dividing line is an uncommon expedient for the organization of the round field. Here it was dictated by Savonarola's need to make his message clear. On the evening of April 5, 1492, the prior was sitting at his desk, seeking inspiration for his sermon in the cathedral next morning, when there burst from his lips the words "Ecce gladius Domini super terram cito et velociter."[6] That same night, at eleven o'clock, lightning struck and split the lantern of the cathedral. Preaching in the damaged structure the following morning, Savonarola repeated the phrase, which he was convinced had been put into his mouth by God. To the awe-struck Florentines the shattered lantern seemed proof that the "sword of the Lord" was indeed hanging over them, and they were newly receptive to Savonarola's call for repentance.

Eleven months later, in December 1492, Savonarola was preparing the last of the Advent sermons he was to deliver in the cathedral when he had a vision of a hand in the heavens wielding a sword, and inscribed on the sword were the same words that had come to him so mysteriously during the previous Lent. The hand and arm holding the sword appeared to be attached to three faces, which the prior took to represent the Holy Trinity. In unison, the three faces threatened vengeance if men failed to repent in time. Then the hand turned the sword downward, and hail, fire, and lightning assailed the earth, bringing plague, war, and famine. The vision ended with a command that Savonarola make known what he had seen.

Medals were evidently one of the means by which Savonarola could obey that command. The present reverse presents an either/or proposition: either repent and enjoy the fullness of the spirit of the Lord, or do not repent, and suffer His sword.

Savonarola's prophecy of the sword had come true in the person of Charles VIII (see cat. no. 38). In the summer of 1495, the prior claimed that he had foretold Charles's coming in a prediction of "someone like Cyrus crossing the Alps into Italy . . . one who would conquer against all resistance."[7] Savonarola accordingly touted himself as a great seer and was hailed as one. At that point the inscriptions of some of his medals were altered, and other new medals cast. In one, for example, the phrase "sainted prophet" replaces "of the Order of Preachers."[8] The altered version was surely cast after 1494, as was a small medal that again speaks of him as a "prophet," and from its rough execution would appear to have been hastily produced so as to capitalize on his enhanced reputation.[9]

The present medal would thus appear to have been produced between December 1492, when Savonarola had the vision of the sword, and late 1494, by which time the French had swarmed into Italy.

Mark Wilchusky

73 obv.

Italy

SIXTEENTH CENTURY

For the convenience of the reader, the dates of religious and political leaders most frequently encountered are provided below. All other life dates appear in the text.

The Papacy

Julius II (Giuliano della Rovere; born 1443, pontiff 1503–13)

Leo X (Giovanni de' Medici; born 1475, pontiff 1513–21)

Adrian VI (Adrian Dedel; born 1459, pontiff 1522–23)

Clement VII (Giulio de' Medici; born 1478, pontiff 1523–34)

Paul III (Alessandro Farnese; born 1468, pontiff 1534–49)

Julius III (Gianmaria del Monte; born 1487, pontiff 1550–55)

Marcellus II (Marcello Cervini; pontiff 1555)

Paul IV (Gianpietro Carafa; born 1476, pontiff 1555–59)

Pius IV (Giovanni de' Medici; born 1499, pontiff 1559–65)

Pius V (Michele Ghislieri, born 1504, pontiff 1566–72)

Gregory XIII (Ugo Buoncompagni; born 1502, pontiff 1572–85)

The Holy Roman Empire

Charles V (born 1500, emperor 1519–56, died 1558)

Ferdinand I (born 1503, emperor 1556–64)

Maximilian II (born 1527, emperor 1564–76)

Rudolf II (born 1552, emperor 1576–1612)

Matthias (born 1557, emperor 1612–19)

Ferdinand II (born 1578, emperor 1619–37)

France

Louis XII (born 1462, king 1498–1515)

Francis I (born 1494, king 1515–47)

Henry II (born 1519, king 1547–59)

Francis II (born 1544, king 1559–60)

Charles IX (born 1550, king 1560–74)

Henry III (born 1551, king 1574–89)

Henry IV (born 1553, king 1589–1610)

England

Henry VIII (born 1491, king 1509–47)

Edward VI (born 1537, king 1547–53)

Mary Tudor (born 1516, queen 1553–58)

Elizabeth I (born 1533, queen 1558–1603)

Ferrara

Ercole II d'Este (born 1508, duke 1534–59)

Alfonso II d'Este (born 1533, duke 1559–97)

Florence

Alessandro de' Medici (born 1510, duke of Florence 1532–37)

Cosimo I de' Medici (born 1519, duke of Florence 1537–69, grand duke of Tuscany 1569–74)

Francesco I de' Medici (born 1541, grand duke of Tuscany 1574–87)

Ferdinando I de' Medici (born 1549, grand duke of Tuscany 1587– 1609)

Cosimo II de' Medici (born 1590, grand duke of Tuscany 1609–21)

Mantua

Federigo II Gonzaga (born 1500, marquess 1519–30, duke 1530–40)

Francesco III Gonzaga (born 1533, duke 1540–50)

Guglielmo Gonzaga (born 1538, duke 1550–87)

Vicenzo Gonzaga (duke 1587–1612)

Ferdinando II Gonzaga (born 1587, duke 1612–26)

Milan

Massimiliano Sforza (born 1493, duke 1512–15)

Francesco Maria Sforza (born 1495, duke 1522–24 and 1529–35)

Ferrante Gonzaga (born 1506, imperial governor 1546–55, died 1557)

Parma

Pier Luigi Farnese (born 1503, duke 1545–47)

Ottavio Farnese (born 1524, duke 1547–86)

Alessandro Farnese (born 1545, duke 1586–92)

Savoy

Emanuel Philibert (born 1528, duke 1553–80)

Charles Emanuel I (born 1562, duke 1580–1630)

Victor Amadeus I (born 1587, duke 1630–37)

Urbino

Guidobaldo Malatesta (born 1472, duke 1482–97, 1503–8)

Francesco Maria della Rovere (born 1490, duke 1508–38)

48 obv.　　　　　　　　　　　　　　48 rev.

Milanese School, between 1518 and 1527
Scaramuccia di Gianfermo Trivulzio, bishop of Como and cardinal (died 1527)
48
Bronze, cast
Diameter 60.2 mm
New York, The Metropolitan Museum of Art, Gift of Ogden Mills, 1926
26.14.5

Obverse: Bust to left, wearing a cap and *mozetta* (a buttoned, hooded cape). Between incised compass lines, the legend: • SCARAMVTIA • TRIVVL[tius] • CAR[dinalis] • COMIH[for COMEN(sis)] • IO[annis] • FIRMI • PRIMI • F[ilius] • (Scaramuccia Trivulzio, cardinal of Como, son of Gianfermo the First).
Reverse: A female figure representing Prudence walking barefoot toward the right, holding a mirror in her raised left hand and compasses in her right. She is looking down at a small dragon to the right of her feet. She wears a version of the antique chiton in the form of a flowing, three-tiered gown fastened at the right shoulder. The gown has long split sleeves, the right one billowing out behind and flowing across beneath her breast, the left one hanging down. The hair and rigid headdress are also classical in style. There are incised compass lines around the edge, but no legend.

48a
Bronze, cast
Diameter 60.2 mm; diameter of the outer perimeter of the inscription, 54.4 mm
Washington, The National Gallery of Art, Samuel H. Kress Collection
1957.14.791

Obverse and reverse as above.

The quality of workmanship in this medal is extremely fine, and for this reason it has been assigned to such eminent masters as Cristoforo Foppa, called Caradosso (after 1452–1527),[1] and Benvenuto Cellini (1500–1571).[2] The early ascription of this medal to Caradosso, an artist of Milanese origin who worked in Rome after 1509, was based on the assertion that he was the only medalist active at the time who could have produced such high-quality work. It was presumably strengthened by superficial similarities between this reverse and the one for the medal of Donato Bramante (cat. no 33), which has heretofore been ascribed, following Vasari, to Caradosso. Although the delicate handling of the Trivulzio medal does suggest the work of a goldsmith such as Caradosso or a plaquette artist, closer relationships can be seen with medals from the circle of the Milanese sculptor and medalist Leone Leoni (cat. nos. 49–52) such as that of Gianfrancesco Trivulzio (cat. no. 53) formerly ascribed to Pietro Paolo Galeotti (cat. no. 57).[3]

Scholars have noted similarities between this work and various other distinguished but unattributed medals, those of John of Lorraine (born 1498, cardinal 1518–50), which has the same reverse; a PIETRO PLANTANIDA (for Piantanida); the Milanese physician Gianfrancesco Martinioni; and Cardinal Pietro Bembo (cat. no. 64). For a time their unknown author was referred to simply as "the Master of the Cardinal Bembo."[4] More recently, scholarly interest has tended to focus on discrepancies in style and dating between these works rather than features they have in common, but attribution of the pieces continues to be elusive, and much remains to be clarified regarding the so-called Milanese school to which they are collectively ascribed.[5]

The subtle characterization of the obverse portrait bears out contemporary descriptions of the subject as a pious and learned man, and the reverse, apparently designed for this medal rather than that of John of Lorraine where it recurs, appears to be perfectly apt. Prudence is one of the four Cardinal Virtues. The mirror she holds in her left hand appears frequently in Renaissance art, and symbolizes the wise man's ability to see himself

48 rev.

as he really is. The compasses represent her measured judgment, and the dragon at her feet is a substitution for a snake, in allusion to the admonition "Be ye wise as serpents" from Matthew 10:16.[6] The figure is ultimately derived from a classical source, either the *Dancing Maidens* from the Villa Borghese in Rome, now in the Louvre,[7] or possibly an antique gem.

Scaramuccia, count of Melzo, was the fourth child of Gianfermo Trivulzio (d. 1491) and a nephew of the famous Giangiacomo (1441–1518).[8] He enrolled in the college of jurisconsults in Milan in 1489, and later taught law in the universities of Pavia and Padua. In 1499, when the duchy of Milan passed into the hands of Louis XII of France (cat. no. 140), Scaramuccia was elected his advisor. At the recommendation of the king, he was consecrated bishop of Como on April 14, 1508, an office he held until January 1518, when he was succeeded by his brother.

Despite his French sympathies, Scaramuccia avoided involvement in the General Council of Pisa, called by Louis XII (cat. no. 140). Instead he went to Rome, where he is said to have distinguished himself at the Lateran Council. Under Pope Leo X, Scaramuccia was elected cardinal of S. Cyriaco on July 6, 1517. He also continued to enjoy French protection under Francis I (cat. nos. 116, 139).

He became a supporter of the Sforza when Duke Francesco Maria united with France against Emperor Charles V (cat. nos. 77, 124–25, 156), and he was one of the first to benefit under the new regime. Scaramuccia remained in Rome until the onset of the sack of the city in 1527, when as a French sympathizer he felt it wise to escape. He took refuge in the monastery of Maguzzano near Verona, where he died on August 3, 1527.

Peta Evelyn

Leone Leoni
(c. 1509–1590)

Leoni was one of the most influential Italian sculptors of the generation that followed Michelangelo (1475–1546); (cat. no. 52). He was also a prolific medalist, coin engraver, and goldsmith.

Nothing is known of his early training. He was born in Arezzo, but it is evident that while still young he was employed in the Ferrara mint.[1] By the late 1530s he was in Venice, working in the circle of Jacopo Sansovino (1486–1570), Titian (born 1487–90, died 1576), and Aretino (cat. no. 70). He portrayed Aretino, who vigorously promoted the younger artist's career, in a 1537 medal,[2] and Titian at about the same date.[3]

In 1537 the artist was in Padua, later Urbino, and finally Rome, where on November 1 he received a first payment for some of his medals from the papal mint.[4] His three known medals for Pope Paul III share the same obverse.[5] Leoni also engraved dies for the papal coinage. His sojourn in Rome was terminated in 1540, when he was imprisoned for assaulting the pope's goldsmith, and his artistic career was only resumed in 1541 in Genoa, where he had been given refuge by Andrea Doria (cat. no. 50). The following year he was appointed to the position of master of the imperial mint in Milan,[6] and in 1543 he is known to have produced a medal of the emperor Charles V (cat. nos. 77, 124–25, 156).[7]

In 1546 Leoni was briefly employed as mintmaster for Pier Luigi Farnese, duke of Parma and Piacenza, but was brought back to Milan by the new imperial governor, Ferrante Gonzaga, who would become an important patron (see cat. no. 51) and was well placed to further Leoni's career. It was probably he who recommended him to the emperor[8] and in 1548 arranged for Leoni to travel to Brussels with the emperor's son Philip, later king of Spain (cat. nos. 58, 156). At Gonzaga's suggestion, Leoni took with him a medal of the young prince as a gift to the emperor.[9] The medal evidently met with imperial approval, for Charles promptly commissioned medals of himself and his former empress Isabella (1503–1536).[10] Other work followed, and in 1549 Leoni traveled to Paris to take casts of ancient statues.

Anxious to escape from "this barbarous country"[11] and return to Italy, Leoni was given permission to leave the Netherlands late in 1549 and arrived back in Milan in December of that year, laden with commissions from the imperial family and the influential bishop of Arras, Antoine Perrenot de Granvelle (cat. no. 159).[12]

Leoni visited Augsburg in 1551, having been commissioned by Charles's sister, Maria of Hungary (cat. no. 124), to execute medals of her brother Ferdinand and nephew Maximilian.[13] At the time, Leoni was also working on bronze statues of both Charles V and Philip[14] as well as fulfilling his obligations at the Milanese mint. Inevitably, delays in completing his many commissions ensued. In August 1555, in an attempt to stem complaints, Leoni suggested that he transport all his imperial works-in-progress to Brussels and finish them there. Accordingly, he set out on his second journey to Flanders in February 1556. Vasari asserts that he then went on to Spain,[15] but as Plon shows, the artist avoided making that journey, sending instead his son Pompeo (c. 1533–1610).[16]

In 1560 the artist again went to Rome, where Pope Pius IV commissioned him to execute the monument to his brother Gian Giacomo de' Medici (1495–1555) in Milan's cathedral. It was during this visit that he produced his famous portrait medal of Michelangelo (cat. no. 52). Also in the early 1560s, Ferrante Gonzaga's son Cesare (1533–1575) commissioned from him a bronze statue of his father. That Leoni remained in favor with Philip II of Spain is shown by work he did in Milan in the 1580s for the Escorial.[17] Payment records show that he was still employed at the mint in Milan in 1589.[18] The doctor's report of his death is dated July 22, 1590.

Philip Attwood

Leone Leoni
Martin de Hanna (1475–1553)
49
Bronze, cast
Diameter 71 mm
Berlin, Staatliche Museen, Münzkabinett, formerly Benoni Friedlaender Collection

49 obv.

him to Leoni during the artist's sojourn there in 1544. It may have been that Leoni executed the models for the present medal along with others for the Hanna family at that time, although Leoni revisited Venice in 1546 and could have made them then.[2] In any event, this is one of Leoni's earliest known cast medals.

The reverse figure reappears as a decorative adjunct to Leoni's 1550–51 statue of the future Philip II of Spain,[3] and would appear to have been suggested by fifteenth-century medals. A similarly draped figure of Hope, her hands held together in prayer and her head turned upward toward a radiant sun, appears on the reverses of a number of Florentine medals executed by an artist from the circle of Niccolò Fiorentino (cat. nos. 42–46).[4] Leoni's version is much more refined than its rather crudely modeled precedents.

The only other signed Leoni medal of a member of the Hanna family is a small portrait of Martin's son Daniel (died c. 1580),[5] and two other medals of Daniel so clearly reflect Leoni's style that they are ascribed to him as well.[6] Daniel was a patron of Titian, and he also appears to have commissioned portraits from other medalists.

Philip Attwood

Obverse: Bust to right, wearing doublet and cloak. Legend, with floral stops: MARTINVS • DE • HANNA.
Reverse: A standing figure of Hope, wearing antique drapery, facing to the right and looking upward, her arms stretched out toward rays of light issuing from a cloud. Legend: SPES • MEA • IN • DEO • EST (My hope is in God). Signed in the exergue: LEO.

De Hanna was one of the wealthiest of the Flemish merchants living in Venice. He arrived from Brussels in the early years of the sixteenth century, and received Venetian citizenship in 1545.[1] A patron of the arts, he engaged Pordenone (1483–1539) to decorate his palace on the Grand Canal, and it was probably Titian (born 1487–90, died 1576) who introduced

50 obv.   50 rev.

Leone Leoni
Andrea Doria (1466–1550)
50
Bronze, cast
Diameter 42 mm
London, The British Museum

Obverse: Bearded bust to right, wearing a square-necked cuirass ornamented with a grotesque mask and a mantle secured with a brooch at the right shoulder. The emblem of the Order of the Golden Fleece hangs around his neck. To the left is a trident; below, a dolphin. Legend: ANDREAS DORIA • P[ater] • P[atriae] • (Andrea Doria, the father of his country). Beaded border.
Reverse: Bust of Leoni, bearded, facing to the right. He too wears a mantle secured with a brooch at the right shoulder. To the left is a galley, and below are a hammer, an opened leg-iron, and a grappling iron. An inner border formed of manacles and chains and an outer one of beading.

49 rev.

51a obv.

This medal can be precisely dated to 1541, and is thus one of Leoni's earliest works in the medium. In May 1540, Leoni had been sent to the galleys for assaulting the goldsmith Pellegrino di Leuti, jeweler to Pope Paul III. He remained in captivity for several months until his release was secured through the intervention of Andrea Doria, the famous admiral and virtual ruler of Genoa, and the Genoese Francesco Doarte. From his refuge in Genoa he announced his freedom to Aretino (cat. no. 70) in a letter dated March 23, 1541.[1] A return letter from July of that year reveals that Leoni had produced a portrait medal of Doria very soon after his release, for in it Aretino urges Leoni to send him a specimen as soon as they are ready and recommends Doria as a longtime patron.[2] A page of Leoni's sketches, including three profile portraits of the admiral, is now in the Pierpont Morgan Library in New York.[3] That the artist was already thinking in terms of a medal is indicated by the circle penned around one of these portraits. The sketches show Doria in contemporary dress, however, while the medal has him wearing the classical cuirass and mantle. Leoni's inclusion of the trident and dolphin, attributes of Neptune, also betrays his classical leanings; the trident is common on Roman republican coins, and both emblems appear in a somewhat similar disposition on silver denarii bearing the portrait of Pompey the Great (106–48 B.C.) and dedicated to the sea-god.[4] The *pater patriae* epithet in the inscription is likewise based on Roman precedent. Leoni had acquired a taste for the antique while in Rome, and it was henceforth an important element of his own art as it was in the medallic art of Italy in the sixteenth century generally. Leoni effectively combines these reminiscences with a vividly characterized portrait of the aged statesman. The emblem of the Order of the Golden Fleece does not appear on some examples of the medal, having been added in the model from which molds were taken for the production of this and other specimens. It seems likely that Doria would have objected to the omission of any reference to the celebrated order, into which he had been received in 1531.

Leoni's self-portrait on the reverse is also classically draped, but the chains and manacles surrounding it, symbols of the captivity from which Doria had procured his release, are unprecedented, as is the inclusion of the galley and the collection of maritime tools. An alternative reverse design shows only the galley with two figures rowing away from it in a small boat.[5] One of the occupants is generally assumed to be Leoni on his way to freedom.

Philip Attwood

Leone Leoni
Ippolita Gonzaga (1535–1563)
51
Bronze, cast
Diameter 67 mm
Berlin, Staatliche Museen, Münzkabinett

Obverse: Bust to left, wearing a loosely draped gown and mantle knotted on the left shoulder. Around the neck a doubled strand

51a obv.

of pearls, from which is suspended a circular jewel ornamented with a cross and a pendant pearl. The hair is braided and adorned with a diadem and ribbons. Legend: HIPPOLYTA • GONZAGA • FERDINANDI • FIL[ia] • AN[no] • XVI (Ippolita Gonzaga, daughter of Ferdinando [Ferrante], in her sixteenth year). Signed on the right: ΛΕΩΝ • ΑΡΗΤΙΝΟΣ (Leone of Arezzo). Beaded border.

Reverse: Ippolita as Diana, wearing antique drapery, a billowing mantle, and sandals, her hair braided and adorned with ribbons. She is moving to the right through a wooded landscape accompanied by three dogs. With her left hand she lifts a horn to her mouth, while in her right she holds a large arrow. To the left, in the arched entrance to a building, Pluto stands carrying Proserpina, both of them nude. At his feet is Cerberus, wearing a collar and with flames issuing from his three mouths. A second building is in the background. Above, the moon and stars. Legend: PAR • VBIQ[ue] • POTESTAS (Her power is everywhere equal). Beaded border.

51a
Bronze, cast
Diameter 68.3 mm
London, Victoria & Albert Museum
A249–1910

Obverse and reverse as above.

Ippolita was the daughter of Ferrante Gonzaga, imperial governor of Milan from 1546 to 1555. At thirteen she was married to Fabrizio Colonna, who died in 1551. In 1554, still only nineteen, she became the wife of Antonio Caraffa, duke of Mondragone.

The obverse legend dates the medal in the sitter's sixteenth year, that is 1550/51. It was probably executed in the months immediately following Leoni's return to Milan from Augsburg in April 1551. Examples were already in circulation by early 1552, as we know from a letter written by Aretino (cat. no. 70) to Onorata Tancredi in January of that year, in which he thanks her for sending him an example.[1]

51a rev.

Famed for her beauty and accomplishments, Ippolita is likened on the reverse to Diana, seen on earth as a huntress and in the heavens as the moon. Pluto, Proserpina, and Cerberus serve to remind us that the ancients also worshipped Diana as Hecate, goddess of the underworld. Affo, writing in the eighteenth century, interpreted the reverse as suggesting that Ippolita was loved in heaven for her piety and on earth for her accomplishments, and that her fortitude on the death of her husband had recommended her to the underworld. She further speculated that the reverse might refer to the three states through which the young woman had passed: virginity, marriage, and widowhood.[2] Given the layering of meanings common in Italian sixteenth-century medallic reverses, all of these suggestions may be accurate.

Philip Attwood

Leone Leoni
Michelangelo (1475–1564)
52
Bronze, cast
Diameter 58.1 mm
New York, private collection

Obverse: Bearded bust facing to the right, wearing a doublet and hooded cape. Legend: MICHAELANGELVS • BONARROTVS • FLO•R[entinus] • ÆT[ati]S ANN[o] • 88 (Michelangelo Buonarroti of Florence, in his eighty-eighth year). Signed on the truncation: LEO. Beaded border.
Reverse: A blind man in the guise of a pilgrim wearing a long cloak and soft hat, walking toward the right behind his dog against a background of trees. In his right hand he holds a staff, a water flask, and the dog's leash. Legend: DOCEBO • INIQVOS • V[ias] • T[uas] • ET IMPII • AD • TE • CONVER[tentur] • ("I will teach transgressors your ways, and sinners shall be converted to you"). The text is from Psalm 51:13 (Vulgate 50:15). Beaded border.

By the time this medal was made, Michelangelo was universally regarded as the greatest living artist, indeed the greatest artist of all time. Works such as the Sistine Chapel ceiling (1508–12), the chapel of S. Lorenzo in Florence (1520–34), the *Last Judgment* (1536–41), and his designs for St. Peter's in Rome had won him a reputation that has remained intact ever since. As an authentic portrait of the great sculptor, painter, and architect, the head on this medal has been frequently copied.[1] A wax model of Michelangelo, attributed to Leoni and quite possibly the model for this portrait, is in the British Museum.[2]

The meaning of the reverse is unclear. It has been suggested that it alludes to the difficulties Michelangelo was then experiencing with the construction of St. Peter's, but it may well be a more general symbol of the earthly pilgrimage.[3] The legend has no obvious application to Michelangelo.

The medal was modeled in Rome in 1560 and cast in Milan, from which city Leoni sent four examples to Michelangelo on March 14, 1561, two in silver and two in bronze. He wrote: "The one which is in the box is all recleaned. Keep it and look after it for love of me. Do with the other three what seems right to you. In my ambition, I have sent some to Spain and Flanders, and likewise through love have sent some to you in Rome and to other places."[4] A letter from April 12, 1561, refers to the medals once again.[5]

52 obv.

52 rev.

52 obv.

Besides furnishing precise documentation for the medal, the passage quoted above is of particular interest for the light it throws on Leoni's attitude to medalmaking. He was evidently quite happy to allow medals to leave his workshop in less than finished state, on the understanding that others could do any necessary chasing. It is also evident that Leoni had distributed the medal far and wide, and this is confirmed by Vasari: " . . . there were so many copies made of it that I have seen a large number of them in many places in Italy and abroad."[6]

The medal's indication of Michelangelo's age is incorrect. Born on March 6, 1475, he would have been only eighty-five when he sat for Leoni. Michelangelo was evidently pleased with the medal—according to Vasari, it was "á compiacenza di lui" (to his satisfaction)—and in gratitude he presented Leoni with a wax model, now lost, of Hercules and Antaeus.

We do not know whether Leoni met Michelangelo during his first stay in Rome in 1538–40, but it is certain that he admired the work of the older artist. This esteem was obviously reciprocated, or Michelangelo would not have recommended Leoni to the pope.[7] The resulting commission, the tomb of Gian Giacomo de' Medici (1495–1555) in Milan's cathedral, shows the definite influence of Michelangelo and may have been based on his design.

Philip Attwood

School of Leone Leoni
Gianfrancesco Trivulzio (1504–1573)[1]
53
Copper alloy, cast
Diameter 60.0 mm; diameter of the outer perimeter of the obverse inscription from the N in REN to the N in FRAN, 54.6 mm
New York, private collection

Obverse: Bearded bust to the right, in cuirass and cloak. Legend, between scribing lines: (leaf stop) IO[annes] • FRAN [ciscus] • TRI[vultius] • MAR[chio] • VIG[evani] • CO[mes] • MVSO[chi] • AC • VAL[lis] • REN[ensis] • ET • STOSA[e]

• D[ominus] (Gianfrancesco Trivulzio, marquess of Vigevano, count of Mesocco, lord of Rheinwald and Stoss). On the bust truncation: AET[atis] 39 (age thirty-nine).
Reverse: Nude female figure of Fortune holding a billowing sail, borne by a dolphin upon a sea blown by the four winds and dotted with struggling, drowning figures. Legend: FVI SVM ET ERO (I was, I am, and I will be).[2]

53a
Copper alloy, cast
Diameter 59.7 mm; diameter of the outer perimeter of the obverse inscription from the N in REN to the N in FRAN, 54.6 mm
Washington, The National Gallery of Art, Samuel H. Kress Collection
1957.14.1099

Obverse and reverse as above.

This medal is usually attributed to Pietro Paolo Galeotti, who signed other medals of Milanese sitters, but stylistically it seems more likely to have originated in the Milanese circle of Leone Leoni. Here the head is more prominent, in relation to both the bust and the field, than in typical Galeotti medals such as that of Francesco Taverna (cat. no. 57). Galeotti's works tend to display a larger portion of the sitters' shoulders, arms, and chest, filling out the lower part of the field; indeed, he often gives almost too much bulk to the sitters' backs, so that they appear almost hunched, an effect missing in the Trivulzio medal. The manner in which the bust intrudes into the area of the inscription is also uncharacteristic. When Galeotti's portraits do cut into the inscription area, it is usually for the whole length of the bust's truncation, while here it is only the front portion that intrudes, allowing the inscription to begin directly under the sitter's arm.

The style of the reverse is more agitated and lively than those of such signed Galeotti pieces as his medal of Francesco Taverna, and those of Franco Lercari, Cassandra Marinoni, and

53a obv.

53a rev.

Chiara Taverna,[3] where great depth is suggested by the contrast between the larger, more important foreground figures and the receding background elements.

The Trivulzio medal has much in common with one of Girolamo Cardano (1501–1576), usually attributed to Leoni himself.[4] Both lack the pearled border usually found on works by Galeotti and both have frenetic reverses with terse inscriptions. Their obverse proportions are equivalent, and the relationship between the inscription and the bust is identical.

Gianfrancesco belonged to a noble Milanese family,[5] the most famous member of which was his grandfather, the *condottiere* Giangiacomo Trivulzio (1441–1518), who is depicted on several medals himself.[6] Giangiacomo, known as "the Great," served the Sforza of Milan before switching his allegiance to Louis XII of France (cat. no. 140), who named him marquess of Vigevano and count of Mesocco,[7] titles that devolved on his heir, Gianfrancesco. The younger Trivulzio also inherited the territories of Rheinwald and Stoss, acquired by his grandfather in 1493. Gianfrancesco served as a general in the French cavalry under Francis I (cat. nos. 116, 139), and later, in 1573, occupied a similar position under Pope Gregory XIII in Avignon. His uncle, Cardinal Scaramuccia Trivulzio (died 1527) is also depicted on a medal by an artist of the Milanese school (cat. no. 48).

The figure on the reverse is standard iconography for the personification of Fortune. Her sail is blown by constantly shifting winds, a reminder of her inconstancy. Here she stands in relation to the several unfortunate figures struggling in the frenzied seas, whipped up by personifications of the four winds. The type has its literary source in the *Odes* of Horace, where Fortune is called the "queen of the waves."[8] It is a recurring motif in Renaissance art, one used on the reverses of numerous other medals.[9]

Fortune's appearance on Trivulzio's medal is probably both a general comment on his life—a generally fortunate one, though not without tribulations—and a reference to a specific event. In 1543, the year this medal was issued, Emperor Charles V (cat. nos. 77, 123–124, 156) rescinded a death sentence imposed on Trivulzio in 1533 for his alleged role in an attempt to poison Francesco II Sforza. Trivulzio had experienced similar trials and reversals before, including having all his properties confiscated by the Sforza and later restored. In keeping with Fortune's fickle nature, Trivulzio's good luck celebrated here was soon followed by new troubles: in 1550 he was condemned anew for an attempted assassination and forced to flee Milan.

Donald Myers

Jacopo da Trezzo
(born c. 1514–19, died 1589)

Born Jacopo Nizzola, the artist always signed himself Jacopo da Trezzo, after his birthplace some twenty kilometers northwest of Milan. He trained as a gem-engraver, sculptor, and architect, and worked in Milan until summoned in 1550 to Florence to serve as gem-engraver to Duke Cosimo de' Medici. A medallic portrait of Isabella Capua is signed, and must belong to the late 1540s or early 1550s,[1] and a signed medal of her daughter, Ippolita, from 1552, seems to have been copied from Leoni's medal of the same sitter (cat. no. 51)

In 1555 da Trezzo traveled to the Netherlands to enter the service of Philip II (cat. nos. 58, 156). He remained there until 1559, when he followed the king to Spain. To this period belong his medals of Philip, Maria of Austria (1528–1603),[2] and Joanna of Portugal (1537–1554).[3] There is some doubt regarding the authorship of the Philip medal, and those of the daughters of Charles V have also been given to Pompeo Leoni (c. 1533–1610), who spent some time in Brussels before accompanying Charles to Spain in September 1556. No doubt attaches to another medal of Philip, signed and dated 1555,[4] or to the medal of Philip's English wife, Mary Tudor (cat. no. 54). Speculation that the artist visited England remains unproved, as does Babelon's argument that he may have been responsible for some of the British coinage of Philip and Mary.[5]

In Spain, da Trezzo worked on architectural and decorative schemes at the Escorial, and was also active as a jeweler, goldsmith, and sculptor. He sometimes worked in collaboration with Pompeo Leoni, as for example on the monument to Joanna of Portugal in Madrid.

Da Trezzo died in Madrid on September 23, 1589. His large cast medals clearly show the influence of Leone Leoni (cat. nos. 49–52), but he was not so skilled at handling complex reverses as was his older contemporary and often restricted himself to single figures. On at least one occasion, however, namely in the medal of Mary Tudor, he produced a masterpiece, and his influence continues to be visible in the cast medals of seventeenth-century France.[6]

Da Trezzo appears on a medal himself (cat. no. 60), a portrait executed by Antonio Abondio while visiting Spain in 1572.

Philip Attwood

Jacopo da Trezzo
Mary Tudor (born 1516, queen of England and Ireland 1553–58)

54

Gold, cast and chased
Diameter 69.0 mm; weight 183.5 g
London, The British Museum

Obverse: Bust facing left, wearing ornately embroidered gown, a brooch with pendant pearl suspended at the breast, and a cap adorned with jewels, with a veil falling down the back. Legend: MARIA • I • REG[ina] • ANGL[iae] • FRANC[iae] • ET • HIB[erniae] • FIDEI • DEFENSATRIX (Mary I, queen of England, France, and Ireland, defender of the faith). Below the bust, the signature IAC TREZ. Beaded border.
Reverse: A figure of Peace, wearing antique drapery and a radiate crown, seated on a throne. In her right hand she holds palm and olive branches, in her left a flaming torch with which she ignites a pile of arms and armor to the right. Below the throne are a cube, with two clasped hands in relief on one of its sides, and a

MARIA·I·REG·ANGL·FRANC·ET·HIB·FIDEI·DEFENSATRIX

IAC·TREZ·

54 obv.

54 obv.

54 rev.

set of scales. To the left, a group of suppliant figures beset by storms. To the right, other figures and a circular temple. Above, rays issuing from a cloud; below, a river. Legend: CECIS VISVS TIMIDIS • QVIES (Sight to the blind, tranquility to the timid). Beaded border.

Mary, daughter of Henry VIII and Catherine of Aragon, followed her half-brother, Edward VI, to the throne on his death at the age of fifteen in 1553. Her initial popularity evaporated rapidly in the face of her persecution of Protestants and her marriage to Philip II of Spain (cat. nos. 58, 156). The matrimonial alliance with a foreign prince and the revival of the influence of the church of Rome, abolished by her father, are both documented by the medal, in the circumstances of its production and the symbolism of its reverse.

This is the most spectacular of da Trezzo's medals. The type of the queen's portrait derives from the three-quarter facing bust painted in 1554 by Anthonis Mor (c. 1512–c. 1576).[1] Da Trezzo may have seen the autograph version now in the Escorial or one of its many copies. The medalist retains the cap, the jewel hanging at her breast, and the general forms of her clothing. The jewel is probably the one Philip sent her in June 1554, since described as "a great diamond with a large pearl pendant, one of the most beautiful pieces ever seen in the world."[2] Da Trezzo introduced the gown's elaborate embroidery, and in accordance with medallic tradition changed the three-quarter view of the face to a profile, permitting a better view of the veil and adding weight to the composition.

The reverse symbolizes the peaceful state of the kingdom under Mary and the blessings enjoyed by her subjects thanks to reconciliation with Rome. The queen herself appears as Peace. Below her throne are symbols of stability (the cube), unity (the clasped hands), and justice (the scales). As an emblem of peace, the motif of an allegorical female figure setting fire to the accoutrements of war can be traced back to ancient Roman coins. The figures beset by storms are Mary's subjects before her accession. Under her reign, they bask in radiant sunlight.

Mary's marriage to Philip had taken place in England on July 25, 1554. The following year Philip was back in the Netherlands, where he received the kingdom of Spain from his father, Charles V (cat. nos. 77, 123–24, 156). In that same year da Trezzo was commissioned to execute a medal of Philip with the reverse legend: IAM ILLVSTRABIT OMNIA (Now he will illuminate all things).[3] It would appear that the medal of Mary was also commissioned at roughly the same time, in all probability by Philip, who intended it, as Hawkins puts it, as "a compliment to Mary upon her government of the kingdom."

Philip Attwood

Jacopo da Trezzo
Gianello della Torre (1500–1585)
55
Bronze, cast
Diameter 81.5 mm
New York, The Metropolitan Museum of Art, Harris Brisbane Dick Fund, 1936

Obverse: Bearded bust facing right, wearing doublet and cloak. Legend: IANELLVS • TVRRIAN[us] • CREMON[ensis] • HOROLOG[iarius] • ARCHITECT[us] (Gianello della Torre of Cremona, clockmaker and architect). Beaded border.
Reverse: A female statue, wearing antique drapery, as the center of a fountain. With her hands she steadies a basin balanced on her head. The basin is decorated with garlands and surmounted by two animal heads, from which water pours forth. A group of seven men, some of them bearded, and a child, all dressed in classical garments, surround the fountain. Four of the men hold vessels. One approaches from the right, one scoops water from the reservoir, one on the left catches the water falling from the basin, and one drinks, while the child tries to get his attention. Another man holds out his hand to catch the water falling on the right. The other two carry a compass and a rule respectively. Legend: VIR TVS NVNQ[uam]: DEFICIT (Virtue never fails). Beaded border.

55 obv.　　　　　　　　　　　　　　　　55 rev.

Della Torre was a celebrated clockmaker and engineer. Born in Cremona, he worked first in Milan, then in the service of Charles V in the Netherlands, and finally for Philip II of Spain.

The medal portrait tends to confirm Leone Leoni's 1556 description of della Torre as "this bull in human form."[1] The reverse shows men of different ages drinking at the fountain of Knowledge. The compass and rule carried by the old men on the left and right indicate that it is specifically scientific knowledge that is here being sought.

The large-scale, skillful modeling and complex reverse composition show this to be the work of one of the great Milanese medalists of the mid sixteenth century, but scholars have long differed on whether to attribute it to Leone Leoni or Jacopo da Trezzo. Central to the problem is the dating of the medal. Babelon argued that the thirst for knowledge depicted on the reverse is a reference to della Torre's raising of the level of the river Tagus, an engineering feat completed in 1568.[2] The apparent age of the subject argues against this hypothesis, for this does not seem to be a man in his late sixties. Moreover, the reverse image may simply allude to della Torre's scientific involvement in general and have nothing to do with his Tagus river project.

The medal is generally thought to date to about 1550, when, like its subject, both Leoni and da Trezzo were working in Milan and either artist could have produced it. It is therefore necessary to determine its authorship on stylistic grounds, and here the evidence favors da Trezzo. His hand is particularly apparent in the somewhat lifeless classicism of the reverse. Leoni's figures have a degree of vivacity and sense of movement in their drapery that is wholly lacking in the work of da Trezzo. The grouped figures of the della Torre reverse, with their monumental symmetry and stiff poses, have much in common with those on the reverse of da Trezzo's Mary Tudor medal (cat. no. 54). The naturalism and asymmetry of the composition and the easy movement of the Diana on the reverse of Leoni's medal of Ippolita Gonzaga (cat. no. 51) are very different. The source

for the fountain design is a cameo that Babelon also attributed to da Trezzo. More recently, it has been suggested that the composition was based on ancient precedents.[3]

Philip Attwood

Milanese School (?)
Ferrante Loffredo, marquess of Trevico (dates unknown)
56
Wax model
Diameter including frame, 98.9 mm; estimated diameter within the frame, 70 mm
New York, private collection

Obverse: Bust to left in Roman-style parade armor with cloak over the right shoulder and knotted on the left. Below the bust, symmetrical stylized vine and acanthus *rinceaux* overlapping in the center and framing a tiny mask. Legend: FERD[inandus] • LOFFREDVS MARCH[io] • TRIVICI (Ferrante Loffredo, marquess of Trevico).
Reverse: Upon a wide and deep platform stand three figures. To the left, facing right, Loffredo, again in Roman-style armor with a long cape, reaches with his right arm across his body, his left hand resting upon the hilt of his sword. In the center, Emperor Charles V, also in cloak and ancient-style armor, with the addition of a laurel-wreath crown. He is facing front but looking to the left. With his right hand he gestures toward Loffredo; his left arm is bent up at the elbow, the hand seeming to beckon to the figure at the extreme right. To the right, a female figure dressed in a thin, flowing dress belted at the waist. She strides forward, carrying in her right hand a lance that she is presumably offering to Loffredo at the behest of the emperor. Her left hand holds up the folds of her dress. Her hair is bound with a fillet. Beneath the platform a symmetrical foliate design with facing serpentlike heads in the center. Legend: • DIVI Q[uinti] • CARO[li] • CAES[ari] • VERITAS • (To the divine emperor Charles V, Truth).

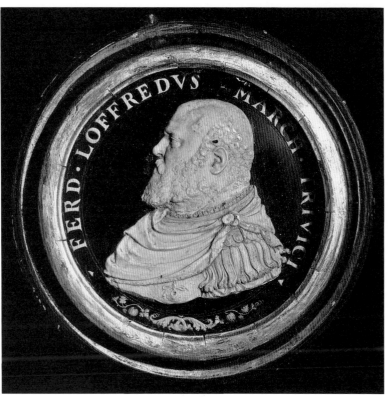

56 obv.

56 rev.

56a
Bronze, cast from the above
Diameter 69 mm
Paris, Bibliothèque Nationale, Cabinet des Médailles
Ital. 466

Obverse and reverse as above.

The medal of Ferrante Loffredo provides a perfect and seldom-encountered example of the development from original model to an early cast to a series of later specimens of varying quality. The model is executed in white wax against a background of black wax (?) over a disc of wood (?), all within a frame of wood and gesso, painted and gilt. With extraordinary virtuosity the artist has rendered in fine detail and jewel-like precision all of the substances and textures present in the subject, finally adding at the base of both obverse and reverse a combination of *rinceaux* and grotesques encountered nowhere else in the medallic art of this period.[1]

According to its internal historical evidence, the medal must have been produced around the middle of the sixteenth century. Charles V, who abdicated his titles in 1556 and died in 1558, is still shown and referred to in his imperial capacity. Loffredo appears from his portrait to be between forty and fifty years old, and one source tells us that he was still alive in 1570, implying that he was then advanced in age.[2] We also know that he was not created marquess of Trevico until 1548.[3]

In Gaetani's catalogue of the Mazzuchelli Collection, Loffredo is described as having distinguished himself in both arms and letters and as being a favorite of Charles V, who chose

him to be governor of Magna Graecia.[4] His only apparent achievement in the field of letters was a history of Pozzuolo (ancient Puteoli), where he had spent some time recovering from ill health.[5]

The Loffredo family was of Norman origin, and one of the oldest and most distinguished in southern Italy. Of this Ferrante Loffredo—there were two; the second died in 1653—we can gather only bits and pieces beyond what Gaetani tells us. He is always described as having been a gallant and courageous soldier. He was one of Charles V's many generals, and was numbered by Croce among "the flower of the Neapolitan nobility," who, after having originally opposed Charles V, could subsequently be counted among his most loyal subjects.[6] In 1555, during the conflict with pope Paul IV, he served in the imperial army under the duke of Alba (cat. no. 163), and in 1557 he fought the Turks in the province of Lecce.[7]

The scene on the reverse could illustrate the conferring of a military title or assignment, or—more likely from the inscription—his appointment to one of the governmental posts already noted. Loffredo wears the Roman style of parade armor that had become so popular at this time. He stands in an expectant pose, looking at his sovereign. The emperor, also wearing armor, indicates to the woman advancing from the right, apparently representing Truth, that the lance she offers is to be given to Loffredo.[8]

In any case, the medal has served its purpose well by giving its subject a certain immortality. It is ironic and rather sad that its creator failed to assure himself of the same by neglecting to sign it, leaving us with an attribution problem. We can eliminate on stylistic grounds many of the centers of production

56a obv.

56a rev.

active at this time. Although it may seem high-handed to dismiss so readily the many important artists whose careers were spent mainly in such cities as Florence, Siena, Rome, Venice, and Padua, there is not one of them whose style matches that of the Loffredo medal, and there was little medallic activity at the time in Naples.[9]

Only when we turn to the works of the Milanese school of sculptors and medalists, not only of those artists at its center, but also those whose stylistic characteristics indirectly connect them with it, do we find an environment in which to place the Loffredo medal.[10] Their works display common themes, figures, and elements of style that are reflected in the Loffredo medal, yet in the end the piece cannot be placed within any single group of works from their hands. Their common features are perhaps best exemplified in the work of Leoni, but the Loffredo piece is in many respects more precise and elegant, less vigorous, less robust than his medals, so that there is no possibility of attributing the Loffredo to him. Many of the same considerations prevent us from considering Jacopo da Trezzo (cat. nos. 54–55), who sometimes drew quite directly upon the work of Leoni—much to the latter's annoyance.

Galeotti (cat. no. 57) is perhaps the most plausible candidate. Not only is his style compatible with the Loffredo medal, but he is known to have made many medals of officials, especially generals, in the court of Charles V. Abondio (cat. nos. 60–63), however, though very proficient in wax carving and also active within the Habsburg court, developed a more rigid, brittle style, one that seems colder, though extremely accomplished. His early work, however, shows influences from the Emilian school (cat. nos. 73–75) and, if one accepts the attributions, from the artists active in Milan and North Italy.

There is, finally, a group of medals that almost all scholars have agreed to put into a general Milanese school of the mid sixteenth century, and it is here that the Loffredo medal must come to rest. These include the very fine medals of Pietro Piantanida, Cardinal John of Lorraine, and Gianfrancesco Martinioni, and if we compare the presentation of their portraits, the lettering, and especially the treatment of the female figure in such works with those of the Loffredo medal, we find a strong resemblance.[11]

Habich places among these medals a portrait of a lady named Faustina Romana. There is also a related wax model of a woman named Barbara, and both were apparently part of a series of portraits of courtesans.[12] There are startling similarities between the faces of this Barbara and the Truth in the wax model of the Loffredo medal. Their profiles are almost identical, and the treatment of their hair is also quite similar. Unfortunately, none of these pieces can be attributed with confidence to a particular artist.

In one respect, however, the Loffredo medal stands by itself. The elaborate decorative *rinceaux* and grotesques included beneath the bust and the reverse scene must be peculiar to the artist who fashioned this remarkable work. They are details that would not lend themselves well to transfer from wax to metal during the casting process, as indeed was the case when later casts were made. Could this suggest the hand of an artist not normally engaged in making medals, more comfortable with goldsmithing or some equally meticulous craft? Though he neglected to sign his work, to our regret, the creator of the Loffredo medal has nonetheless left his signature in such details, a cryptic signature that awaits decoding.

Stephen K. Scher

Pietro Paolo Galeotti, called Romano
(1520–1584)

Galeotti, called Romano, was born in Monte Rotondo, near Rome, the son of Pietro di Francesco Galeotti.[1] He was one of a pair of pupils of Benvenuto Cellini (1500–1571) frequently mentioned in that artist's autobiography, the other being Ascanio de' Mari (died 1566). Cellini relates how he found Galeotti in Rome in 1528. By about 1530, Cellini had brought the boy to Florence, where he worked under the instruction of the goldsmith Bernardonaccio (probably Bernardo Baldini; died 1573), who treated him poorly.[2] Galeotti had returned to Cellini's tutelage by 1535, the year in which Cellini, called away to Rome by the pope, recommended the youth as capable of finishing the dies for a medal of Duke Alessandro de' Medici. In 1540, Galeotti accompanied Cellini to Ferrara and in 1548–49 is found working with Ascanio de' Mari in Cellini's Paris workshop in the Château du Petit-Nesle.[3] He settled in Florence around 1552. From December of that year there is record of a payment to him from Cellini for finishing work he had done on the master's bronze *Perseus* in the Loggia dei Lanzi, Florence.[4] Galeotti entered into the service of the Florentine mint around 1557,[5] and became a citizen of the city in 1560. The Florentine historian and critic Benedetto Varchi (1502–1565), a friend of Cellini's, described Galeotti in a 1555 sonnet as an equal rival of Domenico Poggini, another medalist working at the mint.[6] For a brief time in 1575–76, Galeotti apparently worked as a die-engraver at the papal mint in Rome.[7]

Galeotti was a most prolific medalist, producing some eighty known pieces. Most of his cast medals bear his signature in the form PPR, PETRVS PAVLVS ROM, or some variant of these. His sitters came from many different places in addition to Florence, including Genoa, Turin, Milan, and even cities north of the Alps.[8] His cast medals present elegant and imposing portraits coupled with detailed pictorial reverses. It is a courtly style often enhanced by a pearled border.

Galeotti is also known for a series of struck medals, dating from the late 1560s and early 1570s, depicting Cosimo I de' Medici and commemorating his accomplishments, such as the building of the Florentine aqueducts or the Uffizi.[9] Vasari praised this series, describing the medals as graceful and beautiful, particularly their portraits.[10] Their reverses are more schematic and abbreviated than the artist's cast reverses, in part probably reflecting Cosimo's extensive collection of Roman coins.[11] Several of them were painted as ovals in the courtyard of the Palazzo Vecchio,[12] and some were reproduced as marble tondi on a balustrade that is now in the Palazzo Pitti.[13]

Galeotti's single known monumental work is a signed bronze bust of Ottavio Farnese (1525–1586), second duke of Parma and Piacenza.[14] It is related to Cellini's famous bronze bust of Cosimo I de' Medici in the Bargello, Florence, and may well have been modeled by the master.[15] Galeotti portrayed Farnese in a medal as well, one that also depicts his wife, Margaret of Austria (1522–1586).[16]

A portrait of Galeotti was painted by the Milanese painter Giampaolo Lomazzo (1538–1600),[17] who was himself depicted on one of Galeotti's medals.[18]

Donald Myers

Pietro Paolo Galeotti
Francesco Taverna (1488–1560)
57
Copper alloy, cast
Diameter 57.4 mm; inner diameter of the pearled border from
 roughly 11 to 5 o'clock, 52.0 mm
London, Victoria & Albert Museum
A268–1910

Obverse: Bearded bust to the right, wearing a robe. Legend, set on scribing line: FRA[nciscus] • TABERNA • CO[mes] • LANDR[riani] • MAGN[us] • CANC[ellarius] • STA[tus] • MEDIO[lanensis] • AN[no] • LXVI (Francesco Taverna, count of Landriano, grand chancellor of the Milanese state, in his sixty-sixth year). The inscription is partially obscured by the sitter's head, and its Roman numerals extend across his robe. In the field to the right, the signature: P[ietro] • P[aolo] • R[omano]. Pearled border.

Reverse: In a landscape dominated by various architectural

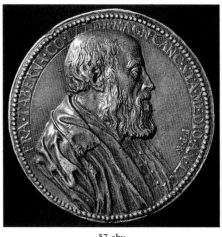

57 obv.

57 rev.

elements, including an obelisk and a broken entablature with three columns, a cityscape—perhaps Rome—in the background, a greyhound seated on a plinth, gazing upward at the constellation Capricorn surrounded by clouds. Legend, set on scribing line: IN CON STANTIA • ET • FIDE • FELICITAS (In constancy and faith is happiness).[1] Pearled border.

57a
Copper alloy, cast
Diameter 56.8 mm; inner diameter of the pearled border from roughly 12:00 o'clock to 6:00 o'clock, 51.2 mm
Washington, The National Gallery of Art, Samuel H. Kress Collection
1957.14.953

Obverse and reverse as above.

This signed medal, featuring a refined, dignified portrait and a detailed, emblematic reverse of high sophistication, is typical of Galeotti's work. Characteristic features are its pearled borders, the inscription lines, and the partial overlapping of the inscription letters with elements of the design. The latter shows that Galeotti probably worked his inscriptions separately from the portraits, then brought the two together, adjusting where necessary. In style, the present piece compares quite closely to Galeotti's 1556 medal of Cardinal Cristoforo Madruzzo, the artist's earliest dated medal.[2] Like the reverse of that earlier work, this one has a large, off-center figure dominating over smaller-scale pictorial elements.

Taverna's age as stated in the inscription indicates that the present medal was made in about 1554. He had received his laureate in law from the university at Pavia, and became a jurisconsult in Milan in 1514.[3] He served as an ambassador for Francesco II Sforza on numerous occasions, representing Milan's interests in Rome in 1526 and in France in 1528, and was also sent to negotiate with Charles V a possible marriage between Sforza and a French princess. In 1533, Sforza named him grand chancellor, and Charles V reconfirmed that honor two years later, when on Sforza's death the Milanese dukedom devolved on him. In 1536, Charles also conferred on him the title count of Landriano, the first of several noble titles acquired by the Taverna family over the next hundred years. Later, Charles named Taverna imperial counselor and senator, and bestowed on him the lordship of Cervesina and S. Gaudenzio.

The medal's reverse is an allegory of stewardship, reflecting Taverna's faithful service to Milan. The greyhound is not only employed as a general symbol of faithfulness (see cat. no. 32),[4] but also specifically denotes Taverna, in whose family arms it appears, staring up and to the left at an eight-pointed star.[5] Here his gaze is fixed on the zodiacal symbol of Capricorn, depicted as a goat dotted with the stars of the constellation. Capricorn was a common symbol of imperial power in the Renaissance, one first associated with the emperor Augustus, who frequently used it on his coins (see the discussion of cat. no. 136).[6]

One famous use of the symbol was in the ancient *Gemma*

Augustea (Vienna, Kunsthistorisches Museum), a large sardonyx cameo depicting the seated Augustus with the astrological sign above and to the left of his profile. This configuration is similar to the relationship between the dog and the constellation on the present medal, and indeed it is possible that Galeotti was consciously emulating the gem, for it was well known in Italy from a description of it by the sculptor and architect Filarete (c. 1400–c. 1470) and from casts made by Filarete and others and painted copies by other Renaissance artists.[7]

The fragments of architecture in the landscape are probably a visual shorthand for Rome, the imperial city, the symbolic seat of power of the Holy Roman Emperor, Charles V.

Galeotti's sophistication is demonstrated by his placement of the Capricorn amid the letters of the word CONSTANTIA. Capricorn was also a symbol of happiness, and is found as such on ancient coins.[8] Here the sign of happiness, or "felicitas," is found quite literally in "constancy," a visual pun reinforcing the inscription.

Donald Myers

Gianpaolo Poggini
(1518–c. 1582)

Poggini spent much of his life outside his native Italy, and is one of those artists who introduced Italian techniques and style to other European countries. He was born in Florence on March 28, 1518, the son of a gem-engraver Michele Poggini. Along with his younger brother Domenico (1520–1590), he trained as a goldsmith. It is probable that both learned the art of gem-engraving from their father, and Gianpaolo would also seem to have worked, like his brother, as a sculptor, although no works of his in this medium are known. The brothers' skill brought them to the attention of Duke Cosimo I of Tuscany, and it was in the context of the Medici court of the 1540s that Cellini (1500–1571) mentions him in his autobiography: "At that time my kidneys began to give me some pain and as I was unable to work I was only too glad to spend my time in the duke's wardrobe, along with some young goldsmiths called Gianpaolo and Domenico Poggini. I got them to make a little gold vessel, decorated in low relief with figures and other beautiful adornments; this was for the duchess. . . . "[1] The brothers evidently had an amicable relationship with Cellini, for in a dispute with Cosimo over the price of a diamond, Cellini named them as witnesses to his truthfulness.[2]

In 1556 Cosimo appointed the two brothers as coin-engravers,[3] in which post they would have been involved in the production of Cosimo's new coinage as duke of Florence and Siena. It was doubtless as a result of this experience and on Cosimo's recommendation that Gianpaolo was called to Brussels in 1557 to work in the mint for Philip II (cat. nos. 58, 156). It is at this point that the careers of the two brothers diverge. Domenico remained in Italy, working in Florence as a sculptor, medalist, and gem- and coin-engraver, until his departure in the mid 1580s for Rome, where he died in 1590. Gianpaolo, on the other hand, never returned to his homeland.

On his arrival in the Netherlands, Poggini was employed to engrave the dies for the new coinage of the provinces handed over to Philip by his father at a ceremony held in Brussels in October 1555. Among the payments made to the artist were one of eighty livres for the dies for Philip's new florin and another of sixty livres for a silver demi-real.[4] But he was also commissioned to produce dies for struck medals, to supplement the larger cast medals of his compatriots Leoni (cat. nos. 49–52) and da Trezzo (cat. nos. 54–55). All of Poggini's medals were originally struck from dies, although the majority of surviving examples are cast copies.

His first known medal dates to 1556, and bears a portrait of Philip as king of the Spains and of England.[5] A medal of the following year commemorates the retirement of Charles V (cat. nos. 77, 123–24, 156) and Philip's assumption of responsibility for Spain and the New World.[6] Both medals are signed.

In 1559, following the Peace of Cateau–Cambrésis, Philip left the Netherlands, never to return. Poggini accompanied the court to Spain. In 1563 he was awarded the title of sculptor to the king and an annual salary of 65,000 maravédis. The following year he received extra payment for dies for coinage.[7] His known medals during his years in Spain are few. All celebrated the achievements of the Spanish king, the earliest commemorating the new peace.[8] Philip is described on the obverse as "king of the Spains and of the New World in the West," while on the reverse a figure of Peace sets fire to a pile of arms (as on the reverse of da Trezzo's Mary Tudor medal, cat. no. 54) in front of a garlanded temple of Janus, its doors firmly closed. Both the reverse legend and image are taken from ancient Roman coins, but Poggini must also have known the reverse of Cellini's 1534 medal of Pope Clement VII, which has a similar figure, also placed in front of a temple of Janus.[9] A medal bearing on one side a portrait of Philip and on the other Elizabeth de Valois (1545–1568), sister of Francis II of France, was probably made in celebration of their marriage in 1560.[10] The medal relating to the Spanish conquest of America (cat. no. 58) followed shortly afterward.

After this burst of activity, Poggini produced few medals. A letter written on October 17, 1571, to Grand Duke Francesco de' Medici[11] shows that a medal celebrating Philip's marriage to Anne of Austria (1549–1580) is also the work of Poggini.[12] A later medal celebrating Philip's triumphal return to Madrid after his Portuguese campaign of 1580 has often been attributed to Poggini and is either by the artist himself or someone working in his style.[13] The medallic work of the Italian artist had a clearly discernible influence on artists working in both the Netherlands and Spain.

Philip Attwood

Gianpaolo Poggini
Philip II (born 1527, king of Spain 1556–98)
58
Gilt bronze, cast
Diameter 40.6 mm
New York, private collection

58 obv.   58 rev.

Obverse: Bearded bust facing left, wearing cuirass, ruff, and mantle fixed with a brooch on the left shoulder. Inner and outer beaded borders. Legend: • PHILIPPVS • II • • HISPAN[iarum] • ET • NOVI ORBIS OCCIDVI REX (Philip II, king of the Spains and of the New World in the West).
Reverse: Female figure, wearing cuirass and antique drapery and with a fillet in her hair, moving to left, holding in her hands a globe. The northern hemisphere has lines of latitude and longitude, the southern hemisphere is left blank. To the left are three Spanish ships. To the right, a group of figures from the New World, one of whom raises her right hand and points upward. Included in the group is a child, and in front of it is a llama carrying silver ingots. Legend: RELIQVVM DATVRA (She will provide the rest). In the exergue: INDIA. Beaded border.

Mexico fell to Spain in the 1520s and Peru in the 1530s, but it was not until the 1550s that Spain began to exploit fully the resources of the New World. By 1560 the Spanish Atlantic economy had been established, a development celebrated by this medal, which also hints at future possibilities. We are fortunate that a letter of Poggini's describing the production of this medal is preserved in the state archive of Florence.[1] It is addressed to his former patron, Duke Cosimo de' Medici, and was written from the Spanish court on February 29, 1562.

The portrait is very similar to earlier representations of Philip on Poggini's medals, but there are differences, particularly in the clothing and the legend. That this portrait was made specifically for this medal is confirmed by Poggini's letter. The same document speaks of the reverse, which the artist described as "a reverse of India, for which I dressed men and women with the clothes they wear in Peru, as you see; and that animal which resembles both a camel and a sheep I have portrayed from one which is alive here, and I have included it because it is a rare animal and a useful one, since like ours it gives wool, milk, and meat, and it bears loads like an ass. I have shown it burdened with bars of silver. The woman who bears the half globe as an offer represents the province of India, as my Lord Gonzalo Pérez is pleased (to interpret it). But I prefer to identify her as Fortune or Providence. The idea was mine in the first place, then I discussed it with my Lord and good friend Gonzalo Pérez; it seemed to him a good idea and he spent much effort working on the motto and refining the representation, with the help of many learned men at this Court. And accordingly I executed it."[2]

58 rev.

The reverse legend was composed by Pérez, secretary of state to Philip II. This is the earliest known medal to attempt a representation of a South American subject. The gesture of the figure with raised hand may allude to the program of conversion to Christianity of the indigenous population. The blank lower half of the globe suggests yet undiscovered areas, including, some have argued, a southern continent that promised to bring still more wealth to Spain.

The medal is known in two versions. One is signed below the bust. The other, an example of which is exhibited here, was produced from the same dies after extensive reworking, possibly by a Netherlandish artist.

Philip Attwood

Milanese School (?)
Carlo Visconti (1523–1565)
59
Copper alloy, cast, gilt
Diameter 70 mm

Boston, Museum of Fine Arts, Theodora Wilbour Fund in memory of Zoë Wilbour, September 21, 1966
66.433.

Obverse: Bust to right, in decorated armor partially evoking ancient Roman forms, with lions' heads for pauldrons and Gorgon heads on the besagews. Around the neck is a heavy chain from which is suspended a portrait medal or large coin. Legend: CAROLVS VICECOMES (Carlo Visconti). Pearled border.
Reverse: Within a pearled border a large piece of branched coral, beneath which is the legend: COR ALIT (discussed below).

59a
Bronze, cast
Diameter 69.8 mm
Washington, The National Gallery of Art, Samuel H. Kress Collection 1957.14.1105

Obverse and reverse as above.

59 obv.

59 rev.

59a obv.

59a rev.

The medal of Carlo Visconti must be numbered among the finest of the sixteenth century. The composition of the obverse is beautifully balanced, the portrait sensitively rendered with character and individuality. The details of the armor are restrained and delicately worked, and the lettering of the inscription is given a carefully measured spacing in proper proportion to the field. On the reverse, the branch of coral is set in dramatic isolation against a barren field, and is anchored by the simple and strong placement of the single word of the inscription.[1]

Although several attributions of authorship have been attempted in the past, none has been comfortably accepted. Armand placed the medal in the active and important Milanese school of the mid sixteenth century, but later cited the opinion of Gaetano Milanesi that the author could have been Francesco Tortorino, a Milanese engraver in rock crystal who did some work for Carlo Visconti. There appears to be no specific evidence to support this theory.[2]

It would seem logical, given the prominence of the Visconti family in Milan, to look to that city for the artist, yet no clear stylistic connection can be made with the most prominent medalists active there in the sixteenth century. Other unsigned medals have been generally lumped together into a Milanese school (e.g., cat. nos. 48, 56), but the real problem lies in the lack of a careful and extensive study of the Italian sixteenth-century medal.[3] The Visconti medal possesses characteristics that could even be linked with an artist such as Pastorino (cat. nos. 67–69), though it is without that artist's distinctively brittle refinement.

Carlo Visconti achieved distinction in several areas. He was a lawyer, a Milanese senator, and a literary man, producing several volumes of letters, speeches, and poetry in both Latin and Italian, along with accounts of his participation in the Council of Trent (1545–47, 1551–52, 1562–63) and his experiences as ambassador from Milan to the court of Spain under Philip II (cat. nos. 58, 156). According to one account, he was not overly impressive in appearance or particularly deserving of great fame.[4] He was attracted to popular celebrations, performances, races, and other entertainments, and since he does not seem to have followed a military career, his involvement in pageants may explain his appearance in a kind of ancient Roman-style parade armor popular at the time.

In fact, his career appears to have developed within the Church, for after his term in Spain he became an ambassador to the court of Pope Pius IV. His contact with the pope led to his appointment as apostolic protonotary and bishop of Ventimiglia. In 1565, after his return from the Council of Trent, he was given a cardinal's hat, but died suddenly that same year at the age of forty-two.

On the medal, Visconti appears as a young man in a completely secular context, with no reference to his eventual ecclesiastical distinction. Since Pius IV ascended to the papal throne in 1559, when Visconti was thirty-six, one can assume that the medal was probably produced sometime between the mid 1540s and the mid 1550s.

On the obverse it is interesting to note, in addition to the armor, the pendant bearing a male portrait in profile around Visconti's neck, an example of the uses to which portrait medals or ancient coins were sometimes put.

In previous literature no attempt has been made to explain the reverse. Red coral (Lat. *corallium*) has long been prized for its amuletic properties. It was believed to guard against the evil eye, to be effective against poisons, and to protect the traveler. To those ends it was frequently incorporated into jewelery and is often seen held or worn by the Christ Child in Italian paintings. In Ovid's telling of the story of Perseus and Andromeda, coral was formed when Perseus covered Medusa's head with seaweed, which hardened upon contact with the head and took on special powers.[5] Whether the coral on the reverse has any connection with the Gorgon heads on the besagews of the armor on the obverse must remain an open question.

Some attention must be given, however, to the form of the word CORALIT and its derivation. It does not correspond to any regular declension of *corallium*, but has been used in the past to designate a very rare form of marble resembling coral. Much more likely, and certainly in keeping with the Renaissance propensity for complicated and obscure meanings, is the possibility that we are to consider the division of the word into two parts, COR ALIT, as it occurs on the medal thanks to the intrusion of the root of the coral. Read thus, it becomes a motto "The heart sustains" (or "nourishes" or "supports"; Lat. *cor, cordis* and *alo, alui, altus*). The concept of the reverse may well have derived from the play on words, rather than the other way around. How all of this relates to Carlo Visconti may never be revealed.

Stephen K. Scher

Antonio Abondio
(1538–1591)

Abondio only appears in available documents after his departure from his homeland. It is presumed that he learned the art of medalmaking in Milan, for one can see in his works influences of Leone Leoni (cat. nos. 49–52) and Pietro Paolo Galeotti (cat. no. 57). In 1566 Abondio entered the service of Emperor Maximilian II (cat. nos. 61–62) in Vienna, and he was kept on by Maximilian's successor, Rudolf II (cat. no. 136), whom he followed when Rudolf transferred his court to Prague. A journey to the Netherlands in 1566 brought him into contact with Jacques Jonghelinck (cat. nos. 158–63), and on a sojourn in Spain in 1571–72 he came to know Jacopo da Trezzo (cat. nos. 54–55). After his return, Abondio received a number of commissions in southern Germany, specifically Munich and Augsburg,[1] which may have put him in touch with Valentin Maler (cat. nos. 129–31). It would have been Maler who had the most to learn from such an encounter. His Spanish sojourn marks a distinct break in Abondio's creative career, as we see in the way he signed his medals. Before he always signed himself A.A., but subsequently he used the more explicit AN.AB.

As a court artist, Abondio created numerous imperial medals

as well as portrait medals of a number of archdukes. In addition, he also produced medals of private persons, most of them connected in some way to the court. He created his models in wax, a technique that he helped to establish in German-speaking regions. At the emperor's behest he also created a model for the first talers coined by Rudolf II. He appears to have been marginally interested in the production of struck medals, for only recently a few carved dies were identified as his.[2] His strength was in portraiture, especially the creation of imposing portraits of princes. When obliged to produce anything for his reverses other than a coat of arms, however, he often relied on the designs of others. We also have a number of polychrome wax medallions by Abondio, created as independent works rather than models for medals, and a few plaquettes. The documents suggest that he may also have created fully three-dimensional works, but none have survived. Abondio is remembered for having integrated the medalmaking styles of Italy and Germany in the waning years of the Renaissance.

Karl Schulz

Antonio Abondio
Jacopo Nizzola da Trezzo (1514?–1589)
60
Bronze, cast
Diameter 69.8 mm; diameter of the outer perimeter of the inscription, 61.2 mm
Vienna, Kunsthistorisches Museum, Münzkabinett
143.996

Obverse: Bearded bust facing to the left, wearing cloak and frilled collar. Legend: IACOBVS NIZOLLA DE TRIZZIA

MDLXXII • (Jacopo Nizzola da Trezzo. 1572). On the right, below the inscription, the signature AN•AB.
Reverse: On the left, a standing Minerva with helmet, lance, and laurel branch. Across from her, Vulcan is seated on an anvil, with a hammer in his hand and a square, compass, and plumb-line, the symbols of architecture, at his feet. Behind him to the right the suggestion of a forge. Legend: ARTIBVS QVAESITA GLORIA (Fame acquired through art).

This medal is of importance in the work of Abondio not only because it is a portrait of one of his colleagues, but also because of the figural scene on its reverse. Reverses of his own design are not very common. Especially on his medals commissioned by the Habsburgs, one most often sees symbolic motifs prescribed by his clients. Thus despite Abondio's very large output there are only two others that compare with the reverse of the Trezzo medal, and these happen to have been created at roughly the same time. They are the medals of Michael Peterle and Johann von Khevenhüller (1538–1606).[1]

Jacopo da Trezzo (cat. nos. 54–55) was from Lombardy, and after sojourns in various cities he ended up working in Madrid beginning in 1560. There he was active as a sculptor, stonecutter, medalist, and architect. Abondio's medal refers primarily to his compatriot's achievements as an architect (most notably in the expansion of the Escorial). The presentation of Vulcan—who may have been given Trezzo's features—is also an allusion to sculpture, and by extension to the art of medalmaking. Antonio Abondio, who probably knew da Trezzo from Milan, was a member of a legation to Spain in 1571–72, and it was on that occasion that he made the artist's portrait.

Karl Schulz

60 obv.

60 rev.

61 obv.

61a obv.

Antonio Abondio
Maximilian II (born 1527, emperor 1564–76)
61
Silver, cast, uniface
Diameter 59 mm
New York, The Metropolitan Museum of Art, Purchase, Gift of
J. Pierpont Morgan, by exchange, 1989

Obverse: Bearded, bareheaded bust facing to the right. The emperor is wearing armor, a draped cloak, a frilled collar, and the chain of the Order of the Golden Fleece. Legend: IMP[erator] : CAES[ar] : MAXIMIL[ianus] : II: AVG[ustus] : (Emperor Maximilian II, Augustus). At the edge, behind the shoulder, is the signature AN:AB:.
Reverse: Plain.

Empress Maria (1528–1603)
61a
Silver, cast, uniface
Diameter 59 mm
New York, The Metropolitan Museum of Art, Purchase, Gift of
J. Pierpont Morgan, by exchange, 1989

Obverse: Bust in bonnet, cloak, and ruffled collar, facing to the left. Legend: MARIA IMPER[atrix] • MDLXXV (vine ornament) (Empress Maria. 1575). At the edge, behind the shoulder, the signature AN•AB.
Reverse: Plain.

The portraits of Maximilian II and Maria are found both cast together and separate. There are various indications that they were not necessarily intended to go together, however.[1] The Maria medal is dated 1575, but it would appear that the one of Maximilian had already been created before 1574—though to judge from the form of the signature, in 1572 at the earliest. It is a copy of the undated Maximilian medal with an eagle on the reverse from the period around 1567, which had shown the emperor with a shorter bust truncation and without the Order of the Golden Fleece. Perhaps this omission was what prompted the newer work, which presents only the slightest changes to the portrait. The medal of the empress Maria might then have

been created as a companion piece. In any case, these are the last of Abondio's portrayals of the imperial couple.

Emperor Maximilian II, the son of Ferdinand I, makes his first medallic appearance in 1543, at the age of sixteen. In 1548, after having been elected king of Bohemia, he married, in Spain, his Spanish cousin Maria, one of the daughters of Emperor Charles V. This marriage had been arranged for Maximilian in the hope of suppressing, with the help of the strictly Catholic Maria, his apparent Protestant leanings. As it happened, he never renounced his Catholic faith, though he retained his sympathy for Lutheranism throughout his life. In 1564 he succeeded his father Ferdinand as emperor, but was forced to divide the Habsburg hereditary lands with his brothers Ferdinand and Charles, who received Tyrol, Styria, and Carinthia. Throughout his reign he sought an accommodation between Catholicism and Protestantism in the empire. He was repeatedly called upon to repel the intrusions of the Turks. On his death in 1576 he was succeeded by his son Rudolf II, who moved the imperial residence from Vienna to Prague. Maria had borne him sixteen children, of whom five sons achieved political prominence. In 1581 she returned to Spain, where she died in 1603.

Karl Schulz

Antonio Abondio
Maximilian II (born 1527, emperor 1564–76)
62
Alloy of lead and tin, cast, uniface
Diameter 105 mm
Munich, Staatliche Münzsammlung

Obverse: Bearded waist-length portrait facing to the left. The emperor is dressed in armor with a cloak, a laurel wreath, and the Order of the Golden Fleece on a ribbon. He carries a commander's baton in his right hand.
Reverse: Plain.

The pattern for this medal is a two-sided colored wax relief decorated with pearls and mounted on a slab of obsidian, in the Kunstkammer of Vienna's Kunsthistorisches Museum.[1] Comparison reveals that the wax medallion cannot have been the

62 obv.

actual model for the lead casting, however, but was conceived as a separate work. The reverse of the wax version refers to the emperor's victories (in fact never achieved) in Siebenbürgen, and that aspect of the work was still stressed in the inventory of Emperor Rudolf II's art collections from 1607–11. As early as 1620, a two-sided medal of this type was published[2]—its material undesignated—bearing an inscription both front and back and identifying the sitter as Rudolf II. Moreover, both front and back are reversed from the pattern of the wax medallion. This medal was published again in 1753 by Marquard Herrgott,[3] who described it as a silver medal preserved in the imperial Münzkabinett, but to this day it has never been found. At about the same time it was correctly illustrated, that is with both sides matching the orientation of the wax medallion, by Köhler.[4] But no such two-sided example has as yet been verified, only the uniface portrait pieces without inscriptions, usually in cast lead.

The splendid presentation of the emperor in a full torso view tends to align the medal more properly with the group of plaquettes. In style, this portrait itself is closely related to the one on the medal from 1575 (cat. no. 61), which suggests that the wax medallion and its descendents were produced toward the end of the emperor's reign. The fact that in 1575 Abondio received a payment of 200 gulden for a work for Emperor Maximilian also tends to support this dating.

Karl Schulz

Antonio Abondio
Archdukes Matthias (born 1557, emperor 1612–19) and Maximilian III (1558–1618)
63
Silver, cast
Diameter 48 mm
Vienna, Kunsthistorisches Museum, Münzkabinett

63 obv.

172

63a obv.

Obverse: Youthful double portrait, both wearing ruff collars, facing to the right. Legend: MATTHIAS [et] MAXIMILIANVS • ARCHI[duces] • AVST[riae] • (Matthias [and] Maximilian, archdukes of Austria). The signature A • A on the arm truncation. In the field, behind the heads, the date 1568.
Reverse: Incuse.

Archdukes Albrecht VII (1559–1621) and Wenzel (1561–1578)
63a
Silver, cast
Diameter 48 mm
Vienna, Kunsthistorisches Museum, Münzkabinett

Obverse: Youthful double portrait, both wearing ruff collars. Legend: ALBERTVS • [et] WENCESLAVS • ARCHIDV[ces] • AVSTRIAE (Albrecht [and] Wenzel, archdukes of Austria). On the arm truncation, the signature AA. In the field, the date 1568.
Reverse: Incuse.

These two matching medals of four of the sons of Emperor Maximilian II (cat. nos. 61–62), each with a double portrait and originally conceived as a single-sided casting,[1] date from the year 1568. They were thus created at the time when Abondio was also producing important portrait medals of Maximilian II and approaching his zenith as a portraitist. While these are portraits of children—still extremely rare at the time—Abondio also produced a number of medallic portraits of both Matthias and Maximilian III as adults. In these later pieces the distinctive features of the two brothers are more apparent. Here, at the ages of eleven and ten respectively, the boys are not yet shown wearing armor, but are dressed in simple garments with narrow ruff collars. The artist also created individual medals of the emperor's oldest sons, Rudolf and Ernst, but not until nearly ten years later, for in 1568 they were in Spain being educated and thus unavailable for sittings.

Archduke Matthias, Emperor Maximilian II's third oldest living son in 1568, was raised in Austria. During the reign of his brother Rudolf II (cat. no. 136), he served as governor in various Habsburg lands, showing himself to be far more ambitious than his emperor. By 1611 he had in fact taken over all of Rudolf's titles except that of emperor, and on Rudolf's death in 1612 he succeeded him. Matthias died childless in 1619, having witnessed the outbreak of the Thirty Years' War. He was succeeded in turn by his cousin Ferdinand II.

The next oldest, Maximilian III, likewise grew up in Vienna. In 1585 he was elected coadjutor of the grand master of the German Order, and soon took over the order's leadership himself. He was officially declared grand master in 1590. In 1587 he made a bid for the crown of Poland, but saw it go to Sigismund III of Sweden instead. From 1602 on, he also served his brother Rudolf II as vice-regent in the Tyrol, and maintained his residence in Innsbruck. He tried to serve as an intermediary in the struggle between his brothers Rudolf II and Matthias, but

tended to support the latter. He died in 1618 and was buried in Innsbruck.

Archduke Albrecht first embarked on a career in the Church in Spain, but later married his cousin Isabella, a daughter of Philip II, and became with her a governor of the Netherlands. Archduke Wenzel died at the age of seventeen, though he had already become grand prior of the Order of St. John in Castile.

Karl Schulz

Artist Unknown
Pietro Bembo (1470–1547)
64
Bronze
Diameter 56.2 mm; diameter of the outer perimeter of the inscription from the E of PETRI to the C of CAR, 50.0 mm
New York, Michael Hall Collection

Obverse: Bearded bust facing to the right, wearing a hooded robe. Legend: PETRI BEMBI CAR[dinalis] ([portrait of] Cardinal Pietro Bembo).
Reverse: Pegasus rearing and the fountain Hippocrene.

64a
Bronze
Diameter 56.2 mm
New York, private collection

Obverse and reverse as above.

Bembo was one of the most celebrated humanists and writers of his day.[1] A native of Venice, he served as secretary to Pope Leo X from 1513 until the latter's death in 1521, then settled in his villa at Villabonza near Padua, where he devoted himself to literary pursuits. His major philological work, *Prose della volgar lingua*, appeared in 1524, and did much to promote the use of a standardized Italian. He was named official historiographer of the Venetian Republic, and in 1538 was created cardinal by Pope Paul III. Bembo's writings, whether in Latin, Greek, or Italian, are distinguished by their polished classical style and purity of language.

On the medal he is shown wearing a hooded cardinal's robe. The winged horse Pegasus appears on the reverse both as a symbol of fame and because of his association with the Muses. It was on the slopes of Mount Helicon, the home of the Muses, that Pegasus struck a rock with his hoof, causing the sacred fountain Hippocrene to begin to flow.

This medal has often been attributed to Benvenuto Cellini (1500–1571), on the basis of that artist's description of a medal he made for Bembo in 1537: "The next day I went along to kiss the hands of Messer Pietro Bembo, who had not yet been made a cardinal . . . Later on he began to drop delicate hints that he would like me to make his portrait: there was nothing I could have wanted more, and so I mixed some spotless white stucco in a little box and began work on it . . . since he wore his beard short, in the Venetian fashion, it proved very troublesome to

64 obv.

64 rev.

make a head that I was satisfied with. But I finished it . . . he reckoned that after I had made the wax model in two hours I ought to finish the steel one in ten; and there I was only able to complete the wax model in two hundred hours, and asking his permission to leave for France. He was terribly upset at this, and begged that I should at least do a reverse for the medal, showing the horse Pegasus with a wreath of myrtle around it. I did this in about three hours, and made a lovely job of it . . . Then he began pleading with me to execute it in steel . . . I assured him that, although I did not want to do it there, I would certainly do it for him when I settled down to work."[2]

The arguments against the attribution are nevertheless many and convincing. On the medal, Bembo's beard is long; there is no wreath on the reverse; Bembo was not made a cardinal until the following year; and the medal is cast, not struck. Still, some authorities insist that the work is Cellini's. Pope-Hennessy, arguing that the portrait "corresponds reasonably well" with Cellini's medal of Francis I, suggests that this is a modified version of the one the artist describes from 1537. In this he follows Armand and Plon.[3] Cellini's vehement dislike of Bembo's short beard is clear from a letter the artist wrote to Benedetto Varchi (1502–1565),[4] but it seems improbable that Cellini would have returned to the medal at some later stage and lengthened the beard, altered the legend, and removed the wreath from the reverse. Moreover, the possibility of his using a wax as large as that from which the present medal was cast as a model for a struck medal does not accord with what we know of Italian practice at this time.[5]

Cellini is of course famed for his works as a goldsmith and sculptor, but was also active as a designer of coins and medals and a die-engraver for the papal mint. He tells us that he designed a type of screw-press[6] and that his improved technique allowed the bronze to be struck without being pre-cast, and gold and silver without first being softened, yet die flaws and double strikes are not uncommon on extant examples.

Rizzoli argued against assigning the present Bembo medal to Cellini.[7] Habich grouped the medal with others as the work of a "Master of the Cardinal Bembo" working in northern Italy.[8] Yet it does not seem to belong with that group, for its relief is higher and the modeling is less detailed. Moreover, its lettering, though skillfully delineated, lacks the delicacy of that of the other medals in Habich's grouping. It does share certain stylistic similarities with those medals, nevertheless, as well as with the medals of other North Italian artists, for example Danese Cattaneo (c. 1509–1573), which would indicate that the medalist must have worked in either Milan or—more probably—in Bembo's native city of Venice.

It has been suggested that the medal served as the basis for Titian's portrait of Bembo in Naples.[9]

Philip Attwood

Francesco da Sangallo
(1494–1576)

Francesco, son of Giuliano di Francesco Giamberti, was the last of the Sangallo dynasty of architect-sculptors. With his father in Rome at the age of ten, he witnessed the discovery of the *Laocoön,* and he was never thereafter far from where the exciting projects were, whether in Florence, Loreto, or Rome. His first sculpture of importance is the *Virgin and Child with St. Anne* in Orsanmichele, Florence, dated 1526. Its handsome if rather brutal figural style, obtained through a penetrating study of Donatello and the quattrocento, recurs in a handful of other marble images, the most memorable being the bust, now in the Bargello, of Giovanni delle Bande Nere, who died in 1526, and figures of Saints Peter and Paul on the tomb of Piero de' Medici in the Badia at Montecassino, completed in 1547. He brought the same intensity to a medallic activity that spanned the years 1519 to 1570, producing twelve medals in all. Their images are brusque and angular, and they were accomplished in a daring, purely sculptural mode of high relief without numismatic precedent.

James David Draper

Francesco da Sangallo
Self-Portrait with Elena Marsuppini (died 1575)
65
Bronze, cast
Diameter 97.6 mm; inside diameter of obverse inscription, 81.5
   mm; outside, 93.3 mm
New York, The Metropolitan Museum of Art. Ann and George
   Blumenthal Fund, 1950
50.58.9

Obverse: Bust facing left, bearded, wearing a soft turban-like
cap. Legend: FRANCESCO DA SANGALLO SCVLTORE [et]
ARCHITETTO FIOREN[tino] (Francesco da Sangallo, Florentine sculptor [and] architect . . .). Truncation inscribed, *in
cavo*: FACIEBA[t] (. . . made [this]).
Reverse: Bust facing left, wearing gathered chemise, and hair
held in a net. Legend: HELENA MARSVPINI CONSORTE
FIORENT[ina] • A[nno] • M • D • LI (Elena Marsuppini, wife,
Florentine, [in the] year 1551).

Sangallo portrayed himself several times, beginning with a
forceful marble plaque, dated 1542, installed as an *ex voto* in
Santa Maria Primerana in Fiesole.[1] It is essentially the image he
re-used in medals of 1550—two with allegorical reverses, two
of different size with reverses showing the campanile of Santa
Croce, whose architect he was[2]—and in this medal of the
following year, marginally smaller than the larger version of the
Santa Croce medal.

Because of the extraordinarily high relief of both sides, this is
one of the most unwieldy ventures in the history of medals.
Indeed, Francesco's efforts to bring a full and vibrant plasticity
to the portrait medal were so singular in their ambitions that
they inspired almost no emulation before modern times.[3]

Detecting that this medal was intended to fortify Francesco's
relationship with the unprepossessing if intrepid-looking lady
on the reverse, Clausse supposes that their marriage reg-
ularized an earlier attachment, for he notes that in October of
the same year, 1551, Duke Cosimo I de' Medici legitimized
Francesco's natural son, Clemente.[4] However, Francesco's will
of 1574 survives, stating that the legitimization of Clemente (by
now for unknown reasons pressed into service in the grand-
ducal galleys) had taken place in 1559. Francesco's wife is
called throughout Monna Lena, daughter of Christofano Marsuppini, and she is said to have three daughters, nuns to whom
he leaves small endowments. He restores to Monna Lena the
450 florins that she had brought with her as a dowry in 1530 or
thereabouts. He speaks of the love and affection he bears for her,
and one appreciates the medal's hearty strength all the more
when reading these sentiments.[5] Clausse understandably ob-
serves that the piece has the weight and gravity of a marriage
contract, but it might be more apt to say that it reinforces old
vows. The couple lived to within a few months of each other.

Two specimens were found, along with three of those whose
reverses show the campanile of Santa Croce, in the foundations
of that structure when it was demolished in the mid nineteenth

65 obv.

65 rev.

century.[6] Despite the corrosion, all the surviving members of this group belonging to the Museo di Santa Croce—one of the campanile type has disappeared—are of very high quality. Their reverses are all reworked. Early specimens in other locations known to this author bear the word FACIEBAT vigorously incised *in cavo* in the *tranche* on the obverse. This feature is lacking in the Museo di Santa Croce group.

James David Draper

Gaspare Mola
(c. 1580–1640)

Mola was born at Coldrerio in the Ticino, and after training in goldsmithing at Milan went to Florence in 1597 to succeed Michele Mazzafirri (c. 1530–c. 1597) as die-cutter at the mint. In 1601 he was asked by the bronze-founder Portigiani (1536–1601) to sculpt two bronze reliefs for the cathedral in Pisa, one of the Presentation in the Temple for the main portal, the other of the Crucifixion for the right side door. During this period he also produced a series of crucifix figures after a model by Giambologna (1524–1608). Mola then left Florence to work as a medalist and agent for Charles Emanuel I of Savoy, on whose behalf he acquired various works of art for which payment to him is recorded in 1607. In 1608, under Ferdinando I de' Medici, he briefly held the post of die-engraver at the Florentine mint, and from 1609 to 1611, after the accession of Cosimo II de' Medici, that of chief engraver. Magnaguti believes many of the unsigned Florentine coins from this period to be by Mola's hand, as are a number of grand-ducal medals.[1] He left Florence once again in 1611, annoyed by the rivalry of his colleague Kolb and harassed by the mintmasters, and in the years 1613–14 he worked for the Mantuan mint, where he engraved the dies for zecchini and scudi for Ferdinando II Gonzaga, as well as for the mints in Modena, Guastalla, and Castiglione. After another Florentine stay, Mola settled in Rome in 1623. There he was appointed papal mintmaster, a position he retained from 1625 until the end of 1639. His stay in Rome produced a long series of coins and medals, often signed with a variety of abbreviations of his name.

Mola's style betrays not only the fine hand of the goldsmith trained in rendering minute detail, but also some of the sculptural qualities of Guillaume Dupré (cat. nos. 146–50), with whom he was in contact.[2] The initials of both artists appear on a medal of Maria Maddalena of Austria (1589–1631), wife of Grand Duke Cosimo II.[3] Mola's cast medals are of such perfect execution that it is at times difficult to distinguish them from struck pieces. Several of his wax models survive in the British Museum

Mark M. Salton

Gaspare Mola
Charles Emanuel I, eleventh duke of Savoy (born 1562, ruled 1580–1630)
66
Gold, struck

66 obv.　　　　　　　　　　　66 rev.

Oval, 58.5 × 45.5 mm (including integral loop); internal measurement from the top of the A in EMAN to the top of the second P, 43.8 mm; weight 66.58 g
American private collection

Obverse: Portrait to right in high relief, with short hair and trimmed beard. The duke wears damascened armor, ruff collar, pearl-seamed drapery gathered with bolla at right shoulder, and on a broad necklace, doubly inscribed FERT between rosettes, the jewel of the Supreme Order of the Most Holy Annunziata, showing the Virgin and the archangel Gabriel. Legend, between scribing lines: CAROLVS • EMAN[uelus] • D[ei] G[ratia] • DVX • SAB[audiae] • P[ater] • P[atriae] • (Charles Emanuel, by the grace of God duke of Savoy, father of [his] country). Below the truncation, the signature: GASP[are] • MOL[a].
Reverse: The centaur Chiron, bearded and with medium-long hair, prancing to right. He spans a bow with his left hand, aiming an arrow with his right, while his head inclines slightly forward as he focuses on his target. A loosely draped stole circles his loins and is tied in front into a loop, the ends floating out behind the shoulder. Five stars appear on his body in the form of the constellation Sagittarius (the Archer). Below his hooves are clouds and a circular arrangement of eight stars. Legend, between scribing lines: OPOR - TVNE (Timely), and on the outer scribing line, the date: MDCVI.

The reverse recalls the Greek myth of Chiron, son of Chronos and teacher of Achilles, renowned for his skill in hunting. He was mortally wounded by one of Herakles's poisoned arrows and transformed by Zeus into the constellation Sagittarius, his immortality passing to Prometheus.[1] On the medal, in illustration of the duke's motto OPORTVNE, Chiron draws his bow, but awaits the right moment for striking his target. The centaur had already appeared, together with that motto, on several of Charles Emanuel's ducatoni coined in 1588.[2] There the reference was to the duke's having wrested from France in that year the marquisate of Saluzzo. In 1602, following the Treaty of Lyon, Henry IV (cat. nos. 146, 155) mocked the duke on a medal of his own. The king is shown as Herakles smiting a centaur with Charles Emanuel's features, and the inscription reads: OPPORTVNIVS (More timely).[3] The swirl of stars on the reverse of Mola's medal appears to represent the solar system as understood by Copernicus (1473–1543).[4]

FERT, the motto of the House of Savoy, has been explained as standing for "foedere et religione tenemur" (Through unity and religion are we sustained). It appears on Savoyan coins from the late fourteenth century onward,[5] and together with its unabbreviated version on a ten scudi d'oro piece of 1635, minted for Victor Amadeus I.[6] An earlier reading, now generally discarded, was "fortitudo eius Rhodium tenuit" (His valor preserved Rhodes).[7] Muratore[8] understood FERT as the third-person singular of the Latin verb *ferre* (to carry), and thought it meant "he carries the three knots of love," a reference to the knots suspended from the buckle of the original chain of the Order. The "love knot" is a symbol of true friendship and unfailing devotion, thus of the unshakable union implied by the word FOEDERE.

Charles Emanuel I, son of Emanuel Philibert and his wife, Margaret of France (1523–1574), was married on March 11, 1585, to Catherine, the Infanta of Spain (1567–1597), daughter of Philip II (cat. nos. 58, 156). The marriage had been proposed and negotiated by Antoine Perrenot de Granvelle (cat. no. 159), as an attempt to contain the power of France. Charles Emanuel, educated in France and mindful of his Valois ancestry on his mother's side, nourished hopes for the French crown himself.[9] Early in his reign, in 1588, he annexed the marquisate of Saluzzo, an act of piracy that earned him in France the epithet "le duc ladron" (the robber duke). Its possession was ultimately confirmed in the Treaty of Lyon in 1601, but only in exchange for his surrender of the much wealthier Besse, Bugey, and Gex to Henry IV of France. The treaty brought an end to the claims of the house of Savoy to territories on the French side of the Alps.

Mark M. Salton

Pastorino de' Pastorini
(c. 1508–1592)

Pastorino was the most prolific of known sixteenth-century medalists. Largely because his output was so enormous, art historians have tended to dismiss his work as shallow and of little interest. It has even been suggested that his pieces should not be considered as medals at all, as the great majority are one-sided.[1] It is certainly true that one looks in vain for psychological insight into the hearts and minds of his sitters, and with no reverses his medals lack the allegorical or emblematic element that constitutes much of the fascination of the genre. As documentation of Ferrarese court circles in the mid sixteenth century, however, they are invaluable, for Pastorino was highly skilled at portraying a variety of notables as they themselves wished to be seen. He held up a mirror to fashionable and would-be-fashionable society, detailing its elaborate costumes and hairstyles with great skill.

Pastorino was born the son of a shoemaker in Castelnuovo della Berardenga, near Siena. He trained as a painter of glass under the French artist Guglielmo di Pietro de Marcillat, who worked in Arezzo from 1522 until his death in 1529.[2] Pastorino practiced that art through the 1530s and 1540s, first at the cathedral in Siena (1531–37) and later in the Sala Regia in the Vatican and in San Marco (1541–48).

It is clear that he began producing medals in the early 1540s. The earliest of these are unsigned, but they have been attributed to him on stylistic grounds.[3]

Pastorino left Rome to return to Siena in 1548. There he again executed glass for the cathedral[4] and was commissioned by the Ufficiali della Mercanzia to paint the vaults of their loggia. Because he failed to complete work for both the loggia and the cathedral in the allotted time, he was imprisoned on various occasions, and it was doubtless with some relief that in 1553 he accepted an invitation from Duke Ercole II d'Este to work in his mint at Reggio. He stayed only a short time in Reggio, and even while there he was interrupted by work in nearby Parma engraving dies for Duke Ottavio Farnese.[5] In 1554 he moved to Ferrara, where he oversaw the Este mint until 1559. Coins of 1558 and 1559 carry his signature.[6] Most of his medals of the Este family and its circle date from these years. Whereas his earliest pieces had been small—medals of from 35 to 40 mm were usual in the 1540s—his works for the Este grew larger, and he now abandoned his plain borders in favor of showier raised and beaded ones.

Though Pastorino himself executed few reverses, some of his marriage medals do occur as two-sided pieces—the bridegroom on one side, the bride on the other—and many late aftercasts of his works are found spuriously combined with similar-size reverses by either Leone Leoni (cat. nos. 49–52) or Jacopo da Trezzo (cat. nos. 54–55).

Pastorino's movements over the next decades are shadowy, although the large number of Ferrarese subjects portrayed on his medals strongly suggests that he remained based in that city throughout the 1560s. A medal of Francesco de' Medici from 1560 may indicate a journey to Florence,[7] and in 1561 he was clearly in Mantua (see cat. no. 69). In 1574 the artist was working for Camillo Gonzaga (1521–1595) in the mint at Novellara, where he produced medals of both Count Camillo and his younger brother Alfonso (1529–1589).[8] After a brief sojourn in Bologna, he then returned to his native Tuscany and in 1576 entered the service of Francesco de' Medici as a master of stucco work. In the same year he executed a medal bearing portraits of Francesco on one side and his wife Giovanna of Austria (1547–1578) on the other.[9] It is sometimes said that Pastorino's last dated medals are from the late 1570s, yet it is clear from his medal of Cosimo de' Medici's widow Camilla (1545–1590) that he was still active in 1584.[10] He also produced medals in colored wax.

Pastorino was dismissed from his post in 1589, and died at an advanced age in December 1592. He was buried in S. Maria Maggiore in Rome.

Philip Attwood

67 obv.

Italy's Jews were by no means immune to the fashion for medals of the mid sixteenth century. A medal from 1552, apparently of Venetian workmanship, portrays Elia Delatas and his mother Rica, members of a family that had settled in Rome in the late fifteenth century.[3] And just prior to the Nasi medal, Pastorino had executed a medal of the banker Abramo Emanuele Norsa, also of Ferrara.[4] The legend on the obverse of the Delatas medal, ELIA DE LATAS EBREO MD52 (Elia Delatas, the Jew. 1552), and the use of Hebrew letters on the present one — their earliest appearance on a personal medal — reflect the pride these individuals felt regarding their origins and reveal how open they could be about their Jewishness in this period. The absence of later parallels to these medals coincides with, but is not wholly explained by, the increasing success of the Counter-Reformation and the growing intolerance toward Italy's Jews.

Philip Attwood

Pastorino
Lucrezia de' Medici (1545–1561)
68
Lead, cast, uniface
Diameter 69 mm
American private collection

Obverse: Bust facing left, wearing a low-cut gown with bodice, one jewel suspended from a chain lying across her shoulders, another suspended from a row of pearls at her neck, and an earring. Her hair is tied in a bun adorned with a diadem. Legend: LUCRETIA MED[ices] • FERR[ariae] • PRINC[ipessa] • A[nno] • A[etatis] • XIII • (Lucrezia de' Medici, princess of Ferrara, in her thirteenth year). Incised signature P on the shoulder. Incised date 1558 on the truncation. Raised and beaded border.
Reverse: Plain.

Pastorino
Grazia Nasi (born 1540)
67
Bronze, cast, uniface
Diameter 66.0 mm
Paris, Bibliothèque Nationale, Cabinet des Médailles
AV 746

Obverse: Bust to left, wearing a low-cut gown with bodice, a jewel suspended from a necklace adorned with pearls, and an earring. A veil, also adorned with pearls, covers her hair, which is arranged in a bun, and falls down her back. Legend: נשיא • גרציאה • A[nno] • Æ[tatis] • XVIII (Grazia Nasi, in her eighteenth year). The incised signature P on the truncation. Raised and beaded border.
Reverse: Plain.

Grazia was the wife of Samuel Nasi, a member of the widely scattered Jewish family of that name, who resided in Ferrara for a time. Samuel's brother Joseph Nasi (c. 1520–1579) was a Turkish military leader and the duke of Naxos. His aunt, the older Grazia Nasi (1510–1568), was a celebrated philanthropist who fled Lisbon after the death of her husband and traveled to Antwerp and Venice and subsequently, about 1550, to Ferrara. She later settled in Constantinople, as did her niece, the subject of this medal.[1]

It has often been claimed that this is a portrait of the older Grazia. However she would have been eighteen — the age given on the medal — in 1538. That was ten years before Pastorino's first dated medal and some fifteen years before his first medals of this size. Moreover, the style of the dress and the arrangement of the hair tend to place the work in the 1550s. It is therefore more likely that this is the niece. The medal may have been commissioned in celebration of her marriage, for Pastorino executed a number of medals of brides.[2]

68 obv.

68 obv.

69 obv.

itself to large-scale production, or that their medals lacked the reverses exploited so energetically for their propaganda potential by the sixteenth-century popes and by the Medici from Cosimo on.

For the Este, Pastorino was the ideal medalist. He was an effective portraitist who had no interest in the subtle riddles of reverses. His likenesses provide no insight into his sitters' personalities, but they are also unaffected by the mannerist artificiality of an artist like Ruspagiari (cat. nos. 73–74), who also produced a medal of Duke Ercole II.[1]

Philip Attwood

Pastorino
Camillo Castiglione (1520–1598)
69
Bronze, cast, uniface
Diameter 68 mm
Washington, The National Gallery of Art, Samuel H. Kress
   Collection
1957.14.914

Obverse: Bearded bust facing right, wearing an elaborately decorated cuirass and ruff. Legend: CAMILLVS DE CASTILIONO BAL[dassari] • F[ilius] • (Camillo Castiglione, son of Baldassare). On the truncation, the incised date and signature: 1561 • P.
Reverse: Plain.

The son of the diplomat and man of letters Baldassare Castiglione (1478–1529), author of *The Book of the Courtier,* Camillo was himself a writer. Yet it is not inappropriate to find him portrayed wearing armor—albeit a decorative type that can have seen little fighting—for he had previously served in the army of Charles V (cat. nos. 77, 124–25, 156).

Camillo was born in Mantua, as was his father.[1] The elder Castiglione had been in the service of Lodovico Sforza, duke of Milan, and more recently that of Guidobaldo Malatesta and Francesco Maria della Rovere, dukes of Urbino. Returned to Mantua, he married Ippolita Torelli, and in the years 1516–18 completed his book of observations on life at court. In 1519 he again took up diplomacy, first for Mantua's Duke Federigo II Gonzaga, then from 1524 until his death as papal nuncio to Spain. He kept close ties to Mantua, nonetheless, and in the 1540s we already find his son Camillo at the Mantuan court of Duke Francesco III.

Pastorino, though still based in Ferrara at the time, sojourned in Mantua in 1561, perhaps summoned by Duke Guglielmo I, whose marriage in that year to Eleonora (1534–94), daughter of Emperor Ferdinand I, is recorded in a pair of portrait medals.[2] The artist also produced a medal of the duke's mother, Margarita (1510–1566), the widow of the elder Castiglione's former employer.[3] This medal of Camillo dates from that same visit.

Philip Attwood

Lucrezia was the daughter of Cosimo I de' Medici. At thirteen she was married to Alfonso d'Este, the son of Ercole II, duke of Ferrara. Pastorino's medal commemorates the occasion.

This marriage was arranged as part of the peace treaty concluded in May 1558 between Philip II of Spain (cat. nos. 58, 156), an ally of Duke Cosimo, and Ercole II d'Este. It took place some six weeks later. Alfonso was less than enthusiastic about the arrangement, and soon after the wedding he returned to France, where he held an honored position at the court of his cousin Henry II (cat. no. 145). Lucrezia remained in her native Florence. On the death of his father in 1559, Alfonso returned to Ferrara to assume the dukedom, and early in the following year his uncle Francesco d'Este (1516–1578), marquess of Massalombarda, escorted Lucrezia from Florence to her husband's capital, where her processional entry on February 14 was the occasion for prolonged public festivities. Only a little over a year later, on April 21, 1561, she died, possibly poisoned by her husband. In 1565, Alfonso married Barbara of Austria (1539–72), the daughter of Emperor Ferdinand I (cat. no. 124).

Pastorino had been mintmaster in Ferrara since 1554. He had also served as court medalist to Duke Ercole II, portraying members of the extensive Este family and its retainers. His earliest medals of Este family members are a pair of portraits of Alfonso's younger sisters, Lucrezia (1535–1598) and Eleonora (1537–1581), from 1552, at seventeen and fourteen respectively. Within a few years he had also produced medals of his employer, Ercole II, the duke's younger brothers Ippolito (1509–1572) and Francesco, and his sons Alfonso and Luigi (1538–1586). Together, these medals form a portrait gallery of Ferrara's ruling family. They are in no way political propaganda in the way that papal medals were beginning to be at the time or those of Cosimo de' Medici would shortly become. The Este saw medals as personal keepsakes, miniatures in bronze that might on occasion serve a diplomatic purpose, but were primarily intended as mementos for family, friends, and courtiers. It did not matter to them that the technique of casting did not lend

Alessandro Vittoria
(1525–1608)

Vittoria is one of the most important names in sixteenth-century Venetian sculpture, being responsible also for a number of medals.

Born in Trent, he may have received some training from the sculptors Giovanni Girolamo (c. 1510–1562) and Vincenzo Grandi. On his arrival in Venice in 1543, he began work under Jacopo Sansovino (1486–1570), training as an architect and sculptor. He remained there until 1547, when, following a disagreement with the older man, he left Venice and worked for a time in Vicenza. In 1550 he received payment from Sansovino for four river gods for the library of San Marco. In 1552 he was commissioned by Duke Ercole II d'Este to produce a model for a colossal statue of Hercules. This placed him in direct competition with Sansovino, for the duke had asked him for an identical work two years before. In the following year the sculptor left Vicenza to return to Venice, and apart from a visit to Padua in 1555 and a period in 1576–77 when he worked in Brescia and Vicenza so as to avoid the plague, he remained there until his death. He died in Venice on May 27, 1608, and was buried in the church of S. Zaccaria. A marble self-portrait bust forms part of the sculptor's monument in that church, and there is also a terra-cotta self-portrait bust in London's Victoria & Albert Museum.

Portrait busts comprise a large part of Vittoria's œuvre. He also executed life-size figures for the altars and tombs of Venetian churches and a certain amount of architectural sculpture, for example the statues of Iustitia and Venetia for the façade of the ducal palace. He also produced numerous small bronzes and reliefs, as well as works in stucco.

His known medals date from the early 1550s, a particularly fruitful period for the Venetian medal. Six are signed AV. Others have been attributed to the artist with more or less certainty. A medal bearing a portrait of the sculptor on one side and the Veronese painter Bernardino India (c. 1528–1590) is stylistically close to the signed works,[1] and probably belongs to the period in the early 1550s when Vittoria was providing stucco decoration for the Thiene Palace in Vicenza, and India was executing the palace's wall paintings.

Philip Attwood

Alessandro Vittoria
Pietro Aretino (1492–1557)
70
Bronze, cast
Diameter 58 mm
University of California at Santa Barbara, University Art Museum, Sigmund Morgenroth Collection

Obverse: Bearded bust facing right, wearing a gown with a fur collar and a chain. Legend: • DIVVS • PETRVS • ARETINVS (The divine Pietro Aretino). Below, the signature A.V.
Reverse: Four men presenting vessels to Aretino, who is seated on a raised throne and holding a book. All are dressed in the antique manner, the principal figure wearing a plumed helmet. Legend: • I PRINCIPI TRIBVTATI DAI POPOLI • IL SERVO LORO TRIBVTANO (The princes, having received tribute from the people, pay tribute to their servant).

The works of the satirist Pietro Aretino made him one of the most celebrated and notorious writers of his time. His lampoons first attracted attention in the Rome of Pope Leo X and his successors, but in 1524 the circulation of his sonnets based on the engravings of the erotic drawings of Giulio Romano (1499–1546) forced him to leave Rome, and in the following year his anti-papal satires necessitated a more permanent absence. He settled in Venice in 1527, and his political, religious, and humorous works won him an international reputation. Ariosto (1477–1533), in his *Orlando Furioso* of 1532, called him "il flagello de' principi." He never lost his notoriety, and his works

70 obv.

70 rev.

were included on the index of prohibited books. His love of self-publicity naturally attracted him to the medium of the medal.

Vittoria's medal shows the writer at the age of sixty. Leoni had portrayed him in 1537,[1] and there is also an anonymous Venetian medal of him.[2] Vittoria's portrait, the latest of the three, shows the vivacity that illuminated the writer's somewhat bovine features. The chain may be the one presented him by Francis I (cat. nos. 116, 139).

The reverse, showing the princes of the world paying tribute to Aretino, was intended to flatter the poet's vanity. In this it succeeded, as we know from a letter he wrote to Vittoria in January 1553: "These two medals, which represent in your style my likeness, together with the letter that you wrote to me on this matter, have been delivered to my house. Certainly the reverse, like every other that you have made, pleases me. Of the casting I will not speak, because it does not deserve too much in the way of praise. It is enough for me that in return you make for me several of them in bronze and in silver, because from Rome and elsewhere they are besought with eager insistence, for which I rejoice rather for your glory than mine."[3]

Aretino's criticism of the casting seems somewhat harsh, given the reasonable quality of surviving examples. Typically, Aretino did not allow his dissatisfaction with it to interfere with the distribution of his portrait.

The two medals to which Aretino refers would appear to have been sent from Vicenza on January 2, 1553.[4] It is possible, however, that the portrait may have been modeled somewhat earlier.

Philip Attwood

Giovanni di Bartolommeo dal Cavino, called Giovanni Cavino
(1500–1570)

Cavino was born in Padua,[1] where most of his work was produced and where he died. His first master was probably his father, Bartolommeo di Giovanni (died 1517), a goldsmith from San Giorgio delle Pertiche in Cavino d'Arsego,[2] from which the name Cavino derives. Cavino's brother Battista (died 1561) was also a goldsmith, as was his father-in-law, Bernardino da Trento, whose daughter, Romana, Cavino married in 1517. Cavino's will from May 16, 1570, mentions two sons: Camillo, who received his laureate in jurisprudence from the University of Padua, and to whom Cavino left his estate, and Giandomenico, who had followed his father in his career and predeceased him.[3]

A close connection between Cavino and the Paduan sculptor Andrea Riccio (1470–1532) suggests that Cavino may have trained under the latter after his father's death.[4] Riccio's sepulchral monument included a bronze portrait tondo, lost by the eighteenth century and replaced by a marble portrait, which Cavino is assumed to have made.[5]

Cavino's first documented works were two silver candlesticks, now lost, made c. 1527–29 for the Duomo in Padua. His only known signed works are his 1554–55 medal of Pope Julius III[6] and two medals of Jesus Christ,[7] one of which is dated by the artist 1565. These three pieces are atypical of Cavino, not only because they are signed, but also because of their subject matter. His sitters were usually either his Paduan contemporaries or figures from antiquity.

Cavino's medals are struck from steel dies, a large number of which survive.[8] His rather meticulous, dry style[9] is partly a result of the engraving process employed in making these dies. The artist worked in fairly low relief, often with great subtlety of detail, but he was not consistently successful in his compositions. His œuvre consists of over a hundred medals,[10] and the range of his abilities can be seen by comparing two medals dated 1540. In the medal of Girolamo Cornaro (flourished 1499–1540),[11] the beautiful bust, with curly hair and a flowing beard, neatly fills the obverse field, joining elegantly with the inscription to form a satisfying solution to the circular format. In the obverse of his Marco Antonio Contarini (died 1548),[12] however, the sitter's head perches on too small a bust, while the inscription crowds him from behind.

Cavino's best known and most notorious works are his medals of ancient subjects, Roman emperors for the most part, made in emulation or imitation of ancient coins. His friend Alessandro Bassiano, a noted antiquarian scholar and collector of ancient coins, is believed to have played an important advisory role in the production of these pieces.[13] Cavino's intention in creating them has been widely debated. His reputation swings from that of a shameless forger, who supplied spurious ancient objects to gullible collectors, to that of an intelligent creator of medals evoking the classical world.[14]

What we can perceive of Cavino's character tends to exonerate him. He was associated with the most learned men of Padua, many of whom were involved in the city's government or its famous university. A document of 1542[15] notes that he was asked to be an arbitrator in a dispute between two other goldsmiths. Both points suggest a character above reproach.

In addition, evidence shows that some Renaissance collectors would have known the difference between Cavino's medals and genuine antique coins. There are physical differences: some lettering forms in Cavino's pieces differ from those on ancient coinage, and also the Cavinos are regularly made on thinner flans and are of different weights than their ancient counterparts.[16] Since weights were a carefully controlled constant in ancient coinage (as they are in today's), any discrepancy could serve to alert the Renaissance collector that a Cavino piece was not a genuine coin.[17] On some of Cavino's restitutions the reverse was struck with the same die used on his medals of contemporary Paduans, so any collector familiar with those medals would also be able to recognize Cavino's authorship of the restitutions.[18]

Most important for Cavino's defense are contemporary descriptions that speak positively of his work. The earliest seems to have been in the engraver Enea Vico's 1555 study of ancient coins, where Cavino is called an imitator—as opposed to a forger—and excellence is cited as the reason for discussing him along with such artists as Cellini or Leone Leoni. A celebratory verse by Francesco Savonarola, published in 1560, couples Cavino and Bassiano, and says "your life, O Caesar, will always be illuminated through their numismatic art."[19]

Vilification of Cavino seems ultimately to be based on a misunderstanding of the manner in which ancient coins were appreciated in the Renaissance. For the sixteenth-century collector, it was the subject and type that usually mattered most. The genuineness of the coin was not the primary focus. Therefore, if a coin of a certain emperor was not available, a modern restitution by Cavino was deemed an acceptable substitute, one moreover having the advantage of greater clarity of detail, a rarity in genuine coins.[20]

Cavino's will stipulated that he was to be buried in the Paduan church of San Giovanni di Verdara. His tomb was later moved to the novitiate cloister in the Santo, not far from Riccio's monument, where it stands today.

Donald Myers

71 obv.   71 rev.

Giovanni Cavino
Alessandro Bassiano (born 1503–4, died 1587) with the Artist
71
Copper alloy, struck
Diameter 36.35 mm; diameter of outer perimeter of the inscription from the H of IOHAN through the stop before ALEXAND, 32.50 mm
Washington, The National Gallery of Art, Samuel H. Kress Collection
1957.14.982

Obverse: Bearded jugate busts of Bassiano and Cavino to the right (Cavino behind Bassiano), both robed in tunics *all'antica*. Legend, with floral or foliate designs as the first and third stops: • ALEXAND[er] • BASSIANVS • ET • IOHAN[nes] • CAVINEVS • PATAVINI (Alessandro Bassiano and Giovanni Cavino, Paduans).
Reverse: The semi-nude male figure of Genius sacrificing at a flaming altar, a patera in his right hand, a dolphin under his left arm. The inscription begins in the exergue, then continues counterclockwise around the circumference: GENIO BENEVEOLENTIAE DVLCIS (To the spirit of sweet benevolence).[1]

Alessandro Bassiano came from an important Paduan family originally from Bassano. He was considered one of the most passionate of Padua's antiquarian scholars.[2] A collector of ancient coins himself, he was the author of a treatise on the coinage of the twelve Caesars, one that included drawings of the coins and interpretations of their iconography and inscriptions.[3] Bassiano was therefore extremely well equiped to advise Cavino and is often thought of as a virtual partner.[4] The two men lived near one another,[5] and were coexecutors for the estate of the sculptor Andrea Riccio.[6] The importance of their friendship is clearly indicated by this medal's dual portrait, Cavino's only known essay into self-portraiture.[7]

Based on the appearance of the two men, the medal has been thought to date from around 1538, when Bassiano would have been about thirty-five, Cavino about thirty-eight.[8]

The Cavino and Bassiano medal is infused with classical feeling, testimony to the artist's interest in the ancient world, its coinage in particular. Both men wear tunics in the antique style. Cavino depicts himself realistically, with a long, hooked nose, a long beard, and hair parted in the middle. His treatment of Bassiano's profile is less harsh, though undoubtedly accurate. The use of the double bust motif derives from ancient coins or medallions and was uncommon in Renaissance medals before this time.[9]

This obverse is also found in other combinations, the most interesting of which bears as its reverse a portrait of the Paduan antiquarian Marco Mantova Benavides (1498–1582). Benavides was also an important influence on Cavino, and in keeping with his antiquarian interests he too is garbed *all'antica*.[10]

The genius figure on the reverse of this medal is derived from types used on ancient coins. The concept of a contrapposto figure gesturing to the right while holding an object in his left hand was found in many permutations, and served as the formula for a great number of allegories.[11] A possible model for Cavino is a coin of Nero, whose reverse is very similar to this one and whose inscription specifically describes the figure as a genius.[12] In both, the male figure is making a sacrifice at an altar, his right hand holding a patera above the flames. The figure and the altar are placed on an exergue line, a common device in Roman coins and one used regularly in Cavino's medals.

The dolphin, here replacing the cornucopia more commonly held by such figures, is probably meant to be a symbol of benevolence. The animal's amiable nature was well known to the Renaissance, especially through such works as Pliny's *Natural History*.[13] Cesare Ripa's 1593 study of iconography notes that the dolphin was the sign of a peaceful, loving spirit[14] and that a child on a dolphin was a symbol of gentleness because of the dolphin's instinctive love for mankind.[15]

Cavino's placement of the reverse inscription underscores this meaning. The three words are carefully lined up with their pictorial counterparts: GENIO appears directly below the figure; BENEVOLENTIAE continues around the medal's circumference to touch the dolphin's tail, and DVLCIS appears above the altar, calling to mind the sweet aroma of the incense or wine

72 obv.

being poured on the flames. The counterclockwise direction of the inscription that allows for this labelling effect is most atypical; it is rarely used by other Renaissance medalists, and rarely does it appear anywhere else in Cavino's œuvre or on the ancient coins and medallions that inspired him.

Cavino's medal of Giovanni Melsi (died 1559)[16] features a similar reverse, but with a portrait of Melsi himself as Genius, this time holding a cornucopia. The die for the obverse is in the Cabinet des Médailles of the Bibliothèque Nationale in Paris. The reverse die is presumably lost.

Donald Myers

Giovanni Cavino
Luca Salvioni (died 1536)
72
Copper alloy, struck
Diameter 38.45 mm; diameter of outer perimeter of the inscription from the V of SALVIONVS to the R of IVR, 32.70 mm
Washington, The National Gallery of Art, Samuel H. Kress Collection
1957.14.990

Obverse: Bust to right, wearing a robe. Legend: SALVIONVS • • IVR[is] • CON[sultus] • (Salvioni, jurisconsult).[1]
Reverse: Ceres wearing a mantle and holding a book and a cornucopia, a boar's head lying at her feet. Legend: LEGIFERAE CERERI (To Ceres, who gives the laws).

This medal couples a classically-derived reverse with a dignified portrait of the elderly Salvioni in a veristic style of astonishing depth and penetration. The old man's face is sunken and wrinkled, but his firm mouth and steady eyes reveal the vigorous force of his personality. Salvioni was a member of the Gallina family, originally from Milan.[2] The family sepulcher in the church of the Eremitani in Padua includes a carved stemma surmounted by a hen (Italian *gallina*), a fitting symbol for a family that made its living from agriculture. Luca did not follow this tradition, choosing to study law instead and becoming a jurist in 1497. He was also interested in antiquity and owned an effigy of Cicero.[3]

The medal is usually dated to about 1536, the year of Salvioni's death. It may have been made somewhat earlier, however, since Cavino must have known the sitter by 1532 at the latest. In May of that year, Salvioni served as lawyer for the aging sculptor Andrea Riccio,[4] who had named Cavino a coexecutor of his estate two months before.[5] It is more than likely that the two would have met in connection with this matter.[6] A further link between the two was Cavino's close friend Alessandro Bassiano (cat. no. 71), who praises the lawyer in his manuscript on Roman coins as "excellentissimum iurisconsultum civemque nostrum."[7]

The Ceres reverse nicely combines reference to Salvioni's legal career and to his family's interests. The goddess is generally thought of in connection with agriculture,[8] yet here she is to be understood primarily as a symbol of jurisprudence.[9]

72 obv.   72 rev.

Ancient myth relates that it was she who first taught men to plant crops. The need to regulate the demarcation of fields then led to the development of law. In his *Metamorphoses,* a well known iconographical source in the Renaissance, Ovid acknowledges the goddess's double nature.[10] On the medal, Ceres proffers a book of law, an illustration of the term LEGIFERAE further emphasized in that the book penetrates between the letters of the word itself. She also holds a cornucopia, the traditional symbol of agricultural abundance, and the boar's head represents her vigilance against wild animals that might destroy ripening crops.[11]

Ceres frequently appears on the reverses of ancient coins and medallions, sometimes with the designation LEGIFERA, which inspired Cavino's reverse. A denarius of the Syrian governor Gaius Pescennius Niger (A.D. 193–94) features a standing Ceres on the reverse, with the inscription CERERI FRVGIFERAE (To Ceres who bears fruit), a formulation very similar to the one on the present medal.[12]

Cavino used this reverse in two other combinations: with the obverse portraying Alessandro Bassiano and the medalist himself (cat. no. 71) and with a portrait of Niccolò Verzi, a jurist like Salvioni.[13]

Cavino's Salvioni obverse is also found in combination with a portrait of Marco Mantova Benavides (1489–1582)[14] and again with a third reverse depicting a female figure restraining a rearing horse, an allegory of Padua.[15] The dies for the Salvioni portrait and the Ceres reverse are in the Cabinet des Médailles of the Bibliothèque Nationale, Paris.

Donald Myers

Alfonso Ruspagiari
(1521–1576)

Ruspagiari was baptized at Reggio Emilia on July 28, 1521. About fifty years later he was named superintendent (*soprastante*) of its mint, and it was in that city that he died between August and October 1575.[1] Almost nothing is known of his activity as an artist, although it would appear to extend from about 1536 to 1575. His work from the earlier years of this period remains to be clarified.

The Ruspagiari family was well established in the environs of Reggio.[2] Alfonso married Ippolita Bonzagno (died 1578),[3] not the woman named Lucia portrayed on a medal generally attributed to him.[4] Ippolita also seems to have belonged to a cultivated family.[5] Their first child was born in 1541, an early point of reference in the artist's chronology and one close to the date of 1536 proposed for the medal of Ercole II d'Este attributed to Ruspagiari.[6] The medalist surely knew the painter and sculptor Alessandro Ardenti (died 1595), of whom he did a medal, and it seems likely that he knew Lelio Orsi (c. 1511–1587; see the discussion of cat. no. 74).

Ruspagiari is referred to as a repairer or curator of sculptures (*conservator statuorum*) and assessor of foodstuffs (*judex victualium*) in 1572.[7] From 1570 to 1574 he was engaged to determine the solidity of a bridge and an aqueduct affected by new construction of the fortifications of Reggio. From his will it appears that he died a wealthy man, which attests to a certain measure of success as artist and civil servant.[8]

Although the artists of the Emilian school have often been discussed as a group, little attempt has been made to distinguish their respective styles. The limited amount of information known about these medalists is partly responsible for such neglect. A systematic analysis of the actual production of the Emilian mints and their professional organization and structure would address the need for such fundamental documentation. The present exhibition provides an opportunity to compare the work of two of these artists, Ruspagiari and Bombarda.

In contrast with the portrait medals signed BOM, those attributed to Ruspagiari are less often identified by inscriptions. The latter have a more pictorial quality and a sense of heightened drama, their figures turning vigorously within the limited depth of the medal. They also show a greater variety of formats than those attributed to Bombarda or Signoretti. The agitated, ambiguous, and truly mannered vocabulary of these Emilian artists challenge any curious scholar to further research.

Mary L. Levkoff

Alfonso Ruspagiari
Bust of a Woman Viewed by a Face in Profile
73
Lead alloy, hollow uniface cast
Diameter 69.5 mm; horizontal measurement inside the frame,
    47.8 mm
New York, Michael Hall Collection

Obverse: Bust of a woman, shown in three-quarter profile, as though floating in the oval field of the relief. The truncation of the bust is bound by a narrow rigid girdle, through which a light veil is intertwined. The veil is bunched at the center under a grotesque mask that seems to be attached to the girdle, while the rest of it is swept behind the bust and knotted over the left shoulder. A pendant on a ribbon hangs from the woman's neck. Her hair is elaborately wound with a twisted cord and a veil. Her right shoulder is raised. Both arms have been truncated just below the shoulder. This is given arresting emphasis by the bold position of the truncation of the proper right arm, with the signature A • R appearing in the cut presented directly to the

73 obv.

viewer. The woman's face, in profile facing right, is confronted by the profile of another face looking in from a scrolled frame cast integrally as part of this relief. There is a trace of drapery at the base of the neck of this second face.
Reverse: Plain.

This object is not, technically speaking, a medal. It portrays no known person, nor does it commemorate an identifiable place or event.[1] It has usually been classified as a medal, however, and indeed it is one of the most compellingly romantic images in medallic art from the Renaissance. The very anonymity of its figures, their abstract reduction, their ambiguous spatial relationship, and the unknown function and purpose of this relief are the basic ingredients of mystery.

Still elusive, the subject of this relief calls to mind the fifteenth-century *Double Portrait* by Fra Filippo Lippi in The Metropolitan Museum of Art, New York,[2] which may show a suitor come to admire his beloved. In the medal, however, the intruding face seems to be staring at a sculptured bust, so that it is perhaps an allusion to the story of Pygmalion, gazing at his sculpture and wishing it to come to life. If, on the other hand, the second face is female, then the subject of the encounter could become an illustration of *vanitas* (see cat. no. 134).[3]

Because of its format and signature, this relief was once associated with a number of other medals with integrally cast voluted frames, some signed AA, others AR and AAR. Hill suggested attributing a coherent group of those signed AA to the sculptor Agostino Ardenti, who, he suggested, was the brother of the painter Alessandro Ardenti.[4] Of that group, only the portrait of Agostino himself was unsigned, and an example of it occurs as the reverse of a medal of Alessandro. The absence of a signature led Hill to conclude that Agostino was the author of that medal, because the artist would have had no need to sign his own portrait. This, however, would be in contrast with the interpretation given here to the word IDEM on the large self-portrait by Ruspagiari (cat. no. 74).

74 obv.

Furthermore, Burckhardt demonstrated in his study of the Demoulin Collection at Basel[5] that another group had to be by Alessandro, because his name is listed in the inventory of that collection drawn up in 1576 by Basilius Amerbach, the purchaser of Demoulin's medals. These were signed with the A and R bound together, and they were almost all portraits of figures from the court of Savoy, where Alessandro was painter to the duke. In conjunction with this, it is useful to recall that Baudi di Vesme quoted sources describing Alessandro as a sculptor, and that he had had considerable practice as a portraitist.[6] Burckhardt's critical eye turned, as had Hill's, to the heavier, more sculptural character of the medals with the elaborately scrolled borders and signed AA, dating from around 1563.[7] These, Burckhardt agreed, were to be attributed to Agostino Ardenti rather than Ruspagiari. The present medal would be considered their source. Its frame, of a much more subdued design, with only one turn and break in the lateral volutes, also occurs in the unsigned (and unattributed) medal of Pierre Bey in the British Museum,[8] but not among those published by Hill or Burckhardt.

While the portrait busts in the medals attributed to Agostino are almost as abbreviated as that of Ruspagiari's small self-portrait,[9] some truncated just below the base of the neck, they have neither the sense of movement, the subtly contrasting textures, nor the challenging manipulation of depth and illusion that distinguish his compositions. Even in the small self-portrait the delicate swag adds a gracefully curving note to the composition and with brilliant economy suggests the illusion of the third dimension. The medals attributed to Agostino lack the elegance of Ruspagiari's.

The fascination of the present medal lies not only in its juxtaposion of a smoothly classical bust, a rigid metal band, and a filmy veil, but also in its enigmatic confrontation between the animate and the ambiguously inanimate.

Mary L. Levkoff

Alfonso Ruspagiari
Large Self-Portrait
74
Lead, cast, uniface
Diameter 79 mm
Washington, The National Gallery of Art, Samuel H. Kress Collection
1957.14.1042

Obverse: Bust from the front, the face turned sharply to the right, with only a hint of the contour of the brow and moustache mitigating the severe linearity of the profile. The thick, short hair is richly textured. The medalist wears a filmy shirt belted at the waist and caught at the center of his chest in a lion's-head brooch. A thin strap, clipped with another little mask, crosses his chest from the left shoulder. A cloak is thrown about his right arm and shoulder, re-emerges under his left arm, and then sweeps across the front of his body. His right hand grasps a reed pipe.[1] The left arm is severed above the elbow with a twisted cloth tied above the cut. Legend: ALF[onsi] RUSPAGIARII REGIEN[sis] ([Portrait of] Alfonso Ruspagiari of Reggio). Below the bust, the word IDEM and the signature AR.
Reverse: Plain.

This is one of two medallic self-portraits by Ruspagiari. The other, smaller one is a clear profile subtly terminated along the ridge of the collarbone and draped by a single looped swag that adds an illusion of depth to the design.[2] In the present medal, the full upper torso of the artist is shown from the front. The flesh of his prominent chest is rendered with a disturbingly female amplitude. Another arresting feature that contributes to the ambiguity of this figure is the drastic amputation of the left arm.

The design of this figure has a breadth and freedom unusual even for the Emilian school, and the drapery is handled with the

74 obv.

fluidity of a consummate modeler. The inscription, with letters of minimal size and broad spaces between them, lacks the graphic density of those on more classic medals. The medallic character of this portrait is thereby undermined, and indeed its overall design seems to be virtually independent of the circular format. This portrait medal is truly pictorial in conception.

In virtually all aspects save the face, the composition of the medal corresponds to a drawing attributed to Lelio Orsi in the Galleria Estense in Modena.[3] The drawing's small size and circular format are appropriate to the form of a medal. It was apparently first identified by Giulio Bariola, who suggested that it was either the sketch for the medal or copied from it.[4] Salvini and Chiodi published it as a study for the medal in 1951, suggesting that the traces of the face were added later.[5] Pirondini has more recently noted that the drawing appears to have been "destined for a female figure," but that Ruspagiari nevertheless joined it to his profile self-portrait for the purpose of the medal.[6]

It is impossible to know why Ruspagiari would have taken the drawing of another artist (complete with syrinx, the presence of which is otherwise unexplained) as the basis for his own self-portrait, or why he should have chosen a figure of such ambiguous sex. Such ambiguity occurs elsewhere in Orsi's œuvre. The Christ in his *Resurrection* (Modena, Galleria Estense) and the figure of the boy in his *Sacrifice of Isaac* (Naples, Museo di Capodimonte) are no less equivocal, while neither Orsi nor Ruspagiari's female figures compare to the one on the medal. Of course it may be that Ruspagiari deliberately chose Orsi's design because of its very ambiguity. The confusion that it causes in the viewer's eye is part of the spell cast by the mannerist artists, whose motives still resist the scientific dissection practiced in modern scholarship.

Ruspagiari's presumed use of the drawing by Orsi may have to do with the latter's involvement with the Novellara mint, which is documented in two letters written by Gian Antonio Signoretti (active 1540–1602) to Alfonso Gonzaga, count of Novellara (died 1596), in December 1569, describing for the count the coins to be struck at Novellara under Orsi's supervision.[7] There are other works by Orsi that bear a distinct similarity to those of Ruspagiari, such as his painted busts in grisaille from the Casino di Sopra at Novellara, but it is important to note that it was the medalist, not the painter, who developed the concept of the portrait. There seem to be no portraits in Orsi's known œuvre.[8]

Orsi is but one artist whose relationship to Ruspagiari needs to be clarified. Because Ruspagiari's vocabulary and designs are quite varied, with ever-shifting relationships to the work of his contemporaries, his œuvre should not be studied in isolation, but rather in the context of Emilian art as a whole, especially sculpture. His treatment of the varied textures in his medal of Ercole II d'Este (c. 1536?) may show his awareness of the terracotta sculpture of his near-contemporary Antonio Begarelli (born c. 1484–1500, died 1565), specifically the figure of John the Baptist in Begarelli's *Deposition* (Modena, S. Francesco, 1531) or the shepherds in his *Adoration* (Modena, Duomo,

1527). Ruspagiari's female portraits bear a similarity to the female figures in Begarelli's terra-cotta sketch for the *Deposition* (London, Victoria & Albert Museum), with their soft fullness and decorative impulses.

The strong affinities between Ruspagiari's medals and those of some of his contemporaries must be taken into account before defining his artistic personality. The scrolled pedestal in his medal of Camilla Ruggeri,[9] for example, is quite like the one in Bombarda's medal of Leonora Cambi (cat. no. 75), but we have no idea which of them used it first. Although their compositions may be similar, Ruspagiari's works are more distinguished; his figures have an alertness and nobility of carriage absent from the designs of Bombarda.

Ruspagiari's relationship to Alessandro Ardenti, court painter (and sculptor) to the dukes of Savoy, would be better understood if more of the latter's works had survived.[10] This might have indicated the origin of Ruspagiari's design for his medal of Ardenti,[11] in which he is portrayed from the back as though arrested in the act of painting. Furthermore, the framed format of the medal showing a bust of a woman and a second face (cat. no. 73) may be either the source or a copy of a work by another Ardenti, a medalist whose signature may take the form of either AA or AR.

Perhaps it was because his own signature tended to be confused with that of this second Ardenti that Ruspagiari took such pains to identify himself on the present self-portrait, even though he may have borrowed its design from Orsi's drawing. Ruspagiari refers to himself three times in the medal: once in the legend, again with his initials in the free-form exergue, and yet again with the word IDEM (the same). In this way he asserts that this is his own portrait, not that of some other medalist using the same initials. While this leaves no doubt about Ruspagiari's identity in the medal, it paradoxically deepens the contradiction in the origin, purpose, and authorship of the drawing attributed to Lelio Orsi, unless of course it is in fact a drawing by Ruspagiari for his self-portrait medal.

Mary L. Levkoff

Bombarda
(active 1540–1575)

The signature BOM or BOMB, universally assumed to be an abbreviation of the word Bombarda (in Italian related to words signifying "bombardment" or "bombardier"), appears on a fairly coherent group of some seventeen medals,[1] a number of which portray women dressed as fantasies *all'antica,* often represented as sculptured portrait busts supported on scrolled brackets. For reasons that are still unclear, the cognomen Bombarda was attached to members of a Cremonese family of sculptors and goldsmiths named Cambi. Cognates of the name Bombarda would suggest that members of this family were involved in the production of munitions. The casting of cannon immediately brings to mind, of course, another product of major foundries: full-scale bronze sculptures. Indeed, "Bombarda" is attached

75 obv.

definitively to the name Cambi by the end of the sixteenth century; it occurs in documents as a surname of Belisario Cambi, active as a sculptor of bronzes.[2]

An artist named Cambi worked in the mint at Reggio Emilia beginning in 1540, taking the post held there by Pastorino (cat. nos. 67–69) after the latter moved on to the mint in Ferrara in 1554. There seems to be no consensus in modern scholarship, however, on whether this artist was named Andrea or Giovanni Battista Cambi.[3]

Medals signed BOM or BOMB place the artist in Ferrara around 1560. That of Lucrezia de' Medici (cat. no. 68), duchess of Ferrara,[4] probably dates from 1560, the year Lucrezia arrived there to join her husband, Alfonso II d'Este, who succeeded to the dukedom following the death of his father Ercole II in 1559. It is assumed that the unsigned medal of Alfonso was also done by Bombarda, and can be dated to the year of his accession.[5] The signed medal of Violante Brasavola Pigna,[6] wife of Alfonso's secretary Giambattista Pigna (of whom Bombarda also executed a medal with a reverse attributed to the humanist Achille Bocchi),[7] evokes the cultured world the medalist may have known in the Emilian courts.

Much remains to be clarified, discovered, and identified in the œuvre of the medalist (or medalists) called Bombarda. There appear to be no consistent similarities between the production of the mint at Reggio[8] and the medals signed by Bombarda. Furthermore, it has been thought that Ruspagiari's work was influenced by Bombarda's because one of the Cambi family preceded Ruspagiari at the Reggio mint, although other arguments have suggested that the direction of influence was instead from Ruspagiari (and Signoretti; active c. 1540, died 1602) to Bombarda.[9] In addition, the discovery of casts of Emilian and Milanese medals in the excavations of Bernard Palissy's ateliers in the Tuileries[10] will contribute to a further understanding of the important transmission of North Italian style to France in the sixteenth century. It is hoped that the archival research necessary to identify the artist(s) known as Bombarda, outside the scope of the present study, will be stimulated by this exhibition.

Mary L. Levkoff

Bombarda
Leonora Cambi
75
Lead, cast, uniface
Diameter 69 mm
London, The British Museum, formerly Lanna Collection 1911.6.9.2

Obverse: Bust in three-quarter view with the face in profile to the right. The sitter wears a diaphanous blouse with vertical slashes caught by bands and above her right shoulder by a grotesque head. The upper edging of her costume is held together by an articulated jewel in the form of a mask with a spiked aureole. The drapery slips away to leave her left breast exposed. A fringed scarf flutters lightly about her left shoulder. A doubled rope of pearls encircles her neck. Her hair is arranged in curls and braids intertwined with a bit of veil that is knotted at the back. Her arms are truncated above the elbow, and a pedestal sets the bust high in the medal's field. The front of the pedestal is itself sculptured with a human figure of indeterminate sex supporting a shield or coat of arms. In small, broadly spaced Roman letters, the legend: LEONORAE CAMB • VXORIS ([Portrait] of Leonora, wife of Cambi). In smaller letters below the arm truncation, the signature BOM[barda]. *Reverse*: Plain.

Inasmuch as the lady portrayed here is identified as the wife of Cambi, surely the medalist himself, this medal may yet hold the key, still undiscovered, to the secure identification of this artist, because any civil document relating to her would probably reveal the name of her husband.

As in other medals signed BOM, Leonora's face is described in a pure profile facing right.[1] The elaborateness of her costume is the salient characteristic of a group of medals produced in Emilia in the second half of the sixteenth century, not only by Bombarda, but also by Ruspagiari (cat. nos. 73–74) and the artist who signs himself S, assumed to be Gian Antonio Signoretti (active c. 1540, died 1603). The origins and development of the distinctive style of the Emilian school of medalists have yet to be firmly traced. Its portrait style may have grown out of that of its Lombard neighbors Leone Leoni (cat. nos. 49–52), Pompeo Leoni, and Jacopo da Trezzo (cat. nos. 54–55), and it is also surely indebted to a type favored by Pastorino (cat. nos. 67–69), several of whose portraits show the arms cut abruptly, with the truncations exposed. The Emilian style is also probably allied in its decorative sense to the work of Abondio (cat. nos. 60–63). The Emilians nevertheless treated the portrait medal with much greater fluidity and idiosyncrasy. The types and locations of the truncations diverge widely and arbitrarily from conventional formulas; inscriptions are reduced in importance, and borders are rare. The likeness is treated with a heightened mannerism that often represents it as a sculptured portrait bust, at two removes from reality. Physically, the portrait is rendered with an ineffable delicacy, stretched to the limits of imagination. In the thinnest lead examples the image appears as if pressed in silk sarcenet the color of anthracite, and the costumes, animated by such whimsical details as slashes, bands, jewels, and scarves as in the present example, are as fabulous and eccentric as any worn later by English masquers.

This gossamer fantasy has not always been appreciated. Physically insubstantial, these medals were condemned by Hill,[2] and Habich referred to them as "Boudoir-Medallistik."[3] They seem to be conjured, not modeled. An instructive contrast in style can be observed in the medals of Lucrezia de' Medici by Bombarda and Pastorino (cat. no. 68).

The medals produced by the Emilian school cannot have been as incidental as Habich's disparaging remarks would imply, for they show that their subjects were content to be memorialized in a classically heroic mode and clothed in fantasy, in images full of the honeyed mannerism of the Emilian style.[4] These arbitrary combinations of semi-nudity, fantasy, and contemporary dress reflect an extremely high level of sophistication.[5]

It can be said that in the third quarter of the sixteenth century, after the death of Parmigianino (1503–1540) and the departure of Niccolò dell'Abbate (1512–1571) for France in 1552, Emilian portraiture would be conveyed not in the primary vehicles of painting or freestanding sculpture, but rather in the medium of medals.

Mary L. Levkoff

Jacopo Primavera
(c. 1544–c. 1600)

As early as 1875, in his study of Primavera, Chabouillet noted that medalists had rarely been the subjects of the kind of intensive art historical investigation routinely accorded to painters, sculptors, and architects.[1] Not the least of the problems confronting any student of these artists is that they frequently migrated from court to court in search of employment, and documentation of their wanderings is sorely lacking. Pri-

mavera is a perfect case in point, for though he left a significant number of signed medals, only a single contemporary reference to him has come to light, a literary mention of him from 1588.[2]

Undaunted, Chabouillet proceeded to suggest a probable birth date for the medalist, probe into his origins and formative influences, and review his possible itinerary. He did so solely on the basis of the medals themselves. These are uniface pieces, most of them signed, some indicating the age of the sitter at the time the work was cast. Since his subjects include members of the French nobility and prominent French poets and religious leaders whose birth dates are known, it is therefore possible in many cases to date his medals precisely. They span the years from 1568 to 1585. Among his few non-French subjects are the rival queens Elizabeth I and Mary Queen of Scots (cat. no. 76).

A medallic self-portrait at the age of thiry-six suggests that Primavera was born around 1544. His name alone establishes his Italian origin, but as further proof of it, Chabouillet points out the way the artist spelled the name Stuart on his medal of the Scottish queen.[3] In some respects the hybrid style of his medals reflects that of the distinguished Italian medalists Jacopo da Trezzo (cat. nos. 54–55) and Leone Leoni (cat. nos. 49–52), intimating that he may have received his early training in Milan or elsewhere in Lombardy.[4] There is also a similarity between his medals and those of the Siena-born artist Pastorino (cat. nos. 67–69). To judge from the majority of Primavera's subjects, much if not all of his working career was conceivably spent in France. It has often been assumed that he also worked in the Netherlands, but since there is no documentary evidence, this is mere conjecture. In all probability he died around 1600; it is not known where.

Primavera appears to have played a considerable role in the dissemination of the humanistic art of the portrait medal beyond Italy. It was through the migration to France of this medalist and others like him that a taste for the Italian form gradually came to replace to a great extent that country's struck and coinlike medals of Gothic character. Total acceptance of the Italian tradition was only later expressed in the large, double-sided medallions by France's native son Guillaume Dupré (cat. nos. 146–50), combining portraits with allegorical reverses of supreme technical achievement. Interestingly enough, Dupré's career began in about 1600, at the very time Primavera is presumed to have died.

An exhaustive reappraisal of this innovative, individualistic, and influential artist is long overdue.

Joseph R. Bliss

Jacopo Primavera
Mary Queen of Scots (1542–1587)
76
Bronze, cast, uniface
Diameter 67 mm
London, The British Museum
M6880

Obverse: Bust to the right, with dainty features and tautly curled

76 obv.

hair. The sitter is dressed in sombre funerary garments. A wired headband partly covers her coiffure, from which rises a hooded and veiled mourning train that billows in loosely cascading folds to envelop her right side. Her plain bodice is relieved only by a small ruff with an underlying collar and buttons extending from the throat to a lace barbe. Legend: MARIA STOVVAR REGI[na] SCOTI[ae] ANGLI[ae] (Mary Stuart [or Stewart], queen of Scotland [and] England). In an arc to the left of the portrait, the signature: IA[cobus] • PRIMAVE[ra]. Pearled border.
Reverse: Plain.

Mary Stuart was the daughter of King James V of Scotland and Mary of Guise (1515–1560).[1] She inherited the Scottish crown in infancy after the death of her father. Through her grandmother, Margaret Tudor, sister of Henry VIII and wife of James IV of Scotland, she was also next in line after Henry's children to the throne of England. Sent to France at the age of five, the young queen enjoyed an idyllic childhood at the court of Henry II (cat. no. 145) and Catherine de' Medici. At sixteen, in 1558, she was married to the Dauphin, and on his accession as Francis II in 1559 she became the queen consort of France. In the following year she was widowed, and in 1561 she returned to Scotland, then under the control of a league of Protestant lords.

Though she had been raised a staunch Catholic, she managed to rule without too much interference, yet she was clearly preoccupied with the notion of becoming queen of England as well. To that end she married in 1565 her cousin Henry Stewart, Lord Darnley (1545–1567), who was also a Tudor and a Catholic. Together they plotted to take the English throne by force, mistakenly assuming that English Catholics would support them. In 1566 Mary gave birth to a son, and in 1567—possibly with her connivance—Darnley was murdered. Within three months she then married James Hepburn, fourth earl of Bothwell (1536?–1578), the chief suspect in Darnley's assassina-

tion. Having alienated the Scottish nobles by this marriage, Mary was forced to send Bothwell into exile and abdicate in favor of her son, who thus became James VI at the age of one in 1567. She herself sought refuge in England, where she spent the remaining years of her life in comfort, but a prisoner of Elizabeth I. Various Catholic attempts to overthrow Elizabeth in favor of Mary were uncovered over the years, and finally, in 1587, the English queen was persuaded to have her rival beheaded. Always a stoic and worldly, at her trial Mary aptly responded: "Look to your consciences and remember that the theater of the world is wider than the realm of England."[2] Shortly before her own death, ironically enough, Elizabeth named as her heir Mary's son, James VI, who thereby became the first sovereign to rule a unified Scotland and England.

In this medal the artist has produced a highly descriptive, sensitive, and psychologically evocative portrayal of the exiled queen. Her tiny and sharply angled features convey her strength of character, singularity of purpose, and lofty ambition. No one, as yet, has managed to establish a firm date for the work.[3] It would appear that only Chabouillet and Mazerolle have correctly noted that the queen is dressed in widow's weeds.[4] This, coupled with her apparent age in the portrait, would suggest that the medal was produced shortly after the death of her last husband in 1578. By that time Mary had long been in exile in England, and though the inscription identifies her as such, she was in fact no longer queen of Scotland and by no means queen of England. It seems probable that the piece was commissioned by a Catholic sympathizer. The dating proposed above is further supported in that the costume and profile on this medal coincide stylistically with at least one of the portraits of Mary printed in an early history of Scotland, *De origine, moribus et rebus gestis Scotorum,* first published in Rome in 1578, by John Leslie, bishop of Ross and Mary's ambassador during her English captivity.[5]

Joseph R. Bliss

192

56 obv.

56 rev.

59 obv.

59 rev.

194

58 rev.

69 obv.

62 obv.

72 obv.

73 obv.

77 obv.

80 obv.

84 obv.

83 obv.

85 obv.

91 obv.

91 rev.

93 obv.

94 obv.

93a obv.

96 obv.

95 obv.

200

Germany

SIXTEENTH CENTURY

For the convenience of the reader, the dates of
political leaders most frequently encountered are
provided below. All other life dates appear in the text.

The Holy Roman Empire
Maximilian I (born 1459, emperor 1493–1519)
Charles V (born 1500, emperor 1519–56, died 1558)
Ferdinand I (born 1503, emperor 1556–64)
Maximilian II (born 1527, emperor 1564–76)
Rudolf II (born 1552, emperor 1576–1612)
Matthias (born 1557, emperor 1612–19)

France
Charles VIII (born 1470, king 1483–98)
Louis XII (born 1462, king 1498-1515)
Francis I (born 1494, king 1515–47)
Henry II (born 1519, king 1547–59)

England
Henry VIII (born 1491, king 1509–47)

Saxony (Ernestine line)
Frederick III, "the Wise" (born 1463, elector 1486–1525)
Johann, "the Steadfast" (born 1468, elector 1525–32)
Johann Friedrich, "the Magnanimous" (born 1503, elector
1532–47, died 1554)

Saxony (Albertine line)
Maurice (born 1521, duke 1541–47, duke and
elector 1547–53)
Augustus I (born 1526, elector 1553–86)
Christian I (born 1560, elector 1586–91)

77 obv.

77 rev.

Hans Krafft
(1481–1542)

Hans Krafft was trained in Nuremberg as a goldsmith, but apparently none of his works survive. In 1502 he was engaged as a die-cutter at the municipal mint, where he worked until 1512. Subsequently he appears to have worked on his own. In 1510 he began experimenting with the production of large coins and medals, for which he developed his own striking procedure. He was first employed by Frederick the Wise of Saxony and then by the city of Nuremberg.

Hermann Maué

Hans Krafft
Charles V (born 1500, emperor 1519–1556, died 1558)
77
Silver, cast planchet with struck images
Diameter 71.5 mm
Nuremberg, Germanisches Nationalmuseum, on permanent
  loan from the City of Nuremberg, Kress Collection
Med K 6

Obverse: Bust of the young, beardless emperor facing to the right. He wears a breastplate, above which hangs the chain of the Order of the Golden Fleece. On his head sits a delicate stirrup crown, its circlet adorned with stylized lilies. Legend: CAROLVS • V • RO[manorum] • IMPER[ator] • (Charles V, emperor of the Romans). The inner field is set off by a narrow, stylized laurel wreath, and a second such wreath circles the outer edge. At the top, between these two wreaths, the emperor's motto PLVS VLTRA (More beyond) appears on a ribbon that winds around the two Pillars of Hercules, the symbol of the Straits of Gibralter.[1] Two links of the chain of the Order of the

Golden Fleece are stretched between the pillars beneath a crown. The remainder of the space between the two wreaths is filled with a series of fourteen crowned coats of arms.[2]
Reverse: In a similar, slightly concave field is the double-headed eagle of the Empire, each head wearing a halo. On its breast is a shield with the coat of arms of Austria impaled with Burgundy. The date 1521 appears beneath the bird's heads in the spaces within the curves of its outspread wings. Circling the eagle is a series of thirteen coats of arms representing the new emperor's Spanish inheritance.[3] Inserted between the seventh and eighth in the series is the letter N (for Nuremberg) enclosed in a wreath.

We know more about the creation of this medal than that of almost any other medal of the German Renaissance, perhaps because it was Albrecht Dürer who produced the design.[4]

Charles was elected to succeed his grandfather, Emperor Maximilian I, in 1519, and was crowned in Aachen in 1520. Since it was traditional for a new emperor to convene his first Diet in Nuremberg,[5] the city council assumed that the Diet would be held there in 1521. It was planned that 100 copies of this medal would be presented to the emperor on his arrival. But as it happened, Nuremberg suffered an outbreak of the plague, so at the last minute Charles convened his Diet in Worms instead.[6] The preparations for the dedication medal were already completed. The council debated whether it was appropriate to present the medal to the emperor in Worms, since the work included such an obvious reference to Nuremberg. Ultimately the presentation was never made, for reasons that are unexplained. From the documents we learn that the council sought advice in matters of heraldry from Johannes Stabius (cat. no. 86) in Augsburg. We are not told, however, who carved the die from Dürer's design and struck the unusually large and heavy medal in silver. P. Grotemeyer came to the conclusion that the only person in Nuremberg with the technical experience required to strike a medal of this sort was Hans Krafft.[7] Krafft had gained such experience in years of experimentation when producing a struck medal of Frederick the Wise of Saxony. U. Timann was recently able to confirm Grotemeyer's thesis by producing the record of payment to Hans Krafft by the City of Nuremberg for the preparation of this die and the cost of producing 167 medals.[8]

The blank for the medal was first cast and then overstruck. Traces of the dies suggest that in order to reduce the pressure, two dies were struck on each side. Two dies were used for the emperor's portrait and the imperial eagle, and two additional, ring-shaped ones for the two wreaths of coats of arms. The dies for the reverse must have cracked before the contract was completed, for it survives in two different types.

In terms of the technique employed in its production, the dedication medal for Charles V is one of a kind. The medal of Frederick the Wise mentioned above is much smaller and thinner. The price paid for the preparation of the dies was 150 gulden, an extraordinary amount when one considers that Hans Schwarz (cat. nos. 81–84) and Matthes Gebel (cat. nos. 109–13) generally received only from two to five gulden for their models. Clearly an enormous amount of work was required in the creation of this technical masterpiece. With this medal, Nuremberg hoped to show the emperor something of the proficiency of its craftsmen. Given the elaborate technique involved, and even the minute detailing of the imperial eagle, it is odd that the portrait of the emperor is so lacking in personal characteristics. One must bear in mind, however, that Charles had grown up in the Spanish Netherlands, and served as king of Spain since 1516. In Germany there were few who knew what he really looked like. In preparing his design for the portrait side of the medal, Dürer was obliged to rely on prints and oral descriptions that were anything but flattering.

The medal is extremely rare. In 1537 the majority of these "thick silver groschen" were melted down. Apparently the council had meanwhile become convinced that it would not have another opportunity to present the medals to the emperor. The unusual presses were preserved in the city hall until the nineteenth century, when they were taken to Munich. They have since been lost. An inventory of Nuremberg's city hall from 1613 lists, in addition to the dies themselves, a total of twenty-four medals. At some later date that number was corrected with the notation: "Nunc 16 Stuck" (now 16 copies). Fewer than ten are in existence today.

Hermann Maué

Hans Daucher

(c. 1485–1538)

Hans Daucher has long been considered one of the most important sculptors of the early German Renaissance. We know of enough signed and thus assured works of his to give us a clear idea of his individuality as an artist. A total of ten reliefs in Solnhofer stone and two epitaphs bear his signature. On the basis of this certain œuvre, scholars have attributed a number of other works of sculpture to him as well, doubtless the most important of which being the altarpiece in the Fugger Chapel at St. Anne's in Augsburg, Daucher's home town.

His birth date is unknown, but it is thought to be circa 1485, for in the year 1500 he began his training as an apprentice to his uncle, the sculptor Gregor Erhart (born c. 1470–75, died 1540). In about 1491, the very young Hans had moved to Augsburg from the nearby Swabian city of Ulm on the Danube with his father, Adolf Daucher (born c. 1460–65, died 1523–24). His father was a "chestmaker," or joiner, as we know from the records relating to Augsburg craftsmen. He was the head of a very successful workshop, producing among other things large altarpieces in wood and stone. It is certain that his son Hans was also employed in this concern after having completed his training.[1]

Hans Daucher became a master sculptor in 1514, but remained in his father's workshop, which was dissolved on Adolf's death. In the following years Hans changed residences in the city with some frequency. His decreasing tax payments— under the municipal tax laws these were always based on income and property—indicate that his career was languishing. His wife, caught up in the confessional turmoil of the early Reformation, was banished from the city in 1527, after which his social standing seems to have fallen as well. He spent the last two years of his life in the service of Ulrich, duke of Württemberg. From the little we now know of his career, it would seem that in about 1520 Daucher chose to specialize in a new type of portable sculpture closely associated with the medium of medals, small bas-reliefs in Jurassic limestone, most of them depicting prominent contemporaries in scenic or allegorical portraits. As with medals, casts of these reliefs were often produced in either metal or plaster. The largest and most ambitious of these is in New York's Metropolitan Museum, and presents an elaborate procession led by Emperor Charles V (cat. nos. 77, 124–25, 156) and his grandfather Maximilian (cat. nos. 37, 79), followed by the imperial entourage. All discussion of Daucher's possible medal production is based on this and similar reliefs.

The "medalist" Daucher is an invention of art historians, and this must be stressed, for no single source refers to Daucher as a *Conterfetter*, the contemporary term for a medal portraitist. Nor are there any signed or monogrammed medals from his hand.[2] Thus any scholar wishing to attribute a given medal to Daucher must do so on the basis of its style alone. Yet there are a number of indications that Daucher did in fact work as a medalist. Two round limestone portraits of the counts Palatine Ottheinrich (1502–1559) (cat. no. 121) and Philipp (1503–1548) (cat. no. 78), best described as "medallions," are very close to the genre of the commemorative medal.[3] Daucher included his monogram on the Philipp portrait. The two are dated 1522, and stylistically they are very similar to two medal portraits of the young counts from the year 1520.[4] A second pair of medals of the brothers was then produced some seven years later (see cat. no. 78). The two sets serve as guideposts in the known work of Daucher the medalist.

Daucher's style is much less distinctive than that of either Hans Schwarz or Christoph Weiditz (cat. nos. 87–91). His work already mentioned is dominated by borrowed forms. His two reliefs of the Virgin, for example, one in Vienna and one in Augsburg, reproduce figures from Dürer prints.[5] A limestone relief from 1522, signed with the initials HD, presents the "pictor Germanicus," Albrecht Dürer, as the victor in a hypothetical duel. Here Daucher borrowed from the Dürer portrait by his contemporary Hans Schwarz (cat. no. 84), reproducing down to the smallest detail the profile, the deep eye sockets, and the curly hair. Because Daucher was so skilled at copying and because he frequently used the works of other medalists as patterns, it is difficult to identify a personal style. For this reason, a number of the medals heretofore thought to be his must be reexamined.

Thomas Eser

78 obv.

Hans Daucher
Philipp, count of the Rhenish Palatinate (1503–1548)
78
Silver, cast
Diameter 51.9 mm; from the bottom of the left shoulder truncation to the tip of the nose, 32 mm
Berlin, Staatliche Museen, Münzkabinett

Obverse: Beardless bust facing to the right. Philipp is wearing a broad, feathered biretta and a fluted breastplate with high neck guards on the shoulders. The extremely flat, sharp letters of the inscription, which rise directly from the field, have been cut on the model in a full circle. The inscription is subordinate to the portrait, and because it is so delicate, one sees a few minor casting errors at the bottom. A thin raised line forms the edge. Legend: PHILIP[u]S • CO[m]ESPA[latinus] • RENI • DUX • INFE[rioris] • + • SVP[er]IOR[is] • BAVAR[iae] • (Philipp, count of the Rhenish Palatinate, duke of Lower [and] Upper Bavaria). In the field: 1527 / 24 (1527, at age 24).
Reverse: Plain.

The medal is modest in format, with rather flat relief and an unobtrusive inscription. The subject's face takes up an astonishingly small percentage of the medal's surface. His cap and body are more than simple decorative additions; they expand the profile portrait into an imposing bust. It is not so much the sculptural three-dimensionality of the portrait that makes it so effective, but rather the dramatic placement of its forms, the way the viewer's attention is focused on the subject's small, but unusually detailed and subtle profile. Without any hint of caricature, the profile seems severely vertical. The strong nose, pointed chin, and straight, fixed gaze are those of a forthright, energetic young man. His distinctive features are overlaid with an element of idealized nobility.[1]

In most of the large number of medals of Philipp he appears together with his brother Ottheinrich (cat. no. 121).[2] Their favorite medalist in the 1520s was Hans Daucher, since there are no fewer than four pairs of medals of them by his hand.[3] Daucher had produced separate medal portraits of each of them seven years earlier. The small medal of Philipp from the year 1520 presents the same sharp profile and much the same style of lettering as the one shown here. The large limestone medallion from 1522, signed by Daucher, depicts the eighteen-year-old wearing armor and clutching at his sword in readiness for battle. In its relief style, its pose, and its approach to the portrait, it is quite similar to the present medal portrait from 1527. The counts Palatine were apparently so pleased with Daucher's work that they approached him once again for a new double medal in 1527.

Though he is here depicted full of self-confidence, Philipp was destined for failure. In 1505, together with his brother, he acquired the newly-created principality of Pfalz-Neuburg, a scattering of holdings in the vicinity of Neuburg on the Danube and in the upper Palatinate. At first it was ruled by their uncle, Duke Frederick II, who served as their guardian. The two brothers assumed their inheritance in 1522. They had little money to work with, and soon, owing to their mismanagement, the new principality was hopelessly in debt. It was ultimately divided between the two brothers in 1535, but in 1541 Ottheinrich was forced to take over his brother's portion as well, for Philipp's mountain of debt had risen from 80,000 to an alarming 416,392 gulden. As a settlement, Ottheinrich paid his brother a lump sum and granted him an annuity of 1,200 gulden, which was Philipp's sole income for his remaining years.

All his life Philipp had tried to make a name for himself. He repeatedly offered his services as soldier or courtier to Emperor Charles V (cat. nos. 77, 124–25, 156), to the king of France, Francis I (cat. nos. 116, 139), and to England's Henry VIII. He also hoped to improve his fortunes by making an advantageous marriage—one that he felt worthy of himself. He was almost completely unsuccessful.[4] Ottheinrich wrote a touching biography of his brother under the title *Philipsen Klag* ("Philipp's Lament"), in which he complains: " . . . no prince of recent years has died so miserably; regardless of the many adversities he suffered, he had to end in misery and poverty."[5]

Thomas Eser

78 obv.

79 obv.

Hans Daucher (?)
Maximilian I (born 1459, emperor 1493–1519)
79
Lead, cast, uniface
Diameter 75 mm; internal measurement from the brim of the
    cap to the heel of the boot, 57 mm
London, Victoria & Albert Museum
78-1867

79 obv.

Obverse: Full figure on horseback in profile facing to the left.
Maximilian is wearing a fluted breastplate and fald—the so-
called "Maximilian armor"—a cloak, and a broad, flat, feathered cap. Spurs, a dagger, and a commander's baton in his left
hand complete his equipment. In his right hand he holds the
reins. The horse is in complete armor adorned with heraldry as
follows: on the peytral or poitrel, an orb bearing a St. George's
cross; on the crupper, a heater-shaped shield with the arms of
Austria (gules, a fess argent) set inside a wreath. At the lower
edge of the medal there is a row of finely etched lines curving
from the horse's front hoof to the tip of his tail. Perhaps this
represents the grass through which Maximilian is riding.
Reverse: Plain.

Full-figure equestrian portraits are extremely rare in the early
medals of German-speaking countries. One encounters them
much more frequently in quattrocento Italy (see cat. nos. 4, 21,
24, 25). As a consequence, it is difficult to relate the style of this
highly detailed depiction of Maximilian on horseback to other
works. The attribution to Hans Daucher was first based not on
the style of the work, but rather on a comparison of the iconography with that of a monogrammed limestone relief in
Vienna.[1] That work depicts the emperor as St. George, riding
his horse across the vanquished dragon, and corresponds to the
medal portrait in every detail, though the group here faces the
other direction. If one takes into account the dating of the medal
to the year 1513, as seems assured by the inscription from a lost
variant,[2] one can assume it to be the pattern for Daucher's relief,
which was certainly executed at a later date. This does not
preclude the possibility that Daucher produced that medal as
well, but it is unlikely. Daucher's earliest known works date
from the year 1518, and his first products as a medalist only
from 1520. There is a simple explanation for the reversal in the
direction of the group. Daucher had as a pattern only a reversed
negative casting of the medal. Just such a specimen survives in
the Germanisches Nationalmuseum in Nuremberg.[3]

The medalist's pattern for the rider was not his own relief, but
rather a woodcut produced in 1508 by the Augsburg painter
and printmaker Hans Burgkmair (1473–1531), in which St.
George appears on horseback in a Renaissance hall.[4] As a
companion piece, Burgkmair created a print portraying the
Emperor Maximilian,[5] and here one finds iconographic parallels to the medal. Georg Habich had reservations about dating
the medal to the year 1513.[6] That would make the work one of
the very first South German cast medals of a ruler. Yet various
arguments do suggest such an early date. Given the historical
situation, and Maximilian's tendency to use art to glorify himself and for propaganda,[7] it is quite plausible that this depiction
of the "ultimate knight" should have been produced precisely in
the period 1510–15, making it an incunabulum in the history
of the German medal.

In 1509, Gregor Erhart began work on an equestrian monument of the emperor that would have certainly been the first
statue of its kind north of the Alps. It was never completed.
These are also the very years in which Maximilian commissioned the major biographies of himself, the *Weiskunig* and
Theuerdank, and Dürer planned and executed the huge prints of
the *Triumphal Procession* and the *Triumphal Arch*. These too are
highly unusual examples of their genre. In these five years there
are also historical reasons for the emperor's seemingly blas-
phemous identification with St. George, apparent in the medal
in the use of the St. George cross on the horse's armor. In 1511,
Maximilian had joined the Order of the Knights of St. George,
which was committed to the reconquest of the Holy Land and
the rebirth of a European Christian empire.[8] Moreover, the year
1513 saw a major military triumph for the Holy Roman Empire
of the German Nation. In league with Henry VIII of England,
Maximilian defeated the French at the battle of Thérouanne.

Maximilian is known to have commissioned medals of himself to use as gifts.[9] In about 1517 the ambassador Hieronymus
Cassola requested from him some "numismata effigiei ma-
jestatis" (medal portraits of His Majesty), for a number of
princes and noblemen had requested such tokens. Cassola
assured the emperor that these likenesses would, in their wide
distribution, contribute to his glory ("cum gloria sua erunt
bene distributa").[10]

Thomas Eser

80 obv.

surrounded by a simple border. In accordance with the fashion of the late 1520s, the king is wearing a simple disk-shaped cap ornamented with a brooch above a page-boy haircut. He is richly dressed in a cloak with a fur collar over a vest. A shirt with a high collar of alternating lace and ribbons covers his neck up to his chin. The only attribute suggestive of his exalted position is the chain of the Order of the Golden Fleece, which is draped across his shoulders.

Reverse: Plain. Ink inscriptions "[v]an Layden" and "169."

Hans Daucher (?)
Ludwig II (born 1506, king of Hungary and Bohemia 1516–26)

80

Stone model for a cast medal

Diameter of reverse 72.6 mm; diameter of obverse 70.9–71.0 mm; diameter of outside of circular band, 66.5 mm (inside 60.5 mm); internal measurement from upper right corner of cap to lower left edge of bust truncation, 58 mm

Boston, Museum of Fine Arts, Theodora Wilbour Fund in Memory of Zoë Wilbour

69.1150

Obverse: Bearded bust portrait in profile facing to the right,

80a

Bronze, cast

Diameter 60.7 mm; internal measurement from upper right corner of cap to lower left edge of truncation, 48.4 mm

New York, private collection

Obverse: Bearded bust portrait in profile facing to the right as above. Legend: LVDOWIG • V[on] • GO[ttes] • GN[aden] • KOENIG IN VNG[arn] • V[nd] • BO[ehmen] • A[nno] • 15Z6 (Ludwig, by the grace of God king of Hungary and Bohemia. 1526).

Reverse: Bearded bust of Count Stephan Schlick (born 1487, died c. 1526) in profile, facing to the left. Legend: HERR • STEFFAN • SChLICK • GRAF • ZV • BASSAN[o] • HER • ZV • WEISKIRCHEN • ELBO[gen] • V[nd] • SCHLACREN[werth] (Lord Stephan Schlick, count of Bassano, lord of Weiskirchen, Elbogen, and Schlackenwerth).

The king's portrait on the medal corresponds in outline and overall appearance to that of the Boston model. Yet there are differences in details, which lead to the certain conclusion that the medal was cast from another model produced especially for the purpose. The profile is more compressed, the line of the nose more curved. The beard is the same shape as that of the surviving stone model, but is much less detailed, as one can see by comparing the two strands of curls beneath the chin. The bust truncation has become more angular, and has been shifted

80a obv.

80a rev.

80 obv.

to the left into the medal's edge and cut off at the bottom, so that the pendant of the Golden Fleece hangs free. The treatment of the clothing—the trimming on the cap, the collar seam, the texture of the fur—is altogether less exacting. Of course this may be due to the medal's much smaller size. The internal measurement differs by more than a centimeter. This can hardly be the result of shrinkage in the casting process, and must be considered further proof that the medal was a separate undertaking.

The portrait of Count Schlick on the reverse is somewhat awkwardly composed, but its relief structure and the treatment of its fabrics reveal the same hand. The chest and shoulder are turned toward the viewer, so that the position of the head, twisted into strict profile, seems cramped. The flat cap, quite similar to the one the king wears on the obverse, is tipped to the back, and looks as though it had been pasted on. Schlick has gathered his hair into a cube-shaped net at the back of his head, an upper-middle-class fashion encountered in a number of medal portraits after 1518. His short beard and sideburns underscore the angularity of his profile. His shirt is richly pleated and trimmed, with what appears to be a silk collar, along with the ornamented collar of his coat and an imposing chain around his neck, it serves as an indication of his wealth.[1] The rim of the reverse, unlike that of the obverse, is ornamented with a delicate line of pearling. Due to an error either in the casting or in the mold, this line does not completely enclose the image, but disappears on the left edge.

There are many questions regarding the iconography, function, and attribution of the stone model in Boston and the surviving medals related to it. Any investigation must begin with the model, for it is the most distinguished specimen of the group. Among the surviving models for South German medals from the sixteenth century, the one in Boston occupies an unusual position.[2] On it the hair and fur are executed with such subtlety, the skin with such smoothness, that the work may have been intended as a showpiece in itself, rather than a routine step in the production of a medal. For this reason Georg Habich attributes the piece to a "goldsmith," and refers to it as a "goldsmith's model." He credits the high quality of the piece to this artisan's virtuosity, insisting that in terms of style his goldsmith "oriented" himself on Daucher.

The flat relief and exquisite details are specific elements of the Daucher style. On closer inspection, however, differences between this relief style and that of Daucher become apparent. Daucher has difficulty suggesting depth, and only rarely does he do so convincingly. By contrast, the artist who produced the Boston model has carved his cap quite logically. It is seen at an angle from below and is clearly three-dimensional. Daucher never exhibits such refined manipulation of space, yet it is difficult to attribute this work to anyone else, unless it was made at a later date after Daucher's medal.[3] It is likely that this is in fact an isolated work by an artist who produced nothing else in the medium of the medal.

In 1512, extensive silver deposits were discovered in a rugged, thinly populated valley in the southern Erzgebirge, a region in the northwestern corner of the kingdom of Bohemia. Newly wealthy, Count Schlick encouraged the subsequent "silver rush" into his territories by founding the city of St. Joachimsthal (St. Joachim's Valley, modern Jáchymov, Czech Republic) in 1516. Silver was mined there on a grand scale, and beginning in 1520 it was minted into highly profitable "Joachimsthaler," commonly called simply "thalers."[4] These coins were readily accepted as an international currency. Their name survives to this day in the English word "dollar."[5] From the start, the Bohemian Diet decreed that such coins were to bear the likeness of the country's ruler, King Ludwig II.[6]

All of the medals deriving from the Boston model happen to include in their inscriptions the date 1526, the year of Ludwig's death, and thus it would seem that the model was commissioned as a pattern for a medal to commemorate the deceased king. In the modeling of its profile, though by no means in style, it corresponds to a reversed medal portrait from 1524, when the king was still alive.[7]

There is also an historical reason for combining portraits of Ludwig II and Stefan Schlick, for the king and the wealthy count shared the same fate. In the spring of 1526, Ludwig turned to Schlick for help in defending his native Hungary against the powerful army of Sultan Suleiman II (born 1494–95, died 1566), then pressing westward. The forty-year-old Schlick rushed to the king's aid with twenty-eight cavalrymen, eight footsoldiers, and three baggage-wagons. Even so, the defending forces were only a tenth the size of the invading host. In the battle of Mohács, on August 29, 1526, the Turks completely destroyed the king's army. Ludwig, trying to escape, died a miserable death by drowning beneath his horse in a swamp. Count Schlick was never seen again, and the circumstances of his death were never discovered.

Thomas Eser

Hans Schwarz
(born c. 1492, died after 1521)

Born in Augsburg in about 1492, Hans Schwarz apprenticed there with Stephan Schwarz, probably a relative. Habich surmises that Hans was a great-grandson of the burgomaster Ulrich Schwarz, who was executed in 1478.[1] His earliest known works date from about 1512. They are small-format, rectangular reliefs or round medallions in wood. Theodor Müller has also attributed to him three large-format, relieflike altar side-panels, which he dated to the year 1515. According to Müller, Schwarz was at that time employed in sculpture workshops along the Danube.[2] In 1518 we find the artist in Augsburg, where he produced his first medals. His patrons were the nobles and their retainers attending the imperial Diet, as well as the city's native patricians and burghers. Schwarz's Augsburg works mark the beginning of a "medal madness" in Germany.[3] In the latter part of 1519, Schwarz moved to Nuremberg at the invitation of Melchior Pfinzing (cat. no. 82).[4] While in Nuremberg, Schwarz again created portraits for members of the city's patrician and mercantile classes. Given the large number of medals he produced there, it is astonishing to learn that he only stayed in Nuremberg for less than a year, for as the result of a nighttime brawl with the imperial mayor of the castle, he was asked to leave the city by March 1, 1520. Later that same year and in the following one Schwarz was active in Worms,[5] where the Diet originally planned for Nuremburg ultimately met (see cat. no. 77). Hans Schwarz based his medals on preliminary charcoal sketches, of which some 136 are preserved, mainly in Berlin and Bamberg. They have lost a great deal of their original appearance, however, for most of them have been cut out along their outlines and even traced over at a later date.[6]

In keeping with his training, Hans Schwarz executed all of the models for his medals in wood. He preferred large, unpretentious forms; sharp distinctions and wealth of detail—in the depiction of clothing, for example—are not his forte. His chief concern in his portraits was the line of the profile. He frequently glossed over individual peculiarities—doubtless in part owing to the speed that allowed him to produce such an extraordinary quantity of work. He was nevertheless an accomplished sculptor, as his medal of Albrecht Dürer (cat. no. 84) clearly shows.

There were no imitators of Hans Schwarz's highly individual style. His restless life, and perhaps his youthfulness as well, made it difficult for him to establish a workshop of his own. In the further development of the German Renaissance medal, refinement and perfection would become all-important. Hans Schwarz's straightforward approach was not the wave of the future.

Hermann Maué

Hans Schwarz
Christoph of Braunschweig, church administrator and bishop (1487–1558)
81
Bronze, cast
Diameter 88 mm
Vienna, Kunsthistorisches Museum, Münzkabinett
78 bβ

Obverse: Bust in profile, wearing a stylish, broad-brimmed hat and a high-necked shirt buttoned at the throat, where it forms a number of creases. His coat boasts a wide fur collar. A scarcely visible chain hangs down along the edge of his lapel. An ornament consisting of crescents and stars serves as a border for the field. The inscription is set off by a line of beading on the inside and a simple molding on the outside. Legend: [Imago] D[omini] • CHR[ist]OPHOR[i] • PREM[ensis] • ET VERD-[ensis] • ECCL[esiae] • ADM[inistratoris] • DVC[i]S • BRVNS-[wiecensis] • ET • LVNEB[u]R[gensis] • ([Likeness] of Lord Christoph, administrator of the Churches of Bremen and Verden, duke of Braunschweig and Lüneburg).
Reverse: Plain.

The medal of Christoph of Braunschweig is one of the first five

81 obv.

works by Hans Schwarz, all of which have the crescent and star motif.[1] Schwarz later abandoned this signature ornament, as it was apparently too delicate to cast—something he could not have known while carving the model. In these earliest Schwarz medals the portraits appear to burst out of the field: the points of caps and bust truncations extend right up to the row of beading. The letters of the inscription are carved out of the surface and lack all three-dimensionality. Their tops merge with a narrow outer strip, into which the abbreviation symbols have been engraved. Schwarz later does away with this outer strip, so that the letters stand out more clearly. The early works all present this imbalance between high relief in the portrait and very flat letters level with the surface of the field.

Historians have drawn an extremely negative portrait of Christoph of Braunschweig.[2] At the age of twelve he was appointed coadjutor by the archbishop of Bremen, Johann Rhode (1497–1511), a move intended to secure the support of Christoph's father, Duke Heinrich VIII of Braunschweig-Wolfenbüttel (born 1463, ruled 1495–1514), in the archbishop's quarrels with his neighbors. The duke nevertheless decided to pursue his own political ends, and his son Christoph would later subject the concerns of Bremen to these as well. In 1502, Christoph was named administrator of the bishopric of Verden on the Aller, with the injunction that he would only join the government when he reached the age of twenty-one. In 1511 he took over the archbishopric of Bremen, though the pope insisted that he be regarded only as its administrator, not archbishop, until he was thirty. It is evident he had no sense of calling to his clerical offices. He was a bitter opponent of the Reformation and had its leaders executed, for he saw it only as a threat to his own power. Nevertheless, he was unable to prevent

81 obv.

the introduction of reform to his two bishoprics. By the time he died, both were in total economic disarray, and irreconcilable differences had developed between the bishop and his flock.

Christoph attended the Diet of Augsburg in 1518, and while there he was one of the first notables to commission work from Hans Schwarz. Since the inscription speaks of him only as an administrator and not a bishop, though he was consecrated as such in Augsburg at the very time the medal was executed, it is not surprising that Christoph is not shown in the vestments of an ecclesiastic.[3]

Hermann Maué

Hans Schwarz
Melchior Pfinzing (1481–1535)
82
Bronze, cast, formerly gilt
Diameter 67.8 mm; diameter of outer perimeter of the inscription from the I in MELCHIOR to the B in ALB, 53.6 mm
Nuremberg, Germanisches Nationalmuseum
Med 8904

Obverse: Bust portrait in three-quarter profile, the head in full profile. Pfinzing is wearing the costume of a provost. A large biretta with the flap folded down almost completely covers his hair, which falls to just over his ears. He has pushed up the long full sleeves of his fur-lined coat so that they form deep folds. The cuffs are turned back to reveal the lining and expose his hands, which hold a rosary. The provost also wears a close-pleated linen choir robe (*superpelliceum*) over his coat. The portrait extends almost to the edge of the medal, leaving little room for a highly abbreviated inscription in uncommonly small letters. Legend: MELCHIOR PFINCZIG PRE[positus] EC-[clesiarum] S[ancti] ALB[ani] MO[guntinensis] ET SEB[aldi] N[orimbergensis] (Melchior Pfinzing, provost of the churches

of St. Alban in Mainz and St. Sebald in Nuremberg). His age is given in the field: AET ANNO XXXVIII (age 38 year). A narrow lip runs around the edge.

Reverse: An allegorical female figure identified as Spes (Hope) standing in front of a gently rolling landscape with little vegetation. She lifts her hands in prayer and gazes upward toward God, suggested by pointed rays radiating outward from wavy clouds. A thin guideline serves to align the letters of the inscription. Legend: SPES MEA IN DEVM (My hope rests in the Lord).

Portraits on German Renaissance medals rarely include the hands. Hans Schwarz only shows them on three other occasions.[1] The Pfinzing medal clearly shows the difficulties such a view presents, for unlike the majority of painted portraits, the head is here depicted in profile, while the body turns slightly toward the front. The left arm is required to extend well out from the body, while the right one is considerably foreshortened. In compositional terms the hands fingering the beads of a rosary tend to draw the viewer's attention away from the face, and constitute a second focal point. Here they are balanced by the arm slit on the left shoulder.[2]

There is no precedent for the figure of Spes in the art of Nuremberg around 1520. It has been suggested that with this Pfinzing commission Hans Schwarz was attempting to demonstrate the range of possibilities in the portrait medal, a genre still quite new to Germany, as a medium between painting and sculpture.[3]

Melchior Pfinzing was born in 1481, the second of six sons of the Nuremberg councilman and architect Seifried Pfinzing (1444–1517).[4] In 1494 he entered the university at Ingolstadt, where he studied under the great humanist Konrad Celtis (1459–1508). Subsequently he moved to Vienna, presented himself at the court of Emperor Maximilian I (cat. nos. 37, 79), and there, as the emperor's private secretary, acquired a knowl-

82 obv.

82 rev.

edge of diplomacy.[5] In his secretarial post, Pfinzing was largely responsible for arranging and editing the *Theuerdank*, a rhymed epic that had occupied the emperor since 1505. In it, a strange mixture of factual narrative and allegorical scenes, the emperor describes his bridal journey to the court of Burgundy. While working on the book, Pfinzing came to know all of the prominent scholars and artists close to the emperor. In 1512, thanks to Maximilian's influence, he was appointed provost of St. Sebald's in Nuremberg and later became a canon of the cathedral chapter in Trient and of St. Stephen's in Bamberg. In 1517 he was named provost of the knightly Order of St. Alban's in Mainz. Pfinzing had no sympathy for the teachings of Luther (cat. no. 101) and accordingly resigned his post in Nuremberg when the city sided with Luther after the Diet of Worms in 1521. The council welcomed his removal, as it was felt that with his numerous offices, requiring frequent absences in the service of the emperor, Pfinzing had neglected his duties in Nuremberg. Pfinzing then moved to Mainz, where he took up his duties as provost of St. Alban's. In 1528 he became dean at St. Viktor's in Mainz, and there he was buried in 1535.

Melchior Pfinzing had come to know Hans Schwarz at the Diet of Augsburg in 1518, and had commissioned a first medal from him there. In Nuremberg he introduced the artist, who lived in his house, to members of his family and other notables, serving in effect as Schwarz's patron. Nevertheless, his intervention with the city council did not prevent Schwarz's expulsion from Nuremberg in March of 1520. Once Schwarz had gone, Pfinzing proceeded to commission still another medal of himself from Matthes Gebel[6] (cat. nos. 109–113).

Hermann Maué

Hans Schwarz
Katharina Starck, née Imhoff (1493–1557)
83
Boxwood model for a medal
Diameter 50.3–51.2 mm
London, Victoria & Albert Museum
181–1867

Obverse: Bust of Katharina Starck facing left, her hair in a plait, one lock over her cheek. She wears a hat with a divided, upturned brim and badge, a high collar, and a broad chain around her neck.
Reverse: Plain.

Schwarz's 1519 charcoal drawing for this model is in the Bamberg Staatsbibliothek.[1] The sketch was conclusively identified as a portrait of Katharina Starck by Hermann Maué, who recognized that in addition to the actual inscription its features resemble those of Katharina Starck as she is depicted with her husband Ulrich in a medal dated 1519.[2] Although broader in treatment, and possibly suffering from additions by a later hand, the drawing is clearly a preparatory study for the present piece.[3] The fine carving of this model, seen particularly in the hair, make it one of Schwarz's most important works. No medal

83 obv.

after it is known, but it is likely that it served as the model for either a pendant to Schwarz's medal of Ulrich Starck or the reverse of that work.[4] Given the dates of the drawing and the medal showing Katharina Starck with her husband, the model is likely to date from about 1519–20.

Katharina's father, Ludwig Imhoff, left Nuremberg to settle in Bari, where he founded the so-called Italian branch of the Imhoff family. She remained in Nuremberg, however, where she married the Nuremberg patrician Ulrich Starck on February 7, 1513. Exceptionally, for a woman, she helped her husband run his copper industry at Eisleben.[5] Ulrich Starck was an important early patron of medalists, commissioning medals from Matthes Gebel as well as from Schwarz.[6] That of 1519 depicting the pair together seems to be the first double portrait on a medal of non-aristocratic sitters.

Marjorie Trusted

Hans Schwarz
Albrecht Dürer (1471–1528)
84
Bronze, cast from a boxwood model without inscription, now in the Anton-Ulrich Museum, Braunschweig
Diameter 57 mm
Vienna, Kunsthistorisches Museum, Münzkabinett
12481 bß

84 obv.

84 obv.

85 obv.

Obverse: Portrait bust facing to the left. Dürer's most striking features are his distinctly curved nose, which draws inward above the bridge, and his long, curling hair. The painter is dressed as a man of means. On top of his pleated shirt with a ruffle at the neck he wears a broad cloak with a fur-trimmed collar. The inscription follows a thin guideline inscribed into the mold. Legend: ALBERTVS DVRER PICTOR GERMANICVS (Albrecht Dürer, German painter). In the field the medalist's initials: H • S. The bust truncation follows the curve of the medal's edge, leaving a narrow empty strip.
Reverse: Plain.

The Albrecht Dürer medal is one of Hans Schwarz's best works. It is small wonder that Schwarz took particular pains in portraying the pre-eminent painter of his age, especially since Dürer himself had already prepared a design for his medal.[1] At times Schwarz's portraits follow established stereotypes, with large hats or elegant netlike caps, but in the Dürer medal he concentrates intently on the rendering of individual features, and even attempts to capture something of the artist's character. Dürer's appearance is similar to his more idealized self-portraits, though none of these is presented in pure profile. Hans Daucher borrowed Schwarz's Dürer portrait as early as 1522, in a relief of the so-called duel between Dürer and Lazarus Spengler.[2] Hans Petzold used it on his own Dürer medals,[3] and Melchior Lorch reproduced the Schwarz medal in an etching dated 1550.

Albrecht Dürer, who was born in Nuremberg in 1471 and died there in 1528, is considered the greatest creative personality in German art. He was highly respected during his lifetime, enjoyed the favor of Emperor Maximilian I (cat. nos. 37, 79), and was a member of the Nuremberg city council. In 1490 he traveled to the Upper Rhine, in 1494 to Venice, in 1505–7 once again to Venice and other cities in Italy, and in 1520–21 to the Low Countries. Dürer had set himself up as a master in Nuremberg in 1495. He owed his fame in large part to his printmaking, an art that he brought to a first flowering in Germany. Toward the end of his life he wrote a number of theoretical works, notably *The Principles of Measurement* (i.e. perspective), from 1525, *The Theory of Fortification*, from 1527, and *Four Books on Human Proportions*, from 1528.

Scholars are divided about whether various reliefs and medals bearing the initials AD are in fact Dürer's own work. Regardless of whether Dürer created medals himself, one can assume that he followed closely the progress of Hans Schwarz's work on his own medal. In September 1520, in the diary he kept on his tour of the Low Countries, he noted that he had had the Fugger branch in Antwerp forward two gulden to Augsburg in the name of Hans Schwarz for the model.

Hermann Maué

Augsburg School
Unknown Youth (member of the Löffelholz von Colberg family?)
85
Boxwood model

85 obv.

Diameter 58.4–58.9 mm
London, Victoria & Albert Museum
180–1867

Obverse: Bust of a young man facing left, clean-shaven, and wearing a cap, probably with a looped and tassled brim, and a slashed doublet or jerkin.[1] No inscription.
Reverse: Blank, with only concentric circles left by the lathe. A later inscription in ink: CWL a K.

This is a closely observed portrait with a deft handling of details. The irregular line of the cap and the slashes in the costume give a sense of liveliness to what is otherwise a composition of simplicity and clarity.

The purpose of the piece is unknown. It may have been the model for a medal, although no medals after it are known. It has a raised rim, but one that would not have afforded protection for the carved image, and this alone suggests that it is unlikely to have been a gaming-piece. Perhaps it was intended as a small-scale piece of sculpture in its own right. The holes drilled at top and bottom suggest that at one time it was hung up for display.

The fineness of the carving suggests that it was done by a medalist working slightly later than Schwarz. Boxwood medallions by Weiditz, such those of Joachim Rehle (cat. no. 89) or Lux Meringer (cat. no. 87), are analogous, but not sufficiently similar to allow an attribution to this artist. Trusted ascribed the work to an anonymous Augsburg medalist,[2] but in his review of her catalogue Maué put forward the idea that the piece could have been carved in Nuremberg.[3] Maué noted that the inked initials on the reverse may denote a member of the Löffelholz von Colberg (Kolberg) family of Nuremberg, and that the CW probably stands for Christoph Wilhelm. Two members of the family bore that name; one lived from 1624 to 1664, the other from 1692 to 1769. Maué suggested that the initials are more likely to be those of the second, who could have owned the medallion. A number of members of this family were depicted on medals during the sixteenth century,[4] and it is possible that the young man seen here was also a Löffelholz.[5] Given the provenance of the work, an attribution to Nuremberg is certainly possible. Yet since the piece is of wood, and would appear on the basis of its style to date from about 1525–30, it would be an exceptional work if from Nuremberg. The leading Nuremberg medalist at that time, Matthes Gebel, used stone for his models, whereas those working in Augsburg, such as Weiditz and Hagenauer, were using wood.[6]

Marjorie Trusted

Nuremberg School (Stabius Group)
Johannes Stabius (1462–1522)
86
Bronze, cast, uniface
Diameter 72 mm
Munich, Staatliche Münzsammlung

Obverse: Portrait bust in profile facing to the left. A laurel wreath encircles the head and is tied at the back with a tassled ribbon. He wears a cloak with a wide collar open at the front. The inscription is set off on the inside by a slightly irregular circle of dots, which is interrupted at the bottom by the bust. Legend: IOHANNES • STABIVS • POETA • LAVREATVS • ET • HISTORIOGRAPHVS • (Johannes Stabius, poet laureate and writer of history).
Reverse: Plain.

Johannes Stöberer, who would later take the humanist name Stabius, was born in 1462 in Hueb, near Steyr in Upper Austria.[1] In 1482 he enrolled in the university at Ingolstadt, in Bavaria, where he received his baccalaureate in 1484. In 1494 he is documented as being in Nuremberg, where toward the close of the fifteenth century the natural sciences were enjoying a remarkable flowering thanks to the researches of Johann Müller (1436–1476), better known as Regiomontanus. In the following years he was in Vienna on a number of occasions,

86 obv.

where he hoped for an appointment to the university. He retained his professorship in Ingolstadt, however, until 1503.

In 1501, at the urging of his friend and teacher Konrad Celtis (1459–1508), Maximilian I had endowed a humanist "collegium poetarum et mathematicorum" in Vienna. The emperor granted the college's directors the right to choose an imperial poet, and in the winter of 1502/3 Stabius received the laurel crown.

In 1503, Maximilian appointed Stabius one of his court historians, which meant that the scholar had little time to pursue his studies in natural science. His first assignment was to assist with research into the Habsburg family tree, which he attempted to trace back to the time of Noah.

Stabius now spent his time at Maximilian's court, accompanying the emperor on his travels and endeavoring to establish an extensive court archive. In 1512 he was in Nuremberg for an extended stay, and there he renewed friendships with Nuremberg's astronomers dating from his Ingolstadt years. His chief assignment, however, was to advise Albrecht Dürer in the creation of his *Triumphal Arch*, only completed in 1517, a monumental series of woodcuts commissioned by the emperor. In addition, two maps were the fruit of this collaboration with Dürer, one of the sky and one of the world, both drawn by Dürer. Stabius had sought fame as poet laureate at Maximilian's court, but produced nothing remarkable there. Nevertheless he had a certain standing in both Germany and Italy as a cosmographer, geographer, and mathematician.

In 1519 Stabius moved to Augsburg. Maximilian had died early in that year, naming him his literary executor. The poet's attempt to awaken an interest in the continuation of his employment on the part of Maximilian's successor, Charles V, was unsuccessful. Charles entrusted him with the administration of his grandfather's literary remains, but for this service he was not to receive any pay. The death of his patron had brought Stabius's brilliant career to an abrupt halt. He died quite suddenly on New Year's Day in 1522, in Graz.

The medal of Johannes Stabius is the only authentic portrait of the scholar, a fact that was long overlooked.[2] His striking head, idealized somewhat, was used as a model by various artists of his time, and there are those who claim to recognize Stabius in Dürer's monumental portrait of Charlemagne.[3]

We can assume that Albrecht Dürer created the design for this medal, but there is no way of knowing who it was that transformed his preliminary drawing into a relief model. Interestingly enough, the medal was cast from a wax model, a technique very seldom used in Germany in the early sixteenth century, though common enough in Italy.[4] Habich dates the Stabius medal to "circa 1520." Yet it is difficult to imagine that after Maximilian's death in early 1519, Stabius, no longer attached to the imperial court, would have continued to use the title "Historiographus." Moreover, the years 1519–20 were the period when Hans Schwarz was working as a medalist in Nuremberg. Dürer had commissioned Schwarz to create his own medal, and one would assume that he would have recommended this medalist to Stabius as well.

219

One can therefore conclude that the Stabius medal was produced in Nuremberg before Hans Schwarz arrived. This means that it was created at roughly the same time as the Pirckheimer medal, dated 1517, which was likewise cast from a model in wax.[5] Accordingly both medals date from the very beginning of medalmaking in Germany.

Hermann Maué

Christoph Weiditz
(c. 1500–1559)

Christoph Weiditz came from a family of sculptors. His father was the Freiburg sculptor Hans Weiditz (or Wydyz). Christoph may have been trained originally as a goldsmith.[1] Only one signed work is known, a dagger-case in the Historisches Museum in Dresden. Partly on the basis of this, other small-scale pieces of sculpture have been ascribed to him as well.[2] A reference in a letter from 1531 to the medal of Christoph Mülich by "Christoff Bildhauer" (Christoff the sculptor) was what led Habich to attribute over a hundred medals to the artist, basing his judgments on stylistic and documentary evidence.[3] Grotemeyer subsequently added two more groups of medals previously thought to be by the anonymous "Master of the Cardinal Albrecht" and "Master of the Simon Pistorius," respectively.[4]

Weiditz is recorded in Strassburg from 1523 to about 1525, and his first series of medals is made up predominantly of humanists and theologians of that city. He then seems to have traveled throughout Europe. On the basis of the medals and Weiditz's own *Trachtenbuch*, an illustrated account of his travels of which a manuscript (perhaps a slightly later copy) survives in Nuremberg, Habich suggested the following chronology of his activity. On leaving Strassburg in 1525, Weiditz went by way of Ulm and other German cities to Augsburg, where he resided until 1529. He then left that city, possibly because of rivalry between himself and Friedrich Hagenauer (cat. nos. 92–100), and traveled to Spain, where he joined the entourage of Emperor Charles V (cat. nos. 77, 124–25, 156). He was there befriended by Bishop Johannes Dantiscus, through whom he met the explorer Hernán Cortés (cat. no. 90). In late 1529 he traveled with the emperor to Italy, visiting Genoa and Bologna, then returned with the court to Augsburg for the Diet in 1530. Later that year he was in Mainz, Cologne, Aachen, and Brussels. He may also have visited England at this time.[5] In 1532 he was again in Augsburg, probably after first visiting Nuremberg. Hagenauer had left Augsburg by this date, and perhaps for this reason Weiditz seems to have settled there. The later groups of medals attributed to him by Grotemeyer imply that in the later 1530s he was based in Saxony, where he may have been active until 1543–44.

Weiditz made his models of wood, and some of these seem to have survived without examples of the medals cast after them.[6] His inscriptions are evenly and widely spaced, with the words often separated by small triangles. His portraits are carved in relatively low relief in a manner that seems to imitate the wax

reliefs used as models for medals in Italy. His sitters are frequently seen from the front or in three-quarter view. A strong Italian influence can be seen in some of his reverses, no doubt a reflection of his visit to Italy, as well as an indication of his interest in small-scale figure carving.[7]

Marjorie Trusted

87 obv. 87 rev.

Christoph Weiditz
Lienhard (Lux) Meringer (died 1549?)
87
Boxwood model
Diameter 45.3–46.3 mm
London, Victoria & Albert Museum
A505–1910

Obverse: Bust portrait facing left, clean-shaven and wearing a cap with a folded brim and a jacket over a shirt. Legend: • LVX • – MERINGER •
Reverse: Shield with monogram, inscribed with the date • M • D • XXVI.

This carving was first published in 1911, when it was noted that "the cost [of the piece] to Mr. Salting . . . was no less than £500."[1] It was intended as a model for a medal, casts of which are in the British Museum and the Münzkabinett in Berlin. Its style strongly supports an attribution to Weiditz, and it is likely to be one of the artist's earliest works, executed soon after his arrival in Augsburg from Swabia. As Habich noted, Weiditz's carved wood models have a cleanness of outline and composition that distinguish them from the works of his contemporary Schwarz (cat. nos. 81–84), who also worked in wood.[2] Typical of Weiditz are the widely spaced letters of the inscription and the triangles used to separate its words.

Habich tentatively identifed the sitter as Lienhard Meringer, a goldsmith who worked in Augsburg, though originally from Ulm in Swabia, and who died in 1549.[3] The medal may form a pair with the medal of Katharina Meringer, an Augsburg citizen and almost certainly Lienhard's wife.[4]

The monogram on the reverse shield is probably made up of the sitter's initials, but this is uncertain.

Marjorie Trusted

87 obv.

88 obv.

88 obv.

88 rev.

Christoph Weiditz
Magdalene Rudolff, née Honoldt (born 1495)
88
Boxwood model
Diameter 67.9–69 mm; diameter of inner perimeter of obverse
 inscription, 58.8–61.0 mm
Berlin, Staatliche Museen, Münzkabinett
810/1876

Obverse: Bust of a woman to the left. Her hair is drawn back tightly, though a few locks hang over her temples, and falls in a long, thin braid down her back. She has full features, a small mouth, and a protruding chin. She is wearing a large, folded bonnet that projects well out from her head, a delicately pleated blouse tied at the neck, a gown that is also pleated, and a long ornamental chain. Legend: MADALENA • HONOLDTIN • ANTHONI • RVDOLFFS • HAVSFRAV • XXXIII (quatrefoil rosette) M • D • XXVIII • (Magdalena Honoldt, wife of Anton Rudolff, [age] 33. 1528). Small triangles serve as stops. Slightly raised edge.
Reverse: Small shield with coat of arms.[1] Legend: DAS • WORT • GOTZ • BLEIBT • IN • EWIGKAIT (quatrefoil rosette) ("God's word endures forever"). Small triangles as stops. Smooth edge.

This thin wood model, slightly convex on the obverse and with a very flat but extremely lively portrait, was produced during Weiditz's sojourn in Augsburg in 1527–29. It depicts a daughter of the Augsburg patrician Hans Honolt vom Luchs and his wife, Elisabeth Rehlinger. In 1517, Magdalena Honolt had married the Augsburg burgher Anton Rudolff, who was a member of the merchant guild in later years and helped to chart the city's course as a member of the city council and ultimately burgomaster. The lynx is the emblem of the Honolt vom Luchs family. The reverse legend, taken from Psalm 119:89, wäs a

motto of the Reformation, to which both Anton Rudolff and his wife subscribed.

This medal, with its pleasing composition, is one of Weiditz's most successful works. Portrait, field, and inscription are nicely balanced, details are reproduced with accuracy, but not obsessiveness, and though extremely flat, the relief suggests a fully three-dimensional form. Weiditz has captured the dignity of this self-assured woman without resorting to coquetry.

Lore Börner

Christoph Weiditz
Joachim Rehle (born 1490–91)
89
Boxwood model
Diameter 56–58 mm
London, Victoria & Albert Museum
A 504–1910

Obverse: Bust in three-quarter view facing to the left, bearded and wearing a flat, feathered cap and a tunic over a shirt with a low collar. Legend: • IOACHIM • REHLE – ALT • XXXVIII • (Joachim Rehle, thirty-eight years old).
Reverse: Coat of arms.[1] Legend: ES – STAT • ALS ZU • GOT • M • D • XXVIIII (All belongs to God. 1529).

Habich was the first to attribute this work to Weiditz, and his opinion is generally accepted.[2] Like other pieces linked to Weiditz, it depicts the sitter facing the viewer but looking slightly to the side.[3] Also typical of Weiditz are the small triangles serving as stops between some of the words in the inscription and the simple, but naturalistic portrayal of costume, including the detailing of the feather and the linen shirt.

Habich also calls attention to a painting of Rehle in the Dresden gallery, dated 1524, by Hans Maler of Ulm (active

223

89 obv.

89 rev.

1510–29),[4] which depicts the sitter without a beard, posed differently, and wearing different clothes, yet with features that appear to be those of the man in the present portrait. Interestingly, the painting is inscribed with a legend of the sort more commonly found on medals.[5] Rehle's date of birth is clear from the inscriptions on this medal and the information given on the painting. His death date is unknown. Little is known of his life, although Habich records that he belonged to a family that was originally from Nördlingen and speculates that he might have conducted business in Augsburg and outside of Germany as well. Weiditz, who is known to have journeyed to Spain and probably Italy, could have executed Rehle's portrait while both he and his subject were abroad.[6] There is also a miniature of Rehle in the Kupferstichkabinett in Berlin.[7]

Domanig noted that there is a poor bronze cast of this work in the Münzkabinett in Vienna,[8] so it is apparent that it was indeed intended as the model for a medal.

Marjorie Trusted

Christoph Weiditz
Hernán Cortés (1485–1547)
90
Bronze, cast
Diameter 55.7 mm; diameter of outer perimeter of inscription, 55.7 mm
Berlin, Staatliche Museen, Münzkabinett, formerly Andreas Rudolphi Collection, 1831

Obverse: Bust portrait, the body frontal, the head facing the viewer with a slight turn to the left. Cortés wears a doublet with full, slashed sleeves, slightly open at the neck, and a cap. Legend: DON FERDINANDO CORTES MD XXIX ANNO [a]ETATIS XXXXII (Don Ferdinando Cortés, 1529, at age forty-two).
Reverse: On top, an arm in a cloud from which rain is falling, the fist clenching part of the cloud. Below, the five-line inscrip-

tion: IVDICIVM • D[omi]NI APREHENDIT • EOS ET • FORTITVDO • EIVS CORROBORAVIT BRACHIUM • MEVM (The justice of the Lord touches all, and His power has strengthened my arm).

Hernán Cortés, the conqueror of Mexico, was born in 1485 in Medellín, Extramadura, and died on December 2, 1547, in Catilleja de la Cuesta, near Seville. He was a member of the minor nobility. He left for the West Indies in 1504, took part in the capture of Cuba by Velasquez in 1511, and set off from there in 1519 on an expedition to Mexico. He first founded the colony of Veracruz, then pushed farther inland, conquered Mexico, and captured the Aztec ruler Montezuma II, forcing him to recognize Spanish supremacy. After "la noche triste" of June 30/July 1, 1520, he lost Mexico, but managed to reconquer it on August 13, 1521, subjecting the Aztec empire once and for all to the Spanish throne. From 1528 to 1530 Cortés was in Spain, where Emperor Charles V (cat. nos. 77, 124–25, 156) received him with honors and named him Marqués del Valle de Oaxaco. Back in Mexico, he led exploratory expeditions into Honduras and California. In 1540 he returned to Spain, and in 1541 took part in the unsuccessful campaign against Algiers under Charles V.

Christoph Weiditz was in Spain in the service of the emperor from 1529 to 1530, and during that sojourn he produced various portrait drawings, including one of Cortés. These drawings are found in his so-called *Trachtenbuch*, in the Germanisches Nationalmuseum in Nuremberg.[1] There is some doubt about whether Weiditz himself was the creator of the book. Perhaps it was only compiled by his son Hans after sketches that have not survived.[2] While in Spain, Weiditz also produced the medal of his patron, Bishop Johann Dantiscus (1485–1548),[3] and the drawing of Andrea Doria (see cat no. 50)[4] that he transformed into a medal in 1533.

The present medal shows Cortés facing forward. Such portraits, though more powerful, are relatively rare on Renaissance medals, since they are more difficult to carve than straight

89 obv.

90 obv.

90 obv.

90 rev.

profiles. Beginning in 1529,[5] the majority of Weiditz's portraits are *en face*. Presumably he was inspired by the paintings of Hans Holbein the Younger. His trip to Spain brought Weiditz into closer contact with the medallic art of Italy, the influence of which is above all apparent in his reliefs for the reverses of his medals.

Ingrid S. Weber

Christoph Weiditz
Charles de Solier, lord of Morette (1480–1547)
91
Boxwood model
Diameter 56.6–58 mm; diameter of outer perimeter of obverse inscription, 53.7 mm
London, Victoria & Albert Museum
A507–1910

Obverse: Bust portrait facing slightly to the left, bearded and wearing a low hat with a badge and a gown with a fur collar. Legend: CAROLVS • DE • SOLARIO • D[omi]N[v]S • MORETY • ANNV • AGENS • L • (Charles de Solier, lord of Morette, at the age of fifty).

Reverse: Allegorical scene of a horse prancing on a rocky foreshore, its reins held by a dolphin in the water. Legend: VIRTVS • ET • FORTV[n]A • VIROS • EXERCET • ET • ORNAT • (Fortune schools men, and virtue adorns them).

The portrait on this wood model, after which no medal is known, is linked with a painting of the same sitter by Hans Holbein the Younger (born 1497–98, died 1543) in Dresden. That work, along with Holbein's preparatory drawing for it, also in Dresden, has been dated to about 1534, when Charles de Solier was serving as the French ambassador in London and could have sat for Holbein, then court artist to Henry VIII.[1] The present boxwood image and inscription served to identify the subject of the painting. Problems of dating, however, and of the precise relationship between the boxwood piece and the Hol-

91 obv.

91 rev.

bein works remain.[2] Charles de Solier was born in 1480, and the carving gives his age as fifty. If the inscription is accurate, this would mean that the work was made in about 1530–31, at least two years before the date proposed for the works by Holbein.[3] There are evident minor differences between the Holbein image and the boxwood, notably in the pose. Nevertheless, it seems likely that Weiditz used Holbein's image as the basis for his piece.[4] This suggests either that Holbein's painting must be dated earlier, to 1531 at the latest, or that de Solier's age as given on the boxwood has been rounded down to fifty, when in fact he would have been about fifty-four. Inaccurate ages were indeed sometimes recorded on medals.[5]

This is the only known piece by Weiditz based on the work of another artist.[6] It is unknown why or under what circumstances he carved it. Weiditz was widely traveled, and it may be that he visited England and was given the commission there.[7]

Charles de Solier was from a Piedmontese family. In his youth he served as a page at the court of Charles VIII of France, and later became a courtier to Francis I. He first visited England as a member of the French embassy in 1518, and in the following year he was one of four French noblemen taken hostage by Henry VIII. After returning to France, he came back to England in 1527 to help negotiate the proposed marriage between Princess Mary and Francis I, and in 1534 he was Francis's ambassador at the court of Henry VIII. He died in Paris only months after the accession of the new king, Henry II.[8]

The allegorical scene on the reverse is an unusual feature in a German medal, but typical of Weiditz's use of Italianate features.[9] Suhle suggested that the horse symbolizes virtue, while the dolphin represents fortune. The reins thus imply constraint, in illustration of the verb "exercet."[10] Weiditz used a dolphin in the image of Fortune on the only work he is known to have signed, his dagger-case in Dresden. There, the relief on the outer case shows a dolphin in the sea beneath a female figure. It is closely comparable to the one depicted here.[11]

Marjorie Trusted

Friedrich Hagenauer
(active 1525–1546)

Friedrich Hagenauer was probably the son of the sculptor Nikolaus Hagenauer (Niclas Hagnower) and is likely to have been born in Strassburg and trained as a sculptor in the region of the Upper Rhine or Alsace.[1] He is recognized as the author of about 250 medals,[2] many of which are signed with his distinctive monogram impressed into the field.

As a *Conterfetter*, or portrait carver, Hagenauer was not tied to a guild, and had more freedom to travel and gain commissions in different German cities.[3] His first known signed work, dated 1525, depicts the goldsmith and die-cutter Matthias Zaisinger, and was probably executed in Munich.[4] He seems to have stayed in Munich until 1527, producing medals of its ruler Wilhelm IV, duke of Bavaria, and his brother Ludwig X, who resided in Landshut, and members of their court.[5] In 1527, Hagenauer went to Augsburg, perhaps attracted by the prospect

of more commissions due to the celebration there of the marriage of Anton Fugger with Anna Reichlinger von Horgau. Thirty-nine medals by Hagenauer date from this year.[6] The Augsburg Diet of 1530 gave rise to further opportunities for medals, and about twenty can be dated to that time. In 1532, Hagenauer returned to his native region of Alsace, possibly for religious reasons,[7] and was active in Strassburg and perhaps Baden. He went north to Cologne in 1536, where he executed perhaps his most important series of medals, portraying predominantly scholars and leading figures in the Lutheran Reformation such as Philipp Melanchthon (cat. no. 99).[8] Hagenauer's last dated work, a medal of Archbishop Hermann von Wied, is from 1546, and in that year he may have journeyed to the Lower Rhine and the Netherlands. The date of his death is unknown.

Hagenauer's models were almost always of wood, and his medals exhibit a dry, linear clarity, partly due to his use of this material. The medals frequently show the sitter's head in profile while the shoulders are turned frontally, with the date sunk into the field. This format is also seen in a number of the anonymous "Nuremberg 1525–27" medals, and in a recent article Hermann Maué has convincingly suggested that Hagenauer could have been the author of some of that group.[9] Hagenauer may have known the painter Hans Baldung Grien (1480–1545) in Strassburg, and was later a friend of the Cologne painter Bartel Bruyn (1493–1555). The portrait styles of these two artists possibly influenced Hagenauer's own portrayal of his sitters.[10] Many of Hagenauer's portraits were copied later on in the sixteenth century for wooden gaming-pieces, which were usually painted and often incorporated gesso additions.[11]

Marjorie Trusted

Friedrich Hagenauer
Augustin Loesch von Hilgertshausen (1471–1535)
92
Lead, cast, uniface

92 obv.

228

93 obv.

Diameter 69 mm; diameter of the outer perimeter of the inscription from the D in DOC to the A in AVGVSTINI, 65.2 mm
Munich, Staatliche Münzsammlung

Obverse: Bust facing to the right, beardless and with medium-length hair. The sitter wears a wide cap with a neck flap, and an outer garment in a raised floral pattern with plain wide lapels. In the field beside the head is the date: M • D • — XXVI. Around the edge, between two raised borders, is the legend: (leafy stop) EFFIGIES • AVGVSTINI • LESCH • DE • HILKERS[hausen] • I[urarum] • V[triarum] • DOC[tor] • BAIO[ariae] • DVCVM • CANCELLA[tor] (Portrait of Augustinus Loesch von Hilgertshausen, doctor of both laws, chancellor to the dukes of Bavaria).
Reverse: Plain.

Augustin Loesch was born in Rothenburg ob der Tauber in 1471. He studied in Italy, and was graduated as a doctor of both Roman and modern law in Siena on September 1, 1494. Emperor Maximilian I (cat. nos. 37, 79) appointed him to the supreme court in Worms, which he presided over from 1503 until 1508, when Duke Wilhelm IV of Bavaria summoned him to serve as his chancellor. The duke ultimately rewarded him for his services with an estate in the Altmühltal. In addition, Loesch purchased the palace at Hilgertshausen on the Ilm in

1518, and had it rebuilt. He died on October 11, 1535, and was buried in the Franciscan Church in Munich.[1]

In 1499, Loesch married Anna von Thann, a lady-in-waiting at the margravial court at Ansbach. She bore him four sons and five daughters. She died on September 11, 1534, and was buried in the cathedral in Freising.

This appears to be the only original specimen of this medal. It was acquired by the Royal Münzkabinett in Munich in 1895 from the Eugen Felix Collection in Leipzig. As early as 1848, Beierlein noticed the stylistic connection between this medal and a group that Hagenauer signed with the initials F • H, and accordingly ascribed the unsigned work to Hagenauer as well.[2] Beierlein's attribution has been accepted without criticism by later scholars. The medal fits in convincingly enough with other Hagenauer works of this time. It would even appear to be one of his best creations.

Ingrid S. Weber

Friedrich Hagenauer
Sebastian Ligsalz (1483–1534)
93
Wood relief
Diameter 123 mm
Munich, Bayerisches Nationalmuseum
R 466

93 obv.

Obverse: Bust to the right of an older man with sideburns. The head is in profile, while the body is turned toward the front in three-quarter view. He wears a net cap, beneath which his short-cropped hair is barely visible. He is dressed in a shirt, the high collar of which has an ornamental border, and a fur-lined cloak with a broad collar. Legend, with small triangles as stops: SEBASTIANS • LIGSALCZ • GESTALT • WAR • IM • XXXXIIII • IAR • ALT: (leafy stop) (Likeness of Sebastian Ligsalz at age forty-four). The date M • D • XXVII appears in the field, the first two letters to the left of the portrait, the remaining ones to the right. The inscription appears between two fine guidelines.
Reverse: The monogram FH in red ink. Below this, a vine with a heart-shaped leaf and the date 1527. In black ink, in a sixteenth-century hand, the inscription: "Lauß xro + 1527 jar + han ich mich Sewastian ligsalcz in dyß holcz lassen ab guntter vetten vnd schneyden. Da ich 44 jar alt waß. wie auff der ain Seytten statt" (Praise be to Christ + I, Sebastian Ligsalz, had my likeness drawn and carved in this wood in the year 1527. When I was forty-four, as it says on the other side).

Ursula Ligsalz (1499–1551)
93a
Wood relief

Diameter 124 mm
Munich, Bayerisches Nationalmuseum
R 467

Obverse: Bust of a young woman to the left, the head in profile and the torso turned toward the front in three-quarter view. Her long straight hair falls down her back in a braid that is twisted so that we see it from the top. She wears an elaborately worked cap with the brim turned up. Her high-necked shirt has an embroidered border. Above it she wears a close-fitting, finely pleated bodice, it too edged with embroidery. Legend, between two fine guidelines with small triangles as stops: VRSVLA • SEBASTI[ani] • LIGSALCZ • HAVSFRAV • WAS • IM • XXVIII • IAR • ALT • (leafy stop) (Ursula, the wife of Sebastian Ligsalz, in her twenty-eighth year). In the field, the date M • D • XXVII, the first two letters to the left of the portrait, the remaining ones to the right.
Reverse: The monogram FH in red ink. Below it, a vine with a heart-shaped leaf and the date 1527.

These two carvings were clearly meant to be a pair. Habich considered them both to be portrait pieces unsuited for use as models for medals both on account of their unusual size and

93a obv.

94 obv.

their deeply incised inscriptions.[1] We know that these are Hagenauer's works from the monograms in ink on their backs.[2] They were carved toward the end of the artist's stay in Munich, probably a short time before his departure for Augsburg. His medal of the Augsburg painter Lukas Furtenagel (cat. no. 94) also dates from 1527.

These flat reliefs, with sharply modeled faces in silhouette-like profile and torsos turned slightly toward the viewer, are altogether characteristic of Hagenauer and are carved with the greatest accuracy. Sebastian Ligsalz was a member of one of Munich's oldest and most respected patrician families. For many years he sat on the councils of the city of Munich. At that time each of the twelve members of the Inner Council served a month each year as burgomaster, so he would have held that office as well.[3]

Ligsalz was first married to a Magdalena von Rosen. Ursula, née Sänftl, was his second wife. She was the daughter of another Munich patrician. Sebastian must have concluded this second marriage in 1522, for in that year he paid a tax on his second wife's dowry. Ursula appears in the tax records for the last time as a widow in 1551, and was already dead by October 17 of that year.[4]

Susanne Wagini

Friedrich Hagenauer
Lukas (Laux) Furtenagel (1505–after 1556)
94
Wood model
Diameter 66 mm
Munich, Bayerisches Nationalmuseum
R 3461

Obverse: Beardless bust of a young man, the head in profile to the left, the torso turned slightly toward the front. He wears a cap with a broad, curving brim, to the bottom of which jewels

94 obv.

have been pinned. He is dressed in a high-necked shirt with a richly pleated standing collar and a cloak with broad lapels, the sleeves apparently caught up by ribbons. There are inner and outer guidelines setting off the area of the inscription, but the space is left blank.
Reverse: In blurred ink the drawing of a teetotum. Around the outside in Latin capitals: ALLAIN WAS OBLIGT DAS GILT (It is only what is shown on the top that matters).

It is clear from the casts that this was the model for a medal of the painter Lukas Furtenagel. The lead cast in Paris has the legend: LVCAS FVRTENAGEL MALER VON AVGSPVRG SEINES ALTERS XXII (Lukas Furtenagel, painter in Augsburg, at age twenty-two).[1] In its field, separated by the portrait, are the letters of the date: M • D • XXVII.[2] Below the date on the left is the ligature monogram FH.[3] The inscription was only added on the casting model, probably by means of punches. The reverse shows a teetotum and the same inscription as the one on the model, this time inside a laurel wreath.[4]

Even if there were no monogram on the cast to identify it, there would be no question that the wood model is Hagenauer's work, for it is altogether typical of him in style and composition.[5] Scholars have never questioned the attribution.

Lukas Furtenagel was born in Augsburg in 1505, the son of the painter Jörg Furtenagel.[6] In 1515 his father apprenticed him to the painter Leonhart Hamer in Augsburg. Hagenauer's medal tells us that the young Furtenagel must have stayed in Augsburg until 1527. It would appear that he subsequently worked as a journeyman for an extended period of time, for the next documentary mention of him is from 1542, in Halle. It is thought that he spent some time in the workshop of Lucas Cranach in Wittenberg.[7] In 1546 he returned to Augsburg as a married man. In that year his daughter Maria was born, and he was accepted into the painters' guild. Two painted frontispieces from the two volumes of the Council Bible in Halle from 1542 are the only works known to be his, though it is documented that he also painted a portrait of Martin Luther on his deathbed in Eisleben in 1546.[8] Furtenagel must have died sometime after 1556, for in that year he presented his apprentice Wilhelm Meitting to the guild.[9]

Susanne Wagini

Friedrich Hagenauer
Margarete von Frundsberg (1509–?)
95
Lead, cast
Diameter 65 mm; diameter of the outer perimeter of the inscription from the G in MARGARITA to the G in FRVNT-SPERG, 61.5 mm
Berlin, Staatliche Museen, Münzkabinett

Obverse: Bust portrait facing left, with feathered hat on top of a net cap. The lady is wearing a stylish gown with wide, puffed sleeves. Beneath it one can see a blouse with ornamental edging closed at the neck. A double chain hangs around her neck and

95 obv.   95 rev.

shoulders. Legend: MARGARITA A FIRMIAN D • GASPARIS A FRVNTSPERG VXOR • ANNO ETATIS SVE XX • (Margarete Firmian, wife of Kaspar von Frundsberg, at age 20). In the field on the left, the ligature of the artist's initials FH.

Reverse: The five-line inscription is from Ecclesiasticus 26:16: GRATIA MVLIERIS SEDVLAE DELECTABIT VIRVM SVVM ET OSSA ILLIVS INPINGVABIT M • D • XXIX • ("A wife's charm is the delight of her husband, and her womanly skill puts flesh on his bones." 1529).

The subject of this medal was the daughter of Baron Georg von Firmian zu Kronmetz. Her husband, Kaspar von Frundsberg (1500–1536), was descended from one of the oldest and wealthiest ministerial families in the Tyrol, with an ancestral Freundsberg Castle near Schwaz.[1]

Habich found this portrait to be "the quintessential image of a German noblewoman," adding: "her pose is so graceful, her expression so full of intelligence, yet not without a degree of piquant charm, that connoisseurs consider this lovely piece one of Hagenauer's triumphs."[2]

Hagenauer produced this small work of art during his Augsburg period, between 1527 and 1532, a time in which he perfected his relief style so as to be able to render the most delicate decorative details. His arrangement of the silhouette portrait with its exquisite relief against the neutral field is masterful.

Wolfgang Steguweit

Friedrich Hagenauer
Christoph, count of Nellenburg and Thüngen (died 1539)
96
Maplewood model
Diameter 88.5–89.5 mm
Munich, Staatliche Münzsammlung

96 obv.

96 obv.

97 obv.

Obverse: Full torso facing to the right. The count's shirt is pleated and trimmed, with a vest, also pleated, slit below the waist, and laced. Above these he wears an outer garment open in front and a cap, to which a feather has been attached by means of a floral brooch. A whistle hangs at the level of his waist on a chain.

Reverse: Ink spot, numbers, and letters from the nineteenth century.

The Staatliche Münzsammlung in Munich also owns a uniface lead medal of this same subject. It depicts the count in armor, and is dated 1534.[1] Habich attributed that specimen, like the wood model, to Friedrich Hagenauer, and dated the wood model to 1534 as well.

By clever politicking, the counts of Nellenburg and Thüngen had managed to amass considerable property holdings, but by the beginning of the sixteenth century the family was in decline. Feuds, family quarrels, and a fire at Thüngen castle only hastened its fall. Count Christoph stood in particularly high regard with Emperor Charles V on account of his enormous size. "Since the emperor already had at court the tallest and shortest men known, he determined to have the fattest one as well, and to that end he invited the count to attend him. The latter arrived in Augsburg for the Diet of 1530, and when the emperor and his Spanish and Italian princes saw him they were all mightily amazed."[2]

It is related that when the count was courting his second wife, Countess Helene von Zollern, "he would occasionally climb onto a wagon at nightfall and have himself driven from Werstain, not far from Haigerloch (the countess's seat), to the church that stands across the valley from her castle. Together with his drummers, bagpipers, and other such folk he would then serenade the Fräulein on the other side of the valley. . . ."[3] If it is true that the wood model depicts the count at the time of his wooing of the countess—which the courtly costume would tend to support—he could have had Hagenauer carve the portrait in Augsburg either during or after the Diet of 1530, thinking of it as a present for his fiancée, who married him on July 23, 1531. As there is no noticeable change in Hagenauer's style over the course of the years, an earlier dating is nevertheless possible.

Ingrid S. Weber

Friedrich Hagenauer
Sibylla von Aich, née von Ried (or Reidt; 1483–1553)
97
Silver, cast
Diameter 43.0 mm; diameter of the outer perimeter of the inscription from the G in IMAGO to the D in DOMINI, 41.5 mm; weight 29.19 g
Berlin, Staatliche Museen, Münzkabinett, formerly Dannenberg Collection, 1892

Obverse: Bust facing forward in a plain garment with necklace and winged cap. Legend: IMAGO SIBILLAE A RIED • VXORIS

97 obv.　　　　　97 rev.

DOMINI IOANNIS AB AICH (Likeness of Sibylla von Ried, the wife of the worthy Johann von Aich).

Reverse: Coat of arms on a shield.[1] Legend: MODVS OMNIBVS IN REBVS OPTIMVS • M • D • XX[x]VII (Moderation in all things is best. 1537).

In the wealthy trading metropolis of Cologne, on the Rhine, Hagenauer found clients not only among the clergy, led by the aging archbishop Hermann von Wied, but most especially among the bourgeoisie, as is evidenced by this tribute to the wife of the burgomaster Johann von Aich (1468–1519).

The medal, known only in this Berlin specimen, presents the portrait of an older woman. She is posed *en face* in a plain, high-necked gown. Her likeness forms a distinct contrast to the delicate, tasteful profile of the young and beautiful Margarete von Frundsberg (cat. no. 95). Hagenauer usually produced profiles, and this pose is a departure. The frontal pose is not so well suited to the two-level image of relief and field as Hagenauer developed it. It is tempting to assume that the work was modeled after a secondary source rather than produced *ad vivam*, and it is probable that Hagenauer based his work on a painting of Sibylla von Aich and her four daughters by Bartholomäus Bruyn in the Alte Pinakothek in Munich.[2] Habich dates the medal to Hagenauer's Cologne years between 1536 and 1546,[3] the period in which he also produced one of his masterpieces, the medal of Philipp Melanchthon (cat. no. 99).

Wolfgang Steguweit

Friedrich Hagenauer
Michael Mercator (born c. 1491, died after 1539)
98
Silver, cast
Diameter 49.2 mm; diameter of the outer perimeter of the inscription from the N in VENLO to the M in ANGLORVM, 45.6 mm
London, The British Museum

Obverse: Bust in three-quarter view facing to the left. The subject is clean-shaven and wears a brimmed cap and a broad fur collar over a shirt and jerkin. Around his neck hangs a double chain with pendant. Legend: (leafy stop, star) A REGE ANGLORVM PRIMI MILITIS CREATI EX VENLO EFFIGIES

98 obv.

98 rev.

(Portrait of the first [man] from Venloo created a knight by the king of the English).
Reverse: Legend: MICHAEL • MERCATOR • ÆTATIS SVÆ XLVIII • GRATIA • DEO ET (as ligature) REGI • M • D • XXXIX • (three leafy stops) (Michael Mercator at the age of 48. Thanks be to God and the king. 1539).

Michael Mercator, no relative of the famous cartographer Gerardus Mercator (1512–1594), was a native of Venloo, in that time in the Netherlands duchy of Guelders. He was born into a respected family[1] and became a diplomat under the protection of Floris d'Egremont, count of Buren. In 1528 a "Michael the Geldrois" (almost certainly Michael Mercator) is recorded as having been sent on a confidential mission respecting the Netherlands to Henry VIII.[2] Letters from Floris d'Egremont from 1538 imply that Mercator was then in England on another diplomatic mission.[3] The date of his death is unknown. The present medal is one of three known medallic portraits of Mercator. All are dated 1539 and seem to be by the same medalist, although none is signed.[4] When first published in 1630, the present medal was thought to have been produced by Mercator himself, who was also credited with a pendant medal of his wife, Elizabeth, from the same year.[5] This attribution was maintained until 1904, when Julius Cahn ascribed all three of the Mercator medals and the one of his wife to Hagenauer.[6] The medal is clearly cast from a wood model, and in other respects has much in common with the works of medalists active in Augsburg. Certain features do recall the work of Hagenauer, who appears to have been active in the region of the Lower Rhine and the Netherlands at around this time.[7] The lettering and spacing of the inscription on the obverse are especially reminiscent of his style,[8] and the treatment of the facial features and costume broadly echo the few other known three-quarter-view portraits by the artist. Certain aspects of this piece would appear to argue against an attribution to Hagenauer, however. The format of the incised inscription on the reverse and its style of lettering are not seen elsewhere in his work.[9] This particular three-quarter view recalls some of the portraits of notables at the court of Henry VIII by Hans Holbein the Younger (born 1497–8, died 1543).[10] It is even possible that the medalist

based his model on a Holbein drawing brought from England. Mercator himself left England in 1539, the date of the medal.[11]

Marjorie Trusted

Friedrich Hagenauer
Philipp Melanchthon (1497–1560)
99
Boxwood model
Diameter 46.6–49.1 mm; internal measurement from the tip of the biretta to the bottom edge of the bust truncation, 39.0 mm
Berlin, Staatliche Museen, Münzkabinett
369/1876

Obverse: Bearded bust in biretta and gown facing to the left. No inscription or signature.
Reverse: Plain.

99 obv.

99a
Silver, cast
Diameter 46.3 mm; internal measurement from the tip of the biretta to the bottom edge of the bust truncation, 38.0 mm; weight 28.61 g
Berlin, Staatliche Museen, Münzkabinett

Obverse: As above, but with the legend: PHILIPPVS MELAN[ch]THON • A° [= anno] ÆTATIS SVÆ • XLVI •

99a obv.

99a rev.

238

(Philipp Melanchthon in his forty-sixth year). Below the biretta, the figure or letter • l • and a leaf. In the field to the left, the monogram signature FH (as ligature).

Reverse: The five-line inscription: PSAL[m] • 36 • SVBDITVS ESTO DEO ET ORA EVM • ANNO • M • D • XLIII • (leaf) (Psalm 37:7, King James Version; Vulgate 36:7]: "Rest in the Lord, and wait patiently for him." 1543).

Because of the spiritual fervor expressed in the portrait of the reformer Philipp Melanchthon, this wood model is one of the most valuable of the twenty or so Hagenauer models to survive. "The delicate likeness of the gaunt, aging, bloodless scholar seems especially true to life, yet not without a certain unpretentious nobility."[1] As is typical in Hagenauer's models, mere ornamental details are avoided. The inscription and signature, as in others of the master's medals, were only impressed into the mold by means of punches.[2]

The medalist created two different portraits of Philipp Melanchthon in 1543, and we can only assume that the "praeceptor Germaniae" sat for them himself. Hagenauer produced portrait medals of a whole series of churchmen that Archbishop Hermann von Wied had summoned either to Cologne or to his residence in Bonn to help him carry out his plans for reform. In addition to the archbishop himself, the series includes Martin Butzer, Johannes Pistorius, Kaspar Hedio, and Johannes Sturm.[3] Hagenauer also portrayed noted opponents of the Reformation, like the members of the cathedral chapter Count Thomas von Rheineck and Count Johann von Isenburg-Grenzau.[4] His medals thus provide a portrait gallery of the participants in the religious controversy at Cologne.

After Martin Luther, Philipp Melanchthon was the most important of the German reformers. On completion of his studies in Heidelberg and Tübingen, Melanchthon received an appointment to the university at Wittenberg in 1518. Under Luther's influence he became increasingly involved in the theological debates of the period. In 1521 he wrote the first systematic theology of Protestantism, thereby placing the Reformation

on a theoretical foundation. For the Augsburg Diet in 1530 he prepared the "Augsburg Confession," a summary of the articles of faith for the evangelical church. In the following decades he attempted to serve as a mediator in quarrels between the Protestant and Catholic churches. It was in that capacity that Melanchthon found himself in discussion with the adherants of the Archbishop of Cologne in the Rhineland in 1543.

Wolfgang Steguweit

Friedrich Hagenauer
Johann Thewen (Zhewen?; 1516–1577)
100
Lead, cast
Diameter 58 mm
St. Petersburg, State Hermitage Museum
17744

Obverse: Bust to right with beard and moustache, wearing a flat cap with its brim turned down and a coat with a fur collar over a pleated shirt. Legend: IOHANNES THEVVEN DE DVPLETO ANNO ÆTATIS SVÆ XXVIII (Johann Thewen de Dupleto, in his twenty-eighth year). In the field in the lower right, the monogram FH (as ligature).

Reverse: The four-line inscription: SALVS POPVLI SVPREMA LEX ESTO A[nno] • M • D • XLIIII (The well-being of the people is the highest law. 1544).

According to the medal, Johann Thewen (Theuven) de Dupleto was born in 1516. He may be identical with the Johannes Dulpetensis who was a jurist at the University of Cologne and pupil of Ludwig Falkenberg. After sojourns in Paris and Orleans, Dulpetensis served from 1566 to his death on April 24, 1577, as regent of the crown college.[1]

In the section of his corpus labeled "Manner of F. Hagenauer," Habich published a wood model presenting the portrait of an unknown man with the comment that the sitter's costume was identical to that of the Thewen medal. Unfortunately, Habich

100 obv.

100 rev.

only knew the Hermitage example from a photograph of a poor-quality plaster cast. If one compares the medal itself with the lovely likeness on the wood model, it becomes clear that both portraits are indeed of the same man.[2]

The Thewen medal has many features in common with other Hagenauer works from around 1540. His famous medal of Melanchthon (cat. no. 99) is designed in the same way, again with only a brief inscription on the reverse. The smallest details of the portrait are rendered in a literal, somewhat dry, and very flat relief. Babelon refers to his style as a "very positive realism."[3] Hagenauer's portraits are distinctly individualized, and this is in fact their chief virtue.

Yevgenia Shchukina

Unknown Artist with the Initials HG (?)
Martin Luther (1483–1546)
101
Silver, cast, uniface
Diameter 60.8–63.3 mm; diameter of the inner perimeter of the
    inscription, 53.4 mm; width of the bust from the tip of the
    nose to the back edge of the cap, 40 mm; weight 76.76 g
Berlin, Staatliche Museen, Münzkabinett
463/1874

Obverse: Bust to the left wearing a beret and a monk's habit with hood. Legend: HERESIBVS • SI • DIGNVS • ERIT • LVTHERVS • IN • VLLIS • ET • CRISTVS • DIGNVS • CRIMINIS • HVIVS • ERIT (small cross as stop) (If Luther is guilty of heresy, Christ too is guilty of this crime). In the empty space to the left, roughly at the height of the chin, is the sunken date 1521. Upside-down below the truncation, just above the small cross in the inscription, are the tiny intaglio initials HG.
Reverse: Plain, with casting holes. Scratched at the bottom in a later hand, the letters I C R.

Martin Luther, the founder of the German Reformation, was born into a well-to-do mining family. He studied philosophy and law in Erfurt before entering a monastery and being ordained in 1507. In 1511 he was asked to teach at the newly founded university in Wittenberg, where he worked as a theologian until his death. His study of the Bible led him to recognize "justification through faith alone" and to reject the idea of ecclesiastical indulgences. He was excommunicated for his numerous tracts against the papacy in 1521. At the Diet of Worms he refused to recant, but was nevertheless placed under imperial safe conduct. On his homeward journey he found refuge for a few months in the Wartburg in Eisenach, where he began his translation of the Bible, a labor that would occupy him for many years.

Luther continued to be active as a theologian, teacher, and pastor in Wittenberg, where in 1525 he married Katharina Bora and established the first Protestant rectory. Lucas Cranach was also a respected citizen of the town and produced portraits of the reformer at various stages of his life, thereby creating the

101a obv.

prototypes for countless medallic portraits executed over the following centuries.

The present portrait is based on the Lucas Cranach engraving *Luther with Doctoral Hat*.[1] The date 1521 refers to the year in which the engraving was done and is not necessarily the date of the medal, though it was probably executed soon afterward. The medalist is unknown, and the initials HG have yet to be deciphered. It may be that the letters do not even stand for the medalist's name. In addition to the uniface example in Berlin, there is a uniface lead casting in Gotha in which the date and the letters HG are raised and part of the casting. Because of their technical quality, these two examples are thought to be the originals. To judge from the countless subsequent repetitions of the piece, there must have been an immediate demand for copies. In these aftercasts, the portrait, legend, and date are often combined with various reverses, for example Christ carrying the Cross or Christ with a fourteen-line inscription COELESTIS • PATER • AETERNE. . . .[2]

Lore Börner

101a
Gold, cast
Diameter 60.5–61.0 mm; diameter of the inner perimeter of the
    obverse inscription, 53.7 mm; diameter inside the reverse
    border, 58.0 mm; weight 87.84 g
New York, American Numismatic Society, Gift of Alastair
    Bradley Martin, 1955
1955.30.[1]

Obverse: As above, but lacking the initials below the bust.
Reverse: Bust of Christ to the right, draped, his hair falling in long curls onto his shoulders and back, his beard of moderate length composed of rows of curls. Above his head the dove of the Holy Spirit on a ribbonlike cloud. Flanking the top of his head, the relief letters CRIS TVS. In the left field, the legend: ICH • BIN •/DAS • LEM/LEIN • DAS/DER • WE/LT •

101a rev.

SVND/TREGT • IO/HANES ./ • AM (I am the lamb who takes away the sin of the world. John, at the . . .). In the right field: I CAP[i]T[el] • NIMANT • KVMPT/ZU • DEM/VATER • D/AN • DVRCH/MICH • IO[hanes] •/AM • XIIII (. . . first chapter. No one comes to the Father except through me. John, at the fourteenth). The quotations are from John 1:29 and 14:60, respectively. Border of tiny birds, possibly again the dove of the Holy Spirit, on a raised ring.

This medal is probably composed of two joined shells—it has a hollow sound, and its specific gravity is 12.96—but there are no join marks visible on the edge. The image of Christ on the reverse is identical with one on medals signed PF and universally attributed to Peter Flötner.[2] It is also known as a cut-out lead casting, trimmed a bit too closely in the back of the head.[3] The reverse as a whole has the same legend as the Flötner version, but differs from it in the size and style of the lettering, the shape of the cloud under the bird, the absence of curls over Christ's forehead, the form of the border, the lack of a signature, and the fact that the word CRISTVS is in relief rather than intaglio. The version shown here appears to be unique.[4] Since the Christ figure is identical while the other elements diverge, it would appear that an original model comprising only the head was used for both the Flötner medal and the present one.

The pairing of this head of Christ with the Luther obverse was certainly done before 1706, the date of the first publication of either side,[5] and this gold specimen, with its sharp casting of both faces, may have been produced as early as any of the other known versions.

Alan M. Stahl

Hans Kels

One of the first writers to concern himself with Hans Kels was Albert Ilg. His essay on the so-called Ambras Gaming-Board, dated 1537 and signed HANS KELS ZV KAUFBEIREN,[1] points out stylistic similarities between that work and a number of medals.[2] Georg Habich expanded this oeuvre with countless attributions.[3] At that time Hans Kels was still thought of as a single person, and it was only Theodor Hampe, working from newly discovered documents, who finally identified two separate artists: Hans Kels the Elder and his son Hans Kels the Younger, also a sculptor.[4]

Hampe was able to provide the following details about Hans Kels the Elder. He worked in Kaufbeuren, and as early as 1507 he is documented as receiving a sum of money for "ettlich bild" (possibly relief portraits) he was creating for Emperor Maximilian I.[5] The documents suggest that this Hans Kels married Anna Müller, a Kaufbeuren girl, in 1506 or 1508.[6] Hampe therefore conjectured that Hans the Elder might have been born in about 1480–85. He must have died in about 1559, for in that year his sons paid a tax on his estate.[7]

Hans the Younger was apparently the oldest of three sons.[8] Given the date of his parents' marriage, he is generally assumed to have been born between 1508 and 1510.[9] The first documentary mention of him is his acceptance into the Augsburg guild as a master sculptor in 1541. Shortly before he had married Barbara Flicker, a daughter of the Augsburg goldsmith Hans Flicker. Hans Kels the Younger acquired his own house in Augsburg in 1554,[10] and it was there that he died in 1565,[11] his wife in the spring of 1568.[12]

Various commissions are spoken of in connection with Hans Kels the Younger,[13] though the works mentioned in the documents either were never completed, have not survived, or have not been definitely identified.[14]

The only two works that can be associated with *one* Hans Kels with certainty are the gaming-board mentioned above, created for King Ferdinand I, and a wooden medal with bust portraits of Emperor Charles V, his wife Isabella, King Ferdinand I, and his wife Anna, which is also signed and dated 1537.[15] It is still unclear, however, whether the signatures on these two pieces are to be ascribed to the father or the son.

Other works are readily associated with the two signed pieces in question. Two wooden medals, for example, one with bust portraits of Charles V, Ferdinand I, and Maximilian I, dated 1540,[16] and another of Georg Fugger the Younger from 1541,[17] reveal the same stylistic characteristics. Several small reliefs with allegorical figures of the Arts and Virtues in Vienna and in Nuremberg—the latter bearing the monogram HK—are clearly related.[18]

Yet as was the case with the two signed works, the authorship of this small related oeuvre cannot be definitely assigned to one Hans Kels rather than the other. Given the guild regulations and workshop customs of the time, it is more plausible to attribute the group related to the gaming-board to Hans Kels the Elder as the director of the Kaufbeuren workshop.

Moreover, the large group of medals collected under the name Hans Kels the Younger in Habich[19] is so heterogenous, quite apart from the question of distinguishing between father and son, that it is in need of critical reexamination.[20]

Susanne Wagini

101a obv.

102 obv.

102 obv.

102 rev.

Hans Kels (?)
Barbara Reihing (1491–1566)
102
Boxwood model
Diameter 51 mm
New York, The Metropolitan Museum of Art, Gift of J. Pierpont
    Morgan, 1917
17.190.472

Obverse: Bust to left of a middle-aged, heavy-set woman. She wears a bonnet of double woven strands and a blouse of tight, parallel pleats with an elaborate ruff collar and an unpatterned bodice. A moderately heavy chain circles her neck and disappears at the truncation. Legend: (rosette) BARBARA REIHINGIN VXOR AETATIS AN[no] XXXXVII (Barbara Reihing, wife, age 47). Leaf border.
Reverse: Scrolled shield with the Reihing arms.[1] Legend: (rosette) IN DOMINO CONFIDO ANNO MD XXXVIII (I trust in God, in the year 1538). Leaf border.

In addition to this wood model there are cast examples of this piece in Munich and Augsburg and various modern forgeries.[2] A smaller version (39 mm), in which the sitter wears a different hat and her hair falls in a braid, exists in the form of a two-sided wooden medal and in cast examples.[3] There are wooden models of the subject's husband, Georg Hermann (see cat. no. 110) bearing this same date of 1538 and with his own arms as their reverse, one the same size as this piece (51 mm) and another considerably smaller (29 mm).[4] Cast examples combining portraits of husband and wife as obverse and reverse of a single medal are known from as early as the eighteenth century.[5] Since the present medal identifies Barbara as a wife (*uxor*) but does not name her husband, such a pairing was probably intended when the piece was originally conceived.

Barbara Reihing was born in 1491, the daughter of a wealthy citizen of Augsburg, Ludwig Reihing. In 1516 she married Georg Hermann, a native of Kaufbeuren.[6] Hermann became a representative for the Fugger family in 1524, then entered the service of Emperor Ferdinand I in 1536. He was a humanist,

and carried on correspondence with Erasmus (cat. no. 157), Melanchthon (cat. no. 99), and others. He kept a house in Kaufbeuren, and in 1537 bought the castle at Gutenberg. He died in 1552, and was buried in Gutenberg, as was Barbara. Earlier medals of Hermann are known from 1527, 1529, and 1531.[7] Those of 1529 are documented to be the work of Matthes Gebel (cat. nos. 109–113).

None of the medals of Barbara Reihing or her husband are signed. The general pose of the 1538 portraits of Hermann is so close to that of the earlier Gebel as to suggest that they are copied from it; the regularization of the somewhat wild hair of the early version supports this idea. The heraldic reverses of the 1538 Hermann pieces also follow the 1529 versions so closely as to suggest copying. It is unlikely that Gebel himself was the author of the 1538 Hermann medals or those of Barbara Reihing, since he was known throughout his long career as a stone carver, and these are carved in wood.

The Barbara Reihing medals bear stylistic similarities to some of the pieces Habich attributes to Kels, also unsigned.[8] There are also close parallels to medals attributed to the Augsburg medalist Christoph Weiditz (cat. nos. 87–91)—most notably to the one of Magdalene Rudolff-Honolt (cat. no. 88)—whom Habich identified as the teacher of Hans Kels the Younger.[9] The medals of Barbara Reihing are certainly the work of an expert wood carver with a fine eye for portraiture. Whether they are the work of either Hans Kels, father or son, or for that matter of another artist in Kaufbeuren or elsewhere is uncertain. In view of their originality and the formulaic nature of the corresponding depictions of her husband, it appears that they were the main focus of the 1538 cycle, and that the Hermann portraits from that year were copied from earlier medals as pendants to them.

Alan M. Stahl

Artist Unknown (from the Upper Rhine?)
Laux Kreler (c. 1486–1552)
103
Hardwood relief
Diameter 59 mm

103 obv.   103a obv.

Munich, Bayerisches Nationalmuseum
R 468

Obverse: Bearded bust in profile facing to the right. A cap covers much of the hair, though a few locks curl around its flaps. On top of the cap sits a flat beret with a narrow brim. The sitter is dressed in a high-necked, richly pleated shirt. His coat has a tall collar with a serrated edge, and from its yoke the fabric falls straight down in even folds. Legend: (foliate stop) M · D · XX [several numerals removed] · (rosette) LAVX · KRELER · WAS (the W and A as a ligature) · ALT · LI · (In 152–, Laux Kreler was fifty-one years old). A simple narrow molding circles the edge of the relief.
Reverse: In black ink on the flat, unworked surface, an old inventory number 83.

Elisabeth Kreler (born c. 1490, died after 1535)
103a
Hardwood relief
Diameter 58 mm
Munich, Bayerisches Nationalmuseum
R 469

Obverse: Bust of a woman in profile facing to the left. Her hair is entirely hidden beneath a smooth bonnet pulled well down on her forehead. A piece of ornamental trimming has been affixed to her bonnet with a pin. She is wearing a high-collared shirt, her square-necked bodice is inset with delicate pleating and has an embroidered border. On top of this she wears what appears to be an open, brocaded jerkin with a leafy vine design in high relief. Two little hooks have been provided in place of buttons. Legend: · ELISABET · KRELERIN · [several numerals deleted] HET (the E and T as a ligature) · ICH · DIEGE STHALT · VND · WAS · 47 · IAR · ALT (Elisabeth Krelerin. I looked like this and was forty-seven years old). A simple raised molding forms the border.
Reverse: In black ink, an old inventory number 82.

The portrait of Laux Kreler once bore the date 1537, but the Roman numerals XVII have been cut away.[1] The entire date has been removed from the portrait of his wife Elisabeth, but it too read (in Arabic numerals) 1537. The two were intended to form a pair. They were long considered to be the work of the medalist Hans Kels the Younger. The first to raise doubts about this universally accepted attribution was Alfred Schädler,[2] who suggested that the date originally read 1535.[3] He compared the works to Kels's signed portrait medal of Emperor Charles V, Isabella, King Ferdinand I, and Anna,[4] also executed in 1537, and found that there is nothing in Kels to match their anatomically correct modeling with its delicate nuances, the precise linear outlines, the sovereign placement of their busts and inscriptions in the circle, the features that constitute their striking pictorial effect.[5]

Friedrich Kobler took up Schädler's argument and filled in the historical background. As Anabaptists, Laux Kreler and his wife emigrated from Augsburg to Strassburg in 1528. Kobler therefore concluded that the two Kreler portrait medals were executed in the region of the Upper Rhine. Friedrich Hagenauer, whose influence is apparent in the two wood models, worked in that region from 1532 to 1536.[6]

Habich questioned whether the two reliefs were in fact intended as models for medals.[7] Because of their high relief, he preferred to think of them as ornaments for a piece of furniture, perhaps a chest.[8]

Born in c. 1486, the goldsmith Laux Kreler probably moved to Augsburg from Landsberg am Lech.[9] In Augsburg he attained master status shortly before 1509. He must have acquired Augsburg citizenship beforehand, for it was a prerequisite to membership in the guild. Kreler lived at Maximilianstrasse 6,[10] and in 1509 he was commissioned, along with other goldsmiths, to produce silver prizes for the Great Shooting-Match. In 1521 he had either completed a silver service for Jakob Fugger or was working on one.[11] None of these pieces have survived, nor have any of his other works—or at least nothing has been identified as his. In 1527 he and his wife became embroiled in the Anabaptist controversy. Though required by the Augsburg council to renounce all ties to that congregation, the Krelers persisted in playing leading roles in it.

103 obv.

103a obv.

Once their continuing affiliation was discovered, they were placed under arrest, but they were permitted to leave the city unharmed, probably thanks to the intercession of Count Georg of Württemberg.[12] They then moved to Strassburg, a haven for many of Augsburg's Baptists. As late as 1528, Kreler asked the Augsburg council to be permitted to retain his Augsburg citizenship and his guild membership until the situation became normalized,[13] but apparently the council refused his petition, for shortly afterward, in October 1528, he bought citizenship in Strassburg and became a member of the guild responsible for that city's goldsmiths.[14] A document from 1530 identifies him as an Anabaptist and shows him to be living in Predigergasse.[15] Kreler died in Strassburg in 1552.[16]

Susanne Wagini

Hans Kels
Johann Scheubel (1494-1570)
104
Boxwood model
Diameter 78.0–79.0 mm; diameter of the outer perimeter of
    the inscription from the I in IOAN to the D in DITIONIS,
    73.5 mm
Berlin, Staatliche Museen, Münzkabinett
355/1876

Obverse: Bearded bust in cap and gown with loop closure facing to the right. Running from the upper left to the lower right of the field, the diagonal inscription: AETATIS — SVAE 45 (in his 45th year). Above this, in the right side of the field, a small tablet with a combination of numbers connected by curves (a horoscope?). Legend: EFFIGIES • IOAN[nes] • SCEVBELII • EX • KIRCHHAYM • SVB • TECKH • DITIONIS •

WIRTENB[ergensis] (Likeness of Johann Scheubel of Kirchheim unter Teck, in the domain of Württemberg). At the end of the legend there is a recessed rectangle.
Reverse: Between twining ribbons with tassles above and below, the two-line inscription: VIVITVR INGENIO • CAETERA MORTIS ERVNT. (One lives from the spirit, the rest is transitory). High-profile border in the form of a wreath, with small fruits (laurel berries?) at top and bottom.

As is apparent from the uncompleted section of the legend at the bottom of the obverse, this model was left unfinished. It is possible that the artist had no intention of reproducing it in metal from the start. The style of the relief, somewhat dry, but skillfully carved, gives the model the appearance of a gem. Its attribution to Hans Kels has been disputed by some scholars, most notably Habich. Julius Ebner was the first to publish it, along with a comprehensive description. It was he who convincingly compared the work to the medal of Adam Oefner, which is signed with the ligature HK.[1] In 1916, Habich praised Ebner's essay as "a substantial contribution to our knowledge of Kels," but chose to present the Johann Scheubel medal himself under the rubric "after the manner of Kels."[2] In his exhaustive corpus Habich relegates both the Scheubel and Oefner medals in his text to a "Ganzhorn group," yet definitely ascribes it to Kels on the plate.[3] Since there is no reason to doubt the attribution of the signed Oefner medal to Kels, we must consider the Scheubel piece to be a work by the same master. Both subjects were active in the years 1539–40 at the university in Tübingen—Scheubel as professor of mathematics—and various details, such as the shape of their beards and the treatment of their clothing, suggest the hand of a single medalist.

Wolfgang Steguweit

104 obv.

104 rev.

The Master of the Beltzinger Group (Martin Schaffner?)

A series of ten models for medals and lead casts from the years between 1522–23 and 1529–30 are traditionally grouped under the heading "Master of the Beltzinger Group." They are related in format, design, and technique, as well as by their subjects' association with Ulm. In an illuminating argument, Habich attributed the models to the Ulm painter and woodcarver Martin Schaffner, basing his assumption on a model bearing the legend M • S • M. He assumed that the letters stood for "Martin Schaffner, Maler" (Martin Schaffner, painter), and suspected that the image was a self-portrait.[1]

Martin Schaffner was born in 1478 or 1479 and died between 1546 and 1549—probably of the plague that struck Ulm in the autumn of 1547. In 1526 he was apppointed Ulm's official painter.

The painting of portraits was an important part of Martin Schaffner's work. He created independent portraits of considerable distinction, and even in his religious panels he tended to incorporate portraits of himself. The latter allow us to identify the image on the M • S • M model as the painter's self-portrait[2]

Though Schaffner always identified himself as a painter, there are surviving examples of his woodcarving that show him to be altogether familiar with wood as a medium and with the design of reliefs. Portrait medals were just then becoming "fashionable" in Germany, especially in Franconia and Swabia. Thus it is not surprising that Schaffner, with his skill as a craftsman and his ability to capture a specific personality in a portrait, would have wished to experiment in the new medium, yet there are no surviving documents confirming the painter's involvement in medalmaking.

The medallic portraits ascribed to him represent a close circle of burghers in Ulm. Six of the ten surviving pieces are of members of the Beltzinger family; one presents the artist himself; one is a portrait of Anna Rotengater of Ulm; and of the remaining two, H • E and Christoph Hengel, nothing is known.[3]

Almost all of Schaffner's medallic work is preserved only in models rather than metal casts, suggesting that perhaps he produced them only as gifts for his own circle of friends. It is perfectly apparent that Schaffner was no routine medalist, for he tended to ignore certain of the elements that constitute perfection in the medium. One cannot help but notice the casual placement of these portraits in the field, for example, the crude forms of his letters, and especially the haphazard alignment of his inscriptions. Yet his subtle command of relief form, his obviously affectionate surrender to the personalities of his subjects, and his ability to design highly convincing portraits are what make these medals so charming.

Lore Börner

The Master of the Beltzinger Group
Christina Beltzinger (born 1500)
105
Boxwood model

105 obv.

Diameter 54.8–55.2 mm; diameter of the inner perimeter of the inscription, 45 mm
Berlin, Staatliche Museen, Münzkabinett
836/1914

Obverse: Bust portrait of a young woman seen from the right. Her hair is gathered in a braid and falls down her back. She wears an embroidered headband and a stylish hat that is slashed and laced and that cuts into the inscription on the left. Beneath her dress one can see her blouse, which has a decorative edging. A knotted cord hangs around her bare neck. Legend: • M • D • IOR • VND • XXII • KRISTINA BELCINGERE XXII ([In the year] 1522, Christina Beltzinger, 22).
Reverse: Two old house or workshop marks along with two small crosses in black ink on a smooth surface.

According to the inscription, Christina Beltzinger was born in 1500, but we know nothing more about her. The left-hand house mark on the reverse could be a crude approximation of the Beltzinger device: a horseshoe-shaped staff bent upward, ending on the left in a small cross and on the right in a P, and enclosing the Gothic letter b or perhaps a lily. That device belonged to a Heinrich Beltzinger, originally from Memmingen, in the Allgäu, who became a citizen of Zurich in 1484.[1] The Beltzinger family that settled in Ulm had also come from the Allgäu.

Lore Börner

The Master of the Beltzinger Group
Erasmus Beltzinger (born 1501)
106
Boxwood model

106 obv.

105 obv.

106 obv.

Diameter 49.9–50.9 mm; diameter of the inner perimeter of the inscription, 41.2 mm

Berlin, Staatliche Museen, Münzkabinett

835/1914

Obverse: Bust portrait of a young man. He is wearing a large slashed and laced hat and a robe that falls from the yoke in folds. Legend: • A[smus] • B[eltzinger] • XXI • M • D • XXII • (Asmus Beltzinger, 21. 1522). Faint, recessed line in the inner circle of the legend.

Reverse: On a smooth surface the name Erasmus Beltzinger in black ink in an early hand.

Nothing is known about Erasmus Beltzinger but what the medal tells us about the date of his birth. His clothing and the Latinized form of his name in the inscription on the back suggest that he was a student or scholar.

Obviously this model was meant to form a pair—the portraits facing each other—with the one of Christina Beltzinger (cat. no. 105), carved in the same year. The similarity in their delicate features suggests that they were not husband and wife, but rather brother and sister. The style of the lettering on the two pieces is also identical, though the few letters on the Erasmus medal are not altogether pleasing because of their inconsistent spacing. The lettering on the Christina medal is unbalanced as well, with more spacing on the left where it is interrupted by the hat and more compressed letters on the right.

Little is known of the status of the Beltzinger family in Ulm. It was certainly not one of the "best families." In this group of medals there is a model dated 1530 with a portrait of the fifty-five-year-old Apollonia Beltzinger. She appears in documents in 1541 as the widow of Erasmus Beltzinger the Elder and could be the mother of these two siblings born in 1500 and 1501.

Lore Börner

"Nuremberg 1525–1527"

After Hans Schwarz's departure from the city in 1520 the first Nuremberg medalist we know by name is Matthes Gebel, whose work is documented beginning in 1527. In the years between 1525 and 1527, however, some sixty medals were produced in the city. The majority of them are two-sided and in bronze, though some are in silver. In most cases their obverses and reverses are stylistically interrelated, though it is often clear that the two were not created by a single artist. We must assume that these medals were produced by one workshop, whose overseer allowed his colleagues to work out their own ideas rather than forcing them to follow a uniform style.

We know from his own testimony that Friedrich Hagenauer (cat. nos. 92–100) worked as a medalist in Nuremberg,[1] and it is possible that some of these anonymous pieces could be his work. Some one-sided, relatively large bronze medals, on which the portrait bust extends down to the bottom edge, were produced in Nuremberg in the years 1525–26. Their subjects are portrayed either in profile or in three-quarter view. The back

shoulder often forms a nearly horizontal line, a feature found in medals known to be by Hagenauer.[2] The modeling of the heads in this group is quite powerful, and the clothing is varied, even in its details.

Matthes Gebel, who had been granted Nuremberg citizenship as early as 1523, but who only appears as an independent medalist in 1527, must also have worked in this unknown workshop. The medals attributed to him are either silver or bronze, and for the most part double-sided. Their portraits clearly reveal Gebel's hand, while the inscriptions and reverse coats of arms are presumably the work of a colleague.

We still have no idea of just how many different medalists might have been connected with this short-lived workshop. Yet we can definitely assume that Friedrich Hagenauer and Matthes Gebel were both associated with it, if only briefly. One must also bear in mind that Nuremberg accepted the Reformation in 1525, as a result of which, suddenly and quite unexpectedly, its sculptors and goldsmiths no longer had commissions from the Church. In order to have work it is likely that some of these artists tried their hand at making medals. The first works certain to be Gebel's are from 1527, and it is at just this time that the workshop "Nuremberg 1525–1527" was dissolved.

Hermann Maué

107 obv.

"Nuremberg 1525–1527"

Barbara Ketzel (1505–1540)

107

Bronze, cast

Diameter 49 mm

Berlin, Staatliche Museen, Münzkabinett

Obverse: Bust portrait in strong relief of a young woman of twenty in three-quarter profile facing to the left. She is dressed as a bride in a high-necked, pleated blouse embroidered at the neck and over this a sumptuous bridal cloak. A double chain with a pendant hangs around her neck, and an additional chain hangs down to her breast. Her hair is caught up in a cap crowned with a wreath of flowers—another sign that she is a bride. The bust extends to the medal's bottom edge. The inscription, set off by a double line, runs from shoulder to shoulder. Legend: WARBARA (leaf stop) GEBORNE (leaf stop) KECZLIN (leaf stop) M • D • XXV (Barbara née Ketzel. 1525).

108 obv.

Reverse: Plain.

From this workshop, whose members were heretofore un-differentiated, this medalist is the only one who chooses the three-quarter profile for his portraits.[1] In the present instance his choice is not especially flattering, though one cannot know whether this is due to the medalist's own awkwardness, the actual appearance of the sitter, or the ideal of beauty at the time.

We know very little about Barbara Ketzel. She was the only daughter of Wolf Ketzel (1472–1544), who also had himself portrayed by the same medalist in 1525.[2] Wolf Ketzel was a wholesale merchant in Nuremberg and was appointed a member of the city's Greater Council in 1504. In 1517 he was dismissed from the council owing to various misdemeanors and even forced to leave the city. The medal of Barbara Ketzel was created at a time when the family had lost its prestige, though her clothing is that of a wealthy woman still. Her presentation as a bride, as well as the wording of the inscription, referring to her as a Ketzel by birth, would suggest that the medal was commissioned on the occasion of her marriage. For unknown reasons, however, her wedding never took place, for the record of deaths from the parish church of St. Sebald in Nuremberg indicates that she died unmarried. Under the year 1540 we find the notation: "Junckfrau Barbara, Wolf Ketzels Tochter am Marckt" (the maiden Barbara, Wolf Ketzel's daughter on the marketplace).[3] Apparently the family had returned after a time to its house in town, a prestigious address in the center of the city.

Hermann Maué

"Nuremberg 1525–1527"
Cardinal Albrecht, margrave of Brandenburg (born 1490, Archbishop of Mainz and elector 1514–45)
108
Bronze, cast, uniface
Diameter 107 mm
Nuremberg, Germanisches Nationalmuseum
Med 3871

Obverse: The thirty-seven-year-old cardinal is depicted in profile facing to the right. He is wearing a soft shirt, the standing collar of which forms a number of horizontal folds around his neck, and a damask coat with large, plain lapels. The only thing that serves to identify Albrecht as a cleric is his wide, flat biretta. The inscription, formed of very beautiful and carefully formed letters, is set off both inside and out by two inscribed circles. Legend: DOMINVS MIHI ADIVTOR • QVEM TIMEBO • ANN[o] AETAT[is] • XXXVII • ("The Lord is my helper." "Whom shall I fear?" At the age of thirty-seven). The first part of the inscription is taken from Psalm 118:6 (Vulgate 117:6), the second from Psalm 27:1 (Vulgate 26:1).

This is the only surviving specimen of this medal. It resembles an engraving that Albrecht Dürer produced shortly before, in 1523, when the cardinal was attending the Diet in Nuremberg.[1] The clothing is not the same, and the medal portrait is more idealized than the engraving. Nevertheless, the medalist may well have patterned his work after Dürer's.

There are two contemporary reproductions of the medal in smaller format, one with a diameter of 44 mm, the other 28 mm, but with distinctly higher relief. Both have the cardinal's coat of arms, a listing of his titles, and the date 1526 on the reverse.[2] It is conceivable that the larger medal was produced as some sort of pattern, after which the two smaller versions, which are unquestionably works of the above-mentioned Nuremberg group, were to be cast in larger quantities. Hans Reinhart (cat. nos. 125–27) would also use this medal, virtually without changes, as the pattern for the obverse of still another medal of Albrecht of Brandenburg eight years later.[3]

The use of a wax model causes one to think of the Vischer workshop (see cat. no. 86), and indeed a year earlier, in 1525, Peter Vischer the Younger had created, on commission from Albrecht himself, the bronze slab for the cardinal's tomb in Halle, now in the collegiate church in Aschaffenburg.[4]

Albrecht of Brandenburg, born in 1490 in Neukölln, near Berlin, was to have a brilliant career in the Church. In 1508–9 he was made a prebendary in Magdeburg, Mainz, and probably Trier as well. Chosen archbishop of Magdeburg and administrator of the bishopric of Halberstadt in 1513, he became archbishop of Mainz only a year later. With this latter office he became an elector and arch-chancellor of the Reich. At the age of twenty-four Albrecht had thus attained the highest ecclesiastical office in the Empire. He was elevated to cardinal four years later. To amass all of these offices and benefices he had to pay large sums to the Curia for dispensation. These payments were financed by the Fuggers and paid back with indulgence monies earmarked for the building of St. Peter's in Rome.

At sixteen, together with his older brother, the elector Joachim I of Brandenburg, Albrecht had founded and also attended Viadrina University in Frankfurt an der Oder. While there he made his first acquaintance with the humanist movement, which would be a strong influence on his later life. Thanks to his humanist leanings and his contacts with leading members of the movement, Albrecht first appears to have felt a certain sympathy with the ideas of the Reformation, but toward the end of his life he distanced himself further and further from its teachings. Initially he had intended to deal with abuses by reforming the clergy, but later he gave his support to the efforts of the Counter-Reformation.

The cardinal was fond of lavish display, a weakness that led him into repeated financial difficulty. As a champion of humanism he sought to emulate the princes of the Italian Renaissance in their patronage of artists and scholars. Among those who worked for him were the most important artists of his age, notably Lucas Cranach, Albrecht Dürer (cat. no. 84), Matthias Grünewald, and Hans and Peter Vischer.

Hermann Maué

Matthes Gebel
(active 1523–1574)

Matthes Gebel is thought to have been the most prolific medalist of the German Renaissance. Georg Habich attributes more than 350 works to him, and sees the large number of inferior pieces among them as an indication that Gebel headed a large workshop.[1] The differences in quality among the medals attributed to Gebel are obvious, yet there is no record of a workshop with many assistants. For this reason it seems more probable that various goldsmiths who only dabbled in medalmaking adopted Gebel's style, which represents a definite trend within German Renaissance medalmaking. Thus it becomes a matter of distinguishing Gebel's own works from those of his imitators.

In terms of technique, his medals in gold, silver, bronze, and also doubtless in lead, all of them cast from stone models, are masterpieces. They are distinguished by a wealth of detail in their often lavish costumes, their strongly modeled hair and beards, their often very high relief, and a nice balance between portrait and inscription. In many of his works Gebel also manages to capture something of the specific personality of his subject. With few exceptions his reverses present coats of arms of a fairly standard design together with highly ornamental crests and occasionally trophies as well. Scenic and narrative or figural portrayals are rare.

Gebel's known works begin with two medals of Albrecht Dürer from 1527 and 1528.[2] It is relatively certain that prior to 1527 Gebel worked in the still somewhat shadowy workshop known as "Nuremberg 1525–1527" (cat. nos. 107–8). What role he played in that organization is not yet clear. It was not until much later that Gebel placed his initials on the bust truncations of his medal portraits—in fact, with but a single exception, only in the years 1542 and 1543.[3] Gebel produced no medals after 1555, though he was to live for another twenty years.

A large number of Nuremberg burghers and patricians appear on Gebel's medals. Those of the nobility are chiefly limited to the families of the margraves of Baden and of the margraves of Brandenburg in Franconia, the dukes in Bavaria, and the counts of the Rhenish Palatinate. Gebel had no need to undertake lengthy travels to secure commissions. Nevertheless, it is recorded that he presented himself at the Diet in Speyer in 1529 and in Augsburg in 1530, as these occasions were ideal for making useful contacts.

Gebel's birthplace and date of birth are unknown. It is also uncertain where and under whom he received his training. The first mention of him is on the occasion of his being granted Nuremberg citizenship in 1523.[4] Presumably he first worked as a sculptor, but then, after 1525, when the demand for sculptors had fallen off in Nuremberg as a result of the Reformation, turned to making medals instead.

Gebel lived in Nuremberg for fifty years, up until his death in 1574. One encounters his family again and again in the baptismal records and death registers of St. Lorenz parish. His first wife died in 1556—in the death register Gebel is once more identified as a portrait carver—and he remarried the following year. How he managed to feed his new wife and six children is unknown, for after the mid 1550s there are no more medals that can be ascribed to him.

Gebel dominated medal production in Nuremberg for nearly thirty years.[5] He was so successful in the second quarter of the sixteenth century that there was simply no room for other medalists in the city, and many of them left. Among these was Hans Bolsterer (cat. nos. 122–23), who only returned to Nuremberg once Gebel had ceased to be active. Others, like Jakob Hofmann or Joachim Deschler (cat. nos. 118–20), only began receiving commissions at about this same time, although they, like Bolsterer, had produced medals before 1555.[6]

Hermann Maué

109 obv.   109 rev.

Matthes Gebel
Christoph Kress (1484–1535)
109
Silver, cast
Diameter 39 mm; weight 15.49 g
Nuremberg, Germanisches Nationalmuseum, on loan from the
    Friedrich von Praun family bequest
Med 8988

Obverse: Bust portrait in profile facing to the right. Kress is wearing a shirt with a high and richly ornamented collar, buttoned at the front, and over it—largely obscured by an outer garment—hangs a chain. The extremely short bust section is cut off at the bottom by two curving lines. The inscription is set off by two inscribed circular lines. Legend: • CRISTOF • KRES • XXXXII • IAR • ALT • (Christoph Kress, forty-two years old). *Reverse*: The Kress family coat of arms.[1] The legend, set off inside and out by two thin laurel wreaths: CHRISTOFF • KRES • VOM • KRESENSTAIN • M • D • XXVI • (Christoph Kress von Kressenstein. 1526).

This particular medal of Christoph Kress is a key to the early work of Matthes Gebel and his connection to the "Nuremberg 1525–1527" workshop, for there is another Kress medal—also dated 1526—with an identical obverse but variant reverse.[2] The reverse of our medal is unquestionably the work of Matthes Gebel, while its obverse is like that of a number of medals from the "Nuremberg 1525–1527" workshop. Typical features of this group are off-center portraits that bring the face close to the edge, the form of the truncation, and finally the deep circular lines framing the inscription. None of the variants of the reverse is comparable to this one attributed to Gebel, where the com-

position is livelier. The armor bends at the waist and turns to the side, and the crest with the miniature heathen is also slightly turned, while the helmet itself is seen from the side. The design nearly overflows the available space, and in several spots touches against the legend: LAS[s] MIRS • GEFALLEM [*sic.*, for GEFALLEN] • TREW • IN • ALLEN • M • D • XXVI • (I take what comes, honest in all things. 1526). The inscription is not set off from the center panel.

Some have claimed that this is among Gebel's earliest works, but in doing so they make the false assumption that the date of 1526 on the reverse designates the year in which it was made. This cannot be, for Kress was not elevated to the hereditary nobility and given permission to use the appellation "von Kressenstein" until July 15, 1530. His advancement was clearly so important to him that he promptly commissioned a new reverse for his medal with his new coat of arms and his new appellation. The combination of this new reverse with the original obverse meant that his name would appear twice, once in the new form, "Christoph Kress von Kressenstein," and once in the old, simply "Christoph Kress."

Kress, who died at the age of fifty-one, is considered the most important member of an extensive family.[3] He studied in Milan (1497), Antwerp (1500–1502), and London (1502–3), and in subsequent years often served as a soldier under various commanders. In 1513 he was admitted into the Nuremberg city council as a young burgomaster, and in 1526 he was appointed *Septemvir*, one of the leaders of the municipal regiment. In 1532 he became the city's chief military officer. His diplomatic skills were recognized early on. Often he was asked to represent Nuremberg's interests at the imperial court and at various Diets. He was one of the first to subscribe to Luther's ideas and was present as Nuremberg's ambassador at the famous Diet of Worms in 1521, where Luther defended his theses. He also represented Nuremberg's interests at the Diet in Augsburg in 1530, where the *Confessio Augustana* was signed and the nobles and imperial cities supporting the new teachings banded together. The city showed its gratitude for his skillful negotiations by conferring on him a number of municipal offices to which sizable incomes were attached.

Christoph Kress died in Nuremberg in high esteem. His likeness, in the form of a full-length statue dressed in armor, still stands in front of Nuremberg's neo-Gothic city hall, the image of an exemplary Nuremberg councilman and burgomaster. The Kress estate has survived the centuries in the form of an endowment, the chief beneficiary of which is the fortified church of St. Georg in Kraftshof. The structure was heavily damaged in the Second World War. The brothers Samuel and Rush Kress of the American branch of the family financed its rebuilding with funds from the Kress Foundation in New York.[4]

Hermann Maué

Matthes Gebel
Heinrich Ribisch (1485–1544), Georg Hermann (1491–1552), and Konrad Maier (1493–1565)

110 obv.

110 obv.   110 rev.

110

Silver, cast

Diameter 39 mm; diameter of the outer perimeter of the inscription from the N in CUNRA to the O in DOCTOR, 36.1 mm

New York, private collection

Obverse: Superimposed profile portraits of three men facing to the right, each wearing a shirt with an ornamented collar buttoned to the neck and a thick chain largely hidden by a cloak. Legend: HEN[rich] • RIBISCH • DOCTOR • GEOR[g] • HERMAN • CVNRA[d] • MAIR.

Reverse: The coats of arms of the three subjects side by side.[1] Around the margin, set off by two narrow laurel wreaths, the legend: QVAM • IVCVNDVM • HABITARE • FRATRES IN VNVM • M • D • XXXI • ("How pleasant it is for brethren to dwell together in unity." 1531). The text is abbreviated from Psalm 133:1 (Vulgate 132:1).

Matthes Gebel's ability to capture the unique appearance and personality of his subject even in the smallest of likenesses is especially apparent in this group portrait of three men ranging in age from thirty-eight to forty-three. Ribisch, in the foreground, appears to be solid and resolute, Hermann circumspect and cooly calculating, Maier somewhat lighter in spirit, even jolly.

Medals with portraits of more than one person are rare in the Renaissance. Hans Schwarz had presented the five Pfinzing brothers on a single medal in 1519, but he failed to characterize each of his subjects as successfully as Gebel has.[2] Gebel himself may not have been particularly pleased with his solution to the difficult problem of producing three portraits in one, for the medal is unique in his œuvre; of all the medals he created there are only eight others with multiple portraits—all from between 1527 and 1533—and all of these are of two subjects, not three.[3]

The three men on the present piece were business partners in the service of the Fuggers in Augsburg.[4] Ribisch, born in Silesia, had studied law, and worked in the Fugger branch in Breslau. He later became an advisor to Ferdinand I (cat. no. 124) and tax collector general in the duchy of Silesia and the margravate of Lausitz.

Georg Hermann was related to the Fuggers by marriage and represented them first in Antwerp and then, beginning in 1520,

in Schwaz, in the Tyrol. Hermann was a medal enthusiast; no other private individual of his time commissioned as many medallic portraits of himself.[5] One can assume, then, that it was he who had the idea of producing this "friendship medal."

Maier, who was in turn related to Hermann, began his career with the Fuggers in Hall, in the Tyrol, where the Fugger mint and the main office of its Tyrolean mining and smelting operations were located.[6] Later employed in Antwerp, he finally moved to the Augsburg headquarters of the trading house in 1540. There his highly esteemed family was accepted into the patrician class. In 1550, Maier became burgomaster in Augsburg and a member of the municipal court.

Hermann Maué

Matthes Gebel
Johann Fernberger (1494–1553) and his son Ulrich (1525–1573)

111

Model in Kelheim stone

Diameter 39 mm

Berlin, Staatliche Museen, Münzkabinett

831/1876

111 obv.

Obverse: Jugate portraits of the Fernbergers, father and son, facing to the left. On top of his pleated shirt Fernberger is wearing a high-buttoned doublet with lapels and a coat that nearly hides a heavy chain hung around his neck. A fashionable embroidered cap, a flap of which hangs down over his ear, accentuates the curve of his head. His eldest son is shown at the age of seven; like his father he wears a pleated shirt and a coat. The letters of the inscription are set unusually far apart. Legend: HONESTATIS ERGO MDXXXII (For the sake of honor. 1532).

Reverse: Plain.

111a

Bronze, cast

Diameter 39 mm

Nuremberg, Germanisches Nationalmuseum

Med 8371

Obverse: As above.

Reverse: The circle is filled with an eleven-line inscription:

111a obv. 111a rev.

D • FERD • I •
ROMANORVM
HVNG • BOIEM • Q • RE =
GIS • A • CONS • SECŔETAR
PRIMAR • VICEDOMINVS •
AVSTR • VLS • ANASVM • IOAN
FERENBERGER • AB • EGEN =
BERG PATER NATVS
ANN • XXXVII •
VLRICH • EIL • SEP =
TU FNN =

The whole of the inscription is probably to be deciphered as follows: Domini Ferdinandi I Romanorum, Hungariae Bohemiaeque regis Archiconsiliarius Secretarius Primarius Vicedominus Austriae Ulterioris Anasum Johannes Ferenberger ab Egenberg Pater natus annos XXXVII. Ulrich filius septem Annos (The father Johann Fernberger from Egenberg, age thirty-seven, trusted advisor and first secretary to his lord Ferdinand I, king of the Romans, Hungary, and Bohemia, and vice-regent of Austria above the Enns, and his son Ulrich at the age of seven years). It is not entirely clear how we are to read the last two lines. Habich, whose example was apparently in poor condition, read them as: VLRICH • FIL • SE • B[?]TYFNN.

It was not uncommon for Matthes Gebel to place his subject's motto next to the portrait on the obverse of his medals, relegating his name, age, and occasionally his position to the reverse, generally together with a coat of arms. This particular motto is somewhat surprising, for the humanists tended to place *virtus* above the more superficial *honestas*.

This is the first German Renaissance medal to present a child's portrait and the first to depict a father and son together. The occasion for this incunabulum in German portrait medal production is unknown.

The Fernberger family came from the Tyrol, where there is mention of a castle with the Latinized name "Vern mons" as early as 1223.[1] According to the medal's inscription, this Johann, the fifth son of Ulrich Fernberger, was born in 1494. In 1521 he moved to Upper Austria and entered into the service of Ferdinand I.[2] He was appointed councilor and first secretary and in 1530 was given the title of *Vicedominus*—that is to say

the king's highest official—in Upper Austria. He was given the job of enlarging and especially fortifying the king's castle in Linz.[3] In the same year he served as ambassador to the Diet in Augsburg. In 1535 he was awarded the additional office of hereditary chamberlain of Upper Austria above the Enns. Fernberger managed to acquire the Egenberg estate in 1531 and added its name as an appellation to his own.[4] He died in 1553 in Linz.[5] This son Ulrich, his oldest child, inherited the title of chamberlain and died in 1573.

Hermann Maué

Matthes Gebel
Georg Ploed (born 1491–92, died 1532)
112
Bronze, cast
Diameter 38 mm; diameter of the outer perimeter of the inscription from the S in GEORGIVS to the O in ANNO, 34.8 mm
Nuremberg, Germanisches Nationalmuseum
Med 53

Obverse: Nude bust of a young man in profile. Legend: GEORGIVS • PLOED • AETA[t]IS • SVE • ANNO • XXXVI • (Georg Ploed in his thirty-sixth year). In the name Ploed, the E appears within the O. Pearled border.
Reverse: In roughly equal proportions, an inscription and a friezelike allegory of Death. A nude youth is seated on a pile of stones, his right foot extended, his left foot braced beneath him. He gazes upward at an inscription, pointing to it at the same time with his left hand: OMNIA • PERIBVNT • DEVS • ETERNVS • (Everything will pass away; God alone is eternal). With his right hand he grasps a large bone that rests on top of a skull, creating a visual link between the skull and the inscription. Also leaning against this skull is a recumbent, winged putto holding in his left hand a cluster of flames and gazing toward the youth. The outer inscription, in much more compressed letters than those of the obverse, reads: MISERERE • MEI • DEVS • SECVNDVUM • MANNAM [for MAGNAM] • MISERICVRDIAM • TVAM • ("Have mercy on me, O God, according to thy loving kindness"). The text is from Psalm 51:1 (Vulgate 50:1). In the remaining space is the date: MDXXXII (1532). A narrow wreath of stylized leaves serves as a border.

112 obv. 112 rev.

111 obv.

As a rule, Gebel's reverses carry coats of arms rather than figural scenes. The very carefully worked reverse of this medal is of particular interest in the debate about the relationship between German Renaissance medals and those of Italy. Georg Habich repeatedly claims that German Renaissance medals developed altogether independently, yet he himself pointed out that this reverse can be traced back to a medal by Giovanni Boldù from 1458 (cat. no. 27).[1] It is probable that Gebel did not have a Boldù medal at hand, however, but only a drawing of its reverse. Konrad Celtis (1459–1508), one of the most influential German humanists, was convinced that the Boldù was antique and had a drawing made of it. Petrus Apianus (1495–1552) included the motif, reproduced from a drawing, in the compilation of ancient inscriptions he published in 1534.[2] Whoever commissioned the Ploed medal thought of the motif as a reinterpretation, in the light of Christian belief in resurrection, of an ancient, pagan allegory of Death, in accord with one of the basic ideas of humanism.

Simultaneously, and independently of each other, Horst W. Janson and Jean Seznec investigated the motif of the youth and the putto with a skull.[3] They concluded that it was Boldù's own invention, and one that was rarely imitated in full. The putto and skull alone, however, soon took on a life of their own, becoming a familiar motif in Western art. According to Janson, the putto is to be thought of as a genius *all'antica*, suggestive of a Christian angel charged with accompanying the soul of the deceased—symbolized by the flames—into heaven.[4]

We know very little about Georg Ploed. The Ploeds were respected merchants in Nuremberg, who carried on trade with various seaports, especially Lübeck. The family died out in 1596.[5] To judge from the present medal, Georg was thirty-six when he died, which would mean that he was born in 1496.[6] Apparently this is not the case, for there is a variant of this medal with an identical obverse, but a portrait on the reverse, dated 1528, of Ploed's wife, Susanna, at the age of twenty-seven.[7] The model for the obverse of the present medal was thus created in 1528, and was then recombined with this new reverse in 1532. This means that Ploed was born in 1491 or 1492 and died at the age of forty. After Ploed's death, Susanna married an Alexander Weller,[8] and died in 1544.[9]

The nude bust admits no clues to the subject's station in life. This, together with the motif of the putto and skull and the inscription taken from the standard funeral service, would suggest that the medal was commissioned as a memorial to Georg Ploed at his death, using an obverse produced four years earlier.

Hermann Maué

Matthes Gebel
Jacoba, duchess in Bavaria (1507–1580)
113
Silver, cast
Diameter 41 mm
Munich, Staatliche Münzsammlung

113 obv.   113 rev.

Obverse: Bust portrait in profile to the right. Jacoba's hair is almost entirely hidden by an elegant net, around which a ribbon has been wound at the back so that it forms a sort of knot. A flat cap trimmed with a large feather sits on top of the net. She wears a pleated blouse with an embroidered collar beneath a bodice. Around her neck hangs a short pearl necklace with a cruciform pendant and a double chain that disappears beneath the bodice. Legend: IACOBA • PFALLCZGR[äfin] • BEI • RHEIN • HERCZ[ogin] • IN • OB[er] • VND • NI[eder] • BAIREN • I[h]R[e]S • ALTERS • XXVII • (Jacoba, countess Palatine of the Rhine, duchess in Upper and Lower Bavaria, at age 27). A very thin wreath of leaves runs around the edge.
Reverse: Two rampant lions support the arms of the Palatinate-Bavaria-Baden alliance.[1] Below, two hands clasp around a heart that has three flowers growing out of it. This motif is framed by a broad laurel wreath wound top and bottom with ribbons and with three more flowers bound in at the bottom. On the wreath, scarcely visible at 10–11 o'clock, is the date MDXXXIIII (1534).

Matthes Gebel produced a large number of medals with portraits of women, all quite similar. They generally have full, round faces, and their schematic and not entirely logical bust truncation and clothing are virtually identical in their overall forms. The sole variation is in the head covering, for at times he omits the cap. His only attempt to reproduce the subject's actual features is in the line of the profile, yet he takes extreme care with the rendering of jewelry and costume details. Jacoba's cap is ornamented with various baubles, including a portrait medal, each precisely reproduced.

Jacoba, born in 1507, was the oldest daughter of Margrave Philipp I of Baden (1478–1533) and Elisabeth of the Palatinate.[2] In 1522, she married Duke Wilhelm IV of Bavaria (born 1493, ruled 1508–50). Their daughter Mechthilde, born in 1532, married her uncle Philibert of Baden (ruled 1537–69), four years younger than she, in 1557. Jacoba served as guardian for her grandson Philipp II of Baden (1559–1588) until her death in 1580. Given the close family ties between the dukes of Bavaria and the margraves of Baden, it is likely that even as duchess in Bavaria, Jacoba exercized a decisive influence over political developments in the margravate. In the opinion of her contemporaries she was distinguished by uncommon intelligence and determination.

113 obv.

114 rev.

The motif of clasped right hands was known in antiquity as the *dextrarum iunctio*, a symbol of concord, commonly between man and wife. Jacoba would certainly have been familiar with the ancient significance of such a motif. Just what the addition of the blossoming heart might mean is unclear. An identical reverse, complete with the date 1534, appears on the medal of her unmarried cousin, Margaretha, though there Gebel has inserted the coat of arms of Baden-Spanheim.[3]

Hermann Maué

Nuremberg School
Hieronymus Wahl (1510–1573)
114
Wood model (pearwood?)
Diameter 35.2 mm
St. Petersburg, State Hermitage Museum
17559

114 obv.   114 rev.

Obverse: Bust portrait three-quarters to the left, bare-headed with moustache and forked beard. Around his neck a cord with a scythelike pendant. Legend: IHERONIMVS • WHAL SEINES ALTERS XXXIII 15 43 (Hieronymous Wahl in his thirty-third year. 1543).
Reverse: A sleeping putto on the ground in front of a dead tree, leaning against a skull. In the field to the right, a shield with helmet, mantling, and crest.[1] Legend: DER LEIPLICH • DOT • DER • GLAVBIGEN • IST • EIN • SCHLAF • (To the faithful, the death of the body is but a sleep).

Little is known of the subject of this medal. Wahl was a citizen of Nuremberg, and married to Euphrosina, daughter of the Nuremberg legal counsel Dr. Johann Müllner.[2] According to the medal, he was born in 1510. He died in 1573, in which year Valentin Maler portrayed him a second time.[3] In 1553 he is listed as the owner of the house at Theresienstrasse 10, and in 1560 his signature appears with those of some sixty of Nuremberg's most prominent merchants on a petition to the city council for new market ordinances. In 1570 he had a stone erected for himself and his family in Nuremberg's Johannis Cemetery.[4]

Nuremberg medalists generally carved their models in stone, and this wood example is therefore exceptional. Habich relates that there was a specimen of the medal cast from this model in Budapest.[5]

The first appearance in the Renaissance of the subject matter of the reverse is on a medal by Giovanni Boldù (cat. no. 27). The putto with a death's head recurs on various medals of the period (see cat. no. 112), and on a number of the so-called *Todesmedaillen* (death medals) created by masters in the Erzgebirge between 1533 and 1557.[6] On the present medal, the traditional *memento mori* is combined with a family coat of arms.

It is extremely difficult to produce an *en face* portrait on a medal. In this case, the artist has solved the problem with great sculptural freedom. The warm tone of the wood causes the portrait to appear especially lifelike. The high relief is so detailed that one can even see a tiny vein on the sitter's temple. Because of its perfect craftsmanship and its high artistic quality, this model belongs among the masterpieces of German medallic art of the Renaissance.

Yevgenia Shchukina

Ludwig Neufahrer
(c. 1505–1563)

Neufahrer's origins are unclear, but he probably came from Lower Bavaria. We also have no idea where he received his training. His first medals, from about 1530, have an association with Upper Austria and its capital of Linz, where he ultimately settled. A number of commissions from King Ferdinand I for works in gold and silver are documented. The city of Vienna also awarded him such a commission. In 1546 he was named court goldsmith. Neufahrer not only cast medals, he also created a number of struck pieces. Thus it is no wonder that he was appointed warden of the Vienna mint in 1547. This appointment occasioned his move to the capital, and it would appear that it brought his career as a medalist to a close, for with but a single exception there are no dated medals of his, either cast or struck, from this point on.[1] He was awarded Viennese citizenship in 1555. In 1558 he became mintmaster in Prague, an office he filled until forced to retire on account of his health in 1561.

Neufahrer's works are not particularly uniform, and it is not altogether clear whether he should be associated artistically with Augsburg or Nuremberg. It would appear that his style is most influenced by the Nuremberger Matthes Gebel (cat. nos. 109–13). At first he carved the models for his medals in wood, but later increasingly favored stone. One notes the change in the decreasing diameter of his works. In his portraits the main focus is on the head. His busts are generally quite minimal, with only a suggestion of costume. He preferred to use coats of arms for his reverses, which have either smooth edges or a framing laurel wreath. There are a few borders of beading or cording, the latter more typical of his struck pieces. His figural reverses are of varying quality. Most were patterned after the works of others, probably taken from prints or drawings.[2]

Karl Schulz

263

115 rev.

101a obv.

103 obv.

103a obv.

106 obv.

110 obv.

111 obv.

112 rev.

113 obv.

114 obv.

114 rev.

115 rev.

121 obv.

123 obv.

269

126 rev.

127 obv.

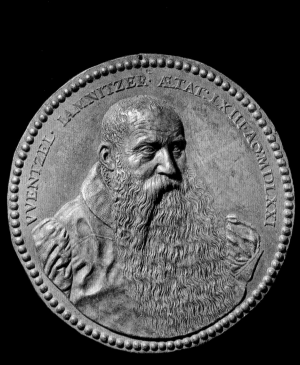

129 obv.

132 obv.

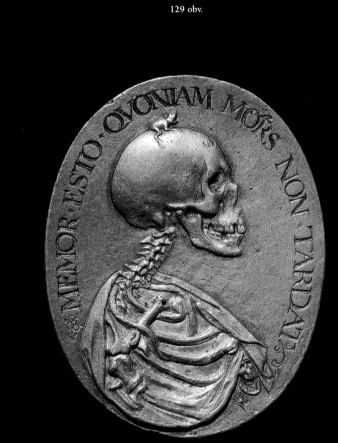

134 rev.

134 obv.

115 obv.   115 rev.

Ludwig Neufahrer
Nikolaus Kolnpock (1500–1579)
115
Silver, cast
Diameter 39.4 mm; diameter of the outer perimeter of the inscription, 39.4 mm; weight 24.44 g
Vienna, Kunsthistorisches Museum, Münzkabinett
14.033bß

Obverse: Bearded bust portrait in hat and chain with pendant facing to the left. Legend: NICLAS KHOLNPOCK AET[atis] XXXI IAR • MDXXXI (Nikolaus Kolnpock in his thirty-first year. 1531).
Reverse: A nude female figure seated on a squared block of stone in the pose of the classical *Boy with a Thorn*, facing to the right.

This is one of the first of Neufahrer's works to reveal his own distinct style, which derives from the Augsburg medal tradition. Although unsigned, it can be attributed to Neufahrer with confidence on the basis of the portrait. Its reverse, however, is disputed, for Neufahrer himself was primarily a portraitist, and his reverses generally carry only a coat of arms with no figures.[1] The motif of the *Boy with a Thorn*, the famous Roman copy of a Hellenistic sculpture, had been especially popular in painting and sculpture since the fifteenth century. In the present medal the boy has been transformed into a girl and the figure reversed. We cannot know just why this image was chosen for the medal of Kolnpock. At roughly the same time, however, it appears in a similar form on two medals by Friedrich Hagenauer.[2] Neufahrer follows the pose of the classical sculpture more closely than does his colleague, so it would not appear that he was copying Hagenauer. Yet the transformation of the figure into a female seems more logical on Hagenauer's medals, the obverses of which carry portraits of women. One must therefore assume that Neufahrer patterned his reverse after Hagenauer after all, even though his actual pattern was different, possibly a print of some kind.[3] In both cases the presentation of the image without inscription and against an empty background is reminiscent of Italian medals.

The family of the sitter, Niklas Kolnpock zu Ottsdorf, lord of Salaberg, came originally from Lower Bavaria and settled as merchants in Upper Austria. Niklas abandoned the merchant

class to take up the life of a landed nobleman. He extended his holdings to Lower Austria as well, where he died in 1570. He was a very wealthy man and repeatedly served as a source of funds for the emperor.

Karl Schulz

Ludwig Neufahrer (?)
Francis I (born 1494, king of France 1515–1547)
116
Silver, cast
Diameter 43.6–44.3 mm; outside diameter of wreath on the reverse, 34.1 mm
New York, private collection

Obverse: Bearded three-quarter-profile bust looking to the left, with feathered cap and embroidered robe. Legend: FRANCISCVS • I • FRANCORVM • REX • C[hristianissimus] 43 (Francis I, most Christian king of the French, age forty-three).
Reverse: A salamander in flames inside a wreath of laurel, above it a crown. Below the salamander, the signature L-N. Legend: DISCVTIT H[an]C FLA[m]MA[m]: FRA[n]CISC[us] ROBORE ME[n]TIS O[m]NIA P[er]VI[n]CIT RERV[m] IMERSABILIS V[n]DIS (Francis destroys this flame, with the power of the spirit he conquers all, in the waves of events he is unsinkable).

The portrait on this medal is definitely modeled after that of a larger (roughly 123 mm) single-sided medal, based in turn on a painting by François Clouet, that bears the date 1537[1] and has been attributed to the medalist Benedetto Ramelli.[2] The attribution to Neufahrer was apparently first made by Forrer.[3] Aside from the fact that the present medal is patterned after someone else's design, there are good reasons to doubt that it is Neufahrer's work. He never signed his other works in this manner; he created only profile portraits, and he left almost no figural reverses. To be sure, the work in question was originally a struck medal (though only casts are known), a fact that has not been pointed out heretofore. Perhaps this explains why it is so different from Neufahrer's other works, and why he was copying someone else, a common practice in the production of struck medals in this period.

116 obv.   116 rev.

116 obv.

Yet it is puzzling why Neufahrer would have produced a portrait of the king of France. Neufahrer worked in Austria, and Francis I was a lifelong enemy of the house of Habsburg. At the very time when the medal was created he was again at war with Emperor Charles V. It is true, of course, that he was internationally admired as a Renaissance prince who generously patronized the arts, and one does find other German medals of this monarch.[4] In future, it would be better to consider this medal as being "attributed to Neufahrer."

The salamander in flames, together with the motto "I live in it and quench it" was the device of Francis I. It can be seen on a medal from as early as 1504, where the Italian inscription translates roughly as "I nourish the good and extinguish the bad."

Karl Schulz

117 obv.

Kunz Peck (died 1535) or Sebald Peck (died 1545)
Kunz Peck with his sons Hans Peter, Linhard, and Sebald
117
Alloy of lead and tin, cast, uniface
Oval, 64.2 × 93.7 mm; vertical measure of the outer perimeter of the inscription, 53.3 mm
London, Victoria & Albert Museum
83–1867

Obverse: Bust of Peck facing front, embracing his sons. Kunz's right forearm and hand and his left hand are visible. Generalized drapery is swathed around the necks of the four men. Wreath border. Legend: • KUNCZ PECK MIT DREIEN SVNEN HANS PE[ter] LINHAR–T SEB • – ALT (Kunz Peck with [his] three sons, Hans Peter, Linhard, and Sebald). Below, in a cartouche: ECCE QVA[m] BONV[m] ET QVAM IOCVNDVM HA • BITARE FRATRES IN VN[um] ("Behold, how good and how pleasant it is for brethren to dwell together in unity"). The text is from Psalm 133:1 (Vulgate 132:1).
Reverse: Plain.

This piece is highly idiosyncratic in composition and style. Habich tentatively assigned it to Hans Peisser (born c. 1500, died after 1571), noting parallels between its oval shape and wreathed border and those of one of Peisser's works. It has also been suggested that the medal might be Netherlandish.[1] Kunz Peck, a sculptor and joiner, was a citizen of Nuremberg, however, and Habich comments that the work could well have been produced by Peck himself. The warmth of the image, together with the unusual oval form, suggest that it may well be a self-portrait of the artist with his sons. Sebald Peck was also a noted sculptor and architect, and it is also possible that it was he who created the piece.[2] His brothers Hans Peter and Linhard (recorded in Nuremberg in 1520 and 1533, respectively) were both joiners.[3] It is worth comparing the present work with the 1519 medal of the five Pfinzing brothers by Hans Schwarz.[4] Their jugate busts are ranged in profile, while here the family grouping is more integrated.

The motto on the cartouche is of the type normally found on reverses of medals (see cat. no. 110), and is a further exceptional aspect of this work.[5] Ingrid Weber classified the piece as a plaquette, suggesting that it exceeds the definition of a medal.[6] It can be tentatively dated to 1530–35, the few years before the death of Kunz Peck.

Marjorie Trusted

Joachim Deschler
(died c. 1571)

The date and place of Deschler's birth are unknown. Similarly, nothing is known about his training. He is first documented in Nuremberg in 1532, on the occasion of his first marriage. He acquired citizenship in that city on May 3, 1537, and at some point during that decade he spent two years studying in Italy, spending most of his time in Venice and Rome. He then appears to have been based in Nuremberg until the late 1550s. He was given the first of many commissions from Archduke Maximilian (later Emperor Maximilian II; cat. nos. 61–62) in 1543, and in 1548 he undertook a portrait in stone of Archduke Ferdinand (later Emperor Ferdinand I; cat. no. 124). A few years later, in 1553, the Nuremberg patrician Hans Ebner (died 1553) delivered an unnamed work for him to Ferdinand in Prague. Deschler had requested 1,000 thalers for the piece, but the archduke paid him only 800. In 1563, Deschler left Nuremberg to enter the service of Maximilian in Vienna, and in 1566 he was named imperial sculptor. He is last documented in Vienna in 1571 and seems to have died at the end of that year.

Deschler was primarily a medalist, but according to the Nuremberg chronicler Johann Neudörfer (1543–1581), he executed small-scale works in various materials, among them cameos, marble portraits, and boxwood carvings.[1] Just over a hundred medals produced between 1540 and 1569 have been attributed to the artist. Among his subjects, in addition to various members of the imperial family, were leading citizens of both Augsburg and Nuremberg.[2]

Deschler seems generally to have used stone models, and in style his medals carry on the tradition of his slightly older contemporary in Nuremberg, Matthes Gebel (cat. nos. 109–13). His portraits combine Gebel's naturalistic observation with a tendency to idealize his subjects. This latter trait, almost certainly a result of his studies in Italy, is especially apparent in works like his portrait of an unknown youth in the Victoria & Albert Museum.[3] His signed medals are incised with his monogram, the interlocked initials ID.[4]

Marjorie Trusted

Joachim Deschler
Georg Tetzel the Elder (1497–1519)
118
Alloy of tin and lead, cast
Diameter 86.2 mm; diameter of the outer perimeter of the inscription, 81.8 mm
London, Victoria & Albert Museum
77–1867

Obverse: Half-length portrait facing to the left, bearded and bare-headed, wearing armor with a lance support fitted to the breastplate, and holding a mace in his right hand. Legend: • GEORG TETZEL • ÆTATIS SV[a]E • XXII • ANNO (Georg Tetzel in his twenty-second year). Beaded border.
Reverse: Coat of arms with helmet, mantling, and crest.[1] Legend: BONITAS DEI IN REBVS OMNIBVS ELVCET (The goodness of God shines out in all things). Wreathed border.

Although this medal is unsigned, Habich first attributed it to

Deschler for stylistic reasons, and it is generally accepted as his work.[2] The relatively unusual half-length portrait format and the bold depiction of the armor and gloved hand grasping a mace give the subject an air of strength, even aggression, that is borne out by his facial expression. The armor is analogous to that found on other medals attributed to Deschler.[3] The stone model for the obverse, dated 1552, is in the Staatliche Münzsammlung in Munich, and provides an approximate date for the present medal.[4] Given this date, it would at first appear that the subject is the younger Georg Tetzel (1529–1595). But inasmuch as his features as they appear on another medal cast in 1556 are clearly unlike the present sitter's, this seems unlikely.[5] Habich pointed out that the older Georg Tetzel, his uncle, was a soldier, and that the family, one of Nuremberg's oldest and most prestigious, may well have commissioned this medal posthumously.

Marjorie Trusted

Joachim Deschler
Hieronymus Paumgartner (1497–1565)
119
Brass, cast
Diameter 69.4 mm
London, Victoria & Albert Museum
171–1867

Obverse: Bust facing front, bearded and bare-headed. Legend: HIERONYMUS • PAVMGARTNER • ANNO • ÆTATIS • 56 (Hieronymus Paumgartner in his fifty-sixth year). On the trun-

118 obv.

118 rev.

119 obv.

119 rev.

cation, the date 1553 and the monogram signature ID. Wreathed border.

Reverse: Coat of arms with helmet, mantling and crest.[1] Legend: • IN • VMBRA • ALARVM • TVARVM • SPERABO • DONEC • TRANSEAT • INIQVITAS (I put my trust under the shadow of your wings until injustice has departed). Wreathed border.

The corpulent Paumgartner is here portrayed facing the viewer with heavy jowls. Deschler handles the varied folds of this sitter's garments with the same sensitivity to texture that is apparent in the soft fur collar of his portrait of Lukas Sitzinger (cat. no. 120). As in that work, the bust, in high relief, overlaps the double incised line that sets off the inscription.

Hieronymus Paumgartner, from a highly influential family, was a prominent Nuremberg citizen. Along with his other civic appointments, he served as *Pfleger* (guardian) of the Sebalduskirche in 1536, and in the following year performed the same function for Nuremberg's other important church, the Lorenzkirche. He was named *Oberster Hauptman* (chief councillor) of Nuremberg in 1553, the year of the present medal, which may have been made in part to celebrate that honor.[2] Other medals of him are illustrated in Habich.[3]

Marjorie Trusted

Joachim Deschler
Lukas Sitzinger the Elder (1482–c. 1554)
120
Silver, cast
Diameter 45.2 mm; diameter of the outer perimeter of the inscription, 42 mm; weight 34.4 g
Berlin, Staatliche Museen, Münzkabinett

Obverse: Bust facing to the right, bearded, wearing a low, broad-brimmed hat over a cap with flaps and a gown with a wide fur collar. Legend: • LVCAS • SYCZINGER • ÆTATIS • SVÆ • 72 (Lucas Sitzinger at seventy-two). On the truncation, the date 1554. Pearled border.
Reverse: Coat of arms with helmet, mantling, and crest.[1] Legend: MEMORIA • IVSTI • ÆTERNA ("The righteous shall be in everlasting remembrance"). The text is from Psalm 112:6 (Vulgate 111:6). Pearled border.

This unsigned medal was first ascribed to Deschler in 1893,[2] and the attribution seems quite certain. The medal is likely to have been issued in the year of the sitter's death. Its pious inscription encircling the coat of arms on the reverse is a feature frequently seen on German medals of the sixteenth century.[3]

120 obv.

120 rev.

Little is known about the subject. Sitzinger was originally from Augsburg, where he had married Hester Fugger, a daughter of Hans and Veronika Fugger, in 1510. He was appointed to Nuremberg's council in 1514 and spent the remainder of his life in that city. In 1518 he is recorded as buying a house in Nuremberg, and in 1524 he bought a stable from Jakob Fugger. In 1534 he bought another house from Hans Decker.[4] Other references to him survive in the Nuremberg archives. His son, Lukas Sitzinger the Younger, is also represented on a medal.[5]

Marjorie Trusted

The Master of the "Ottheinrich of the Palatinate Group"

The sixteen medals from the years 1551 to 1559 published by Habich under the heading "Otto-Heinrich of the Palatinate Group"[1] are among the finest of their time, yet scholars are by no means agreed about their authorship.[2] Most writers consider the creator of the Ottheinrich group to be the sculptor who carved the famous alabaster bust of the prince elector in the Louvre,[3] and accordingly the identity of that sculptor changes with each new attribution of the Ottheinrich medals.

None of the attributions proposed heretofore is altogether convincing. The stone medallion of Ottheinrich above the portal of his wing at Heidelberg Castle, attributed to Alexander Colin,[4] shows none of the mastery of design that we so admire in most of the Ottheinrich medals and the alabaster bust. Moreover, it is by no means certain that Colin, accustomed to working on large sculptures, was also experienced in small forms. The same objections can be raised against the Abel brothers, whose contribution to the Maximilian tomb in Innsbruck is generally considered to be the least imposing of the whole ensemble. Deschler's medals from the years 1551 to 1559—the period here in question—reveal no particular stylistic parallels to the Ottheinrich medals.[5]

There is a remarkable similarity between the coat-of-arms reverse of the Ottheinrich medal exhibited here and Ottheinrich's electoral seal from the year 1556, assumed to be the work of the Heidelberg goldsmith and seal-maker Adelmann.[6] There are also stylistic connections between the Ottheinrich medals and the works of the Nuremberg medalist Hans Bolsterer (cat. nos. 122–23), yet with only a very few exceptions Bolsterer always signed his medals.[7] The last of the contenders is Dietrich Schro. When comparing signed Schro medals with those of the Ottheinrich group, it is best to study his surviving stone models, for the known castings of his medals are of only mediocre quality. One might first consider the single surviving Schro model for the medal of Otto Count of Solms.[8] It is very similar in style to the models for the two small Ottheinrich medals from 1551 and 1559,[9] and their precise rendering of detail is virtually identical, though some of the letters have different shapes. It is striking how the inscription on the model for the medal of Count Solms is preceded by a spray of flowers, just as on the Ottheinrich medal exhibited here.

Like Georg Habich and Paul Grotemeyer, I do not attribute

the medals of the Ottheinrich group—and with them the alabaster bust of the prince elector in Paris—to any known artist. I think of them as having been produced in immediate proximity to Schro. It is still entirely possible that the master of the "Ottheinrich of the Palatinate Group" will one day recover the name he bore in life.

Peter Volz

The Master of the "Ottheinrich of the Palatinate Group"
Ottheinrich, count of the Rhenish Palatinate (born 1502, duke in Lower and Upper Bavaria 1502–59, duke of Palatinate-Neuburg 1505–44 and 1552–59, prince elector of the Palatinate 1556–59)

121
Gold, cast
Diameter 45.0 mm; width of flat cap, 21.7 mm; weight 38.37 g
Heidelberg, Kurpfälzisches Museum
M 301

 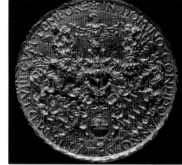

121 obv.   121 rev.

Obverse: Bust portrait facing three-quarters to the left. The prince elector is wearing a flat cap with a medallion, a pleated shirt, a vest, and a richly decorated coat. A double chain hangs about his shoulders. Legend: OTTO HENRICVS • D[ei] G[ratia] • CO • MES PALATINVS RHENI ELECTOR ÆTATIS • LVI (Otto Heinrich, by the Grace of God count of the Rhenish Palatinate, elector, at age fifty–six). A spray of flowers precedes the inscription, and a high circle of laurel leaves forms the edge. *Reverse*: Ottheinrich's three coats of arms.[1] Behind the middle lion crest is a label with the inscription: M[it] • D[er] – Z[eit] (All in good time), and a flower. Legend: IN DOMINO CONFIDO • ANNO • SALVTIS • M • D • LVIII • CVM TEMPORE (I trust in the Lord. In the year of our salvation 1558. All in good time).[2] A flower precedes the inscription, and a high circle of laurel leaves forms the edge.

Ottheinrich was born in Amberg on April 10, 1502. His parents, Count Palatine Ruprecht (1481–1504) and Elisabeth of Bavaria-Landshut (1478–1504), died in the War of the Bavarian Succession (the Landshut Feud) only two years later. With the 1505 Cologne Edict of Emperor Maximilian I (cat. nos. 37, 79), the principality of Neuburg, the so-called "Young Palatinate" was created out of certain Bavarian holdings for

121 obv.

Ottheinrich and his younger brother Philipp (cat. no. 78). Both brothers grew up in Neuburg on the Danube, under the guardianship of an uncle, Count Palatine Frederick II (1482–1556). They were declared of age in 1522, and together assumed authority in Neuburg. Ottheinrich participated in the Sickingen Feud in 1523 and the Peasants' War in 1525. In 1529 he married Susanne of Bavaria (1502–1543), the widow of Margrave Kasimir of Brandenburg-Ansbach (1481–1527). The two brothers divided the heavily indebted principality of Neuburg between them in 1535, but in 1541 Ottheinrich was forced to take over Philipp's portion of the territory in addition to his own. In the following year, Ottheinrich introduced the Reformation into Neuburg, and his troubles soon multiplied. His wife died in 1543, and in 1544, after complete financial collapse, he was forced to abdicate and seek exile in Heidelberg and Weinheim as a landless prince. His beloved brother Philipp died in 1548. It was only in his last years that Ottheinrich achieved success. The principality of Neuburg was returned to him by the Treaty of Passau in 1552, and on the death in 1556 of his uncle Frederick II he finally succeeded him in Heidelberg as prince elector of the Palatinate. One of his first acts was to introduce the Reformation into the Palatinate as well. In 1558, with the help of Melanchthon (cat. no. 99), he gave the University of Heidelberg a new constitution, making it one of the leading humanistic universities in the Empire. He died at the age of fifty-six, after a scant three years as elector. The old electoral line in the Palatinate died out with him, for he left no children.

Ottheinrich was one of the most important collectors and art patrons of his time. He acquired Greek and Roman coins, sculptures, engravings, manuscripts, books, bindings, tapestries, astronomical instruments, weapons, and armor for both men and horses. Many of the objects from his collections are now among the prized possessions of European and American museums. He was especially fond of portrait medals of himself. Between 1520, when he was only eighteen, and his death in 1559, he commissioned some thirty medals from the best German medalists, among them Hans Schwarz (cat. nos. 81–84), Hans Daucher (cat. nos. 78–80), Matthes Gebel (cat. nos. 109–13), and Ludwig Neufahrer (cat. nos. 115–16).[3] One assumes that Ottheinrich commissioned the present specimen in gold either for his own collection or as a gift for some high-ranking personage.

The Ottheinrich medal is extremely important. Artistically, it is one of the best German medals from the second half of the sixteenth century. Moreover, of the gold medals cast by important German masters before 1560, scarcely a handful has survived.

Peter Volz

Hans Bolsterer
(died 1573)

Nuremberg records refer to Hans Bolsterer as a goldsmith and sculptor, and he is listed as the author of various carvings in the inventory of Archduke Leopold Wilhelm.[1] He first appears as a medalist in 1540, and it is clear from his subjects that his first works were created in Nuremberg. After a sojourn in Frankfurt from roughly 1546 to 1548, one of the most productive periods of his life, he appears often in Nuremberg with only brief absences. By 1551 his artistry was so admired that he was given Nuremberg citizenship without having to pay the customary fee, and a year later he there produced a medal of Wenzel Jamnitzer (see also cat. no. 129). After 1555 he created fewer and fewer medals, his last piece dating from 1567. Although it is possible that he gave up his Nuremberg citizenship in 1562, it was there that he died in 1573.

Bolsterer was above all a portrait sculptor. Most of Bolsterer's medals—especially those of his Frankfurt period—are distinguished by a soft, rounded style, with great care given to details, especially in the clothing. They typically employ large letters in their inscriptions and many have a foliate border. In terms of casting technique, Bolsterer's uniface medals are remarkable for their thinness and the exact reproduction of the negative image on the reverse. He carved his models in wood or stone. He produced portraits—most of them in profile—of numerous Nuremberg and Frankfurt burghers and a few princes. In 1547 he even created a medal of Emperor Charles V. His reverses are generally coats of arms, with particular emphasis on mantling and crests. The majority of Bolsterer's works are signed with his initials and an intervening mark that varies considerably, but is basically a cross.

Karl Schulz

Hans Bolsterer
Ursula von Solms (1528–1573)
122
Silver, cast
Diameter 49 mm; diameter of the outer perimeter of the inscription, 46.3 mm
Vienna, Kunsthistorisches Museum, Münzkabinett
4863 bß

Obverse: Bust portrait facing to the left. The subject wears a bonnet and wreath, a necklace with pendant, and two chains. A

122 obv.

122 obv.

laurel wreath runs around the edge. Legend: (Rosette) VRSVLA GEPOREN GREVIN ZV SOLMS Z • IRS ALTERS IM • XVII (Ursula, born countess of Solms, at seventeen years of age). On the arm truncation, the signature H (cross) B.
Reverse: Negative impression of the obverse.

Bolsterer produced this medal in 1546, together with medals of Ursula's mother and sister.[1] The three pieces are among his earliest signed and dated works.

Ursula Countess of Solms was the daughter of Count Reinhard I of Solms-Lich (1491–1562) and Maria Countess of Sayn. In 1563 she married Count Hugo of Montfort (died 1574). It is documented that between 1546 and 1548 Bolsterer worked for at least four months at Castle Rödelheim, near Frankfurt, in the employ of Friedrich Magnus of Solms-Laubach, a nephew of Count Reinhard, creating two coats of arms. It was at this time that the three medals were produced, and it seems odd that there is none of Count Reinhard himself. The other people portrayed by the medalist in this period were almost all friends or employees of either Count Reinhard or Friedrich Magnus. As late as 1551, Hans Bolsterer cast medals for the count, probably from the already existing models.[2]

Karl Schulz

123 obv.

Hans Bolsterer
Ursula Dürr
123
Stone model, uniface
Diameter 46.5 mm; diameter of the outer perimeter of the
  inscription, 42.5 mm
Berlin, Staatliche Museen, Münzkabinett
382/1876

Obverse: Bust wearing braid and flat cap facing forward and to the left. Legend: (Rosette) VRSV[la] D[es]: WOLFG[ang]: DVRRE[n] [el]ICHE HAVSFRAV AN[no]: AET[atis]: SVAE: XLVI (Ursula, wife of Wolfgang Dürr, in her forty-sixth year). On the arm truncation, the signature H (mark) B.
Reverse: Plain.

This piece is in all probability from the period around 1560.

The stone model is all that we have of the medal, for apparently no casts are known.

The subject appears to be the wife of a Nuremberg burgher. According to Habich, the widow of a Wolfgang Dürr is named in documents from 1564, and this could well be our Ursula, though she is not identified as a widow on the medal. On the other hand, there is a 1567 medal of a Wolf Dürr, by an artist who signed himself AE, that portrays him at the age of seventy-two.[1] If Ursula was the widow of this gentleman, as Habich seemed to think, it would mean that she was roughly twenty years younger than he. In this portrait Ursula Dürr appears older than her indicated forty-six years. Bolsterer's ordinarily quite gentle treatment of his subjects is here abandoned in favor of a more pointed naturalism.

Karl Schulz

Peter Flötner
(c. 1485–1546)

Peter Flötner was probably born about 1485. Thurgau in Switzerland is sometimes given as the place of his birth, but this is pure speculation. On August 8, 1523, he swore the oath of citizenship in Nuremberg together with Sigmund Hartman and a messenger named Hans Stengel. The normal fee was waived for all three of them.[1] The relevant resolution on the part of the city council suggests that Flötner moved to Nuremberg from Ansbach.[2] Nothing is known of his career before that date. It is assumed that he had formerly worked in Augsburg.[3] Though the Nuremberg minutes speak of him as "Master Peter," it is doubtful whether he had really produced a masterpiece and passed an examination as a *Bildschnitzer*, for Flötner did not belong to any guild.

He was married three times and was twice a widower. He died on November 23, 1546, and was buried in the Johannis Cemetery in Nuremberg.[4] His only children were from his first marriage. His son Kaspar and several of his descendants worked as "pattern casters" or "lead casters," and one of his grandsons was a goldsmith. None of them attained his stature.

Flötner was one of the more versatile artists of the German Renaissance. His woodcuts, with designs for architectural details, fountains, furniture, jewelry mountings, and ornaments, were revolutionary, as were his relief models for goldsmiths, which were used by all manner of craftsmen. He carved his models in Solnhofen stone. Lead casts of them were widely sought after and used until well into the seventeenth century.

It would appear that all of Peter Flötner's plaquettes have been identified,[5] and that his most important works in sculpture have been thoroughly discussed.[6] Bitter disagreement arose in the 1920s over the attribution of a number of medals to Peter Flötner.[7] There are only two surviving medals signed PF, and it is possible that Peter Flötner did indeed carve the models for these. The Salvator medal[8] fits quite easily into the Flötner oeuvre, and it is documented that the 1537 medal commemorating the refortification of the castle in Nuremberg was cast by Hans Maslitzer from a Flötner model.[9] All attributions of other medals to Peter Flötner are either highly suspect or altogether untenable.

Ingrid S. Weber

Peter Flötner (?)
Charles V (born 1500, emperor 1519–56, died 1558), Ferdinand I (born 1503, emperor 1556–64), and Maria of Hungary (1505–1558)
124
Silver, cast
Diameter 74.0 mm; diameter through the K and I in the rulers' initials, 60.7 mm; weight 146.22 g
Vienna, Kunsthistorisches Museum, Münzkabinett
733 bß

Obverse: Jugate busts of Charles V and Ferdinand I. Charles has a trimmed beard and moustache and curly hair. He is wearing a pleated shirt with a high-standing collar with points, a brocade vest in a raised floral pattern, a cloak, and a chain with the Order of the Golden Fleece. His brother is smooth-shaven, with straight, medium-length hair. He too wears a pleated shirt, a brocade vest, a cloak, and the Order of the Golden Fleece. Above their heads is the five-line inscription: • CAROL[us] • V • ET • FER[dinandus] • I • FR[atr]ES • RO[manorum] • IMP-[erator] • ET • RE[ges] • RE[x] • HISP[aniae] • UTRI[u]SQ[ue] • SICI[liae] • [H]VNG[ariae] • BO[h]E[miae] • Z[= etc.] AR-CHID[uces] • AVST[riae] • D[ux] • BVRG[undiae]: 1 • 5 • 3 2 (Charles V and Ferdinand I, brothers, [the former] emperor of the Romans and [both] kings, [the one] king of Spain and both Sicilies, [the other] of Hungary, Bohemia, etc., [both] archdukes of Austria and [the former] duke of Burgundy. 1532). On the left: [ornament] • K[arolus] • Q[uintus] (Charles V); on the right: • REX • F[erdinandus] • I • (King Ferdinand I).

Reverse: Bust of Maria of Hungary, the sister of Charles and Ferdinand, facing left. She wears a buttoned bodice over a richly pleated gown with puffed sleeves and a high, closed collar. Her hair, gathered into a knot at the back, is covered by a hairnet, on top of which sits a flat cap with a flap at the neck, appliquéd with the letter M. To the side of her head, the incised letters: M[aria] R[egina] / K[önigin von] V[ngarn] (Maria Regina / Queen of Hungary). Double ridge around the edge, overlaid by the bust truncation. Simple incised line as border.

This presentation of three members of the imperial family surely cannot have been commissioned by the court. The portraits and the inscription and its arrangement are too unorthodox. It would appear that there are at least three variants of the obverse. One, with five lines in the inscription, an incised line around the border, and the date 1532, is represented by the present example and the silver example in the Staatliche Münzsammlung in Munich (diameter 74 mm).[1] Another version is the brass cast in the Victoria & Albert Museum, London (75 mm), which lacks the incised border line.[2] A third variant has only a four-line inscription and is dated 1531.[3] Finally, there is a second specimen in the Victoria & Albert Museum, this one in silver (69 mm). On it the top line with CAROL V has been cut off, the 2 in the date 1532 is missing, and the X in REX is incomplete. That example would appear to be not a variant, but only a cut down version of the present specimen, the discrepancies resulting from the reduction from 74 mm to 69 mm.[4]

The situation with regard to the medal's reverses is also puzzling. The brass specimen in London has a wholly different reverse showing the non-noble coat of arms of a certain Christof Arothschiez and the date 1535. The Munich example has the portrait of Maria of Hungary, to be sure, but without the letters flanking the bust; instead, the field is damascened. Habich

124 obv.

124 rev.

questioned whether the models for the obverse and reverse of the Munich copy go together. In terms of iconography, the portrayal of the three siblings in the present manner is justified. In 1532 the two brothers were in fact kings, Charles V was emperor, and their sister, the widow of Ludwig II of Hungary (cat. no. 80), was vice-regent of the Netherlands. The awkward legend, conforming only in part to official usage, and its format, as opposed to the circular inscription a princely patron would certainly have demanded, suggest that all of the examples are but trials or sketches for a medal that was ultimately never executed.[5] Otherwise it could scarcely have been possible for the obverse to be combined with a bourgeois emblem, as in the London brass copy, as early as 1535.

Habich tentatively assigned the medal to Peter Flötner, but with a question mark.[6] He based his conclusion on comparison with the Spott medal and the medal from 1538 celebrating the refortification of Nuremberg's castle,[7] both of which are signed PF. Yet it is known that a whole team of artists worked on the medal of the strengthening of the castle and that Flötner can at most have carved the model. In the extensive Flötner oeuvre there are almost no portraits, yet these three are very precise. Nowhere else in his work does one find this degree of three-dimensionality, figural poses like these, or such sumptuous costumes. Habich's attribution must therefore continue to be questioned.[8]

Ingrid S. Weber

Hans Reinhart the Elder
(c. 1510–1581)

Hans Reinhart the Elder occupies an unusual position among German medalists of the first half of the sixteenth century. Working apart from the medal centers of Nuremberg and Augsburg, this Leipzig artist, in a brief burst of creativity between 1535 and 1544, produced medals with both portraits and Biblical subjects. Habich lists twenty-six signed works. At least thirty-three other medals can be attributed to either the master himself or his workshop on the basis of their style.[1]

Long stretches of the artist's life remain obscure. It is thought that he was born in Dresden in about 1510.[2] In 1539 he appears as a citizen in Leipzig, where he apparently lived without interruption until his death in 1581.

According to one relatively reliable source, Reinhart was originally a cabinetmaker and had worked in the 1530s at castles in Halle, Torgau, and elsewhere as a decorative wood sculptor and furniture maker. Some of his medals were definitely cast from wooden models.[3] Thus it appears that he was at least as familiar with the tools of the woodcarver as he was with the techniques of the gold and silversmith. Nevertheless, it seems that his silver casts did not meet the stringent standards of the guild of gold- and silversmiths in Leipzig, for he was long denied membership in the guild, with the explanation that he was only a cabinetmaker and caster of coins.[4] It was only because the medal was such a new medium that his works were not accepted; the regulations governing the guild made no provision for such objects. After a five year apprenticeship with a master goldsmith by the name of Georg (Jörg) Treutler, Reinhart produced his prescribed masterpiece in 1547.

Reinhart signed roughly half of his works with his monogram HR. It is possible to see precedents for at least some of his medals in the prints of his well-known contemporary, the painter and printmaker Lucas Cranach the Elder (1472–1553).[5] He also appears to have been influenced by the struck medals then being produced in the Erzgebirge region.[6] The Saxon mints at Annaberg and Schneeberg, founded in 1496 and 1471, respectively, as well as at St. Joachimsthal, founded on the south slope of the mountain range by Count von Schlick (cat. no. 80a) in 1519, all employed talented die-cutters who created both portrait and miscellaneous medals.

Unlike his South-German colleagues—Matthes Gebel, Friedrich Hagenauer, and Christoph Weiditz, for example—whose portrait medals are marked by relatively consistent style and design, Reinhart continually experimented with unconventional effects, incorporating miniature three-dimensional sculptures and other details soldered onto the basic casting.[7] Soldering itself was by no means new and was practiced by makers of various kinds of medals, but in all of medallic art it is nowhere employed so masterfully as in Reinhart's work.

Given his astonishing virtuosity and his mastery of technical processes, it is odd that he created no new works in the last thirty years of his life. The Trinity medal from 1544 (cat. no. 127) is his final work—discounting of course the later versions of it dating from 1556, 1561, 1569 and 1574. It is possible that Reinhart lost interest in medalmaking once he gained acceptance into Leipzig's guild of goldsmiths in 1547. His oldest son, Hans Reinhart the Younger (died 1622), continued his father's workshop.[8]

Wolfgang Steguweit

Hans Reinhart the Elder
Charles V (born 1500, emperor 1519–56, died 1558)
125
Silver, cast
Diameter 65.0 mm; internal measurement from the top of the hat to the base of the scepter, 57.5 mm
New York, private collection

Obverse: Bust in three-quarter view to right with the head in profile. Charles wears a flat cap or beret and a pleated shirt with a high figured and ruffled collar tied in front beneath a coat or vest. His outer garment is an elaborately decorated cloak with a wide collar and puffed and slashed sleeves. Around his neck is the collar of the Order of the Golden Fleece, and in his hands he holds the orb and scepter of the empire. Legend: (flower) CAROLVS • V • DEI • GRATIA • ROMAN[orum] • IMPERATOR • SEMPER • AVGVSTVS • REX • HIS[paniae] • ANNO • SAL[vatoris] • M • D • XLIIII • ÆTATIS • SVÆ • XLIIII (Charles V, by the Grace of God forever exalted emperor of the Romans,

125 obv.

125 rev.

king of Spain, in the year of our Savior 1544, at the age of forty-four).

Reverse: Dependent from the conjoined necks of the double headed imperial eagle, between whose heads rests the imperial crown, hangs the shield of arms of Charles V.[1] The collar of the Order of the Golden Fleece emerges from beneath the shield. The eagle's talons stand on a rocky ground, and the tail frames the fleece. Beneath each part of the tail, in perspective on the ground, are the initials of the artist, H R. Flanking the arms, Charles's emblem, the crowned Pillars of Hercules and the motto PLVS OVLTRE (More beyond).

The quality of Reinhart's portraiture is considerably varied, depending on his model. He seems to have worked only rarely *ad vivam*, choosing instead some secondary source such as a painting, drawing, medal, or woodcut. His medal of Johann Friedrich of Saxony, for example (cat. no. 126), was based on a woodcut by Lucas Cranach (1472–1553), which undoubtedly explains why that portrait has so much more character than this somewhat remote and lifeless one of Charles V.

What is lacking in the portrait is more than compensated for by Reinhart's extraordinary facility in the precise handling of detail, the tactile rendering of materials, and the imaginative treatment of space. He achieves a suggestion of three-dimensionality both by his modulation of relief and by positioning the figure so as to break the circular frame of the medal with the base of the scepter.

Both in this medal and that of Johann Friedrich, Reinhart presents on the reverse a masterpiece of heraldic design bristling with energy and strength, yet precise, balanced, and uncluttered. These are perhaps the most successful heraldic reverses in all of Renaissance medallic art.

Two versions exist of the medal of Charles V. The first is dated 1537,[2] and shows the emperor seven years younger than in the present medal. He wears a smaller flat cap, and his hair is more tightly cut, partially covering his ear, while his beard is shorter and more pointed. There are a few additional small differences, such as in the head of the scepter, but in all other respects Reinhart seems merely to have recarved the earlier model to produce the medal of 1544.

It does not appear that either medal was produced to commemorate any specific triumph in Charles's life. On the contrary, this was a particularly difficult and complicated period for him with respect to the major issues of his reign: the wars with France, the efforts to defeat the Turks, and the upheavals occasioned by the spread of the Reformation.

Stephen K. Scher

Hans Reinhart the Elder
Johann Friedrich I (born 1503, elector of Saxony 1532–47, died 1554)

126
Silver, cast
Diameter 65.7 mm; diameter from the E of FECIT to the second I of FRIDERICVS, 63 mm
New York, private collection

Obverse: Bust in three-quarter view to right, wearing a pleated shirt with high embroidered collar under a fur cloak with puffed and slashed sleeve of the right arm showing and with a heavy chain around the neck. Johann bears the electoral sword in his right hand, and the electoral hat with decorated band and ostrich plume in his left. Between two plain borders, the legend: (oak or maple-branch stop) IOANN[e]S • FRIDERICVS • ELECTOR • DUX SAXONI[a]E • FIERI FECIT • ETATIS SVÆ • 32 (Johann Friedrich, elector duke of Saxony caused [this] to be made at the age of thirty-two). Embroidered on the collar, the legend: XRENXALSXINXEREN. This is only a portion of a motto, the remainder obviously appearing on the part of the collar we cannot see. In full it reads: "Alles in Ehren kann niemand wehren" (There is no defense against an honorable

126 obv.

126 obv.

126 rev.

man). In the field beneath the elector's right hand, the engraved signature HR.

Reverse: Johann's full heraldic achievement on an elaborate shield ornamented with scrolls, oak-leaf tendrils, and grotesque birds' heads on the corners.[1] Legend: (oak or maple-branch stops between all words) SPES • MEA • IN • DEO • EST • ANNO • NOSTRI • SALVATORIS • M • D • X • X • X • V (My hope is in God, the year of our Savior 1535).

Of Reinhart's few portrait medals, this one has by far the most character and strength, thanks in part to its reliance upon painted and woodcut portraits by Lucas Cranach the Elder (1472–1553).[2] Yet Reinhart has adapted and modified Cranach's portraits to create an entirely original composition. Johann is shown bare-headed, with only one hand holding the great electoral sword that breaks beyond the circular frame, bringing the hand holding the hilt forward into the viewer's space. In fact, the use of a three-quarter view and the relatively high relief of the head and right hand create an illusion of three-dimensionality that is remarkably successful, a rarity in medallic art. Since the wood models for both the obverse and reverse of this medal existed until recently, one can appreciate Reinhart's skill as a wood carver, by which title he is often referred to in documents.[3]

Johann Friedrich was born in 1503, and as the nephew of Frederick III, "the Wise," and son of Johann of Saxony, "the Steadfast," he was reared in a household that firmly supported the Reformation and its most prominent founder, Martin Luther (cat. no. 101). Unlike his father and uncle, Johann vacillated between pleasing his Protestant colleagues in the League of Schmalkalden and the champion of Catholicism in Europe, Emperor Charles V. His rival Maurice, of the Albertine Saxon line in Meissen, became duke of Saxony in 1541. Casting a longing eye upon Johann Friedrich's electoral dignity, he left the ranks of the Protestant princes and in 1546 came to a secret understanding with the emperor, who was preparing an attack

on the League of Schmalkalden. In July of that year, Maurice invaded Johann Friedrich's lands, but was repelled. Johann pressed his success by overrunning ducal Saxony, but was in turn checked by the interference of Charles V. At the battle of Mühlberg, on April 24, 1547, Johann Friedrich was wounded and taken prisoner by the imperial forces. He was first condemned to death, but the emperor remitted the sentence to life imprisonment. Johann was forced to relinquish the electoral dignity and the territory of Saxe-Wittenberg to Maurice. He refused to make any religious concessions, however, and remained in captivity until May 1552. Upon his release, Johann returned to the remainder of his ancestral lands in Thuringia, where he was received with wild enthusiasm, and shortly thereafter the emperor restored to him all of his former dignities. He died at Weimar on March 3, 1554. Quite apart from his political activities, he had been known as an enthusiastic hunter and a hard drinker, and it was because of his dignified bearing in misfortune that he was given the agnomen "the Magnanimous." He was the last Ernestine elector of Saxony, for he had agreed that on his death the title should pass to Maurice's successor Augustus (cat. no. 128).

Stephen K. Scher

Hans Reinhart the Elder

The Trinity Medal

127

Silver, cast

Diameter 103 mm; height of the separate castings: Cross, 47 mm; Christ figure, 27 mm; dove, 15.5 mm; weight 268.68 g

Berlin, Staatliche Museen, Münzkabinett

Obverse: God the Father sits on a highly ornamented throne, wearing an imperial crown and dressed in a richly embroidered and jeweled cope. In his hands, which rest on the cross-arm of a crucifix standing between his knees, are the orb and scepter of

127 obv.

his dominion over the universe. The dove of the Holy Spirit stands above the crucifix. On either side of his throne are angels standing on strips of cloud, their hands clasped in adoration. In the field above each of these appear three faces of cherubim of graduated size. Legend: PROPTER • SCELVS • POPVLI • MEI • PERCVSSI • EVM • ESAIÆ • LIII ("Stricken to the death for my people's transgression" — Isaiah 53:[8]). At the bottom, on either side of the foot of the cross, are the inscribed initials of the signature, H R.

Reverse: Two angels, standing on strips of cloud, support a tablet, above which appear the arms of Saxony.[1] Legend: REGNANTE • MAVRITIO - D[ei] • G[ratia] • DVCE • SAXONIÆ , ZC • GROSSVM - HVNC • LIPSIÆ H[ans] R[einhart] • CVDEBAT • ANo • M • D • XLIIII • MENSE • IANV[arii] (In the reign of Maurice, by the Grace of God duke of Saxony etc., Hans Reinhart cast this medal in Leipzig in the month of January, 1544). The tablet presents a twenty-two-line Latin inscription: HÆC EST FIDES CATHOLICA, VT • VNVM DEVM IN TRINITATE, ET TRINITATEM, IN VNITATE, VENEREMVR • ALIA EST PERSONA PATRIS, ALIA FILII, ALIA SPIRITVS SANCTI • SED PATRIS ET FILII ET SPIRITVS SANCTI, VNA EST DIVINITAS, ÆQVALIS GLORIA, COETERNA MAIESTAS O VENERA[n]DA VNITAS, O ADORANDA TRINITAS, PER TE

SVMVS CREATI, VERA AETERNITAS, PER TE SVMVS REDEMPTI SUMMA TV CHARITAS, TE ADORAMVS OMNIPOTENS, TIBI CANIMVS, TIBI LAVS ET GLORIA (The Catholic faith is this: That we worship one God in Trinity and Trinity in Unity . . . there is one person of the Father: another of the Son: and another of the Holy Ghost. But the Godhead of the Father, of the Son, and of the Holy Ghost is all one; the Glory equal, the Majesty coeternal. O venerable Unity. O worshipful Trinity. By You we were created, You true Eternity. By You we were redeemed, You greatest Love. We worship You, All-powerful One. We exalt You. To You praise and honor). The first part of this text, ending in the word MAIESTAS, is taken from the Athanasian Creed[2]; the source of the succeeding prayer is unidentified.

The medal of the Holy Trinity from 1544 is rightly considered Reinhart's masterpiece, and the Berlin specimen is held to be the loveliest example of it. An equally beautiful Gotha specimen was lost in the Second World War.[3] In no other work did the artist so convincingly display his mastery. The physical beauty of the separately cast Christ on the Cross enhances the emotional effect of the whole.

There is no clear pattern for the design of this medal either in

127 rev.

paintings or prints from this period, and it is interesting to note that Reinhart also failed to draw on the Trinity medals that had been produced since 1535 by the St. Joachimsthal die-cutter Nickel Milicz and his workshop.[4] Instead, he appears to have borrowed from specific works of architectural sculpture. The motif of the God-Father enthroned appears in a distinctly related form on the portals of two Saxon churches.[5] One of these is the so-called "Schöne Tür" inside the north wall of the Annenkirche in Annaberg, with its sandstone carving by Hans Witten. The other is the same sculptor's portal on the north side of the palace church in Chemnitz.

It is generally assumed that the Trinity medal was produced in support of efforts at reconciliation between the new Protestant church and the church of Rome.[6] In 1539, the year Reinhart became a citizen of Leipzig, that city adopted the Reformation, and the country's ruler, Duke Maurice of Saxony—expressly mentioned in the legend on the medal's reverse—converted to Protestantism. The Athanasian Creed, from which a part of the inscription on the reverse is taken, provided the theoretical foundation for the doctrine of the Trinity in both churches.[7] The reference to Maurice and the appearance of the Saxon coat of arms, significantly placed directly behind God's crown, suggest that the work was a commission. Commonly referred to as the *Moritz-Pfennig*, the medal was obviously popular, for copies of it with four different dates are known, the last one from 1574. Most of these lack something of the high quality of the 1544 specimens, and doubtless many of them were not the work of Reinhart himself.

Wolfgang Steguweit

Tobias Wolff
(second half of the 16th century)

For this medalist, whose name appears in the older literature as Wost,[1] we have no life dates at all. Nor do we know where he came from. Habich suspected that he had some connection to Augsburg,[2] yet it would appear that Wolff spent the greater part of his career in Silesia (Breslau) and Saxony, leading one to suspect that his home town was somewhere in that region. This suspicion is fortified in that the elector of Saxony refers to him in 1576 as a "portrait carver from Breslau,"[3] though to be sure that could have been only his temporary residence. Although he appears in documents as early as 1561, his earliest dated medals were only executed in 1568. His output then proceeds almost without interruption until 1606. Silesian subjects are predominant on Wolff's earlier medals, but after 1574 these are

289

128 obv.

supplanted by Saxon ones. In that year he received—as did Valentin Maler—a commission from the elector of Saxony. The results of this summons were a medal depicting Hartenfels Castle at Torgau[4] and a suite of medals after half-length princely portraits that hung there.[5] Valentin Maler also produced a series of medals from other paintings in that collection. Wolff found these half-length portraits altogether congenial, for even when working from life he tended to portray his subjects in half figure and with their hands showing.[6]

Wolff's extremely extensive œuvre is characterized by a predominance of small-format portrait medals, often *en face*, with very expressive faces. All of them were produced from stone models. Many of his pieces have no reverse, and those that he did execute rarely include figures. Most often they present coats of arms with emphasis on the crest and mantling and generally less attention given to the shield itself.

Wolff appears to have attracted numerous followers, leading Habich to speak of a veritable workshop.[7] Though Jan de Vos (cat. no. 134) created a signed reverse for a Wolff medal early on in his career, his later work has little in common with that of the older artist. It is not easy to imagine what prompted this apparently unique collaboration, or to guess whether the piece was executed in Dresden or in Augsburg, where de Vos was at home.

Karl Schulz

Tobias Wolff
Augustus (born 1526, elector of Saxony 1553–86), and Johann
    Georg (born 1525, elector of Brandenburg 1571–98)
128
Silver, cast, uniface
Diameter 85.5 mm; diameter of the outer perimeter of the
    inscription, 78.5 mm; weight 65.41 g
Vienna, Kunsthistorisches Museum, Münzkabinett
94 bß

Obverse: The elector of Brandenburg, standing in the right-hand foreground, holds a cap in his left hand and has placed his right arm around the elector of Saxony, who is seated beside him. The latter holds a glove and a ring in his hands. Both wear embroidered cloaks. Legend: PAX MVLTA DILIGENTIBVS LEGEM TVAM DOMINE PSA[lmus] 118 / GELOBET SEI GOT ("Great peace have they which love thy law." Psalm 119:165, King James Version; Vulgate 118:165] / Praise be to God). Below is a cartouche with the inscription: D[ei] • G[ratia] • AVGVST[us]: / ET • JOHA[nnes] • GEOR[gius] / VT • ERQVE • ELE / CTORES • IMP[erii] (By the Grace of God August and Johann Georg, both electors of the empire).
Reverse: Plain.

The medal presents full-torso portraits of the two sitters, a view relatively common in the work of Wolff and other Saxon and North-German medalists. As the hands are included, the portraits appear more animated. Medals incorporating multiple portraits in a single image often present their subjects in stiff

128 obv.

poses unrelated to each other. Here, however, the vaunted harmony between the two princes is expressed in their mutual embrace.

Various copies of this medal, unlike the present one, are dated 1581. Most of them cast in bronze, they have the recessed date in the lower right instead of chasing. They also lack the damascening on Johann Georg's shirt. A stone model of the same general type, but altogether different in its execution, is in the Germanisches Nationalmuseum in Nuremberg. Probably it is an earlier version of the present medal. It is dated 1577 and bears the signature TW.[1]

These different datings also suggest the occasion for the medal, namely the two princes' acceptance of the Torgau "Formula of Concord," which was to bring uniformity to evangelical Lutheran doctrine as opposed to the teachings of Calvin. The formula was adopted for their countries by both electors in 1577 and published in 1580 in the *Book of Concord*. Augustus, who also commissioned the medal, was particularly supportive of this line of Lutheran orthodoxy.

Karl Schulz

Valentin Maler
(c. 1540–1603)

Maler was born in Iglau, in Moravia, but nothing is known about his youth and training. He is documented as working in Nuremberg beginning about 1568. In 1569, shortly after becoming a citizen of the city and a master goldsmith, he married one of the daughters of Wenzel Jamnitzer (cat. no. 129). The majority of his extremely large number of medals portray citizens of Nuremberg, yet he also worked for the imperial court in both Vienna and Prague, and at the court of the elector of

129 obv.

Saxony in Dresden. His medals also indicate sojourns in Munich, Würzburg, and Augsburg. On his travels he became acquainted with Antonio Abondio (cat. nos. 60–63), and at the emperor's behest he made struck copies of some of Abondio's cast medals. He entered into fruitful artistic competition with Tobias Wolff (cat. no. 128) in Dresden in 1574–75 and with Balduin Drentwett in Augsburg in 1583–84.

Maler was one of the first German medalists to use wax for his models for cast medals. His early cast pieces are in high relief and often have a pearled border of the sort frequently employed in the Low Countries. Later he reduced the size of his pieces, adopting a flatter style more like that found in medals cast from stone models and sharper contours in emulation of struck medals. He was a master of the *en face* portrait, and his roughly 200 medals provide numerous examples of that pose. He rarely provided reverses, and those he did create are generally coats of arms; only in his late works does one encounter increasing numbers of figural compositions.

Maler set himself up on a commercial basis in 1582, when he managed to secure an imperial license for the production of medals.[1] He thus stands near the beginning of a tradition of medalmaking in Nuremberg that persisted for centuries. He also worked to a lesser extent as a sculptor. The epitaph for his father-in-law Wenzel Jamnitzer is a typical example of his work. We also know of several wax models of his that are painted in polychrome and thus represent independent works of art. He ceased to work as a medalist in 1593, though he lived on in Nuremberg until 1603. His son Christian carried on his work in that city, and among his creations is an oval medal with a portrait of his father in the style of the latter's epitaph medal for Wenzel Jamnitzer.[2]

Karl Schulz

Valentin Maler
Wenzel Jamnitzer (1508–1585)
129
Lead, cast, uniface
Diameter 80 mm
Munich, Staatliche Münzsammlung

Obverse: Bust portrait with long beard, facing forward and to the right. Legend: VVENTZEL · IAMNITZER · ÆTAT[is]: LXIII · A[nn]O: MDLXXI · (Wenzel Jamnitzer at age sixty-three, in the year 1571). Beaded border.
Reverse: Plain.

This is one of the first medals Valentin Maler produced, and it is distinguished from the rest of his work by both its dimensions and its high relief. It was patterned after a medal from 1563 that is probably to be attributed to Jakob Hofmann, but considered by some to be an early work by Maler himself.[1] Subsequently, doubtless as the result of his considerable experience with struck medals, he worked in much flatter relief. The present medal was probably intended as a present to Jamnitzer, the artist's father-in-law. Maler also portrayed him in profile on later medals.[2] The 1585 portrait medallion on Maler's epitaph for Jamnitzer is based on the medal dated 1584.[3] Casts of that medallion also exist as independent plaquettes.[4] There is also a portrait medal of Jamnitzer by Hans Bolsterer (cat. nos. 122–23).[5]

Wenzel Jamnitzer was born in Vienna in 1508. He came from a family of goldsmiths that had worked in the service of the Habsburgs since the mid fifteenth century. He is first mentioned in Nuremberg in 1534, when he became a master goldsmith himself. Influenced in his early work by Peter Flötner (cat. no. 124), he evolved over the next few years into one of the most important goldsmiths of his time. Table centerpieces, goblets, decorative boxes, and figures preserved in numerous collections attest to his remarkable skills. Of his eleven children, three daughters married goldsmiths, and three sons also took up the family craft.

Karl Schulz

Valentin Maler
Dorothea of Saxony (1563–1585)
130
Alloy of tin and lead, cast, uniface
Diameter 48 mm; diameter of the outer perimeter of the inscription from the E in DOROTHEA to the opposite X, 43 mm
Munich, Staatliche Münzsammlung

Obverse: Bust portrait with braided hair, wearing a gown with a ruff collar and puffed sleeves and a double chain with pendant around her neck. Legend: DOROTHEA DVC[issa] SAX[oniae] ÆTA[tis] XI ANNO MDLXXIIII (Dorothea, duchess of Saxony, at age eleven, in the year 1574).

129 obv.

130 obv.

130 obv.

Reverse: Plain.

In 1574 Valentin Maler was summoned to Dresden to the court of the Saxon elector Augustus I (cat. no. 128), where he produced three medals of the elector's children.[1] A Maler medal of the elector himself bears no date, but must have been created at about the same time.[2] All of the portraits are done *en face* in Maler's typical flat style, and all but the one of the elector have plain borders. In the same year Maler also produced a medal of the fourteen-year-old Charles of the Palatinate (1560–1600), the founder of the Birkenfeld-Zweibrücken line.[3] During his stay in Dresden Maler also executed a series of medals based on portraits of various deceased German princes that hung in Hartenfels Castle in Torgau, some of which were attributed to Lucas Cranach.[4] The medallic portraits of the elector's children are of much better quality and are more indicative of Maler's style than his stereotyped copies from paintings. Even so, the expression of the eleven-year-old Duchess Dorothea is not altogether successful. Inasmuch as she is dressed in adult clothing, as was the custom, it is difficult to imagine that this is really only a child.

At the time Maler portrayed her on this medal, Dorothea was the elector's second oldest surviving child. She was depicted on two later medals as well, from 1581 and 1582, by the Saxon court artist Tobias Wolff (cat. no. 128).[5] In 1585 she married Duke Heinrich Julius of Braunschweig-Wolfenbüttel (born 1564, ruled 1589–1613) and two years later she died in childbirth at the age of twenty-four.

Karl Schulz

Valentin Maler
Matthias (1530–1602) and Anna Schilherr (born 1525)
131
Silver, cast
Diameter 51.5 mm; vertical diameter of the outer perimeter of the inscription, 47.0 mm; weight 42.33 g
Berlin, Staatliche Museen, Münzkabinett, formerly Andreas Rudolphi Collection, 1831

Obverse: Bearded bust portrait facing forward and to the right, with ruff collar. Legend: M[agister]: MATTHIAS SCHILHERR

ANNO ÆTA[tis] • XLVIIII (Master Matthias Schilherr at age forty-nine). Incised in the arm truncation is the ligature signature VM.
Reverse: Bust portrait facing forward and to the right, with braid and flat cap, simple dress, and ruff collar. Legend: ANNA M[agistri]: MATTHIAS SCHILHERRIN ANNO ÆT[atis]: LIII (Anna, wife of Master Matthias Schilherr, at age fifty-three). Incised in the arm truncation are the date 1578 and the ligature signature VM.

This is one of Maler's larger pieces, but shows the relatively flat relief and sharp contours typical of his works from this period. The double raised border gives it the appearance of a struck medal. The man's bust is unusual for Maler, in that Schilherr's gaze is directed somewhat away from the viewer as a result of the twist of his torso to the left and that of his head to the right.[1]

Matthias Schilherr was a Nuremberg burgher. His birth date, like that of his wife, née Baldermann, is known only from the inscription on this medal. His death date is documented, but not hers. Matthias was among other things secretary to the city council, and is mentioned as one of Nuremberg's councilmen in 1577. According to the medal, his wife was several years older, yet he certainly appears as old as she.

Karl Schulz

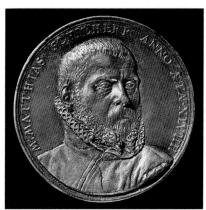

131 obv.

131 rev.

132 obv.

132 rev. of case

Artist Unidentified (circle of Georg Holdermann, c. 1585–1629)

Nuremberg Patrician

132

Wax medallion, uniface

Approximate dimensions of the portrait, 55 × 55 mm. Oval capsule 150 × 94.8 mm, including integral loop ring and pendant-shaped bottom ornament.

American private collection

Obverse: Half-length bust, almost facing front, with short hair, long smooth beard, and moustache, wearing large ruff collar and buttoned gown with two parallel rows of ornamentation in front and on upper sleeves. The portrait is polychromed and mounted on a background of blackened glass, with spiral-shaped gold wire border, enclosed in a contemporary gilded bronze capsule. Engraved on the cover of the capsule is a seated putto surrounded by floral and fruit volutes on stippled ground,

and on its back elaborate scrollwork on stippled ground. Unepigraphic.

The use of wax in the arts can be traced back to antiquity. At the time of Alexander the Great (356–323 B.C.) it served for sculptured busts, and from the inception of the Renaissance medal Italian masters created their models in that medium (cat. no. 56). In the medallic art of Germany it found application about the mid sixteenth century, gradually superseding the formerly favored stone and wood model.[1] Medalists in the Low Countries had already adopted the wax technique from their Italian colleagues, and they in turn provided impetus to the medallic schools of Germany as well. A decisive stimulus was added by the arrival north of the Alps of the Milanese medalist Antonio Abondio (cat. nos. 60–63),[2] whose influence would have a lasting effect on German medallic art. The function of the wax model also soon underwent a change; it no longer served merely as a preparatory stage in the production of a medal, but devel-

296

oped into an independent work of art in its own right. Nuremberg, Augsburg, and Prague were among the centers where the new art form was acknowledged. In Nuremberg toward the end of the sixteenth century *Wachskonterfetter* (wax portraitists) and *Bossierer* (wax modelers), engaged in fashioning portrait medallions, statuettes, and figurines, formed a distinct professional brotherhood within the goldsmiths' guild. Like medals, wax medallions were small, intimate mementos that might be given to one's family and friends, or by princes and prelates to their contemporaries to perpetuate their memory. Soft and infinitely malleable, wax was an ideal portrait medium, one in which the artist could achieve the most subtle gradations and detail, and one possessing the luminous transparency of skin. Ceroplastics invited a high degree of naturalism, coinciding with contemporary tendencies toward greater freedom from conventions and custom. To further enhance the effect, portraits could be polychromed in the very colorings of the sitter. Wax is not a durable material, however; aside from its vulnerability to changes in temperature and to physical shock, it tends to shrink and become brittle over time. For this reason the survival rate of such medallions is low, and even fewer have come down to us intact and unrestored.

Our medallion, like most in the medium, does not bear a signature. Its stylistic characteristics are consistent with those of the Nuremberg school of the early seventeenth century, and there is some justification for considering a possible association with the œuvre of the distinguished wax modeler Georg Holdermann (active 1606–29). While similarities in the treatment of the attire are undeniable,[3] the modeling of the facial features is more refined and contrasts with Holdermann's somewhat heavy-handed style. This is evident especially in the rendering of the eyes, which do not show the rigid stare encountered in his facing portraits, and in the subtle execution of nose and mouth. Authorship may have to be sought with an artist close to Holdermann, but one whose name has so far eluded us.

The identity of the sitter also remains undetermined. He appears to be between forty and fifty years of age; his dress, relatively frugal, displays neither brocade nor fur or jewelry or any other adornments that might suggest his station in life. Apparently no medal bearing this or a corresponding portrait has been recorded.

Mark M. Salton

Johann Philipp von der Pütt
(born c. 1560–62, died 1619)

Jan Philip van der Put moved in 1586 from Dordrecht, Holland, to Nuremberg, where he acquired residency on December 13, 1589.[1] In the civic register his name is Germanicized, and his craft is given as "*Bossierer*" (wax modeler).[2] On March 22, 1594, the city council urged the goldsmiths' guild to admit the journeyman von der Pütt as a master, even though he had not yet worked the requisite amount of time in Nuremberg. The city fathers confessed that in view of his artistic ability they had already commissioned work from him.[3] Most likely this re

ferred to his tableau of 1593 with wax medallions of eight Nuremberg councilmen.[4] The guild apparently granted their request, for between 1595 and 1612 von der Pütt employed four apprentices, among them Georg Holdermann (1585–1629) and, from 1602 to 1606, his son "Hans von der Pitt."

During the years of his medallic activity between 1591 and 1611, von der Pütt produced some sixteen pieces.[5] None are signed, and only one has a reverse design,[6] the remainder being uniface. His medals portray exclusively Nuremberg patricians and their wives, all presented in frontal or almost frontal view. Von der Pütt was one of the main exponents of the *en face* portrait, as contrasted to the more linear profile image. In the frontal view he was able to achieve a very high relief facilitated by the wax technique. Prominent beards, reflecting the Spanish-Italian fashion, and voluminous ruff collars are dominant features of his male portraits. His style, like that of several of his contemporaries, blends Netherlandish and Franconian elements into a distinctly Nuremberg decorum.

Mark M. Salton

133 obv.

Johann Philipp von der Pütt
Julius Geuder von Heroldsberg (1531–1594)
133
Silver, cast, uniface
Diameter 47.5 mm; internal measurement from the low point of the first V in IVLIVS to the low point of the G in HEROLTZBERG, 40.0 mm; weight 68.20 g
American private collection

Obverse: Bare-headed bust of Geuder in very high relief, facing front, with short-cropped hair, moustache, and long forked beard. He wears a large ruff collar and fur-trimmed coat open in front to reveal a small rosette-shaped jewel suspended from a necklace. Legend: • IVLIVS • GEVDER • V[on] • HEROLTZBERG • Æ[tatis] • 60 • (Julius Geuder von Heroldsberg, at age sixty).
Reverse: Plain.

This undated portrait of Geuder is one of von der Pütt's earliest medallic accomplishments. Geuder's age as given in the inscrip

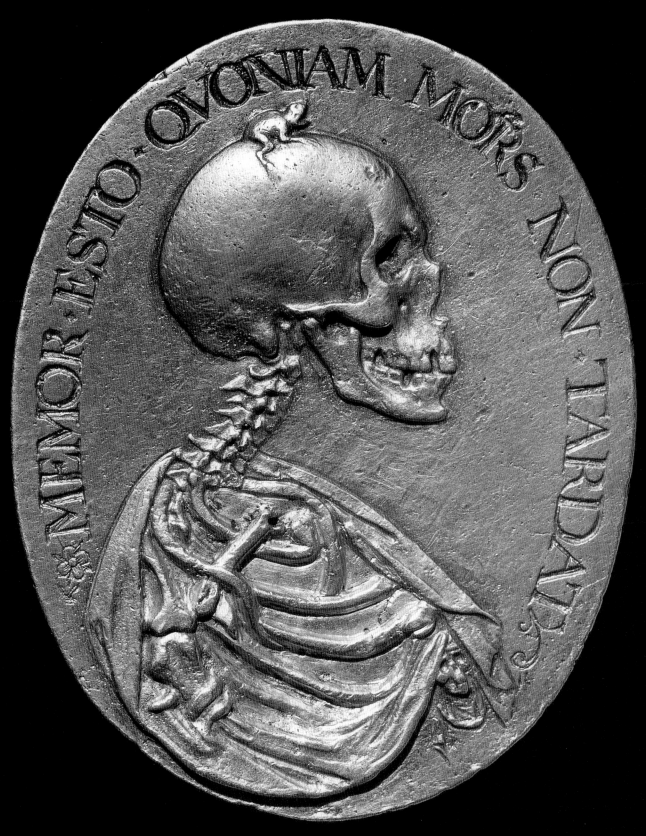

134 rev.

tion indicates that the work dates from 1591. Characteristic of von der Pütt's style are the massive three-dimensional portrait, barely contained by the tondo of the medal, and the keen gaze of the eyes with distinct round pupils, their lids indicated by simple curved ridges.

Julius Geuder was the scion of an old Nuremberg patrician family, one of seven children of Hans Geuder von Heroldsberg zu Heroldsberg und Neuhof and his wife, Brigitta Hirsch-vogelin. The Neuhof line, a side branch of the main stem von Heroldsberg zu Heroldsberg, Neuhof und Stein, became extinct on Julius's death.[1] Geuder was a member of the Elder Council and third-highest captain of the city. In 1561 he married Maria Hallerin von Hallerstein (1534–1583), and in 1588 Ursula Tucherin von Simmelsdorf (1556–1603). He lies buried in the church at Heroldsberg.[2] The Geuder family is known to have owned an important collection of woodcuts, copper etchings, and plaquettes.[3]

Mark M. Salton

Jan de Vos
(born 1578, died after 1619)

The Augsburg goldsmith registers list Jan de Vos as a native of Cologne. However, his contemporary Philipp Hainhofer relates that he was originally from the Netherlands, and there is reason to think him correct.[1] In any case, de Vos arrived in Augsburg at the age of twelve and apprenticed there for six years with a relative, the goldsmith Andreas Attemstett (Adamstetter). It then appears that he worked as a journeyman. In the year 1596 he may have been in Dresden, for a medal from that date of the two Saxon physicians Johann and Kaspar Neefe presents an obverse attributed to the Dresden medalist Tobias Wolff (cat. no. 128) together with a reverse bearing de Vos's signature.[2] This is his first known medal. His silver plaquette depicting the equestrian statue of Archduke Maximilian III by Hubert Gerhard must have been executed in Innsbruck shortly after 1600.[3] In 1602 de Vos received Augsburg citizenship and married there. He then worked in Augsburg until 1619. In 1605, however, he was appointed court goldsmith to Emperor Rudolf II (cat. no. 136) in Prague, and as late as 1614 he created medals of Rudolf's successor, Matthias, and his wife Anna (1585–1618). De Vos apparently left Augsburg after 1619, for subsequently there is no definite documentary mention of him.

Most of de Vos's medals bear a monogram formed of the letters IDV. Thanks to a misreading of that monogram all of them were at one time attributed to the Prague silversmith Paulus van Vianen.[4] Today his works are unquestioned, while there is increasing doubt about whether van Vianen worked as a medalist.[5] De Vos made his models in wax, and his medals are generally oval in form. His portraits have sharp outlines and appear to have been set down on the flat field. In only a few instances does the image blend into the background.[6]

The other surviving works by de Vos are mainly chased silver pieces, often copying the designs of others.

Karl Schulz

Jan de Vos
Allegory of *Vanitas*
134
Silver, cast
Tall oval, 58.6 × 48 mm; measurement from the top of the N in IN to the bottom edge of the bust truncation, 54.1 mm; weight 37.80 g
University of Vienna, Institut für Numismatik, Brettauer Collection
5005

Obverse: Female bust facing to the left, with diadem and pearls in her hair, earrings, necklace, and wearing a dress that leaves her breasts exposed. Engraved legend: (flower) NE GLORIERIS • IN • CRASTINVM (vine ornament) • (Do not boast of the morrow). The monogram IDV is engraved in the breast trunca-tion between the numbers of the date 1612.

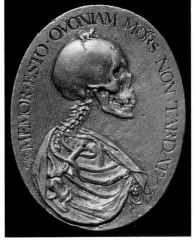 

134 rev.   134 obv.

Reverse: Bust of a skeleton facing to the right, draped in a cloak and with a toad sitting on the skull. Engraved legend: (flower) MEMOR • ESTO • QVONIAM MORS NON • TARDAT (vine ornament) • (Be mindful that Death does not delay).

Since the Middle Ages, artists had eagerly provided frightening images of death, either as a skeleton, a collection of bones, or some other symbol of decay. Less drastic motifs are the infant playing with a skull (cat. nos. 27, 112, 114) or the hourglass. Here the motif of *vanitas* is added to the *memento mori* of the inscription. Together, the obverse and reverse of the medal provide graphic illustration of the transitoriness of life. The vanity of the flesh is symbolized by a heavily jeweled woman, death by a skeleton with a snake winding between its ribs.[1] The highly adorned hairdo of the living beauty is contrasted with a toad, the symbol of death. The woman's sunburst brooch be-comes a death's head hanging in front of the skeleton's rib cage. Perhaps it was deliberate that the woman's earring resembles a fly, another symbol of decay.

Heinrich Modern claimed that the female figure is in fact a portrait of one of the mistresses of Emperor Rudolf II (cat. no. 136), a woman who bore him a daughter the day before he died. Though such an identification seems improbable, it may well be that de Vos was inspired to create the work by the emperor's death in 1612. The inclusion of that date would seem to be of some significance, though there is a variant of the medal with the date 1614.[2] If the piece does have to do with Rudolf's death, the presence of a toad in place of a crown takes on a special significance.

Karl Schulz

Severin Brachmann
(second half of the 16th century)

It was only relatively recently that Severin Brachmann was identified as the author of a group of medals notable for the broad form of the letter H in their inscriptions.[1] Their subjects are chiefly from Bohemia and Austria, especially Vienna. Given the medals attributed to him, it would appear that he first worked in Prague, with brief interruptions,[2] from 1564 to 1580, and indeed his name has been discovered in documents in Prague dating from 1568.[3] After producing a few pieces in Graz, he then appears in Vienna beginning in 1581. A series of medals of subjects from that city and its environs extends from 1581 to 1590. He married a Maria Khelner in Vienna in 1583. Stylistically Brachmann has been called a follower of Joachim Deschler (cat. nos. 118–20), though he only took up residence in Vienna some ten years after Deschler's death.

The majority of Brachmann's subjects are members of the bourgeoisie or the lesser nobility. His medals, almost all of them small, present their portraits either in strict profile or *en face* — the latter pose becoming more frequent in his late works. They are distinguished by their treatment of costume and a particular emphasis on head coverings, especially in portraits of women. In his profile portraits, the line of the back is quite rounded, and the bust truncation always extends down to the medal's edge. His men tend to wear long, full, pointed beards. With only a single exception,[4] Brachman's reverses — when he provided them — present coats of arms. His shields are generally pointed with concave sides and completely devoid of scroll-work. In his earlier medals he often provided borders of laurel wreaths, but later contented himself with a simple raised molding.

Brachmann worked in the old German tradition, creating his models in stone. Some of these survive, painted in bright colors.

Karl Schulz

Severin Brachmann
Eva Glueknecht (died c. 1605)
135
Silver, cast
Diameter 38.5 mm; diameter of the outer perimeter of the inscription, 36.5 mm; weight 26.33 g

135 obv.   135 rev.

Vienna, Kunsthistorisches Museum, Münzkabinett
13.847bß

Obverse: Bust portrait with high bonnet and ruff collar, facing to the left. Legend: EVA GLVEKNECHTINE: GEBO[rene] FRAVNBERGERIN (Eva Glueknecht, née Frauenberger).
Reverse: Coat of arms, a swan between bars, with a crowned helmet with mantling and swan crest. Legend: SIHE FVR DICH TREW IST MISLICH (Provide for yourself, loyalty is unreliable).

This medal is the companion piece to one of Eva's husband, Michael Glueknecht, dated 1586.[1] Though unsigned, both are attributed to Severin Brachmann on the basis of their style and in fact belong among his last works. The woman's high ruff collar and large but rather plain bonnet prevent us from seeing much of her face. Her round shoulder is emphasized by a broad seam on her sleeve in the foreground. On the reverse, the mantling and crest overwhelm the shield. The medal's edge is formed of a simple molding. On the reverses of the two medals, especially, one notes the broad letter forms typical of Brachmann, notably his wide letter H.

According to Eva Glueknecht's will, dated 1605, Michael Glueknecht was a Viennese merchant. The coats of arms on the reverses of these medals are therefore not noble. Interestingly enough the two arms are different. Hers may well be that of the Frauenbergers, about whom nothing further is known. Eva's will also makes it clear why she chose to wear such a large bonnet when sitting for her portrait, for in it she bequeaths to each of her three daughters a Genoese damask cap, two of them with marten-fur lining. She obviously had a special fondness for such showy costume accessories.[2]

Karl Schulz

Artist Unidentified (Prague, beginning of the seventeenth century)
Rudolf II (born 1552, emperor 1576–1612)
136
Gold, cast
Oval 41.6 × 33.3 mm; internal measurement from the low point of the first V in RVDOLPHVS to that of the V in HVNG, 26.06 mm; weight 20.74 g
Malibu, The J. Paul Getty Museum

136 obv.   136 rev.

Obverse: Laureate bust of Rudolf, facing three-quarters to right, with trimmed beard and long moustache. He wears cuirass, ruff collar, drapery *all'antica* gathered with a bolla at right shoulder, and around his neck the collar and jewel of the Order of the Golden Fleece. Legend: RVDOLPHVS II ROM[anorum] IMP[erator] AVG[ustus] REX HUNG[ariae] BO[h]E[miae] (Rudolf II, exalted emperor of the Romans, king of Hungary [and] Bohemia). Pearled border and raised rim.
Reverse: The constellation Capricorn, represented as a beast half goat and half fish, rising toward the right above a globe showing the outlines of the Mediterranean, Europe, and North Africa. Above, an eagle winging toward the sun. In the field a small star. Legend: ASTRVM FVLGET CÆS[aris] (The emperor's star shines). Pearled border and raised rim.

136a
Silver, cast, gilt
Oval 46.5 × 37.8 mm (excluding integral loop, ring, and pearl);

internal measurement from the low point of the first V in RVDOLPHVS to that of the V in HVNG, 29 mm; weight 17.52 g
American private collection

Obverse: As above.
Reverse: Essentially as above, but with the legend: FIRMAVIT OMEN (The omen has strengthened).

Both of these medals are undated, but their legend still identifies Rudolf as king of Hungary, indicating an origin before 1608, the year the title passed to his brother Matthias. Assigning authorship of these two works, part of a group of nine unsigned and undated Rudolf medals, has proven to be somewhat problematic.[1] Fine as these medals are in their minute detail, they reveal but little assertion of artistic individuality. Stylistically they follow the Italianizing mannerism of the period around 1600. Their relative uniformity may be the result not only of reciprocal influences within the circle of medalists working at court, but beyond that of the involvement of the emperor himself, for Rudolf took an active interest in virtually every aspect of artistic endeavor, impressing on his craftsmen his own personal tastes and preferences.

The imagery of the reverse would seem to have been selected by him after a Typotius design.[2] His imperial ambitions are manifested by the globe, emblem of ever-extending power, while the star and the triumphant rising eagle suggest the glorious future of the house of Habsburg. The symbolism of the Capricorn is more complex. In Greek myth Capricornus fought on the side of Zeus, crushing the Titans who attempted to storm Mount Olympus, a parallel to Rudolf's struggle against his numerous adversaries. In astrology, the creature appears as the tenth sign of the zodiac, signifying December, or winter in general, and on coins of Augustus (ruled 31 B.C.–A.D. 14), according to Suetonius, it represents his conception constellation (December 23, 64 B.C.), not that of his birthday (September 23, 63 B.C.), one that had assured him a long and successful reign.[3] Rudolf was in fact born under the sign of Virgo, but he too chose to appropriate this more auspicious augury, to partake in the Roman emperor's prestige and in the presage of rising fortune that had eluded him during his own troubled reign.

Rudolf II, son of Emperor Maximilian II (cat. nos. 61–62) and Maria (cat. no. 61a), the infanta of Spain and daughter of Charles V, was born in Vienna, but educated at the Spanish court as possible successor to his uncle Philip II (cat. nos. 58, 156). Early in life he displayed the essential traits of his character; he was haughty, distrustful, and superstitious. At the age of twenty he was recalled from Spain to be crowned king of Hungary. In 1576, on his father's death, he inherited the imperial crown.

While he attended to some extent to matters of state during the first two decades of his reign, his involvement gradually

136a obv.   136a rev.

136a obv.

subsided, most affairs being delegated to his courtiers. Unwisely he reversed Maximilian's policy of religious tolerance and gave open support to the forces of counter-reformation, thereby alienating the loyalty of many of his subjects. Rudolf increasingly directed his attention to collecting art; his gallery of paintings and a *Kunst- und Wunderkammer* (art and curio chamber) became focal points of his interest, and to satisfy his ravenous collecting appetite his agents scouted all over Europe for suitable objects. Among the arts that flourished at his court were architecture, goldsmithing (at which the emperor himself tried his hand), painting, and sculpture, revealing a blend of Italian, Netherlandish, and German influences. Over the years, Rudolf became more and more taken with the occult, dabbling in alchemy, astronomy, and astrology. It was on his invitation that Tycho Brahe (1546–1601) took up residence in Prague in 1599, to be followed a year later by Johannes Kepler (1571–1638).[4] In 1606, alarmed by Rudolf's indifferent leadership and chronic attacks of a melancholy bordering on insanity, a Habsburg family council declared him incapable of ruling, recognizing as regent one of his younger brothers, Archduke Matthias. Though ultimately forced to surrender the Habsburg lands to Matthias, Rudolf managed to hold onto his imperial title until he died, a virtual prisoner, at the Hradcany castle in Prague.

Mark M. Salton

137 obv.   137 rev.

Unknown German Master
Elisabeth, duchess of Braunschweig-Calenberg (1510–1558)
137
Silver, struck
Diameter 44.3 mm; weight 64.16 g
St. Petersburg, State Hermitage Museum
17728

Obverse: Bust facing front, wearing a widow's bonnet topped with a broad cap. Her wide-open eyes look out from a full, round face. In the field, the date 1545. Foliage border, doubled at the top.
Reverse: The Brandenburg coat of arms, with a crest of a lion to the right between two horns.[1] To the left of the helmet the

figure 3, to the right the figure 4. Between a line of pearling and the foliage border, the legend: ELISABET[a] - MAR[chionessa] PRI[ncipissa] BRVN[suicensis] - E[t] - LVNE[burgensis] (Elisabeth, marchioness [and] duchess of Braunschweig and Luneburg).

The visible defect in the obverse is the result of a double strike. The numbers 3 and 4 on the reverse are meant to be read together as 34, the sitter's age. Elisabeth, the second daughter of the elector Joachim I of Brandenburg (1484–1535) and Elisabeth, daughter of King Frederick I of Denmark, was born in 1510. On July 7, 1525 she married Duke Erich the Elder of Braunschweig-Calenberg. That marriage produced four children. Elisabeth was widowed on July 26, 1540, and on May 30, 1546, she took as her second husband Count Poppo of Henneberg. Since her son Erich was only twelve at the time of his father's death, Elisabeth ruled as his guardian. It was she who introduced the Reformation into her territories.

She died at Ilmenau Castle on May 25, 1558, and was buried in the ducal vault at Bessra, a Premonstratensian abbey.[2] A pair of medals with portraits of the deceased duke and Elisabeth was cast in Braunschweig in 1544. The coats of arms of Braunschweig and Brandenburg appear on the reverses of both. In the following year the medal of Elisabeth was repeated—this time as a struck piece—with the date 1545, possibly the year in which Prince Erich attained his majority and his mother placed the government in his hands.

The South German cities of Nuremberg and Augsburg were the centers of medal production in Germany in the mid sixteenth century, and it was from them that the art spread to the rest of the country. Virtually every secular and ecclesiastical prince aspired to have his portrait on a *Verehrungspfenning*, certain that it would enhance his prestige. Such pieces were struck in their official mints, though there were not always trained and gifted masters on hand to design them. Nevertheless, these struck medals are of great interest for the history of portraiture in Germany.

The Elisabeth medal, one of the first examples of the medallic portrait in Braunschweig, was the work of an inexperienced but ambitious master. One sees how intent he was on reproducing textures, such as the smooth skin of the face or the fur on the collar and the cap. Despite its visible imperfections, the medal is filled with a certain charm. The duchess's lively face is portrayed with an expressive naiveté.

The medal is known in two weights, depending on the thickness of the flan. Although their weights correspond to those of the thaler, these commemorative pieces were not intended to be circulated as coinage. They were produced solely as showpieces, and represent prototypes of the *Gnadenpfenninge* that would become common in Braunschweig in the later sixteenth and seventeenth centuries.[3]

The medal of Elisabeth of Braunschweig is an indication of the rapid spread of the new art and of its development at different levels of artistry.

Yevgenia Shchukina

151 obv.

France

SIXTEENTH AND EARLY SEVENTEENTH

CENTURIES

For the convenience of the reader, dates of
political leaders most frequently encountered are
provided below.
All other life dates appear in the text.

France
Charles V, "the Wise" (born 1337, king 1364–80)
Charles VI, "the Well-Beloved" (born 1368,
king 1380–1422)
Charles VII (born 1403, king 1422–61)
Louis XI (born 1423, king 1461–83)
Charles VIII (born 1470, king 1483–98)
Louis XII, "Père du Peuple" (born 1462, king 1498–1515)
Francis I (born 1494, king 1515–47)
Henry II (born 1519, king 1547–59)
Francis II (born 1544, king 1559–60)
Charles IX (born 1550, king 1560–74)
Henry III (born 1551, king 1574–89)
Henry IV, "Henry of Navarre" (born 1553, king 1589–1610)
Louis XIII (born 1601, king 1610–43)
Louis XIV, "the Great" (born 1638, king 1643–1715)

England
Henry VIII (born 1491, king 1509–47)
Edward VI (born 1537, king 1547–53)
Mary Tudor (born 1516, queen 1553–58)
Elizabeth I (born 1533, queen 1558–1603)
James I (born 1556, king 1603–25)
Charles I (born 1600, king 1625–49)

Navarre
Henry II d'Albret (born 1505, king 1516–55)
Jeanne d'Albret (born 1528, queen 1555–72)

Savoy
Philip of Bresse (born 1438, duke 1496–97)
Philibert II (born 1480, duke 1497–1504)

Tuscany
Ferdinando I de' Medici (born 1549, grand duke 1587–1609)
Cosimo II de' Medici (born 1590, grand duke 1609–21)

138 obv.

138 rev.

French School
Louise of Savoy (1476–1531) and Marguerite of Angoulême (1492–1549)
138
Bronze, cast
Diameter 63 mm
London, Victoria & Albert Museum, Salting Collection

Obverse: Bust of Louise to right, with *chaperon* falling at the sides and back. Legend: LOYSE · DVCHESSE · DEVALOIS · COMTESSE · DANGOLESME · (Louise, duchess of Valois, countess of Angoulême).
Reverse: Bust of Marguerite to right, wearing *coiffe à templette* beneath a small *chaperon*. Legend: MARGVERITE · FILLE · DE · CHARLES · COMTE · DANGOLESME · (Marguerite, daughter of Charles, count of Angoulême).

138a
Bronze, cast
Diameter 68 mm
London, The British Museum (ex Rosenheim Collection)

Obverse: As above, but with a *bandeau* visible across her forehead.
Reverse: As above.

The medal of Louise of Savoy and her daughter Marguerite of Angoulême belongs to a group of early sixteenth-century medals of important figures at the court of France long associated with Giovanni Candida (see cat. nos. 37–38).[1] In their general format, many of these pieces do recall Candida's medals of the mid 1490s, but they are probably the work of French artists for whom Candida's late work furnished a stylistic point of departure. They tend to show higher relief than Candida's work; they lack his incisive rendering of facial features, and their lettering is less fine.

Louise of Savoy was born into a high-ranking family fallen

upon hard times.[2] Her father was Philip of Bresse, "Sans Terre," who became duke of Savoy in 1496. Through her mother, Marguerite de Bourbon, she was closely related to Louis XI and Charles VIII. On her mother's death in 1483, Louise was sent to be educated at the court of the regent Anne of France (1462–1522), and in 1488 she was married to Charles d'Orléans, count of Angoulême (1460–1496), from a cadet branch of the royal house of Valois. Their daughter Marguerite was born in 1492, and their son, the future Francis I, two years later. Louise was widowed in 1496.

When Francis became king in 1515, his mother and sister received important new titles and holdings, and Louise came to serve as his most trusted counselor and most energetic partisan. On her death in 1531, Marguerite stepped into her mother's place. Though never officially regent, she too exercised great power in France during her brother's absences, spending more time at his court than at her own. In 1509, Marguerite had married Charles, duke of Alençon (1489–1525). When Francis was imprisoned by the emperor Charles V in 1525, she journeyed to Spain and petitioned for his release. A second marriage, in 1527, to King Henry d'Albret of Navarre, made her life a balancing game as her opportunistic husband allied himself by turns with both Francis and Charles V. Marguerite herself drew continual fire from conservatives over her role in ecclesiastical and monastic reforms. In the decade before her death in 1549, as her appeals for reform became less outspoken, Marguerite came increasingly under the influence of Florentine Neoplatonism.

The present medal is undated, but it must be contemporary with its pendant, a medal of Francis of Angoulême bearing the date 1504.[3] The apparent ages of Louise and Marguerite on their medal seem to accord with that date, when they were twenty-eight and twelve, respectively.[4]

Louis XII had failed to produce a male heir, and when the king was stricken by a near-fatal illness in January 1504, Louise prepared to see her son Francis mount the throne. She may well have commissioned the medals of herself and her children at

138 obv.

this time in order to impress the features of the new royal family upon the minds of the court.[5] The king then recovered, and lived on until 1515. His final hopes for an heir were dashed when his last child, a son, died immediately after birth in 1512, and it was in that year that Francis was definitively appointed to succeed him. It can hardly be coincidental that another pair of medals depicting Louise and Francis date from that pivotal year in Francis's road to the throne (see cat. no. 139).

Earlier writers have doubted that the present medal is contemporary with its counterpart of Francis because of the titles it attributes to Louise. She only became duchess of Valois in her own right in 1515, after her son's coronation as king of France. The source of the confusion is that Francis was legally a minor until his emancipation in 1512, and until that date his mother held his titles for him *en tutelle*.[6] She had fought bitterly to retain guardianship of her children in her widowhood, and one of her reasons for commissioning a medal of herself to match the portrait of her son may well have been a desire to advertise the titles—and the concomitant power and influence—that that struggle had brought her.

Louis Waldman

French School
Francis of Angoulême, later Francis I (born 1494, king of France 1515–47)
139
Bronze, cast
Diameter 98 mm
Paris, Bibliothèque Nationale, Cabinet des Médailles

Obverse: Laureate bust to left, with long hair and wearing plate armor over a mail shirt. Legend: MAXIMVS FRANCISCVS FRANCORVM DVX 1512 (The supreme Francis, duke of the French. 1512).
Reverse: Plain.

This large 1512 medal of Francis of Angoulême, together with its pendant representing his mother Louise of Savoy,[1] has been assigned to the "school" of Giovanni Candida—a case of guilt by association with the Candidesque medals of the same subjects from 1504 (see cat. no. 138). But even setting aside the questionable concept of a "Candida school," there is little evidence that the medalist of 1512 was significantly influenced by any single Italian master.[2] He was an artist of much more independent character than the medalist of 1504. The finesse and elaboration with which the specimen in this exhibition was worked after casting may point to a goldsmith employed in court circles.

Having inherited Angoulême on the death of his father in 1496, Francis became heir presumptive to the throne of France at the accession of the childless Louis XII in 1498.[3] He was created duke of Valois in the following year. Louis's continuing inability to produce a son led to the young duke's recognition as Dauphin in 1505, and to his engagement in 1507 to the king's daughter, Claude de France, whom he married in 1514. Louis died on the last day of 1514, and Francis d'Angoulême was

crowned king. In the early years of his reign he busily forged a string of alliances with neighboring states and prosecuted a regime of governmental and clerical reforms at home. His chief rival in Europe was the Spanish emperor, Charles V, and the two fought each other with only brief intermissions for the next thirty years. In 1525, after the French defeat at the battle of Pavia, the emperor took Francis as a prisoner to Spain, where he languished for a year (see cat. no. 145), yet in 1530, as one of the terms of the Peace of Cambrai, Francis married the emperor's sister Eleanora (1498–1558).

139 obv.

For all its bellicosity, his reign saw little expansion of France's territory, but the cultural gains of his rule were enormous. His legacy includes the Collège de France and the Bibliothèque Royale, as well as the countless châteaux that he built or enlarged, among them Chambord, Fontainebleau, Blois, and the Louvre. His agents scoured Italy for antiquities and masterpieces of Renaissance art. His opulent court attracted such artists as Leonardo, Giulio Romano, Cellini, and Clouet, and writers of the stature of Marot and Budé.

There can be little doubt that the present medal was commissioned specifically to spotlight Francis in his triumph on being named heir to the throne, and all the evidence points to one likely patron. As in the case of the 1504 medals (cat. no. 138), it was probably Louise of Savoy.[4]

Louis Waldman

140a obv.

Nicolas Leclerc and Jean de Saint-Priest

Louis XII (born 1462, king of France 1498–1515) and Anne of
    Brittany (1476–1514)

140

Bronze, cast

Diameter 113 mm; diameter of inner perimeter of inscription,
    105 mm

Boston, Museum of Fine Arts, Elizabeth M. and John F. Para-
    mino Fund

Obverse: Bust of Louis to right, wearing his crown over a cap.
Around his neck is the collar of the Order of St. Michael. Field
semé of fleur-de-lis.[1] In the margin below the bust, a lion
passant, the symbol of the city of Lyon. Legend: + FELICE •
LVDOVICO • REGNA[n]TE • DVODECIMO • CESARE •
ALTERO • GAVDET • OMNIS • NACIO • (In the blessed reign of
Louis XII, a second Caesar, the entire nation rejoices).
Reverse: Bust of Anne of Brittany to left, wearing crown, veil, a
small necklace, and a long cord with a jewel pendant. Field
semé of fleurs-de-lis and ermine tails.[2] In the margin below the
bust, a lion passant. Legend: + LVGDVN[ensi] • RE • PUBLICA
• GAVDE[n]TE • BIS • ANNA • REGNANTE • BENIGNE • SIC •
FVI • CONFLATA • 1499 (The commune of Lyon rejoicing in
the second reign of good Queen Anne, I was cast. 1499).

140a

Bronze, cast

Diameter 114 mm

New York, The Metropolitan Museum of Art, Gift of George and
    Florence Blumenthal, 1935

Obverse and reverse as above.

This medal of Louis XII and his wife Anne of Brittany is one of
the milestones in French medallic art. Commissioned by the
city of Lyon on March 18, 1499,[3] it was the collective effort of a
small group of local artists who, under the influence of the
Italians, helped to introduce medalmaking into France. The
modeling was done by Nicolas Leclerc and Jean de Saint-Priest,
while the casting was entrusted to Jean Lepère, his brother
Colin, and an unidentified founder. Nicolas Leclerc was a master engraver and mason active in Lyon from 1487 to 1507.[4] Jean
de Saint-Priest, also a master engraver, lived in Lyon from 1490
to 1516.[5] The Lepère brothers were the sons of the goldsmith
Louis Lepère (died 1500), and were goldsmiths themselves.

The effigies of the royal couple are somewhat ponderous, and
their faces look rather like those of minor gentry. One would not
know from the starched portrait of Anne of Brittany that she
was a spirited, intelligent, pugnacious woman. Lacking in ele-

140a rev.

gance and crowded with heraldic devices, the piece is medieval in spirit. Its creators had yet to learn the virtues of reducing a design to its essentials. Moreover, to its detriment, the medal was recast again and again, and consequently decent specimens are hard to find. Most of the existing recastings are coated with an artificial patina that conceals the luster of the metal, which is admittedly often of an inferior grade.

A specimen in gold, now lost, was quickly produced and presented to Queen Anne to commemorate Louis's second state entry into Lyon. Such royal visits to the cities of the realm were the occasions for great festivities, and gifts to the monarchs were in order.[6]

Anne was the daughter of Francis II, the last duke of Brittany, whom she succeeded at the age of twelve in 1488. In 1490, in an attempt to preserve the independence of the duchy, she was married by proxy to Emperor Maximilian I (cat. nos. 37, 79). But Maximilian was never able to claim his bride and was unable to defend her. Soon afterward she was forced to marry instead the king of France, Charles VIII, who had in turn renounced an alliance with Margaret of Austria (1480–1530), daughter of Maximilian and Mary of Burgundy (cat. no. 37). Widowed in 1498, Anne then married Charles's successor, Louis XII. Her greatest concern was to avoid any alliance that risked the separation of Brittany from France, especially since the country was just then in a period of expansion.

Louis XII was thirty-six when he assumed the throne in 1498. The son of the poet Charles d'Orléans (1394–1465) and great-grandson of Charles V, "the Wise," he established an enlightened reign in support of the arts and literature, but was less successful at protécting his kingdom. His internal policy was carried on with much prudence, earning him the soubriquet "the father of his people." He did not have the spirit of Charles VIII, but like him he felt the lure of Italy and the Renaissance. Rather than attempting conquests there, he cultivated the friendship of the country's great artists such as Leonardo da Vinci (1452–1519). His fondness for literature induced him to support booksellers, publishers, and translators of the classical authors.

Jean-Baptiste Giard

Jean Marende (active c. 1502)
Philibert II, "the Fair" (born 1480, eighth duke of Savoy 1497–1504), and Margaret of Austria (1480–1530)

141
Bronze, cast
Diameter 103.5 mm
St. Petersburg, State Hermitage Museum
26470

Obverse: Rising from behind a wattle palisade, the confronted

141 obv.

141 rev.

busts of Philibert the Fair and Margaret of Austria against a field sown with Savoy knots and marguerites. Legend: PHILIBERTVS • DVX • SABAVDI[a]E • VIII • MARGVA[rita] • MAXI[miliani] • CAE[saris] • AVG[usti] • FI[lia] • D[ucissa] • SA[baudiae] (Philibert, eighth duke of Savoy, Margaret, daughter of Maximilian, Caesar Augustus, duchess of Savoy).
Reverse: Shield with the coat of arms of Austria impaling Savoy[1] on a field sown with Savoy knots and marguerites. The letters FE to the left of the shield, and the letters RT to the right.[2] Legend: GLORIA IN ALTISSIMIS • DEO ET IN TERRA • PAX • HOMINIBVS • BVRGVS : (Glory to God in the highest, and on earth peace to men: Bourg). The text is abbreviated from Luke 2:14.

The medal of Philibert the Fair and Margaret of Austria was made by Jean Marende, a goldsmith in Bourg-en-Bresse.[3] Marende's family came from Bresse, but his name appears only in an account ledger and book of minutes of the syndics and council of Bourg, where it is recorded that he was commissioned by the city to make a gold medal in honor of Margaret of Austria. Aside from these documents we know nothing about his life.

The medal was made in two stages. One of the two existing versions was probably the trial proof, of which the most distinctive feature is the fact that fleurs-de-lis, symbols of the kingdom of France, were mistakenly placed around Margaret's portrait.[4] We could speculate that Marende chose fleurs-de-lis instead of marguerites because he lacked specific instructions regarding

the ornamentation of his medal and may have patterned it after the one of Louis XII and Anne of Brittany (cat. no. 140). The other, final version appears in two variants: in one the field is sown with eleven Savoy knots and eleven marguerites,[5] in the other with ten Savoy knots and nine marguerites.[6]

The gold specimen of this medal, now lost, was presented to the duchess when she made her state entry into Bourg on August 2, 1502. We do not know if the portraits are true to life, but the workmanship seems somewhat crude. While the composition is skilled enough, with confronted effigies in the tradition of ancient coins, there is little in the way of attention to detail or elegance of line. Even so, the engraver did manage to convey the youthfulness of his subjects, which is further underscored by the marguerites—homonyms in French of the duchess's name—and Savoy knots, or love knots.[7] The wattle fence is probably a reference to the enclosed garden of the Song of Solomon (4:12): "A garden enclosed is my sister, my spouse; a spring shut up, a fountain sealed." Normally applied to the Virgin Mary and seen also enclosing the unicorn as the symbol of Christ, in secular terms the fence enclosed the garden of Love, certainly appropriate here in reference to the newlywed couple's pledge of fidelity and purity. It would also relate to the meaning of the marguerites as symbols of innocence.[8] Marende was clearly a capable local craftsman, but one whose work was not up to the high standards of the great medalists of the Italian Renaissance. Like the medal of Louis XII and Anne of Brittany his design still contains Gothic elements.

Philibert the Fair, eighth duke of Savoy, died at twenty-four, and did not have time to achieve fame. His second wife, however, Margaret of Austria, the daughter of Emperor Maximilain I and Mary of Burgundy (cat. no. 37), was an outstanding figure. She proved an able administrator while regent of the Netherlands, and was a patron of art and literature.

Jean-Baptiste Giard

Jacques Gauvain
(born before 1501, died after 1547)

Jacques Gauvain was probably born in Picardy.[1] From 1515 to 1547 he lived in Lyon, where he married twice. His first wife was the daughter of Jean Lepère, a master goldsmith active in Lyon and the author of the medal of Anne of Brittany (cat. no. 140). His second wife was a daughter of Guillaume Carme, called Augustin, another local goldsmith. He had two sons—we do not know by which wife—both of whom also became goldsmiths in Lyon. From 1521 to 1524 Gauvain served as die-engraver to the mint at Grenoble, but relinquished that post because he refused to give up his lucrative activities in Lyon. He also made medals, including three self-portraits from 1523 that reflect the contemporary Germanic style.[2] The artist even made a point of copying the flamboyant German fashion of the time with its hairnets and broad, flat caps. His only documented medals were commissioned by the consulate of Lyon as presents for Queen Eleonore, the wife of Francis I, the Dauphin, and Antoine Duprat, cardinal legate and chancellor of France, on the occasion of their entry into the city in May 1533. The one of the Dauphin is the only one of the three to have survived.

Jean-Baptiste Giard

Jacques Gauvain
Antoine, duke of Lorraine and Bar (1489–1544), and Renée de Bourbon
142
Silver, struck
Diameter 41.5 mm
St. Petersburg, State Hermitage Museum
17731

Obverse: Bust of Antoine to right, his hair in a net, wearing a hat with the letter A in a medallion under the brim. Legend: (cross of Lorraine) • ANTHONIVS • D[ei] • G[ratia] • LOTHOR

142 obv.   142 rev.

142a obv.   142a rev.

[ingiae] • ET • Bar[i] • DUX • (Antoine, by the grace of God, duke of Lorraine and Bar).
Reverse: Bust of Renée to left, wearing a light cloth coif covering the ears and hanging down her back. Legend: RENATA • DE BORBO[n]IA • LOTHOR[ingiae] • ET • BAR[ri] • DUCISSA (Renée de Bourbon, duchess of Lorraine and Bar).

142a
Silver, struck
Diameter 41.5 mm
Paris, Bibliothèque Nationale, Cabinet des Médailles
Ancien fonds 189

Obverse and reverse as above, except for addition of pearled borders.

The medal of Antoine de Lorraine was probably engraved between 1521 and 1525, since he wore a beard, following the example of Francis I, only after 1521,[1] and since the doublet he wears was popular during that period.[2] Its attribution to Gauvain is based on its similarity to the artist's self-portrait.[3]

Antoine, duke of Lorraine and Bar (Barrois), was the son of duke René and Philippe de Gueldre. He lived at the court of Louis XII (cat. no. 140) from 1501 to 1508. When his father died in 1508, he returned to Lorraine, where he was declared of age by the States General. He married Renée de Bourbon on the advice of Louis XII in 1515. Antoine was also close to Louis's successor, Francis I (cat. nos. 116, 139), until shortly before his wife's death in 1539. In April of that year their friendship was strained when Francis I laid down new and more stringent terms of subinfeudation on the inhabitants of Bar living on the left bank of the Meuse. The Meuse had served as the approximate boundary between the kingdom of France and the Holy Roman Empire since the Treaty of Verdun in 843, yet the French king had been repeatedly tempted to ignore this line of demarcation.[4] In November 1541, Francis forced the duke and his son to acknowledge that they held jurisdiction over subinfeudated Bar solely at the king's pleasure, and Antoine was obliged to cede to the king the fortified town of Stenay in exchange for his continuing good will. This was the event that pushed Antoine into the camp of Francis's adversary, Charles V.

Jean-Baptiste Giard

Pierre II Woeiriot de Bouzey
(1532–after 1596)

Born at Neufchâteau (Lorraine) about 1531–32, Pierre II Woeiriot de Bouzey came from a family with a strong background in the fine arts.[1] His grandfather was a sculptor and architect, his father a goldsmith. His mother, Urbaine de Bouzey, came from an old Lorraine family with a knightly pedigree. Since the Bouzey line was about to die out, she stipulated in her will that her children were to add the name and coat of arms of Bouzey to their own.[2] We do not know exactly when Pierre Woeiriot left Lorraine, but he settled in Lyon and probably spent some time in Italy. A humanist, he maintained close ties with Protestant circles in Lyon and worked for publishers in the city. Although his book engravings are not highly accomplished, in certain instances, notably those of Flavius Josephus's *Antiquities of the Jews*,[3] they show genuine ability. His engraved illustrations of Roman coins grace Antoine Le Pois's *Discours sur les médailles et graveures antiques, principalement romaines . . .* , published in Paris in 1579. Some are not lacking in elegance, and compare favorably with contemporary work by Enea Vico and Hubert Goltzius, who were famous for their consummate drawings of ancient coins.

Jean-Baptiste Giard

Pierre II Woeiriot
Simon Costière (1469–after 1562)
143
Bronze, cast, uniface
Diameter 67.0 mm
Washington, The National Gallery of Art, Samuel H. Kress Collection
1957.14.1139

Obverse: Bust to left, wearing a doublet and a round hat with a cord at the base of the crown and a flap covering the ears and neck. Legend: SIMON • COSTIERE • AN[no] • ET (as ligature)• Æ[tatis] • 97 • (Simon Costière, in his ninety-seventh year). The word ET would appear to be superfluous. The date 1566 appears on the truncation.
Reverse: Plain.

Simon Costière was born in Lyon in 1469, and was over 102 when he died in 1572. In addition to being a goldsmith, jeweler, and lapidary, he served as the head of the guild of money changers in 1534–35, 1541–42, and 1546–47.[1] He was well-to-do himself, and clearly belonged to the enterprising class that turned Lyon into a thriving commercial and literary center during the sixteenth century. A solid bourgeois, he is represented on the medal in his ninety-seventh year, still alert and wearing a plain but snug round hat. This portrait medal of a simple private citizen is an exceptional occurence, one that presages a new era. Heretofore in France, only kings and princes felt entitled to have themselves portrayed on medals, but now we find a member of the middle class to some extent usurping

143 obv.

that right. Only a bold individual accustomed to a certain level of authority would have had the presumption to commission such a work.

There are three different versions of this medal: (1) the present type, with the word ET in the legend and the date on the truncation; (2) a version in lead with the same legend and portrait, but framed; (3) a version in bronze without the ET and with the date immediately following Costière's age in the inscription.[2] A single example of the last version bears a faint impression of Woeiriot's monogram.[3] The artist's crisp, spare technique infuses this portrait with realism and considerable presence.

Jean-Baptiste Giard

Germain Pilon
(c. 1525–1590)

Germain Pilon is generally considered the greatest sculptor of the French Renaissance. The surviving documents, covering the period between 1540 and his death, allow us only faint glimpses of his involvement in the events of his turbulent century. That his talents had been recognized by the late 1550s is evident from his collaboration, in a minor way, on the tomb of Francis I under the direction of Philibert de l'Orme (born c. 1510–15, died 1570).[1] We next find him engaged on a number of the projects commissioned by Catherine de' Medici to commemorate her late husband, Henry II, and glorify the house of Valois. Sometime between 1560 and 1566 he carved the statues of the Three Graces for the monument to the heart of the deceased king, originally located in the church of the Céléstins,[2] and during these same years, and continuing to 1573, he worked on one of the most important projects of his career, producing all of the major sculpture for the tomb of Henry II in Saint-Denis.[3]

By 1572, Pilon was already *Sculteur ordinaire* to Henry's successor, Charles IX. In that year he was also appointed to a newly created post, that of *Conducteur et Controleur Général en l'art de sculture sur le faict de ses monnoyes et revers d'icelles*.[4] The introduction of portraiture on coins had necessarily placed much greater demands on the designers of coin types and on the engravers themselves. The king's decision to place aesthetic control of the coinage and production of medals in the hands of his chief sculptor reveals that these new demands had not been adequately met. Pilon was expected to provide models in wax of the portraits to be placed on coins and medals, to supervise the quality of the dies produced from these models, to participate in decisions regarding the choice of die-engravers, and, finally, if all else failed, to carve the dies himself.[5]

Pilon served as *Controleur Général* until his death, but it is impossible to determine whether he in fact provided the models for all of the coinage produced during this period. The coins themselves vary in quality, as might be expected, since the dies would have been carved by a number of hands and might not always have been submitted to his scrutiny. In a document dated February 3, 1575, we learn that Pilon was involved in the striking of coronation jetons or medals for Henry III, yet it is difficult to recognize his style in the type that has survived.[6] With one very notable exception (see the discussion of cat. no. 144), this is true of most of the struck medals produced during his tenure as *Controleur Général*.

Two groups of medals appear to be the work of Pilon himself or one of his immediate followers. These are the series of portraits of prominent members of the Valois dynasty (see cat. no. 145) and a group of small struck pieces centering around the coronation medal of Henry III, documented to Pilon.[7] Except for the medals of René de Birague—both those in the latter series and the cast medallion included in this exhibition (cat. no. 144)–these medals have little in common with the cast Valois series, and shed only faint light on their possible authorship.

Stephen K. Scher

Germain Pilon
René de Birague (1507–1583)
144
Bronze, cast and gilt
Diameter 164 mm
Paris, Bibliothèque Nationale, Cabinet des Médailles, formerly the Chevalier de Stuers Collection
AF 5085

Obverse: Bust in profile to right. Birague wears a heavy outer cloak with a fur collar and edging over a high-necked shirt with a ruff. Legend: RENATVS • BIRAGVS • FRANCIA • CANCELARIVS • ANNO • [a]ETATIS • SVAE • LXX • (René de Birague, chancellor of France, in his 70th year).
Reverse: Inscription engraved after casting as follows: HIC, EST QVI LATIIS DVM RES DECLINAT IN ORIS (flower) GALLICA, FORTVNAE, QVAE TRANSFVGIEBAT AD HOSTES (flower) NOLVIT ESSE COMES SED AVITOS LAETVS HONORES (flower) ET PATRIAS LINQVENS SEDES, SVPERESSE

RVINAE (flower) AMISSIS VBI PROQVE BONIS ET HONORIB[us], AMPLIS (flower) ADSPIRANTE DEO REPERIT MAIORA RELICTIS (flower) FACTVS APVD GALLOS SACRI CAPVT IPSE SENATVS (leafy branch) (This is he who, while Gallic affairs declined in the Latin lands, did not wish to be companion to a fortune that was deserting to the enemy. Leaving behind, even joyfully, ancestral honors and the dwelling place of his forefathers, refusing to remain in a homeland in ruins, he took refuge in the Gallic kingdom where, after having lost, by the grace of God, considerable possessions and honors, he obtained in exchange more than he had lost: He was appointed, in France, the leader of the Senate [or Ministry of Finance, i.e. chancellor]).[1]

There can be no doubt that this particular medallion is from the hand of Germain Pilon. The agitated, nervous folds of the robe and the ruff, the tense, spiky textures of hair and fur, and the lean, taut planes of the face are pure manifestations of the style of the master who produced the famous *priant* for Birague's tomb, sculpted seven or eight years later. In terms of medallic art, Pilon has here created a unique type on a scale previously unknown. This example of the Birague medal is especially fresh and sharp, and it is probable, since it exists with its original tooled leather box, that this is the very example given to Birague by the artist.[2]

In 1577, in the reign of Henry III, a small medal was struck apparently to commemorate the convening of the Estates General at Blois. Its obverse bore a portrait of the king's chancellor René de Birague identical to the one seen here. Just how that small struck medal relates to this large cast piece is not entirely clear. The present work is almost certainly cast from a wax model, the lettering on the reverse subsequently cut into the surface. It may reflect the sort of wax model Pilon supplied to the engravers, who would then have carved a die for striking the smaller piece.[3] Both were done in the same year, 1577. Five years earlier, Birague had commissioned Pilon to fashion his wife's tomb.[4] We would like to suggest that the artist, having prepared a wax model for the mint, decided to make a cast from it for presentation to his client. The medal may also serve as something of a preliminary study for the great kneeling tomb figure of Birague done around seven years later.

There is another specimen in the British Museum that bears at the end of the reverse inscription the words G PILLON FECIT.[5] On the obverse of the British Museum example the lettering is not as fine, and the details of the bust are not quite as sharp. Its reverse inscription, cast from a broken mold rather than cut into the cold metal as in the Paris example, differs in several places, and does not have the flower stops or the leafy branch at the end.[6] It is Mark Jones's theory that the London specimen was possibly a trial piece prepared for Birague's inspection.[7] Although this is open to question, the authenticity of the London medal, and therefore the validity of the signature, are undisputed.

A final proof of Pilon's authorship of the Birague medal is the conformity between the style of the lettering on the reverse of

144 obv.

the Paris specimen and that of the inscriptions on Pilon's drawing for the Birague tomb.[8] Taking into consideration the differences in material and technique, the similarities are striking, even to the use of the leafy scroll at the end.

Among the *fuorusciti*, the exiled Italians who flocked to the French court in the sixteenth century, René de Birague was certainly one of the most successful and powerful.[9] Born on February 2, 1507, to a prominent Milanese family that supported France's claim to the duchy, Birague was forced to flee with the rest of his family to Piedmont after the French relinquished Milan to Charles V in 1522. Francis I had established in Piedmont a fully functioning state, and it was there that René laid the foundations of a career devoted to the house of Valois and to France. Advancing quickly through several important positions, Birague became president of the Parlement of Turin

in 1543, and held that position until the return of the duke of Savoy in 1562. During this period he became known for his championship of the Catholic faith and harsh punishment of reformers.

In 1563, Birague was named to the privy council of Charles IX, and in the following year he became governor of Lyon. His efficient administration caught the attention of Catherine de' Medici, and by 1571 Birague had been advanced to keeper of the royal seals in Paris. Within a year, he became involved in the planning of one of the bloodiest events of the century, the massacre of the Protestants on the night of August 23/24, 1572, the feast of St. Bartholomew. By March of 1573, Birague had become chancellor of France, the most powerful judicial officer in the kingdom.

After his wife's death in 1572, Birague gave further evidence

of his religious fervor by becoming a priest, and in February 1578 Pope Gregory XIII named him a cardinal. For his devotion to the French crown, he was awarded the rank of commander of the Order of the Holy Ghost on December 31, 1579. Although he had managed to accumulate a substantial income in the service of the crown and the Church, he lived in a very lavish style, and died virtually penniless.

Stephen K. Scher

Germain Pilon
Henry II (born 1519, king of France 1547–59)
145
Bronze, cast
Diameter 164 mm
New York, private collection

Obverse: Bust in three-quarter view facing right. The king wears a soft cap decorated with pearls, a cord above the brim, and ostrich feathers on the left side. He is dressed in an embroidered, high-collared shirt with an elaborate necklace, and a jacket. He also wears a pearl drop earring. Legend: HENRICVS • II • GALLIAR[um] • REX • CHRISTIANISS[imus] P[ater] P[atriae] 1559 (Henry II, most Christian king of the French, father of the people).
Reverse: Incuse.

This medal is one of a series dedicated to the last members of the house of Valois: Henry II; his queen Catherine de' Medici; their sons Charles IX and Henry III; and Charles's queen Elizabeth of Austria. Although one occasionally encounters hesitant doubts about their attribution in the literature, these works

145 obv.

are generally presented as impressive examples of Pilon's portraiture and numbered among his most significant works. In the inventory of Pilon's estate there are many references to sculpted and painted portraits and medals, but nothing that could be specifically associated with these large pieces.[1] There are no contemporary documents that mention these medallions, and so far the earliest date that can be assigned to them is provided by a specimen of the medal of Henry II owned by the École des Beaux-Arts. Stamped onto the lower right-hand portion of its obverse field is a crowned letter C, a mark that was used on all bronzes in commerce between 1745 and 1749 and thus provides a terminus post quem of around 1745.[2]

The style of the Valois pieces is not at all the same as that of the Birague medallion, and we cannot assert with confidence that they are directly from the hand of Pilon. Because of certain similarities with Pilon's sculptured portraits of these same subjects and because the medallions are based on contemporary paintings or drawings, we have concluded that they should be attributed tentatively to Pilon himself or to one of his immediate followers. On the basis of their style and of historical logic, it would seem that the Valois series was probably commissioned by Catherine de' Medici sometime around 1575, perhaps in conjunction with Henry III's accession to the throne.

These portraits differ not only in style but also in presentation, profile in the case of Birague, three-quarter view for the Valois. Although not always the case, it can often be demonstrated that the source for the three-quarter format is a drawing, painting, or engraving, and this is certainly true for the Valois medallions, whose portraits are based on paintings and drawings by, or attributed to, François Clouet (c. 1510–1572) and his followers.[3] Indeed, it is the very closeness of the relationship between the medals and the Clouet works that has occasioned doubts about dating the medals to the sixteenth century. One must consider the possibility that at a later date, especially in the seventeenth century when such series were popular, an enterprising sculptor put together a group of Valois medallions using the Clouet portraits as a source and taking the Birague medal and the later medals of Guillaume Dupré as patterns for their size and format.

If we place next to the portrait on the present medal Pilon's various renderings of Henry II such as the *priant* of his tomb, the marble *gisant* in coronation robes, and the bronze bust in a private collection, it is difficult to deny that there are strong similarities in many details, such as the modeling of the eyes, the carving of the hair, the handling of the planes of the face, and the general expression.[4] Differences exist as well, perhaps resulting from the artist's use of painted portraits as models.

The elements of concurrence are sufficient in number and strong enough in character to support the traditional attribution of the Valois series to Germain Pilon or one of his immediate followers—his son, perhaps, or Mathieu Jacquet.[5] The entire question of Pilon's activities as a medalist clearly requires further study.

Henry II is most often described as a man of limited intelligence, whose weak character and single-mindedness place him among the more mediocre of French kings, but this judgment is certainly too severe and is not entirely sustained by historical reality.[6]

When only seven and eight, respectively, Henry and his older brother Francis were sent to the court of Charles V in Spain, there to be held as hostages on the release of their father Francis I. At first they were well treated, but once their father repudiated the terms of his treaty with the Habsburg monarch and continued to oppose him, the princes' confinement grew increasingly harsh. They were only returned to France in 1530. Henry never forgot his experience and nourished a lifelong hatred of Charles V.

It was clear to Henry in his early years that his father, of so very different a temperament, favored his first son, Francis, and this was to mold even further the boy's taciturn, melancholy, and guarded personality. In maturity, Henry was tall, handsome, and well built. Strong and athletic, he was devoted to the hunt, to tournaments, and sports. He is said to have smiled but rarely, and there were those at court who maintained that they had never seen him laugh. In most of his portraits there is a sadness and cynicism permeating his features, even when, as in the present medal, he seems to project a certian *bonhomie*.

He was well educated and was said to have an extraordinary memory, but his narrow-minded opinions and his obstinacy

with respect to his decisions set in motion events that would stain the remaining years of the sixteenth century in France. All in all, however, he was a gentle and gracious prince, an attentive and appreciative husband, who did not follow his father's lubricious habits—except for one notable exception–and a devoted father.

In 1530, at age eleven, Henry had been placed in the care of one of the ladies of the court, Diane de Poitiers (1499–1566), wife of the grand senechal of Normandy. Diane was widowed the following year, and what began as a maternal relationship with the prince seems fairly certain to have become sexual by around 1536, definitely before he succeeded to the throne in 1547. Throughout his reign Henry was virtually ruled by his mistress, who shared her dominance over him only with the constable of France, Anne de Montmorency (1493–1567) and possibly the brothers de Guise, Duke Francis (1519–1563) and Charles, Cardinal of Lorraine (1525–1574).

In 1533 Henry was married to Catherine de' Medici, who thus became a partner in an interesting *ménage à trois*. The self-effacing Catherine accepted Diane as a member of the family intimately involved in all aspects of the household.

With the death of his brother Francis in 1536, Henry became heir to the throne, and by the time his father died in 1547 he was well prepared for his accession. His reign was dominated by continued conflict with the hated Habsburgs and the stirrings of internal unrest occasioned by the rise of Protestantism. Henry unwisely set out on yet another military adventure against the Empire in Italy, whereupon Philip retaliated by invading France. At the battle of Saint-Quentin on August 10, 1557, the French lost all that had been gained over three-quarters of a century of struggle for Mediterranean hegemony. The subsequent Treaty of Cateau-Cambrésis (April 2–3, 1559) was to lay the foundations of conflict for at least the next 120 years.

The treaty specified that Henry's daughter Elizabeth would marry Philip II and his sister Marguerite the duke of Savoy. During the wedding celebrations on June 30, 1559, Henry engaged in one of his favorite pastimes, tilting. He was struck by the shattered lance of his opponent and several splinters were driven into his forehead over his right eye. He died ten days later and was succeeded by his young son Francis, but the real power passed into the capable and determined hands of the queen regent, Catherine de' Medici.

Stephen K. Scher

Guillaume Dupré
(c. 1579–1640)

The work of Guillaume Dupré represents the last flowering, in France, of the tradition of medallic portraiture first developed and brought to perfection in sixteenth-century Italy.

Dupré was the first French medalist fully to appreciate and exploit that tradition. Unlike his predecessors, he was superbly competent at modeling in wax, capable of translating his sitters' features into dignified and characteristic images in exquisite low relief. Moreover, he understood more clearly than they the

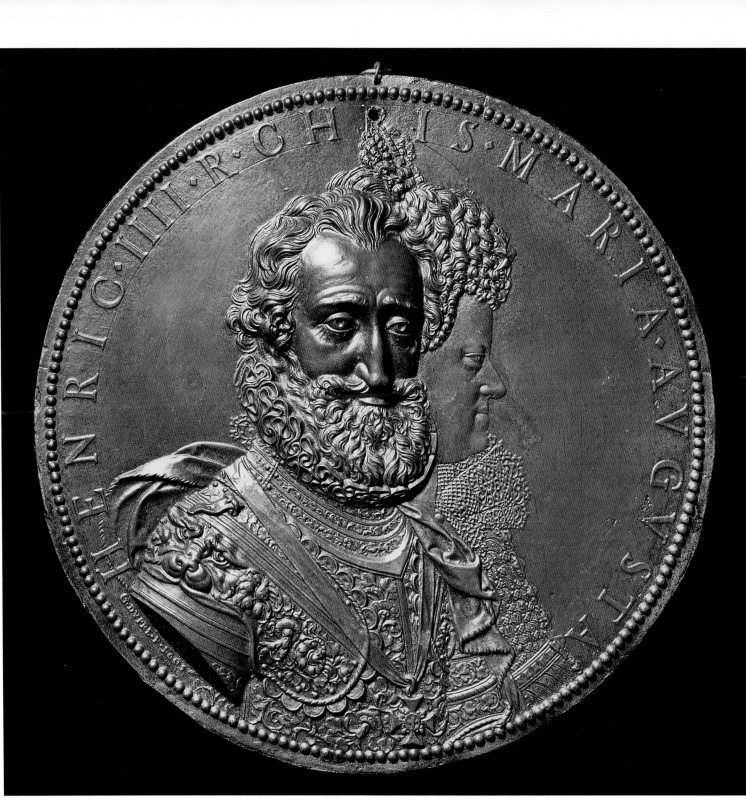

146 obv.

purpose and potential of the medallic reverse. Finally, Dupré was a supreme technician, perhaps the best bronze-founder ever to have made medals.

Like the majority of sculptors and engravers in late sixteenth and early seventeenth-century France, Dupré was a Protestant. It appears that he was a native of Sissonne near Laon, and he is recorded as having come to the attention of Henry IV in the late 1590s. It is likely that he trained under Barthelémy Prieur (died

1611), a Protestant sculptor settled in Paris who had himself studied with Germain Pilon (cat. nos. 144–45), at the time when the latter was responsible for modeling the king's portrait for the coinage of the realm.[1]

In 1600, Dupré married Prieur's daughter Madeleine, and he seems to have been jointly responsible with Prieur for the large quantity of decorative bronzes emanating from Prieur's workshop in the first decade of the seventeenth century. The two

138 obv.

138 rev.

140 obv.

140 rev

144 obv.

147 obv.

143 obv.

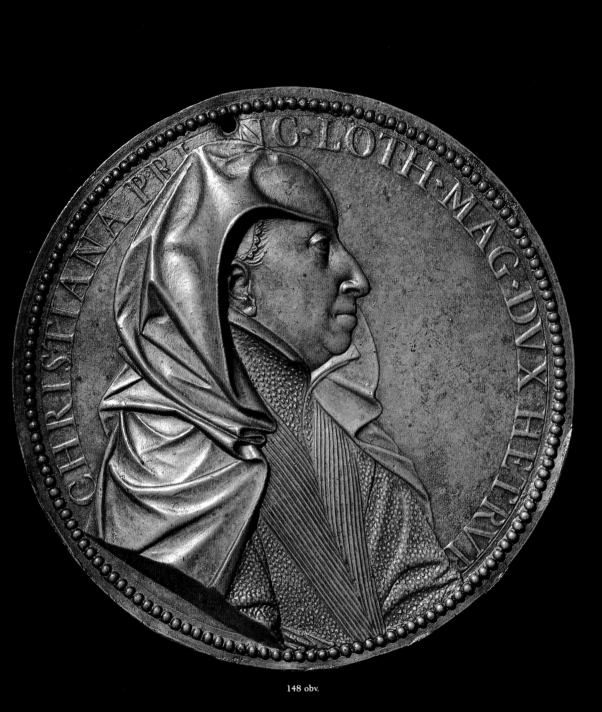

148 obv.

149 obv.

151 obv.

152 obv.

150 obv.

152 rev.

155 obv.

153 rev.

146a obv.

artists also collaborated with Barthelémy Tremblay on the decoration of the Louvre.

It was Dupré's medals, however, rather than bronzes or sculptures, that made his reputation.

In 1602 or 1603, Dupré produced a medal celebrating the birth of the Dauphin,[2] a later version of which is included in this exhibition (cat. no. 146). The king followed his progress on the piece with interest, visiting Dupré's workshop, and ordered

the finished work cast in gold and silver. More important, he gave the medalist the privilege of casting as many variants of the piece as he wished, along with legal protection against reproduction of his work.

When the Paris guild of goldsmiths attacked this privilege in the courts, asserting that the casting of medals was their traditional prerogative and hinting that Dupré might make use of his access to precious metals to forge coins, Dupré returned to the king and gained the right to set up his furnace in the Louvre, under direct royal protection. He thus became the first of what was to become an entire colony of artists working for the king outside the guild system in the *galérie du Louvre*.

In 1604, Dupré was appointed, jointly with Germain Pilon's son Jean (died 1606), *Controleur Général des Poinçons et Effigies des Monnoyes de France*. This gave him responsibility for modeling the king's portrait for the coinage and ensuring the quality of its reproduction throughout the country.

After the assassination of Henry IV in 1610, Dupré had to find his way in a climate increasingly hostile to Protestants. His brilliant portraits of Marie de' Medici (cat. no. 146a) found favor with her, and it was probably at the queen regent's request that he set off to Italy in 1612. There he traveled first to Mantua, where he produced a marvelous medallic portrait of the young Francesco IV Gonzaga (1586–1612), who had just succeeded to the dukedom.[3] He then went to Venice to create a similar work for the new doge, Marcantonio Memmo (cat. no. 147), before visiting Florence.

There Dupré undertook a series of portraits, notably of Grand Duke Cosimo II, Francesco de' Medici (died 1614), Maria Maddalena of Austria (1587–1629), and Christine of Lorraine (cat. no. 148), widow of Grand Duke Ferdinando I, before returning to Paris in 1613.

Back in France, he produced his two finest medals of Marie de' Medici in 1615 and 1625. He also attracted the patronage of Cardinal Richelieu (cat. no. 153), who found him the ideal man to improve the manufacture of cannon for the French army.[4]

The post of *Commissaire Générale des Fontes de l'Artillerie de France* may not seem to us a suitable one for any medalist, let alone one noted for the refinement of his modeling and the subtlety of his allegorical compositions. In the early seventeenth century, however, cannon were still extensively decorated and immensely sculptural objects that relied for their effectiveness on the skill of the founder and for their prestige on the quality of their modeling. Unfortunately, they were regularly thrown back into the pot and remade, so early seventeenth-century French pieces are rare indeed. We know from examples that do survive, however, that the modeling skills employed in the creation of their dolphin handles and exquisite lettering were precisely the ones at which Dupré excelled, and it is possible that some of his late masterpieces, dating from the 1630s, remain unrecognized in the armories of French châteaux or, perhaps more likely, some foreign arsenal.

Mark Jones

Guillaume Dupré
Henry IV (born 1553, king of France 1589–1610) and Marie
 de' Medici (1573–1642)
146
Bronze medallion, cast
Diameter 186 mm
Los Angeles County Museum of Art
79.4.147

Obverse: Jugate busts of Henry IV and Marie de' Medici, he in three-quarter view, she in profile behind him. The king wears richly decorated armor with a lion's head on the shoulder, a ruff, a cape thrown over his left shoulder, and the cross of the Order of the Holy Ghost suspended from a ribbon around his neck. The queen wears a standing lace collar and two jewels in her elaborately coiffed hair. Legend: HENRIC[us] • IIII • R[ex] • CHRIS[tianissimus] • MARIA • AVGVSTA (The most Christian king Henry IV, empress Maria). Incised in the truncation of the king's right arm, the date 1605. Below the truncation, the signature and date: G[uillaume] • DVPRE • F[ecit] • 1605.
Reverse: Plain.

146a
Bronze medallion, cast
Diameter 185 mm
Los Angeles County Museum of Art
79.4.146

Obverse: (designed as the reverse of no. 146): The royal couple as Mars and Minerva, between them the Dauphin as a plump naked boy. The king is dressed in Roman armor, with an antique sword at his waist, sandals, and the *paludamentum* over his left shoulder; the queen in a plumed helmet, an ornamented breastplate, and classical drapery. He holds a staff in his left hand, she a shield on her left arm. The Dauphin holds his father's plumed helmet with both hands. His right foot rests on the head of a dolphin, behind which lie a shield and a spear. An eagle with a crown in its beak hovers above the Dauphin's head. Legend: PROPAGO IMPERI (the imperial line). In the exergue, the signature: G[uillaume] • DVPRE • F[ecit]. Below the king's right foot, the date 1605.
Reverse: Plain.

This medal is a variant of the piece executed early in 1603 to celebrate the birth of the Dauphin, a work that so pleased the king that he granted Dupré the right, for ten years, to make as many examples as he liked and sell them or have them sold throughout France. That Dupré made full use of his privilege is demonstrated by the large number of surviving examples of that piece and its variants executed in succeeding years. Jacques de Bie records that these were distributed by the king himself on several occasions.[1]

The reverse is based on an emblem published by Nicholas Reusner in Frankfurt in 1581, showing two female figures holding hands and a standing boy between them.[2] That emblem was derived in turn from coins of Plautilla, the wife of Caracalla, which bear the legend PROPAGO IMPERI and show the emperor and Plautilla holding hands.[3] The image was one well suited to represent the dynastic ambitions of the founder of the Bourbon royal line. The dolphin is the traditional symbol of the Dauphiné, simply identifying the child as the Dauphin, and his gesture in grasping the helmet indicates that he is eager to emulate his father's warlike accomplishments. Finally, the eagle with a crown in its beak suggests the rulers' imperial pretensions. These are echoed in the title AVGVSTA given to Marie on the obverse, and in the reverse legend with its direct reference to the Roman Empire.

Henry IV was the son of Jeanne d'Albret, heiress to the throne of Navarre, and Antoine de Bourbon, duke of Vendôme (1518–1562).[4] He was educated as a Protestant, and as a young man joined in the religious wars on the side of the Huguenots. On the death of his mother in 1572, when he was only nineteen, he succeeded her as king of Navarre. In that same year he married Margaret of Valois, sister of Charles IX of France, and for the next few years he was held a virtual prisoner at court. He escaped in 1576, and again joined the Protestants. In 1584, on the death of Monsieur, brother of King Henry III, he became heir presumptive to the throne of France, but it was not until four years later that the king was forced to recognize him as his heir. Henry then inherited the crown when Henry III was assassinated in 1589, but being Protestant, that is to say a heretic, he was not accepted by a number of the French nobility, and it was in part by converting to Catholicism in 1593 that he managed to quell the opposition. He nevertheless introduced a policy of tolerance, and in 1598 signed the Edict of Nantes, assuring religious liberty to the Protestants. Though a distinct irritant to the papal party, that document allowed France to experience years of peace, a welcome respite after decades of religious wars.

In his foreign policy, Henry never ceased to fight the Habsburgs, whose pretensions of universal monarchy threatened the kingdom of France. He successfully maintained in fragile equilibrium a country subjected to outside pressures from Spain and to internal attack from a nobility ill disposed to pardon his past heresy. With the aid of his excellent advisors, most notably Sully (1560–1641), he soon brought a new prosperity to France, encouraging industry and agriculture, and improving roads and canals. Among his lasting adornments to Paris are the Pont Neuf, the Place Dauphine, the Place Royale (now des Vosges), and the Hôtel-de-Ville.

Henry had had no children by his first wife, Margaret of Valois. After securing an annulment of that marriage from the pope, he married Marie de' Medici, daughter of the grand duke of Tuscany and a distant relative of the late Catherine de' Medici, in 1600. Their first son and heir, the future Louis XIII, was born in 1601.

Henry was assassinated on May 14, 1610, and under the regency of Marie the country experienced a period of uncertainty and disorder that only ended with the entrance of Richelieu (cat. no. 153) into the king's council in 1624. With a firm hand, the cardinal put the nobility in its place and restored the power of the crown.

Mark Jones

Guillaume Dupré
Marcantonio Memmo, doge of Venice (born 1536, ruled 1612–15)
147
Lead, cast, uniface

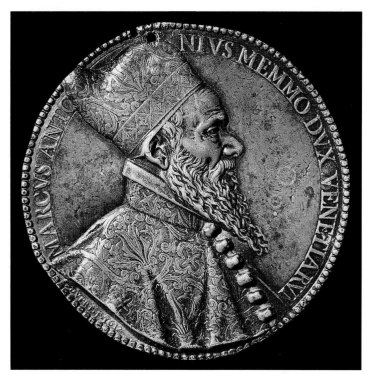

147 obv.

Diameter 89.5 mm
New York, private collection

Obverse: Quarter-length profile bust facing to the right. The sitter is heavily bearded and wears a richly brocaded, high-collared robe closed with toggles. His *corno*, or cap, is ornamented in the same pattern as the robe. Two letters of the inscription are hidden by the doge's hat and his robe. Legend: MARCVS ANT[o]NIUS MEMO DUX VENETIARV[m] (Marcantonio Memmo, doge of Venice). Below the truncation, the signature and date: G[uillaume] DVPRÈ • F[ecit] • 1612.
Reverse: Plain.

This strongly characterized portrait must have been executed in Venice shortly after Memmo's election on July 24, 1612. There appears to be no record of the commission. It is known that Dupré was in Mantua, occupied with the execution of a medal of Francesco IV in the period after the duke's accession in February of that year, so it seems likely that he there received the invitation to come to Venice.

About a dozen examples of this medal are known in public collections, including three in the Cabinet des Médailles, Paris; two in the Hermitage, St. Petersburg; and one in The Metropolitan Museum of Art, New York. The most interesting one is the large (91 mm) and finely chased example in the British Museum, London, which may well have been a presentation piece.

Mark Jones

147 obv.

148 obv.

the different reactions of the two women to the loss of their husbands.

This is not one of Dupré's most successful compositions, though the characterization of the sitter is exceptionally convincing. The veil is a definite formal success, but its emergence on the far side of her head between the nose and mouth seems unfortunate and the treatment of the sitter's waist and left arm, the termination of which follows and appears to rest upon the beaded border, is unconvincing.

At least twenty examples of this medal are known in public collections. The gold specimen in the Bargello in Florence, the best of them, was presumably the one executed for the sitter herself.[2] It is an exceptionally fine and rare survival, a reminder that the primary examples of most of Dupré's medals, indeed of most medals of every period, were made in precious metals, and that the bronze examples we now treasure have survived simply because they were less valuable than the presentation pieces in gold or silver.

Mark Jones

Guillaume Dupré
Christine of Lorraine, grand duchess of Tuscany (1565–1636)
148
Bronze, cast, uniface
Diameter 93.1 mm; outer diameter of pearling, 89.0 mm
New York, private collection

Obverse: Half-length bust in profile to the right. The sitter wears a widow's veil, modeled in exceptionally high relief, beneath which a lace cap can be glimpsed above her right ear. Beneath her plain outer garment with a V-shaped collar she wears a high-collared, beaded doublet. The veil and the sitter's left arm partially obscure the inscription, the abbreviations of which are marked with the diamond-shaped stops typical of Dupré. Legend: CHRISTIANA PRINC[ipissa] • LOTH[eringae] • MA[gna] • DVX HETRVR[iae] (Christine, princess of Lorraine, grand duchess of Tuscany). Unsigned. Beaded border.
Reverse: Plain.

The daughter of Charles III of Lorraine (1543–1608), Christine was brought up at the French court by her grandmother, Catherine de' Medici (1519–1589). In 1589 she married Ferdinando I de' Medici, grand duke of Tuscany (born 1549, ruled 1587–1609).

The widow's display of her state, with the prominent veil and the relative plainness of her dress, is quite unlike the style adopted by Marie de' Medici after the assassination of Henry IV in 1610.[1] This may in part reflect differences in the culture of the two courts, but one suspects that it also has to do with

Guillaume Dupré
Pierre Jeannin (1540–1622)
149
Bronze, cast, uniface
Diameter 194 mm
Boston, Museum of Fine Arts, Elizabeth Marie Paramino Fund
  in Memory of John F. Paramino, Boston Sculptor
1984.531

Obverse: Bust in profile to the right. The sitter wears a high-collared shirt closed by four sets of four buttons each under a full magisterial robe. Legend: PETRVS IEANNIN • REG[is] • CHRIST[ianissimi] • A • SECR[etis] • CONS[iliarius] • ET • SAC[ri] • ÆRA[rii] • PRÆF[ectus] (Pierre Jeannin, member of the private council of the most Christian king, superintendant of finances). The last three letters run over his robe. Upside-down below the edge of the truncation are the inscribed signature and date: G[uillaume] DVPRE F[ecit] 1618. Pearled border.
Reverse: Plain.

Pierre Jeannin was a native of Autun who studied law at Bourges with the great jurist Jacques Cujas. He became an advocate at Dijon in 1569, and was later made councillor and then president of the *parlement* of Burgundy.[1] Throughout his long and distinguished career, Jeannin had a reputation for honesty and fairness, and was revered for his skill as a negotiator and diplomat. Through clever use of the law, he managed to avert the terrible massacre of St. Bartholomew's Day from his province of Burgundy. In 1595, Henry IV took Jeannin into his privy council. After the king's death in 1610 his widow Marie de' Medici turned to Jeannin as an advisor, and he was made superintendant of finances. A large correspondence survives, documenting Jeannin's diplomatic activities and his efforts to

149 obv.

maintain good relations between Louis XIII and the queen mother.[2]

Jeannin was seventy-eight when this medal was made. It may have been commissioned at the time of his retirement from royal service. He is said to have withdrawn from his position of counselor to the king shortly before his death, in order to write a biography of Henry IV.

The Jeannin medal is perhaps Dupré's finest work. It was executed a few years after the sculptor's stay in Italy, and in style it is a synthesis of Italian and northern sixteenth-century

150 obv.

influences, recalling Germain Pilon's magnificent medal of René de Birague (cat. no. 144). The quality of the cast is so fine that it must have been made by Dupré himself, and may be a first proof from the wax model. Of the known examples of this version of the medal, this is the finest. It is interesting to note that there is an unusually high percentage of silver in the alloy, for which there is no known technical explanation.

There seem to be two different models of the Jeannin medal. The Boston specimen is of the first type. A second version, also of superb quality, is found in the Bibliothèque Nationale in Paris.[3] While it too is uniface and dated 1618, it is considerably smaller in size (187 mm) and differs in a number of modeling details. There the sitter's robe is brocaded, and its collar has a decorative double-stitched edge. It would seem that Dupré, for some reason, reworked his first model to create a second version of his most noble composition.

Anne Poulet

Guillaume Dupré
Charles Duret de Chevry (born 1560–65, died 1636)
150
Bronze, cast, uniface

Diameter 180 mm
Paris, Bibliothèque Nationale, Cabinet des Médailles
5060

Obverse: Bust of Duret to the right, with carefully groomed beard and moustache. His curly hair is combed back off his forehead. He wears a shirt with a ruff collar, a sash, and a large cloak with an ermine collar, underneath which the embroidered cross of the Order of the Holy Ghost is visible. Legend: MESSI^RE CHARLES DVRET SEIGNEVR DE CHEVRY (Monsieur Charles Duret, lord of Chevry). Below the truncation, the signature and date: GVIL[laume] • DVPRE F[ecit]• 1630. Pearled border.
Reverse: Plain.

Of all of Dupré's medals, the one of Charles Duret de Chevry is deserving of particular attention. Though its subject is of no particular interest, Dupré has masterfully captured his character. This is the portrait of a conceited elderly officer high in the financial administration.

Charles Duret, lord of Chevry, was probably born between 1560 and 1565. He was raised at court, where his father served as the king's physician. By 1591 he was already *Intendant et Contrôleur Général des Finances*. On January 2, 1610, he was appointed president of the Chambre des Comptes, replacing

Nicolas Lhuillier, but it was only after the death of Henry IV in May of that year that he exercised total control over the state finances. He died of a kidney stone on September 18, 1636, leaving behind the reputation of a boastful and cynical man.[1] In 1621 he had been made commander of the Order of the Holy Ghost.

The medal is extremely rare, in it the artist has captured the character of his sitter with supreme competence. This old man with jowels and a double chin is still intent on presenting himself as a younger gentlemen. All is artifice, clearly betraying the man's vanity and self-esteem with respect to his high office, even though the legend fails to give his titles. This is a delicious piece of characterization.

Jean-Baptiste Giard

Jacob Richier (c. 1585–c. 1645)
Marie de Vignon
151
Bronze, cast, uniface
Diameter 105.7 mm; height of bust, 70.7 mm
Paris, Bibliothèque Nationale, Cabinet des Médailles
AF 5004

Obverse: Quarter-length bust in profile to the right, dressed in a partlet and low-cut dress with elaborate shoulder wings and

151 obv.

hanging sleeves, topped by a standing lace-edged collar. A flowering branch emerges from a jeweled headband worn over upswept hair. Drop earrings and a simple pearl necklace complete the costume. Legend: MARIE DE VIGNON MARQUISE DE TREFFORT. Below the bust, the signature and date: I[acob] • R[ichier] • F[ecit] • 1613.

Reverse: Plain.

This remarkable portrait of an early seventeenth-century French beauty is the only signed medal by the sculptor Jacob Richier.

Richier was born at Saint-Mihiel, in Lorraine, the scion of a well-known family of Lorraine sculptors. In 1611 he moved to Grenoble, where he was employed by François de Bonne, duc de Lesdiguières, on the extensive decorations of the Château de Vizille, including a large bronze bas-relief of the duke on horseback that was placed above the entrance.

In 1612, Lesdiguières commissioned Richier to sculpt the tomb for his first wife, Claudine Bérenger. It is likely that the sculptor was at work on that monument when he created the medal, for its sitter, Marie de Vignon, was the duke's mistress, and was to become his second wife in 1617. According to Tallement des Réaux,[1] it was at about the time of the completion of the medal that Marie persuaded a Colonel Alard to murder her husband, a merchant draper by the name of Aymon Mathel, so that she might be free to marry the duke.

Mark Jones

Jean Warin
(1606–1672)

Jean Warin is the key figure in the history of the medal in France. Ruthless and dishonest, talented and ambitious, he demonstrated to Richelieu (cat. no. 153) Colbert (1619–1683), and Louis XIV himself the medal's potential as a medium that could encapsulate the monarchy's achievements and hold them up both to the contemporary world and to posterity.

Warin's origins lay in the half-world of illegal mints operated in the pocket sovereignties clustered around France's northeastern border. Born in Liège in 1607, he spent his childhood at one mint in Bouillon, closed in 1614 for making light coinage, and another at La Tour-à-Glaire, known to have provided false coin in 1628. His father worked at each of them as an engraver. Beginning about 1617, it seems that Jean Warin was in the service of the count of Rochefort, the director of whose mint at Cugnon was arrested and hanged in 1626.[1]

It may well have been this event that precipitated Warin's removal in the latter year to Paris, where an uncle was a waxmodeler and a cousin a goldsmith, both having connections with the mint. They helped Warin find work there under Pierre Regnier, who happened to be in need of skilled engravers. They also appear to have put him in contact with Guillaume Dupré, whose medallion of Jean Héroard (1551–1628) provided the model for Warin's earliest recorded medal, from 1628. What boosted his career most of all, however, was Warin's seduction

of Jeanne Desjours, the wife of Regnier's co-director at the mint, René Olivier. Olivier was conveniently murdered in January 1629, whereupon his widow was free to nominate Jean to take over the functions her sons had inherited from him. Temporarily, at least, this placed control of a one-third share in the mint in Warin's hands, and over the next twenty years he worked indefatigably to complete his hold on the mint and all its operations.

In 1636, Warin secured a one-fourth share in the mint for himself, and in 1639 he bought out Pierre Regnier. In 1640, poacher turned gamekeeper, he persuaded the government that the only way to deal with the problems of clipping and forgery was to introduce an entirely new, better engraved, and mechanically struck coinage, the regularity and beauty of which would render such practices impossible. The huge success of this project brought Warin the post of *Conducteur Général des Monnaies au Moulin de France et Graveur d'icelles*, and an indemnity against any charges that might arise from the production of light coinage.

In 1646, Warin acquired by nomination and purchase the offices of Engraver of Seals and Engraver General of the Coinage, and in 1647 he obtained the post of Controller General of Puncheons from the grandson of Guillaume Dupré. It was a common bourgeois strategy in seventeenth-century France to acquire multiple offices, thus assuring oneself a regular income and enhanced status, and it was for just such reasons that Warin purchased those of *Conseiller du Roi en ses Conseils d'Etat* and *Intendant des Bâtiments*. Accumulating offices at the mint meant much more, however. It gave Warin effective monopoly over the production of coinage and medals, thereby providing him with very substantial opportunities for making money while attracting the favorable attention of the king.

Ruthlessness alone would not have helped Warin rise so high; he was also extremely talented. His greatest medallic achievement was his invention of a new formula for the medium. This combined low relief with fine detail, presenting beautifully balanced compositions against large areas of perfectly flat field. With carefully spaced and precisely rendered lettering, and surrounded by a perfectly circular raised rim, these medals achieved a level of elegance and technical perfection unsurpassed elsewhere in Europe or for that matter in the history of the struck medal.

The emphasis here must be on the word struck, for elaborate and successful though Warin's cast medals were, it was the struck pieces that provided the greater part of his income, and on which he expended the most thought and labor. The makers of cast medals were unable to imitate his new formula successfully, and accordingly their works fell out of favor in France. Warin's new medallic style was triumphant, not only in France but throughout Europe—with the single, and interesting, exception of Florence.

It was not so much the artistic merit of the new formula that motivated Warin's promotion of it as his appreciation of the financial benefits of monopoly. Struck medals could only be made at the mint, and since the mint was also engaged in

152 obv.

152 obv.

152 rev.

making coinage, it was necessary for the government to permit only a tightly restricted group of engravers to work there. Medalmaking thus became a monopoly of the mint and accordingly of Warin himself, one confirmed by the Conseil d'Etat in 1663 and recognized by the Cour des Monnaies in 1672.

To pursue his personal ends, Warin needed to demonstrate to the state the value of such works. He did so brilliantly in the pioneering medallic history of Louis XIV that he executed, initially under direct orders from Colbert, between 1662 and his death a decade later. These works, demonstrating the superiority of French artists, engravers, and mint machinery, and only with difficulty emulated elsewhere, were the perfect medium through which to spread the message that France was the greatest state in the world.

In this sense, Warin was responsible for the great transformation of the medal in late seventeenth-century France into an art almost wholly devoted to the glory of king and state. The whole meaning of medals was transformed, both for those who made them and those who received them, a development that put at least a temporary end to the artistic tradition that developed in fifteenth-century Italy and thus to the type of medal celebrated in this exhibition.

Mark Jones

Jean Warin
Antoine Coeffier, called Ruzé, marquis d'Éffiat (1581–1632)
152
Silver, cast and chased
Diameter 66 mm; weight 74.48 g
London, The British Museum, George III Collection
Ill.Men.374

Obverse: Quarter-length bust with the upper trunk turned slightly toward the viewer and the head in profile to the right. He is dressed in elaborately decorated armor with a lion's-head shoulder piece and a breastplate bearing a head through which a sash appears to be threaded. A falling collar in fine lace and the

Order of the Holy Ghost, worn on a sash, complete his adornments. Legend: A[ntoine] • RVZE • M[arquis] • DEFFIAT • ET • D[e] • LONIVMEAV • SVR[intendan]T • DES • FINANCES • (Antoine Ruzé, marquis of Éffiat and Longjumeau, superintendant of finances). Incised signature on the truncation: WARIN. *Reverse*: Atlas and Hercules, both bearded and nude, in a landscape. Atlas, leaning against a tree stump, is transferring the weight of the world onto the shoulders of Hercules, who has laid down his club in order to receive it. Atlas wears a protective cloth on his shoulders, and the ends of it flow down between his legs. Hercules wears a lion skin over his right shoulder, one paw and the tail of which fly out behind him while the head rests on the ground beside his club. Legend: QVIDQVID • EST • IVSSVM • LEVE • EST (Whatever is ordered is easy). In the exergue, the incised date: 1629.

Since this is an exceptionally finely worked example of this medal—Hercules' arm stands clear of the field as on no other recorded specimen—and the only signed example known, it seems likely that it was the primary example of the work.

The reverse indicates that Ruzé saw himself as a willing Hercules, onto whose shoulders the king (Atlas) had placed the burden of affairs of state.

Antoine Coeffier was adopted by his uncle, Martin Ruzé, the superintendant of mines. In 1616 he purchased the charge of *Premier Ecuyer de la Grande Ecurie*. He became marquis of Longjumeau in 1621, and of Éffiat in 1624. In 1626, after his return from an embassy to London, where he negotiatied the marriage between the king's sister, Henrietta Maria, and Charles I of England, he was appointed superintendent of finances. He accompanied Louis XIII on his campaigns in Savoy and Piedmont in 1629, and in December of that year he became joint commander of the army in Italy, under Cardinal Richelieu (cat. no. 155). Created *Maréchal de France* in January 1631, he was about to take command of the army sent to the aid of the elector of Trier when he fell ill and died.[1]

Mark Jones

152 rev.

153 obv.

153 rev.

Jean Warin
Armand-Jean du Plessis, Cardinal Richelieu (1585–1642)
153
Bronze, cast
Diameter 78.0 mm
Washington, The National Gallery of Art, Samuel H. Kress
   Collection
1957.14.10

Obverse: Bust facing right, wearing a biretta and cardinal's robes. Legend: ARMANDVS IOHANNES CARDINALIS DE RICHELIEV (Armand-Jean, Cardinal Richelieu).
Reverse: France, represented as a crowned woman with long hair, wearing classical drapery over armor and riding over a rocky terrain in a richly decorated four-wheeled chariot. She holds up a sword in her right hand, a palm branch in her left. The chariot is drawn by four spirited horses and driven by Fame, a nude female figure blowing a trumpet from which hangs a banner bearing Richelieu's coat of arms.[1] Fortune, also a nude female, but provided with wings and carrying a circle of drapery, is chained to the rear of the chariot. A winged Victory flies above, her drapery billowing out behind, and is about to place a crown of laurel on the head of France. Legend: TANDEM VICTA SEQVOR (Conquered at last, I follow). Signed and dated in the exergue: • I[ean] • WARIN • 1630.

Though he became a cardinal, the Church was not Richelieu's original vocation. His father, François du Plessis, seigneur de Richelieu (died 1590), intended him to follow a military career, and accordingly young Richelieu went to a military academy on leaving the Collège de Navarre. It was only his elder brother's renunciation of the family bishopric of Luçon that catapulted him into theological studies at the Collège de Calvi and underage ordination as a priest and bishop by the pope in 1607.

Because he had administered his diocese in an exemplary manner, the clergy of Poitou elected Richelieu to represent them at the Estates General of 1614. While there he attracted the attention of Marie de' Medici with a suitably sycophantic speech in which he called on the young Louis XIII to add the title "Mother of the Kingdom" to her distinctions. The following year he was appointed chaplain to Anne of Austria, the king's child bride, and in 1616, on the recommendation of the king's first minister, Concini (died 1617), he was named Secretary of State for War and Foreign Affairs.

Richelieu followed Marie de' Medici into exile in 1617, and made himself the indispensible mediator between the queen mother and the court. It was on her nomination that he was made a cardinal in 1622 and a member of the king's council in 1624, but she soon learned to her cost that he was his own man. By 1630, when this medal was produced, Richelieu had long since become chief minister, and it is just possible that the piece was occasioned by his triumph on the "Day of Dupes," November 10, 1630, when the king refused to follow the recommendation of his mother and the Keeper of the Seals, Michel de Marillac, that the cardinal be ousted from his offices.

It is not known whether Warin executed this beautiful medal on a commission from Richelieu or as a way of attracting the cardinal's attention. That it won his favor is evident, for in 1633, when Warin was accused of forgery, it was thanks to Richelieu that he escaped the death sentence imposed on his father and brother for similar crimes, and was permitted to continue working at the Paris mint.[2]

The reverse is clearly meant as a celebration of Cardinal Richelieu's conduct of affairs of state. France is armed, and as the palm branch, the laurel crown proffered by the winged Victory, and the mural crown all emphasize, she is victorious in battle and siege. Fortune, whose wheel is suggested by a circle of drapery, is herself in thrall, chained to the chariot of state.

The rocky terrain suggests the perilous path the state must negotiate, and that it has done so successfully, Fame appears to proclaim, is solely to the cardinal's credit.

Mark Jones

Jean Warin
Louis XIV (born 1638, king of France 1643–1715) and Anne of Austria (1601–1666)
154
Silver, cast
Diameter 95.7 mm; inside diameter of the border pearling, 94.3 mm
Paris, Bibliothèque Nationale, Cabinet des Médailles
S. R. 2812a.

Obverse: Half-length portrait of the queen, wearing a widow's veil that falls from the back of her head over both shoulders. Louis XIV, a boy of six, is facing his mother and playing with the fastening of her dress. Both are shown in profile, their bodies turned toward the viewer. Louis wears a lace collar, doublet, and sash. His long, curly hair is held in place by a hair band. Legend: ANNA • D[ei] • G[ratia] • FR[anciae] • ET • NAV[arrae] • RE[gina] • R[egnans] • MATER • LVD[ovici] XIV • D[ei] • G[ratia] • FR[anciae] • ET • NAV[arrae] • REG[is] • CHR[istianissimi] (Anne, by the grace of God queen regent of

France and Navarre, mother of Louis XIV, by the grace of God most Christian king of France and Navarre).
Reverse: The Val-de-Grâce as planned by Mansart: two porticos, one above the other, flanked by niches. The bottom niches contain sculpted figures looking upward, but the upper ones are empty, the sculptures having, as it were, stepped out onto the stone ledge below them. Above the porticos is a colonnade supporting a dome topped by a cupola and a cross. A massive flight of stone steps leads up to the door of the church. Wings of the convent are visible on either side. Legend: • OB • GRATIAM • DIV • DESIDERATI • REGII • ET • SECUNDI • PARTVS (In thanks for the longed-for happy issue of the king). Dated in the exergue: • QVINTO • CAL • SEPT • 1638.

This medal shows Warin in a much calmer and more classical mode than does his earlier one of Richelieu. He employs the flowing drapery of Anne's veil and the enfolding movement of her arm and hands to create an image perfectly adapted to its encircling rim.

Anne had been married to the young Louis XIII in 1615, but for twenty years the marriage had been without issue. At last, on September 5, 1638—the date given on the medal's reverse—the queen was delivered of a son, the future Louis XIV. She had vowed that if only she might produce an heir she would show her gratitude by building a church and convent for the order of Benedictine nuns she had brought to the capital from Dièvre.

154 obv.

154 rev.

155 obv.

155 rev.

The medal was made to commemorate the laying of the foundation stone of the Val-de-Grâce on April 1, 1645, by which time Anne had been widowed for two years. It provides the only record of the plans for the church at that stage by François Mansart (1598–1666), for they were modified four months later and ultimately superceded when Mansart was replaced by Jacques Lemercier (c. 1585–1654) in October 1646.[1]

According to Lemaire, the king arrived for the ceremony in the arms of the duc de Saint-Simon, followed by the queen mother and his brother: "Estant arrivé au lieu destiné à la Ceremonie, on luy donna une Truelle, d'argent . . . pour mettre la première pierre, dans la quelle est encastrée une Médaille d'or massif, de trois pouces et demy de diametre, pesant un marc et trois onces, sur laquelle est en bas relief, d'un costé le portrait au naturel du Roy Louis XIV porté par la Reine Regente sa mére . . . de l'autre côté . . . est aussi en bas relief le Portail et la face de l'Eglise. . . .[2]

Mark Jones

French School
Henry IV (born 1553, king of France 1589–1610)
155
Bronze, cast
Diameter 60 mm
London, Victoria & Albert Museum, Salting Collection
A351–1010

Obverse: Bust three-quarters to the right, in doublet with ruff and a scarf over the right shoulder. The king wears a tall hat with a broad brim turned up at the front to the center of which a badge has been pinned. A feather rises behind the brim. His nose and forehead are prominent, even exaggerated. Legend: HENRICVS IIII D[ei] • G[ratia] • REX FRAN[ciae] • ET NAV[arrae] (Henry IV, by the grace of God king of France and Navarre). Edged in a circle of dots broken by the bust and the hat.
Reverse: Shields of France and Navarre-Béarn, each surmounted by a crown.[1] Below these, the initial H atop the numeral 4—for Henry IV—flanked by palm and laurel branches. All within a collar of the Order of St. Michael,

surrounded by a border of laurels and thunderbolts with a crown at the top.

This piece is unsigned and undated. Though published without attribution,[2] when it was accessioned by the Victoria & Albert Museum in 1910 it was assigned with no supporting evidence to the sculptor Nicolas-Gabriel Jacquet. Stylistically, it does not conform to the medals signed by Jacquet, nor is it included in a listing of those attributed to him by de Foville.[3]

The medal presents several peculiarities. The figure is in three-quarter view rather than the usual profile. Among the medals of Henry IV, this presentation is found only on Dupré's large 1605 version of his medal celebrating the birth of the Dauphin (cat. no. 146) and on the anonymous uniface portrait of the king apparently derived from it.[4] The depiction in the present medal differs from these in its exaggerated rendering of the facial features and especially in its extravagant hat. The obverse legend is unusual, bearing the REX before rather than after the names of the kingdoms, an order not found in the Latin legends of other medals of Henry or on his coins.[5] This medal is also noteworthy for its use of the Order of St. Michael on the reverse rather than the Order of the Holy Ghost, which Henry wears in the Dupré double portrait and the piece apparently derived from it.

The likeness on this medal bears strong similarities to two unsigned portrait paintings, dated 1592 and 1593, and to an engraving by the Dutch artist Hendrik Goltzius, dated 1592.[6] A lost original painting, probably of 1592, is a more likely direct source for the depiction on the medal than either the known paintings or the engraving. The medalist has used the inscription on the painting as the basis for his obverse legend and has placed the collar of the Order of St. Michael on the reverse around the arms of France, to which he has added those of Navarre-Béarn. The medal was probably produced before Henry's coronation in 1594, when he received the Order of the Holy Ghost that he wears in most subsequent portraits and that appears on the reverses of later medals.[7] It presents him in a fully royal context at a time when, though he had inherited the throne in 1589, his claim to it was under serious challenge.

Alan M. Stahl

158 obv.

England
and the
Low Countries

SIXTEENTH AND EARLY SEVENTEENTH

CENTURIES

156 obv.

For the convenience of the reader, dates of political leaders most frequently encountered are provided below.
All other life dates appear in the text.

The Holy Roman Empire

Charles V (born 1500, emperor 1519–56, died 1558)
Ferdinand I (born 1503, emperor 1558–64)

England

Henry VIII (born 1491, king 1509–47)
Edward VI (born 1537, king 1547–53)
Mary Tudor (born 1516, queen 1553–58)
Elizabeth I (born 1533, queen 1558–1603)
James I (born 1566, king 1603–25)

France

Francis I (born 1494, king 1515–47)

Spain

Philip II (born 1527, king 1556–98)

The Low Countries

Margaret of Parma (born 1522, regent 1559–67, died 1586)
Ferdinand, duke of Alba (born 1507, governor-general 1567–73, died 1582)
Luis de Requesens (governor-general 1573–76)
Don John of Austria (governor-general 1576–78)
Alessandro Farnese (born 1545, governor-general 1578–92)

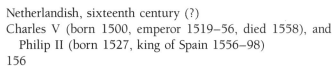

156 rev.

156a obv.

Netherlandish, sixteenth century (?)

Charles V (born 1500, emperor 1519–56, died 1558), and Philip II (born 1527, king of Spain 1556–98)

156

Bronze or brass alloy, cast, with integrally cast suspension loop at the 12 o'clock position

Diameter 100.0 mm; diameter of the outer perimeter of the obverse inscription from the I of IMP to the A of AVG, 89.1 mm; height of bust through center line, 79.1 mm; length of horse from just above curl of tail on a straight line to center of chest, 48.0 mm.

New York, private collection

Obverse: Bust of Charles to right, bearded and laureate, wearing cuirass with shoulder flaps and cloak knotted at right shoulder and gathered at breast by a brooch in the shape of a winged putto's head. Order of the Golden Fleece hanging from a long cord around the neck. Legend: IMP[erator] • CAES[ar] • CAROLVS • V • AVG[ustus] • (The emperor Caesar Charles V Augustus).

Reverse: Philip, in full body armor and holding commander's baton in his right hand, riding to right on a charger with crest of plumes on its head and tail tied in loop. Legend: • PHILIPVS • AVSTR[iacus] • CAROLI • V • CAES[aris] • F[ilius] • (Philip of Austria, son of Emperor Charles V).

156a

Bronze or brass alloy, cast

Diameter 103.5 mm; length of horse from just above curl of tail on a straight line to center of chest, 48.6 mm

American private collection[1]

Obverse: As reverse above.

Reverse: Plain.

The numismatic image of the emperor Charles V spanned a continent and half a century (see cat. nos. 77, 124–25). His features adorned coins from Spain in the west to Austria in the east, from the Netherlands in the north to the kingdom of Naples in the south. Charles, and his courtiers and allies, also exploited the medal's ability to convey a finely-nuanced self-preservation, an ideal image of the ruler that symbolically connected him to the glorious Roman past. The Habsburgs found in the medal the quintessential courtly and diplomatic art form, and their patronage helped bring it to new heights of popularity and prestige.

No ruler since antiquity held sway over such vast territories as Charles V.[2] His domains were the accretion of generations of shrewd marital politics. Charles's father was a Habsburg, Archduke Philip the Handsome (1476–1506), ruler of the Netherlands and son of the emperor Maximilian I and Mary of

Burgundy (cat. no. 37). His mother, Juana the Mad (1479–1555), was the daughter of Ferdinand and Isabella of Spain, and heiress to the kingdoms of Aragon and Castile. Early in childhood, Charles showed some of the traits that would characterize him throughout his life: a love of solitude, great personal piety, and a fondness for the tourney and the hunt. On his father's death in 1506, Charles inherited the Netherlands, ruling the great merchant power through the regency of his aunt, Margaret of Austria (1480–1530). Margaret's regency was unpopular, so Charles was declared of age to rule early in 1515. On the death in 1516 of Ferdinand of Spain, he was crowned king of Castile and Aragon—an inheritance that included the kingdoms of Sicily and Naples as well as the Spanish conquests in America. Aided by enormous bribes and the threat of military force, Charles was elected Holy Roman Emperor in 1519. The early 1520s saw Charles's army victorious against French forces in Italy. Francis I of France (cat. nos. 116, 139) was captured at Pavia in 1525, but a confederation of Italian states under the leadership of the papacy was formed with the aim of driving Charles out of Italy. Imperial troops sent to Rome to intimidate Pope Clement VII in 1527 unexpectedly sacked the Eternal City.

The greatest impediment to European unity was the spread of the Reformation. The growing military might of the Protestant princes of Germany forced Charles to maintain a conciliatory stance toward them for many years. After the German Protestants of the Schmalkaldic League repudiated the Council of Trent, Charles finally went to war against them in 1546. The imperial victory at Mühlberg in April 1547 dissolved the League's resistance. The same year saw the death of Charles's arch-rival, Francis I, and Charles's prospects on the European stage seemed to brighten. The reality, however, was bleak. Plans to forge the Catholic and Protestant states of the empire into a coherent political body fizzled. Reluctantly, Charles was forced to accept in 1555 the Peace of Augsburg, guaranteeing the religious freedom of Europe's Protestant states. At the same time he watched his hopes of preserving the unity of the Habsburg dynasty erode. At last, sick and mentally disquieted, the emperor abdicated in 1556, leaving Spain to his son Philip and the imperial crown and eastern demesnes to his brother Ferdinand. Charles withdrew to the monastery of San Jeronimo at Yuste, where he died in September 1558.

The authorship of the present medal is problematic. The equestrian figure of Philip on its reverse appears to be by the same hand as the portrait of Charles. Both sides show the same broad and somewhat heavy-handed modeling with an abrupt transition between figure and ground. Philip's face is treated in the same blunt manner as Charles's, with heavy, bulbous nose and prominent eyelids.

The obverse is a much-enlarged adaptation of a portrait type created by the Milanese sculptor, medalist, and die-engraver Leone Leoni (cat. nos. 49–52).[3] The closest analogue to the portrait and costume on the present piece is Leoni's medal of Charles with a reverse depicting an allegorical figure of the Tiber.[4] The main discrepancies between the Leoni portrait and its adaptation here are a slightly different draping of the cloak, the substitution of a winged cherub for the Gorgon on Charles's cuirass, some alterations to the detailing of the armor, and the addition of the Golden Fleece.

The equestrian representation on the reverse finds a parallel in a gilt lead plaque in Berlin representing Philip on horseback, possibly fashioned after the medal or deriving from a common prototype.[5] Even closer to the reverse of the medal is a Netherlandish (?) alabaster relief of Frederick II of Denmark in the Wallace Collection, dated 1591.[6]

No. 156a, an unepigraphic uniface cast of the Philip design, is a trial casting made from the original wax model. Like the stone or wooden models favored by German medalists, the bronze trial cast would have served for making molds whenever it was desired to reproduce the medal. Lettering could be added and details of the design changed at will by working directly on the plaster molds made from the trial cast. This process made it easy to produce variants of the same type by working up molds from the same model with minor differences in detail, and explains the different versions of the types that survive.

Hill's suggestion that the piece may be Netherlandish seems plausible on a number of grounds. Besides their importance as a center of courtly and intellectual life under the Habsburgs, the Low Countries were home to a large and varied school of sculptors whose work was heavily influenced by Italian mannerism.[7] The medal's legends suggest that it was made before the accession of Philip as king of Spain and Charles's abdication on January 16, 1556.

Mark M. Salton, Louis Waldman

Quentin Matsys (Metsys, Massys)
(c. 1462–1530)

Quentin Matsys is one of the great masters of the Antwerp school of painting. Little is known about his life, and much relating to his origins, his training, and a possible stay in Italy is only hypothetical. He was born in Louvain about 1462, and his childhood seems to have unfolded in that city. According to a tenacious legend, he first wanted to be a blacksmith, but became a painter to please his sweetheart. It is true that he came from a family of locksmiths and ironmongers, and that his father and older brother worked at those trades.

In 1491 he registered as a painter with the Guild of St. Luke in Antwerp, and to that corporation of artists he gave a self-portrait that was transferred to Paris during the occupation of the French revolutionary armies in 1794 and has since disappeared. He consorted with the small group of humanists in Antwerp associated with Thomas More (1478–1535) and Desiderius Erasmus (cat. no. 157), and during a stay in Louvain in 1517 he painted a portrait of the latter. Matsys married twice. His sons Jan and Cornelis would also become painters. He died in Antwerp in 1530.

A transitional painter, between the great generation that included van Eyck, van der Weyden, and Memling, and the

157 rev.

158 obv.

Romanists of the new age, he excelled not only in portraits, such as those of Erasmus and Peter Gillis, but also in religious compositions. While remaining true to the Flemish primitives of Bruges, Ghent, and Louvain and a traditionalist in the concept of his works, he introduced into northern painting architectural settings of Italian inspiration, romantic landscapes, and an amplitude of forms hitherto unknown.

Matsys also worked in the medium of medals, possibly as a result of his early training in metalworking. No one contests his authorship of the large medal of Erasmus, dated 1519, and he is also credited with the portrait of his sister-in-law, Christina Matsys, from 1491, which seems to have been cast from a wood or stone model in the German fashion. He also produced a medallic self-portrait, dated 1495, based on the painting mentioned above.[1]

Luc Smolderen

Quentin Matsys
Desiderius Erasmus (c. 1469–1536)
157
Bronze, cast
Diameter 105 mm
Cambridge, Fitzwilliam Museum
C.M. 28–1979

Obverse: Bust to left, wearing a cap and a coat with a fur collar. Legend: THN ΚΡΕΙΤΤΩ ΤΑ ΣΥΓΓΡΑΜΜΑΤΑ ΔΕΙΞΙ : IMAGO

AD VIVA[m] EFFIGIE[m] EXPRESSA (His writings will present a better image: portrait executed from life). In the field to the left, ER[asmus]; to the right, ROT[terdamensis] (Erasmus of Rotterdam). Below, the date 1519.
Reverse: On a rocky mound, a bust to left of the god Terminus, set upon a square base. Legend: ΟΡΑ ΤΕΛΟΣ ΜΑΚΡΟΥ ΒΙΟΥ - MORS VLTIMA LINEA RERV[m] (Consider the end of a long life — death is the ultimate limit of things). On the base: TERMINVS. Horizontally in the field, the motto, to be thought of as spoken by the god: CONCEDO — NVLLI (I yield to no one).

Although the piece is unsigned, its attribution is quite definite. In a letter to Willibald Pirckheimer from June 3, 1524, Erasmus relates that he had paid the artist over thirty florins for the "Terminus medal," as much, he adds, as for his painted portrait. In a letter to Henry Botteus from March 29, 1528, he reveals that the piece is the work of Quentin Matsys.[1]

Erasmus of Rotterdam, a leading figure of northern humanism, is best known for his critical mind, his cosmopolitanism, and his tolerance, all of which make him a precursor of the modern intellectual. Though he himself insisted that his best portrait was to be found in his books,[2] Erasmus commissioned likenesses from some of the greatest artists of his day: Matsys, Dürer, and Holbein. Matsys had already painted Erasmus and his Antwerp friend Peter Gillis in 1517 in a sort of diptych intended for the English chancellor Thomas More (1477–1535).

349

Two years later he created this earliest medal of the famous humanist, who happened to pass through Antwerp in that year.

With Erasmus's consent the medal was extensively reproduced in copper, lead, or bell metal by Nuremberg casters from 1524 on, so that today many copies may be found in public and private collections.

The Erasmian character of the medal's legends and inscriptions should be noted. The Greek legend on the obverse echoes the philosopher's statement, noted above, that his truest likeness is to be found in his works. The reverse inscription is explained in a letter of 1528 to Alfonso Valdes, secretary to Charles V. There Erasmus relates that "out of a profane god [Terminus] I have made for myself a symbol exhorting to decency in life. For death is the real terminus that yields to no one."[3]

The style of this medal is monumental, sober, realistic, and at the same time very personal. It is rightly considered one of the very earliest masterpieces of Flemish medallic art.

Luc Smolderen

Jacques Jonghelinck (Jongeling)
(1530–1606)

Jacques Jonghelinck was born into a family of mintmasters in Antwerp on September 20, 1530. His maternal grandfather, Thomas Gramaye, was master of the Antwerp mint and later master-general for Brabant. His father, Peter Jonghelinck, also headed the mint, as did his oldest brother Thomas. Another brother, Jan, was appointed assayer-general. The future medalist did not take up the family craft at once, but chose to yield to his vocation as a sculptor, one favored by the high cultural level of Antwerp in the mid sixteenth century.

Nothing is known about his early training, but he could have been initiated into the technique of the medal by the die-engravers at the mint. Art historians suggest that he may have studied with the sculptor Cornelis de Vriendt (alias Floris; born 1513–14, died 1575), while numismatists insist that he was a pupil of a brass caster by the name of Jan Symons.

It is certain that in 1552 he was in Milan, working as an assistant to the famous Leone Leoni (cat. nos. 49–52). Doubtless he had been introduced to the Italian master thanks to his family's contacts in court circles.

Jonghelinck was probably back in Brussels in 1553, in which year he furnished the pattern for a new silver florin called the carolus, but had certainly returned by the beginning of 1556, when he carved the counter-seal for the chancellery of the Golden Fleece. Charles V had meanwhile abdicated in favor of his son Philip II (cat. nos. 58, 156), who removed with his court to Spain in 1559. Jonghelinck began receiving increasing numbers of court commissions thanks to protectors like Antoine Perrenot de Granvelle (cat. no. 159), the extremely powerful minister of both Charles V and Philip II, and Viglius van Zuichem, president of the privy council. In 1559 he was asked to supervise the construction of the tomb of Charles the Bold, to be erected in Bruges, an enterprise that occupied him until

1563. Philip's governor-general, Margaret of Parma (cat. no. 159), commissioned him to create the bronze ornaments for a fountain in the garden of the Brussels court—a Cupid, a small Neptune, and two grotesques—and subsequently appointed him founder and engraver of the king's seals.

In 1561, the year of his marriage, Jonghelinck acquired a mansion in the vicinity of the court, but his large workshops were located in Granvelle's palace. The city of Brussels exempted him from excises on wine and beer, and he was named a dean of the Great Guild. He seems to have moved in the highest circles.

One of his brothers, Nicolas Jonghelinck, a clever businessman and collector of tolls, was himself a patron of the arts and commissioned from Jacques, probably around 1565, a series of bronze statues to ornament the gardens of his residence outside the city walls of Antwerp. This grouping, which included a fountain with Bacchus and figures of the seven planets, was to become one of the most important bronze ensembles of the sixteenth century. The planet figures now adorn various rooms of the Palacio Real in Madrid, while the Bacchus stands in the royal gardens in Aranjuez.

The departure of Philip II and his court to Spain had deprived the artists of the Low Countries of generous royal commissions, and the increasing religious conflicts, aggravated by the onset of civil war in 1566, caused countless Flemish artists to emigrate. Jonghelinck remained loyal to the Spanish regime, and was dependent on the patronage of the Habsburgs and their governors-general.

In 1567, Margaret of Parma resigned the governorship on the arrival of the dreaded duke of Alba (cat. no. 163), who promptly instituted a reign of terror. By 1568, Alba had crushed much of the resistance against Spanish rule, having executed many of its leaders and driven thousands of prominent citizens into exile. To commemorate his victory, he commissioned a statue of himself from Jonghelinck to be erected in the citadel in Antwerp, showing him standing triumphant over a monster symbolizing Rebellion and Heresy. After Alba's departure, his successor, Don Luis Requesens, quietly had Jonghelinck's statue melted down. We have a good idea what it looked like, however, for the sculptor presented Alba with a bust version—either a working model or a smaller-scale replica—that is now in the Frick Collection in New York.

Jonghelinck was rewarded with the post of keeper of the coins at the Antwerp mint. He was eminently qualified for such a post, given his upbringing, and felt that it would not prevent him from continuing to work as a sculptor, but he soon found himself overwhelmed by his administrative duties. In the remaining thirty years of his life he only twice returned to sculpture: in 1598 to model a new Cupid for the gardens of the court, his earlier one having disappeared during the Troubles, and in 1605 to cast a large crucifix for the Meir Bridge in Antwerp, a work that was interrupted by his death.

He did continue to work as a seal-engraver and medalist. Once settled in Antwerp, he no longer produced large medals in bronze and lead, preferring smaller cast medals in precious

158 obv.

158 rev.

metals. His models are rarely signed, yet it is possible to attribute to him over a hundred pieces with certainty and several dozen that are more than likely from his hand—to say nothing of his numerous copies of Italian works requested by important patrons.

Jonghelinck died in his apartments in the Antwerp mint on May 31, 1616, and was buried in St. Andrew's, the minters' parish church.

Luc Smolderen

Jacques Jonghelinck
Margaret of Austria, duchess of Parma (1522–1586)
158
Silver, cast
Diameter 59.5 mm
Brussels, Bibliothèque Royale

Obverse: Bust to right, wearing a veiled headdress, a gown with puffed sleeves, and a necklace with a pendant cross. Legend: MARGARETA • DE • AVSTRIA • D[ucissa] • P[armae] • ET • P[lacentiae] • GERMANIÆ • INFERIORIS • GVB[ernatrix] (Margaret of Austria, duchess of Parma and Piacenza, governorgeneral of the Low Countries). Engraved on the truncation: ÆT[atis] 45 (at age 45).
Reverse: An allegorical figure standing on a rock battered by wind and waves and turned to the left, wearing a laurel wreath and classical garments, with a sword in the right hand, palm and olive branches in the left. In the background, to the right, are a church and other buildings, partially obscured by shrubbery. To the left, beyond an arm of the sea, is a fortified town, toward which a man is paddling in a small boat. Legend: FAVENTE • DEO (If God so wishes).

Margaret of Parma, the illegimate daughter of Emperor Charles V (cat. nos. 77, 124–25, 156) was born in Flanders in 1522.[1] She was raised by her aunts, Margaret of Austria, duchess of Savoy (cat. no. 141), and Maria of Hungary (cat. no. 124), each of whom served ably as regent in the Low Countries. Her marriage to Ottavio Farnese, arranged for political reasons, was not a success, and when Philip II left for Spain in 1559, he asked her to return from Parma and govern in his stead.

A captain Francesco Marchi, who was attached to the person of the duchess, wrote to Cardinal Farnese from Antwerp in July 1567, informing him that he was sending the first two copies of the present medal, one for the pope, the other for the cardinal. He explains that Jacques Jonghelinck, the medal's author, had managed to reproduce the subject's features "more faithfully than anyone before," and adds that it was he, Marchi, who had the idea for the reverse, on which Margaret is shown "with weapons in hand and as though preaching throughout the country." Clearly the allegorical figure is meant to be Margaret herself, and the motto therefore alludes to her prodigious efforts to control insurrection and the predations of the Iconoclasts. Subsequent reductions of the piece, with the identical motif but the legend A • DOMINO • FACTUM • EST • ISTUD (This has been accomplished by the Lord), would tend to confirm this interpretation.[2]

Margaret of Parma left the Low Countries soon after the arrival of the duke of Alba in November 1567. She should have resumed her role as governor-general in 1580, but she could not get along with her son, Alessandro Farnese (1545–1592), who was then in charge of military operations against the Dutch provinces and had no intention of sharing his power, even with his own mother. She therefore returned to Italy, and died quite alone in Ortona in 1586.

Luc Smolderen

Jacques Jonghelinck
Antoine Perrenot de Granvelle, bishop of Arras (1517–1586)
159
Silver
Diameter 59 mm
Leiden, Rijksmuseum Het Koninklijk Penningkabinet

Obverse: Bust to right, bare-headed and bearded, wearing a surplice. Legend: ANTONII PERRENOT • EPI[scopus] • ATREBAT[ensis] (Antoine Perrenot, bishop of Arras).
Reverse: Aeneas attempting to steer his vessel through a tempest. Several sailors have been thrown into the sea, while others are busy repairing the masts. In the foreground, two sea-dogs rush toward a nude female body floating in the waves. In the background an overcrowded launch. On the right, Neptune in his chariot drawn by a pair of seahorses, brandishing his trident

159 obv.

159 rev.

and threatening the unbridled winds, represented by two chubby faces in the clouds. Hailstones are falling, and a rainbow has appeared. At the top, Granvelle's motto: DVRATE (Carry on).

Antoine Perrenot de Granvelle was the true head of the government of the Low Countries following the departure of Philip II for Spain in 1559. At that time he was the bishop of Arras, but in 1560 he was appointed archbishop of Malines (Mechlin) and in the following year became a cardinal.[1] Though undated, the present medal must have been executed before 1560, for it makes no mention of these later titles.

In March 1564, a group of angry nobles led by William of Orange and counts Egmont and Hoorn forced the cardinal to leave the country, but his political setback in no way diminished his patronage of the arts. He continued to be in touch with Jonghelinck, his former protégé. The sculptor had already created a dozen different medals for him and received further commissions in the following years.[2] Granvelle served as viceroy of Naples from 1570 to 1575, and continued to second Philip II as a minister until his death in Madrid in 1586.

This reverse is perhaps the best known of all those made by Jonghelinck. It was reused on later medals of Granvelle, from 1561 and after, where he is identified as the cardinal archbishop of Malines.[3] The scene is taken from Vergil's *Aeneid*. At the request of Juno, Aeolus has unchained the winds with the object of sinking Aeneas's ship. Neptune then intervenes to calm the waves. Here the vessel is equated with the ship of state, which Granvelle firmly steers through the storms of rebellion and heresy. Calm is restored by the appearance of the king in the guise of Neptune. It was in fact said that Philip would one day return to the Low Countries, but the king had no such intention.

Jonghelinck was inspired by earlier Granvelle medals created by his master, Leone Leoni.[4] The composition and even specific details such as Neptune's gesture and the placement of the tails of the seahorses are direct borrowings from Leoni. The sea-dogs in the foreground are further confirmation of his indebtedness to the Italian master. They have nothing to do with the Aeolus episode, but derive from a Leoni medal illustrating Aeneas's encounter with Scylla.[5] Jonghelinck's fe-

male nude may in fact be the sorceress herself. Granvelle's motto, DVRATE, included on many of his medals and seals, is also taken from the *Aeneid* (Book I, verse 207): "Durate et vosmet rebus servate secundis" (Carry on, and preserve yourself for better times).

Luc Smolderen

Jacques Jonghelinck
Jan Walravens
160
Silver, cast, uniface
Diameter 105 mm
Brussels, Cabinet des Médailles

Obverse: Bust to right, bearded and bare-headed, wearing ruff and doublet with puffed sleeves, a draped toga on the left shoulder. Legend: MAISTRE OOMKEN PRINCE CORONNE DES DOCTEURS A QUATRE ORELLES ÆT[atis] • 56 (Master Uncle, crowned prince of the four-eared doctors. At age 56). In the field to the left: IAN WAL • RAVENZ. To the right: NIET SONDER WIELLE OOM (translation discussed below). Engraved on the arm truncation: 1563.
Reverse: Plain.

Jan Walravens was the jester of the Brussels society known as "De Corenbloem" (The Cornflower), a fraternity that was one of a number of so-called chambers of rhetoric playing a major role in the political life of the Low Countries in the sixteenth century. They served as a kind of safety valve for the expression of public opinion, and at local festivals competed against each other with elaborate floats and plays presenting thinly-veiled criticism of the authorities. Like most artists at the time, Jonghelinck was himself associated with such a group, called the "Olijftak" (Olive Branch), and served as its "prince," or chairman in 1560–61.[1]

At the 1551 "Festival of Fools" in Brussels, a certain Master Oomken was seen strutting beside a donkey and administering justice to his fellow citizens. The same figure reappeared at a similar event in Antwerp in 1561, riding on a treelike float covered with playing-cards. He was accompanied by colleagues dressed in black stockings, white shoes, and blue coats with

159 rev.

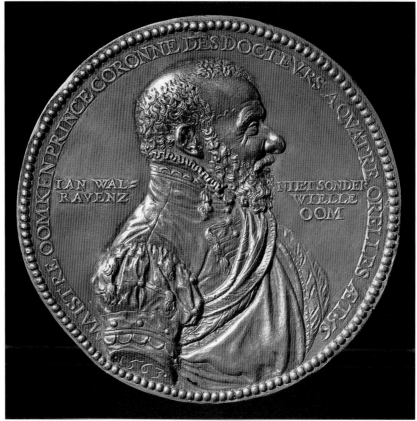

160 obv.

white and red stripes and green sleeves. No one knows just who this Jan Walravens—alias Master Oomken—really was.[2] Some have suggested that he could have been the painter Jan Colyns, who was also branded on such occasions as Prince of Fools or Master Oomken. According to the medal's inscriptions, Jan Walravens would have been born in 1507, but unfortunately we do not know Jan Colyns's birth date.

The Flemish motto NIET SONDER WIELLE OOM appears as though it were issuing from the subject's mouth. Its meaning is obscure, and it was undoubtedly meant to be understood only by the initiated. Some translate WIELLE as "wheel," so that the phrase becomes "nothing without a wheel, my uncle."[3] Others consider it a dialect form of *wil* (will, desire) and

translate the whole as "nothing without [your] will, my uncle."[4] Clearly the message is satirical. One should note that the medal's inscriptions alternate French and Dutch in typical Flemish fashion.

Luc Smolderen

Jacques Jonghelinck
Anthony van Stralen (1521–1568)
161
Silver
Diameter 54.4 mm; diameter of the outside perimeter of the pearling, 44.7 mm
Leiden, Rijksmuseum Het Koninklijk Penningkabinet

161 obv.

161 rev.

354

161 rev.

Obverse: Bust to right, bearded and bare-headed, dressed in a coat with wide lapels and a doublet with a turned-down collar. Legend: ANTONI • A • STRALE • D[omin]VS • DE • MERXEM • ET • DAMBRUGGE • (Antony van Stralen, lord of Merxem and Dambrugge). Engraved on the truncation: ÆT[atis] • XLIII • 1565 (Age 43. 1565).

Reverse: Nude figure of Fortune standing atop a globe set on a conch amid waves, holding a mast and billowing sail. Legend: VIRTVTE • ET • CONSTANCIA (With valor and steadfastness).

This medal is highly characteristic of Jonghelinck's style. The profile is both dignified and realistic, and the reverse presents an allegorical scene of Italian inspiration.

Antony van Stralen (or Straelen) was born in Antwerp, where he served as alderman in 1549, 1552–53, 1558–60, 1562, and 1566–67.[1] In 1554 he held the office of treasurer, and in 1555–57, 1561, and 1565 that of burgomaster. He was greatly respected for his financial skill and in 1557 was asked by the states of Brabant to insure the renewal of their bonds. In the following year, during the war against France, the States General appointed him commissioner general, charging him with the collection of funds voted for the defense of the provinces. In that office he was able to follow military operations quite closely, and by advancing the sum of 400,000 florins from his personal account saw to it that the German mercenaries desolating the country were disbanded. Though he solidified the finances of the provinces, he engendered the wrath of the Spanish authorities. In 1561 he purchased the domains of Merxem and Dambrugge mentioned on the obverse.

The reverse motif, used here to symbolize the role of the burgomaster of a large harbor city, frequently appears in engraving and sculpture of the period. One thinks, for example, of the *Marine Venus* of Danese Cattaneo. It had already been used by a follower of Niccolò Fiorentino on the 1498 medal of Alessandro di Gino Vechietti.[2]

Antony van Stralen came to a tragic end. He was openly hostile to the religious policy of Philip II, fearing that rigorous application of the edicts of the Inquisition could not help but provoke mass emigration of foreign merchants and bring about Antwerp's ruin. His sentiments allied him with the principal leaders of the opposition and brought him great popularity.

On the arrival of the duke of Alba in 1567, he attempted to leave the country. He was arrested in his coach to the north of Antwerp, and his possessions were seized. The inventory drawn up on that occasion mentions eight silver medals bearing his portrait, all of which were returned to his wife.[3] The burgomaster and aldermen of Antwerp tried to effect his release, but in vain. He was soon transferred to Brussels and brought before the notorious "Court of Blood," charged with having conspired with William of Orange and a number of the lesser nobility and publishing seditious writings. The duke of Alba pronounced the death sentence himself. Van Stralen was executed on September 23, 1568. He had been so badly tortured during his interrogation that he had to be beheaded sitting down.

Luc Smolderen

Jacques Jonghelinck
Philip of Croy, duke of Arschot and prince of Chimay (1526–1595)
162
Silver, gilt
Diameter 65 mm
London, The British Museum

Obverse: Bust to right, bare-headed and bearded, dressed in a doublet adorned with diagonal tucks and a frilled collar, and wearing the insignia of the Order of the Golden Fleece. Legend: PHILIPPE DE CROY DVC D'ARSCHOT PRINCE DE CHIMAY • Z [= et] (Philip of Croy, duke of Arschot, prince of Chimay and . . . [contined on the reverse]). The date 1567 engraved on the shoulder truncation.

Reverse: A celestial hand holding a hive, from which seventeen bees have taken flight. Legend: (floral stop) PORCEAN

162 obv.

162 rev.

CONTE DE BEAVMONT Z [= et] SENNINGHEM (. . . [titles continued from obverse] Porcien, count of Beaumont and Senninghem). On a phylactery displayed in the field, the engraved motto: DVLCIA • MIX–TA • MALIS (Sweetness is mixed with pain).

The extension of the obverse legend onto the reverse is a peculiarity found on other Jonghelinck medals as well. The motif of the beehive is a clear illustration of the reverse motto. Several tokens and a small medal of the duke of Arschot dated 1595 reproduce this same reverse composition.[1] The present example of the medal, from the Rosenheim Collection, is undoubtedly the best of those that survive. Most of the specimens encountered elsewhere are rather crude aftercasts in which the portrait is nearly unrecognizable.[2]

Philip of Croy, the third duke of Arschot, was born in Valenciennes, in France.[3] At fourteen he was sent by his father to the court of the king of the Romans and future emperor Ferdinand I (cat. no. 124), to be brought up with the monarch's sons. Throughout his life, Philip enjoyed privileged relations with the empire and on a number of occasions was entrusted with missions or embassies in Germany and Austria.

In 1564–65 he refused to join in the intrigues against Cardinal Granvelle, then acting as prime minister, and for his loyalty was appointed councillor of state. He continued to stand fast during the disturbances provoked by the Iconoclasts and the revolt of the "Beggars" in 1566–67. Accordingly, he was rewarded with a perpetual annuity of 4,000 pounds, to be raised from confiscated properties.

Philip exhibited all the flaws of the nobility of the period. He was debauched, greedy, frivolous, inconsistent, and quarrelsome. Never satisfied, he was jealous of both the Spaniards and many of his fellow countrymen.

In part owing to his rank, but also in part thanks to his outspoken attitude toward the Spaniards, Arschot played a major role when the States General assumed power in 1576, before the arrival of the king's new governor, Don Juan of Austria (1545–1578). In 1577, however, the Calvinist authorities in Ghent, secretly influenced by William of Orange (cat. no. 170), placed him under arrest as he was preparing to take over the governorship of Flanders. The States General intervened, and he was soon released. Furious about the outrage to his person, Arschot was henceforth determined to seek reconciliation with the king of Spain. He found his opportunity at the Conference of Cologne, where he submitted himself to representatives of the new governor-general, Alessandro Farnese, and was reestablished in his properties and charges.

In 1595, despite his great age, he undertook a pilgimage to Italy, where he died unexpectedly in Venice on December 11.

Luc Smolderen

Jacques Jonghelinck
Ferdinand, duke of Alba (1508–1582)
163
Silver, cast

163 obv.   163 rev.

Diameter 39.5 mm
Paris, Bibliothèque Nationale, Cabinet des Médailles
Esp. 646

Obverse: Bust to right, bare-headed and bearded, wearing cuirass, cloak, and ruff and the pendant of the Golden Fleece. Legend: FERDIN[andus] • TOLET[anus] • ALBÆ DVX • BELG[ii] • PRÆF[ectus] (Ferdinand de Toledo, duke of Alba, governor-general of Belgium). The date 1571 is engraved on the truncation.
Reverse: A burning candle supported by a crouching lion and two cranes. In the top of the field, the raised inscription DEO ET REGI, the beginning of a motto completed by the engraved words VITÆ VSVS in the exergue (The purpose of life [is service] to God and the king).

It was in 1571, the year of this medal, that Jonghelinck erected his notorious statue of the duke of Alba in the citadel at Antwerp, presenting to his patron the bust copy now in the Frick Collection in New York. The profile of that bust is virtually identical to the one presented here. These brisk and spirited likenesses are probably the most accurate of all the surviving portraits of this fascinating figure. The reverse presents a rather complicated composition. The burning candle represents the duke's life, being consumed in the service of God and king and sustained by Might (the lion) and Vigilance (the cranes). One notes that the crane on the left holds a stone in its raised foot. The ancients believed that the crane often dozed while balanced on one foot and carrying a stone in the other as a precaution. Should the bird relax too deeply, the falling stone would startle it into wakefulness.

The duke of Alba was raised by his grandfather, Ferdinand of Toledo, one of the heroes of the Reconquista, from whom he acquired a visceral hatred of heretics, unconditional devotion to his sovereign, and iron discipline.[1] In 1531 he accompanied Charles V to Hungary in the war against Suleiman II, then to Tunis in 1535, and in 1538 he was appointed general of the Spanish armies, which he completely reorganized. In 1547, by now generalissimo, he was victorious against the German Protestants at Mühlberg. He then proceeded to London, where he witnessed the marriage of the future Philip II (cat. nos. 58, 156) to Mary Tudor (cat. no. 54) in 1549. He was also present at the abdication of Charles V in Brussels in 1556. His temporizing spirit and icy reserve were extremely agreeable to Philip II, more Spanish than his father.

In 1556, Alba organized the Milanese defense against the French, and was then sent to Naples as viceroy. Recalled in 1559, he took part in the negotiations of the Treaty of Câteau-Cambrésis between France and Spain. After a period at the court in Madrid, he was appointed governor-general of the Low Countries in 1567, for Philip had decided to respond to the excesses of the Protestant Iconoclasts with a show of force. At first the duke's brutal and energetic methods appeared to succeed. In 1568 he ordered the execution of counts Egmont and Hoorn and forced William of Orange (cat. no. 170) into retreat, but he soon overstepped himself. The tribunal he established to deal with the insurrection, officially called the "Council of Troubles" but popularly known as the "Court of Blood," was impossibly cruel. The high taxes he imposed set even fellow Catholics against him, and his arrogance in erecting a monument to himself in the Antwerp citadel—the Jonghelinck statue mentioned above—met with universal scorn. By 1572 the rebellion grew out of hand, and in the following year the duke was recalled to Madrid.

He promptly fell out of favor, but in 1581 was recalled to carry out the conquest of Portugal. Before he died he was thus able to present his master with a new throne.

Luc Smolderen

Nicholas Hilliard
(c. 1537–1619)

Nicholas Hilliard is known primarily as a limner, or painter of miniatures, but was apprenticed in 1562 to Robert Brandon, a goldsmith like Hilliard's father. There is also evidence pointing to early activity as an engraver in collaboration with Jan Rutlinger, later under-engraver at the Tower mint in London.[1] Hilliard's first surviving miniature of Queen Elizabeth I is dated 1572, and portraits of the queen were to employ him until his death.[2] He described a royal sitting in his *Arte of Limning*, from c. 1600.[3] He spent the years 1576–79 in France, where he is thought to have made contact with Germain Pilon (cat. nos. 144–45).[4] In 1584, Hilliard and the sergeant painter George Gower tried, but failed, to gain the monopoly of production of the queen's portraits.[5] Even so, he and his workshop painted her miniature over and over again, following the so-called "Mask of Youth" pattern. He designed her image for one executed great seal of England and one planned one, and a drawing attributed to him survives for the great seal of Ireland.[6]

Hilliard's work at court continued under James I, who in 1617 actually granted him the sole right to produce portraits of the royal family, calling him "our well-beloved servant Nicholas Hilliard, gentleman, our principal drawer for the small portraits and embosser of our medallions of gold."[7] He enjoyed this privilege, leasing out his designs to other artists, until his death in early January 1619. Other payments made to Hilliard by James I show that the artist made a number of medals in

precious metals for the king and his court, but these are now mostly unidentifiable

Despite the documentation from the reign of James I, the precise nature of Hilliard's medal production is still unclear, and the medals ascribed to him remain only attributions to be proved. That Hilliard was capable of modeling is suggested by surviving records of his collaboration on the second and third great seals of England. As a court artist, however, Hilliard was accustomed to providing designs for others. It can only be suggested, therefore, that Hilliard modeled medals and engraved medal dies himself, although the probability is strong.

Luke Syson

Nicholas Hilliard
Elizabeth I (born 1533, queen of England and Ireland 1558–1603)
164
Gold, cast
Oval 56 × 44 mm; weight 57.57 g
London, The British Museum

164 obv.   164 rev.

Obverse: Half-length portrait three-quarters to the left. The queen is crowned and heavily jeweled, and wears a high open ruff and a gown in a diamond-shaped pattern. Legend (with rose stops): DITIOR • IN • TOTO • NON • ALTER • CIRCULVS • ORBE (No other circle in the whole world more rich).
Reverse: A bay tree growing on an islet, threatened but uninjured by a thunderbolt that splashes into the sea in the distance. Two ships are visible in the background to the left. The monogram E[lizabeth] R[egina] appears in the field. On the island is the inscription: NON • IPSA • PERICVLA • TANGVNT (Not even danger affects it). Decorative border of leaves.

The attribution of this medal to Nicholas Hilliard depends on its similarity to his medal of James I.[1] The fact that the James I medal is struck and the present one is cast accounts for some small differences. Similarly, the degree of collaboration within

Hilliard's oeuvre (apart from the Anthonys, he is known to have worked with other engravers, including his son),[2] may explain some stylistic variations. However, the great similarities of design and modeling outweigh the differences. Common to both portraits are the shape of the face, the heavily lidded eyes, the hollow pupils, the detailed rendition of jewels and hair, and the smooth transition between jaw and neck. The shapes of the letters in the two inscriptions, notably the R and the E, are almost exactly the same. The weight of evidence, both documentary and stylistic, suggests that the two medals are by the same hand.

On her accession in 1558, Elizabeth I, the daughter of Henry VIII and Anne Boleyn, inherited a country made uneasy by the marriage of her late sister, Mary Tudor (cat. no. 54), to the Spanish king Philip II (cat. nos. 58, 156), and by the restoration of Catholicism. Though she reinstated the Protestant faith, she initially maintained a fragile peace with Spain and with Philip, one that only faltered during the late 1560s and 1570s. For his part, Philip refrained from action against England until his notably unsuccessful campaign in 1580. Nevertheless, his capture of Portugal at about the same time gave him greater naval power with which to threaten Elizabeth.

During the 1580s, her position grew increasingly precarious. She had few allies, and between 1582 and 1585 there was a series of plots against her life. Philip's decree in May of 1585, confiscating English goods and placing a ban on her shipping in Iberian ports, led Elizabeth to ally herself in August of that year with Dutch rebels against him. In essence, her response was a declaration of war, and in July 1588 he launched the Spanish Armada against her. Its defeat was a tremendous propaganda coup, if not an absolute guarantee of future security.[3]

Elizabeth was always aware of the political potency of portraiture, and exercised great control over her image.[4]

The portrait on the present medal belongs to the pattern unnecessarily divided between an "Armada" type and the so-called "Mask of Youth."[5] These are essentially the same generalized, feminizing image showing the queen with rounded cheeks, large, slightly hooded eyes, and a rosebud mouth, an image probably less accurate, and certainly less bony and angular, than previous ones. The type seems to make its appearance in c. 1579–80 with the engraved frontispiece, attributed to Remigius Hogenberg,[6] for Christopher Saxton's *Areas of England and Wales*, and it survived until the queen's death.

The evergreen bay tree or laurel was one of the devices of Lorenzo de' Medici, with the motto "Ita ut virtus" (This is virtue).[7] It refers more specifically to contemporary belief that the bay tree was immune to lightning.[8] The E and R flanking the tree identify it with Elizabeth. One might therefore interpret the reverse as showing the virtues of the queen as unassailable. The bay could also be seen in a more specifically military context. In Samuel Daniel's *Thetys Festival*, a masque performed in 1610, Anne of Denmark and her gentlewomen placed offerings at a "Tree of Victory, which was a bay erected . . . upon a little mound,"[9] an idea that may even have been derived from the medal.

The medal was evidently intended to be worn or suspended, as can be seen from the attached rings. The lower loops were probably meant to support drop pearls. The iconography of the piece combines the political with the personal, as the lack of identifying legend on its obverse indicates. The obverse inscription seems not to have any wider political significance, but to refer to the object itself: no circle in the world could be richer than this one encompassing the features of the queen.

Luke Syson

Jacob Zagar (Sagarus)
(born c. 1530, died after 1584)

In 1550, Zagar made a portrait medal of Eguinaire Baron, a law professor at Bourges. In its legend he refers to himself as Baron's pupil. If we assume that he was accordingly a student at Bourges in that year, it would mean that he was born around 1530. In 1557 he served as town clerk of Middelburg, in Zeeland, and ten years later as pensionary of that town. He went to Brussels in 1569 to attend a meeting of the States General convened by the Spanish governor of the Low Countries, the duke of Alba (cat. no. 163), there to receive information about a tax measure. In 1571 he visited Brussels again, this time to try to obtain a tax reduction for the inhabitants of Middelburg. He was in Brussels a third time in 1572, recruiting troops and collecting ships and provisions with which to withstand an anticipated siege of his home town by rebels against their Spanish overlord, Philip II (cat. nos. 58, 156). The town was in fact besieged from the end of 1572 until 1574, and finally captured. From that time on there is no further mention of this loyalist administrator, yet portrait medals signed by him and dated 1574, 1578, and 1584 have come down to us.

Zagar is the last representative of a group of erudite, non-professional medalists that also includes Janus Secundus and Antoine Morillon. Of the ten medals so far known to be by his hand, the majority portray natives from Zeeland, often interrelated, who must have been friends of his. Only two medals from 1553 and 1574, both depicting his friend Frédéric Perrenot, betray the influence of Italian medalists, the latter one perhaps that of Jacques Jonghelinck as well (cat. nos. 158–63).

Gay van der Meer

Jacob Zagar
Lieven Bloxsen (c. 1490–1556)
165
Lead, cast, a small suspension hole at top
Diameter 46 mm
Leiden, Rijksmuseum Het Koninklijk Penningkabinet

Obverse: Bust to the right, wearing a beret, a doctor's gown with fur collar and lapels over a garment buttoned in front, and a shirt with a ruffled collar. Legend: LEVINUS • BLOCCENUS • A • BVRGH • (Lieven Bloxsen, [lord of] Burgh). In the exergue, beneath the shoulder, the engraved signature: IAC[ob] ZAG[ar] F[ecit].

165 obv.

Reverse: Plain.

Lieven (Livinus, Levinus) Bloxsen (Bloccenus, Bloxenius), lord of Oudewerve and Burgh, was a son of a burgomaster of Zierikzee in Zeeland, Anthonis Block, or Bloxsen. Lieven was born in about 1490, studied law, became a burgomaster of Zierikzee himself in 1523, and was later, from 1526 until his death in 1556, town clerk. Zagar probably made this medal as a memorial tribute just after Bloxsen died. They were colleagues, moved in the same social circles in Zeeland, and were probably friends.

A portrait of Bloxsen at an earlier age is found on a draft sketch for a window that he donated to a church, probably the church of his patron saint, the St. Lieven minster at Zierikzee. The window itself has disappeared. In the drawing he is depicted in three-quarter view to the right, which makes comparison with the medal portrait difficult.

Gay van der Meer

Steven van Herwijck
(born c. 1530, died between 1565 and 1567)

Born at Utrecht as the son of Cornelis van Herwijck, about whom nothing further is known, Steven van Herwijck first appears in 1558 in the register of St. Luke's guild in Antwerp, where he is listed, among the artists who became masters of the guild in that year, as a sculptor ("beeldsnijdere"). It is assumed that he served his apprenticeship in Antwerp, probably with the sculptor and medalist Jan Symons. No sculptures by van Herwijck's hand are known.

Because van Herwijck's medals show Italian influence, it has been suggested without any supporting evidence that he traveled in Italy in 1557. This may just as well be explained by the presence of several Italian medalists at the Court of Brussels in the fifties, namely Leone Leoni (cat. nos. 49–52), Pompeo Leoni, and Jacopo da Trezzo (cat. nos. 54–55).

In 1558 van Herwijck created five medals of Utrecht citizens. It seems probable, therefore, that he resided in his native city for some time in that year. On December 1, 1559, he became a burgher of Antwerp. In the next three years he portrayed more than ten of his fellow citizens on medals. A number of portrait medals of Englishmen bear the date 1562. He must therefore have stayed in England for some time, but at the end of that year he was back in Utrecht. A portrait painted in 1564 in Utrecht or Antwerp by Anthonis Mor is probably a likeness of the medalist. He must have returned to Antwerp in 1564 or 1565, for in March 1565 he applied for a temporary exemption from his burghership. The reason he gave was that he was going to England with his family for at least three years in order to complete certain works commissioned by Queen Elizabeth. The nature of this commission is unknown, but he may have been referring to sculptures. In his letter he describes himself as a painter and medalist or sculptor ("conterfeytere ende medalyeur oft beeldsnijdere"). The last dated work known to have been made by him is an English medal with a portrait of Queen Elizabeth, dated 1565.

A list of aliens living in London in 1567 contains a reference to a Dutch widow by the name of "Jonekin" (probably a phonetic spelling of Janneken), who had been a resident there for two years with her children, "Abraham and Stephen van Harwick." They were living in a house owned by one of the persons depicted on a van Herwijck medal.

There is a marked difference between the style of his medals made before 1562 in Utrecht and Antwerp and that of his later medals, made mostly in England. The earlier works are much larger and less subtle than the later ones. Curiously, though, his last signed medal, that of Queen Elizabeth from 1565, shows all the characteristics of his early work.

A total of between forty and fifty medals by van Herwijck have been registered. It is not possible to attribute all of them to him with certainty, but most are signed STE[ven] • H[erwijck] • F[ecit].

Gay van der Meer

Steven van Herwijck
Joris van Egmond, bishop of Utrecht (1504–1559)
166
Bronze, cast
Diameter 153 mm
Vienna, Kunsthistorisches Museum, Münzkabinett

Obverse: Bust in three-quarter view to the left, the head in profile. The sitter wears a flat beret and a gown with fur collar and lapels and three buttons visible on the sleeve of his left arm. Underneath this is a garment buttoned in front with eleven buttons over a shirt with a ruffled collar and cuffs. On the fourth finger of his left hand he wears a ring. In his right he holds a pair of gloves. Legend: • D[ominus] • GEORG[ius] • DEGMOND • EP[iscopu]S • TRAIECT[ensis] • A[nn]°, 1558 • AET[atis] • SV[a]E • 54 • (Lord Joris van Egmond, bishop of Utrecht, in the year 1558, at age fifty-four). Between the hands, parallel to the edge, the signature: STE[ven] • H[erwijck] • FEC[it].
Reverse: Plain.

157 obv.

157 rev.

158 obv.

160 obv.

161 rev.

162 obv.

162 rev.

164 obv.

164 rev.

169 obv.

169 rev.

170 obv.

170 rev.

166 obv.

The earliest medals van Herwijck signed are four portrait medals of three Utrecht prelates and a lady of that city, all dated 1558. One of them, a large medal with the portrait of Bishop Joris van Egmond, is so exceptional, both in size and composition, that, were it not dated and signed by him, one might be inclined to date it half a century later and attribute it to another artist.

In 1558, van Herwijck was admitted a master in St. Luke's guild of painters and sculptors in Antwerp. This medal may have served as an example of what he could do. The bishop's own copy may have been a silver one, though no genuine silver specimen has been preserved. He probably commissioned another medal that van Herwijck made in the same year, half as large and combined with an appropriate allegory on the reverse, as a gift to his friends and relatives.

On the large bronze medal the bishop wears the gown and beret of a scholar. The only outward signs of his office are the ring (or perhaps two rings) on the fourth finger of his left hand and the gloves he holds in his right. If official, the ring should have been worn on his right hand. It is also most unusual for a bishop to be depicted with gloves, and moreover they look rather simple, not like the ornate liturgical gloves he would wear during Mass.

Joris van Egmond was the third son of Jan I, count of Egmond and stadholder of Holland (1438–1516). Having first held several important church offices on the recommendation of

369

167 obv.

Emperor Charles V, a distant relative who would later confer on him the Order of the Golden Fleece, van Egmond was enthroned as bishop of Utrecht in 1535. Officially, he had been appointed in 1534, but it was disovered that he had never received Holy Orders and could only be consecrated after that omission had been rectified. Around this time, Jan van Scorel (1495–1562) painted his portrait. There the bishop is again shown dressed in gown and beret, but without ring or gloves, though infrared reflectography reveals that on the underdrawing he does wear a ring on the little finger of his left hand.

Van Egmond was noted for his piety and love of art. He commissioned numerous paintings and stained glass windows for churches in his see. His preferred residence was the Benedictine abbey of St. Amand near Tournai (now in France, but then in the southern Netherlands), of which he enjoyed the usufruct. It is therefore not impossible that it was there that he gave the commission for either one or both medals to van Herwijck, when the artist was working in Antwerp. The two other Utrecht prelates could have commissioned their own medals when visiting their bishop, but it is less probable that the fourth Utrecht native depicted on a medal in that same year, Engelken Tols (cat. no. 167), should have sat for him in Antwerp. Thus it is still quite plausible that van Herwijck was indeed working in Utrecht in 1558, as is generally accepted.

Gay van der Meer

Steven van Herwijck
Engelken Tols (1530–after 1568)
167
Lead, cast
Diameter 77 mm
London, The British Museum

Obverse: Bust of a lady to the left, wearing a cap, a decorated bodice over a shirt, and a ruffled collar. Legend: ENGELKEN • TOLS—AET[atis] • 28 • A[nn]° • 1558 • (Engelken Tols, age twenty-eight, in the year 1558). To the right of her arm, the signature: STE[ven].
Reverse: Plain.

A year after producing this realistic portrait of a lady of rank from his native town of Utrecht, van Herwijck became a burgher of Antwerp and there portrayed the wife of a wealthy merchant, Cecilia Veeselar (cat. no. 168). The portraits are closely related in style and provide a clear impression of the personalities of the two sitters. From a notarial protocol of 1563 we learn that Engelken was the daughter of a minor nobleman, Johan Toll, and Engelberta van Diemen. Her maternal grandfather, Adam van Diemen, had been a burgomaster of Utrecht. His widow, Lysbeth van de Kerck, in whose house Engelken was living in 1563, was a prominent Protestant who was beheaded for her religious convictions in 1568. Engelken Tols was banished, together with a number of other Utrecht Protestants, and all her goods were confiscated. We know nothing about her subsequent fate.

Gay van der Meer

168 obv.

Steven van Herwijck
Cecilia Veeselar (born 1521, died after 1559)
168
Lead, cast
Diameter 72 mm
Leiden, Rijksmuseum Het Koninklijk Penningkabinet

Obverse: Bust to the left, wearing a bonnet with a ruffled edge, a bodice over a figured shirt, tied in front with a lace, and a ruffled collar. Legend: CESILIA • VEESELAR • AET[atis] • 37 • A[nn]º • 1559 • (Cecilia Veeselar, age thirty-seven, in the year 1559). On the truncation of the bust, the signature: STE[ven] • H[erwijck] • F[ecit].
Reverse: Plain.

In style, this piece is related to the portrait medal of Engelken Tols (cat. no. 167), made in Utrecht the year before, though Cecilia's portrait is much more refined. To judge from the freshness of its execution, we can assume that this one-sided lead plaque with two small suspension holes at the top was the artist's first trial cast, straight from the wax model.

Cecilia Veeselar (Veselar, Vezeler) was one of the daughters of Joris Veeselar, a wealthy silversmith and merchant who sold Flemish tapestries all over Europe. He became warden, and later comptroller-general of the Antwerp mint. Cecilia first married Melchior Balde, and after his death (date unknown) contracted a second marriage in 1559 with Floris Allewijn, a minor nobleman from the duchy of Gelderland in the northern Netherlands. There is a companion lead plaque with his portrait, also dated 1559 and signed STE[ven] • H[erwijck]. It seems plausible that these lead casts are the prototypes of obverses for medals commissioned on the occasion of the couple's wedding.

Though the two plaques are uniface, it is quite probable that van Herwijck also made reverses for both. He certainly did for Cecilia's medal. Another lead specimen of this same portrait has been preserved, this time with an allegorical reverse.[1]

It is not known whether Cecilia and her new husband Floris Allewijn were Roman Catholics or Protestants. Her elder sister was definitely a Protestant who left Antwerp, as so many did, to avoid persecution after Spanish troops reconquered the city in 1585, at the beginning of the Eighty Years' War. It seems that Floris Allewijn also went to the northern (Protestant) Netherlands at some time, and that he died in Amsterdam. We are informed of this in a deed of partition from as late as 1638, dividing his estate between a grandnephew and grandniece. It could mean that Cecilia had also converted to the new religion, but she could have done so after 1559.

Gay van der Meer

Steven van Herwijck
Richard Martin (1534–1617) and his wife Dorcas Eglestone (1537–1599)
169
Silver, cast
Diameter 58 mm
London, The British Museum

Obverse: Bust of Richard Martin to the right, wearing a flat beret, a gown with a stiff collar over a garment buttoned in front, and a ruffled collar. Legend: (flower) RICHARD (lozenge) MARTIN (lozenge) AET[atis] (lozenge) 28 (lozenge) A[nn]º 1562 (Richard Martin, age 28, in the year 1562). On the truncation of the arm, the signature: STE[ven] • H[erwijck].
Reverse: Bust of Dorcas Eglestone to the left. She wears a

169 obv.

169 rev.

pointed bonnet over a lace underbonnet and a gown with a fur collar and sleeves faced with fur over a shirt with a small ruff. Legend: DORCAS (lozenge) EGLESTONE VX[or] (lozenge) RICHARD (lozenge) MARTIN (lozenge) AET[atis] 25 (Dorcas Eglestone, wife of Richard Martin, at the age of twenty-five).

In 1562, when van Herwijck created this medal with two beautiful portraits of a London couple, Richard Martin, later Sir Richard, stood on the threshold of a brilliant career. He was a goldsmith, and in this capacity made plate and jewelry for Queen Elizabeth, commissioned for use as gifts. From 1559 on he was employed in an unknown capacity in the London mint. In 1572 he became its warden, and in 1581 its master as well, introducing numerous innovations. His son Richard (died 1616) became his deputy and in 1599 was named joint master with his father. Sir Richard rose to great heights in the city. He served as lord mayor of London twice, in 1589 and 1594, and as prime warden of the Worshipful Company of Goldsmiths in 1592. Nevertheless, he was poorly paid for his work at the mint, and sometimes even had to work at a loss. Moreover, it has been recorded that in 1589 the court owed him some 30,000 pounds, an enormous amount at the time, probably for his work as a goldsmith.

Shortly after his wife's death in 1599, Richard was persuaded to give up his post of warden—he was then sixty-five years old—but he continued to serve as master of the mint together with his son. From then on his fortunes declined. The new warden persecuted him with all sorts of harassments and intrigues, and in 1602 he was dismissed from several important offices owing to his poverty, imprisonment for debt, and unfitting demeanor. In 1604 he appealed to King James I, but the king was partial to the new warden, to whom he gave lands and titles. Even so, Martin kept his job as mintmaster until his death in 1617 at the age of eighty-three.

This is the largest medal van Herwijck made in England, apart from his anomalous portrait of Queen Elizabeth from 1565. It is also his only medal with a portrait on either side. Both are beautifully modeled, full of life and character.

Gay van der Meer

Coenraad Bloc
(born c. 1545, died after 1602)

Very little is known about this medalist, though he produced portrait medals of important sitters throughout Europe. It is thought that he was active in Rome, Vienna, Paris, and Cleves, although as yet no archival evidence has turned up to support that of the medals. His first signed and dated medal is from 1575, his last from 1602. A certain Coenraad Bloc, who may have been our medalist, was exiled from Antwerp in 1566 on the charge of Anabaptism. The only other trace of him in the archives of Antwerp is from 1578, when Coenraad was admitted to the goldsmith's guild with the note that he was "from this city." Compared to that of Jacques Jonghelinck (cat. nos. 158–63), who also came from Antwerp, Coenraad's style lacks refinement. His portraits and images are modeled in a rather straightforward style. His lettering, however, is very elegant. The portrait medal of William and Charlotte (cat. no. 170) is undoubtedly ·one of his best pieces. The expressions of both sitters are more lively than those seen on most of Bloc's other medals.

Marjan Scharloo

Coenraad Bloc
William of Orange (1533–1584) and Charlotte de Bourbon (1548–1581)
170
Gold, cast
Diameter 44 mm; weight 30.465 g
Leiden, Rijksmuseum Het Koninklijk Penningkabinet

Obverse: Bust of William of Orange in profile to the right, wearing a ceremonial cuirass with a drapery around the shoulders and a small ruff collar. Legend: GVILEL[mus] • D[ei] • G[ratia] • PR[inceps] • AVRIACAE • CO[mes] • NASSAVIAE • 1577 (William, by the grace of God, prince of Orange and count of Nassau, 1577). On the arm truncation, the sitter's age: AET[atis] • 44. Below the exergue, the signature: COEN[raad] • BLOC • F[ecit].

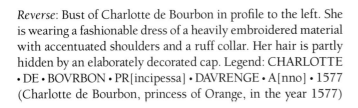

170 obv.

170 rev.

Reverse: Bust of Charlotte de Bourbon in profile to the left. She is wearing a fashionable dress of a heavily embroidered material with accentuated shoulders and a ruff collar. Her hair is partly hidden by an elaborately decorated cap. Legend: CHARLOTTE • DE • BOVRBON • PR[incipessa] • DAVRENGE • A[nno] • 1577 (Charlotte de Bourbon, princess of Orange, in the year 1577)

Comparison with contemporary paintings and prints confirms the quality of these portraits of William and Charlotte, and supports the assumption that they were modeled from life in wax. The portrait of William shows him to be a well-proportioned man with an energetic personality. He is portrayed as a warlord struggling with the most powerful monarch of Europe in an attempt to gain more independence for the Netherlands. This is in sharp contrast with a painted portrait of about three years later by the Antwerp artist Adriaan Key, where he is depicted as an elder statesman, wearing robes and a small cap. Charlotte's prominent nose and fleshy cheeks on the reverse of the medal correspond closely to her image on a print by Goltzius from 1581.

William and Charlotte were married in 1575, to the consternation of many of their relatives. Charlotte de Bourbon was born in 1546 and destined for convent life at the age of twelve. In 1572 she renounced the Catholic faith and left the convent of Jouarre. She fled to the court of the count Palatine, Frederick III the Pious, where William must have met her. At that time he was already estranged from his second wife, Anna of Saxony, who was gradually going mad. After having consulted a number of theologians, who declared his marriage with Anna to be annulled, William invited Charlotte to Holland in 1575, and married her on the very day she set foot on Dutch soil. The duke of Saxony was outraged at the insult to his family, and the political storm that followed William's decision took some time to settle. According to all historical sources, the new couple had a happy life together, and they produced a baby girl each year until Charlotte's early death in 1582. Not surprisingly, Charlotte remained very much in the shadow of her husband, taking care of her large family.

William was to experience alternating fortunes, both in his public career and in his personal life. He was brought up at the court of Charles V in Brussels, and even as a young man he occupied top posts in the government under Philip II (cat. nos. 58, 156). He was the richest nobleman in the Netherlands and enjoyed the good things of life. Philip's efforts to increase his control over executive power in the Low Countries were understandably met with the greatest suspicion by the powerful cities and provinces. The rise of Protestantism was a test case, and soon after the iconoclasm of 1566 a civil war began. William, finally forced to take sides, went into exile in Germany, and his properties were confiscated. In due course he became the leader of the Dutch revolutionaries, who wanted religious freedom and respect for their medieval privileges. Apart from his contribution to the independence of the Netherlands, he is most remembered today for his tolerance, an exceptional virtue in the violent sixteenth century. He married four times and had twelve children. His eldest son was kidnapped by Philip and spent many years at the Spanish court in Madrid. After several failed attempts on his life, William was murdered in 1584 in the city of Delft.

Bloc's portrait medal is the only contemporary image of Prince William in metal, Originally, it was intended to serve as a special gift to relations and courtiers, like the German *Gnadenmedaille*. A portrait has come down to us of François de Virieu (c. 1580), the majordomo of William and Charlotte's court, holding the medal on a small chain in his hand. There are several other courtiers who are known to have received a copy of it as a reward for special missions abroad or for other services.

Many copies of this important medal exist, executed in different metals and with variations in design. One earlier cast in a private collection shows a small but meaningful discrepancy in the obverse legend, in that it lacks the D[ei] • G[ratia]. It is well known that William laid particular stress on his position as an independent prince of Orange, who possessed the right to conduct war against Philip II. The addition of D • G • to the final design may have been meant to underscore his rank.

From 1577 on, as William's influence on the politics of the Netherlands increased, the medal came to be used for different purposes. It evolved from a special gift for notables at court to a public propaganda piece, copied and imitated by other goldsmiths.

Marjan Scharloo

170 obv.

Documentation

Introduction

Notes:

1. In addition to the great early catalogues of medals such as Hill 1930, for Italian medals of the fifteenth century, and Habich 1929–34, for German medals of the sixteenth century, there are a number of good introductions to the subject, for example Fabriczy 1904, Habich 1916, Habich 1924, Hill and Pollard 1978, and Jones 1979. Pastoureau 1982 and 1986 provides interesting and provocative thinking on the origins and nature of medals, as does Trenti Antonelli in *Le Muse* . . . , 1991, pp. 25–35.
2. See the section on medallic technique in Hill and Pollard 1978, pp. 23–35.
3. The theme of the scholarly sessions at the last congress of the Fédération Internationale de la Médaille, held in London in September 1992, was the relation between drawings and medals. The papers delivered at those sessions will be published in the near future.
4. Both Vasari and Cellini provide instructions for preparing the wax and casting bronze. See Vasari 1960 and Cellini 1898. Wax models of the fifteenth century are practically nonexistent, and those of the sixteenth extremely rare. Not included in the category of wax models for medals are the many painted wax portraits that make their appearance in the sixteenth century. See Pyke 1973.
5. See the introductory sections in the various volumes of Habich 1929–34.
6. For a more detailed description of this process, see Tuttle 1987.
7. See Hill and Pollard 1978; Adams 1978, pp. 201–6; Doty 1982; Cooper 1988. The process is also described by Vasari. Hill (Hill and Pollard 1978) mentions that the medalist Gianfrancesco Enzola began making experiments in the striking of medals from dies in the second half of the fifteenth century, but gives no references to support his assertion.
8. See Pastoureau 1982; Pastoureau 1986; Trenti Antonelli, *Le Muse* . . . , 1991, pp. 22–35.
9. Much of the following text is adapted from Scher 1989 ("Immortalitas . . . ").
10. Pastoureau 1982, p. 207, maintains that to credit Pisanello with the invention of the medal is "absurde." On the basis of his argument, any significant artistic innovation would have to be seen as absurd, which is clearly not the case.
11. For Roman medallions, see Toynbee 1986. The development of portrait coins begins in the Hellenistic period with the followers of Alexander the Great and continues with Roman republican and imperial coins. The tradition was suspended in the Middle Ages except for the imitation of Roman coinage by Emperor Frederick II with his famous augustales. See Kowalski 1976. In the early Renaissance there was some confusion regarding the use of several variations of the word "medal" and its application to both coins and medals.
12. For the Sesto medals, see Hill 1930, nos. 10–13. A long and thorough article on this subject by Louis Waldman and Alan Stahl is soon to appear in the *American Journal of Numismatics*. For the Malatesta coin, see Pasini 1983, p. 77.
13. See Scher 1989 ("Immortalitas . . . "), p. 15, note 18.
14. Ibid., p. 17, note 33.
15. See Hill 1930, pp. 154–57.
16. Ibid., pp. 113–14.
17. Ibid., pp. 16–19.
18. Ibid., pp. 76–79.
19. See Horne 1980, pp. 27–29; Pope-Hennessy 1966, pp. 28, 30.
20. See *Splendours* . . . , especially the article by Anthony Radcliffe, pp. 46–49; also Paolucci 1988.
21. *Splendours* . . . , p. 160, no. 109.
22. Ibid.; Cartwright 1926, vol. 1, pp. 166–68.
23. Cartwright 1926, vol. 2, pp. 10–11.
24. Ibid., vol. 1, p. 166.
25. Cartwright 1926, vol. 2, pp. 12–13.
26. *Splendours* . . . , p. 160, no. 109, and especially J. M. Fletcher, pp. 51–63, fig. 49.
27. See Hill and Pollard 1978, p. 86.
28. H. Maué in Nuremberg 1300–1550, p. 105.
29. An article by the author specifically devoted to the subject of connoisseurship in the field of medals has been published in the Autumn 1993 issue of *The Medal*.

Prototypes: The Medals of the Duke of Berry

Notes:

1. Guiffrey, ed. 1894–96. See also Scher 1961 (*Medals*), pp. 2–12; M. Jones 1982–88, vol. 1, pp. 17–24; *Ex aere* . . . , pp. 90–96; and Scher et al. 1986, pp. 81–84.
2. Guiffrey, ed. 1894–96, vol. 1 (1413 inventory), item 199.
3. Most of the duke's collections were supposed to go to his two daughters. Charles VI, however, desperate for funds with which to continue his war against the English, seized most of the precious objects in his late uncle's treasury and melted them down for coinage or sold them at auction. An account of that auction, dated 1417, is in the Bibliothèque Nationale, ms. fr., No. 6747. It is reproduced in full in Guiffrey, ed. 1894–96, vol. 2, pp. 339–44.
4. Guiffrey, ed. 1894–96, vol. 1 (1413 inventory) items 201–2.
5. In the *Très Riches Heures*, the figure of Constantine from the medal appears as a magus (fol. 51v.). In addition, at the top of each of the famous calendar pages (fols. 1v.–12v.), the chariot of the sun is taken from the reverse of the Heraclius medal, and the entire reverse composition of that medal appears in the *Belles Heures* (fol. 156).
6. Guiffrey, ed. 1894–96, vol. 2 (1416 inventory), item 234.
7. Of several seals of the duke of Berry, the one most likely to represent the reverse of the Virgin and Child "medal" is found in Eygun 1938, pl. III, no. 23.
8. Berlin, Staatliche Museen, Skulpturengalerie, inv. no. 2181.

Additional literature: As may be imagined, the literature on the Constantine and Heraclius medals is extensive. Fairly complete bibliographies are found in Scher 1961 (*Medals*); M. Jones 1982–88, vol. 1; and *Ex aere* . . . , pp. 90–96.

1, 1a
Artist Unknown
Constantine the Great (M. Jones 1982–88, vol. 1, no. 1)

Notes:

1. This would also argue for an Italian origin of the original pieces purchased by the duke.
2. A more complete discussion of the female figures may be found in Scher 1961 (*Medals*), pp. 159–69; M. Jones 1979 ("The First"), pp. 35–44; and M. Jones 1982–88, vol. 1, p. 18.

2, 2a
Artist Unknown
Heraclius, emperor of Byzantium (M. Jones 1982–88, vol. 1, no. 5)

Notes:

1. Guiffrey, ed. 1894–96, vol. 1, art. 200, 202.
2. Jacobus de Voragine 1941, pp. 543–45.
3. Hill 1910, pp. 110–16.
4. *Belles Heures*, fols. 156, 156v., 157.
5. See note 2.

Italy, Fifteenth Century
Leon Battista Alberti

Literature: There is an enormous library of writings pertaining to the life and work of Alberti. There are helpful listings in Wilhelm Suida's biography in Thieme-Becker, vol. 1, p. 201, as well as the entries by Bruno Zevi et al. in *The Encyclopedia of World Art*, vol. 1, columns 188–216; by C. Grayson and G. C. Argan in *Dizionario Biografico* . . . , vol. 1, pp. 702–13; and by H. Lorenz and P. von Naredi-Rainer in *Saur, Allgemeines Künstler-Lexikon* . . . , vol. 2, pp. 84–91.

3
Leon Battista Alberti
Self-Portrait in the Roman Style (Hill 1930, no. 16)

Notes:

1. I closely follow Stephen Scher's arguments, suggesting an essentially Italian paternity for at least certain of the duke of Berry's "proto-medals" of c. 1400 and recognize the chronological preeminence of the fourteen Italian "proto-medals" of 1390–1433 (Hill 1930, nos. 1–15). But those incunabula in fact prove the point: their obverses portray only two living men, and their reverses display only familial heraldic devices. The essential concept of the developed Renaissance medal is to represent concisely the dual nature of man through a naturalistic depiction of a specific individual's outward appearance conjoined with a "psychological" portrait of his inner personality. That unifying idea is as conspicuously absent in the proto-medals as it is manifestly struggling to be resolved in this pioneering self-portrait, with its defining hieroglyph hovering in alternate functions along the edge, poised to slip across that metaphoric threshold and thus to establish the classic, emblematic reverse typology of the true medal. Accordingly, I cannot help but wonder whether it may not have been Alberti himself who first (to judge from the imperial iconography of this relief) grasped the significance of meeting and *portraying in this medium* a living emperor, and suggested to Pisanello some of the ingredients of his revolutionary medallic invention of 1438. This comes close to the view of Maria Grazia Trenti Antonelli in *Le muse* . . . , vol. 1, pp. 25–28.
2. Donatello's principal commissions during this Roman sojourn were a Sacrament tabernacle for St. Peter's and a marble tomb slab for the archdeacon Giovanni Crivelli. See Janson 1957, vol. 1, pls. 136–39, and vol. 2, pp. 95–102.
3. Janson 1957, vol. 1, pls. 158–62, and vol. 2, pp. 108–18 (Pulpit); vol. 1, pls. 163–81, and vol. 2, pp. 119–29 (Cantoria). On the bronze heads specifically, ibid., vol. 1, pls. 179–80, and vol. 2, pp. 123–25, where their authorship and iconography are fully discussed.
4. See C. W. King 1872, vol. 1, p. 304, and G. Richter 1971, pp. 99–100, no. 474. Another pertinent gem that anticipates the design of this relief almost exactly is a sardonyx cameo of the head of Apollo in the Museo Archeologico, Florence. See Vollenweider 1966, pp. 69, 118, pl. 76, fig. 1.
5. Hill 1930, no. 161. On the conceptual theory of emblematic reverse *imprese*, see Paolo Giovio's celebrated recommendations as summarized in Hill and Pollard 1978, pp. 16–17.
6. Schneider 1990, summarizes the considerable literature on the "winged eye" and adds some new interpretative hypotheses. The reading given here is essentially my own, developed in part as a result of my conversations with the late Sir Kenneth Clark when we studied the relief together on his visit to the National Gallery of Art in 1970. See also *Le muse* . . . , vol. 1, pp. 166–73, nos. 39–42. I believe it may not have been remarked in this

context that ancient Greek numismatic reverses referring to Zeus at Olympia actually enclosed the god's thunderbolts within wreaths of laurel, exactly as in Alberti's emblem on Matteo's medallic reverse. These provide a clear precedent for the identity of the thunderbolts and confirm the character of the whole device. See King sale, 1992, no. 706, a silver stater of Olympia from c. 416 B.C.

Additional literature: Armand 1883–87, vol. 1, p. 23, no. 28 (attributed to Matteo de' Pasti); Ephrussi 1883, p. 249, illus.; Heiss 1881–92, vol. 4, no. 1, pl. 1 (attributed to Alberti); Müntz 1887, vol. 1, p. 461, illus.; Michel 1888, p. 512, illus.; Venturi 1896, p. 73 (attributed to Pisanello); Fabriczy 1903, p. 17 (dated 16th century); Hill 1905, pp. 192–93; Wilhelm Suida in Thieme-Becker, vol. 1, p. 202; Migeon 1908, p. 6, illus. p. 2 (attributed to Pisanello); Hill 1912 (*Portrait*), pp. 29–31, no. 1, pl. 16; Hill 1920 (*Medals*), pp. 46 and 184, pl. 6, fig. 1; Habich 1924, pp. 44–45 and 151, pl. 12, fig. 1 (attributed to Pisanello [?]); Vaudoyer 1925, p. 252, illus.; Hill 1930, no. 16; S. Ricci 1931, p. 2, no. 1, pl. 1; *The Art of the Renaissance Craftsman*, pp. 38–39, no. 51, illus.; Seymour 1949, p. 180, no. 38, pl. 121; Cott 1951, p. 141, no. A–278.1B; Badt 1958, pp. 78–87, fig. 1; Wind 1958, pp. 187ff. (2nd ed., 1968, pp. 231–35); Watkins 1960, pp. 256–58 (dated c. 1438); Seymour 1961, pp. 46, 207, pl. 40; Pope-Hennessy 1965, pp. 7–8, no. 1, fig. 1; Pope-Hennessy 1966, pp. 66–69, fig. 67; Grayson 1972, p. 154, no. 1, pl. 6; Ames-Lewis 1974, pp. 103–4, fig. 40 (reversed for comparison); Lewis 1975, pp. 620 and 623, fig. 954; Middeldorf 1978, pp. 310–22; Sheard 1978, no. 81, illus. (as c. 1434); Callmann 1981, pp. 51–52, no. 47, pl. 1; Walker 1983, p. 98, fig. 107; Wilson 1983, p. 12, illus. (and cover illus.); Anthony F. Radcliffe entry in *Italian Renaissance Sculpture . . .*, pp. 163–64, no. 48, illus. (*Donatello . . .*, p. 214, no. 82).

Pisanello

Notes:
1. A review of the question of the artist's birth date and first name is found in Paccagnini 1973, pp. 117–20. In contemporary documents he is called variously "Antonius Pisanus," "Antonio dicto Pisanello," "Pisanus pictor," "Pisanellus pictor," "Pisano da Verona," or "Pisanello de Pisis." Some recent references have used the form "Antonio di Puccio, called Pisanello," which would follow a more strict Italian construction referring to the subject's immediate parentage.
2. Woods-Marsden 1988, pp. 32 and 186, note 3.
3. Paccagnini 1973, pp. 129–40; Woods-Marsden 1988, pp. 32 and 186, note 4.
4. Most of the documents concerning Pisanello are cited, if not actually transcribed, in Woods-Marsden 1988, pp. 32–38 and 186–95, notes 1–49.
5. Woods-Marsden 1988, pp. 32 and 186, note 1.
6. Ginevra d'Este was the first wife of Sigismondo Malatesta (cat. no. 14). She was the illegitimate daughter of Niccolò III d'Este and sister to Leonello (cat. no. 5), also illegitimate.
7. There are two drawings recording the emperor and his entourage, one in the Louvre, the other in the Art Institute of Chicago. See Fossi Todorow 1966, pp. 30–31 and 80–81. To the bibliography cited there should be added Vickers 1978, pp. 417–24.
8. Paccagnini 1972; Paccagnini 1973, chapters 1–3; Woods-Marsden 1988.
9. Hill 1930, nos. 21–23.
10. It is as difficult to follow the shifting loyalties of the *condottieri* as it is to understand the changing alliances of the various factions for whom they fought. See Trease 1971 and Mallett 1974.
11. See Sindona 1961, pp. 20–21, also Woods-Marsden 1988, pp. 34–35.
12. Hill 1930, nos. 24–31. The small Leonello medals form a fascinating group both in terms of style and iconography. See Scher et al. 1986, pp. 87–89, and the discussion of cat. no. 5.
13. Hill 1930, nos. 33–35.
14. Hill 1930, nos. 38 (Vittorino), 39 (Cumano), and 40 (Decembrio).

15. For a transcription and translation of the *privilegium* granted to Pisanello by Alfonso, see Woods-Marsden 1988, pp. 37 and 195, note 47.
16. For details relating to the once difficult question of when and where Pisanello died, see Sindona 1961, p. 116, note 57, and Woods-Marsden 1988, pp. 37 and 195, note 49.
17. Pisanello was the subject of an unusually large number of contemporary literary works. They are discussed in Hill 1905 under the names of the various authors. See also Baxandall 1971 and 1972. Praise of the artist continued into the sixteenth century. See Woods-Marsden 1988, p. 37.
18. There is some evidence to suggest that Pisanello collected ancient coins. Several drawings in the *Codex Vallardi*, Louvre, Paris, reproduce ancient coins or heads from them, but these are now generally attributed to hands other than Pisanello's. See Fossi Todorow 1966, nos. 218v, 222, 223r, 224r, and 279r. There is also the amusing passage in Carlo de' Medici's letter to Giovanni de' Medici from October 31 [1455], in which he mentions that he has purchased "about thirty very good silver medals from a pupil of Pisanello, who died a few days ago." Carlo then goes on to say that he was rather forcefully relieved of these pieces by Pietro Barbo (later Pope Paul II), a notoriously voracious collector of ancient coins. It is possible, of course, but unlikely, that the objects were not in fact ancient. See Hill 1905, pp. 212–13, and Woods-Marsden 1988, p. 195, note 49.
19. Among the large number of drawings once attributed to Pisanello and gathered together in the *Codex Vallardi* and other collections there are many that are clearly copied from ancient sculpture. The most exhaustive study of these drawings is found in Fossi Todorow 1966. See also *Da Pisanello. . . .* Much depends on the attribution of the drawings both in the *Codex Vallardi* and in other collections. The attributions found in Fossi Todorow are those most commonly accepted, in which case most of the drawings that have been clearly based on ancient subjects fall into groups that are not attributed to Pisanello. Some could have been copies of drawings by him, but here the situation becomes cloudy. The only drawing of a classical subject given to Pisanello is Fossi Todorow 1966, no. 67. The figure, however, is placed within a purely Gothic frame, and is thus a perfect example of the intermingling of subjects, ideas, and styles found in Pisanello's art and in North Italian quattrocento art in general.

Additional literature: Venturi 1896; Degenhart 1940; Brenzoni 1952; Magagnato 1958.
Though covering much besides Pisanello, the bibliographies in *Le Muse . . .*, vol. 1, pp. 465–516, and vol. 2, pp. 341–90, are exhaustive.

4, 4a
Pisanello
John VIII Paleologus (Hill 1930, no. 19)

Notes:
1. Hill 1930, p. 13, gives a list of medals credited to the artist in the literature, but many of these are doubtful. Hill 1905, pp. 185–91, discusses these "lost" medals at greater length.
2. Head 1977, p. 124, note 2.
3. The standard work on the council in English is Gill 1959.
4. The two drawings most directly linked with the medal are one in the Louvre (Fossi Todorow 1966, no. 57), and another in the Art Institute of Chicago (ibid., no. 58). Three drawings of horses in the *Vallardi Codex* (ibid., nos. 31–33) may also be closely connected with the work. Other related drawings cannot be attributed to Pisanello with confidence. One, from the *Vallardi Codex* (ibid., no. 143), shows a man on horseback seen from the rear, and relates to the page on the medal's reverse. Another in the same collection (ibid., no. 301) is a drawing of John VIII Paleologus in profile. The latter has usually been given to Pisanello and considered a study for the medal; however Fossi Todorow agrees with Manteuffel 1909, p. 159, that the drawing was actually done

after the medal by a Venetian artist of the second half of the fifteenth century. This question remains open, and requires further study. See also Vickers 1978, pp. 417–24.
5. For a fuller study of Alberti and his portrait reliefs, see cat. no. 3. Pope-Hennessy 1963, pp. 66–69, already suggested that Alberti may have had a role in the invention of the Renaissance portrait medal, but made no direct mention of the fact that Alberti was actually present at the council in Ferrara along with Pisanello and John VIII Paleologo. Trenti Antonelli in *Le Muse . . .*, vol. 2, pp. 25–35, carries the argument much further by linking Pisanello with humanist culture in Ferrara and artistic activities in Florence, emphasizing in this context the writings of Alberti. None of these authors mention the important article by Samuel Edgerton that convincingly ties a drawing in the *Vallardi Codex*, Paris, no. 2520 (Fossi Todorow 1966, no. 99), attributed to Pisanello by some, but disputed by others, to Alberti's perspective theories as set forth in his *Della Pittura*. See Edgerton 1966, pp. 367–78, especially pp. 375–77. This discussion also brings up the question of where the medal was actually made, whether in Ferrara or Florence, and at exactly what date, 1438 or 1439. The details are summarized in Lorenzi 1983, pp. 9–13, with additional bibliography, including reference to the important contribution of Fasanelli 1965, pp. 36–47. See also Fossi Todorow 1966, pp. 30–31.
6. On Pisanello's handling of the space and composition of the reverse in relation to Alberti's theories, derived from his *Della Pittura* and from other sources, see Trenti Antonelli in *Le Muse . . .*, vol. 2, pp. 27–28, and Edgerton 1966, pp. 367–78.
7. For a fairly complete listing of works of art using the medallic portrait of the emperor, see R. Weiss 1966.

Additional literature: Hill and Pollard 1967, p. 7, no. 1; Pollard 1984–85, vol. 1, pp. 30–33; Johnson and Martini 1986, p. 94, nos. 413–14.

5, 5a
Pisanello
Leonello d'Este (Hill 1930, no. 32)

Notes:
1. For Leonello, see Gardner 1968 and Gundersheimer 1973.
2. Hill 1930, nos. 24–31.
3. Hill 1905, p. 146; Wind 1968, p. 98; Trenti Antonelli in *Le Muse . . .*, vol. 2, p. 33; Corradini in *Le Muse . . .*, vol. 1, no. 3, p. 62, and no. 8, p. 69.

Additional literature: Armand 1883–87, vol. 1, pp. 3–4, no. 8; Forrer 1904–30, vol. 4, pp. 564–81; Habich 1924, pp. 34–35, pl. III, 1; Hill 1930, no. 32; Venturi 1939, pp. 40–44; *Medaglie del Rinascimento*, pp. 25–26, no. 8; Pope-Hennessey 1966, pp. 69, 156; Salton 1969, p. 3, no. 4; Lorenzi 1983, no. 9; Johnson and Martini 1986, p. 92, nos. 403–4; *Da Pisanello . . .*, p. 105, no. 33.

6, 6a
Pisanello
Domenico Malatesta (Hill 1930, no. 35)

Notes:
1. Yriarte 1882, pp. 300–309, and 315–16.
2. P. Jones 1974; Ettlinger 1989, pp. 20–26.
3. Hill 1930, nos. 33–34 (dated 1445).
4. Ibid., nos. 19 (John VIII Paleologus, cat. no. 4), 20 (Gianfrancesco Gonzaga), 21 (Filippo Maria Visconti), 34 (Sigismondo Malatesta), and 36 (Lodovico Gonzaga).
5. Fossi Todorow 1966, pp. 25, 28, 32 (note 51), 35, 68, 72, and nos. 22, 31–32.

Additional literature: Hill 1905, pp. 165–68; Venturi 1939, pp. 46–47; Degenhart 1940, p. 41; Degenhart 1945, p. 43; Sindona 1961, p. 48; B. Degenhart in *Enciclopedia Universale dell'Arte*, vol. 10, pp. 613–15; Hill and Pollard 1967, no. 15; *Sigismondo . . .*, pp. 105–6; Chiarelli 1972, no. 103; Wixom 1975, nos. 20–21; Lorenzi 1983, no. 11; Pollard 1984–85, vol. 1, pp. 50–

52, no. 12; Johnson and Martini 1986, pp. 85–96, nos. 422–24; *Le Muse . . .* , vol. 1, p. 111, no. 27.

7, 7a
Pisanello
Cecilia Gonzaga (Hill 1930, no. 37)

Notes:
1. Quoted in Simon 1988, pp. 36–37.
2. For an eloquent testimony to her character, see Vespasiano 1963, pp. 411–12. See also *Splendours . . .* , p. 110, no. 16.
3. Ibid. This description is attributed to Francesco Prendilacqua, but without specific references.
4. Fossi Todorow 1966, pp. 24, 64, no. 14.
5. Fossi Todorow 1966, p. 129, no. 185; p. 130, no. 187; and pp. 133–34, no. 195. *Da Pisanello . . .* , pp. 93–97, nos. 23–25.
See also the references to these and other drawings based on classical sculpture and attributed to Pisanello or his workshop in Bober and Rubenstein 1986.

Additional literature: Armand 1883–87, vol. 1, p. 3, no. 12; Hill 1905, pp. 172–75; Habich 1924, p. 37; Venturi 1935 ("Su alcune"), p. 38; Venturi 1939, p. 49; Degenhart 1945, p. 43; Salmi 1957, p. 18; Tervarent 1958–64, vol. 2, p. 236; Magagnato 1958, p. 109, no. 126; Sindona 1961, p. 49; Magnaguti 1965, pp. 7–8, 90, no. 15; Hill and Pollard 1967, p. 10, no. 17; Panvini Rosati 1968, p. 21, no. 17; Chiarelli 1972, p. 101, no. 115; Paccagnini 1972, p. 115, no. 77; Zanoli 1973, pp. 31–32; *Splendours . . .* , p. 110, no. 16; Pollard 1984–85, vol. 1, p. 56, no. 14; Johnson and Martini 1986, p. 94, no. 416; *Da Pisanello . . .* , pp. 101–2, no. 29; Woods-Marsden 1988, pp. 36, 74, and 205, note 57. See also M. L. King 1988, pp. 434–53.

8, 8a
Pisanello
Vittorino Rambaldoni da Feltre (Hill 1930, no. 38)

Notes:
1. For Vittorino, see Woodward 1963; Symonds 1935, vol. 1, pp. 89, 90, 461–65; Bolgar 1964, pp. 258, 331–33; Baxandall 1971, pp. 127–29; Kohl 1988, pp. 14–17; Simon 1988, pp. 32–37; Woods-Marsden 1988, pp. 73–78, 83–84.
2. Vespasiano 1963, p. 410.
3. Ibid., p. 410, 413; Woods-Marsden 1988, p. 75.
4. Male 1984, pp. 44–45, 49.
See also Tervarent 1958–64, cols. 302–3, 304–6. In *Splendours . . .* , p. 109, no. 14, D. S. Chambers introduced the possibility that the bird on the reverse could also be a phoenix, a creature associated with Vittorino in other works of art. Chambers's observation is interesting, but he, too, concludes that the image is more likely a pelican.

Additional literature: Armand 1883–87, vol. 1, p. 8, no. 24; Hill 1905, pp. 175–77; Hill and Pollard 1967, p. 10, no. 18; Gomes Ferreira and Pereira Coutinho 1979, no. 6; Lorenzi 1983, nos. 14–15; Pollard 1984–85, vol. 1, pp. 57–59, nos. 15–15a; Johnson and Martini 1986, p. 98, nos. 435–36.

9, 9a
Pisanello
Don Iñigo de Avalos (Hill 1930, no. 44)

Notes:
1. Azure, a castle triple-towered or, a bordure compony argent and gules.
2. Candida Gonzaga 1875, pp. 101–4; Rastrelli 1896; Ryder 1976, especially p. 170 and note 6; Ravegnani Morosini 1984, vol. 1, pp. 1–3; Garcia Carraffa 1920, vol. 3, pp. 26–34; Bentley 1987, pp. 62–63; Ryder 1990.
3. Candida Gonzaga 1875, p. 101, and other sources mention the existence of an inscribed stone from the Roman period in the plaza at Calahor, on which appears the name of a Marcus Avalus, taken to be the progenitor of the line.
4. Ryder 1976, pp. 26, 273.
5. Ibid., p. 170, note 6, includes a quote from the *Diurnali*

detti del Duca di Monteleone (p. 129), where Don Iñigo is described as "home multo amato et intrinsico suo."
6. Ibid., p. 349.
7. Ibid., pp. 169–70. Although Ryder clearly indicates here that Avalos was named chamberlain on the death of d'Aquino in 1449, he earlier speaks of him (p. 143) as bearing that title in 1445. See also Candida Gonzaga 1875, pp. 101–3.
8. The younger Iñigo, who became fourth marquess of Vasto in 1497, died in 1502. His older brothers Alfonso and Rodrigo had preceded him in death in 1495 and 1497, respectively. It is of course an outside chance that it is he who appears on the medal, but on the one hand he was too young in 1449–50 and on the other there would scarcely have been as much reason to honor him at that time as there was his father.
9. Fossi Todorow 1966, no. 87, p. 93, with full bibliography up to 1966 and a discussion of the attributions.
10. For further references and a full text of the poem, see Friedländer 1880, pp. 17–18. See also Venturi 1896, p. 67, and Hill 1905, pp. 208–10. There are of course elements of the description of the shield that do correspond to Pisanello's globe; however, the shield as described by Homer presented many scenes and would bear no real resemblance to the globe on the Avalos reverse. Castaglione's poem was first published in Parma in 1660. The poet settled in Rome in 1582, and became governor of Corneto in 1598.
11. Hill 1905, p. 210.

Additional literature: Armand 1883–87, vol. 1, p. 2, no. 1; Hill and Pollard 1967, no. 22; Lorenzi 1983, no. 17; Pollard 1984–85, vol. 1, nos. 19–19a; Johnson and Martini 1986, nos. 398–99.

10
Unknown Ferrarese Master
Pisanello (Hill 1930, no. 87)

Notes:
1. Armand 1883–87, vol. 1, p. 9, no. 25.
2. Habich 1924, p. 41.
3. See Heiss 1881–92, vol. 1, p. 9.
4. Friedländer 1882, p. 41, no. 27; Hill and Pollard 1967, no. 32.
5. Armand 1883–87, vol. 1, p. 9, no. 26; Hill 1930, no. 77.

Additional literature: *Catalogue of the Vernon . . .* , no. 73; Zograf 1923, p. 8.

Matteo de' Pasti

Notes:
1. Pasini 1987, p. 156. For Pasti in general, see that article, pp. 143–59; C. Ricci 1974, pp. 35–60; Hill 1930, pp. 37–43.
2. For the letter, see Gilbert 1980, p. 6; Ames-Lewis 1984, pp. 351–61.
3. Pasini 1987, pp. 154–55.
4. On these issues see Middeldorf 1978, pp. 310–22 (1979–81, vol. 3, pp. 192–201); Pope-Hennessy 1985 (*Italian Renaissance*), pp. 73, 309, 312, 313–14, 361; Mitchell 1978, pp. 75, 80.
5. See C. Ricci 1974, p. 256.
6. Raby 1987, pp. 175–76, 187–88.
7. C. Ricci 1974, pp. 45 and 59, n. 51; the death date of c. 1490 given in Johnson and Martini 1986, p. 80, is unexplained.
8. Middeldorf 1978, p. 311 (1979–81, p. 193).

11, 11a
Matteo de' Pasti
Guarino da Verona (Hill 1930, no. 158)

Notes:
1. Pasini 1987, pp. 152 and 159, n. 37. On the development of fifteenth-century lettering, see Covi 1963, pp. 1–17, and Sperling 1989, pp. 221–28.
2. For Guarino, see Grendler 1989, especially pp. 29, 119–23, 133, and 167–69. The foundation of studies on him is Sabbadini 1896, of which Grendler, p. 457, cites later editions.
3. For Guarino's letters, see Sabbadini, ed. 1919. For

Guarino on the arts, see Baxandall 1971, pp. 78–96 and pl. 9b.
4. Gilbert 1980, pp. 171–73. See also Baxandall 1971, pp. 89–90, and *Le Muse . . .* , especially the essays by Antonia Tissoni Benvenuti, vol. 1, cat. 37, pp. 158–61, and vol. 2, pp. 322–23.
5. Baxandall 1971, p. 90.
6. Hill 1930, vol. 1, p. 37.
7. Sabbadini 1896 (1933, p. 27).
8. Ideal nudity and a Roman mantle had been used to exalt the subject of the earliest portrait medals, Francesco I Carrara of Padua, in 1390. See *Natur und Antike . . .* , cat. 33, pp. 343–44.
9. Pope-Hennessy 1966, p. 70, suggested this.
10. Tervarent 1958–64, col. 50.
11. Pasini 1987, p. 152, noted the influence of Ghiberti and Donatello on this medal.
12. Ghiberti says in his *Commentaries* that he set this gem about the same time he made the reliquary of Saints Protus, Hyacinthus, and Nemesius. For the quotation and date, see Krautheimer 1970, vol. 1, pp. 13 and 138–39.
13. F. Rossi 1989, p. 58, argues for continued Florentine ownership. Douglas Lewis, in his forthcoming catalogue of plaquettes in the National Gallery of Art, finds stronger evidence that it passed through the collection of Pope Paul II before coming to Lorenzo.
14. See Maffei 1731–32, vol. 2, pp. 137, 144, who cites this to explain the medal's reverse. His suggestion was traced by Nancy Brown Colvin, National Gallery of Art intern, in 1981.
15. See, for example, Tervarent 1958–64, cols. 231–32, and Trapp 1958, pp. 234ff.
16. Hill 1930, no. 161.
17. Pope-Hennessy 1966, p. 311, note 9, notes arguments for dates c. 1440–44, 1446, and c. 1452. Hill 1930, vol. 1, p. 38, favored c. 1446 in Ferrara. Pasini 1987, pp. 150–52, argues for c. 1455, in relation to Matteo's Riminese medals.
18. Hill 1931 ("A Lost Medal"), pp. 487–88.

Additional literature: Migeon 1908, p. 10, no. x, p. 15; Hill 1931 (*Dreyfus*), p. 34, no. 55, pl. XVI; Cott 1951, pp. 103, 164; Hill and Pollard 1967, pp. 15–16, no. 55; Baxandall 1971, pl. 9b; Sheard 1978, no. 83; Wilson 1983, p. 23.

12, 12a, 13
Matteo de' Pasti
Isotta degli Atti of Rimini (Hill 1930, nos. 167 and 187)

Notes
1. For the *giornea*, see Levi Pisetzky 1964–69, vol. 2, p. 249 and pls. 101, 136; for the *gamurra* or its lighter summer version, the *cotta*, ibid., pp. 230, 246–47, 252; and for the hairstyle, ibid., pp. 288–92. See also Herald 1981, pp. 47–48, 50, 105.
2. For Isotta, see Augusto Campana's "Atti, Isotta degli," in *Dizionario Biografico . . .* , vol. 4, pp. 547–56. For Sigismondo as an early patron of the art of the medal, see Ettlinger 1989, especially pp. 173–87, 256. See also Pasini 1987.
3. Hill 1930 illustrates nine different types, nos. 167–71, 173, and 187–89. Hill no. 169 is dated 1447, the year in which Isotta's first child Giovanni was born. Campana (see note 2), p. 554, alludes to two dated 1447.
4. On the dating, see Pope-Hennessy 1985 (*Italian Renaissance*), p. 313, and Pasini 1987, p. 147. For Isotta's tomb and its inscription, subsequently covered by a different inscription in bronze, see C. Ricci 1924, pp. 436–37, 446, fig. 534. Pasini dates this medal to 1453, but the date 1449/50, as a counterpart to face Hill 174 (for instance) of Sigismondo in nearly identical costume, seems equally likely. Ettlinger 1989, pp. 182–84, has argued that designs for Hill nos. 163, 165, and 174 of Sigismondo must predate December 1447, after which date Sigismondo ceased to act as captain general of the Church.
5. Polissena probably died of plague rather than being murdered. See P. Jones 1974, pp. 201–2.
6. Ettlinger 1989, pp. 2–3, 151–52.
7. Pasini 1983, pp. 144 (the tower) and 143 (Mengozzi's collection); Campana (see note 2), p. 548.

8. Pasini 1987, p. 147. Elephants occur frequently on Greek and Roman coins. See Vermeule 1987, pp. 272–74, or the coin of Scipio Africanus in Belloni 1977, p. 91, no. 272.
9. Tervarent 1958–64, cols. 153–54; Pasini 1987, p. 147.
10. Hill 1930, no. 178. On the elephant as symbol of fame thanks to its longevity, excellent memory, and ability to trumpet, see White 1974, p. 209. For a connection with Sigismondo's putative descent from the Roman hero Scipio Africanus, see Pasini 1987, p. 147.
11. Pasini 1983, p. 144.
12. See Tervarent 1958–64, col. 154. Also Börner 1976, pp. 199–200, and Elena Corradini in Le Muse . . . , vol. 1, pp. 106–7.
13. C. Ricci 1924, pp. 314–15.

Additional literature: Migeon 1908, p. 10, no. viii, and p. 15; Hill 1931 (Dreyfus), p. 36, no. 59, pl. VII; Cott 1951, pp. 103, 164; Hill and Pollard 1967, p. 16, no. 59; Pasini 1992, nos. 2.22 and 6.13–14.

14, 14a
Matteo de' Pasti
Sigismondo Pandolfo Malatesta (Hill 1930, no. 186)

Notes:
1. Gabel, ed. 1959, pp. 110–11, 184–85. Ettlinger 1989, chapter 1, offers a good synopsis of the historical treatment of Sigismondo. For further biographical material, see P. Jones 1974. Somewhat out of date, but still useful, is Yriarte 1882.
2. Ettlinger 1989, pp. 20ff.
3. Ibid., pp. 86–108. Above the main entrance of the castle Sigismondo placed an inscription on a marble plaque that is still *in situ*: It reads: "This fortress, the glory of Rimini, Sigismondo Pandolfo Malatesta, son of Pandolfo, has newly erected and constructed from the foundations. And furthermore, he has ordered the castle to be called by his name, Sismundum. 1446."
4. On the foundation medals, see Pasini 1983, pp. 140–47; A. Turchini in *Castel Sismondo*, pp. 131–45; Woods-Marsden 1989, pp. 387–414, especially pp. 400–402 and notes 65–72; Ettlinger 1989, pp. 170–87.
5. For more detailed discussions of these differences, see Hill 1930; Pasini 1983 and 1987; Ettlinger 1989; and Woods-Marsden 1989.
6. See also M. A. Lavin 1974, pp. 345–74.

Additional literature: Le Muse . . . , vol. 1, pp. 108–9, no. 25, and vol. 2, pp. 25–35; Pasini 1992, no. 2.20–21.

Bartolo Talpa

Notes:
1. D'Arco 1857, pp. 32, 36.
2. Hill 1930, nos. 204–5.

15
Bartolo Talpa
Federigo I Gonzaga (Hill 1930, no. 204)

Notes:
1. Commissioned by Lodovico III. Begun in 1465 and completed in 1474, they depict scenes from the life of Lodovico, his wife Barbara of Brandenburg, and their family. The *Meeting Scene*, to the left of the entrance door, was probably the last to be completed.
2. Constructed between 1395 and 1406 by Bartolino da Novara (active 1368–c. 1410).
3. Francesco was elevated to cardinal in 1461, at the age of seventeen, and appointed papal legate to Bologna in 1471. He is portrayed on a medal by Sperandio (Hill 1930, no. 390) considered by several writers to be a memorial from 1483.
4. Thode 1897, pp. 63, 66.
5. *Corpus Nummorum Italicorum*, vol. 4, p. 235, no. 1, pl. XX, no. 14: ducato (the only coin struck for Federigo) by an unidentified die-engraver.
6. Ibid., pl. XXIII, no. 14.
7. Hill 1930, no. 203.
8. Ibid., no. 205.
9. Armand 1883–87, vol. 1, pp. 82–83.
10. For the Gonzaga, see Schivenoglia 1857; Hofmann 1881 (Barbara of Brandenburg); Lanzoni 1898;

Brington 1927; Amadei 1955; Coniglio 1967; *Splendours . . .* , was introduced to Italian language and culture by no less a luminary than Vittorino Rambaldoni da Feltre (cat. no. 8).
11. Schivenoglia 1857, pp. 153, 157.]
12. Gianfrancesco, together with Cardinal Francesco, was given Bozzolo, Gazzuolo, Isola Dovarese, Rivarolo, Sabbioneta, San Martino dell'Argine, and Viadena, while Rodolfo and Lodovico, a "pronotario apostolico," succeeded to Canneto, Castelgoffredo, Castiglione delle Stiviere, Ostrano, Redondesco, and Solferino. Solferino, however, was to remain under Federigo's military control.
13. Federigo's appointed administrators were Eusebio Malatesta, his brother-in-law Francesco Secco, and Evangelisto Gonzaga, a natural son of his uncle Carlo.
14. Isabella's portrait appears on a medal by Giancristoforo Romano (Hill 1930, no. 221) and, together with Francesco II, on another by an unidentified Mantuan artist (Hill 1930, no. 239).

Additional literature: Supino 1899; Forrer 1904–30, vol. 4, pp. 9–13; Fabriczy 1904, p. 49; Habich 1924, pp. 76–77.

Pier Jacopo di Antonio Alari Bonacolsi, called Antico

Note:
1. U. Rossi 1888. ("I medaglisti").

Additional literature: Thieme-Becker, vol. 1, pp. 555–56; M. Chiarini in *Dizionario Biografico . . .* , vol. 1, columns 580–82; L. Börner in *Saur, Allgemeines Künstler-Lexikon*, vol. 4, pp. 262–64.

16, 16a
Antico
Gianfrancesco Gonzaga (Hill 1930, no. 206)

Notes:
1. For the role of the Gonzaga as patrons of the arts, see *Splendours . . .* . For the Antico medals included in that exhibition, see nos. 49–50, by Anthony F. Radcliffe.
2. Regarding the life and career of Gianfrancesco Gonzaga, see Litta et al. 1819–83, vol. 4, pl. 14; *Splendours . . .* , nos. 47–50; and Allison 1986, pp. 9–13.
3. See U. Rossi 1888 ("I medaglisti"), pp. 161–94 and 433–38, and Hermann 1910, pp. 202–5, 209, 217–19, and 221–30.
4. Allison 1986, pp. 9–13.
5. Ibid., fig. 6, pp. 10–11.
6. For these medals, see Hermann 1910, pp. 223–24 and 227–28, and Hill 1930, nos. 207–10. For the Gonzaga *imprese*, see Mario Praz in *Splendours . . .* , pp. 64–72.
7. Hermann 1910, pp. 222–23, chooses to see the figures as Minerva and probably Mars. Hill 1930, no. 206, is more cautious, and questions both identifications. Subsequent authorities categorically refer to the figures as Mars and Minerva. This reverse served as the source for a marble relief on the portal of the Palazzo Stanga in Cremona, now in the Louvre. See U. Rossi 1888 ("I medaglisti"), p. 163, and Hermann 1910, fig. 6, pp. 223 and 230.
8. I am indebted for this tentative interpretation to Professors Jennifer Neils and Donald R. Laing, Jr., of Case Western Reserve University in Cleveland, who also assisted with the translation of the legends on these medals.

Additional literature: Armand 1883–87, vol. 1, p. 62, no. I; Hill 1931 (Dreyfus), no. 71; Cott 1951, p. 165; Hill and Pollard 1967, no. 71; Lewis 1987, fig. 1, pp. 78, 80, 82, 84, 89, 93 (note 11), 94 (note 27), and 95 (note 41).

17, 17a
Antico
Diva Giulia (Hill 1930, no. 214)

Notes:
1. See Hill 1920 (*Medals*), p. 51; Hill 1923 ("L'ecole"), p. 16; and Hill 1930, no. 214.

2. Allison 1986, p. 12.
3. Ibid. The sarcophagus was formerly in the church of Saints Cosmas and Damian in Rome.
4. Illustrated and discussed in Bober and Rubinstein 1986, p. 154, and Paolucci 1988, p. 50.
5. Lewis 1987, pp. 77–97.
6. Ibid., p. 95, note 50. I am grateful to Paul Connor of the Library of Congress, Washington; Stephen N. Fliegel and Bruce Christman of The Cleveland Museum of Art; and Donald Myers and especially Dr. Douglas Lewis of The National Gallery of Art, Washington, for helping me to compile these entries on Antico's medals.

Additional literature: His de la Salle sale, 1880, lot 174; Hill 1931 (Dreyfus), no. 73; Cott 1951, p. 165; Pope-Hennessy 1965, no. 186; Hill and Pollard 1967, no. 73; Lewis 1989, pp. 109, 134, note 45, and 134, note 46.

Galeazzo Mondella, called Moderno

Literature: Rognini 1975, pp. 95–119; Lewis 1987, pp. 77–97; Lewis 1989, pp. 105–141.

18, 18a
Attributed to Moderno
Magdalena Mantuana (Hill 1930, no. 215)

Notes:
1. Hill 1930, no. 215, refers to this as "the verge of a folliot balance (?)."
2. Ibid.; Hill and Pollard 1967, p. 19, no. 73a.
3. Lewis 1987, pp. 77–97.
4. An uninscribed uniface plaquette of the allegory alone (in a unique example) is in the Staatliche Museen, Berlin. See Bange 1922, p. 73, no. 532, pl. 49, and Lewis 1989, p. 122, fig. 2. Hill 1930, no. 215, described the allegory thus: "Occasion . . . *fronte capillata*, . . . attempting to seize . . . Time." His reference is to a famous distich by Cato: "Rem tibi quam nosces aptam dimittere noli: Fronte capillata, post est occasio calva." See Wittkower 1977, pp. 97–106 and 207–8, especially p. 207, note 11. On the advice of Virginia W. Callahan, to whom I am indebted—as so often—for the translation of the inscription at the head of this entry, I have followed Cicero (De Inventione I, 27) in choosing the term "Opportunity."
5. Lewis 1987, p. 88, fig. 17; Lewis 1989, p. 122, fig. 24.
6. Pope-Hennessy 1965, p. 51, no. 165, fig. 161; Lewis 1989, p. 123, fig. 26.
7. Pope-Hennessy 1965, p. 47, no. 150, fig. 176; Lewis 1989, pp. 120–21, fig. 18.
8. Pope-Hennessy 1965, p. 49, no. 159, fig. 162; Lewis 1989, p. 123, fig. 27.
9. The sitter for this portrait has not been identified; but the resulting work of art is so important (in addition to having been so costly to produce), and so clearly displays the hand of a major artistic intelligence, that I am tempted to ask why it might not represent the noble lady Magdalena de' Gonzaga, who in 1489 married Giovanni Sforza (1466–1510), lord of Pesaro from 1483 to 1500 and again from 1503 to 1510. Her fully documented likeness on a medal signed by Melioli (Hill 1930, no. 197) is close enough to make the hypothesis plausible, and the circumstances of her husband's having been ousted by Cesare Borgia in the years 1500–1503 and his opportune return just before the creation of this medal seem well worth considering in this context.
10. Hill 1930, no. 215; Lewis 1987, p. 87, fig. 13.
11. Hill 1930, no. 216. A "fine old cast" reappeared at Sotheby's, London, on April 10, 1992, lot 453, and is now in a private collection in the United States.
12. Hill 1930, no. 236; Hill and Pollard 1967, no. 82.
13. Hill 1930, no. 237.
14. Hill 1930, nos. 234–35, notes, and no. 236, note (the source of the formula quoted here); Lewis 1987, pp. 88–89.

Additional literature: Armand 1883–87, vol. 1, pp. 100–

101, no. 11; Keary 1893, p. 36, no. 84; *Catalogo delle . . . Medaglie*, no. 380; Supino 1899, no. 667, pl. 51, fig. 1; Hermann 1910, pp. 226–27, no. 7, pl. 34, fig. 6; *Select Italian Medals*, pl. 19, fig. 3; Hill 1923 ("L'ecole"), p. 17, pl. 3, fig. 1; Habich 1924, p. 88, pl. 63, fig. 5; *Erwerbungsberichte 1924–26*, pl. 4, fig. 2; Cott 1951, p. 165; Pollard 1984–85, vol. 1, p. 145, no. 57.

19, 19a
Mantuan School ("manner of Antico")
Giulia Astallia (Hill 1930, no. 218)

Notes:

1. For the *gamurra*, see Levi Pisetzky 1964–69, vol. 2, pp. 246–47, and for closely related costumes, p. 230, pl. 98, and especially p. 233, pl. 100.
2. Hill and Pollard 1978, pp. 49–50.
3. Friedländer 1880, p. 129, suggests that the time and place connect with Talpa, but that the portrait is too good and individual for him.
4. Armand 1883–87, vol. 1, p. 83, no. 3; U. Rossi 1890, pp. 30–31; and Fabriczy 1904, p. 49, give the work to Talpa without hesitation, while Bode 1904, p. 37, voices doubts.
5. Hill and Pollard 1978, pp. 49–50 ("by or very near Antico"); Hill 1930, no. 218 ("Mantuan school in the manner of Antico"); M. Jones 1979 (*Art*), p. 32, illus. 61b, pl. 61a ("attributed to Antico").
6. Bode 1904, p. 37, singling out "the style of Sandro and Ghirlandaio"; Hill and Pollard 1978, p. 49. For the pose, see especially the portrait of a lady in yellow, sometimes attributed to Baldovinetti, c. 1465, in Levi Pisetzky 1964–69, vol. 1, pl. 131, and Davies 1971, p. 42, no. 758, as well as the portrait in the Staatliche Museen, Berlin, controversially attributed to Antonio del Pollaiuolo, c. 1465 (Busignani 1970, pp. 44–45).
7. *Chantilly, Musée Condé*, pp. 118–20, no. 62, the "Simonetta" as an early work of Piero, c. 1480.
8. Bode 1904, p. 37 follows this line of thinking.
9. Friedländer 1880, p. 129. U. Rossi 1890, pp. 30–31, cited Friedländer, yet claimed this proposal as his own. For Giulia of Gazzuolo, see Bandello 1928–31, vol. 1, pp. 114–20. As Habich noted, the story is retold in Baldassare Castiglione's *Il Cortegiano*, with the implication that it occurred shortly before the death of Lodovico Gonzaga, and that the girl's name was already forgotten. See Castiglione 1901, pp. 214–15 and 403, note 16.
10. In a hand annotation on p. 54 of his copy of Hill 1930, now in the National Gallery of Art library, Pollard observed that the Astalli are a Roman family. On the Astalli, see Amayden 1979, vol. 1, pp. 85–88, and Pietrangeli 1968, pp. 6–13. Tacchi-Venturi 1899, p. 308, mentions a fifth-century ancestor called Iulio de Astallis, and on p. 310 relates that by 1526 at least twelve Astalli had been buried in the church of S. Maria degli Astalli, or della Strada, formerly on the site of the Gesù. Frommel 1973, vol. 1, p. 130, reports that a Giulia Astalli (widow d'Aragona) was still living in 1590. Notes from the Biblioteca Vaticana, D. Iacovacci, *Repertorii di Famiglie*, Ott. Lat. 2548, part 2, p. 899, relate to the settlement of a lawsuit involving a Iuliana de Astallis in 1482. I am grateful to Deborah Wilde for bibliographic guidance on the above.
11. See Shearman 1986, pp. 45–47. The costume and coiffure would generally accord with the 1470s or 1480s (Bode proposed c. 1475). The style corresponds tantalizingly to that of the young girl in a red gown at the left of Ghirlandaio's *Calling of the Apostles*, ibid., p. 60.
12. Tervarent 1958–64, cols. 305–6, and van Broek 1972, pp. 146–47, 357–58.
13. Sigismondo della Stufa, the grieving fiancé of Albiera degli Albizzi, who died aged fifteen in 1472, gathered poems in tribute to her, including one on her marble portrait bust. See I. Lavin 1970, pp. 214 and 226, notes 46, 47. The medal could have been a tribute to Giulia Astallia under similar circumstances.

Additional literature: Migeon 1908, p. 13, no. xxii; Hill 1920 (*Medals*), pp. 49–50; Habich 1924, pl. lv, 1; Hill 1931 (*Dreyfus*), p. 45; Cott 1951, p. 165; Hill and Pollard 1967, p. 19, note 75; Pollard 1984–85, vol. 1, pp. 145–47.

20
Mantuan School
Jacoba Correggia (Hill 1930, no. 234)

Notes:

1. Hill 1920 (Hill and Pollard 1978, p. 51) viewed it with "unalloyed pleasure," and found it "delicious." Hill 1930, no. 234, calls it "one of the loveliest of medals."
2. Hill 1930, no. 236, note.
3. Ibid., nos. 992 and 1011; Lewis 1987, p. 88, fig. 16.
4. Pope-Hennessy 1965, p. 53, no. 175, fig. 190; Lewis 1987, p. 88, fig. 17; Lewis 1989, p. 122, fig. 24.
5. Hill 1930, no. 233. The Melioli attribution was first proposed in Foville 1908, pp. 385–93. Hill 1920 (Hill and Pollard 1978, p. 52) doubted that suggestion, but I would tentatively propose reviving it. For Melioli, compare Hill 1930, vol. 2, pls. 36–37.
6. Hill 1930, no. 235; Hill and Pollard 1967, p. 128, and fig. 81.
7. Specifically, the portrait type is a direct descendent of Antico's medal of Antonia del Balzo. See Hill 1930, no. 212; Lewis 1987, p. 88.
8. Hill 1930, no. 236, note.
9. This was suggested to the author by William S. Heckscher.
10. In letters to the author, Virginia W. Callahan suggested this preferred reading. I am extremely grateful for her help, together with that of William S. Heckscher, in solving this puzzle. It has only now come to my attention that Foville 1908, p. 387, note 1, arrived at precisely this same reading "pro meritis" as a probable translation of the ancient Greco-Roman glyptic inscription ΔΙΚΑΩΣ on gems depicting "captive Love."

Additional literature: *Trésor des Numismatiques . . .* (Italian) vol. 1, p. 28, pl. 34, fig. 4; Friedländer 1880, pp. 166–68, no. 4, pl. 32, fig. 4; Keary 1881, p. 36, no. 82; Heiss 1881–92, vol. 9, p. 45, pl. 5, fig. 1; Armand 1883–87, vol. 1, p. 118, no. 1; Fau sale, 1884, no. 440; Supino 1899, no. 239; Migeon 1908, pp. 1–32, pl. 12, fig. 4; *Select Italian Medals*, pl. 19, fig. 2; Hill 1923 (*Guide*), p. 17, fig. 15 (from a cast); Hill 1923 ("L'ecole"), pp. 19–20, pl. 3, fig. 5; Habich 1924, p. 93, pl. 58, fig. 6; Cott 1951, p. 166; Pollard 1984–85, vol. 1, p. 151, no. 63, illus. p. 152; Lawe 1990, pp. 233–45, figs. 32–33;

Costanzo da Ferrara

Notes:

1. For discussion of a typical misattribution, see Klinger and Raby 1987.
2. "Uno pictore de quelli dal Canto di qua."
3. Venturi 1891, pp. 374–75. For Costanzo's biography, see G. F. Hill's article in Thieme-Becker; Andaloro 1980, pp. 185–212; and A. S. Norris's article in *Dizionario Biografico. . . .*
4. Filangieri 1883–97, vol. 6, pp. 198, 230, and 236; Nicolini 1925, pp. 246–49.
5. Andaloro 1980, p. 188, note 18; Fabriczy 1897, p. 97. On La Duchesca, see Hersey 1969, pp. 70–71.
6. Andaloro 1980. But see Raby 1980 for different attributions.
7. Gray 1932, pp. 4–6; Atil 1973, pp. 104–20; Raby 1980.
8. Fabriczy 1907, pp. 149–59.
9. Karabacek 1918; Atil 1973, pp. 104–20; Meyer zur Capellen 1985, pp. 97, 168–70, nos. E 5–8 and E 12–14; Raby in *Circa 1492 . . .* , p. 212, no. 108.
10. Sarre 1906, pp. 302–6; Sarre 1907, pp. 51–52.
11. F. R. Martin 1910, pp. 5–6; Atil 1973; Canby 1983, pp. 5–13, especially p. 11.

21
Costanzo da Ferrara
Mehmed II (Hill 1930, no. 321)

Notes:

1. Meyer zur Capellen 1985, pp. 128–28, no. A 10.
2. Hill 1930, no. 322; Raby 1987, pp. 176–78; *Eredità . . .* , no. 62.
3. For the Mantuan ambassador, see Pastor 1959, vol. 3, p. 259; regarding Giovio and Vasari, see A. S. Norris's

article "Costanzo" in *Dizionario Biografico . . .* , vol. 30, pp. 395.
4. Sakisian 1939, pp. 172–81; *Gli Uffizi*; Kenner 1898.

Additional literature: Venturi 1891, pp. 374–75; Hill 1926, pp. 287–98; Gray 1932, pp. 4–6; Hill and Pollard 1967, no. 102; Raby in *Circa 1492 . . .* , p. 211.

Adriano Fiorentino

Literature: Fabriczy 1903, pp. 71–98; Draper 1992, pp. 43–52.

22, 22a
Adriano Fiorentino
Elisabetta Gonzaga (Hill 1930, no. 344)

Notes:

1. Fabriczy 1903, p. 82.
2. Hill 1930, no. 345.
3. Settis 1985, p. 237, notes 89–90.

Additional literature: *Splendours . . .* , no. 83.

Sperandio of Mantua

Notes:

1. Venturi 1888 ("Sperandio"), p. 386, notes 3–4.
2. Ibid., pp. 391–92, and Malagola 1888.
3. Venturi 1888 ("Sperandio"), pp. 391–92, note 6.
4. U. Rossi 1886–87, pp. 89–90.
5. Foville 1914, p. 433.
6. Venturi 1888 ("Sperandio"), p. 385.
7. Venturi 1889, p. 229.
8. Venturi 1888 ("Sperandio"), p. 387, notes 1–3.
9. "Per Sperandio da Mantova," pp. 143–44.
10. Venturi 1885, pp. 278–79.
11. Ruhmer 1960, pp. 20–21.
12. Malaguzzi Valeri 1896, pp. 84–86.
13. Ibid., p. 86.
14. Hill 1930, p. 90.
15. Ibid., nos. 400–401.

Additional literature: Mackowsky 1898; Foville 1910; Forrer 1904–30, vol. 5, pp. 592–93; Hill 1930, pp. 89–103; Weinberger 1930, pp. 293–318; Cora 1950, pp. 108–10; Gans 1969; Middeldorf and Stiebral 1983, pp. xxxi–xxxiii; *Splendors . . .* , p. 130; Boccolari 1987, pp. 68, 76, 82; Lloyd 1987, pp. 99–113. For drawings (questionably) attributed to Sperandio, see Hill 1909–10, pp. 24–25; Williamson 1918, pp. 64–66; and *Recent Acquisitions . . .* , p. 48, no. 13.

23, 23a
Sperandio
Bartolommeo Pendaglia (Hill 1930, no. 356)

Notes:

1. Pardi, ed. n.d., p. 34, note 1.
2. Dean 1988, p. 136.
3. *Quattro Canti del Magnifico Sgr Bartolomeo Pendaglia* (Ferrara, 1563), pp. 9–10.
4. Tagliati 1977, p. 66, note 26.
5. Dean 1988, p. 60.
6. Tagliati 1977, p. 66, note 26.
7. Ibid., p. 11.
8. Gundersheimer 1973, p. 153. For sources on the wedding, see Pardi, ed. n.d., pp. 34–35, and Maresti 1681, who gives a surprisingly complete bibliography for the event.
9. Ibid., p. 41.
10. Piromalli 1975, p. 94.
11. Lloyd 1987, p. 101.

Additional literature: Middeldorf and Goetz 1944, p. 8, no. 45; Hill and Pollard 1967, no. 112; Pollard 1984–85, vol. 1, no. 95; Johnson and Martini 1986, p. 114, nos. 513–14.

24, 24a
Sperandio
Giovanni Bentivoglio (Hill 1930, no. 391)

Notes:

1. Per bend indented or and gules, called in Bologna the

"sega rossi di setti denti" (red saw with seven teeth), and this *sega* or *sera* was the family badge. I am grateful to Stephen K. Scher for blasoning these arms.

2. See, for example, Hill 1930, no. 391.

3. Bentivoglio's bibliography is surprisingly short. The most recent and complete account of his life is G. de Caro's article in the *Dizionario Biografico* . . . , vol. 8, pp. 622–32, on which the present summary is largely based. See also Bocchi 1970.

4. Frati 1900.

5. Fabriczy 1904, p. 92.

6. Foville 1910, p. 56.

7. Hill 1930, no. 391

8. See, for example, the bas-relief portrait in the Bentivoglio chapel at San Giacomo Maggiore. For an analysis of that portrait, see Roversi 1982, pp. 322–23. For later medals, see Hill 1930, nos. 605–7.

Additional literature: Hill and Pollard 1967, no. 128; Pollard 1984–85, vol. 1, p. 224, no. 110; Johnson and Martini 1986, p. 106, nos. 466–70; and C. Johnson 1990, vol. 1, p. 48, no. 27.

25, 25a
Sperandio
Federigo da Montefeltro (Hill 1930, no. 389)

Note:

1. The most recent life of Federigo is Tommasoli 1978. Contemporary biographies include Paltroni 1966; Guerrino da Gubbio 1902; and Vespasiano da Bisticci 1951. See also Dennistoun of Dennistoun 1909. For Federigo as patron, see Clough 1973.

Additional literature: Reposati 1772, vol. 1, pp. 251–52; Cicognara 1824, vol. 5, p. 411; Cucci 1968; Franceschini 1970, p. 480; Pollard 1984–85, vol. 1, p. 220, no. 108; Johnson and Martini 1986, p. 113, nos. 509–11; C. Johnson 1990, p. 52, no. 30; *Eredità* . . . , no. 55.

26
Sperandio
Carlo Grati (Hill 1930, no. 392)

Notes:

1. For Giacomo Grati, see Malvezzi 1879. Dolfi 1670, p. 400, makes it clear that the change of name was at the suggestion of the emperor, though it is true that such changes were always permitted with knighthood.

2. Dolfi 1670, p. 399. Cuppini 1974, p. 299, discusses the family's actual origins and the construction of its palace.

3. Roversi 1982, p. 374, provides information about Andrea di Giacomo Grati.

4. Roversi, ibid., makes the point that the tomb inscription for Giacomo and Andrea Grati emphasizes their ties to the Bentivoglio family and to Giovanni II Bentivoglio in particular.

5. L. A. Muratori, ed. n.d., p. 107, lines 41–42.

6. Ibid., p. 115, lines 4–6.

7. Dolfi 1670, p. 402.

Additional literature: Lorenzi 1983, no. 38.

Giovanni (Zuan) di Pasqualino Boldù

Notes:

1. Hill 1930, p. 110.

2. Hill 1930, pp. 110-11, nos. 416 (Pietro Bono), 417 (Filippo Maserano), 418 (Nicolas Schlifer), 419 (Filippo de' Vadi), 420 (self-portrait), and 421 (self-portrait *all'antica*); Gruyer 1897, vol. 1, pp. 611-12.

27
Boldù
Self-portrait *all'antica* (Hill 1930, no. 421)

Notes:

1. See Scher et al. 1986, pp. 90–91. Page 80 of that article presents a table showing the exact X-ray fluorescence analysis.

2. Hill 1930, no. 420.

---

3. See F. P. Weber 1910, pp. 65–67; Janson 1937, pp. 423–49; Levin 1975, p. 118, no. 84; Sheard 1978, no. 80.

4. Hill 1930, no. 407.

5. See Tervarent 1958–64, col. 374; F. P. Weber 1910, p. 118.

6. Tervarent 1958–64, col. 374.

7. Hill 1930, no. 423.

8. See Morscheck 1978, pp. 244–50.

Additional literature: Hill and Pollard 1967, no. 142; Pollard 1984–85, vol. 1, pp. 246–52, no. 119; Himmelmann 1985, pp. 1–28; Johnson and Martini 1986, pp. 12–14, nos. 46–56.

Vettor Gambello

Notes:

1. Hill 1930, p. 115.

2. Thieme-Becker, vol. 13, p. 140.

3. Hill 1930, nos. 437, 444, and 445.

4. Ibid., nos. 439 and 438.

5. Ibid., p. 115: "*Gambello* is the Venetian dialect form for *camelus* (camel); the artist signs himself *Camelius* (not *Camelus*, as often stated)."

6. Cited in McCrory 1987, p. 119.

7. Ibid.

8. Hill 1930, no. 446.

9. Thieme-Becker, vol. 13, p. 140.

28
Vettor Gambello
Giovanni Bellini (Hill 1930, no. 438)

Notes:

1. All three are discussed in Rapp 1987, pp. 365–68.

2. Hill 1912 (*Portrait*), p. 39.

3. Habich 1924, p. 94.

4. Rapp 1987, p. 368.

5. Quoted in Wilde 1974, p. 42.

6. Quoted in the "Bellini" entry of the *Enciclopedia italiana*, vol. 6.

7. See Cunnally 1984, pp. 117–18.

Additional literature: Hill 1931 (*Dreyfus*), no. 146; Goldschneider 1952, p. 7; Terverant 1958–64, vol. 1–2, p. 96; Hill and Pollard 1967, no. 146; G. Robertson 1968, p. 75; Salton 1969, no. 19; Pastoureau 1986, p. 4; Goffen 1989, p. 293, note 7.

Fra Antonio da Brescia

Notes:

1. Hill 1930, pp. 123–24; Hill 1933, pp. 483–85; Peroni 1963, vol. 2, pp. 819 and 825–27; and F. Rossi 1977, pp. 122–23.

2. Hill 1930, p. 124. Papafava died in 1487, and Savorgnan defended Osopo in 1514, an event to which the reverse of his medal refers.

3. Ibid., nos. 471–74.

4. Ibid., p. 125.

5. Habich 1924, p. 59, suggests he may have been trained as a sculptor, a conjecture that awaits confirmation by the discovery of works bearing signatures like those on the medals.

29
Fra Antonio da Brescia
Niccolò Michiel and Dea Contarini (Hill 1930, no. 471)

Notes:

1. Fabriczy 1903, p. 37.

2. Peroni 1963, p. 826.

3. Moureyre-Gavoty 1975, no. 162, presents a marble relief believed to have been carved in Venice in the early sixteenth century after Fra Antonio da Brescia's medal of Niccolò Michiel. It is more likely that Niccolò is portrayed on the companion relief (no. 161), which Moureyre-Gavoty identifies as a likeness of his son Simone.

4. Sanuto 1879–1903, vol. 25, p. 426, praises his wisdom and describes his humanist burial in SS Giovanni e Paolo "with books above his head and at his feet."

5. Douglas Lewis has kindly shared this information from his unpublished *Preliminary Research on Subjects of Venetian Medals*, 1983.

---

6. Sanuto 1879–1903, vol. 3, p. 471.

7. Ibid., p. 176.

8. Ibid., pp. 172–75.

9. Newton 1988, p. 59.

10. Sanuto 1879–1903, vol. 11, pp. 796–99.

Additional literature: M. Jones 1979 (*Art*), p. 35.

Maffeo Olivieri

Notes:

1. Passamani 1967, p. 127.

2. Sanuto 1879–1903, vol. 46, p. 405. The candlesticks are now in the left transept of San Marco.

3. The crucifix has been restored, and was published in Redona 1985.

4. Papaleoni 1913, p. 76. Excellent photographs of the Condino altarpiece are in Castelnuovo 1989.

5. Bode 1907–12, pp. 79–81; Planiscig 1932, pp. 34–55.

6. F. Rossi 1977, pp. 115–34; Boselli 1977, vol. 2, pp. 34–35; Redona 1985, p. 8.

7. Hill 1930, pp. 126–30.

8. Boselli 1977, vol. 2, pp. 74–75.

30
Maffeo Olivieri
Altobello Averoldo (Hill 1930, no. 486)

Notes:

1. Bode 1904, p. 40.

2. Max Rosenheim in *Catalogue of the Winter* . . . , p. 50; Hill in *Catalogue of a Collection* . . . , p. 100.

3. Sanuto 1879–1903, vol. 1, p. 826.

4. Gaeta in *Dizionario Biografico* . . . , pp. 667–68.

5. Pialorsi 1989, p. 16, no. 6.

6. Sanuto 1979–1903, vol. 25, p. 610, and vol. 28, p. 273.

7. Ibid., vol. 25, pp. 268, 420, 295, and 522.

Additional literature: Planiscig 1932, p. 54; Pialorsi 1991, pp. 81–86.

31, 31a
Maffeo Olivieri
Jacopo Loredano (Hill 1930, no. 487)

Notes:

1. Loredano's death date is recorded in an eighteenth-century manuscript copy of Marco Barbaro's *Genealogie delle famiglie patrizie venete*, preserved in the Biblioteca Nazionale Marciana, Venice.

2. Hill 1930, nos. 482–83.

3. Davenport 1948, p. 495

4. Cicogna 1827–34, vol. 2, p. 283, where Marco Barbaro's *Alberi* is given as a source.

5. Pope-Hennessy 1985 (*Review*), p. 55.

6. Jacopo di Giovanni should not be confused with two other contemporary Venetians who bore the name Jacopo Loredano and also held offices.

7. Cicogna 1827–34, vol. 2, p. 283.

8. Ibid.

9. Sanuto 1879–1903, vol. 8, pp. 156, 162, and 461.

10. Cicogna 1827–34, vol. 2, p. 283.

11. Ibid., vol. 4, pp. 668–669.

Additional literature: Peroni 1963, p. 818.

32
Venetian School
Eustachio di Francesco Boiano (Hill 1930, no. 525)

Notes:

1. Ostermann 1888, p. 206.

2. Hill and Pollard 1967, no. 495.

3. Further information may be discovered in the Boiani family archives, which are preserved in the Museo del Cividale, see Fogolari 1906, p. 106, or E. del Torso's *Fam. Boiani*, cited in *Dizionario Biografico* . . . , p. 205.

4. On the placement of medals in walls as a guarantee of immortality, see Ettlinger 1989.

5. Hill 1930, no. 281.

6. Ibid., no. 884.

7. Ostermann 1888, p. 205, identifies it as a greyhound.

8. M. A. Lavin 1974, p. 364.

Additional literature: *Catalogue of the Vernon* . . . , no. 94.

Donato Bramante

Note:

1. This biography is drawn from the full account in the article by A. Bruschi in the *Dizionario Biografico . . .* , vol. 13, pp. 712–25. For Bramante's plans for St. Peter's, see Wolff-Metternich 1975.

33, 33a
Bramante
Self-Portrait *all'antica* (Hill 1930, no. 657)

Notes:

1. See most recently, Wolff-Metternich and Thoenes 1987, pp. 30–33.
2. For a complete bibliography, see G. F. Hill's article "Caradosso" in Thieme-Becker, vol. 5, pp. 563–65. See also Hollanda 1918.
3. Brown and Lorenzoni 1982, E3.
4. Ibid., E7. For the plaquettes Caradosso executed for this inkstand, see Molinier 1886, vol. 1, pp. 99–109; Bode 1922, pp. 145–55 (as designed by Bramante); Bange 1922, pp. 34 and 85–86 (as Bramante); and Pope-Hennessy 1965, pp. 17–19.
5. Martinori 1918, p. 54.
6. Plon 1884, p. 29; Hill 1930, no. 662.
7. Theseus Ambrosius 1539, p. 183.
8. Lomazzo 1844, vol. 3, p. 214.
9. Ibid., p. 216.
10. Vasari 1878–85, vol. 4, p. 161: " . . . che sentendolo avere volunta di buttare in terra la chiesa di Santo Pietro per rifarla di nuovo, gli fece infiniti disegni; ma fra gli altri ne fece uno che fu molto mirabile dove egli mostro quella intelligenza che si poteva maggiore con due campanile che mettono in mezzo la facciata, come si vede nelle monete che batte poi Giulio II e Leon X, fatte da Caradosso eccellentissimo orefice che nel far coni non ebbe pari, come ancora si vede la medaglia di Bramante fatta da lui molto bella."
11. Shearman 1974, pp. 567–73, especially p. 572.
12. Hill 1930, no. 876.
13. R. Weiss 1965, pp. 163–82. Hill 1930, no. 868, attributes the medal to Pier Maria Serbaldi da Pescia.
14. Hill 1930, nos. 870, 659–60. The former is claimed by Hill to be a later hybrid. For the inscription on nos. 659–60 see Murray 1974, pp. 27–34.
15. For good, detailed illustrations of the British Museum impression, see Suida 1954, pl. VI–IX.
16. The arrangement of the neck and shoulders is very similar, suggesting Bramante had seen the medal.
17. See E. Förster's "Euklid" in *Reallexikon zur Deutschen Kunstgeschichte*, vol. 6, pp. 256–66.
18. Hermania 1934, pp. 7 and 47; E. Carli 1960, p. 43.
19. Hill 1930, nos. 659–61. See also Armand 1883–87, vol. 3, pp. 36–37.
20. Hill 1930, no. 663.

Additional literature: Hill and Pollard 1967, no. 193; Pollard 1984–85, vol. 1, no. 140; Johnson and Martini 1986, nos. 73–74; C. Johnson 1990, p. 9, no. 4.

34, 34a
Artist Unknown
Marguerite de Foix (Hill 1930, no. 711)

Notes:

1. Specifically, the shield is blazoned as follows: Argent, a chief azure (*Saluzzo*); Quarterly, 1 and 4, Gules, three pales or (*Foix*); 2 and 3, Or, two cows in pale passant gules, collared, armed and belled azure (*Béarn*) (*Counts of Foix*).
2. Gabrielli, ed. 1974, p. 233.
3. *Corpus Nummorum Italicorum*, vol. 2, p. 71. Fava 1974 includes a special section on the coins of Saluzzo. See also Ravegnani Morosini 1984, vol. 3, p. 107.
4. The wall above the fireplace in the great hall of the Casa Cavassa in Saluzzo presents a painting of the Saluzzo arms with helmet, crest, and mantling beneath a tree in full leaf. Perhaps Marguerite had such an image in mind in relation to the barren tree of her medal.
5. Ravegnani Morosini 1984, p. 107.
6. Hill 1930, no. 711; Pollard 1984–85, vol. 1, p. 286, no. 145. Hill also interprets the T C at the end of the obverse inscription as ETC. Here it might make sense as the

continuation of the titles of the ruler, but the alternative interpretation cited in the text seems more reasonable.
7. Armand 1883–87, vol. 2, p. 123, no. 14, and vol. 3, p. 204; Forrer 1904–30, vol. 1, p. 442.
8. Roggiero 1901, pp. 13, 16–17; Fava 1974, pp. 246–47; Ravegnani Morosini 1984, pp. 105, 107.

Christoforo di Geremia

Notes:

1. Magnaguti 1921, p. 30.
2. Fabriczy 1903, p. 78.
3. Bertolotti 1890, pp. 268–71.
4. Giovannoni and Giovetti 1992, p. 59.
5. Yatsevich 1925, p. 89.
6. Hill 1930, pp. 195–96.
7. Hill 1930, nos. 756, 755; Habich 1924, p. 80.

35
Christoforo di Geremia
Alfonso of Aragon (Hill 1930, no. 754)

Notes:

1. Heiss 1881–92, vol. 1, pp. 29–30.
2. Habich 1924, pp. 39–40.
3. Fabriczy 1903, p. 78; Hill 1930, p. 197.
4. Hill 1930, nos. 41–43, 45.
5. Habich 1924, p. 80.
6. Panvini Rosati 1968, p. 34.
7. Giovannoni and Giovetti 1992, p. 59. The Nereids riding on sea-centaurs are portrayed as in the painting by Mantegna.
8. Hill 1930, no. 304.

Additional literature: Armand 1883–87, vol. 1, p. 8, no. 1; Middeldorf and Goetz 1944, no. 77; *Catalogue of the Vernon . . .* , no. 110.

Lysippus the Younger

Notes:

1. Quoted in full in Hill 1930, p. 205.
2. Ibid., no. 788.
3. Ibid., no. 789.
4. Ibid., no. 806.
5. R. Weiss 1969, p. 162.
6. See Hill 1930, pp. 211–21.
7. Hill 1908, pp. 274–86, was the first to develop such a theory.

Additional literature: Hill and Pollard 1967, nos. 217–21; Pollard 1984–85, vol. 1, nos. 174–82; Johnson and Martini 1986, nos. 280–302.

36
Lysippus the Younger
Self-Portrait (?) (Hill 1930, no. 796)

Notes:

1. I am indebted for this translation to M. Jones 1979 (*Art*), p. 38. There is also an English verse translation: "This side the likeness of your slave displays/Turn me, your own fair face will meet your gaze."
2. Hill 1930, no. 125, the surviving example in the Ashmolean Museum, Oxford.
3. Ibid., no. 808.
4. M. Jones 1979 (*Art*), p. 38.
5. Campbell 1990, p. 67.
6. *Lo specchio e il doppio*, p. 145.
7. Pliny 1857, pp. 174–77.

Additional literature: Hill 1908, pp. 274–86; Hill 1912 (*Portrait*), p. 35.

Giovanni Filangieri Candida

Notes:

1. On the phenomen of humanists dabbling in medals, see Middeldorf 1978.
2. Bernardo Candida Gonzaga, cited in de la Tour 1895, pp. 13–14, states that the medalist was the son of Salvatore Filangieri Candida, a noble of Benevento. But according to Erasmo Ricca, cited in Pontieri 1969, p. 593, note 1, his father was a certain Niccolò Candida of the branch of Lucera. The letters patent granted Can-

dida by Maximilian of Austria in 1480 refer to the artist as a native of the kingdom of Naples. See Tourneur 1919 ("Jehan . . . [suite et fin]"), p. 298, note 7. His approximate birth date is deduced from his own statement that he was a boy (*puer*) at the siege of Troia in August 1462, and from the fact that he was employed at the court of Charles the Bold in 1467.
3. Stein 1928, p. 236, note 1; Tourneur 1914, p. 385. Contemporary chroniclers record that many of the duke of Calabria's Italian retainers became attached to Charles's court (ibid., pp. 390–92).
4. Tourneur 1919 ("Jehan . . . [suite]"), p. 47.
5. Ibid., pp. 24–28.
6. Samaran 1944, p. 189.
7. Tourneur 1919 ("Jehan . . . [suite]"), p. 28.
8. Tucked into the space beside Miette's portrait is a tower labeled CARCER CANDIDE INSVLIS (Candida's prison at Lille). Near Gruthuse is a large A, perhaps for "Assertor" (liberator), and the love-knot below his bust with the letters A A may have a related meaning. See Tourneur 1919 ("Jehan . . . [suite et fin]"), pp. 272–74.
9. Tourneur 1919 ("Jehan . . . [suite]"), pp. 44–46.
10. Porcher 1921–22, p. 320; Stein 1928.
11. Pontieri 1969, p. 604.
12. Porcher 1921–22; Couderc 1924, pp. 326–29 and 336–41; Pontieri 1969, pp. 618–22 and 642–51. The manuscript, contained in Vatican MS lat. 7578, contains Candida's autograph rubrics.
13. Delisle 1890, p. 310, and Heiss 1890, p. 454. De la Tour 1895, pp. 11–12, doubts that Candida actually produced a seal matrix for Briçonnet, but this is probably unjustified. De la Mare's letters are dated; de la Tour 1895, pp. 58–60, discusses internal evidence for their chronology.
14. The portrait on one (Hill 1930, no. 837) shows him in a plain cap and robe, the other (Hill 1930, no. 838) with the tonsure of the regular clergy and wearing a rochet. Some writers have seen the earlier medal as representing a man several years younger than the one portrayed on the later medal (Heiss 1890, p. 455; de la Tour 1895, p. 62), but Hill is probably correct in suggesting that the later portrait was made by retouching an impression of the earlier one not long after the first medal was made. The reverses of the two medals are identical.
15. Hill 1930, nos. 819–21.
16. Ibid., nos. 845–52.
17. Ibid., no. 823. Hill doubted the attribution of the Kress medal to Lysippus, seeing in it "a broader conception" than in his other works. But Lysippus is rather uneven, and his best works—e.g. the large medals of Alvise Toscani (nos. 812–13) and the so-called self-portrait (cat. no. 36)—definitely approach the quality of the Candida medal. The treatment of the planes of the face and the format of the bust are distinctly Lysippean. Judging by the age of the sitter, the Candida medal was probably made at the very end of Lysippus's career, in the late 1470s to mid 1480s. The authorship of the other portrait medal of Candida (no. 822) is uncertain.
18. Two Laurana medals from 1464 probably commemorate the Neapolitan campaign in which Candida had participated. One of these (Hill 1930, no. 61) represents Candida's leader, John of Calabria. The other (no. 60) depicts Ferry II of Lorraine, count of Vaudemont. A previously unrecognized variant of the latter is in the Kress Collection (Hill 1930, no. 137; Hill and Pollard 1967, no. 51).

37, 37a
Giovanni Candida
Maximilian I and Mary of Burgundy (Hill 1930, no. 831)

Notes:

1. Hill 1930, no. 819.
2. Ibid., no. 821.
3. Baldass 1925, pp. 248–49. The piece is reproduced in Hill and Pollard 1967, no. 616.
4. Tourneur 1919 ("Jehan . . . [suite]"), p. 9.
5. Cazaux 1967, p. 246.
6. Rausch 1880, p. 175.
7. Wiesflecker 1991, p. 47. The letter dates from the winter of 1477/78.

8. Hill 1930, no. 830.
9. Hommel 1951, p. 328, and Cazaux 1967, p. 309.
10. Hommel 1951, p. 328.
11. Ibid., p. 87; Tourneur 1919 ("Jehan . . . [suite et fin]"), p. 278.

Additional literature: Middeldorf and Goetz 1944, no. 85; Goldschneider 1952, no. 58; *Maximilian I. 1459–1519*, no. 658; Hill and Pollard 1967, no. 225; Salton 1969, no. 27; *Maximilian I*, no. 317; Norris and Weber 1976, no. 21; M. Jones 1979 (*Art*), p. 36; Pollard 1984–85, vol. 1, no. 187; Johnson and Martini 1986, nos. 59–62; *Hispania-Austria*, p. 263, no. 91.

38, 38a
Giovanni Candida
Giuliano and Clemente della Rovere (Hill 1930, no. 843)

Notes:
1. Hill 1930, no. 838.
2. See the "Candida" entry in *Dizionario Biografico . . .*, p. 775.
3. O. Ferrara 1940, p. 127.
4. Cloulas 1990, p. 103.

Additional literature: Hill and Pollard 1967, no. 230; Pollard 1984–85, vol. 1, no. 191; Johnson and Martini 1968, nos. 640–41.

Bertoldo di Giovanni

Notes:
1. Bode 1925.
2. Hill 1930, nos. 913 (Gratiadei), 914 (Filippo), and 917 (Leticia Sanuto).

Additional literature: Hill 1930, vol. 1, pp. 238–43; Draper 1992.

39, 39a
Bertoldo di Giovanni
Mehmed II (Hill 1930, no. 911)

Notes:
1. Hill 1930, no. 432.
2. Piazzo 1956, p. 104
3. Jacobs 1927, pp. 1–17.
4. Draper 1992, fig. 55.
5. Hill 1930, no. 917. See Draper 1992, cat. 6.

Additional literature: Friedländer 1881–82, pp. 33–34; Bode 1895, pp. 152–53; Bode 1925, pp. 18–20; Middeldorf and Goetz 1944, no. 94; Babinger 1953, pp. 425–28; Hill and Pollard 1967, no. 248; Jestaz 1974, pp. 96–98; Raby 1987, pp. 180–83; Vermeule 1987, pp. 245–67.

40
Bertoldo di Giovanni
Frederick III (Hill 1930, no. 912)

Notes:
1. Meiss 1961, pp. 65–66.
2. Draper 1992, cat. 2.
3. Draper 1992, fig. 42.
4. His portraiture is surveyed in Kemmerich 1910, pp. 52–54.

Additional literature: Bode 1895, pp. 156–57 and note 2; Bode 1925, pp. 35–37; Middeldorf and Stiebral 1983, no. 8; Pollard 1984–85, vol. 1, nos. 220–220a; Johnson and Martini 1986, nos. 30–31; *Eredità . . .*, no. 61.

41
Bertoldo di Giovanni
The Pazzi Conspiracy (Hill 1930, no. 915)

Notes:
1. Bode 1895.
2. Draper 1992, appendix 4.
3. Lorenzo de' Medici 1977, pp. 3–4.
4. Poliziano 1958, edited by Alessandro Perosa. Perosa tirelessly collates the various contemporary accounts.
5. Ibid., p. 30, note.
6. Draper 1992.

7. Ibid., figs. 48–50.
8. Ibid., fig. 52.

Additional literature: Vasari 1878–85, vol. 3, p. 297; Bode 1925, pp. 26–28; Langedijk 1981–87, vol. 1, p. 27, and vol. 2, pp. 1072, 1168; Pollard 1984–85, vol. 1, nos. 223, 223a; J. D. Draper in *Donatello . . .*, no. 110; Johnson and Martini 1986, nos. 41–43; *Eredità . . .*, no. 26.

Niccolò Fiorentino

Notes:
1. Hill 1930, p. 244, based on manuscripts of Gaetano Milanesi, formerly in the Biblioteca comunale, Siena.
2. J. P. Richter, ed., 1970, vol. 2, p. 183, no. 1008.
3. Armand 1883–87, vol. 3, p. 21a, quoting from Adolfo Venturi: "Mo. Niccolò Forzore di Spinelli da Fiorenze per havere composto una medaglia de arzento a lo illustrissimo don Alphonso."
4. A Memling in Antwerp shows a young man holding a sestertius of Nero, and probably represents a member of a Florentine banking family, either the Neroni or Del Nero. This suggestion was made by Roberto Weiss in a private communication. McFarlane 1971, pp. 40–41, also suggests that the sitter is a Neroni. The second portrait is a Botticelli in the Uffizi, Florence, of a young man holding a gilt gesso roundel of Cosimo de' Medici the Elder. The young man is probably the sculptor Bertoldo (cat. nos. 39–41). See Middeldorf 1978 (1979–81, vol. 3), pp. 186–91.

Additional literature: Hill in Thieme-Becker, vol. 31, pp. 387–88; Hill and Pollard 1978, pp. 74–79.

42
Niccolò Fiorentino
Lorenzo de' Medici (Hill 1930, no. 926)

Notes:
1. Hook 1984.
2. Langedijk 1981–87, vol. 1, p. 30, and vol. 2, p. 1154, no. 26.

Additional literature: Armand 1883–87, vol. 1, p. 85, no. 4, vol. 2, p. 289, and vol. 3, p. 20, no. D; Hill and Pollard 1978, pp. 75–76; *Eredità . . .*, no. 29.

43
Niccolò Fiorentino (?)
Girolamo Ridolfi (Hill 1930, no. 940)

Note:
1. St. Geminianus was celebrated for his powers as a healer. When Attila the Hun attacked the city that would later become San Gimignano, the saint appeared to Attila in a vision and prevented the city's destruction. In consequence, he was adopted as the city's patron.

Additional literature: Armand 1883–87, vol. 2, p. 52, no. 22, and vol. 3, p. 173, 1.

44
Niccolò Fiorentino (?)
Filippo Strozzi (Hill 1930, no. 1018)

Notes:
1. (*Strozzi*) Or, on a fess gules three moons increscent argent. I am grateful to Stephen K. Scher for blasoning these arms.
2. Friedländer 1882, p. 141, no. 1.
3. The others in this group are Hill 1930, nos. 978 (Giovanni Antonio de' Conti Guidi), 982 (Pietro Machiavelli), and 991 (Maria de Mucini).
4. Hill 1930, no. 1018 *bis*. For the wax model, see Sambon sale, 1914, no. 11, and Babelon 1921, pp. 203–10. There is also an iron plaque of the portrait type, now in the Walters Art Gallery, Baltimore, for which the wax model was probably the prototype. See Ross 1943, pp. 151–53. No other fifteenth-century wax portrait model exists. A wax portrait of Vittorio Pavoni (?) from the Gaettens Collection, ascribed to Pisanello, recently reappeared in the Tietjen sale, 1992, lot 763, but to judge

from its style and technique it is patently an antiquarian confection.
5. Nickel 1974, pp. 229–32.

Additional literature: Armand 1883–87, vol. 1, p. 98, no. 6; Migeon 1908, p. 11, no. v; Hill and Pollard 1978, pp. 74 and 78; *Eredità . . .*, no. 44.

45, 46
Niccolò Fiorentino (?)
Giovanna Albizzi Tornabuoni (Hill 1930, nos. 1021–22)

Notes:
1. Hill 1930, no. 1011. On the one of Nonina Strozzi, wife of Bernardo del Barbigia (Hill 1930, no. 957), the husband's name precedes that of his wife, as here. Simons 1988, p. 8, suggests that the large number of profile painted portraits of women surviving from the Renaissance were produced for patriarchal display rather than as intense personal records of the sitters.
2. Pope-Hennessy 1966, pp. 24 and 28, figs. 24–25.
3. In the Thyssen-Bornemisza Collection, Lugano. Pope-Hennessy 1966, fig. 25.
4. Wind 1958, pp. 49, 67, and 72, redated the medal of Pico to precede that of Giovanna, so that the version on Giovanna's medal constituted a compliment to Pico. On his, the legend reads "Beauty, Love, Pleasure," a combination taken from Ficino and referring to a trinitarian philosophy of love. See Panofsky 1962, pp. 168–69.
5. As suggested by Hill 1930.
6. Wind 1958, pp. 26–30.
7. A group of the Three Graces now in the Vatican Collection has the same poses and gestures as the figures on the medal. See Reinach 1906, p. 340. The only sculpture group of the Graces that appears with certainty to have been known in the fifteenth century is the one now in Siena, in which the gestures do not match those on the medal. See Bober and Rubinstein 1987, pp. 95–97, fig. 60. The range of the group in various mediums is given in Deonna 1930, pp. 274–332.
8. See Spencer 1987, pp. 202–3.
9. Wind 1958, pp. 91–94.

Additional literature: Armand 1883–87, vol. 1, p. 88, no. 20; Hill and Pollard 1978, pp. 27 and 78; *Eredità . . .*, no. 41.

47
Florentine school
Savonarola (Hill 1930, no. 1079)

Notes:
1. Villari 1888, p. 760.
2. Vasari 1878–85, p. 181.
3. Middeldorf 1979, p. 270, pl. XVII, fig. b (Wicar Collection, diameter 7.5 cm). See also Hill and Pollard 1967, no. 282, p. 53.
4. See the "della Robbia" entry in *Dizionario Biografico . . .*, pp. 268–69.
5. Reproduced in M. Ferrara 1952, pl. XIV and p. 446.
6. The outburst combines the phrase "gladius Domini" from the Old Testament books of Isaiah and Jeremiah with the formula "cito et velociter" from Joshua and Joel. See Antonetti 1991, p. 79.
7. Quoted in Weinstein 1971, p. 71.
8. See Hill 1930, nos. 1077 and 1076.
9. Ibid., no. 1073.

Additional literature: Fabriczy 1904; Pollard 1984–85.

Italy, Sixteenth Century

48, 48a
Milanese School
Scaramuccia Trivulzio (Hill 1930, no. 703)

Notes:
1. Fabriczy 1904, pp. 171–72.
2. Hill 1911, pp. 14–19.
3. A similar, though less close example, is the Pietro Aretino medal. See Scher 1989, pp. 4–11. The example in the Victoria & Albert Museum shows virtually identical constituents. I am indebted to Josephine Darrah for the analysis.

4. See Hill 1930, nos. 703–5; Habich 1924, pp. 121 and 157; and Hill and Pollard 1967, nos. 424 and 423.

5. See Dworschak 1958, p. 50; Hill and Pollard 1967, nos. 198 and 484b; Scher 1986, pp. 15–21, especially pp. 18 and 21, note 30. I would like to thank Lucy Cullen, Luke Syson, and Donald Myers for their helpful ideas and suggestions, as well as Anthony Radcliffe and Paul Williamson.

6. Hall 1979, pp. 254–55.

7. Bober and Rubinstein 1986, nos. 59a and 59b; Haskell and Penny 1981, no. 29, pp. 195–96.

8. See Litta et al. 1819–83, vol. 1, fasc. 4. Additional information from Hill 1930, p. 180; *Enciclopedia Italiana di Scienze . . .*, vol. 34, p. 391; and the *New Catholic Encyclopedia*, vol. 14, p. 313.

Additional literature: Robinson 1856, no. 474, pp. 137–38; Bode 1904, p. 42; Hill and Pollard 1978, pp. 85 and 177, note 220; Pollard 1984–85, vol. 3, p. 1465.

Leone Leoni

Notes:

1. He left Ferrara after having been accused of forgery. See Venturi 1888 ("Leone"), pp. 327–28.

2. Armand 1883–87, vol. 1, p. 162, no. 3; Plon 1887, p. 253, pl. 29, no. 10; Pollard 1984–85, vol. 3, no. 716. For an early instance of his endeavors on Leoni's behalf, see Aretino 1957–60, vol. 1, p. 37.

3. Armand 1883–87, vol. 1, p. 166, no. 21; Plon 1887, p. 253, pl. 29, nos. 8 and 9; Hill and Pollard 1978, p. 97.

4. Müntz 1884, pp. 322–23.

5. Armand 1883–87, vol. 1, p. 165–66, nos. 16–18, and vol. 3, pp. 69–70, nos. t–v; Plon 1887, p. 255, pl. 29, nos. 4–7; Hill and Pollard 1976, no. 434; Pollard 1984–85, vol. 2, nos. 520–21.

6. He held the post from 1542 to 1545 and again from 1550 to 1589.

7. Letter from Antonio Patanella to Granvelle dated May 1, 1547. See Plon 1887, pp. 43 and 354. This medal may be the one published in Armand 1883–87, vol. 1, p. 162, no. 2, and Plon 1887, p. 259, pl. 30, nos. 7–8.

8. Leoni's letter of November 1, 1546, probably to Gonzaga. See Ronchini 1865, p. 24, and Plon 1887, p. 41.

9. Ronchini 1865, pp. 25–26; Plon 1887, p. 44. For the medal, see Armand 1883–87, vol. 1, p. 164, no. 11; Plon 1887, p. 159, pl. 30, nos. 9–10; and Pollard 1984–85, vol. 3, no. 714.

10. Armand 1883–87, vol. 1, p. 162, no. 1, and p. 168, no. 25; Plon 1887, p. 260, pl. 31, nos. 1–4; Hill and Pollard 1976, no. 426d.

11. See Campori 1855, p. 286, and Plon 1887, p. 46.

12. Van Durme 1949, pp. 653–78.

13. Plon 1887, pp. 72–78. For the medals, see Armand 1883–87, vol. 2, p. 236, no. 1, and p. 237, no. 4.

14. Plon 1887, pp. 281–84.

15. Vasari 1878–85, vol. 7, p. 538.

16. Plon 1887, pp. 125–26, 128–30, and 180–81.

17. Ibid., pp. 202 and 210–11.

18. Ibid., p. 226.

Additional literature: Casati 1884; Ilg 1887, pp. 65–88; Kenner 1892, pp. 55–93; Simonis 1904, pp. 27–42; Forrer 1904–30, vol. 3, pp. 398–411, and vol. 7, p. 549; Schottmüller and Hill in Thieme-Becker, vol. 23, pp. 84–87; Planiscig 1927, pp. 544–67; Tribolati 1955, pp. 94–102; Pope-Hennessy 1985 (*Italian Renaissance*), pp. 400–403.

49
Leone Leoni
Martin de Hanna

Notes:

1. For merchants in Venice, see Brulez 1965.

2. Plon 1887, p. 257, suggested 1544. Proske 1943, p. 54, argued for 1546.

3. Proske 1943, p. 54, fig. 2.

4. See Hill 1930, nos. 960 and 966.

5. Armand 1883–87, vol. 1, p. 165, no. 14; Plon 1887, p. 257. For the signed version, see Greene 1885, p. 149, no. 1.

6. Armand 1883–87, vol. 1, p. 169, nos. 29–30; Greene 1885, p. 150, nos. 3–4.

Additional literature: Bergmann 1844–57, vol. 2, p. 1; *Trésor de Numismatique . . .* (German), pl. 31, no. 10; Armand 1883–87, vol. 1, p. 165, no. 13; Habich 1924, pl. 92, no. 4; Hill and Pollard 1978, p. 97, pl. 18, no. 5; Pollard 1984–85, vol. 3, no. 715.

50
Leone Leoni
Andrea Doria

Notes:

1. Bottari and Ticozzi 1822–25, vol. 1, p. 525, and vol. 5, p. 251.

2. Aretino 1957–60, vol. 1, pp. 192–93. For Doria, see Arnolfini 1598; *Elogi storici . . .*; Luzzati 1943; Cadenas y Vicent 1977; and Lingua 1984.

3. Drawing no. 1960.11. Reproduced in M. Jones 1979 (*Art*), p. 60.

4. See Grueber 1970, vol. 2, p. 564. The galley reverse suggests a classical source for Leoni's alternate reverse for the Doria medal.

5. Armand 1883–87, vol. 1, p. 164, no. 9; Plon 1887, p. 256; Hill and Pollard 1967, no. 431; Pollard 1984–85, vol. 3, no. 712.

Additional literature: Armand 1883–87, vol. 1, p. 164, no. 8; Ilg 1887, p. 88; Fabriczy 1904, pl. 39, no. 1; Hill 1912 (*Portrait*), p. 53, no. 30; Habich 1924, pp. 130–31, pl. 92, no. 1; Panvini Rosati 1968, no. 174; Middeldorf and Stiebral 1983, pl. 53; Pollard 1984–85, vol. 3, p. 711; *Fitzwilliam . . .*, pl. 22, no. 1.

51, 51a
Leone Leoni
Ippolita Gonzaga

Notes:

1. Aretino 1957–60, vol. 2, pp. 390–91.

2. Affo 1787, pp. 104–5.

Additional literature: Gaetani 1761–63, vol. 1, pl. 70, no. 4; van Loon 1732–37, vol. 1, p. 266; Armand 1883–87, vol. 1, p. 163, no. 7; Plon 1887, p. 263, pl. 32, nos. 7–8; Ilg 1887, p. 76; Habich 1924, pl. 92, no. 6; Hill and Pollard 1967, no. 432; *Splendours . . .*, no. 148; Pollard 1984–85, vol. 3, no. 709; Barocchi and Gallo 1985, no. 145.

52
Leone Leoni
Michelangelo

Notes:

1. See Steinmann 1913, pp. 51–52, also Duchamp 1988, pp. 10–16.

2. Fortnum 1875, pp. 7–9; Forrer 1904–30, vol. 3, p. 100; Hill 1912 (*Portrait*), pl. 26; M. Jones 1979 (*Art*), p. 61, fig. 135.

3. Various interpretations are discussed in Vasari 1962, vol. 4, pp. 1736–38.

4. Plon 1887, p. 165; Vasari 1962, vol. 4, p. 1736.

5. Plon 1887, p. 178; Vasari 1962, vol. 4, p. 1736.

6. Vasari 1962, vol. 1, p. 109.

7. Plon 1887, p. 155. For the tomb, see Pope-Hennessy 1985 (*Italian High*), pp. 401–2.

Additional literature: Lochner 1737–44, vol. 3, p. 281; Gaetani 1761–63, vol. 1, pl. 73, no. 4; Fortnum 1875, pp. 1–15; Armand 1883–87, vol. 1, p. 163, no. 6; Forrer 1904–30, vol. 3, p. 405; Habich 1924, pl. 92, no. 2; Hill and Pollard 1967, no. 429; Pollard 1984–85, vol. 3, no. 719.

53, 53a
School of Leone Leoni
Gianfrancesco Trivulzio

Notes:

1. Earlier writers, including Hill 1923 (*Guide*), p. 39, gave 1509 as Trivulzio's date of birth, which meant that to them the medal was produced in roughly 1548 rather than 1543.

2. I would like to thank Alessandra Galizzi for her assistance with translations of the Latin inscriptions.

3. Armand 1883–87, vol. 1, p. 230, no. 13, p. 232, no. 27, and p. 235, no. 39; Hill and Pollard 1967, nos. 351, 356, and 359. All three are signed PPR.

4. Armand 1883–87, vol. 2, p. 162, no. 21; Hill and Pollard 1967, no. 436a. Habich 1924, p. 135, also connects the Trivulzio medal with the one of Cardano, citing the spirit of Leone Leoni in both but not attributing either directly to him. In the margin of his copy of Armand 1883–87, now in the library of the National Gallery of Art, Washington, Hill made the simple annotation: "Leone Leoni." In addition to Graham Pollard's discussion in Hill and Pollard 1967 regarding the Cardano medal's connection to Leoni and its similarities to Leoni's medals of Michelangelo and Martin de Hanna (cat. nos. 52 and 49, respectively), see Greene 1913, pp. 413–21, who records an example of the Cardano signed LEO (p. 417). I would like to thank Philip Attwood for his correspondence regarding this issue, pointing out that the British Museum owns an example of the Cardano with scratches on the truncation of the arm only vaguely like a signature, and quite different from Leoni's signature on the medal of Michelangelo.

5. For Gianfrancesco's biography, see the Trivulzio entry in *Enciclopedia Italiana di Scienze . . .*, vol. 34, pp. 390–91; Giuseppe Coniglio in *Enciclopedia Cattolica*, vol. 12, columns 559–60; and Litta et al., vol. 14.

6. Hill 1930, nos. 655 and 706; Hill and Pollard 1967, nos. 192 and 199, attributed to Caradosso and "Milanese 16th century," respectively. See also the related pieces, Hill 1930, nos. 656 and 707–10.

7. Gianfrancesco ceded the rights to Mesocco, for payment, in 1519. See *Enciclopedia Italiana di Scienze . . .*, vol. 34, pp. 390–91, and *Storia di Milano*, vol. 9, pp. 213ff.

8. See Tervarent 1958–64, vols. 1 and 2, columns 145, 358, and 410.

9. Ibid., columns 145 and 410. Among those cited are Hill 1930, nos. 857, 958, 968, 981, 993, 1027, 1065, and 1070–71. See also the present catalogue, no. 161.

Additional literature: Keary 1881, p. 54, no. 170; Armand 1883–87, vol. 2, p. 302, no. 13 bis; de Rinaldis 1913, p. 229; Habich 1924, p. 135, pl. XCVI, no. 5; Hill and Pollard 1967, p. 67, no. 360a; Panvini Rosati 1968, p. 54, no. 212; Salton 1969, no. 42; Norris and Weber 1976, p. 20, no. 33; Middeldorf and Stiebral 1983, fig. LI; Pollard 1984–85, vol. 2, pp. 800–805, nos. 432 and 432a.

Jacopo da Trezzo

Notes:

1. Armand 1883–87, vol. 1, p. 242, no. 7; Babelon 1922, p. 192, no. I; Hill and Pollard 1976, no. 439.

2. Armand 1883–87, vol. 2, p. 237, no. 6; Babelon 1922, p. 215, no. VI; Pollard 1984–85, vol. 3, no. 738.

3. Armand 1883–87, vol. 2, p. 247, no. 15; Babelon 1922, p. 219, no. VII.

4. Armand 1883–87, vol. 1, p. 241, no. 2; Babelon 1922, p. 200; Hill and Pollard 1976, no. 437; Pollard 1984–85, vol. 3, no. 723.

5. Babelon 1922, p. 72.

6. For an example, see M. Jones 1982–88, vol. 2, p. 88.

Additional literature: Bolzenthal 1840, pp. 148–50; Forrer 1904–30, vol. 6, pp. 132–39, and vol. 8, pp. 240–42; Thieme-Becker, vol. 33, pp. 392–93; Tribolati 1955, pp. 94–102; Panvini Rosati 1968, pp. 49–50.

54
Jacopo da Trezzo
Mary Tudor

Notes:

1. Strong 1969, pp. 210–12.

2. Hume 1908, p. 86, quoted in Strong 1969, p. 212.

3. Van Loon 1732–37, vol. 1, p. 4; Armand 1883–87, vol. 1, p. 241, no. 2; Babelon 1922, p. 200; Hill and Pollard 1976, no. 437; Pollard 1984–85, vol. 3, no. 723.

Additional literature: Luckius 1620, p. 165; van Loon 1732–37, vol. 1, p. 10; Hawkins 1885, vol. 1, p. 72, no. 20; Armand 1883–87, vol. 1, p. 241, no. 3; Forrer

1904–30, vol. 6, p. 137; Babelon 1922, p. 201; Habich 1924, p. 134, pl. 94, no. 2; Hill 1927, pp. 37–38; Tribolati 1955, pl. 4, no. 7; V. Johnson 1975 ("La medaglia italiana"), pp. 8–9, fig. 4; M. Jones 1979 (*Art*), p. 65; Pialorsi 1982, pp. 22–23, fig. 29; Middeldorf and Stiebral 1983, pl. 72; Pollard 1984–85, vol. 3, no. 725.

55
Jacopo da Trezzo
Gianello della Torre

Notes:
1. Ronchini 1865, p. 38.
2. Babelon 1913.
3. Vermeule 1987, p. 278.

Additional literature: Gaetani 1761–63, vol. 1, pl. 49, no. 1; Armand 1883–87, vol. 1, p. 170, no. 38, vol. 3, p. 74, no. nn, and p. 115, no. c; Plon 1887, p. 273; Herrera 1905, pp. 266–70; Babelon 1913, pp. 269–78; Habich 1924, p. 135, pl. 93, no. 8; Eidlitz 1927, no. 998; Hill and Pollard 1967, no. 441a; V. Johnson 1975 ("La medaglia italiana"), fig. 5; Gimeno Rua 1976, pp. 80–81; Hill and Pollard 1978, p. 97, pl. 18, no. 8; M. Jones 1979 (*Art*), p. 62, fig. 140; Pollard 1984–85, vol. 3, no. 721.

56, 56a
Milanese School
Ferrante Loffredo

Notes:
1. For obvious reasons, wax models from this period are extremely rare. In the latter part of the sixteenth century, colored wax portraits begin to be produced as an end in themselves. Antonio Abondio (cat. nos. 60–63) was particularly adept at this art, and many of his wax portraits still exist. See Habich 1929–34, vol. 2, 2, pp. 486–507.
2. Gaetani 1761–63, vol. 1, p. 365, pl. 81, no. 3.
3. A full bibliography of all references to the family is gathered in Candida Gonzaga 1875, vol. 5, pp. 92–98. Trevico (or Trivico; Lat. Trivicum) is now a tiny town in the province of Avellino, to the east of Naples. In the Middle Ages it was the center of a large feudal complex, and before coming to Loffredo it belonged to Gonzalo di Córdoba (1453–1515), known as "el Gran Capitan."
4. Gaetani 1761–63, p. 365; Rizzini 1892, p. 87, no. 607.
5. *Antiquitas Puteolorum cum Baleneorum, Agnani, Puteolorum, et Tripergolarum descriptionibus . . .*, included in *Thesaurus antiquitatum . . .*, vol. 9, part 4a, cols. 1–28.
6. Croce 1970, chapter 2, especially pp. 104–5.
7. Candida Gonzaga 1875, vol. 5, p. 96.
8. Elaborate parade armor became very popular in the second half of the sixteenth century, and one of the forms it took was in imitation of that of a Roman officer, derived, in part, from ancient reliefs showing members of the imperial Praetorian Guard. A suit of such armor was made for Charles V in 1546, and can still be seen in the Real Armeria, Madrid. See Blair 1958, p. 117, fig. 42.
9. As all who study medals are painfully aware, there is no pendant to Hill 1930, which only includes works produced before 1530. The only reference work covering the remainder of the sixteenth century is Armand 1883–87, which has no illustrations. Yet by using Hill and Pollard 1967, Hill and Pollard 1978, Pollard 1984–85, and available monographs, one can develop an adequate understanding of individual styles and general stylistic patterns in the medallic art of this period.
10. See the entries for cat. nos. 48 and 59. For a fuller discussion of the Loffredo medal and its resemblances to works of various artists of the Milanese school, see Scher 1986, pp. 14–21.
11. Hill and Pollard 1967, pp. 80–81, nos. 423–25. The reverse of the Cardinal of Lorraine medal is also found on a medal of Scaramuccia Trivulzio (cat. no. 48), who died in 1527.
12. Hill 1909, pp. 31–35; Habich 1924, p. 122, pl. 83, no. 7; Pollard 1984–85, vol. 3, p. 1411, no. 816. The wax model of BARBARA BO . . . has been in the Metropoli-

tan Museum of Art, New York, since 1936. See also Hill and Pollard 1978, p. 24, pl. 2.2.

Additional literature: Armand 1883–87; Rinaldis 1913; Alvarez-Ossorio 1950; Gonzales-Palacios 1981.

Pietro Paolo Galeotti

Notes:
1. See Thieme-Becker, vol. 13, pp. 91–92, for a summary of Galeotti's life. See also Vasari 1878–85, vol. 5, p. 390; vol. 6, p. 251; and vol. 7, pp. 542–43. For Cellini's references to the artist, see the index in vol. 3 of Cellini 1828–29 under "Galeotti, Pietropaolo da Monteritondo," "Paolo, Romano, allievo di Benvenuto," and "Pietro Paolo romano." Additional references are in Pini, ed. 1869, dispensa 9, no. 209; Campori 1864, pp. 289–97, especially pp. 295–97; and Plon 1883, especially pp. 66–70.
2. Cellini 1828–29, vol. 1, pp. 350–51. The same in English translation by John Addington Symonds in Cellini 1949, p. 150. Symonds suggests, without giving reasons, that Bernardonaccio was Bernardo Sabatini. Cellini 1828–29, vol. 1, p. 351, no. 2, notes that the Poirot manuscript of the autobiography has a marginal notation identifying Bernardonaccio as Bernardo Baldini, a Florentine goldsmith favored by Cosimo I. Baldini, master of the Florentine mint from September 1560 to February 1562, was soundly disliked by Cellini, who includes a derogatory, scatological verse about him in his autobiography (Cellini 1828–29, vol. 2, p. 478; in English: Cellini 1949, p. 385). Thieme-Becker repeats the identification, and it is supported by Charles Hope's abridgment of Symonds's translation (Oxford, 1983, p. 84, no. 188).
3. For a discussion of work done in Cellini's workshop in Paris, see Campori 1864, pp. 295–97, and Plon 1883, especially pp. 60–70.
4. Cellini 1828–29, vol. 3, p. 49. Compare Plon 1883, p. 69, which records a document that would seem to place Galeotti still in Paris in 1556, though Thieme-Becker, vol. 13, pp. 91–92, argues that the document is mistaken.
5. For this date, and for a discussion of Galeotti's coins, see C. Johnson 1976, pp. 14–46, especially pp. 18–19 and figs. 4 and 6. See also Martinori 1913, p. 101, no. 985, pl. XIII (piastra of Cosimo I).
6. Varchi 1555, vol. 1, p. 252.
7. Bertolotti 1885, p. 109.
8. Forrer 1904–30, vol. 2, pp. 190–94, for a listing of most of Galeotti's sitters. For the cast medals, see also Armand 1883–87, vol. 1, pp. 227–36, and vol. 3, pp. 106–8 and 111–12.
9. For a discussion of this series, see C. Johnson 1976, pp. 14–46. See also Armand 1883–87, vol. 2, pp. 198–99, and vol. 3, pp. 108–12, and Langedijk 1981–87, vol. 1, pp. 485–91, nos. 146–49.
10. Vasari 1878–85, vol. 7, pp. 542–43.
11. C. Johnson 1976 compares Galeotti's reverses to those of Roman coins. On p. 28, for example, he discusses the reverse celebrating the fortification of Elba and a related reverse by Domenico Poggini (Armand 1883–87, vol. 3, p. 110, V, and vol. 1, p. 256, no. 10, respectively), both of which relate to the reverse of a sestertius of Nero. Galeotti uses this same composition in a more pictorial cast version for the reverse of one of his medals of Cristoforo Madruzzo (Armand 1883–87, vol. 1, p. 231, no. 17; Hill and Pollard 1967, no. 353), a useful indication of how his style in cast medals differs from that of his struck ones.
12. See Langedijk 1981–87, vol. 1, p. 140, note 5.
13. See *Firenze . . .*, pp. 338–44, nos. 686–93, and Langedijk 1981–87, vol. 1, p. 140, note 5. Fabriczy 1904, p. 182, refers to marble replicas of Galeotti's reverses on a sculpture pedestal he had seen in the refectory museum for the church of Ognissanti in Florence. He was probably referring to these tondi.
14. Humphris sale, 1990; Sotheby Parke Bernet sale, 1980, lot 1154; and Sotheby's sale, New York, 1988, lot 119.
15. As suggested by Cyril Humphris.
16. Armand 1883–87, vol. 1, pp. 228–29, no. 6.
17. Hill 1912 (*Portrait*), p. 63. See also Casati 1884, p. 82.
18. Armand 1883–87, vol. 1, p. 230, no. 15.

57, 57a
Pietro Paolo Galeotti
Francesco Taverna

Notes:
1. I would like to thank Alessandra Galizzi for her assistance with translations of the Latin inscriptions.
2. Armand 1883–87, vol. 1, p. 231, no. 20; Hill and Pollard 1967, no. 352. The date on this medal has been read variously as 1552, 1556, or 1561. The Kress example reads 1556.
3. For information on Taverna and his family, see *Enciclopedia Italiana di Scienze . . .*, vol. 33, pp. 340–41; *Storia di Milano*, vols. 8, 9, and the index volume, p. 727; and Calvi 1882.
4. This association, reflected in the common use of the name Fido (from Lat. *fides*) for dogs, is already evident in Pliny's *Natural History*. See Pliny 1940, pp. 101–5.
5. Illustrated in *Enciclopedia Italiana*, vol. 33, p. 340.
6. See Stevenson et al. 1982, pp. 171–72. An example is illustrated in Belloni 1977, no. 323. The Capricorn was also used on coins of the emperors Nero, Vespasian, Titus, Domitian, Hadrian, and Antoninus Pius. See also Tervarent 1958–64, columns 59–60. Galeotti would have known of the adoption of the symbol by Cosimo I from the many uses of it in Florentine art of the time. See Middeldorf and Kriegbaum 1928, pp. 9–17.
7. See Bober and Rubinstein 1986, no. 168, p. 200.
8. As in a coin of Gallienus; see Stevenson et al. 1982, p. 172.

Additional literature: Armand 1883–87, vol. 1, pp. 234–35, nos. 37–38; Hill and Pollard 1967, p. 67, no. 360; C. Johnson 1976, pp. 14–46.

Gianpaolo Poggini

Notes:
1. Cellini 1886, p. 388. English translation from Cellini 1956, p. 319.
2. Cellini 1886, p. 402; Cellini 1956, p. 329.
3. Vasari 1878–85, vol. 5, p. 391, note 2.
4. Pinchart 1870, p. 19. For Poggini in the Netherlands, see also Simonis 1904, pp. 38, 58, 105, 110.
5. Armand 1883–87, vol. 1, p. 238, no. 2; Pollard 1984–85, no. 403.
6. Armand 1883–87, p. 238, no. 1; Hill and Pollard 1967, no. 338; Pollard 1984–85, no. 402.
7. Babelon 1922, p. 94. On pp. 95–96 Babelon prints a list from 1602 of punches and dies formerly in the possession of Poggini.
8. Armand 1883–87, vol. 1, p. 238, no. 5; Pollard 1984–85, no. 404.
9. Armand 1883–87, vol. 1, p. 248, no. 9; Pollard 1984–85, no. 516; Pope-Hennessy 1985 (*Cellini*), pp. 52–54, pl. 18, 29–32.
10. See Armand 1883–87, vol. 1, p. 239, no. 7; Pollard 1984–85, no. 405.
11. Gaye 1839–40, vol. 3, p. 303.
12. Armand 1883–87, vol. 1, p. 240, no. 15.
13. Ibid., vol. 3, p. 281, E.

Additional literature: Bolzenthal 1840, pp. 152–55; Heiss 1881–92, vol. 8, pp. 27–40; Forrer 1904–30, vol. 4, pp. 632–35, and vol. 8, p. 141; Grotemeyer in Thieme-Becker, vol. 27, p. 188.

58
Gianpaolo Poggini
Philip II

Notes:
1. See Kubler 1964, pp. 149–52.
2. Ibid.

Additional literature: van Loon 1732–37, vol. 1, p. 238; Armand 1883–87, vol. 1, p. 239, no. 10; Heiss 1881–92, vol. 9, p. 40, no. 18, pl. 3–4; Dompierre de Chaufepié 1903–6, vol. 1, no. 332; Hill 1920–21, no. 315; Habich 1924, pl. 80,6; Brooke and Hill 1924, p. 99, no. 23; Alvarez-Ossorio 1950, p. 151, no. 230; Pollard 1984–85, no. 407; Gimeno 1987, p. 35.

59, 59a
Milanese School
Carlo Visconti

Notes:
1. See Scher et al. 1986, pp. 94–95. A detailed analysis of the metal by X-ray fluorescense may be found on p. 80 of that article.
2. Armand 1883–87, vol. 2, p. 206, no. 15, and vol. 3, p. 255, c.
3. The entire question of a "Milanese school" requires extensive examination. Early, but brief, treatments of this material may be found in Hill and Pollard 1978, pp. 95–100, and Habich 1924, pp. 131–37.
4. Gaetani 1761–63, pp. 73–74, pl. 117, no. II.
5. Ovid 1975, p. 114.

Additional literature: Hill and Pollard 1967, no. 510; Pollard 1984–85, vol. 3, no. 876.

Antonio Abondio

Notes:
1. Lietzmann 1989–90, pp. 327–49, has confirmed that Abondio did not make this stop in Munich on his trip back from Spain, but rather went there some months later from Vienna.
2. Schulz 1989–90, pp. 155–61.

Additional literature: Fiala 1909; Habich 1929–34, vol. 2, 2, pp. 486–88; Dworschak 1958; Schulz 1988.

60
Antonio Abondio
Jacopo Nizzola da Trezzo (Habich 1929–34, no. 3363)

Note:
1. Habich 1929–34, nos. 3354 and 3356. Jacopo da Trezzo also produced a medal of Khevenhüller in 1577.

Additional literature: Armand 1883–87, vol. 1, p. 273, no. 30; Hill 1912 (*Portrait*), p. 70, no. 52; Babelon 1922, p. 76; Dworschak 1958, pp. 78–79.

61, 61a
Antonio Abondio
Maximilian II and Empress Maria (Habich 1929–34, no. 3412)

Note:
1. See Habich 1929–34, nos. 3412 and 3411, respectively.

Additional literature: *Prag um 1600*, vol. 1, no. 459.

62
Antonio Abondio
Maximilian II (Habich 1929–34, no. 3397)

Notes:
1. See *Prag um 1600*, vol. 2, p. 261, no. 744.
2. Luckius 1620, p. 379.
3. Herrgott 1752–53, vol. 2, p. 90.
4. Köhler 1750, p. 262.

63, 63a
Antonio Abondio
Archdukes Matthias and Maximilian, Albrecht VII and Wenzel (Habich 1929–34, no. 3410)

Note:
1. This is clear from the fact that both are dated. Had they been intended as the obverse and reverse of a single medal, only one side would be dated.

Additional literature: *Prag um 1600*, p. 579, no. 462.

64, 64a
Artist Unknown
Pietro Bembo

Notes:
1. See C. Dionisotti in *Dizionario Biografico . . .* , vol. 8, pp. 133–51.
2. Cellini 1886, pp. 204–6. English translation from Cellini 1956, pp. 176–77.

3. Pope-Hennessy 1985 (*Cellini*), p. 80; Armand 1883–87, vol. 1, p. 150; Plon 1883, pp. 328–34.
4. From September 9, 1536. See Bottari and Ticozzi 1822–25, vol. 1, pp. 14–16.
5. Models for struck (as for cast) medals seem to have been made in the same size as the finished piece, as for example Mazzafirri's reverse of his medal of Ferdinando de' Medici of 1588 (see Hill 1914, p. 217). A later and better-known example is Morone Mola's wax model based on Bernini's design for the reverse of a medal of Pope Alexander VII from 1662 (M. Jones 1979 [*Art*], p. 89). It was beyond the technical capabilities of Cellini's age to produce a struck medal the size of the Bembo piece, and Trento 1984, p. 26, is incorrect in saying that the silver example in the Bargello is struck, an assertion repeated in Pope-Hennessy 1985 (*Cellini*), p. 301, note 22. It is cast and heavily tooled.
6. Cellini 1888, pp. 77–78.
7. Rizzoli 1905, pp. 276–80.
8. Habich 1924, p. 121.
9. Wethey 1971, vol. 2, p. 154.

Additional literature: Gaetani 1761–63, vol. 1, pl. 57, no. 1; van Mieris 1732–35, vol. 3, p. 188; Durand 1865, p. 16; Armand 1883–87, vol. 1, p. 146, no. 1; Heiss 1881–92, vol. 7, p. 197, and vol. 8, p. 114; Rinaldis 1913, nos. 93–94; Camesasca 1955, p. 67; Alvarez-Ossorio 1950, p. 107, no. 132; Hill and Pollard 1967, no. 484b; Veit 1976, p. 111; Hill and Pollard 1978, p. 85; Avery and Barbaglia 1981, no. 16; Pollard 1984–85, vol. 3, no. 818.

Francesco da Sangallo

Literature: Clausse 1902, pp. 139–261; Middeldorf in Thieme-Becker, vol. 29, pp. 404–6; Venturi 1935 (*Storia*), pp. 243–59; Middeldorf 1938, pp. 109–38; Pollard 1984–85, vol. 2, pp. 633–46; Pope-Hennessy 1985 (*Italian High*), pp. 355–56, 456.

65
Francesco da Sangallo
Self-Portrait with Elena Marsuppini

Notes:
1. Venturi 1935 (*Storia*), p. 254, fig. 193.
2. The campanile, commissioned in 1549, was never completed. For the medals, see Pollard 1984–85, nos. 314–15.
3. An exception is a Sangallo-inspired medal of a boy of the Pio di Savoia family now in The Metropolitan Museum of Art, New York, modeled in such adventuresome depth that the North Italian artist responsible abandoned it before supplying the obverse inscription. See Avery 1985, no. 40.
4. Clausse 1902, p. 236.
5. Darr and Roisman 1987, p. 790.
6. See Ruschi 1986, pp. 18–38, especially p. 37, note 10.

Additional literature: Hill 1912 (*Portrait*), no. 37; Pollard 1984–85, nos. 316–17.

Gaspare Mola

Notes:
1. Magnaguti 1918, p. 103.
2. Dupré had been invited to Mantua by Francesco IV Gonzaga, son-in-law of Charles Emanuel I and nephew of Marie de' Medici.
3. M. Jones 1986, p. 35, illus. 30; Domanig 1896, no. 160, pl. 22.

Additional literature: Bertolotti 1877; Reymond 1900, p. 181; Anton Küchler in *Schweizerisches Künstler-Lexikon*, pp. 414–15; Forrer 1904–30, vol. 4, p. 117; Thieme-Becker 1931, vol. 25, p. 28; Hill and Pollard 1967, p. 68; Panvini Rosati 1968, p. 54; Pollard 1984–85, vol. 3, p. 854.

66
Gaspare Mola
Charles Emanuel I

Notes:
1. For Sagittarius as the ninth sign of the zodiac, see Tervarent 1958–59, vol. 2, col. 332. Charles Emanuel was born under the sign of Capricorn, not Sagittarius.
2. *Corpus Nummorum Italicorum*, vol. 1, pp. 263–64, nos. 148–53, pl. 17.10.
3. M. Jones 1982–88, vol. 1, no. 193, "presumably by Philippe II Danfrie (c. 1572–1604)."
4. Copernicus's heliocentric theory, presented in his *De orbium coelestium revolutionibus*, Nuremberg, 1543, postulated the circular movement of the planets.
5. FERT appears from about 1391 on anonymous coins of Savoy. See *Corpus Nummorum Italicorum*, vol. 1, p. 31, nos. 1ff. Also on coins of Amedeo VIII (born 1383, ruled 1391–1451), ibid. p. 33, nos. 1ff, pl. III.17/18. See also cat. no. 138.
6. Ibid., p. 321, no. 63, pl. XXII.1.
7. The allusion to Rhodes recalls the bravery of Amedeo V (born c. 1253, ruled 1285–1323) at the siege of Rhodes in 1310. In memory of that hero, Amedeo VI (born 1334, ruled 1343–83) founded in 1362 (or 1364?) the Ordine Supremo della Santissima Annunziata, also called the Order of the Necklace, with a membership of fifteen, symbolizing the fifteen mysteries of the rosary. The design of the pendant, attached to the necklace by three short chains as shown on this medal, is the one introduced in 1518 by Duke Charles II (born 1486, ruled 1504–53), who also raised the number of knights to twenty. I am grateful to James C. Risk for kindly supplying literature on the Order of the Annunziata.
8. Muratore 1909–10, quoted in José 1952.
9. He was the grandson of Francis I. For more on Charles Emanuel, see Raulich 1896–1902; Rua 1905; E. Rott 1902–9; and Bergadani 1927.

Additional literature: Forrer 1904–30, vol. 4, illus. p. 113; Salton 1969, no. 43.

Pastorino de' Pastorini

Notes:
1. Pastoureau 1990.
2. Mario Salmi in Thieme-Becker, vol. 15, pp. 260–61.
3. Specifically those of Marzio and Livia Colonna, Durante Duranti, and Titian. The first of these must have been produced at the time of the couple's marriage in 1540 or shortly thereafter. Armand 1883–87, vol. 2, p. 169, no. 28, lists it as anonymous, while Hill 1906–7, p. 387, recognizes it as Pastorino's. The second is also listed as anonymous by Armand (vol. 3, p. 223, H), yet it is certainly the work of Pastorino. It describes the sitter as bishop of Cassano, making no mention of his being a cardinal, and must therefore date from 1541–44. The Titian medal may be dated to the painter's stay in Rome from September 1545 to June 1546. See Armand 1883–87, vol. 1, p. 208, no. 122; Heiss 1881–92, vol. 9, p. 164; and Hill 1912 (*Portrait*), pp. 56–57, no. 35.
4. *Guido storico-artistica . . .* , pp. 120, 122; della Valle 1786, vol. 3, p. 335.
5. Ronchini 1870, p. 41.
6. *Corpus Nummorum Italicorum*, vol. 10, pp. 456–57 and 461, "Collezione di Vittorio Emanuele III," pp. 121, 123, and 125.
7. Heiss 1881–92, vol. 9, p. 145; Pollard 1984–85, vol. 2, p. 353.
8. Armand 1883–87, vol. 1, p. 199, nos. 65–66; Heiss 1881–92, vol. 9, pp. 134–35.
9. Pollard 1984–85, vol. 2, no. 355, records it as the work of an anonymous artist, but its inferiority is probably a reflection of the decline in Pastorino's artistic abilities.
10. Armand 1883–87, vol. 1, p. 201, no. 81; Heiss 1881–92, vol. 9, p. 145; Pollard 1984–85, vol. 2, p. 352.

Additional literature: Vasari 1878–85, vol. 4, pp. 433–40; U. Rossi 1888 ("Nuovi"), pp. 229–30; Kenner 1891, pp. 84–164; Gruyer 1897, vol. 1, pp. 672–90; Hill 1906, pp. 408–12; Forrer 1904–30, vol. 4, pp. 408–22; G. F. Hill in Thieme-Becker, vol. 26, p. 289; Hill and Pollard 1967, pp. 60–63; Hill and Pollard 1978, pp. 85–87.

67
Pastorino
Grazia Nasi

Note:

1. For information on the family, see Grunebaum-Ballin 1968.

2. For example, those of Lucrezia de' Medici, on the occasion of her marriage to the future Alfonso II d'Este in 1558 (cat. no. 68), and Eleonora of Austria, who married Duke Guglielmo I of Mantua in 1561 (Armand 1883–87, vol. 1, p. 199, no. 64; Hill and Pollard 1967, no. 326).

3. Armand 1883–87, vol. 2, p. 231, no. 10; Hill 1913, p. 21; Cecil Roth in Friedenberg, ed. 1963, pp. 12–13; Friedenberg 1970, p. 42; Pollard 1984–85, vol. 3, no. 847.

4. Armand 1883–87, vol. 3, p. 87, U; Cecil Roth in Friedenberg, ed. 1963, p. 13; Friedenberg 1970, pp. 42–44.

Additional literature: Longpérier 1858, pp. 89–104; Armand 1883–87, vol. 1, p. 202, no. 86; Heiss 1881–92, vol. 9, p. 147; Habich 1924, pl. 85, no. 6; Middeldorf and Goetz 1944, no. 141; Pollard 1984–85, vol. 2, no. 356.

68
Pastorino
Lucrezia de' Medici

Note:

1. Armand 1883–87, vol. 1, p. 218, no. 14.

Additional literature: Armand 1883–87, vol. 1, p. 195, no. 40; Heiss 1881–92, vol. 2, p. 119; Hill and Pollard 1967, no. 325; Salton 1969, no. 38; Langedijk 1981–87, vol. 2, p. 1302, no. 7a.

69
Pastorino
Camillo Castiglione

Notes:

1. For the lives of Baldassare and Camillo, see G. de Caro and C. Mutini in *Dizionario Biografico . . .* , vol. 22, pp. 53–68 and 75–76.

2. Armand 1883–87, vol. 1, p. 199, nos. 63–64.

3. Ibid., vol. 1, p. 198, no. 62; Heiss 1881–92, vol. 9, p. 132.

Additional literature: Armand 1883–87, vol. 1, p. 191, no. 17; Heiss 1881–92, vol. 9, p. 108; Rizzini 1892, no. 287; Hill and Pollard 1967, no. 321.

Alessandro Vittoria

Note:

1. Armand 1883–87, vol. 2, p. 274, no. 5, and vol. 3, p. 118, B; Hill 1912 (*Portrait*), pp. 77–78; Cessi 1960, pp. 62–64. See Schweikhart 1990, pp. 123–30.

Additional literature: Heiss 1881–92, vol. 7, p. 137–41; Forrer 1904–30, vol. 6, pp. 288–91; H. V. in Thieme-Becker, vol. 34, pp. 438–40; Habich 1924, pp. 128–29; Cessi 1961; Cessi 1961–62; Pope-Hennessy 1985 (*Italian High*), pp. 415–18; Pollard 1984–85, vol. 3, pp. 1296–99.

70
Alessandro Vittoria
Pietro Aretino

Notes:

1. Armand 1883–87, vol. 1, p. 162, no. 3, and vol. 3, p. 65, f; Plon 1887, p. 254; Pollard 1984–85, vol. 3, no. 716; Scher 1989, p. 8.

2. Armand 1883–87, vol. 2, p. 153, no. 11; Plon 1887, p. 254; Hill and Pollard 1967, no. 484a; Pollard 1984–85, vol. 3, no. 760; Scher 1989 (*Veritas*), pp. 4–11; Waddington 1989, pp. 12–13.

3. Aretino 1957–60, vol. 2, p. 427–28. Cessi 1960, p. 96.

4. Bottari and Ticozzi 1822–25, vol. 8, p. 354; Cessi 1960, p. 95.

Additional literature: Gaetani 1761–63, vol. 1, pl. 63, no. 4; van Mieris 1732–35, vol. 3, p. 50; Armand 1883–87, vol. 1, p. 159, no. 1, and vol. 2, p. 297, no. 1; Heiss 1881–92, vol. 7, p. 140; Forrer 1904–30, vol. 6, p. 288; Habich 1924, p. 128; Hill and Pollard 1978, p. 94; Pollard 1984–85, vol. 3, no. 756.

Giovanni Cavino

Notes:

1. Most of the documents relating to Cavino's life are published in Sartori 1976, pp. 336–39, and many are discussed in Gorini 1987, pp. 45–54. See also Cessi and Caon 1969, and Andrea Norris in *Dizionario Biografico . . .* , vol. 23, pp. 109–12.

2. Now called Camposampiero (Norris, as in note 1, p. 109).

3. Giandomenico seems to have died before June 11, 1561, since a document of that date discusses Cavino's son Camillo with no mention of any other. See Sartori 1976, p. 339.

4. A further connection between the two artists is provided by a document from November 6, 1527, noting that Riccio's brother Battista, a goldsmith, was asked to evaluate candelabra finished by Cavino. See Sartori 1976, p. 280.

5. Planiscig 1927, p. 474.

6. Armand 1883–87, vol. 1, p. 183, no. 27; Johnson and Martini 1989, nos. 1172–73.

7. The first is Armand 1883–87, vol. 1, p. 182, no. 19, and Johnson and Martini 1989, no. 1171. The second is Lawrence 1883, no. 113; Armand 1883–87, vol. 3, p. 79, C; and Cessi and Caon 1969, p. 45, no. 13.

8. They are grouped together in the Cabinet des Médailles of the Bibliothèque Nationale, Paris, and include 53 obverse and 51 reverse dies, a few of which may or may not be by Cavino. I would like to thank Jean-Baptiste Giard for allowing me access to them and for sharing his inventory list.

9. Hill 1923 (*Guide*), p. 43, evidently antipathetic to Cavino, rather overstates the situation, describing Cavino's style as "desperately arid."

10. Lawrence 1883 lists 76 medals of ancient subjects and 37 of contemporary ones, for a total of 113.

11. Armand 1883–87, vol. 1, p. 180, no. 11; Hill and Pollard 1967, no. 391; Johnson and Martini 1989, nos. 1165–66.

12. Armand 1883–87, vol. 1, p. 180, no. 12; Johnson and Martini 1989, nos. 1163–64.

13. See the entry for cat. no. 71, below, for discussion of Bassiano's role and the relevant bibliography.

14. Armand 1883–87, while noting that the medals of ancient subjects are Cavino's most famous pieces, only catalogues his medals of Renaissance sitters. Hill 1912 (*Portrait*), p. 52; Hill 1920 (Hill and Pollard 1978, p. 93); and Hill 1923 (*Guide*), p. 43, repeatedly stresses that Cavino's pieces were forgeries. However Lawrence 1883, p. 5, insists that "Cavino's imitative medals were not originally designed as forgeries." Gorini 1987 also judges the medalist positively. See also J. R. Jones 1965, vol. 232–33, who leans toward a condemnation of the artist. Cavino's pieces were so famous that all Renaissance copies after ancient coins, regardless of where they were produced, the artist responsible, or the artist's intention, became known simply as "Paduans."

15. Sartori 1976, p. 338.

16. See Lawrence 1883, p. 6; Klawans 1977, pp. 7–13; and Gorini 1987, p. 46, for discussions of these differences.

17. Many of the earliest Renaissance scientific publications on numismatics dealt with the subject of metrology, or the value of coins and their weights. One example is Guillaume Budé's well-known *De asse et partibus ejus*, first published in 1515 and reprinted in sixteen editions by 1550. See Clain-Stefanelli 1965, p. 18, and R. Weiss 1969, pp. 177–78.

18. Such as the medal of Cosimo Scapti (Armand 1883–87, vol. 1, p. 184, no. 33; Hill and Pollard 1967, no. 398; and Johnson and Martini 1989, no. 1200), which has the same reverse as the medal of Commodus (Hill and Pollard 1967, no. 409; Cessi and Caon 1969, pp.

89–90, no. 71; and Johnson and Martini 1989, nos. 1774–78).

19. Published in Scardeone 1560, p. 376 and cited in Zorzi 1962, p. 87.

20. Cunnally 1984, p. 19. For further discussion of coin collecting in the Renaissance, see Gorini 1987, pp. 46–47; Clain-Stefanelli 1965, especially pp. 15–21; and R. Weiss 1969, especially Chapter 12. Gorini contends that coin collecting in the period was largely uncritical, and Cunnally, Clain-Stefanelli, and Weiss provide ample support for that contention.

Additional literature: Montigny 1842–46, vol. 1, pp. 385–414, and vol. 2, pp. 9, 30; Rizzoli 1902, pp. 69–76; Forrer 1904–30, vol. 1, pp. 366–73; Thieme-Becker, vol. 6, pp. 236–37; Chowen 1956, pp. 50–65; Cessi 1965; Gorini 1973, pp. 110–130; Davis 1978, pp. 331–34.

71
Giovanni Cavino
Alessandro Bassiano with the Artist

Notes:

1. I would like to thank Alessandra Galizzi for her assistance with translations of the Latin inscriptions.

2. According to Hubert Golzius in 1563; see Cessi and Caon 1969, p. 37. For Bassiano's biography, see also Zorzi 1962, pp. 41–98, and for information on his family, see Joost-Gaugier 1983, pp. 113–24, especially pp. 120ff.

3. *Interpretatio historiarum ac signorum in numismatibus excussarum excussorumqve duodecim primorum Caesarum. . . .* The unpublished manuscript is preserved in the Biblioteca del Seminario Vescovile (ms. 663) in Padua. See Zorzi 1962, pp. 51ff.

4. As noted by Cessi and Caon 1969, p. 37, du Molinet 1692, pp. 92–118, considered Cavino's medals based on Roman pieces to be joint productions of the two men.

5. Gorini 1987, p. 45.

6. For the Italian version of Riccio's will of March 8, 1532, see Rigoni 1970, pp. 230–31; for the Latin one of March 18, see Sartori 1976, p. 202.

7. The friendship was also commemorated in a poem by the historian Francesco Savonarola. See note 19 from the Cavino biography, above.

8. Gorini 1987, p. 49.

9. A Roman medallion of the third century features a portrait of Postumus coupled with a profile of Hercules behind him, both facing right. See Dressel 1973, p. 269, no. 161, pl. XIX, no. 9, and Toynbee 1986, p. 157, note 130, p. 162, note 166, and pl. XLVI, no. 8. There are also double-bust medallions of Commodus coupled with Roma or Minerva; see Fröhner 1878, p. 140, or Dressel 1973, p. 154, no. 86, pl. XII, no. 1. This latter piece is perhaps more likely to have been known to Cavino, since he himself made medals of Commodus; however, the medallion of Postumus is closer to Cavino's design.

10. Armand 1883–87, vol. 1, p. 180, no. 7, and Johnson and Martini 1989, no. 1152. Cavino also made two other dies of Benavides (Armand 1883–87, vol. 1, p. 179, nos. 5 and 6, and Johnson and Martini 1989, nos. 1158 and 1160). Other reverses combined with the present obverse include Ceres, as in the reverse of cat. no. 72, below, and an eagle with the inscription VIRT • KÆT • CONS (Armand 1883–87, vol. 1, p. 180, no. 8). For Benavides, see Davis 1976, pp. 472–84, and Davis 1978, pp. 331–34.

11. See Belloni 1977, vol. 1, and the reverses of coins of Hadrian, no. 418; Maximianus, nos. 696–97 and 718; Galerius Maximianus, no. 702; and Diocletian, no. 736.

12. The inscription of this reverse reads GENIVS AVGVSTI. See Mattingley et al. 1923, vol. 1, no. 87.

13. Book 9, VII.20–XI.34; Pliny 1940, pp. 177–87. See also the discussion in *Paulys Realencyclopädie der classischen Altertumswissenschaft*, vol. 4, part 2, columns 2504–2510.

14. Ripa 1992, pp. 23–25, cites several ancient authors, including Pausanius and Pliny, who wrote of the dolphin's nature. Cavino's use of the dolphin as a positive symbol also occurs in a medal he made of Vitellius, the

reverse of which was copied from a genuine sestertius. See Klawans 1977, p. 58, no. 1.

15. The motif appears on a limited number of Roman coins. See Stevenson et al. 1982, pp. 338–39. See also Tervarent 1958–64, columns 143–45.
16. Armand 1883–87, vol. 1, p. 182, no. 20; Hill and Pollard 1967, no. 393.

Additional literature: Keary 1881, p. 46, no. 116; Lawrence 1883; Armand 1883–87, vol. 1, p. 180, nos. 7–10; Hill 1923 (*Guide*), p. 43; Habich 1924, p. 110, pl. LXXVI, no. 14; Hill and Pollard 1967, p. 73, no. 389; Panvini Rosati 1968, p. 46, no. 160; *Medaglie del Rinascimento*, p. 92, no. 161; Pollard 1984–85, vol. 3, pp. 1313–14, no. 763.

72
Giovanni Cavino
Luca Salvioni

Notes:

1. Other specimens carry the longer inscription: LV CAS SALVIONVS PAT[avinus] IVR[is] CON[sultus] (Luca Salvioni, jurisconsult in Padua). I would like to thank Alessandra Galizzi for her help with the translations of the Latin inscriptions.
2. A useful summary of Salvioni's life is found in Cessi and Caon 1969, pp. 66–67. For his eulogy, see Scardeone 1560, p. 191.
3. See Zorzi 1962, p. 62.
4. See Sartori 1976, p. 203.
5. See cat. no. 71, note 6.
6. Davis 1978, pp. 331–34, apparently assumes that there was no personal contact between the medalist and Salvioni, for he suggests that Cavino must have based his portrait on a death mask. Although it is possible that such a mask may have been employed as an aid in making the medal, I cannot agree with Davis's opinion that the Salvioni portrait is only superficially individualized, that it was not based on direct observation or an understanding of the sitter's character—whether or not it was made posthumously.
7. Zorzi 1962, p. 62. I would like to thank Thomas McGill for assistance with the Latin passages.
8. As in Virgil's *Georgics*, especially the first two books. See Virgil 1942, pp. 81–237.
9. As noted by Cessi and Caon 1969, p. 36, who cite Labus 1837, pp. 27–31, especially p. 29.
10. Book Five, lines 341–44. See Ovid 1955, p. 118.
11. Stevenson et al. 1982, p. 195, note that animals that ate seeds, above all sows, were sacrificed to Ceres.
12. Ibid., pp. 195–97; the author does not cite specific coins of Ceres Legifera. See also the discussion in Davis 1985, pp. 241–42. For other coins with reverses featuring Ceres, see Belloni 1977, vol. 1, no. 433 (a sestertius of Hadrian) or nos. 439 and 440 (aurei of Faustina Senior).
13. Johnson and Martini 1989, nos. 1203–4; Armand 1883–87, vol. 1, p. 185, no. 35.
14. Armand 1883–87, vol. 1, p. 184, no. 32.
15. Johnson and Martini 1989, no. 1199.

Additional literature: Lawrence 1883; Armand 1883–87, vol. 1, p. 184, nos. 31–32; Cessi 1965, pp. 13–18; Hill and Pollard 1967, p. 74, no. 397; Gorini 1987, pp. 45–54.

Alfonso Ruspagiari

Notes:

1. Balletti 1901, pp. 107ff., Balletti 1904, pp. 44–46, and Balletti 1914, pp. 46–48, form the basis of our knowledge of the artist. Forrer 1904–30, vol. 5, pp. 272–75, gives a good, though out-of-date resumé. See also Baudi di Vesme 1968, vol. 3, pp. 948–54.
2. Balletti 1904, p. 44.
3. Balletti 1914, p. 46.
4. Ibid., and Balletti 1904, p. 44. The medal is Armand 1883–87, vol. 1, p. 217, no. 6, and vol. 3, p. 100, no. 6. This portrait also occurs, for example, in the Molinari Collection (Norris and Weber 1976, no. 63), as the reverse of the image of an unidentified woman that has always been attributed to Ruspagiari. See Armand

1883–87, vol. 1, p. 216, no. 4. An aftercast of it was discovered in the excavations of Palissy's workshop in the Tuileries. See Dufay et al. 1987, fig. 77, type 26. In the Molinari version it is circular, while in the Kress example (Hill and Pollard 1967, no. 449) and the one in the Museum Mayer van den Bergh (de Coo 1969, no. 2439) it is oval.
5. Balletti 1914, p. 46.
6. Balletti 1904, p. 44. Norris and Weber 1976, no. 62, propose the date 1534. This would only be possible if Ruspagiari was indeed precocious enough to have produced the work when only thirteen years old. A slightly later date of 1536 is suggested here, as that is the year of Ercole d'Este's triumphal entry into Reggio, the occasion for Lelio Orsi's first documented work in that city (see *Lelio Orsi*, nos. 147 and 147b). Ercole died in 1559, a reasonable if somewhat extended terminus for this medal.
7. Balletti 1904, p. 44.
8. Ibid., pp. 44–45; Balletti 1914, p. 46, note 1.

73
Alfonso Ruspagiari
Bust of a Woman

Notes:

1. Habich 1924, p. 139, describes these medals of the Emilian school, most of which have no reverses, as "bits of portraiture, not medals" ("Porträtstücke also, keine Medaillen"). Because this object is pierced and cast integrally with a frame, it also resembles a pendant badge or a reproduction in lead of a locket or jewel.
2. Pope-Hennessy 1966, p. 41, points out that this painting is unusual for a fifteenth-century profile portrait of a woman in that it is a double profile.
3. The abbreviated profile also brings to mind the reflection of a sitter's face in a mirror, as in the sixteenth-century painting *Dame à sa toilette* (versions in the Musée des Beaux-Arts, Dijon, and the Worcester Art Museum), which may allude to marriage or Vanity. See also Vasari's *Toilet of Venus*, c. 1558, Stuttgart, Staatsgalerie (Markova 1992, p. 239). Our medal would seem to be a conflation of various elements from this picture, namely the face of Venus, the reflection in the mirror, and the mirror's scrolled frame.
4. Hill and Rosenheim 1907, pp. 141–47. Hill 1928, pp. 11–12, continues his identifications. For further bibliography, see also Hill and Pollard 1967, no. 450, and Hill and Pollard 1978, p. 180, note 271.
5. Burckhardt 1918, pp. 45–49, with his own references to Hill and Rosenheim.
6. Baudi di Vesme 1968, vol. 1, pp. 46, 49.
7. Burckhardt 1918, p. 49, suggested this date based on the age of one of the sitters and the evident stylistic coherence of the group. The complexity of the scrolled frames (especially in the two examples illustrated in Burckhardt) recalls certain designs by Lelio Orsi. See *Lelio Orsi*, nos. 104–5.
8. Mark Jones 1982–89, vol. 1, no. 249: French, lead, 63 mm.
9. Pollard 1984–85, vol. 3, no. 784.

74
Ruspagiari
Large Self-Portrait

Notes:

1. This object is identified as such in the description of the example in the British Museum.
2. Pollard 1984–85, no. 784.
3. Inv. no. 914, 88.0 × 75.0 mm. I am grateful to Jadranka Bentini for providing a photograph and correct dimensions. Previous publications have misreported the latter, suggesting that the drawing is ten times larger than it really is. In the drawing one can see that the figure's right leg crosses in front of its left. This is omitted on the medal to make room for the word IDEM and the artist's initials.
4. Balletti 1914, p. 46.
5. Salvini and Chiodi 1950, no. 10.
6. M. Pirondini in *Lelio Orsi*, p. 171. Bonsanti 1990 also subscribes to this theory.
7. E. Monducci in *Lelio Orsi*, document nos. 201–2. See

also document no. 86, a letter from Count Gonzaga, dated June 5, 1555, discussing medals in gold, silver, and "metal" (lead?): "gli stucchi li manderó per Lelio che presto se ne verràin [sic] questi paesi."
8. There are no portraits in either Salvini and Chiodi 1950 or *Lelio Orsi*, nor do any appear in the latter in the listing of known works destroyed or missing.
9. Hill and Pollard 1967, no. 447.
10. Baudi di Vesme 1968, vol. 1, p. 46. In this context it may be useful to draw attention to a bronze bust of Carlo Emanuele as a boy, attributed to Leone Leoni, Philadelphia Museum of Art, which has a curiously medallic quality.
11. Balletti 1914, p. 46.

Bombarda

Notes:

1. The most recent discussion of the group is provided by Graham Pollard in his article "Cambio" in *Dizionario Biografico . . .*, vol. 17, pp. 140–44.
2. Bertolotti 1890, pp. 28 and 54. Belisario was acquainted with Giambologna.
3. Armand 1883–87, Habich 1924, Hill 1930, and M. Jones 1979 (*Art*), p. 64, identify him as Andrea, however Malaguzzi Valeri 1910, p. 186, insists that he was called Giovanni Battista. Pollard (see note 1) presents the medalist as "Andrea (o Giovanni Battista)."
4. Langedijk 1981–87, vol. 2, pp. 1202–3.
5. Habich 1924, p. 139; Boccolari 1987, nos. 137–38.
6. Hill and Pollard 1967, no. 459. Violante was in all probability related to Girolamo Brasavola (1536–1594), court physican to Alfonso d'Este and son of Antonio Musa Brasavola, famed for his medical studies.
7. Bernhart 1925–26, p. 83. Bocchi dedicated to Pigna a sequel to his 1555 treatise *Symbolicarum Quaestionum de universo Genere*, and is thought to have been the author of a design Bombarda used for a reverse found coupled both with his portrait of Pigna and his signed portrait of the gem-cutter Miseroni (Kris 1929, p. 88, note 15; Hill 1912 [*Portrait*], pp. 73–74; and Hill 1916, p. 59). For a more thorough examination of the interaction between this humanist patron and the artists who worked for him, see Lugli 1982.
8. See Ravegnani Morosini 1984. I am grateful to Dr. Alan Stahl of the American Numismatic Society for this reference.
9. See Balletti 1904, p. 45, and Pollard 1984–85, p. 1345.
10. Dufay et al. 1987.

75
Bombarda
Leonora Cambi

Notes:

1. Compare those of Lucrezia de' Medici (Langedijk 1981–87, vol. 2, pp. 1202–3) and Violante Pigna (Hill and Pollard 1967, no. 459). I am grateful to Mme S. de Turckheim-Pey of the Cabinet des Médailles in Paris for having made that collection's example of the Lucrezia medal available for examination. M Jean-Baptiste Giard of the same institution kindly provided a photograph of the specimen of the Violante medal preserved in the State Hermitage Museum, St. Petersburg.
2. Hill 1912 (*Portrait*), p. 17.
3. Habich 1924, p. 139.
4. For a fine discussion of the style, see Wilson 1983, p. 172.
5. See the analysis of a parallel development in Emilian frescoes in Boschloo 1984, pp. 85–86.

Additional literature: Armand 1883–87; Hill and Pollard 1967, no. 454.

Jacopo Primavera

Notes:

1. Chabouillet 1875, p. 21.
2. As mentioned in M. Jones 1982–88, vol. 1, p. 159, citing the earlier study, d'Espezél 1925 ("Le médaille"), pp. II–III, that initially brought this document to light.
3. Chabouillet 1875, p. 32.
4. Ibid., pp. 34–35, provides an insightful discussion of

the fundamental contrast between the more sculptural and meticulously detailed medals by these two medalists and the more painterly and broader handling of the details in Primavera's medallic output.

Additional literature: *Trésor de Numismatique . . .* (Italian) vol. 3, part 1, pp. 33–38; Bolzenthal 1840, vol. 4, pp. 160–61; Mazerolle 1902–4, vol. 2, pp. XC, XCI, and 63–67; Forrer 1904–30, vol. 4, pp. 691–96; G. K. Nagler in *Neues Allgemeines Künstler-Lexicon*, vol. 13, pp. 286–87; Hill 1912 (*Portrait*), pp. 69–70; Hill 1920 (*Medals*), pp. 146–47; G. F. Hill in Thieme-Becker, vol. 27, p. 403; M. Jones 1979 (*Art*), p. 56; M. Jones 1987, pp. 62–63.

76
Jacopo Primavera
Mary Queen of Scots

Notes:
1. The literature on Mary Stuart is voluminous. A convenient directory is Tannenbaum and Tannenbaum 1944–46; see especially vol. 2, pp. 25–30 for citations pertaining to the portraits, and entries 566, 669–70, 908, 963, and 1200 for the medals. Fraser 1970 remains the essential biography, however other useful sources are Donaldson 1983; Lynch, ed. 1988; Wormald 1991; and Angus, duke of Hamilton 1991.
2. Quoted in Maxwell-Scott 1912, p. 35.
3. For various dates, ranging from Mary's residency in France to after her death, see Chabouillet 1875, pp. 44–50, especially p. 47; Hawkins 1885, pp. 52–54; Cust 1903, pp. 121–22; A. Lang 1906, pp. 32–33; Forrer 1904–30, vol. 4, p. 695; Hill 1920 (*Medals*), pp. 146–47; Hill 1922, p. 67; and Strong 1969, p. 215.
4. Chabouillet 1875, pp. 44 and 50; Mazerolle 1902–4, vol. 2, p. 299. For specific details of the mourning attire of Mary Stuart, see Taylor 1983, pp. 81–83 and 85–86.
5. For discussion of this book and its engraving of Mary see Hind 1955, pp. 47–48, pl. 19a, and Smailes and Tomson 1987, pp. 40–42 and 53. The latter hint at a correlation between the medal and the print, but without drawing any conclusions regarding the medal's date. Strong and Oman 1972, p. 42, reproduce a woodcut of Mary supposedly taken from the 1578 edition of Leslie's book. Fraser 1970, pp. 450–51, seems to imply that the profile frontispiece portrait in Leslie's history was based on the medal, but this may or may not be the case. I personally viewed a copy of the book in the Cleveland Public Library, and it, like other copies examined at my request in the Johns Hopkins University Library, Baltimore; the University of Michigan Library, Ann Arbor; and the library of St. Borromeo Seminary, Philadelphia, contains only an engraving in three-quarter view. I wish to thank the librarians of the facilities named for their time-consuming efforts, also James Roan and the Numismatic Division of the Smithsonian Institution Libraries and Ann B. Abid and her staff at The Cleveland Museum of Art Library for their general helpfulness.

Additional literature: Brooke and Hill 1924, pp. 21–23, fig. 11; M. Jones 1982–88, vol. 1, no. 159.

Germany, Sixteenth Century

Hans Krafft

77
Hans Krafft
Charles V (Habich 1929–34, no. 18)

Notes:
1. E. Rosenthal 1971, pp. 204–28.
2. These are blasoned as follows, reading clockwise from the top: Gules, a castle triple-towered or (*Castille*); Or, four pallets gules (*Aragon*); Argent, a lion rampant gules, crowned and armed or (*Leon*); Quarterly, 1 and 4 Aragon; 2 and 3, Hungary-ancient, which is Gules, four bars argent (prior descriptions have called this Catalonia, which is simply Or, four pallets gules) (*Naples*); Argent, an eagle displayed sable, membered gules, crowned or (*Sicily*); since there are so many arms with

eagles that could be associated with Charles V, this identification is tentative); Per saltire: in chief and base, Aragon; in flanks, Sicily (*Kingdom of the Two Sicilies* [or Aragon/Sicily]); Argent, a cross-potent between four crosslets or (*Jerusalem*); Azure, a king crowned or, seated on a throne of the same, holding in one hand a scepter or and in the other a sword (*Seville*); Gules, a castle triple-towered or (*New Castille*); Azure, semé of cross crosslets, a chalice or covered cup or (*Galicia*: [shown as a simplification of the actual arms]); 1. Gules, a five-towered fortified city above flowing water argent; or 2. Azure, a walled city argent, with walls, towers, and masonry sable, and surrounded by water (*Valencia-ancient:* [two versions]); Azure, an imperial crown or (*Toledo*); Argent, a pomegranate gules (originally vert) seeded and slipped proper (*Granada*); Gules, a cross, saltire, and double orle of chains linked together or (*Navarre*). At the top, on a banderole, Charles's motto: PLVS VLTRA, and his devices: the Pillars of Hercules and the steel and flints of the Order of the Golden Fleece. I wish to thank Stephen K. Scher for the entire blasoning of these arms and those in note 3, below.
3. (Austria) Gules, a fess argent; (Burgundy ancient) Bendy of six azure and or, a bordure gules (abbreviated on this medal). Reading clockwise from the top: Argent, a cross gules between four moor's heads couped sable banded (or crowned) of the first (*Sardinia*); Gules, three bars or (*Cordoba*); Argent, a moor's head sable, banded of the first (*Corsica*); Gules, six open crowns or (*Murcia*); Azure, a bust of a king or crowned of the same (*Jaén*); Argent, three moor's heads sable (*Algarve*); Quarterly: 1 and 4, argent, a moor's head couped sable, banded of the first; 2 and 3, argent, a crowned, bearded head proper (also, azure, a bust of a king or crowned of the same) (*Algeciras*); three open cups (?) (*Mazzarón*; this identity has not been confirmed); an empty shield (*New World*); a turtle (?) (*Minorca*; this identity has not been confirmed); Gules, four pallets or, overall a bend (tincture uncertain) (*Mallorca*); Rhinoceros with signs of the zodiac: Cancer, Leo, Virgo, Libra, flanked dexter and sinister by a star (on the medal not all of these charges are present, and the tinctures are uncertain) (*Indian and Oceanic Islands*); Party per fess, in chief a leopard or, in base an elephant argent (*Islas y Tierra Firme* [the Islands and the Continents]; these arms have also been identified as Gibraltar, which has as arms Vert, a castle over rocks in the sea, the castle or). It is striking that on both the obverse and reverse the sequence of coats of arms is in no way aligned with the center image. Neither the emperor's motto on the front nor the N for Nuremberg on the back appears to relate to the vertical axis. At first glance one might wonder why only an initial is used instead of the Nuremberg coat of arms, but doubtless it was felt that the latter did not fit in with a series of Spanish emblems.
4. Petz 1889, pp. 44–45, nos. 5829, 5831–32.
5. This tradition had been established by the Golden Bull, issued by Charles IV in 1356. See Zeumer 1908, p. 45.
6. This was the famous Diet of Worms at which Luther was required to defend himself. It is not entirely certain, according to some scholars, that there actually was a plague in Nuremberg at this time.
7. Grotemeyer 1970, pp. 143–66.
8. Timann 1990, p. 104.

Additional literature: Lochner 1743, vol. 7, pp. 41–48; Herrgott 1752, no. 7 and pl. 19; Imhof 1782, pp. 7–9, no. 6; Bernhart 1919, pp. 8–10; Habich 1929–33, vol. 1, 1, p. 5, no. 18; Mende 1983, pp. 50–57 and 182–86; Maué 1987, pp. 227–44; Trusted 1990, nos. 91–92.

Hans Daucher

Notes:
1. Regarding the relationship between sculptor and joiner, see Baxandall, 1980, p. 112.
2. This is in distinct contrast to contemporaries of his like Hans Schwarz, Christoph Weiditz, Matthes Gebel, Friedrich Hagenauer, or Hans Kels the Younger. We can confirm either from contemporary documents or their signatures that all worked as portraitists. Out of his vast

experience, Georg Habich felt justified in attributing as many as fifty (!) medals to Daucher, but the historical facts are so vague that they in no way bear him out. See Habich 1929–34, nos. 38–90 and 92–99. Domanig 1907, p. 11, was much more circumspect in his attributions to Daucher.
3. Wittelsbacher Ausgleichsfonds; Munich, Schloss Nymphenburg. See Habich 1929–34, vol. 1, 1, nos. 48–49.
4. Habich 1929–34, vol. 1, 1, nos. 46 and 47.
5. Comparative illustrations in Eser 1991, pp. 1770–73, illus. 2f.

Additional literature: Bode 1887, pp. 3–10 and 169–71; Habich 1903 ("Beiträge"), pp. 53–76; Theodor Demmler in Thieme-Becker, vol. 8, pp. 427–31; Fries 1919; Halm 1920, pp. 283–343; Feuchtmayr 1952, pp. 433–71; H. Müller 1958, pp. 131–65; Schindler 1985.

78
Hans Daucher
Philipp, count of the Rhenish Palatinate (Habich 1929–34, no. 51)

Notes:
1. Compare the slightly smaller version of this medal with a wide rim framed by a laurel wreath (Habich 1929–34, no. 53; Trusted 1990, no. 9). It was probably produced—also by Daucher—as a later "edition" of the present piece. It also bears the date 1527. A matching one with the portrait of Philipp's brother Ottheinrich is also preserved.
2. See Gaettens 1956, pp. 62–85.
3. Habich 1929–34, nos. 46–47, pl. VI,1 and VI,2 (the 1520 pair); nos. 48–49, pl. VII, 2 and illus. 20 (the large medallion pair, 1522); no. 50, pl. VI, 3 (counterpart to the medal exhibited here, 1527); and nos. 52–53.
4. See Robert Salzer in *Allgemeine Deutsche Biographie*, vol. 26, pp. 18–27.
5. H. Rott, ed. 1912, pp. 21–191. Ottheinrich's biography of his brother appears on pp. 160–85.

Additional literature: Erman 1885, p. 44; Habich 1903 ("Beiträge"), pp. 72f., illus. 29; Habich 1914–15, p. 212; Habich 1916, p. 18; Fries 1919, pp. 88–90; Bernhart 1937, pl. X, 3.

79
Hans Daucher (?)
Maximilian I (Habich 1929–34, no. 70)

Notes:
1. Kunsthistorisches Museum, inv. no. KK 7236. See Domanig 1907, p. 11, no. 47.
2. Herrgott 1752–53, vol. 1, pl. XII, presents a specimen of this medal with the date 1513 on the reverse.
3. Grotemeyer 1953 investigated a homogenous group of forty-three negative molds of German Renaissance medals, now distributed in various collections. Though their dating and function continues to be disputed, it was Grotemeyer's thesis that these were from the holdings of contemporary (casting) workshops, and Daucher's use of the reversed mold of the Maximilian medal as a pattern for his Vienna relief tends to confirm this.
4. Bartsch 1803–21, no. 32.
5. Ibid., no. 23. A good interpretation of Burgkmair's woodcuts is in Silver 1985, pp. 9–29.
6. Habich 1919–34, vol. 1, 1, no. 70.
7. The literature relating to the life of Maximilian I is extensive. Hermann Wiesflecker recently published a selected bibliography in his article on the emperor in *Neue deutsche Biographie*, vol. 16, pp. 458–71. For the iconography of the portraits of Maximilian I, see Baldass 1913–14.
8. See Giehlow 1988, pp. 30–112. For Maximilian's championship of the Order of St. George, see especially p. 38ff.
9. See the imperial instructions regarding the creation of new works from the year 1512 in Zimermann, ed. 1883, extract 295, p. LII.
10. Ibid., extract 489, p. LXXVII.

Additional literature: Habich 1903 ("Beiträge"), p. 75, illus. 38; *Exhibition of Early . . .* , D 17, p. 143, pl. 53; Habich 1916, p. 18; Bernhart 1937, pl. XX, 1; *Maximilian I, 1459–1519*, no. 656; *The Medal — Mirror of History*, no. 35; Trusted 1990, p. 24, no. 7.

80, 80a
Hans Daucher (?)
Ludwig II of Hungary (Habich 1929–34, nos. 75 and 79)

Notes:
1. Count Schlick appears in even more splendid clothing on a mother-of-pearl medallion in Berlin apparently patterned after the medal. See Bange 1928, p. 40, pl. 35. The Victoria & Albert Museum in London has a similar round image of Schlick in the same material (inv. no. 80–1929), without inscription.
2. For the roughly 5,000 known medals, there are after all over 100 surviving models in stone, wood, or wax.
3. We are now in a position to propose a new grouping of the surviving medals and molds relating to the model. In doing so, it is important to make a definite distinction between the larger, more carefully executed portraits of Ludwig, his consort Maria, and Schlick—the best being the Boston model—and smaller, somewhat sketchier reductions. Only one specimen in lead, now in London (Victoria & Albert Museum, 115–1867), can be identified as having been produced directly after the stone model in Boston. Its inscription was added later by cold engraving: LVDOVIC • REX • HVNGARIAE • OBIIT Aᵒ • 1526. The raised edge of the model has been removed, though traces are still visible on the rim. This change was probably made on the casting mold. Negative molds in Hannover (Kestner-Museum) and Nuremberg (Germanisches Nationalmuseum) are directly related to the London specimen. They are somewhat smaller, owing to shrinkage during cooling. Also belonging to this group are the portraits of Maria and Schlick preserved only in negative molds in Nuremberg (Germanisches National-museum) and a mold of the Schlick portrait in Hannover (Grotemeyer 1953, p. 115, nos. 22–24). The leading specimen from the second group, smaller in format and produced from separate models, is the medal shown here. A silver version with the same obverse and reverse images was in the Rosenheim Collection in London around the turn of the century (compare a re-worked silver version in the Hohenkubin Collection, Lanz sale, 1985, no. 369). A matching copy is in Vienna's Münzkabinett, and Habich mentions an additional example in Budapest. These were doubtless created after the pattern of the "Boston group." The somewhat unfortunate shortening of Ludwig's bust—we have noticed how the "Golden Fleece" is left hanging in space—and the considerably smaller format make it clear that this was a reduced variant produced independently and at a somewhat later date. Stylistically, most notably in their letter forms and their flat relief, unlike that of the Boston model, these are close to the known medals of Hans Daucher. If one compares them to his medals of the counts Palatine, however, especially the one of Philipp, also dating from c. 1527 (cat. no. 78), one can see differences in modeling technique. Of course the reduced detail, especially noticeable in the face of Count Schlick, could be the result of a loss of contrast in the casting.
4. Regarding minting and medalmaking in the Joachimsthal, see the bibliography in Kratzsch 1972, pp. 130–33. On the struck medal of Stefan Schlick, ibid., pp. 132 and 164, and Katz 1932, pl. VII.
5. See *Vom Taler . . .* , pp. 93 and 202f.
6. There is a listing of sources in Palacky 1865, vol. 5, 1, p. 413.
7. Habich 1929–34, no. 66.

Additional literature: For the stone model, see Lanna sale, 1911, no. 40; Habich 1916, pp. 18f., illus. 4; Grotemeyer 1953, p. 115, no. 22, also nos. 23–24; Hirsch sale, 1969, no. 259; Scher et al. 1986, no. 8, pp. 95f. Trusted 1990, pp. 25f., no. 10. For the Ludwig/Schlick medal, see *Exhibition of Early . . .* , no. D 12, p. 141; Habich 1916, pp. 18f.; Peus sale, 1989, p. 52, no. 844.

Hans Schwarz

Notes:
1. Habich 1929–34, vol. 1, 1, p. 23. The frequent occurrence of the name Hans Schwarz makes the evaluation of the sources relating to the artist considerably more difficult.
2. T. Müller 1950–51, pp. 25–30.
3. Zeitler 1951, pp. 77–95; Volz 1972.
4. Maué 1988, pp. 12–17. Pfinzing invited him to the dedication of the tomb of St. Sebald by Peter Vischer, and it was in Pfinzing's house that the artist resided while in Nuremberg.
5. Gaettens 1951–58, pp. 8–17.
6. These drawings were first thought to be by Albrecht Dürer, and accordingly scholarly interest in them was intense. The entire collection is published and reproduced in Bernhart 1934, pp. 65–89, with a survey of the older literature. Bernhart attempted to identify the sketches on the basis of completed medals; however, a large number of these identifications are either false or purely hypothetical.

Additional literature: Stetten 1779, pp. 451–52; Bolzenthal 1840, pp. 129–31; Neudörfer 1875, pp. 124–25; Erman 1884, pp. 20–27; Habich 1906, pp. 30–69; Bernhart 1937, pp. 44–48.

81
Hans Schwarz
Christoph of Braunschweig (Habich 1929–34, no. 114)

Notes:
1. Zeitler 1951, p. 81.
2. Krause in *Allgemeine deutsche Biographie*, vol. 4, pp. 235–39; F. Prüser in *Neue deutsche Biographie*, vol. 3, pp. 243–44; Schwarzwälder 1975, pp. 140–46, 171–84, and 212–34; Heyken 1983, pp. 95–110.
3. Volz 1972, p. 132, note 9, identifies the collar seen here as the generic clerical collar of the period, not a liturgical vestment. For the ceremony, ibid., pp. 82–85.

Additional literature: Brockmann 1985, p. 35, no. 27.

82
Hans Schwarz
Melchior Pfinzing (Habich 1929–34, no. 176)

Notes:
1. Habich 1929–34, nos. 167 (this medal has the same dimensions as the Pfinzing medal), 171, and 259.
2. Löcher 1985, pp. 40–41.
3. Zeitler 1951, pp. 89–90.
4. Biedermann 1748, table 405. A brother Paul died young. Schwarz also produced a highly unusual medal of the remaining five Pfinzing brothers, Habich 1929–34, no. 177. See also Maué in *Schatzhaus . . .* , p. 222, no. 12.8.
5. D. Weiss 1991, pp. 14–29.
6. Habich 1929–34, no. 970.

Additional literature: Will 1764–67, vol. 1, p. 7, no. 17; Imhoff 1782, vol. 1, 2, p. 623, no. 5; Maué in *Nürnberg 1300–1500*, p. 416, no. 215 (with false dimensions).

83
Hans Schwarz
Katharina Starck (Habich 1929–34, no. 188)

Notes:
1. Maué 1988, p. 15, fig. 6.
2. Habich 1929–34, vol. 1, 1, pl. XXIV, 1. One version of this medal is in the Germanisches Nationalmuseum, Nuremberg. See Maué 1988, p. 14 and p. 15, fig. 7.
3. Ibid., p. 14.
4. For the medal of Ulrich Starck, for which the wood model survives, see Habich 1929–34, no. 168.
5. Biedermann 1748, table 219; Burger 1972, p. 222, no. 5956. I am grateful to Dr. Hermann Maué for these references.
6. Dr. Maué kindly pointed this out in correspondence. For Gebel's medals of Ulrich Schwarz, see Habich 1929–34, nos. 966–67.

Additional literature: *Exhibition of Early . . .* , p. 132, pl. XLIX; Maskell 1911, pl. XXVIII, 2; *The Medal — Mirror of History*, no. 14; Trusted 1990, p. 104, no. 157.

84
Hans Schwarz
Albrecht Dürer (Habich 1929–34, no. 201)

Notes:
1. Mende 1983, pp. 37–46. A page dated 1519 and presenting two designs for the reverse of the medal is in the British Museum, London.
2. Berlin, Staatliche Museen, Skulpturengalerie. See Decker 1981, pp. 97–100, no. 47, a catalogue that includes additional examples of later borrowings from Schwarz's Dürer medal.
3. Mende 1983, pp. 265–75, nos. 65–67. See also Gaettens 1958, p. 6, pl. 2.

Additional literature: Imhoff 1782, vol. 1, 1, p. 724, no. 35; Erlanger 1965, pp. 145–172; Gaettens sale, 1966, p. 10, no. 45; *Selbstbildnisse . . .* , pp. 88–90.

85
Augsburg School
Unknown Youth (Habich 1929–34, no. 291)

Notes:
1. I am grateful to Linda Woolley for her advice on the costume.
2. Trusted 1990, p. 109.
3. Maué 1991, p. 108.
4. See Habich 1929–34, nos. 203, 1191–93, 1216–18, 1220, 1222, 1593, 1673, and 2699.
5. The sitter could have been Wilhelm Löffelholz (1502–1551), who was represented on a medal by Matthes Gebel in 1541 (Habich 1929–34, no. 1191), and who attended the Diet in Augsburg in 1530. Perhaps the boxwood model was carved there during his visit.
6. See Trusted 1990, p. 6.

Additional literature: Maskell 1911, pl. XXVIII, 1; *The Medal — Mirror of History*, no. 15.

86
Nuremberg School (Stabius Group)
Johannes Stabius (Habich 1929–34, no. 318)

Notes:
1. For Johannes Stabius, see Grössing 1968, pp. 239–64, and Wiesflecker 1986, especially pp. 321, 323–39, 362–80.
2. A compilation of the idealized portraits is in Grössing 1968, pp. 260–62.
3. Eye 1860, p. 341.
4. Habich 1929–34, vol. 1, 1, pp. XXIV–XXV.
5. Habich 1929–34, no. 17, considers a connection between this medal and the master of the Stabius medal. The reverse is also cast from a wax model—despite Habich, who assumes a model in wood. The copy in the Historisches Museum, Basel—doubtless original—makes this quite clear. See Beatrice Schärli in *Erasmus . . .* , p. 111, no. A 2.5.

Additional literature: Bezold 1910, pp. 125–26; Mende 1983, pp. 46–50 and p. 178, no. 11; Maué in *Nürnberg 1300–1550*, p. 406, no. 219.

Christoph Weiditz

Notes:
1. Zeitler 1951, p. 99, note 12.
2. The dagger-case is signed "Christof Weyditz." See Schädler 1987, p. 162 and fig. 2.
3. Habich 1929–34, vol. 2, 1, p. C.
4. Cited in Schädler 1987, p. 161. See also Grotemeyer 1958, pp. 317–27.
5. See the entry for cat. no. 91.
6. For example the Charles de Solier (cat. no. 91).
7. For example the reverse of the Andrea Doria medal. See Grotemeyer 1958 and Schädler 1987, p. 173, fig. 17.

Additional literature: Habich 1913, pp. 1–35; Hampe, ed. 1927; Grotemeyer in Thieme-Becker, vol. 35, pp. 267–68; Trusted 1990, p. 117.

87
Christoph Weiditz
Lienhard Meringer (Habich 1929–34, no. 346)

Notes:
1. Maskell 1911, p. 182 and pl. XXVIII.
2. Habich 1929–34, vol. 2, 1, p. CV.
3. Ibid., vol. 1, 1, p. 56. See also Trautmann 1869, p. 146.
4. Habich 1929–34, no. 347. This medal has a later reverse, and is falsely inscribed LK, the initials of Ludwig Krug.

Additional literature: Habich 1913, pp. 9–10 and pl. III, 3; *The Medal — Mirror of History*, no. 17; Trusted 1990, p. 117, no. 179.

88
Christoph Weiditz
Magdalene Rudolff (Habich 1929–34, no. 361)

Note:
1. *Luchs* (Brandenburg): Gules, a lynx proper seated on a terrace vert (on the wood model there is no terrace); helmet with mantling, orle, and crest, a lynx sejant. I thank Stephen K. Scher for blasoning these arms.

Additional literature: Erman 1884, p. 40; Bode 1888, p. 188; Habich 1913, pl. 4.2; Habich 1916, p. 32; Suhle 1952, p. 32, pl. 9.1; Börner and Steguweit 1990, pp. 18f.

89
Christoph Weiditz
Joachim Rehle (Habich 1929–34, no. 371)

Notes:
1. *Rehlen* (Nuremberg): Azure, a stag springing proper (in the case of the wood model the shield is party per bend-sinister with only the upper part of the stag showing in the dexter part and the tinctures uncertain); helmet with mantling, crown, and crest of a stag issuant. I am grateful to Stephen K. Scher for blasoning these arms.
2. Habich 1929–34, no. 371.
3. See cat. no. 91 and Habich 1929–34, vol. 1, 1, pl. XLIX, 1, pl. L, 4, and pl. LI, 2.
4. The painting is illustrated in Menz 1962, p. 282.
5. The inscription reads: DOM AN M • D • XXIIII • ZALT • WAS ICH • IOACHIM REHLS • XXXIIII • IAR ALT • AVFF ADI • XIII LVIGO (In the year 1524, I, Joachim Rehle, was thirty-four years old on the 13th day of July). See *The Picture Gallery Dresden*, p. 66.
6. Habich 1913, p. 13, and Habich 1929–34, vol. 1, 1, p. 60.
7. Habich 1929–34, vol. 1, 1, p. 60. The writer has not had an opportunity to see the work.
8. Domanig 1895, p. 60.

Additional literature: Maskell 1911, pl. XXVIII, 4; *Exhibition of Early . . .*, p. 132, and pl. XLIX, LII; Trusted 1990, p. 118, no. 180.

90
Christoph Weiditz
Hernán Cortés (Habich 1929–34, no. 376)

Notes:
1. Hampe, ed. 1927. For the Cortés portrait, see p. 77, pl. IV. See also Suhle 1950, illus. 13.
2. Grotemeyer in Thieme-Becker, vol. 35, p. 268.
3. Habich 1929–34, nos. 374–75.
4. Grotemeyer 1958, pp. 317–27.
5. The only three-quarter-profile portrait Weiditz produced before this time was the one of Hieronymus Rotengater, Habich 1929–34, no. 348.

Additional literature: Zeitler 1951, p. 106; Grotemeyer 1957, p. 50, illus. 29–30; I. Weber in Kauffmann, ed. 1970, p. 327, no. 324 c.

91
Christoph Weiditz
Charles de Solier (Habich 1929–34, no. 398)

Notes:
1. Rowlands 1985, p. 142.
2. Habich 1929–34, vol. 2, 1, p. CVII, noted that the boxwood and Holbein's portrait were inextricably

linked. In his earlier article on Weiditz from 1913, p. 18, Habich had dated the boxwood to c. 1530–31 because of de Solier's age, and remarked that the painting was slightly later. In 1929–34, vol. 2, 1, p. CIII, he tentatively suggested a date of about 1530, when Weiditz visited the Rhineland and the Netherlands and possibly made a trip to England as well.
3. Charles de Solier's date of birth is given in the unsigned article "Das Porträt Moretts in der Dresdener Galerie," *Kunstchronik* 17, no. 7 (1881), column 98.
4. The drawing for the painting is less detailed and shows slight changes in the costume. De Solier's frown is also more prominent in both the painting and the boxwood. For the drawing, see Ganz 1937, no. 38, pl. XXIV, 3.
5. The inscription on Weiditz's own medal of Hernán Cortés (cat. no. 90) is a case in point. See Habich 1929–34, no. 376, and note 9, below.
6. Weiditz's medal of Hernán Cortés is probably based on the full-length watercolor portrait of the navigator he made while in Spain. See Hampe, ed. 1927, p. 77 and pl. IV.
7. See Habich 1929–34, vol. 2, 1, p. CIII.
8. See Hampe, ed. 1927, pp. 10–11.
9. Habich 1929–34, vol. 2, 1, p. CV, noted that no other German medalist betrays Italian influence so strongly as does Weiditz. This is quoted in Schädler 1987, p. 166.
10. Suhle 1950, pp. 34–35..
11. This is illustrated in Schädler 1987, p. 173, fig. 16.

Additional literature: Domanig 1900, p. 259; Habich 1913, p. 18 and fig. 19; Rowlands 1985, p. 87, fig. 17 and p. 142; Trusted 1990, p. 119, no. 183; Starkey, ed. 1991, p. 117, no. VII.25.

Friedrich Hagenauer

Notes:
1. A limewood relief in Berlin may be by Hagenauer. See Trusted 1990, p. 57. Habich attributed two wood busts in the Bayerisches Nationalmuseum in Munich to him, but these are no longer thought to be his. See Habich 1907, pp. 192–93, figs. 67–68.
2. Habich 1929–34, vol. 1, 1, pp. 70–99.
3. See Trusted 1990, pp. 8–9.
4. Habich 1929–34, vol. 2, 1, p. CX.
5. Zeitler 1951, pp. 113, proposed that the medals of Wilhelm and Ludwig were made to aid their candidacy for the throne of Bohemia following the death of Ludwig II in August 1526.
6. Habich 1929–34, vol. 2, 1, pp. CX–CXI.
7. Ibid., p. CXI.
8. For a range of such sitters, see Habich 1929–34, vol. 1, 1, pp. 94–95.
9. Maué 1989, pp. 27–28.
10. See Habich 1929–34, vol. 2, 1, p. CXI.
11. Trusted 1990, pp. 122ff.

92
Friedrich Hagenauer
Augustin Loesch von Hilgertshausen (Habich 1929–34, no. 457)

Notes:
1. Beierlein 1848, pp. 5f.
2. Ibid. It is certain that this lead medal was the one Beierlein published, but he makes no mention of its whereabouts at that time, so that we do not know who Eugen Felix acquired it from.

Additional literature: Felix sale, 1895; Habich 1906, pp. 19f., pl. G 8.

93, 93a
Friedrich Hagenauer
Sebastian and Ursula Ligsalz (Habich 1929–34, nos. 465–66)

Notes:
1. Habich 1929–34, no. 465.
2. Beierlein 1848, pp. 175–78, no. V, was the first to ascribe them to Hagenauer, and no one has ever questioned his attribution.
3. He was a member of the Outer Council from 1506 to

1512 and again in 1516, and of the Inner Council in 1513–15, 1517–19, and in 1522. I am indebted to Dr. Helmuth Stahleder for this information from the Council records. Dr. Stahleder is preparing an essay on the Ligsalz family.
4. For these details about Ursula Ligsalz I am again indebted to Dr. Stahleder.

Additional literature: Beierlein 1851–52, p. 176; T. Müller 1959, p. 291, nos. 307–8.

94
Friedrich Hagenauer
Lukas Furtenagel (Habich 1929–34, no. 492)

Notes:
1. Bibliothèque Nationale, Cabinet des Médailles. See *Trésor de Numismatique . . .* (German), p. 11, no. 10, and pl. VI, no. 10, with reverse.
2. In the above publication, the date appears as MDXXVI. There the MALER of the inscription is also misread as MAYER.
3. Compare Habich 1929–34, no. 492.
4. It is unclear just when and why the drawing on the back of the wood model was made. Possibly it was simply a sketch from which the model for the reverse was to be carved. Or it may be that it was done after the carving of the reverse model as an aid toward the alignment of the two.
5. Compare the wood reliefs of Sebastian and Ursula Ligsalz (cat. nos. 93 and 93a).
6. For biographical information, see the Furtenagel article in Thieme-Becker, vol. 12, p. 602–3. Also Wilhelm 1983, p. 476, no. 78, with further bibliography.
7. Thieme-Becker, vol. 12, p. 602.
8. Ibid., pp. 602–3. Also Rolf Biedermann in *Welt im Umbruch*, pp. 199–200.
9. *Augsburger . . .*, p. 122.

Additional literature: Habich 1903, p. 10 and note 1; T. Müller 1959, p. 292, no. 309.

95
Friedrich Hagenauer
Margarete von Frundsberg (Habich 1929–34, no. 540)

Notes:
1. Bergmann 1844–57, vol. 1, p. 63.
2. Habich 1907, p. 239. Sallet 1884 says much the same thing, finding the work "one of the most beautiful female portraits to be found on German Renaissance medals."

Additional literature: Suhle 1950, p. 39, pl. 16, 1.

96
Friedrich Hagenauer
Christoph, count of Nellenburg and Thüngen (Habich 1929–34, no. 605)

Notes:
1. Habich 1929–34, no. 604.
2. Barack, ed. 1881, p. 76.
3. Ibid., p. 80.

Additional literature: Felix sale, 1886, no. 968; Habich 1906, pp. 19f., pl. E 7; Suhle 1950, pl. XVII, 1; Grotemeyer 1957, p. 49, no. 15; *Spätgotik . . .*, no. 430, illus. 261; I. Weber in Kauffmann, ed. 1970, p. 327, no. 324 d; *Die Renaissance . . .*, vol. 2, K 15.

97
Friedrich Hagenauer
Sibylla von Aich (Habich 1929–34, no. 615)

Notes:
1. *Reidt, Ryth*, or *Riedt* (these names with similar arms found in Cologne and Holland and with various arrangements of shells and stars): The arms for the Cologne family are: Party per fess, 1. Gules, a star argent flanked by two shells of the same; 2. Argent, a shell gules flanked by two stars of the same; for the family in Holland: Party per fess, 1. Gules, a star sable flanked by two shells argent; 2. Argent, two stars gules flanked by a shell of the same. I thank Stephen K. Scher for the blasoning of these arms.

2. Habich 1907, p. 255. Hagenauer also produced an impressive medal of the painter Bartholomäus Bruyn, see Habich 1929–34, no. 630.
3. In that case the date MDXXVII should be changed to MDXXXVII.

98
Friedrich Hagenauer
Michael Mercator (Habich 1929–34, no. 627)

Notes:
1. C. P. Serrure 1850, p. 116.
2. Letter from Sir Thomas More to Cardinal Wolsey from March 16, 1528, cited in Hawkins 1885, vol. 1, p. 42.
3. Ibid.
4. Habich 1929–34, nos. 625, 627 (the present version), and 628.
5. E. Puteanus, *Genealogia Puteanaea Bamelrodiorum Venlonensium*, Louvain, 1630, cited in C. P. Serrure 1850, p. 116. The engraving of the medal of Michael Mercator, taken from Puteanus, suggests that the work may be a slightly different version from this one in the British Museum. The inscription starts with a leaf and a cross rather than a leaf and a star as here. This may be an error, or it may mean that at least one other version survived until 1630. The present piece now seems to be unique. For the medal of Elizabeth Mercator, see Habich 1929–34, no. 626.
6. See Hawkins 1885, vol. 1, pp. 41–43. For Cahn's attribution, see Forrer 1904–30, vol. 4, pp. 32–34.
7. See the medals of Heinrich Joham and Matthias Steffli, Habich 1929–34, vol. 1, 1, pl. LXXIII, 7 and LXXIII, 5, respectively. He was active in Cologne from 1536 on. His later work of the 1540s suggests that he may have journeyed to the Netherlands. See the biographical introduction.
8. See the signed medal of Melanchthon, cat. no. 99.
9. The present author is unaware of any parallel examples, although some reverses, including the present one, were not always illustrated in Habich 1929–34.
10. See the *Young Man in a Beret, An unknown Man in a Beret*, and *Sir Henry Guidford* in Ganz 1937, pl. XVI, 1; I, 1; and XIII, 7, respectively.
11. See the discussion of the medal of Charles de Solier, cat. no. 91.

Additional literature: Habich 1907, p. 257 and fig. 116.

99, 99a
Friedrich Hagenauer
Philipp Melanchthon (Habich 1929–34, no. 652)

Notes:
1. Habich 1907, p. 252.
2. Regarding these punched inscriptions, see Habich 1929–34, vol. 1, 1, p. XXIII.
3. Ibid., nos. 656 (Butzer), 655 (Pistorius), 654 (Hedio), and 657 (Sturm).
4. Ibid., nos. 642 (Rheineck) and 648 (Isenburg).

Additional literature: Suhle 1950, pp. 49f., pl. 17, 2; Börner and Steguweit 1990, p. 20.

100
Friedrich Hagenauer
Johann Thewen (Habich 1929–34, no. 668)

Notes:
1. Habich 1929–34, no. 668, mistakenly read Thewen's age as thirty-eight, though the medal clearly reads XXVIII. Many of his assumptions regarding Thewen's biography are therefore unlikely.
2. Ibid., no. 694.
3. Babelon 1966, p. 32.

101
Unknown Artist with the Initials HG (?)
Martin Luther (Habich 1929–34, no. 721)

Notes:
1. Sallet 1875, pl. 7.2, was the first to point out the connection. The Cranach engraving is reproduced in Hollstein 1954–80, vol. 4, no. 9.
2. Juncker 1706, pp. 58–59.

Additional literature: Erman 1884, p. 48; Michaelson 1900, p. 274; Domanig 1907, no. 283, note; Habich 1916, p. 7; Bernhart 1933, p. 150, pl. a.4; Ficker 1934, pp. 103ff., no. 50; Grunthal 1954, p. 201, pl. 21; Schnell 1983, no. 5; *Kunsthandwerk . . .*, p. 118; *Kunst der Reformationszeit*, p. 329.

101a
Unknown Artist with the Initials HG (?)
Martin Luther (Habich 1929–34, no. 721)

Notes:
1. This is possibly the same specimen as the one described by Habich and Bernhart as being at Klosterneuberg. See Habich 1929–34, vol. 1, 1, no. 721, and vol. 1, 2, no. 1829; Bernhart 1933, p. 156, no. 4.I.a and pl. a, 4.
2. Erman 1884, p. 34; Domanig 1895, pp. 9–10; Lange 1897, p. 106; Merzbacher 1899, pp. 32–36; Bezold 1907, p. 6; Hill 1920 (*Medals*), p. 71, fig. 44; Habich 1929–34, nos. 1829–30.
3. Vöge 1910, p. 234, no. 541 and pl. XII.
4. It corresponds to the engraving of a silver specimen, also with the Luther obverse, illustrated by Juncker and van Mieris.
5. Juncker 1706, p. 59.

Additional literature: Grunthal 1954.

Hans Kels

Notes:
1. Now in the Kunsthistorisches Museum, Vienna.
2. Ilg 1885, pp. 53–78.
3. Habich 1903 ("Hans"), pp. 9–19.
4. Hampe 1918–19 ("Geneologie"), pp. 42–39. There was still another sculptor in the Kels family as well, namely Veit Kels, a brother of Hans Kels the Younger and a master documented in Augsburg beginning in 1546. For biographies of the whole family, see Karl Simon in Thieme-Becker, vol. 20, pp. 127–29. For a summary of the family's dates and the works spoken of in documents in association with its three artists, see Mengden 1973, pp. 1–11.
5. Hampe 1918–19 ("Geneologie"), pp. 43–44.
6. Based on the dates and other information provided by his sons Veit and Georg in their suit to prove their legitimacy. See Hampe 1918–19 ("Geneologie"), pp. 42–43.
7. Ibid., p. 47, note 171.
8. Followed by the sculptor Veit and the shoemaker Georg. See Hampe 1918–19 ("Geneologie"), pp. 42–45.
9. Karl Simon in Thieme-Becker, vol. 20, p. 128; Mengden 1973, p. 1.
10. Mengden 1973, p. 5.
11. Between May 24 and October 15, 1565. See Mengden 1973, p. 10.
12. Guardians were appointed for the couple's four minor children. One of these was Veit Kels, the brother of Hans Kels the Younger. See Mengden 1973, p. 10.
13. See the listing in Mengden 1973, pp. 6–10.
14. For example, the reliefs in Ottobeuren attributed to Hans Kels the Younger in Lieb 1937–38, pp. 50–64.
15. Hamburg, Museum für Kunst und Gewerbe, inv. no. 1891.280. See Rasmussen 1975, no. 12, pp. 89–90, with additional bibliography.
16. Vienna, Kunsthistorisches Museum, no. 4251; Habich 1903 ("Hans"), p. 14; Habich 1929–34, no. 785. Mengden 1973, p. 124, note 404, relates that it has been destroyed.
17. Babenhausen, Fugger-Museum. Habich 1929–34, no. 789; Schädler in *Welt im Umbruch*, vol. 2, p. 187, no. 550.
18. High-relief carvings, probably goldsmith's models, in the Kunsthistorisches Museum, Vienna, dated 1545. See Schlosser 1910, vol. 2, p. 8, pl. XVII. Closely related to these are the four reliefs in the Germanisches Nationalmuseum, Nuremberg, one of which, a depiction of Calliope, bears the monogram HK. See Josephi 1910, pp. 296–97, and Schädler in *Welt im Umbruch*, pp. 187–88, nos. 551–54.
19. Habich 1929–34, vol. 1, 1, pp. 111–18 lists forty medals for Hans Kels the Younger and Veit Kels.
20. As urged by Schädler in *Welt im Umbruch*, p. 189.

102
Hans Kels (?)
Barbara Reihing (Habich 1929–34, no. 777)

Notes:
1. *Reihing or Reiching* (Ulm, Augsburg): Gules, three arrows without feathers argent, two in saltire, the third in pale (these charges have more accurately been described as *Zainhaken*, or wicker hooks; see Habich 1929–34, no. 777). I am grateful to Stephen K. Scher for blasoning these arms.
2. See Habich 1929–34, no. 777.
3. Ibid., no. 774a.
4. Ibid., nos. 776a and 775.
5. Ibid., nos. 774 and 776a; Imhof 1780–82, vol. 1, part 2, pp. 786–7, F.
6. Köhler 1745, no. 17; Hampe 1918–19 ("Kaufbeurer").
7. Habich 1929–34, nos. 967, 1000–1003, and 1061 (cat. no. 110).
8. Ibid., nos. 789 (Georg Fugger), 767 (Kolman Helmschmid), and 790 (Carchesius).
9. Habich 1916, pp. 56–57, and Habich 1929–34, vol. 2, 1, p. CXX.

Additional literature: Ilg 1885, pp. 71–77; *La Collection Frédéric Spitzer*, vol. 3, p. 262, no. 34, pl. VII; Spitzer sale, 1893, lot 2156; Habich 1903 ("Hans"), pp. 9–19; Hampe 1918–19 ("Kaufbeurer"), p. 35, note 113.

103, 103a
Artist Unknown
Laux and Elisabeth Kreler (Habich 1929–34, no. 781)

Notes:
1. Using a stereomicroscope, Rudolf Göbel was able to determine the letters that had been removed. Using the same process, he discovered what the missing date was on the relief of Elisabeth Kreler. The approximate birthdates given for the couple are deduced from the date 1537 originally provided on both reliefs.
2. See Alfred Schädler in *Welt im Umbruch*, pp. 188–89, no. 555.
3. Ibid., p. 189. Also Kobler 1985, p. 410. Habich 1903 ("Hans"), p. 17, was the first to note the missing letters. Habich 1929–34, no. 781, proposed that the original date may have been 1540, while T. Müller 1959, p. 289, preferred to read it as 1524.
4. Hamburg, Museum für Kunst und Gewerbe. See Rasmussen 1975, pp. 89–90, no. 12.
5. Alfred Schädler in *Welt im Umbruch*, p. 189.
6. See Kobler 1985, p. 410.
7. See Habich 1903 ("Hans"), p. 17, and Habich 1929–34, vol. 1, 1. p. 115.
8. Kobler 1985, pp. 410 and 412, note 21, also refers to them as "portrait medals" rather than "models for medals."
9. For a more detailed biography of Kreler, see Kobler 1985, pp. 409–10 and 412, note 1 (with earlier bibliography). Ibid., p. 412, note 4, refers to Kreler's supposed origin in Landsberg am Lech.
10. Ibid., p. 412, note 4.
11. Lieb 1952, vol. 1, pp. 70, 264.
12. Kobler 1985, p. 409.
13. Ibid., p. 410. Kreler's letter is reproduced in an appendix.
14. Ibid., pp. 109–10.
15. Ibid., p. 409.
16. H. Rott 1936, p. 285. In the listing of Strassburg goldsmiths between 1400 and 1600, Laux Kreler appears for the years 1528–52. I am grateful to Dr. Friedrich Kobler for this information.

Additional literature: *Augsburger . . .*, p. 95, no. 531.

104
Hans Kels
Johann Scheubel (Habich 1929–34, no. 783)

Notes:
1. Habich 1929–34, no. 782. See Ebner 1908–9, pp. 101–4.
2. Habich 1916, pp. 56 and 58.
3. Habich 1929–34, nos. 782–83.

The Master of the Beltzinger Group

Notes:

1. Habich 1915, p. 153, no. 1; Habich 1929–34, no. 824. The wood model is in the Staatliche Münzsammlung, Munich. Regarding Schaffner in general, see K. Feuchtmayr in Thieme-Becker, vol. 29, p. 562, and Lustenberger 1959.

2. Examples of his self-portraits are the man facing outward on the left side of his panel *Christ's Farewell from Mary* and the accusing man holding a page of writing in the center of his so-called *Wettenhaus Altar*, where Christ appears before Pilate. See *Altdeutsche Meister*, vol. 1, p. 104, illus. 59, and p. 106, illus. 67.

3. The group as assembled by Habich includes: nos. 822 (Christina Beltzinger, 1522, wood), 823 (Erasmus Beltzinger, 1522, wood), 824 (M.S.M. [M. Schaffner], 1522, wood), 825 (unknown "H.E.," 1523, wood and lead), 826 (Johannes Beltzinger, Protestant clergyman in Ulm, 1523, wood), 827 (Christoph Hengel, 1523, lead), 830 (unknown, possibly Erasmus Beltzinger the Elder, 1529, wood), 831 (Anna Rotengater, 1529, wood), 832 (Apollonia Beltzinger, 1530, wood), and 833 (Amalie Beltzinger, 1530, wood). One must exclude the Martin Schall, no. 828, the Jakob Hofmann, no. 834, and another unknown, no. 835, attributed to the same master solely on the basis of their similar lettering, as well as the Albrecht Dürer, no. 829, a later reproduction of the medal by M. Gebel from 1527–28.

Additional literature: Habich 1916, p. 63; Suhle 1952, p. 56, pl. 18, 2 and 3.

105
The Master of the Beltzinger Group
Christina Beltzinger (Habich 1929–34, no. 822)

Note:

1. Siebmacher 1885–1904, vol. 5, pt. 7, p. 79, pl. 81, and vol. 5, pt. 9, p. 69, pl. 81.

Additional literature: Habich 1915, p. 154, no. 2; Suhle 1952, p. 56, pl. 18.2.

106
The Master of the Beltzinger Group
Erasmus Beltzinger (Habich 1929–34, no. 823)

Additional literature: Habich 1915, p. 154, no. 3; Suhle 1952, p. 56, pl. 18.3.

"Nuremberg 1525–1527"

Notes:

1. Habich 1907, pp. 181–84 and 269–72; Maué 1989, pp. 27–28.

2. Compare, for example, the medals of Johann von Guttenberg and Augustin Lösch, both from 1526 (Habich 1929–34, nos. 920 and 457).

107
"Nuremberg 1525–1527"
Barbara Ketzel (Habich 1929–34, no. 907)

Notes:

1. Habich 1929–34 identifies nine medals with portraits in three-quarter view: nos. 895–900, 902, 905, and 907.

2. Ibid., no. 905.

3. Burger 1972, p. 1540, no. 2210.

Additional literature: Will 1767, pp. 187–94; Imhoff 1782, vol. 1, 2, p. 811, no. 19; Aign 1961, pp. 79–80; Kohlhaussen 1968, p. 436, attributing the medal to Ludwig Krug; Maué in *Nürnberg 1300–1550*, p. 418, no. 219.

108
"Nuremberg 1525–1527"
Albrecht of Brandenburg (Habich 1929–34, no. 922)

Notes:

1. *Albrecht Dürer*, p. 296, no. 548.
2. Habich 1929–34, nos. 923–24.
3. Ibid., no. 1941.
4. Stafski 1962, pp. 42–44; Reber 1990, pp. 14–17, illus. 4–6.

Additional literature: Cahn 1906, pp. 159–67; Kohlhaussen 1968, p. 436, no. 456; Maué in *Nürnberg 1300–1550*, p. 418, no. 218.

Matthes Gebel

Notes:

1. Habich 1929–34, vol. 1, 2, p. 140. Bernhart 1936, p. 13, even proposes that Gebel's workshop was so specialized that the portraits, coats of arms, and inscriptions were all assigned to different craftsmen, Gebel reserving the portrait work for himself. See also Suhle 1950, pp. 52–62.

2. Habich 1929–34, nos. 959 and 968.
3. See Erman 1884, p. 31.
4. The biographical facts are in Bauch 1898, pp. 470–75.
5. Maué 1989, pp. 28–29.
6. Habich 1929–34, nos. 250, 221–36, and 350–51.

109
Matthes Gebel
Christoph Kress (Habich 1929–34, no. 957)

Notes:

1. Gules, a sword in bend argent garnished or; Crest: bust of a savage issuant from five peacock plumes proper habited gules wearing a bonnet sable bordered ermine and crowned with five additional peacock plumes, holding in his teeth a sword in fess debruised by a small crescent argent at the level of the mouth. I thank Stephen K. Scher for blasoning these arms. The original letter patent, including a precise description of the coat of arms and an illustration of it, is preserved in the Germanisches Nationalmuseum, Kress Archive, Signature XXIII D 3. Christoph Kress was given it at the Diet in Augsburg. The document is reproduced in Frank zu Döfering 1936, column 278, note 26. In addition, the emperor presented him with a cap decorated with ostrich feathers and a gilt sword designed by Peter Flötner. These are also preserved in the Germanisches Nationalmuseum. See B. Moeller in *Martin Luther . . .*, p. 158, no. 189. Kressenstein is a fourteenth-century manor in Kraftshof, near Nuremberg. It was expanded in half-timber as a summer house in 1449; however, by 1530 it was no longer the family's chief residence.

2. Habich 1929–34, no. 945. On the relationship between this medalist and Matthes Gebel, ibid., pp. 131 and 138. See also Trusted 1990, p. 40, no. 30. There are smaller copies of both medals: Habich 1929–34, nos. 944 and 957.

3. Frank zu Döfering 1936, columns 263–303.
4. Kress von Kressenstein 1985, pp. 10–11.

Additional literature: Will 1765, pp. 153–60; Imhoff 1782, vol. 1, 2, p. 464, no. 3; Suhle 1950, p. 56; J. C. Smith 1983, p. 240, no. 144.

110
Matthes Gebel
Heinrich Ribisch, Georg Hermann, and Konrad Maier (Habich 1929–34, no. 1061)

Notes:

1. Left to right: *Ribisch* (Silesia): Shield: Per fess, 1. sable, a lion's face or, ringed of the same, chaperonné-ployé of the last; 2. or, a fess sable. Crest: The head of a lion between two horns or on sable. *Hermann* (Hermann von Mondthal, Saxony): Shield: Per pale, 1. or on a fess sable a star of the first; 2. sable, a crescent moon with profile face or. Crest: A pyramidal hat sable crowned with a button or between wings, the dexter with the arms of 1., the sinister with the arms of 2. *Maier* (Mayer, Dortmund): Shield: Quarterly, 1 and 4, Azure, a star or; 2 and 3, quarterly, or and gules. Crest: Wings, the dexter, azure, a star or; the sinister, quarterly, or and gules. See Rietstap 1968. I am grateful to Stephen K. Scher for blasoning these coats of arms.

2. Habich 1929–34, no. 177.
3. Ibid., nos. 962, 980, 989, 992, 1039, 1069, 1076, and 1101.
4. Lieb 1958, especially pp. 81–85 and 90–95.
5. Hampe 1918–19 ("Kaufbeurer"), pp. 9–41.
6. Lenger 1967.

Additional literature: Theuerkauff 1977, no. 14; Maué in *Nürnberg 1300–1550*, no. 229.

111, 111a
Matthes Gebel
Johann and Ulrich Fernberger (Habich 1929–34, no. 1076)

Notes:

1. K. H. Lang, ed. 1825, vol. 3, p. 202.

2. For the history of the family, see Hoheneck 1747, pp. 159–164. There we read that Johann Fernberger was the seventh son of Ulrich Fernberger. It is possible that the end of the reverse inscription refers to this rather than to the age of the younger Ulrich. For additional information about the family, see Wissgrill 1797, pp. 31–36.

3. Wied 1977, pp. 488 and 490. According to Wissgrill (see note 2), Johann Fernberger was not named *Vicedominus* until 1532.

4. The medieval Egenberg castle (now Eggenberg, in the jurisdiction of Gmunden) no longer survives. Johann Fernberger acquired the property from the Kirchbergers, and expanded Egenberg into a splendid palace. The Fernberger family died out in 1671. Though it is frequently claimed that the family came from Bavaria, there is no proof of this. See Grüll 1963, pp. 13–14 and 148. According to Hoheneck and Wissgrill (see note 2), the family had moved to the Tyrol from a seat of the same name—no longer traceable—in the margravate of Ansbach. There is however a Balthasar Fer vom Berge, knight, documented there in 1453 and 1454. See Ortmann 1967, p. 59. For more on the origins of the Fernberger family, see Siebmacher 1885–1904, vol. 4, part 5, pp. 44–45.

5. He was buried in Linz in the church of the Bürgerspital, which was demolished in 1885. His tombstone has not survived, but its inscription is preserved, according to which Fernberger zu Egenberg bore the titles imperial councilor, first secretary, and hereditary chamberlain. See Schmidt 1964, p. 57. Wissgrill 1797 gives 1554 as the date of his death.

Additional literature: Maué in *Nürnberg 1300–1550*, no. 230.

112
Matthes Gebel
Georg Ploed (Habich 1929–34, no. 1082)

Notes:

1. Habich 1929–34, vol. 1, 2, pp. XLIII–IL.
2. Apianus and Amantius 1534, p. 385.
3. Janson 1937, pp. 423–49; Seznec 1937–38, pp. 298–303.
4. Janson 1937, p. 440.
5. Kress 1640.
6. Zahn 1972, p. 88. The inscription on the tombstone—now lost—in Nuremberg's St. Johannis Cemetery read: "Brigitha Ploed and sons. 1534 / The mortal remains of the honorable Georg Ploed were buried here. 1532." Georg Ploed's parents were Hans and Brigitta, née Fuchshard. See Wölcker MS, vol. 3.
7. P. Volz in Peus sale, 1975, lot 19, p. 12. Also Volz 1981–82, p. 143, no. 2.
8. Schornbaum 1949, p. 15, line 203.
9. Burger 1972, p. 116, line 2971.

Additional literature: Imhoff 1782, vol. 1, 2, p. 867, no. 22; Maué in *Nürnberg 1300–1550*, no. 231; Maué 1992.

113
Matthes Gebel
Jacoba, duchess in Bavaria (Habich 1929–34, no. 1109)

Notes:

1. Per chapé, 1. Sable, a lion rampant or (*Palatinate*); 2. Or, a bend gules (*Baden*); 3. Fusilly in bend, argent and

azure (*Bavaria*). I am grateful to Stephen K. Scher for blasoning these arms and those in note 3.
2. Weech 1890, especially pp. 101–39.
3. Quarterly, 1 and 4, Or, a bend gules (*Baden*); 2 and 3, chequy, argent and gules *or* azure and or (*Spanheim*).

Additional literature: Beierlein 1897, no. 276; Wielandt and Zeitz 1980, no. 10 (geneological chart, p. 10); P.-H. Martin in *Die Renaissance . . .* , no. K 22.

114
Unknown Nuremberg Master
Hieronymous Wahl (Habich 1929–34, no. 1304)

Notes:
1. *Wahl*: Argent, two hooks in saltire gules with two roses in pale of the same; with helmet, mantling, and a crest of two wings argent, each wing charged with a rose gules. Siebmacher 1885–1904, vol. 5, p. 68. I am grateful to Hermann Maué for this reference, and to Stephen K. Scher for blasoning the arms.
2. Habich 1929–34, no. 1304.
3. Ibid., no. 2454.
4. Hermann Maué kindly provided these biographical details from the Landeskirchliches Archiv, Nuremberg, and Zahn 1972, no. 301, no. 1184.
5. Habich 1916, p. 57.
6. Katz 1932, nos. 95, 135–36, 217, 360, 378.

Ludwig Neufahrer

Notes:
1. Katz 1932, pp. 162f., excludes the two medals of Christoph Gendorf from Neufahrer's œuvre. See Habich 1929–34, nos. 1394–95.
2. Probszt 1960, p. 54.

Additional literature: Habich 1916, pp. 114f.; Dworschak 1926, pp. 213–14; Habich 1929–34, vol. 1, 2, p. 181; Dimt and Dimt 1990, pp. 38f.

115
Ludwig Neufahrer
Nikolaus Kolnpock (Habich 1929–34, no. 1332)

Notes:
1. The closest similarities are the reverses of his medals of Friedrich II of the Palatinate and Wolfgang Thenn (Habich 1929–34, nos. 1329 and 1331, respectively). Both were produced the year before the Kolnpock medal and suggest Italian precedents, though none have been discovered.
2. Habich 1929–34, nos. 505 (Katharina Neumann) and 553 (Magdalena Diem).
3. Dworschak 1926, p. 218, had considered Peter Flötner to be Neufahrer's model, if not in fact the actual creator of the reverse of the Kolnpock medal, an assumption that must be rejected.

Additional literature: Probszt 1960, no. 51; Trusted 1990, no. 123.

116
Ludwig Neufahrer (?)
Francis I (Habich 1929–34, no. 1397)

Notes:
1. *Trésor de Numismatique . . .* (French), vol. 1, pl. 11, no. 3. The British Museum also has an aftercast with the date 1544. See M. Jones 1982–88, vol. 1, no. 32.
2. Rondot 1904, p. 85. Mark Jones 1982–89, vol. 1, no. 32, emphasizes that Rondot's attribution is purely hypothetical.
3. Forrer 1904–30, vol. 4, p. 249, sees the pattern for the reverse in a medal of François Thevenot from 1533 (Mazerolle 1902–4, vol. 2, p. 16, no. 57).
4. For more about the life of Francis I, see cat. no. 139. For other German medals of the king, see Habich 1929–34, Registerband, under "Frankreich, Franz I."

Additional literature: Probszt 1960, no. 25.

117
Kunz Peck (or Sebald Peck?)
Kunz Peck with his Sons (Habich 1929–34, no. 1435)

Notes:
1. Habich 1929–34, no. 1435.
2. Habich 1929–34, vol. 1, 2, p. 201.
3. Ibid., pp. 200–201.
4. Habich 1929–34, no. 177.
5. A slightly abbreviated form of the same verse is found on the reverse of Matthes Gebel's medal of Heinrich Ribisch, Georg Hermann, and Konrad Maier (cat. no. 110), and also that of Tobias Wolff's medal of the three brothers Christian II, Johann Georg, and August of Saxony, dated 1600. See Habich 1929–34, no. 2140.
6. I. Weber 1975, vol. 1, p. 100, no. 90, and vol. 2, pl. 31.

Additional literature: Trusted 1990, p. 87, no. 133.

Joachim Deschler

Notes:
1. Cited in Thieme-Becker, vol. 9, p. 118.
2. Habich 1929–34, nos. 1557–58 (Ferdinand and Maximilian), 1606 (Marx and Anna Stengl of Augsburg), 1596 (Georg Tetzel; cat. no. 118), and 1611 (Hieronymus Paumgartner; cat. no. 119).
3. Ibid., no. 1562, and Trusted 1990, no. 12.
4. See, for example, the medal of Hieronymus Paumgartner, cat. no. 119.

118
Joachim Deschler
Georg Tetzel the Elder (Habich 1929–34, no. 1596)

Notes:
1. *Detzel* (Nuremberg): Gules, a cat rampant gardant argent; crest: On an open crowned helmet with mantling a cat issuant gardant. See Siebmacher 1885–1904, vol. 6, part 1, p. 94, pl. 92. I am grateful to Stephen K. Scher for blasoning these arms.
2. Habich 1929–34, no. 1596.
3. Ibid., pl. CLXX, nos. 7–7a.
4. Grotemeyer 1957, fig. 43.
5. Habich 1929–34, no. 1628.

Additional literature: Trusted 1990, no. 13.

119
Joachim Deschler
Hieronymus Paumgartner (Habich 1929–34, no. 1611)

Notes:
1. *Baumgarten* (Augsburg): Sable, a fleur-de-lis argent, in chief, argent a parrot vert; crest: On a closed helmet with mantling a fleur-de-lis upon which perches a parrot. I am grateful to Stephen K. Scher for blasoning these arms.
2. Habich 1929–34, vol. 1, 2, p. 228. The term is difficult to translate, but it is important to note that this was a civil office, even though a *Hauptmann* is generally a military captain.
3. Ibid., pl. CLXXIII. See also Grotemeyer 1957, no. 59, for a silver example in Nuremberg with a different reverse.

Additional literature: Hill and Pollard 1967, no. 608; Salton 1969, no. 90; Trusted 1990, no. 14.

120
Joachim Deschler
Lukas Sitzinger the Elder (Habich 1929–34, no. 1620)

Notes:
1. *Sitzinger* (Augsburg): Party per bend sinister gules and argent, the bust of a man in profile wearing a conical bonnet countercharged. Crest: a man issuant, clothed gules, coiffed with a bonnet of the same bordered argent holding a spear (or club) resting on his shoulder. See Siebmacher 1885–1904, vol. 6, part 1, p. 94, pl. 92. I am grateful to John Coast for locating this reference, and to Stephen K. Scher for blasoning the arms.
2. Domanig 1893, p. 31, no. 20, and pl. IV, no. 20.
3. Trusted 1990, p. 5.
4. Habich 1929–34, vol. 1, 2, p. 229.
5. Domanig 1893, p. 31; Habich 1929–34, vol. 1, 2, p. 229, pl. CLXXVII, 3.

Additional literature: Domanig 1907, no. 163.

The Master of the "Ottheinrich of the Palatinate Group"

Notes:
1. Habich 1929–34, nos. 1695–1710. In addition to these, there are two further medals from the year 1559, nos. 1711 and 1712, in which Habich sees a connection to the earlier medals of the Ottheinrich group on the basis of their presentation of coats of arms. There is some doubt whether all of the medals Habich presents of persons close to Ottheinrich are by the same hand.
2. See, for example, Exter 1759–75, part 2, p. 329, no. 59 (1988, pl. 40); H. Rott 1905, p. 106; Habich 1914–15, pp. 72f.; Habich 1916, p. 150; Habich 1920–21, p. 33; Gessert 1921–22, pp. 53f.; Habich 1929–34, vol. 1, 2, pp. 237f.; Bange 1933, p. 366; Grotemeyer 1937, p. 17; Gaettens 1956, pp. 77f.; H.-P. Martin in *Die Renaissance . . .* , no. K12.
3. Habich 1914–15, pp. 67f., illus. 1–4; Habich 1929–34, vol. 1, 2, p. 240, illus. 211–12.
4. Rossmann 1956, p. 270; Gaettens 1956, p. 84, illus. 25. Gaettens does not feel that Colin did the work himself. The stone medallion above the portal of the Ottheinrich Wing, from 1556 at the earliest, is based on the medal portrait by the Ottheinrich Master from 1555. See Habich 1929–34, no. 1702.
5. Habich 1929–34, nos. 1588–1651.
6. Gessert 1921–22, p. 54.
7. Habich 1929–34, vol. 1, 2, pp. 250f.
8. Trusted 1990, no. 154.
9. Habich 1929–34, nos. 1698 and 1705.

121
The Master of the "Ottheinrich of the Palatinate Group"
Ottheinrich, count of the Rhenish Palatinate (Habich 1929–34, no. 1706)

Notes:
1. Left to right: 1. Sable, a lion rampant or (*Palatinate*); crest: On an open helmet with mantling a crowned golden lion sejant between horns charged fusilly-bendy (*Bavaria*). 2. Gules, an orb or (*prince elector of the Palatinate and archsteward*); crest: On an open helmet with mantling a golden lion sejant. 3. Fusilly-bendy argent and azure (*Bavaria*); crest: On a crowned open helmet with mantling a crowned lion sejant between a pair of wings charged fusilly-bendy (*Bavaria*). I am grateful to Stephen K. Scher for blasoning these arms.
2. "Mit der Zeit" (All in good time) and "in domino confido" (I trust in the Lord) are frequently recurring Ottheinrich devices.
3. Habich 1929–34, index vol., p. 22, with an additional medal by Utz Gebhart that was probably not commissioned by Ottheinrich himself; ibid., vol. 2, 1, no. 1919.

Additional literature: Exter 1759–75, part 2, p. 329, no. 59 (1988, pl. 40); Habich 1914–15, pp. 72f., no. 7, pl. 1, no. 4; Habich 1916, p. 150; Gaettens 1956, no. 22; H.-P. Martin in *Die Renaissance . . .* , no. K12.

Hans Bolsterer

Note:
1. See Schlosser 1910, p. 8, pl. XVII, no. 2.

Additional literature: Cahn 1903, pp. 181–98; Domanig 1907, pp. 20f.; Habich 1929–34, vol. 1, 2, p. 250.

122
Hans Bolsterer
Ursula von Solms (Habich 1929–34, no. 1773)

Notes:
1. Habich 1929–34, nos. 1774–75.
2. Solms 1956, pp. 11f.

Additional literature: Bergmann 1844–57, vol. 2, p. 153.

123
Hans Bolsterer
Ursula Dürr (Habich 1929–34, no. 1801)

Note:
1. Habich 1929–34, no. 1551.

Additional literature: Imhof 1782, vol. 2, p. 728, no. 46.

Peter Flötner

Notes:
1. Lange 1897, p. 8.
2. Ibid., p. 9.
3. Bange 1923, pp. 107–17.
4. Lange 1897, pp. 4f.
5. I. Weber 1975, pp. 56–85.
6. Most recently Pechstein 1984, pp. 91–100.
7. Sponsel 1924, pp. 121–84 and 214–76; Sponsel 1925, pp. 38–90; Habich 1925–26, pp. 26–45; Sponsel 1927, pp. 139–83; Habich 1929.
8. Habich 1929–34, no. 1829.
9. Ibid., no. 1830.

Additional literature: Domanig 1895, pp. 1–80; Leitschuh 1904; Haupt 1905, pp. 116–35 and 148–68; Falke 1916, pp. 121–45; Habich 1916, pp. 101–3; Bange 1921–22, pp. 45–52; Bange 1926, pp. 38–90; Bange 1928; Falke 1928, pp. 206–9; Habich 1929–34, vol. 1, p. 1, p. 257; Kris 1931, pp. 496–99; Bange 1938, pp. 231–32; *Peter Flötner . . .* ; Troche 1947, pp. 123–33; Bange 1949; Braun 1951, pp. 195–203; C. L. Kuhn 1954, pp. 109–15; Schadendorf 1954–59, pp. 143–69; Zimmermann 1955, pp. 15–19; Pfeiffer 1956, pp. 53–56; Braun 1957, pp. 172–75; Weihrauch 1967; Kohlhaussen 1968; I. Weber 1970, pp. 521–25; Pechstein 1971; Rasmussen 1976, pp. 96–98; Lühmann-Schmid 1976–77, pp. 65–68; Geissler 1980, pp. 20–21; Angerer 1984.

124
Peter Flötner (?)
Emperor Charles V, King Ferdinand I, and Maria of Hungary (Habich 1929–34, no. 1823)

Notes:
1. Habich 1929–34, no. 1823.
2. Trusted 1990, no. 28.
3. Habich 1929–34, no. 1824; Löbbecke sale, 1908, pl. XXII, no. 355.
4. Habich 1929–34, no. 1824, mistakenly includes this specimen, though its inscription is clearly different.
5. Compare the rectangular plate with a reproduction of these same heads and necks in Herrgott 1752, pl. XXIV, no. LXI.
6. Habich 1929–34, no. 257.
7. Ibid., nos. 1829–30.
8. Trusted 1990, no. 27, nevertheless accepts it without qualification.

Additional literature: Habich 1916, pp. 102f.; Bernhart 1919, p. 52, no. 73; Mai 1970, no. 18; Reber 1990, pp. 126–27.

Hans Reinhart the Elder

Notes:
1. Habich 1929–34, vol. 2, 1, pp. 278–87. The works signed with either the ligature HR or simply H-R are presented in Habich under the following numbers: 1926–29, 1931–35, 1937, 1941, 1942, 1947–50, 1962–64, 1968–71, and 1973–75.
2. For biographical details in addition to those presented in Habich and in H. Kuhn 1941, pp. 169–84, see Junius 1935, pp. 64–112.
3. Habich 1929–34, nos. 1935 and 1968.
4. This despite the fact that Reinhart was capable of embellishing his "originally quite simple models with all manner of curlicues and luxuriant added detail in the spirit of late Gothic goldsmithing. . . . " Habich 1929–34, vol. 1, 1, p. XIX.
5. Pick 1905, pp. 33–36, thinks it possible that Reinhart was in fact a pupil of Lucas Cranach the Elder. H. Kuhn 1941, p. 173, refuses to accept any direct influence from Cranach.
6. Cahn 1928, pp. 121–22, attempted to show such borrowings in the case of a religious medal presenting the Sacrifice of Isaac and the Crucifixion. Katz 1932, p. 21,

stretches the point in his insistence that Reinhart was only imitating the medals of the Erzgebirge. It is more probable that both Reinhart and those anonymous artists patterned their works after some common precedent, as Kuhn 1941, p. 176, suggests.
7. Habich 1929–34, vol. 2, 1, p. 285.
8. Regarding Hans Reinhart the Younger, see Habich 1929–34, vol. 2, 1, pp. 289–91.

125
Hans Reinhart the Elder
Charles V (Habich 1929–34, no. 1927)

Notes:
1. Parti per fess: In chief, Spain: parti per pale, A. quarterly 1 and 4, Gules, a castle triple towered or (*Castille*); 2 and 3, Argent, a lion rampant gules, crowned or (*Leon*); B. Or, four pallets gules (*Aragon*) impaling the Kingdom of the Two Sicilies: Per saltire, in chief and base, Or, four pallets gules (*Aragon*); in flanks, Argent, an eagle-displayed sable (*Sicily*); enté en point of Granada. In base, quarterly: 1. Gules, a fess argent (*Austria Modern*); 2. Azure, semé of fleurs-de-lis or, a bordure-compony argent and gules (*Burgundy Modern*); 3. Bendy of six, or and azure, a bordure gules (*Burgundy Ancient*); 4. Sable, a lion rampant or (*Brabant*). En surtout, Or, a lion rampant sable (*Flanders*) impaling Argent, an eagle displayed gules, crowned or (*Tirol*). Around the base of the shield, the collar of the Order of the Golden Fleece composed of double fusils (originally the device of the dukes of Burgundy, beginning with the founder of the Order of the Golden Fleece, Philip the Good) placed facing each other to form double B's alternating with stylized flowers (instead of the usual flint stones), from this depending the Golden Fleece. Flanking the arms, the emblem and motto of Charles: the crowned Pillars of Hercules (representing the Strait of Gibraltar) and "Plus Oultre" (More beyond).
2. Bernhart 1919, no. 93; Habich 1929–34, no. 1926; Trusted 1990, no. 143.

126
Hans Reinhart the Elder
Johann Friedrich I, elector of Saxony (Habich 1929–34, no. 1935)

Notes:
1. It is blazoned as follows: Quarterly of eleven, three, two, two, three, one. 1. Barry of ten sable and or, over all a crancelin vert (*Saxony*); 2. Azure, a lion rampant, barry argent and gules, crowned or (*Thuringia*); 3. Or, a lion rampant sable, crowned gules (*Meissen*); 4. Azure, an eagle displayed, crowned or (*Saxon Palatinate*); 5. Or, two pallets azure (*Landsberg*); 6. Argent, three nenuphar leaves gules (*Brehna*); 7. Sable, an eagle displayed or (*Thuringia [Palatinate]*); 8. Or, semé of hearts gules, a lion rampant sable, crowned sable (*Orlamünde [or Weimar]*); 9. Argent, a rose gules, barbed and seeded or (*Altenburg*); 10. Azure, a lion rampant per fess or and azure (*Pleissen*); 11. In base, gules, the *Blut-Fahne or Regalien*. En surtout, per fess, sable and argent, over all two swords in saltire gules (the *Arch-Marshalship of the Holy Roman Empire*). Above, three crests on helmets and mantling: 1. Two horns, each ornamented with five little batons in fess, carrying trefoils (*Thuringia*); 2. Out of a coronet a pyramidal chapeau, charged with the arms of Saxony, topped with a panache of peacock's feathers, and between two horns, each ornamented with five little batons bearing banner flags (*Saxony*); 3. Bust of a bearded man in profile, on the vestment a pale, wearing a pointed cap also charged with a pale, and having a large tuft (*Meissen*).
2. Specifically the portrait in Berlin, Staatliche Museen, c. 1535, and the woodcut, undated but usually placed around 1533, in the Landesmuseum in Gotha. See van der Osten and Vey 1969, p. 208, fig. 186; Hollstein n.d., vol. 6, p. 106, no. 131; Geisberg 1974, p. 602; *Land im Mittelpunkt*, pp. 389–90, no. E12.
3. The wood model was in the Herzögliches Museum, Gotha, and is illustrated in Habich 1929–34, vol. 2, 1, pl. CCIV, no. 3a. For reference to the documents, ibid., p. 178.

Additional literature: Habich 1916, pp. 126–27; Scher 1961 ("Doppeltaler"), pp. 332–34; Mai 1970, no. 19; Frese and Datow 1983, p. 47; Trusted 1990, p. 90, no. 139.

127
Hans Reinhart the Elder
The Trinity Medal (Habich 1929–34, no. 1962)

Notes:
1. Barry of ten sable and or, over all a crancelin vert. I thank Stephen K. Scher for blasoning these arms.
2. The full text of the Creed, in English, may be found in the Episcopal *Book of Common Prayer*.
3. Special studies on the Trinity medal and its imitations are Cahn 1905, columns 3339–43, and Domanig 1913, 69–73.
4. Katz 1932, nos. 351 and 411–15.
5. Habich 1929–34, vol. 2, 1, p. 278, refers to this as well.
6. See Cahn 1905; Domanig 1913; and Habich 1929–34, vol. 2, 1, p. 283.
7. Athanasius (A.D. 295–373), one of the four fathers of the Greek church, originated the doctrine of the unity of God and the divinity of Christ. The doctrine of the Trinity was a significant issue in the religious debates of the period. Duke Maurice of Saxony, himself a Protestant prince, was drawn more and more into the sphere of imperial (Catholic) policy, which necessarily placed him in conflict with his cousin, the elector Johann Friedrich of Saxony (cat. no. 126), and with other supporters of Protestantism.

Additional literature: Tentzel 1705, pp. 85–87; Bolzenthal 1840, pp. 137–40, pl. XII; Börner and Steguweit 1990, pp. 21f.

Tobias Wolff

Notes:
1. Tentzel 1705, p. 158, even notes the existence of a medal with a self-portrait of "Wost."
2. He noted that Wolff produced a medal of members of the Wolff family in Augsburg in 1588–92, one of the Augsburger Philipp Ulstat in 1595, and that the artist collaborated on one occasion with the Augsburg medalist Jan de Vos (cat. no. 134). See Habich 1929–34, nos. 2115, 2120, and 2125.
3. Ibid., p. 310.
4. Ibid., no. 2050.
5. Regling 1928, p. 100; Habich 1929–34, nos. 2167–79.
6. Habich 1929–34, vol. 2, 1, pp. 310f.
7. Ibid., pp. 293 and 311.

128
Tobias Wolff
Augustus of Saxony and Johann Georg of Brandenburg (Habich 1929–34, no. 2083)

Note:
1. Habich 1929–34, no. 2050. The casting from this model is combined with a reverse on which the Saxon elector is portrayed along with a suggestion of Hartenfels Castle, near Torgau. The date of 1574 on this reverse suggests that it did not originally belong to the obverse from 1577. The 1564 medal of Joachim II, Sigismund, Johann Georg, and Friedrich of Brandenburg (Habich 1929–34, no. 2267) may have served as a pattern for the woodcut. Habich places that work under the name of the medalist Hans Schenck with the "group of Brandenburgish and Saxon stone models." On it the four princes are arranged in opposing pairs.

Additional literature: *Schaumünzen . . .* , nos. 41a and 42.

Valentin Maler

Notes:
1. From this point on, one encounters reference to this privilege—chiefly on his struck medals—in the abbreviated form C[um] P[rivilegio] C[aesaris].
2. Habich 1929–34, no. 2853. Maler's age is given here as sixty-two. Since one can assume that Christian Maler produced the portrait of his father as a memorial at the time of his death or shortly before, it would appear that the older artist was born in 1541.

Additional literature: Habich 1916, pp. 195ff; Regling 1928, pp. 93–101; Habich 1929–34, vol. 2, 1, p. 352; Schulz 1988, pp. 14f. and 25f.

129
Valentin Maler
Wenzel Jamnitzer (Habich 1929–34, no. 2442)

Notes:
1. Habich 1929–34, no. 2409. This medal also presents an *en face* portrait, but is stylistically related to a medal with a profile portrait of Jamnitzer from 1563 (ibid., no. 2404), also attributed to Jakob Hofmann.
2. Ibid., nos. 2529, 2530, and 2563.
3. Ibid., no. 352; *Wenzel Jamnitzer*, no. 526.
4. Habich 1929–34, no. 2564; I. Weber 1975, no. 303; Trusted 1990, no. 102.
5. Habich 1929–34, no. 1793.

Additional literature: Bernhart 1936, pp. 38ff.

130
Valentin Maler
Dorothea of Saxony (Habich 1929–34, no. 2475)

Notes:
1. Habich 1929–34, nos. 2472, 2475, and 2473.
2. Ibid., no. 2471.
3. Ibid., no. 2476.
4. Ibid., nos. 2630–41. Regling 1928 distinguished these twelve medals, for some of which the wax models are preserved in the Germanisches Nationalmuseum in Nuremberg, from those of the series produced by Tobias Wolff at the same time.
5. Habich 1929–34, nos. 2082 and 2091.

131
Valentin Maler
Matthias and Anna Schilherr (Habich 1929–34, no. 2520)

Note:
1. One finds this same feature, though less pronounced, in Maler's medals of Augustus I of Saxony and Georg Johann of the Palatinate. See Habich 1929–34, nos. 2471 and 2540.

Additional literature: Imhof 1782, vol. 2, p. 900, no. 19.

132
Unidentified Artist
Nuremberg Patrician

Notes:
1. Habich 1929–34, vol. 1, 1, p. XXV, dates the beginning of this evolution to around 1560, in connection with a group of medals tentatively assigned to the goldsmith and *Pildschneider* (portrait carver) identified (ibid., vol. 2, 1, pp. 350–51) as "Meister des Jakob Hofmann" (possibly Hofmann himself; c. 1512–1564).
2. For Abondio's career, see the biography preceding cat. no. 60.
3. Our medallion was known to Habich only from the Spitzer catalogues (*La Collection Frédéric Spitzer*, vol. 5, p. 191, no. 10; Spitzer sale, 1893, vol. 2, no. 2959, pl. LVI), on the basis of which he tentatively placed it after "workshop or school of Georg Holdermann."

Select bibliography on wax models and technique: Vasari 1878–85; Cellini 1898; Schlosser 1911; Hill 1909, pp. 31–35; Hill 1914, pp. 212–17; Hill 1917, pp. 178–83; Habich 1924, pp. 11–15; Habich 1929–34, vol. 1, 1, pp. XXIV–XXVIII; Reilly 1953; Büll n.d., 1959, and 1963; Pyke 1973, pp. XXXVI–XLV; Büll 1977; Hill and Pollard 1978, pp. 23–25.

Johann Philipp von der Pütt

Notes:
1. Hampe 1904, no. 1024.
2. He appears in Nuremberg records under various names, among them "von der Butt" and "von der Pith."

3. Hampe 1904, no. 1316, as quoted by Gessert 1923–24, pp. 127–8.
4. Habich 1929–34, no. 2750; Pyke 1973, no. 229; Ursula Erichsen-Lehre, *Die Nürnberger Ratsherren-Tafel* (unpublished MS.).
5. Habich 1929–34, nos. 2740–49 and 2751–56.
6. Ibid., no. 2742 (Balthasar Paumgartner, 1592).

133
Von der Pütt
Julius Geuder von Heroldsberg (Habich 1929–34, no. 2740)

Notes:
1. Geuder had only one daughter, Maria Magdalena, who died in 1593, only two years after marrying Seigfried Pfintzing von Heuchling, Heroldsberg, Güntersbühl, Nuschelberg und Weigelshof (1568–1617).
2. Biedermann 1748, table LI, A and B.
3. I. Weber 1975, p. 15.

Additional literature: Imhof 1780–82, vol. 2, p. 340, no. 9; Erman 1885, pp. 14–102; Bezold 1913, p. 13, fig. 15 [*sic*].

Jan de Vos

Notes:
1. Habich 1927, p. 129.
2. Habich 1929–34, no. 2125. Bernhart 1937, p. 77, exaggerates when he speaks of "a number of signed medals . . . of Saxon notables," for that of the two Neefe brothers is the only one. There is no proof of further collaboration with Wolff, so one must not give too much credence to a possible Dresden sojourn for the artist.
3. *Prag um 1600*, vol. 2, p. 67, no. 537.
4. In Modern 1894, for example, Habich suggested de Vos as early as 1901, yet scholars were slow to accept the attribution. Accordingly, in subsequent articles and catalogues one finds both artists credited with the works in question. The controversy was only laid to rest by Habich's 1927 essay.
5. In his monograph on the van Vianen family, ter Molen presents only two medals as possible works of Paulus van Vianen, one on the reconquest of Raab and one of Hans Petzold. See ter Molen 1984, nos. 199 and 200.
6. For example, the medal of August and Clara Maria of Brunswick, Habich 1929–34, no. 3070.

Additional literature: Habich 1929–34, vol. 2, 1, p. 442; Bernhart 1937, pp. 41–98; ter Molen 1984, vol. 2, pp. 53–55.

134
Jan de Vos
Allegory of *Vanitas* (Habich 1929–34, no. 3069)

Notes:
1. The snake is only clearly visible in the specimen from the Schulman sale, 1956, no. 875, indicating that it is a superior cast.
2. Lanna sale, 1911, no. 479 (attributed to Paulus van Vianen). The Schulman specimen (see note 1) is said to bear the date 1618, but I suspect that this was a misreading of the medal itself or a misprint in the catalogue.

Additional literature: Modern 1894, p. 95, pl. X, no. 1; Habich 1927, p. 126, no. 12; Holzmair 1937, no. 5005; ter Molen 1984, vol. 2, no. 214; *Prag um 1600*, vol. 2, p. 303, no. 823.

Severin Brachmann

Notes:
1. Dworschak 1923–24, pp. 78f. Only two medals bear the signature S.B. See Habich 1929–34, nos. 3288 and 3299.
2. It appears that he spent some time in Silesia in 1571 and in Germany (Nuremberg and Saxony) in 1578–79.
3. Nohejlová 1938–39, pp. 72 and 116.
4. Habich 1929–34, no. 3274; Nohejlová 1938–39, p. 87, no. 15.

Additional literature: Dworschak 1926, pp. 213–44; Habich 1929–34, vol. 2, 2, p. 475.

135
Severin Brachmann
Eva Glueknecht (Habich 1929–34, no. 3323)

Notes:
1. Habich 1929–34, no. 3322.
2. Dworschak 1927, pp. 101f.

Additional literature: Dworschak 1927, pp. 91–104; *Renaissance . . .*, p. 134, no. 342.

136, 136a
Unidentified Artist
Rudolf II (Habich 1929–34, nos. 3553 and 3555)

Notes:
1. For attribution to Paulus van Vianen: Modern 1894, pp. 60ff.; Domanig 1907, p. 163; Dworschak 1925–26, p. 67; and Habich 1929–34, vol. 2, 2, who ascribes nos. 3549–55 to van Vianen and nos. 3547–48 to "the van Vianen workshop." Ter Molen 1984, vol. 2, pp. 52–53, no. 204, lists these medals because they had been attributed to Paulus in the past, but he himself does not subscribe to the attribution. Regarding the possible authorship of Alessandro Abondio: Habich in Thieme-Becker, vol. 1, p. 26, and Habich 1927, p. 124. For a possible association with the œuvre of Jan de Vos: Schütte in *Prag um 1600*, vol. 1, pp. 576 and 585–86.
2. Typotius 1601–3, vol. 1, pl. 25, no. XXXVIII (the variant Habich 1929–34, no. 3553).
3. Grueber 1910, vol. 3, pl. CVI, nos. 3–4, and pl. CVIII, no. 4. Suetonius 1903, p. 94, relates that when Augustus visited Apollonia in 45 B.C., he went together with Agrippa to the astrologer Theogenes. When Agrippa's horoscope appeared to be unbelievably brilliant, Augustus, for fear of a less favorable augury, hesitated. Upon some urging, he declared Capricorn to be his sign, resulting in a horoscope even more brilliant than Agrippa's. Two further Rudolf medals depict the Capricorn: one derives from Augustan sestertii, with two intertwined Capricorns resting atop a globe, the other shows the constellation within its tropic (Habich 1929–34, nos. 3549–50).
4. Tycho Brahe's compilation of 777 fixed stars, later expanded to 1,005 by Kepler, was published in 1627 as the *Rudolfine Tables*.

137
Unknown German Master
Elisabeth, duchess of Braunschweig-Calenberg

Notes:
1. Quarterly of nine: 1. Argent, an eagle displayed gules, with "Klee Stengeln" on its wings or, and armed of the last (*Margravate of Brandenburg*); 2. Or, a lion rampant sable, crowned of the field within a bordure compony argent and gules (*Burgravate of Nuremberg*); 3. Argent, a griffin segreant gules, crowned or (*Stettin*); 4. Argent, a griffin segreant gules (*Pomerania*); 5. Azure, a scepter or (*Electoral shield*); 6. Or, a griffin segreant sable (*Cassuben*); 7. Argent, a griffin segreant, bendy gules and vert (*Wenden*); 8. Quarterly argent and sable (*Hohenzollern*); 9. Illegible. Above, helmet and mantling with a crest of a crowned lion rampant between horns (possibly Nuremberg). I am grateful to Stephen K. Scher for blasoning these arms.
2. Brockmann 1985, p. 29.
3. Ibid., nos. 7, 31, 44, 52; Börner 1981, p. 150.

Additional literature: Madai 1765, no. 1083; Knyphausen 1872–77, no. 78; Fiala 1904, no. 15.

France, Sixteenth and Early Seventeenth Centuries

138, 138a
French School
Louise of Savoy and Marguerite of Angoulême (Hill 1930, no. 852)

Notes:

1. Hill 1930, nos. 845–62.
2. Among the works consulted for this entry: Louise de Savoie 1851, pp. 83–93; Maulde la Clavière 1895; Jourda 1930; Tilley 1932, pp. 519–31; Terrasse 1943–70; D. M. Mayer 1966; and Lembright 1974.
3. Hill 1930, no. 848. The artist who produced the Marguerite/Louise and Francis medals is also responsible for the medals of Thomas Bohier (no. 845) and Pierre Briçonnet (nos. 846–47), all of which present the same bust format, modeling, and epigraphy. The identity of this medalist is uncertain. Rondot 1904, p. 186, note 1, and 188, mentions names of jeton-engravers employed by Louise of Savoy.
4. Clothing styles appear to be of little help in confirming or denying such a dating. On a medal of Margaret of Austria (Hill 1930, no. 719, probably from 1501–4), the sitter's costume is nearly identical to Marguerite's on the present medal; yet Marguerite de Foix (cat. no. 34) wears a *chaperon* very like Louise's on her tallero of 1516 (Hill 1930, no. 711).
5. The salamander, symbolizing the kingly virtue of justice, makes its first appearance in Francis's iconography on the reverse of his medal (see also cat. no. 116). On its meaning and origin, see Terrasse 1943–70, vol. 1, pp. 34–36.
6. Poilleux 1842, p. 222; Maulde la Clavière 1895, p. 314; Terrasse 1943–70, vol. 1, pp. 11–12, 18.

Additional literature: Alvarez-Ossorio 1950; M. Jones 1979 (*Art*), p. 52; Pollard 1984–85, vol. 1, no. 195; and Johnson and Martini 1986, nos. 621 22.

139
French School
Francis of Angoulême, later Francis I of France (Hill 1930, no. 851)

Notes:

1. Hill 1930, no. 850.
2. D'Espezél 1925 ("Sur un médaillon"), p. 5, saw no stylistic connection to Candida. But Hill 1930 catalogued the medals as "French school of Candida," because he erroneously believed the Louise of Savoy (no. 850) to have been the visual source for the Candidesque Louise of Savoy medal from 1504 (cat. no. 138).
3. For the life of Francis I, see especially Maulde la Clavière 1895; Terrasse 1943–70; Seward 1973; and Knecht 1982.
4. A manuscript illuminated for Louise in 1512 (Bibliothèque Nationale, lat. 8396, reproduced in Maulde la Clavière 1895 opposite p. 304) gives a more intimate view of her jubilation over recent events. It contains a miniature representing St. Agnes leading Francis toward the crucified Christ—a private but definite allusion to the death of Louis XII's last son on St. Agnes's Day. Her journal records her jubilant remarks on that occasion (Louise de Savoie 1851, p. 87): "Anne, queen of France, had a son at Blois on the day of St. Agnes, 21 January; but he could not retard the exaltation of my Caesar, because he was stillborn."

Additional literature: M. Jones 1979 (*Art*), pp. 52, 54, and fig. 116; Pollard 1984–85, no. 195.

140, 140a
Nicolas Leclerc and Jean de Saint-Priest
Louis XII and Anne of Brittany (M. Jones 1982–88, vol. 1, no. 15)

Notes:

1. On the trinitarian symbolism of the fleur-de-lis, see Lecoq 1987, p. 396.
2. The ermine, considered a symbol of purity, was the emblem of Brittany. See Tervarent 1958–64, columns 212–13.
3. Rondot 1885 ("médaille"), p. 29; Rondot 1904, p. 77.
4. Rondot 1884, p. 21, no. 38. I shall not raise here the thorny issue of the possible involvement of the painter Jean Perréal in the making of the medal. See Sterling 1963, p. 5.
5. Rondot 1884, p. 21, no. 41.
6. On state entries into cities, see Konigson 1975, pp. 57–69, and Guenée and Lehoux 1968, pp. 7f.

Additional literature: Luckius 1620, pp. 1–2; *Inventaire . . .* , pp. 5–6; *Trésor de Numismatique . . .* (French), pl. V, 1; Mazerolle 1902–4, vol. 2, p. 9, no. 27; Tricou 1958, p. 5, no. 4; *La Bretagne . . .* , pp. 174–75, nos. 210.6–8.

141
Jean Marende
Philibert II and Margaret of Austria (M. Jones 1982–88, vol. 1, no. 16)

Notes:

1. Gules, a cross argent (*Savoy*): Quarterly, 1. Gules, a fess argent, (*Austria*); 2. Azure, semé of fleurs-de-lis or, a bordure-compony argent and gules (*Burgundy-modern*); Bendy of six or and azure, a bordure gules (*Burgundy-ancient*); 4. Sable, a lion rampant or, armed and langued gules (*Brabant*); Overall, or, a lion sable, armed and langued gules (*Flanders*). I am grateful to Stephen K. Scher for blasoning these arms.
2. Blanchet 1930, p. 394, interprets it as standing for "Fortitudo eius rodum tenuit" (Through courage he stood his ground). See also cat. no. 66.
3. Rondot 1883.
4. Examples are preserved in Paris, Bibliothèque National; the same, Collection Armand-Valton 1926; and Lyon, Musée des Beaux-Arts.
5. Of this variant there are specimens in Washington, National Gallery of Art, Kress Collection; the collection of Umberto di Savoy (U. di S. 1980, vol. 1, p. 91, no. 1); and New York, The Metropolitan Museum of Art.
6. Of this variant there are specimens in Paris, Bibliothèque Nationale, Collection Armand-Valton 1927; and London, Victoria & Albert Museum (U. di S., vol. 1, p. 91, no. 2).
7. On the symbolism of Savoy knots, see Tervarent 1958–64, columns 284 and 286, and Lecoq 1987, p. 416.
8. For these suggestions I am indebted to Stephen K. Scher.

Additional literature: Guichenon 1650, p. 98; Köhler 1743, vol. 15, pp. 121–28 (inaccurate illustration?); Greene 1883, pp. 288–96; Mazerolle 1902–4, vol. 2, nos. 29–30.

Jacques Gauvain

Notes:

1. Rondot 1887, pp. 11f; M. Jones 1982–88, vol. 1, pp. 49–50.
2. Habich 1929–34, no. 284; Rondot 1887, pp. 11f.

142, 142a
Jacques Gauvain
Antoine, duke of Lorraine and Bar, and Renée de Bourbon (M. Jones 1982–88, vol. 1, no. 29)

Notes:

1. E. Duvernoy in *Dictionnaire de biographie française*, vol. 3, column 11. See also Philippe 1928, pp. 38–43.
2. M. Jones 1982–88, vol. 1, p. 53.
3. Ibid., no. 26.
4. Dion 1947, pp. 79f.

Additional literature: Luckius 1620, p. 56 (with a different reverse, see de la Tour 1910, no. 3885); de Saulcy 1841; Lepage 1875, pp. 44 and 219; Armand 1883–87, vol. 2, p. 190, no. 18; de la Tour 1897, pp. 84–87; Mazerolle 1902–4, vol. 2, p. 21, no. 75; Calmet 1973, vol. 5, columns 463f.

Pierre Woeiriot de Bouzey

Notes:

1. Marot 1952, pp. 136–45.
2. Firmin-Didot 1872, p. 283.
3. *F. Iosephi Antiquitatum Iudaicarum. . . .* Lyon, 1556.

143
Pierre II Woeiriot
Simon Costière (M. Jones 1982–88, vol. 1, no. 97)

Notes:

1. Tricou 1958, pp. 16–17.

2. Tourneur 1925 ("Simon"), p. 87, proposes that the medal was produced at three different times: Type 2 in 1566, Type 1 in the early seventeenth century, and Type 3 after the seventeenth century. While it is true that Type 3 probably resulted from a late (nineteenth-century) recasting, there is no reason to rule out the possibility that the first two versions were cast at about the same time.
3. Brussels, Bibliothèque Royale Albert Ier, Cabinet des Médailles. See Tourneur 1925 ("Simon"), p. 86. I am indebted to Mr. Yves Landrain, a researcher in the Brussels collection, for checking the accuracy of the monogram.

Additional literature: Mazerolle 1902–4, vol. 1, pp. 94–95; Rondot 1902, pp. 271–87; L. Rosenthal 1909, p. 172; Firmin-Didot 1872, p. 279f.

Germain Pilon

Notes:

1. Ciprut 1969 ("Chronologie"), pp. 333–34; Babelon 1927 (*Germain*), pp. 33, 35, and 57–58.
2. Ciprut 1969 ("Chronologie"), pp. 334–35; Babelon 1927 (*Germain*), pp. 35–36, 58–59. For the sculptures, see Beaulieu 1978, nos. 197–98.
3. Ciprut 1969 ("Chronologie"), pp. 334–37; Babelon 1927 (*Germain*), pp. 36, 46, and 59–61. For the sculptures, see Vitry and Brière 1925, pp. 173–78.
4. All of the relevant documents are given in Mazerolle 1902–4, vol. 1. See also Babelon 1927 (*Germain*), pp. 33–56, and Ciprut 1969 ("Nouveaux"), pp. 337–38, 340, and 343–44.
5. Mazerolle 1902–4, vol. 1, pp. 130–31. Much of the material discussed here and in the following two entries on Pilon's medals was presented by the author in a paper given at the Pilon colloquium held at the Louvre, Paris, on October 26–27, 1990, the proceedings of which will be published in the near future.
6. Ibid., no. 204.
7. The struck medals are Mazerolle 1902–4, vol. 2, nos. 242–96; M. Jones 1982–88, vol. 1, nos. 122–42.

Additional literature: Terrasse 1930; Gaehtgens 1967; Blunt 1953, pp. 98–102; and M. Jones 1982–88, pp. 128–58.

144
Germain Pilon
René de Birague (M. Jones 1982–88, vol. 1, no. 121)

Notes:

1. The translation is based on that found in M. Jones 1982–88, vol. 1, p. 142.
2. The medal is accompanied by its original presentation box covered in engraved red leather with the cipher RB divided between the two sides of the box. See Babelon 1920, pp. 165–72.
3. We offer this only as a suggestion, because of the close correspondence between the small struck medal and the large cast piece. As we understand the process, it was more normal for the sculptor to provide a wax model on the same scale as the eventual struck coin or medal. An indication of this is given in a document dated July 10, 1573, where Pilon is asked to submit "ung modelle en paste ou cire de l'efigie du Roy, de la grandeur d'ung teston, avec le revers d'icelluy et lettres y necessaires. . . ." See Mazerolle 1902–4, vol. 1, no. 200.
4. Babelon 1927 (*Germain*), pp. 29–30 and 66–67; Grodecki 1981, pp. 61–78.
5. M. Jones 1982–88, vol. 1, pp. 138–42.
6. See M. Jones 1982–88, vol. 1, p. 142, where one must beware the many typographical errors, some of them in the transcription of the legend.
7. Ibid.
8. Paris, Bibliothèque Nationale, MS Clairambault 1111, fols. 240–41.
9. For further information on the life of Birague, see Litta et al. 1852, fasc. LXXI, and the entry in *Dizionario Biografico. . . .*

Additional literature: Armand 1883–87, vol. 1, p. 252, no. 19; Mazerolle 1902–4, vol. 2, no. 241; Babelon and Jacquiot 1950, no. 53, pl. X; M. Jones 1979 (*Art*), p. 56 and pl. 3

145
Germain Pilon
Henry II (M. Jones 1982–88, vol. 1, no. 114)

Notes:
1. Coyeque 1940, p. 56. One also finds a reference to medals in a document dated April 26, 1616, in the Minutier Central, referring to Pilon's widow, Germaine Durand: "Dans la somme de 216 livres 2 sols est comprise la part de la veuve Leblond [Germain Durand's stepdaughter, Claude Pilon] dans une enseigne de diamants baillée en gage par le sieur de Saint-Phal, et sa part des 106 médailles promises à défunt Germain Pilon par Claude de Héry." See Fleury 1969, vol. 1, pp. 550–51.
2. See Verlet 1987, pp. 268–71. If further proof were needed that the Valois medals are not a romantic fabrication of the nineteenth century, one can visit the courtyard of the École des Beaux-Arts and see there a grille with a gate, the lock-plates of which are fashioned from two of the Valois series: medallions of Charles IX and his queen Elizabeth of Austria. The grille, originally from Saint-Denis, was used by Alexandre Lenoir to close the chapel containing the tomb of Francis I in the Musée des Monuments Français at the Petits-Augustins. Lenoir had mounted on this grille "plusiers médaillons représentant Catherine de' Medici, Henry III, Charles IX, la reine sa femme et Henry IV." He had purchased the medallions in 1802 (the receipt is dated "8 frimaire an XI"), and had considered them all—excepting, no doubt, the one of Henry IV—"modelé et fondu dans le seizième siècle." I wish to expresss my gratitude to M. Fédéric Chappey, formerly conservateur des sculptures, Ecole Nationale Supérieure des Beaux-Arts, for directing me to these medals and to the reference in Lenoir. See Courajod 1878–87, vol. 2, pp. 44ff, especially pp. 48–49.
3. Moreau-Nélaton 1908; Moreau-Nélaton 1924; Adler 1929, pp. 201ff; *Les Clouet et La Cour des Rois de France*; Broglie 1971, pp. 258–336. Among these paintings are the standing figure of Charles IX in the Musée Carnavalet, Paris, and the portraits of Elizabeth of Austria and Charles IX in the Musée Condé, Chantilly.
4. The first two are of course in the abbey church of Saint-Denis. The bust appears in Babelon 1927 (*Germain*), p. 63, no. 11, pl. XXXVI, fig. 41. At that time it was in the collection of the Comte d'Hunolstein, Paris, and it is now in a private collection in the United States.
5. Raphael Pilon, the artist's eldest son by his first wife, Marguerite Alain, was born in 1559, and eventually worked with his father. He died in March 1590, a mere six weeks after his father. Pilon married his third wife, Germaine Durand, on May 11, 1567, and she bore him six more sons. Very little research, if any, has been done on the question of successors to Pilon. The silence of the past is perhaps an indication that his sons produced nothing of significance, if indeed any of them followed their father's profession. See Ciprut 1969 ("Chronologie"), pp. 333–44. On the other hand, Mathieu Jacquet did work in Pilon's atelier, and on April 26, 1574, his master held Jacquet's son Germain at his baptism. See Ciprut 1969 ("Chronologie"), p. 337, and Ciprut 1967.
6. A full bibliography on the life of Henry II may be found in the latest biography of him, Baumgartner 1988. See also Batiffol 1909, pp. 118–55.

Additional literature: *Trésor de Numismatiques . . .* (French), vol. 1, pl. XVI, no. 1; Armand 1883–87, vol. 2, p. 249, no. 4; Mazerolle 1902–4, vol. 2, no. 232; Babelon 1926, pp. 111–15; Babelon and Jacquiot 1950, no. 48, pl. VII.

Guillaume Dupré

Notes:
1. For a fuller treatment of Dupré's life, see M. Jones 1982–88, vol. 2, pp. 37–47.
2. Mazerolle 1902–4, vol. 2, no. 639; M. Jones 1982–88, vol. 2, no. 18.

3. M. Jones 1982–88, vol. 2, no. 36.
4. Richelieu 1853–77, vol. 7, pp. 277, 300.

146, 146a
Guillaume Dupré
Henry IV and Marie de' Medici (M. Jones 1982–88, vol. 2, nos. 19a–19b)

Notes:
1. Bie 1636, pl. 95, no. 78, and pp. 287–88.
2. Reusner 1581, p. 12.
3. Mattingly et al. 1923–62, vol. 2, p. 235, no. 405, and pl. 38, no. 2.
4. For the reign of Henry IV, see Mousnier 1964 and Babelon 1982.

Additional literature: Neugebauer 1619, p. 99; *Recueil . . .*, p. 12; *Trésor de Numismatique . . .* (French), vol. 2, pl. 20, 20 bis; Mazerolle 1902–4, vol. 1, no. 470, vol. 2, no. 643; Migeon 1904, nos. 587–88; Reichmann sale, 1921. no. 633; Mann 1931, p. 138; Maumené 1935, pp. 28–39; Hill and Pollard 1967, no. 556; Knoedler sale, 1968, no. IIB; Bardon 1974, pp. 8, 168, and 218, pl. LXVIII H; *Catalogue of the Vernon . . .*, no. 170; *Sculpture from the David . . .*, no. 13; Marrow 1982, p. 58 and fig. 27.

147
Guillaume Dupré
Doge Marcantonio Memmo (M. Jones 1982–88, vol. 2, no. 37)

Additional literature: *Trésor de Numismatique . . .* (French), vol. 2, pl. IX; Mazerolle 1902–4, vol. 2, no. 669; Alvarez-Ossorio 1950, p. 103.

148
Guillaume Dupré
Christine of Lorraine (M. Jones 1982–88, vol. 2, no. 45)

Notes:
1. See M. Jones 1982–88, vol. 2, nos. 33, 48.
2. Pollard 1984–85, vol. 2, no. 475.

Additional literature: *Trésor de Numismatique . . .* (French), vol. 2, pl. x, no. 2; Supino 1899, no. 846; Mazerolle 1902–4, vol. 2, no. 678; Migeon 1904, no. 593; Reichmann sale, 1921, no. 634; Hamburger sale, 1924, no. 62; *Medaljen . . .*, pl. 4; Alvarez-Ossorio 1950, p. 178, no. 388; V. Johnson 1975 ("barocca"), pp. 14–15; Langedijk 1981–87, vol. 1, p. 670, no. 34.

149
Guillaume Dupré
Pierre Jeannin (M. Jones 1982–88, no. 50)

Notes:
1. On the life of Jeannin, see Saumaise 1623 and *Négociations . . .*, vol. 1, pp. 9–42.
2. *Négociations . . .*, vol. 1, pp. 9–24, and the article "Pierre Jeannin" by Hippolyte de Laporte in *Biographie Universelle Ancienne et Moderne*, vol. 21, pp. 24–26.
3. Illustrated in Babelon 1946, pl. XXX.

Additional literature: *Trésor de Numismatique . . .* (French), vol. 2, pp. 12–13, pl. XVI, no. 2; Mazerolle 1902–4, vol. 2, no. 683; Forrer 1904–30, vol. 1, p. 657; Hill 1923, p. 77, no. 11; Löbbecke sale, 1929, no. 147, illus. pl. XXXII; Hill 1931, no. 564, pl. CXXIII; Oppenheimer sale, 1936, no. 320; Babelon 1948, p. 40, pl. XXI; Cott 1951, p. 128, illus. p. 178; Hill and Pollard 1967, p. 106, no. 564; M. Jones 1979 (*Art*), p. 77, no. 189; Christie's sale, London, 1985, no. 95; M. Jones 1986; Scher et al. 1986, pp. 80, 100–101.

150
Guillaume Dupré
Charles Duret de Chevry

Note:
1. For Duret, see Tallement des Réaux 1960, vol. 1, p. 170.

Additional literature: Mazerolle 1902–4, no. 703.

151
Jacob Richier
Marie de Vignon (M. Jones 1982–88, vol. 2, no. 87)

Notes:
1. Tallement des Réaux 1862, vol. 1, pp. 91–94.

Additional literature: *Trésor de Numismatique . . .* (French), vol. 1, p. 155, no. 5; Rondot 1885 (*Jacob*); Mazerolle 1902–4, vol. 2, no. 759; Charvet 1907, pp. 280–82; Tricou 1953, no. 22.

Jean Warin

Note:
1. For all references, see M. Jones 1982–88, vol. 2, pp. 177–87.

152
Jean Warin
Antoine Coeffier, called Ruzé (M. Jones 1982–88, vol. 2, no. 180)

Note:
1. Pinard 1760–78, vol. 2, pp. 493–502; Jacquart 1959, pp. 298–313.

Additional literature: Bie 1636, pp. 143–44, no. 125; *Recueil . . .*, p. 30; *Trésor de Numismatique . . .* (French), vol. 2, pl. 14, no. 2; Mazerolle 1902–4, vol. 2, no. 702; Foville 1913, pp. 155–56; Mann 1931, p. 139; Middeldorf and Goetz 1944, no. 287; Hill and Pollard 1967, no. 569.

153
Jean Warin
Cardinal Richelieu (M. Jones 1982–88, vol. 2, no. 182)

Notes:
1. Or, three chevrons gules; above, a ducal crown. I am grateful to Stephen K. Scher for blasoning these arms.
2. Mazerolle 1932, vol. 1, p. 23, and vol. 2, document 38; M. Jones 1982–88, vol. 2, p. 178, and note 46.

Additional literature: Bie 1636, pl. 45, no. 25 (reverse only, and in a different size, with the same legend and date and similar composition, but with Louis in the chariot); *Recueil . . .*, p. 32; Gaetani 1761–68, vol. 2, pl. 108, no. 1; *Trésor de Numismatique . . .* (French), vol. 2, p. 21, nos. 2–3; Rizzini 1892, vol. 2, p. 97, no. 8; Mazerolle 1932, vol. 1, no. 5; Pény, 1947, no. 6 (obverse only); Hill and Pollard 1967, no. 575a; Salton 1969, no. 84; Fischer 1969, nos. 165–66; Norris and Weber 1976, no. 250.

154
Jean Warin
Louis XIV and Anne of Austria (M. Jones 1982–88, vol. 2, no. 208)

Notes:
1. Blunt 1953, pp. 149–50; Dumolin 1930, pp. 106–7; Blunt 1941, pp. 14–16; Braham 1963, pp. 351–63, fig. 5; P. Smith 1964, p. 115.
2. Lemaire 1685, vol. 2, pp. 314–16.

Additional literature: Menestrier 1691, p. 5; Perrault 1700, p. 86; *Trésor de Numismatique . . .* (French), vol. 2, pl. 22, no. 2; Migeon 1904, no. 612; Blanchet 1920, pp. XXXIV–XXXVI; Mazerolle 1932, vol. 1, no. 60; Jacquiot 1970, p. 277; Norris and Weber 1976, no. 276.

155
French School
Henry IV

Notes:
1. To the left, Azure, three fleurs-de-lis or (*France Modern*). To the right, Quarterly, 1 and 4: Gules, a cross, saltire, and double orle of chains, linked together or (*Navarre*). 2: Or, two cows passant in pale gules, collared, armed and belled azure (*Béarn*). 3: Azure, three fleurs-de-lis or (*France Modern*). I thank Stephen K. Scher for blasoning these arms.
2. *Trésor de Numismatique . . .* (French), vol. 1, pl. XXVII, no. 6; Armand 1883–87, vol. 2, p. 279, no. 6; Mazerolle

1902–4, vol. 2, p. 78, no. 373. Mazerolle describes the piece in the Bibliothèque Nationale as being provided with a loop; the one illustrated in the *Trésor*, like the one exhibited here, has no such loop.

3. Mazerolle 1902–4, vol. 2, p. 144, nos. 720–24; Foville 1915, p. 775.
4. M. Jones 1882–88, vol. 2, p. 17, and nos. 19a and 21.
5. Of necessity, this order does occur on the few medals and coins of Henry with legends in French: Mazerolle 1902–4, vol. 2, p. 78, no. 372; Lafaurie and Prieur 1951–56, vol. 2, p. 154, no. 1112.
6. Laprade 1953, pp. 89–92; Maumené and d'Harcourt 1929, vol. 1, pp. 209 and 224–25, nos. 311–12; van Thiel et al. 1976, p. 157, no. A1400; Strauss, ed. 1977, vol. 1, pp. 554–55, no. 308.
7. Teulet 1864, p. 12.

England and the Low Countries, Sixteenth and Early Seventeenth Centuries

156, 156a
Netherlandish, sixteenth century (?)
Charles V and Philip II

Notes:

1. Formerly in a Zurich collection. See Habich 1923–24, p. 178, illus. pl. XVII.
2. Useful surveys of the life and times of Charles V are provided by: Robertson 1857; Brandi 1939; Fernández Alvarez 1975; and Rady 1988. A good general history of the intellectual climate in Charles's empire is in Trevor-Roper 1976, pp. 11–43. For a fundamental and profound study of the Habsburgs' use of the arts, see Eisler 1983.
3. The prime sources on Leoni's sculptural and medallic work remain Plon 1887 and Kenner 1892. For Leoni's coinage, see *Corpus nummorum italicorum*, vol. 5, pl. XVI, nos. 7, 9–10, 12–13, and Crippa 1992.
4. Plon 1887, p. 259, pl. XXX, nos. 7–8; Kenner 1892, p. 56, pl. III, 1–2; Bernhart 1919, no. 161. An unpublished paper by Braden K. Frieder, "A Matter of Technique: An Unusual Portrait Medal of Charles V," a copy of which is on file at the American Numismatic Society, New York, argues that this medal, known from cast specimens, was originally struck.
5. 225 × 170 mm. See Bange 1922, no. 14, pl. VII, and Habich 1923–24 (Review), p. 178. Bange's attribution to Giampaolo Poggini (cat. no. 58)—based on the head's indebtedness to Poggini's medallic portraits of Philip—is hardly likely, and Paul Grotemeyer doubted it in his "Giampaolo Poggini" in Thieme-Becker, vol. 27, p. 188. A lead plaquette in the Schlossmuseum, Gotha, which seems to reproduce the horse from the Berlin plaquette (without rider or trappings), is published in I. Weber 1975, no. 659.6, pl. 178. Van Mieris 1732–35, vol. 2, p. 442, illustrates our medal without legends and with numerous variations. In his engraving, Philip is beardless, his horse walks upon a grassy plot of ground, and the armor of Charles is somewhat modified. No specimen of this type is now known. Van Mieris may have relied for his illustration upon a vague sketch from memory or an illegible example of the medal. Although the features of the bust on the obverse are unmistakably those of Charles V, van Mieris describes the sitters as Francis I of France and his son Henry II. An adaptation of the Charles/Philip medal depicting Francis and Henry is indeed known (Armand 1883–87, vol. 2, p. 188, no. 12; Neuburg sale, 1938, no. 71, pl. XII). The types are generally identical to the original work, with the heads of the French monarchs substituted for those of Charles and Philip. Both figures face left instead of right. Since this piece names Henry as king, it must date from after his accession in 1547. Armand's assertion that the Charles V and the Francis I are by the same medalist is far from certain; the lettering on the latter is similar, but not identical to that on our no. 156. A uniface bronze variant of the Francis I obverse, apparently made from the same model, but given a different border and style of lettering, is also recorded (*Trésor de Numismatique . . .* (French), vol. 1, p. 7, pl. X, 2). A uniface variant of the Charles V obverse exists in a New York private collection, evidently made from the same model but with minor changes, particularly in the decoration of Charles's cuirass. An old label on the reverse reads "Louvre 544." It may be identical with a uniface bronze specimen of this type in the Vidal Quadras y Ramón Collection, Barcelona (Vidal Quadras y Ramón sale, 1892, vol. 4, no. 13531).

6. Mann 1931, no. S13, pl. 2.
7. Hill 1921, pp. 159–60.

Additional literature: Merzbacher sale, 1900; Lanna sale, 1911; Bernhart 1919, no. 178, pl. XVI; Alvarez-Ossorio 1950; Norris and Weber 1976; C. Johnson 1990, vol. 1.

Quentin Matsys

Note:

1. Tourneur 1920 ("Quentin"), p. 157; Smolderen 1969 ("Quentin"), pp. 520–22.

Additional literature: Simonis 1900, pp. 49–52; de Bosque 1975.

157
Quentin Matsys
Desiderius Erasmus

Notes:

1. Allen 1906–47, vol. 5, no. 1452, and vol. 7, no. 1985.
2. In a letter of May 15, 1520, to Cardinal Albrecht of Brandenburg (cat. no. 108). Allen 1906–47, vol. 4, no. 1101.
3. Allen 1906–47, vol. 7, no. 2018.

Additional literature: van Mieris 1732–35, vol. 2, p. 94; Köhler 1740, vol. 12, pp. 116–20; Picqué 1882, pp. 107–8; Simonis 1900, pp. 31–32 and 80–85, pl. II, no. 3; Dompierre de Chaufepié 1903, vol. 1, nos. 40–41; Tourneur 1920 ("Quentin"), pp. 139–60; Hill 1920 (*Medals*), p. 125; Habich 1923–24 ("Erasmus"), pp. 119–22; Babelon 1927 (*La médaille*), pp. 116–17 and pl. XVI, 2; Wind 1937–38, pp. 66–69; Gerlo 1944, pp. 33–45; Gerlo 1950, pp. 17–26; Baillion 1958, pp. 35–36; Treu 1959, pp. 26–28, fig. 9; Wellens-de Donder 1959 (*Médailleurs*), nos. 19–20 and pl. IV; Hill and Pollard 1967, no. 629a; *Erasme . . .*, no. 83; Smolderen 1969 ("Quentin"), pp. 513–25; Theuerkauff 1977, pp. 105 and 109, no. 17; Hill and Pollard 1978, pp. 118–21 and pl. 22, no. 2; Toussaint 1986, pp. 120–30; *Erasmus . . .*, pp. 113–15, no. A 2.10.

Jacques Jonghelinck

Literature: Baert 1848, pp. 55–56, 559–62, and 1849, p. 209; Visschers 1853; Pinchart 1854, pp. 209–39; Pinchart 1868, pp. 21–26, 30–31, and 37–38; Marchal 1895, pp. 329–33; Simonis 1904, pp. 43–186; Forrer 1904–30, vol. 2, p. 82–85, and vol. 7, pp. 487–89; Motta 1908, pp. 75–76; Tourneur 1920 ("La maison"), pp. 209–13; Tourneur 1927, pp. 79–93; Thieme-Becker, vol. 19, pp. 135–37; Baillion 1956, pp. 93–94, 101–13, and 1957, pp. 13, 22–24; Wellens-de Donder 1960, pp. 295–305; Smolderen 1969 ("Jacques"), pp. 83–147; Pope-Hennessy and Hodgkinson 1970, pp. 28–33; Becker 1971, pp. 75–115; Smolderen 1972; Smolderen in *Biographie nationale*, vol. 38, columns 370–88; Smolderen 1977, pp. 102–43; Meijer 1979, pp. 116–35; Smolderen 1980–81, pp. 21–53; Smolderen 1984, pp. 119–39; Buchanan 1990, pp. 102–13.

158
Jacques Jonghelinck
Margaret, duchess of Parma

Notes:

1. For Margaret's biography, see Rachfahl 1898, De Jonghe 1965, Lefevre 1986, and Puaux 1987.
2. Van Loon 1732, vol. 1, p. 97, nos. II and III.

Additional literature: Herrgott 1752–53, vol. 1, 2, pl. XX-VIII, no. 135; Litta et al. 1868, tavola XXII and pl. II, no. 17; Armand 1883–87, vol. 2, p. 211, no. 40; U. Rossi 1888, pp. 333–350; Ambrosoli 1891, pp. 389–92 and pl. XVIII, no. 1; Simonis 1904, vol. 2, pp. 58–60 and pl. VIII, no. 1; Dompierre de Chaufepié 1903–6, vol. 1, no. 214; Babelon 1927 (*La médaille*), p. 120 and pl. XVII, no. 2; Wellens-de Donder 1959 (Médailleurs), no. 121; Weiller 1979, p. 116, no. 128 and pl. XVI; Maijer 1988, p. 136 and fig. 115.

159
Jacques Jonghelinck
Antoine Perrenot de Granvelle

Notes:

1. For biographical details, see van Durme 1953.
2. See Bernhart 1920–21, pp. 109–11, nos. 8–19, and Tourneur 1927, pp. 83–92.
3. Van Loon 1732, vol. 1, p. 58; Simonis 1904, vol. 2, pl. IX, no. 1; Bernhart 1920–21, pl. VI, no. 14.
4. Van Loon 1732, vol. 1, p. 47, no. IV; Plon 1887, pl. XXXII, nos. 2 and 4; Bernhart 1920–21, pl. IV, no. 3, and Pl. V, no. 5.
5. Van Loon 1732, vol. 1, p. 47, no. II; Plon 1887, pl. XXXIV, no. 2; Bernhart 1920–21, pl. VI, no. 13.

Additional literature: Gaetani 1761–63, vol. 1, pl. LX-XVI, no. 5; Armand 1883–87, vol. 2, p. 255, no. 37; Plon 1887, p. 275 and pl. XXXIV, no. 3; Simonis 1904, vol. 2, p. 109 and pl. IX, no. 2; Lanna sale, 1911, no. 465, pl. 26; Bernhart 1920–21, no. 12, p. 115 and pl. VII; Tourneur 1927, p. 85; M. Hoc in *Exposition-concours . . .*, p. 128; *Anvers . . .*, no. 217; *De triomf . . .*, no. 401; *Antwerpens . . .*, no. 346; *Médailles des anciens . . .*, no. 43; Salton 1969, no. 142; Jacquiot 1989, pp. 97–109.

160
Jacques Jonghelinck
Jan Walravens

Notes:

1. De Beer 1930, p. 136.
2. Regarding the jester, see van Even 1861, p. 58; van Eeghem 1936, pp. 75–78; and Roobaert 1961, pp. 83–100.
3. Van Loon 1732, vol. 1, p. 63.
4. Van Eeghem 1936, p. 76.

Additional literature: Dompierre de Chaufepié 1903–6, vol. 1, no. 186; Simonis 1904, vol. 2, p. 118 and pl. XI, no. 1; Baillion 1956, no. 5; Wellens-de Donder 1959 (Médailleurs), no. 113 and pl. XIV.

161
Jacques Jonghelinck
Antony van Stralen

Notes:

1. On van Stralen, see Génard 1871, pp. 1–321; van der Linden in *Biographie nationale*, vol. 24, columns 131–43; and Cosemans 1933, pp. 599–663.
2. Hill 1930, no. 1027.
3. See Génard 1865, p. 266.

Additional literature: van Loon 1732, vol. 1, p. 95; Armand 1883–87, vol. 2, p. 241, no. 29; Dompierre de Chaufepié 1903–6, vol. 1, no. 190; Simonis 1904, vol. 2, p. 126 and pl. X, no. 4; Baillion 1956–57, no. 7; Wellens-de Donder 1959 (*Médailleurs*), no. 116; Hill and Pollard, 1978, pl. 23, no. 5; M. Jones 1979 (*Art*), pp. 47–48, figs. 98a–98b.

162
Jacques Jonghelinck
Philip of Croy

Notes:

1. Van Loon 1732, vol. 1, p. 450.
2. Van Loon 1732, vol. 1, p. 91, no. 1, and Simonis 1904, vol. 2, pl. V, no. 4.
3. On the duke, see Gachard 1890, vol. 3, pp. 489–98, and Born 1981, pp. 175–350.

Additional literature: Rosenheim sale, 1923, no. 510, pl. 25; Weiller 1979, no. 157, p. 121 and pl. XX.

163
Jacques Jonghelinck
Ferdinand, duke of Alba

Note:

1. For his biography, see Ossorio 1669; Astorga 1697; Duquessa de Berwick y de Alba 1891; Duque de Berwick y de Alba 1919; Alba 1952; Kirchner 1968; Grierson 1969; Parker 1977, pp. 99–163; and Maltby 1983.

Additional literature: van Loon 1732–37, vol. 1, p. 134, no. 1; Armand 1883–87, vol. 2, p. 246, no. 12; Dompierre de Chaufepié 1903–6, vol. 1, no. 249; Simonis 1904, vol. 2, p. 143, and pl. XV, no. 1; Lanna sale, 1911, no. 470, pl. 27; Smolderen 1972, pp. 75–76, pl. XXV.

Nicholas Hilliard

Notes:

1. Edmond 1983, pp. 30, 50–51. For Hilliard's activity as a goldsmith, see Auerbach 1961, pp. 169–97.
2. Strong 1963, pp. 90–91; Strong 1969, p. 101; Edmond 1983, p. 39; Strong and Murrell 1983, p. 117.
3. Strong 1963, p. 8.
4. Edmond 1983, pp. 61–64.
5. Madden 1852, p. 238.
6. M. Jones 1979 (*Art*), pp. 68–69.
7. Ibid., p. 178.

Additional literature: Farquhar 1908, pp. 324–56; Reynolds 1952–54; Barclay and Syson 1993.

164
Nicholas Hilliard
Elizabeth I

Notes:

1. First described in Corkran 1867, pp. 45–46.
2. For his collaboration with Abel Feckeman, see Challis 1978, p. 290; for that with his son Lawrence and his former apprentice Rowland Lockey, see Edmond 1983, p. 143.
3. Martin and Parker 1988.
4. Auerbach 1953, pp. 197–205; Strong 1963, p. 7; Strong 1987, p. 16.
5. Strong 1963, pp. 72–75, 90–97, and 102–3.
6. Ibid., pp. 107–9, no. E11.
7. Hall 1974, p. 190.
8. Hawkins 1885, vol. 1, p. 154.
9. Strong and Murrell 1983, p. 124, no. 197.

Jacob Zagar

Literature: Pinchart 1871, p. 75; Picqué 1879, pp. 292–93 and 302–3; de Man 1895, pp. 502–7; Simonis 1900, pp. 111–14; de Munter 1914, pp. 173–80; Tourneur 1919 ("Société"), pp. 368–70; van Kerkwijk 1919, p. 5; Wellens-de Donder 1959 (*Médailleurs*), pp. 53–57; *Encyclopedie van Zeeland*, vol. 3; *Kunst voor de beeldenstorm*, pp. 341–42, nos. 223–24.

165
Jacob Zagar
Lieven Bloxsen

Literature: de Man 1895, pp. 502–7; Simonis 1900, pp. 111–14; de Munter 1914, p. 175; de Vos 1931, pp. 2–3, no. 1; Vroom 1942, pp. 171–78; Wellens-de Donder 1959 (*Médailleurs*), p. 55, no. 48; *Kunst voor de beeldenstorm*, no. 223.

Steven van Herwijck

Literature: Simonis 1904, pp. 187–220; Tourneur 1921, pp. 27–55; Muller 1922, pp. 24–31; Tourneur 1922 ("Steven"), pp. 91–132; Tourneur 1922 ("Le médailleur"), pp. 209–11; Tourneur 1925 ("Jan"), pp. 45–55; Majkowski 1937, pp. 1–37; Wellens-de Donder 1959 (*Médailleurs*), pp. 83–95; Wellens-de Donder 1959 ("La médaille . . . "), pp. 165–70; van Dorsten 1969, pp. 143–45; *Kunst voor de beeldenstorm*, pp. 338–41.

166
Steven van Herwijck
Joris van Egmond

Literature: van Loon 1723, vol. 1, p. 47; Simonis 1904, pp. 192–93; Dompierre de Chaufepié 1903–6, no. 153; *Catalogus . . .* , no. 149; Tourneur 1921, p. 39; Tourneur 1922 ("Steven"), p. 111; *Lexikon für Theologie und Kirche*, vol. 2, column 376, vol. 4, columns 814–15, and vol. 8, columns 374 and 902; Wellens-de Donder 1959 (*Médailleurs*), no. 52; van de Ven 1959, pp. 87–99; Hill and Pollard 1967, no. 564; Pollard 1971, pp. 325–29; *Kunst voor de beeldenstorm*, no. 66.

167
Steven van Herwijck
Engelken Tols

Literature: Simonis 1904, p. 197; S. Muller 1911, p. 179; *Catalogus . . .* , no. 153; Tourneur 1921, p. 40, no. 5; S. Muller 1922, p. 7; *Kunst voor de beeldenstorm*, no. 219.

168
Steven van Herwijck
Cecilia Veeselar

Note:

1. Both the two-sided medal of Cecilia Veeselar and the lead portrait plaque of Floris Allewijn are preserved in the collection of the Royal Dutch Academy of Sciences in Amsterdam. Simonis 1904, pp. 200–202, erroneously gave the Royal Coin Cabinet, then at The Hague, as the reference for Cecilia's two-sided medal, but that collection never possessed it. Tourneur 1922 ("Steven") repeats the error.

Additional literature: de Voogt 1867, pp. 347–49, pl. VII and VIII; Nahuys 1867, pp. 506–10; C.-A. Serrure 1882, pp. 3–6; Dompierre de Chaufepié 1903–6, no. 170; van Zuiden 1913, p. 160; Hill 1918, p. 58, pl. B; van der Heijden 1948, pp. 12–13; Wellens-de Donder 1959 (*Médailleurs*), pp. 86–87, no. 87; Henkel and Schöne 1978, columns 637–39 and 1569; Hofman 1983, p. 23.

169
Steven van Herwijck
Richard Martin and Dorcas Eglestone

Literature: Hawkins 1885, pp. 107–8, no. 33, pl. VII, 9; Simonis 1904, p. 214, pl. XXV, 3 and 4; Hill 1907–8, p. 363, pl. II, 2; Hill 1918, p. 58; Tourneur 1922 ("Steven"), p. 120, no. 20; Craig 1953, pp. 123–24, 126–29, 135, and 142; *Spink & Son's . . .* , p. 71, no. 1492; Auctiones sale, 1985, no. 1123.

Coenraad Bloc

Literature: Tourneur 1925 ("Conrad"), pp. 199–211; Mazerolle 1927, pp. 95–98; van Kerkwijk 1929, pp. 103–4; Smolderen 1991, pp. 159–64.

170
Coenraad Bloc
William of Orange and Charlotte de Bourbon

Literature: Bizot 1690, p. 27; van Loon 1732–37, vol. 1, p. 236; Dompierre de Chaufepié 1903–6, no. 304; Tourneur 1925 ("Conrad"), pp. 199–211; Mazerolle 1927, pp. 95–98; van Kerkwijk 1929; Flohil 1953, pp. 49–70; Flohil 1968, pp. 65–70; *Mauritshuis . . .* , no. 448; de Werd 1977, pp. 49–51; den Besten 1983; *Willem van Oranje . . .* , pp. 21–22; van der Meer 1983, pp. 5–14.

Adams, Nicholas. "New Information about the Screw Press as a Device for Minting Coins: Bramante, Cellini and Baldassare Peruzzi." *American Numismatic Society Museum Notes* 23 (1978): 201–6.

Adler, Irene. "Die Clouet." *Jahrbuch der Kunsthistorischen Sammlung in Wien,* new series 3 (1929): 201f.

Affo, I. *Memorie di tre celebri principesse della famiglia Gonzaga.* Parma, 1787.

Aign, Theodor. *Die Ketzel, ein Nürnberger Handelsherren- und Jerusalempilger-Geschlecht.* Freie Schriftenfolge der Gesellschaft für Familienforschung in Franken, vol.12. Neustadt/Aisch, 1961.

Alba, Duque de. *Epistolario del III Duque de Alba, don Fernando Alvarez de Toledo.* 3 vols. Madrid, 1952.

Albrecht Dürer 1471–1971. Exhibition catalogue, Germanisches Nationalmuseum, Nuremberg. Munich, 1971.

Alckens, August. *München in Erz und Stein. Die Epitaphien der Altstadt-Kirchen.* Mainburg, 1974.

Allen, P. S. *Opus epistolarum Des. Erasmi Roterodami.* Oxford, 1906–47.

Allgemeine Deutsche Biographie [1875–1912]. Reprint Berlin, 1967–71.

Allison, Ann Hersey. "Antico's Medals for the Gonzaga." *The Medal* 9 (special issue 1986): 9–13.

Altdeutsche Meister. Catalogue of the Staatsgalerie Augsburg, vol. 1. Munich, 1978.

Alvarez-Ossorio, Francisco. *Catalogo de las Medallas de los Siglos XV y XVI Conservadas en el Museo Arqueológico Nacional.* Madrid, 1950.

Amadei, F. *Cronaca Universale di Mantova.* Mantua, 1955.

Amayden, Teodoro. *La Storia delle Famiglie Romane.* Edited by Carlo Augusto Bertini. 2 vols. Rome [1914?]. Reprint Bologna, 1979.

Ambrosoli, S. "Una medaglia inedita di Giacomo Jonghelinck." *Rivista italiana di Numismatica* 4 (1891): 389–92.

Ames-Lewis, Francis. "A Portrait of Leon Battista Alberti by Uccello?" *The Burlington Magazine* 116 (1974): 103–4.

———. "Matteo de' Pasti and the Use of Powdered Gold." *Mitteilungen des Kunsthistorischen Institutes in Florenz* 28 (1984): 351–61.

Andaloro, M. "Costanzo da Ferrara. Gli anni a Costantinopoli alla corte di Maometto II." *Storia dell'Arte* 38–40 (1980): 185–212.

Angerer, Martin. *Peter Flötners Entwürfe. Beiträge zum Ornament und Kunsthandwerk in Nürnberg in der 1. Hälfte des 16. Jahrhunderts.* Dissertation, Munich, 1983. Kiel, 1984.

Angus, Duke of Hamilton. *Maria R., Mary Queen of Scots: The Crucial Years.* Edinburgh, 1991.

Antonetti, P. *Savonarole: Le prophète désarmé.* Paris, 1991.

Antwerpens Gouden Eeuw. Exhibition catalogue. Antwerp, 1955.

Anvers, ville de Plantin et de Rubens. Exhibition catalogue, Galerie Mazarine. Paris, 1954.

Apianus, Petrus, and Amantius, Bartholomäus. *Inscriptiones sacrosanctae vetustatis non illae quidem Romanae, sed totius fere orbis summo studio ac maximis impensis Terra Mariq: conquisitae feliciter incipiunt.* Ingolstadt, 1534.

Archibald, M. M. *Sylloge of Coins of the British Isles.* Vol. 34. London, 1986.

d'Arco, Carlo. *Delle arti e degli artefici di Mantova.* Mantua, 1857.

Aretino, Pietro. *Lettere sull'Arte.* Edited by Fidenzio Pertile and Ettore Camesasca. 3 vols. Milan, 1957–60.

Armand, Alfred. *Les médailleurs italiens des quinzième et seizième siècles.* 3 vols. Paris, 1883–87.

Arnolfini, Pompeo. *Della Vita et fatti di Andrea Doria, principe di Melfi.* Genoa, 1598.

The Art of the Renaissance Craftsman. Exhibition catalogue, Fogg Art Museum, Harvard University. Cambridge, 1937.

Astorga, Marquis de. *Histoire de Ferdinand Alvarez de Tolede.* Translated by J. Guignard. 2 vols. Paris, 1697.

Atil, E. "Ottoman Miniature Painting under Sultan Mehmed II." *Ars Orientalis* 9 (1973): 104–20.

[Auctiones sale, 1985]. Auction catalogue, Auctiones AG, Basel, September 18–19, 1985.

Auerbach, E. "Portraits of Queen Elizabeth I," *The Burlington Magazine* 95 (1953): 197–205.

———. *Nicholas Hilliard.* London, 1961.

Augsburger Renaissance. Exhibition catalogue. Augsburg, 1955.

Autelli, F. *Pitture Murali a Brera.* Milan, 1989.

Avery, Charles. *Studies in European Sculpture.* London, 1981.

———. *Plaquettes, Medals and Reliefs from the Collection L[ederer].* London, 1985.

Avery, Charles, and Barbaglia, Susanna. *L'Opera completa del Cellini.* Milan, 1981.

Babelon, Jean. "Gianello della Torre horloger de Charles-Quint et de Philippe II." *Revue de l'Art ancien et moderne* 34 (1913): 269–78.

———. "Le médaillon du Chancelier René de Birague par Germain Pilon à la Bibliothèque Nationale." *Gazette des Beaux-Arts* (March–April 1920): 165–72.

———. "Un médaillon de cire du Cabinet des Médailles. Filippo Strozzi et Benedetto da Maiano." *Gazette des Beaux-Arts* 4 (1921): 203–10.

———. *Jacopo da Trezzo et la construction de l'Escurial.* Paris, 1922.

———. "A propos du médaillon d'Henri II attribué à Germain Pillon." *Aréthuse* 3 (1926): 111–15.

———. *La médaille et les médailleurs.* Paris, 1927.

———. *Germain Pilon.* Paris, 1927.

———. "Portraits en Médaille." In *Encyclopédie Alpina Illustrée.* Paris, 1946.

———. *La Médaille en France.* Paris, 1948.

———. *Great Coins and Medals.* London, 1959.

———. *Das Menschenbild auf Münzen und Medaillen von der Antike bis zur Gegenwart.* Leipzig, 1966.

Babelon, Jean, and Jacquiot, J. *Histoire de Paris d'après les médailles.* Paris, 1950.

Babelon, J.-P. *Henri IV.* Paris, 1982.

Babinger, Franz. *Mehmed der Eroberer und seine Zeit.* Munich, 1953.

Badt, Kurt. "Drei plastische Arbeiten von Leone Battista Alberti." *Mitteilungen des Kunsthistorischen Institutes in Florenz* 8 (1958): 78–87.

Baert, P. "Mémoires sur les sculpteurs et architectes des Pays-Bas." *Bulletin Commission Royale d'Histoire* 14 (1848): 55–56 and 559–62; and 15 (1849): 209.

Baillion, F. "Jacques Jonghelinck, célèbre médailleur anversois, 1530–1606." *Alliance numismatique européenne* 11 and 12 (1956): 93–94, 101–3; and 1 and 3 (1957): 1–3, 22–24.

———. "Quentin Metsys." *Alliance numismatique européenne* 5 (1958): 35–36.

Baldass, Ludwig von. "Die Bildnisse Kaiser Maximilians I." *Jahrbuch der kunsthistorischen Sammlungen des allerhöchsten Kaiserhauses* 31 (1913–14): 247–334.

———. "Die Bildnisse Kaiser Maximilians I." *Jahrbuch der kunsthistorischen Sammlungen in Wien* 31 (1925): 248–49.

Balletti, Andrea. "Alfonso Ruspagiari e Gian Antonio Signoretti, medaglisti del secolo XVI." *Rassegna d'Arte* (1901): 107ff; (1904): 44–46; and (1914): 46–48.

Bandello, Matteo. *Le Novelle.* Edited by Gioachino Brognoligo. 3 vols. Bari, 1928–31.

Bange, Ernst Friedrich. "Zur Datierung von Peter Flötners Plakettenwerk." *Archiv für Medaillen- und Plakettenkunde* 3 (1921–22): 45–52.

———. *Die Italienischen Bronzen der Renaissance und des Barock.* Vol. 2, *Reliefs und Plaketten.* Katalog des Kaiser Friedrich-Museums in Berlin. Berlin and Leipzig, 1922.

———. "Peter Flötners Augsburger Aufenthalt." *Jahrbuch der Preussischen Kunstsammlungen* 44 (1923): 107–17.

———. *Peter Flötner.* Meister der Graphik, vol. 14. Leipzig, 1926.

———. *Die Kleinplastik der deutschen Renaissance in Holz und Stein.* Florence and Leipzig, 1928.

———. "Literaturübersicht. Georg Habich, Die deutschen Schaumünzen des XVI. Jahrhunderts." *Zeitschrift für Kunstgeschichte* (1933): 357–68.

———. "Eine unbekannte Zeichnung Peter Flötners." *Jahrbuch der Preussischen Kunstsammlungen* 58 (1938): 231–32.

———. *Die deutschen Bronzestatuetten des 16. Jahrhunderts.* Berlin, 1949.

Barack, Karl August, ed. *Zimmersche Chronik.* 2nd ed. Freiburg and Tübingen, 1881.

Barclay, C., and Syson, L. "A medal die rediscovered: a new work by Nicholas Hilliard." *The Medal* 22 (Spring 1993): 3–9.

Bardon, F. *Le Portrait Mythologique à la cour de France sous Henri IV et Louis XIII.* Paris, 1974.

Barocchi, Paolo, and Gallo, Daniela. *L'Accademia etrusca.* Exhibition catalogue. Cortona, 1985.

Bartsch, Adam. *Le Peintre-Graveur.* Vienna, 1803–21.

Batiffol, Louis. *Le Siècle de la Renaissance.* Paris, 1909.

Bauch, Alfred. "Der Nürnberger Medailleur M. G." *Historisches Jahrbuch* 19 (1898): 470–75.

Baudi di Vesme, A. *Schede Vesme.* 3 vols. Turin, 1968.

Baumgartner, Frederic J. *Henry II, King of France, 1547–1559.* Durham, North Carolina, and London, 1988.

Baxandall, Michael. *Giotto and the Orators. Humanist Observers of Painting in Italy and the Discovery of Pictorial Composition 1350–1450.* Oxford, 1971.

———. *Painting and Experience in Fifteenth-Century Italy.* Oxford, 1972.

———. *The Limewood Sculptors of Renaissance Germany.* New Haven and London, 1980.

Beaulieu, Michèle. *Description raisonnée des sculptures du Musée du Louvre.* Vol. 2, *Renaissance française.* Paris, 1978.

Becker, J. "Hochmut kommt vor dem Fall. Zum Standbild Albas in der Zitadelle von Antwerpen 1571–1574." *Simiolus* 5 (1971): 75–115.

Beierlein, J. P. *Medaillen auf ausgezeichnete und berühmte Bayern.* Offprint from the *Oberbayerisches Archiv für vaterländische Geschichte* 10, no. 2. Munich, 1848.

———. "Medaillen auf ausgezeichnete und berühmte Bayern, Nachträge und Berichtigungen zur ersten Lieferung. Zu Nro. V und VI. Sebastian und Ursula Ligsalz." *Oberbayerisches Archiv* 12 (1851–52): 176.

———. *Die Medaillen und Münzen des Gesamthauses Wittelsbach.* Vol. 1, *Bayerische Linie.* Munich, 1897.

Belloni, Gian Guido. *Gabinetto Numismatico.* Musei e Gallerie di Milano, vol. 1. Milan, 1977.

Bentley, J. H. *Politics and Culture in Renaissance Naples.* Princeton, 1987.

Bergadini, R. *Carlo Emanuele I.* Turin, 1927.

Bergmann, Joseph. *Medaillen auf berühmte und ausgezeichnete Männer des Österreichischen Kaiserstaates vom XVI. bis zum XIX. Jahrhunderte.* 2 vols. Vienna, 1844–57.

Bernhart, Max. *Die Bildnismedaillen Karls des Fünften.* Munich, 1919.

———. "Die Granvella-Medaillen des XVI. Jahrhunderts." *Archiv für Medaillen- und Plakettenkunde* 2 (1920–21): 101–20.

———. "Nachträge zu Armand." *Archiv für Medaillen- und Plakettenkunde* 5 (1925–26): 83.

———. "Reformatorenbildnisse auf Medaillen der Renaissance." *Numismatik* 2 (1933): 148–60.

———. "Die Porträtzeichnungen des Hans Schwarz."

Münchner Jahrbuch der bildenden Kunst, 2nd series 11 (1934): 65–89.

———. "Die Porträtzeichnungen des Hans Schwarz." *Münchner Jahrbuch der bildenden Kunst*, 2nd series 11 (1934–36): 93.

———. "Kunst und Künstler der Nürnberger Schaumünze des 16. Jahrhunderts." *Mitteilungen der Bayerischen Numismatischen Gesellschaft* 54 (1936): 1–61.

———. "Augsburger Medailleure und Bildnisse Augsburger Kunsthandwerker auf Schaumünzen des 16. Jahrhunderts." *Mitteilungen der Bayerischen Numismatischen Gesellschaft* 55 (1937): 41–98.

Bertolotti, A. "Testamento e Inventarii di Gaspare Mola." *Rivista Europea*, July 16, 1877.

———. *Artisti Bolognesi, Ferraresi ed Alcuni altri del già Stato Pontificio in Roma nei Secoli XV, XVI e XVII*. Rome, 1885. Reprint New York, 1972.

———. *Figiuli, Fonditori e Scultori in relazione con la Corte di Mantova nei secoli XV, XVI, XVII*. Milan, 1890.

Berwick y de Alba, Duque de. *Contribución al estudio de la persona del III Duque de Alba*. Madrid, 1919.

Berwick y de Alba, Duquessa de. *Documentos escogidos del Archivo de la Casa de Alba*. Madrid, 1891.

Bezold, Gustav von. "Die Medaillen Peter Flötners." In *Festschrift herausgegeben vom 'Verein für Münzkunde in Nürnberg' bei der Gedenkfeier seines 25-jährigen Bestehens*. Nuremberg, 1907, pp. 3–48.

———. "Der Meister des Stabius." *Mitteilungen aus dem Germanischen Nationalmuseum* (1910): 125–26.

———. "Der Nürnberger Wachsbossierer Georg Holdermann." *Mitteilungen aus dem Germanischen Nationalmuseum* (1913): 1, 12 13.

de Bie, J. *La France Métallique*. Paris, 1635.

———. *Les familles de la France illustrées par les monuments des médailles anciennes et modernes*. Paris, 1634.

Biedermann, Johann Gottfried. *Geschlechtsregister der Hochadelichen Patriziats zu Nürnberg*. Bayreuth, 1748.

Biographie nationale. Brussels.

Biographie Universelle Ancienne et Moderne. 2nd ed. Paris, n.d.

Bizot, [Abbé]. *Medalische Historie der Republyk van Holland*. Amsterdam, 1690.

Blair, Claude. *European Armour*. London, 1958.

Blanchet, A. "Catalogue du Cabinet de M. Bailly (1766)." *Revue Numismatique*, 4th series 23 (1920): XXXIV–XXXVI.

———. *Manuel de numismatique française. . . .* Vol. 3, *Médailles, jetons, Méreaux*. Paris, 1930.

Blunt, Anthony. *Art and Architecture in France 1500 to 1700*. London, 1953.

———, *François Mansart*. London, 1941.

Bober, Phyllis Pray, and Rubenstein, Ruth. *Renaissance Artists and Antique Sculpture*. Oxford and London, 1986 (New York, 1987).

Bocchi, F. *Il patrimonio beatiolesco alla meta del '400*. Bologna, 1970.

Boccolari, G. *Le Medaglie di casa d'Este*. Modena, 1987.

Bode, Wilhelm von. "Ein Altar in Kelheimer Stein vom Augsburger Meister Hans Daucher in den Königlichen Museen zu Berlin." *Jahrbuch der Kgl. preussischen Kunstsammlungen* 8 (1887): 3–10, 169–71.

———. *Geschichte der deutschen Plastik*. Berlin, 1888.

———. "Bertoldo di Giovanni und seine Bronzebildwerke." *Jahrbuch der Kgl. preussischen Kunstsammlungen* 161 (1895): 18–20.

———. "Zur neuesten Forschung auf dem Gebiete der italienischen Medaillenkunde." *Zeitschrift für bildende Kunst*, new series 15 (1904): 37–42.

———. "Caradossos Plaketten und Bramantes Anteil daran." *Zeitschrift für Numismatik* 33 (1922): 145–55.

———. *Bertoldo und Lorenzo dei Medici: Die Kunstpolitik des Lorenzo il Magnifico im Spiegel der Werke seines Lieblingskünstlers Bertoldo di Giovanni*. Freiburg im Breisgau, 1925.

———. *The Italian Bronze Statuettes of the Renaissance* [1907–12]. Revised by James David Draper. New York, 1980.

Bolgar, R. R. *The Classical Heritage*. New York, 1964.

Bolzenthal, Heinrich. *Skizzen zur Kunstgeschichte der modernen Medaillen-Arbeit*. Berlin, 1840.

Bonsanti, G. "Lelio Orsi per Novellara: linee di ricerca su affreschi e medaglie." In *Lelio Orsi e la cultura del suo tempo*. Atti del Convegno internazionale di studi, Reggio Emilia/Novellara, 1988. Reggio Emilia, 1990.

Bora, G. "Donato Bramante." In *Pinacoteca di Brera: scuole Lombarda e piemontese 1300–1535*. Edited by F. Zeri et al. Milan, 1988, pp. 118–25.

Born, R. *Les Croy*. Brussels, 1981.

Börner, Lore. "Der Elefant als Sinnbild auf Medaillen." *Forschungen und Berichte der Staatliche Museen zu Berlin* 17 (1976): 199–200.

———. *Deutsche Medaillen-kleinode des 16. und 17. Jahrhunderts*. Leipzig, 1981.

Börner, Lore, and Steguweit, Wolfgang. *Die Sprache der Medaille*. Berlin, 1990.

Boschloo, Anton. *Il fregio dipinto a Bologna da Niccolò dell'Abbate ai Carracci (1550–1580)*. Bologna, 1984.

Boselli, C. "Regesto artistico dei notai roganti in Brescia dall'anno 1500 all'anno 1560." In *Supplemento ai Commentari dell'Ateneo di Brescia per il 1976*. Brescia, 1977.

Bottari, G., and Ticozzi, S. *Raccolta di lettere sulla pittura, scultura ed architettura*. 8 vols. Milan, 1822–25.

Braham, A. "Mansart Studies I: The Val-de-Grâce." *The Burlington Magazine* 105 (1963): 351–63.

Brandi, Karl. *The Emperor Charles V: Growth and Destiny of a Man and of a World-Empire*. Translated by C. V. Wedgwood. London, 1939.

Braun, Edmund Wilhelm. "Ein Nürnberger Bronzebrunnen von 1532/33 im Schlosse zu Trient." *Münchner Jahrbuch der bildenden Kunst*, 3rd series 2 (1951): 195–203.

———. "Der Kleopatrabrunnen des Berliner Museums, seine Nürnberger Herkunft und sein Besteller." In *Festschrift für Erich Meyer zum 60. Geburtstag*. Hamburg, 1957, pp. 172–75.

Brenzoni, R. *Pisanello*. Florence, 1952.

Brington, S. *The Gonzaga, Lords of Mantua*. London, 1927.

British Museum Catalogue of Greek Coins. London, 1888.

Brockmann, Günther. *Die Medaillen der Welfen*. Vol. 1, *Linie Wolfenbüttel*. Cologne, 1985.

de Broglie, Raoul. "Les Clouet de Chantilly, catalogue illustré." *Gazette des Beaux-Arts* (May–June 1971): 258–336.

Brooke, G. C., and Hill, G. F. *A Guide to the exhibition of historical medals in the British Museum*. London, 1924.

Brown, C. M., and Lorenzoni, A. M. *Isabella d'Este and Lorenzo da Pavia: Documents for the history of Art and Culture in Renaissance Mantua*. Geneva, 1982.

Brulez, Wilfrid. *Marchands flamands à Venise 1568–1605*. Etudes d'histoire économique et sociale, vol. 6. Brussels and Rome, 1965.

Buchanan, I. "The Collection of Niclaes Jonghelinck, I. Bacchus and the Planets, by Jacques Jonghelinck." *The Burlington Magazine* 132 (1990): 102–13.

Büll, Reinhard. "Vom Wachs. Beiträge zur Kenntnis der Wachse." *Farbwerke Höchst A.G.* 1 (n.d.); 3 (1959); and 7, no. 2 (1963).

———. *Das grosse Buch vom Wachs*. Munich, 1977.

Burckhardt, Rudolf. "Über die Medaillensammlung des Ludovic Demoulin. . . . " *Anzeiger für Schweizerischer Altertumskunde*, new series 20 (1918): 45–49.

Burger, Helene. *Nürnberger Totengeläutbücher*. Vol. 3, *St. Sebald 1517–1572*. Neustadt/Aisch, 1972.

Busignani, Alberto. *Pollaiuolo*. Florence, 1970.

de Cadenas y Vicent, Vicente. *El Protectorado de Carlos V en Génova*. Madrid, 1977.

Cahn, Julius. *Frankfurter Medailleure im 16. Jahrhundert*. Frankfurt, 1903.

———. "Die Dreifaltigkeitsmedaille Hans Reinharts." *Blätter für Münzfreunde* 40 (1905), columns 3339–43.

———. "Die Medaillenporträts des Kardinals Albrecht von Mainz, Markgrafen von Brandenburg." In *Studien aus Kunst und Geschichte. Friedrich Schneider zum siebzigsten Geburtstag gewidmet*. Freiburg im Breisgau, 1906, pp. 159–67.

———. "Das Vorbild zu einer Medaille Hans Reinharts." In *Georg Habich zum 60. Geburtstag*. Munich, 1928, pp. 121–22.

[Cahn sale, 1926] Auction catalogue, Adolph E. Cahn, Frankfurt, October 26, 1926.

Callmann, Ellen. *Beyond Nobility: Art for the Private Citizen in the Early Renaissance*. Exhibition catalogue, Allentown Art Museum. Allentown, Pennsylvania, 1981.

Calmet, Dom A. *Histoire de Lorraine. . . .* 2nd ed. [1745]. Reprint Paris, 1973.

Calvi, F. "Il Gran Cancelliere Francesco Taverna e il suo process secondo nuovi documenti." *Archivo Storico di Lombardo* 9. Milan, 1882.

Camesasca, E. *Tutta l'opera del Cellini*. Milan, 1955.

Campbell, L. *Renaissance Portraits*. New Haven and London, 1990.

Campori, Giuseppe. *Gli Artisti italiani e stranieri negli stati estensi*. Modena, 1855.

———. "Documents Inédits sur les Relations du cardinal Hippolyte d'Este et de Benvenuto Cellini." *Gazette des Beaux-Arts* 17 (1864): 289–97.

Canby, S. R. "The Al-Sabah Collection. Islamic Art in the Kuwait National Museum." *Art International* 26 (November-December 1983): 5–13.

Candida Gonzaga, Conte Berardo. *Memorie delle famiglie Nobili delle Provincie Meridionali d'Italia*. Naples, 1875.

Carli, E. *Il Pinturicchio*. Milan, 1960.

Cartwright, Julia. *Isabella d'Este*. New York, 1926.

Casati, Carlo. *Leone Leoni d'Arezzo scultore e Giov. Paolo Lomazzo pittore milanese*. Milan, 1884.

Castelnuovo, E. *Imago lignea*. Trento, 1989.

Castel Sismondo e Sigismondo Pandolfo Malatesta. Edited by Carla Tomasini Pietramellara and Angelo Turchini. Rimini, 1985.

Castiglione, Baldassare. *The Book of the Courtier*. Edited and translated by Leonard E. Opdycke. New York, 1901.

Catalogo delle . . . Medaglie. Catalogue of the Museo Civico Correr. Venice, 1898.

Catalogue of a Collection of Italian Sculpture and Other Plastic Art of the Renaissance. Burlington Fine Arts Club. London, 1912.

Catalogue of the Vernon Hall Collection of European Medals. Elvehjem Museum of Art, University of Wisconsin. Madison, 1978.

Catalogue of the Winter Exhibition. Burlington Fine Arts Club. London, 1910.

Catalogus van het Historisch Museum der stad. Utrecht, 1928.

Cazaux, Y. *Marie de Bourgogne*. Paris, 1967.

Cellini, Benvenuto. *Vita di Benvenuto Cellini* and *Ricordi, Prose e Poesie di Benvenuto Cellini con Documenti, la Maggior Parte Inediti*. Edited by Francesco Tassi. 3 vols. Florence, 1828–29.

———. *La Vita di Benvenuto Cellini*. Edited by B. Bianchi. Florence, 1886.

———. *The Treatises of Benvenuto Cellini on Goldsmithing and Sculpture*. Translated by C. R. Ashbee. London, 1898. Reprint New York, 1967.

———. *La vita di Benvenuto Cellini sequita dai trattati dell'oreficeria e della scultura e dagli scritti sull'arte*. Edited by A. Jahn Rusconi and A. Valeri. Rome, 1901.

———. *The Life of Benvenuto Cellini Written by Himself*. Translated and edited by John Addington Symonds. London, 1949.

———. *Autobiography*. Translated by George Bull. Harmondsworth, 1956.

Cessi, Francesco. *Alessandro Vittoria medaglista*. Trent, 1960.

———. *Alessandro Vittoria bronzista*. Trent, 1961.

———. *Alessandro Vittoria architetto e stuccatore*. Trent, 1961.

———. *Alessandro Vittoria scultore*. 2 vols. Trent, 1961–62.

———. "Pezzi editi e inediti di Giovanni da Cavino al Museo Bottacin di Padova." *Padova*, new series 11 (1965) no. 1, pp. 13–18; no. 2, pp. 13–18; no. 3, pp. 26–32.

Cessi, Francesco, and Caon, Bruno. *Giovanni da Cavino, Medaglista Padovano del Cinquecento*. Padua, 1969.

Chabouillet, A. *Notice sur une médaille inédite de Ronsard par Jacques Primavera, suivie de recherches sur la vie et les œuvres de cet artiste*. Orleans, 1875.

Challis, C. *The Tudor Coinage*. Birkenhead, 1978.

Chantilly, Musée Condé, Peintures de l'Ecole italienne. Paris, 1988.

Chiarelli, R. *L'opera completa del Pisanello*. Milan, 1972.

Chowen, Richard H. "Paduan Forgeries of Roman Coins."

Renaissance Papers (University of South Carolina) 3 (1956): 50–65.

[Christie's sale, London, 1985] Sale catalogue, Christie's, London, July 3, 1985.

Cicogna, E. *Delle inscrizioni veneziane.* Venice, 1827–34.

Cicognara, L. *Storia della Scultura.* Prato, 1824.

Ciprut, Edouard-Jacques. *Mathieu Jacquet, sculpteur d'Henri IV.* Paris, 1967.

———. "Nouveaux Documents sur Germain Pilon." *Gazette des Beaux-Arts* 74 (May–June 1969): 257–76.

———. "Chronologie Nouvelle de la Vie et des Œuvres de Germain Pilon." *Gazette des Beaux-Arts* 74 (December 1969): 333–44.

Circa 1492. Art in the Age of Exploration. Exhibition catalogue, National Gallery of Art. Edited by Jay A. Levenson. Washington, New Haven, and London, 1991.

Cittadella, N. *Notizie relative a Ferrara.* Ferrara, 1864.

Clain-Stefanelli, Elvira Eliza. *Numismatics—An Ancient Science. A Survey of its History.* Contributions from The Museum of History and Technology, bulletin 229, paper 32. Washington, 1965.

Clausse, Gustave. *Les San Gallo, architectes, peintres, sculpteurs, médailleurs.* Vol. 3, *Florence et les derniers Sangallo.* Paris, 1902.

Clough, C. H. "Federico da Montefeltro's patronage of the arts." *Journal of the Warburg and Courtauld Institutes* 36 (1973).

Cloulas, I. *Jules II Le pape terrible.* Cher, 1990.

"Collezione di Vittorio Emanuele III, Zecca di Ferrara, Parte 1." *Bollettino di Numismatica* 3, no. 1. Rome, 1987.

Coniglio, Giuseppe. *Il Regno di Napoli al Tempo di Carlo V.* Naples, 1951.

———. *I Gonzaga.* Varese, 1967.

Cooper, Denis R. *The Art and Craft of Coinmaking.* London, 1988.

Cora, G. "'• Opus • Sperandei •'." *Faenza* 36 (1950): 108–10.

Corkran, S. "On two gold medals of Queen Elizabeth." *Numismatic Chronicle,* new series 7 (1867): 45–46.

Corpus Nummorum Italicorum. 20 vols. Rome, 1910–43.

Cosemans, A. "Antoon van Stralen, burgemeester van Antwerpen, commissaris der Staten-Generaal by den aanvang der regeering van Philip II, 1521–1568." *Verslagen en mededeelingen· van de Koninklijke Vlaamsche Academie voor taal- en Letterkunde* (1933): 599–663.

Cott, Perry. *National Gallery of Art, Washington, D. C. Renaissance Bronzes: Statuettes, Reliefs and Plaquettes, Medals, and Coins from the Kress Collection.* Washington, 1951.

Couderc, C. "Jean de Candida, historien." *Bibliothèque de l'Ecole des Chartes* 55 (1894): 564–67.

———. "Jean de Candida, historien," *Bibliothèque de l'Ecole des Chartes* 85 (1924): 323–41.

Courajod, Louis. *Alexandre Lenoir, Son Journal et le Musée des Monuments Français.* Paris, 1878–87.

Covi, Dario A. "Lettering in Fifteenth-Century Florentine Painting." *Art Bulletin* 45 (1963): 1–17.

Coyeque, Ernest. "Au domicile mortuaire de Pilon." *Bibliothèque d'Humanisme et Renaissance* 7 (1940): 56, 80–84.

Craig, J. *The Mint. A History of the London Mint from AD 287 to 1948.* Cambridge, 1953.

Crippa, Carlo. *Le monete di Milano durante la dominazione spagnola dal 1535 al 1706.* Milan, 1992.

Croce, Benedetto. *History of the Kingdom of Naples.* Edited by H. Stuart Hughes, translated by Frances Frenaye. Chicago and London, 1970.

di Crollalanza, G. B. *Dizionario Storico-Blasonico delle Famiglie Nobili e Notabili Italiane Estinte e Fiorenti.* Bologna, 1965.

Cucci, C. *Medaglie, placchette e monete del Risorgimento.* Bologna, 1968.

Cunnally, J. *The Role of Greek and Roman Coins in the Art of the Italian Renaissance.* Dissertation, University of Pennsylvania, 1984.

Cuppini, G. *I palazzi senatorii a Bologna: architettura come immagine del potere.* Bologna, 1974.

Cust, Lionel. *Notes on the Authentic Portraits of Mary Queen of Scots, Based on the Researches of the Late Sir George Scharf.* London, 1903.

Da Pisanello alla nascità dei Musei Capitolini. L'antico a Roma alla vigilia del Rinascimento. Exhibition catalogue. Rome, 1988.

Darr, Alan P., and Roisman, Rona. "Francesco da Sangallo: a rediscovered early Donatellesque 'Magdalen' and two Wills from 1574 and 1576." *The Burlington Magazine* 129 (1987): 790.

Davenport, M. *The Book of Costume.* New York, 1948.

Davies, Martin. *National Gallery Catalogues. The Earlier Italian Schools.* 2nd ed. London, 1971.

Davis, Charles. "Ammannati, Michelangelo, and the Tomb of Francesco del Nero." *The Burlington Magazine* 118 (1976): 472–84.

———. "Aspects of Imitation in Cavino's Medals." *Journal of the Warburg and Courtauld Institutes* 41 (1978): 331–34.

———. "Working for Vasari: Vincenzo Danti in Palazzo Vecchio." In *Giorgio Vasari: Tra Decorazione Ambientale e Storiografia Artistica, Convegno di Studi (Arezzo, 8–10 Ottobre 1981).* Florence, 1985.

Dean, T. *Land and Power in late medieval Ferrara. The rule of the Este, 1350–1450.* Cambridge, 1988.

De Beer, J. "Mereaux anversois." *Revue belge de Numismatique* 81 (1929): 53–173; 82 (1930): 5–236.

De Bosque, A. *Quentin Matsys.* Brussels, 1975.

Decker, Bernhard. *Dürers Verwandlung in der Skulptur zwischen Renaissance und Barock.* Exhibition catalogue, Liebieghaus Museum alter Plastik. Frankfurt am Main, 1981.

De Coo, Jozef. *Beeldhouwkunst, Plakketten, Antiek.* Catalogues of the Museum Mayer van den Bergh, vol 2. Antwerp, 1969.

Degenhart, B. *Antonio Pisanello.* Vienna, 1940.

———. *Pisanello.* Torino, 1945.

De Jonghe, J. *Madama. Margaretha van Oostenrijk, hertogin van Parma en Piacenza, 1522–1586. Regentessen der Nederlanden,* vol. 3. Amsterdam, 1965.

Dekker, A. M. M. *Janus Secundus (1511–1536).* Nieuwkoop, 1986.

De la Tour, H. *Jean de Candida: Médailleur, sculpteur, diplomate, historien.* Paris, 1895.

———. "Médailles Modernes. Récemment Acquises par le Cabinet de France (suite)." *Revue numismatique* (1897), pp. 84–87.

———. *Bibliothèque nationale, Catalogue de la collection Rouyer légué en 1897 au département des médailles et antiques.* Part 2, *Jetons et méreaux de la Renaissance et des temps modernes.* Paris, 1910.

Delisle, L. "Le Médailleur Jean de Candida." *Bibliothèque de l'Ecole des Chartes* 51 (1890): 310–12.

della Valle, Guglielmo. *Lettere Sanese.* Rome, 1786.

De Man, M. "Médaille uniface de Levinus Bloccenus à Burgh." *Revue belge de Numismatique* 51 (1895): 502–7.

———. "De latere bezitters van een gouden Zierikzeesche noodmunt, vermoedelijk in 1575 aan admiraal Hollaer geschonken." *Jaarboek voor Munt- en Penningkunde* 14 (1927): 133–36.

den Besten, A. *Wilhelmus van Nassouwe. Het gedicht en zijn dichter.* Leiden, 1983.

Dennistoun of Dennistoun, J. *Memoirs of the Dukes of Urbino.* Edited by E. Hutton. London and New York, 1909.

Deonna, W. "Le Groupe des trois Graces nues et sa descendance." *Revue Archéologique* 31 (1930): 274–332.

De triomf van het Maniërisme. Exhibition catalogue, Rijksmuseum. Amsterdam, 1955.

Dictionnaire de biographie française. Paris, 1939.

Die Renaissance im deutschen Südwesten. Exhibition catalogue, Badisches Landesmuseum, Karlsruhe. 2 vols. Karlsruhe, 1986.

Dimt, Heidelinde, and Dimt, Gunter. *Der Linzer Taler.* Linz, 1990.

Dion, Roger. *Les frontières de la France.* Paris, 1947.

Dizionario Biografico degli italiani. Rome.

Dolfi, P. S. *Cronologia delle famiglie nobili di Bologna.* Bologna, 1670.

Domanig, Karl. "Älteste Medailleure in Österreich" *Jahrbuch der Kunsthistorischen Sammlungen des allerhöchsten Kaiserhauses* 14 (1893): 31.

———. "Peter Flötner als Plastiker und Medailleur." *Jahrbuch der Kunsthistorischen Sammlungen des allerhöchsten Kaiserhauses* 16 (1895): 1–80.

———. *Porträtmedaillen des Erzhauses Österreich.* Vienna, 1896.

———. "Peter Flötner als Médailleur." *Numismatische Zeitschrift* 32 (1900): 257–66.

———. *Die deutsche Medaille in kunst- und kulturhistorischer Hinsicht. Nach den Beständen der Medaillensammlung des allerhöchsten Kaiserhauses.* Vienna, 1907.

———. "Die Hans Reinhart'sche Dreifaltigkeitsmedaille." *Mitteilungen der Österreichischen Gesellschaft für Münz- und Medaillenkunde in Wien* 24, new series 9 (1913): 69–73.

de Dompierre de Chaufepié, H. J. *Catalogus der Nederlandsche en op Nederland betrekking hebbende Gedenkpenningen.* 2 vols. The Hague, 1903–6.

[Donabauer sale, 1899] Auction of the Max Donabauer Collection, Adolph Hess, Frankfurt, May 22, 1889.

Donaldson, Gordon. *All the Queen's Men, Power and Politics in Mary Stewart's Scotland.* New York, 1983.

Donatello e i suoi: scultura fiorentina del primo Rinascimento. Exhibition catalogue, edited by Giorgio Bonsanti and Alan P. Darr. Florence and Milan, 1986 (Revision of *Italian Renaissance Sculpture in the Time of Donatello).*

Doty, Richard G. *Encyclopedic Dictionary of Numismatics.* London, 1982.

Draper, James David. *Bertoldo di Giovanni, Sculptor of the Medici Household.* Columbia, Missouri, 1992.

Dressel, Heinrich. *Die Römischen Medaillone des Münzkabinetts der Staatlichen Museen zu Berlin.* Dublin and Zurich, 1973.

Duchamp, Michel. "G. A. Santarelli, modeleur de cires: L'histoire de deux camées retrouvés." *The Medal* 12 (Spring 1988). 10–16.

Dufay, B., et al. "L'atelier parisien de Bernard Palissy." *Revue de l'Art* 78 (1987): 33–60.

Dumolin, Maurice. "La Construction du Val-de-Grâce." *Bulletin de la Société de l'histoire de Paris* (1930): 106–7.

du Molinet, Claude. *Le Cabinet de la Bibliothèque de Sainte Geneviève.* Paris, 1692.

Durand, A. *Médailles et jetons des numismates.* Geneva, 1865.

Dürer, Albrecht. *Dürers Schriftlicher Nachlass.* Edited by Hans Rupprich. Berlin, 1969.

Dworschak, Fritz. "Bemerkungen und Nachträge zum Meister des Heidegger und zum Monogrammisten S.B." *Archiv für Medaillen- und Plakettenkunde* 4 (1923–24): 63–79.

———. "Der Manierismus in der deutschen Medaille." *Archiv für Medaillen- und Plattenkunde* 5 (1925–26), p. 67.

———. "Die Renaissance Medaille in Österreich." *Jahrbuch der kunsthistorischen Sammlungen in Wien,* new series 1 (1926): 213–44.

———. "Wiener Porträtmedaillen des XVI. Jahrhunderts." *Mitteilungen des Vereins für Geschichte der Stadt Wien* 7 (1927): 91–104.

———. *Antonio Abondio, Medaglista e ceroplasta (1538–1591).* Trento, 1958.

Ebner, Julius. "Zum Werk des Hans Kels." *Mitteilungen der Bayerischen Numismatischen Gesellschaft* 26/27 (1908–9): 101–4.

———. "Peter Flötner oder Matthes Gebel?" *Frankfurter Münzzeitung* 9 (1909): 472–79.

Edgerton, Samuel Y., Jr. "Alberti's Perspective: A New Discovery and a New Evaluation." *Art Bulletin* 48 (1966): 367–78.

Edmond, M. *Hilliard and Oliver.* London, 1983.

Ehrend, Helfried. *Speyerer Münzgeschichte.* Speyer, 1976.

Eidlitz, R. J. *Medals of Architects.* New York, 1927.

Eisler, William Laurence. *The Impact of Charles V upon the Visual Arts.* Dissertation, University of Pennsylvania, 1983.

Elogi storici di Cristoforo Colombo e di Andrea D'Oria. Parma, 1781.

Enciclopedia Cattolica. Vatican City, 1948–54.

Enciclopedia italiana. Rome, 1930.

Enciclopedia Italiana di Scienze, Lettere ed Arti. Rome, 1929–39.

Enciclopedia Universale dell'Arte. Rome, 1963.

Encyclopedia of World Art. New York, 1959.

Encyclopedie van Zeeland. Middelburg, 1984.

Ephrussi, Charles. "Les médailleurs de la Renaissance." *L'Art* 34 (1883): 243–52.

Erasme et la Belgique. Exhibition catalogue, Bibliothèque Royale. Brussels, 1969.

Erasmus von Rotterdam. Exhibition catalogue, Historisches Museum. Basel, 1986.

Eredità del Magnifico. Exhibition catalogue, Museo Nazionale del Bargello. Florence, 1992.

Erlanger, Herbert J. "The Medallic Portrait of Albrecht Dürer." *Museum Notes* X (1965): 145–72.

Erman, Adolf. *Deutsche Medailleure des 16. und 17. Jahrhunderts.* Berlin, 1884.

———. "Deutsche Medailleure des sechzehnten und siebenzehnten Jahrhunderts." *Zeitschrift für Numismatik* 12 (1885): 14–102.

Erwerbungsberichte 1924–26. Staatliche Münzsammlung, Munich.

Eser, Thomas. "Augsburger Kalksteinreliefs des frühen 16. Jahrhunderts. Hans Daucher—ein Zeitgenosse Dürers." *Weltkunst* 61 (1991): 1770–73.

d'Espezél, P. "Sur un médaillon de Louise de Savoie, mère de François I." *Aréthuse* 2 (1925): 1–10.

———. "La médaille de Ronsard." *Aréthuse* 3 (January 1925): II–III.

l'Estoile, Pierre de. *Mémoires-journaux de Pierre de l'Estoile.* Paris, 1875.

———. *Journal.* Edited by L. R. Lefevre. Paris, 1948–60.

Ettlinger, Helen S. *The Image of a Renaissance Prince: Sigismondo Malatesta and the Arts of Power.* Dissertation, Berkeley, 1988. Ann Arbor, 1989.

Evelyn, John. *A Discourse of Medals.* London, 1697.

Ex Aere Solido. Bronzen von der Antike bis zur Gegenwart. Exhibition catalogue. Berlin, 1983.

Exhibition of Early German Art. Exhibition catalogue, Burlington Fine Arts Club. London, 1906.

Exposition-concours de Numismatique à l'Hôtel des Monnaies. Exhibition catalogue. Paris, 1949.

Exter, Friedrich. *Versuch einer Sammlung von Pfälzischen Münzen und Medaillen* [1759–75]. 2 vols. with supplement. Reprint Munich, 1988.

Eye, August von. *Leben und Werk Albrecht Dürers.* Nördlingen, 1860.

Eygun, François. *Sigillographie du Poitou jusqu'en 1515.* Poitiers, 1938.

Fabriczy, Cornelius von. "Toscanische und oberitalienische Künstler in Neapel." *Repertorium für Kunstwissenschaft* 20 (1897): 97.

———. "Adriano Fiorentino." *Jahrbuch der Kgl. preussischen Kunstsammlungen* 24 (1903): 71–98.

———. *Medaillen der italienischen Renaissance.* Leipzig, 1903.

———. *Italian Medals.* London, 1904.

———. "Summontes Brief an M. A. Michiel." *Repertorium für Kunstwissenschaft* 30 (1907): 149–59.

Falke, Otto von. "Peter Flötner und die süddeutsche Tischlerei." *Jahrbuch der Kgl. Preussischen Kunstsammlungen* 37 (1916): 121–45.

———. "Die Flötnerkassette im Züricher Kunsthaus." *Pantheon* 1 (1928): 206–9.

Farquhar, H. "Portraiture of our Tudor monarchs on their coins and medals." *British Numismatic Journal* 4 (1907): 79–143.

———. "Nicholas Hilliard, 'Embosser of Medals in Gold'." *Numismatic Chronicle,* 4th series 8 (1908): 324–56.

Fasanelli, James. "Some Notes on Pisanello and the Council of Florence." *Master Drawings* 3 (1965): 36–47.

[Fau sale, 1884] Auction catalogue, Hôtel Drouot, Paris, March 3, 1884.

Fava, A. S. *Monete e Medaglie.* Exhibition catalogue. Turin, 1963.

———. "Le monete della zecca di Carmagnola." In *Arte nell'Antico Marchesato di Saluzzo.* Edited by Noemi Gabrielli. Turin, 1974.

[Felix sale, 1886] *Die Kunstsammlung des Herrn Eugen Felix in Leipzig.* J. M. Heberle, Cologne, October 25, 1886.

[Felix sale, 1895] *Sammlung Eugen Felix, Kunstmedaillen hauptsächlich aus der Periode der deutschen Renaissance.* Adolf Hess Nachfolger, Frankfurt am Main, September 23, 1895.

Fernandez Alvarez, Manuel. *Charles V: Elected Emperor and Hereditary Ruler.* Translated by J. A. Lalaguna. London, 1975.

Ferrara, M. *Savonarola.* Florence, 1952.

Ferrara, O. *The Borgia Pope Alexander the Sixth.* New York, 1940.

Feuchtmayr, Karl. "Die Bildhauer der Fuggerkapelle bei St. Anna zu Augsburg." In *Die Fugger und die Kunst.* Vol. 1. Edited by Norbert Lieb. Augsburg, 1952, pp. 433–71.

Fiala, Eduard. *Münzen und Medaillen der Welfischen Lande.* Vol. 1. Vienna, 1904.

———. *Antonio Abondio.* Prague, 1909.

Ficker, J. "Die Bildnisse Luthers aus der Zeit seines Lebens." *Luther Jahrbuch* 17 (1934): pp. 103ff.

Filangieri, G. *Documenti per la storia, le arti e le industrie nelle provincie napoletane.* Naples, 1883–97.

Firenze e la Toscana dei Medici nell'Europa del Cinquecento. Exhibition catalogue, Palazzo Vecchio. Florence, 1980.

Firmicus [Maternus Julius Firmicus]. *Libri VIII Matheseos.* Edited by W. Kroll and F. Skutsch. Leipzig, 1897–1913.

Firmin-Didot, A. *Étude sur Jean Cousin, suivie de notices sur Jean Leclerc et Pierre Woeiriot* [1872]. Reprint Geneva, 1971.

Fischer, J. *Sculpture in Miniature: The Andrew S. Ciechanowiecki Collection of Gilt and Gold Medals and Plaquettes.* Exhibition catalogue, J. B. Speed Art Museum. Louisville, Kentucky, 1969.

Fitzwilliam Museum Annual Report. Cambridge, 1987.

Fleury, Marie-Antoinette. *Documents du Minutier Central concernant les peintres, les sculpteurs et les graveurs au XVIIe Siècle (1600–1650).* Paris, 1969.

Flohil, M. "Het penning- en muntportret van Willem van Oranje." *Jaarboek voor Munt- en Penningkunde* 40 (1953): 49–70.

———. "Eerste en tweede staat van Coenraad Bloc's portretpenning van Willem van Oranje." *Jaarboek voor Munt- en Penningkunde* 48 (1968): 65–70.

Fogolari, G. *Cividale del Friuli.* Bergamo, 1906.

Forrer, L. *Biographical Dictionary of Medallists.* 8 vols. London, 1904–30.

Fortnum, C. D. E. "On the original portrait of Michel Angelo by Leo Leoni, 'il cavaliere aretino'." *Archeological Journal* 32 (1875): pp. 1–15.

Fossi Todorow, M. *I Disegni del Pisanello e della sua Cerchia.* Florence, 1966.

de Foville, Jean. "Le médailleur 'à l'Amour Captif'." *Gazette des Beaux-Arts* 39 (1908): 385–93.

———. *Sperandio.* Paris, 1910.

———. "Francesco da Brescia." *Revue numismatique.* 4th series 6 (1912): 419–28.

———. "Les premières oeuvres de Jean Varin en France." *Revue de l'art* 34 (1913): 155–56.

———. "Notes sur le médailleur Sperandio de Mantova." *Revue Numismatique* 16 (1914): 432–33.

———. "La médaille française au temps de Henri IV et de Louis XIII." In *Histoire de l'art.* Edited by André Michel. Vol. 5, part 2. Paris, 1915.

Fox, Stephen Paul. "Medaglie Medicee di Domenico di Polo." *Bollettino di Numismatica* 19 (1988): 189–219.

Franceschini, G. *I Montefeltro.* Varese, 1970.

Frank zu Döfering, Karl Friedrich von. *Die Kressen, eine Familiengeschichte.* Schloss Senftenegg, 1936.

Fraser, Antonia. *Mary Queen of Scots.* New York, 1970.

Frati, L. *La vita privata di Bologna del secolo XIII al XVII.* Bologna, 1900.

Frese, Inge, and Datow, Joachim. *Martin Luther und seine Zeit auf Münzen und Medaillen.* Schwetzingen, 1983.

Friedenberg, Daniel M. *Jewish Medals.* New York, 1970.

———, ed. *Great Jewish Portraits in Metal.* New York, 1963.

Friedländer, Julius. *Die italienischen Schaumünzen des fünfzehnten Jahrhunderts 1430–1530* [1880]. Reprint Sala Bolognese, 1976.

———. "Die italienischen Schaumünzen des fünfzehnten Jahrhunderts. 8, Florenz, Fortsetzung." *Jahrbuch der Kgl. preussischen Kunstsammlungen* 3 (1881–82): 33–34.

———. *Die italienischen Schaumünzen des fünfzehnten Jahrhunderts 1430–1530.* Berlin, 1882.

Fries, Walter. *Hans Daucher.* Dissertation, Freiburg im Breisgau, 1919.

Fröhner, W. *Les Médaillons de l'Empire Romain.* Paris, 1878.

Frommel, Christoph L. *Der Römische Palastbau der Hochrenaissance.* 3 vols. Tübingen, 1973.

Gabel, Leona C., ed. *Memoirs of a Renaissance Pope, The Commentaries of Pius II.* Translated by Florence A. Gregg. New York, 1959.

Gabrielli, Noemi, ed. *Arte nell'Antico Marchesato di Saluzzo.* Turin, 1974.

Gachard, L. "Recherches historiques sur les princes de Chimay et les comtes de Beaumont, 1415–1843." In *Études et notices historiques concernant l'Histoire des Pays-Bas.* Brussels, 1890.

Gaehtgens, Th. W. *Zum frühen und reifen Werk des Germain Pilon.* Bonn, 1967.

Gaetani, Pietro Antonio. *Museum Mazzuchellianum seu numismata virorum doctrina praestantium.* 2 vols. Venice, 1761–63.

Gaettens, Richard. "Der Konterfetter Hans Schwarz auf dem Reichstag zu Worms 1521." *Der Wormsgau* 3 (1951–58): 8–17.

———. "Die Dürer-Medaillen," *Blätter für Münzfreunde und Münzforschung* 781–83 (1954–56): 557–64.

———. "Das Bildnis des Pfalzgrafen und Kurfürsten im Spiegel der Medaille und Grossplastik." In *Ottheinrich. Gedenkschrift zur vierhundertjährigen Wiederkehr seiner Kurfürstenzeit in der Pfalz (1556–1559).* Edited by Georg Poensgen. Heidelberg, 1956, pp. 62–85.

———. *Zur Ikonographie Albrecht Dürers.* Heidelberg, 1958.

[Gaettens sale, 1966] *Kunstmedaillen u. Plaketten 1400–1837.* Auction catalogue no. 21, Richard Gaettens, Jr., Lübeck, April 1, 1966.

Gans, E. *Goethe's Italian Medals.* San Diego, 1969.

Ganz, P. *Die Handzeichnungen Hans Holbeins d. J.* Berlin, 1937.

Garcia Carraffa, Alberto, and Garcia Carraffa, Arturo. *Enciclopedia Heraldica y Genealogica Hispano-Americana.* Madrid, 1920.

Gardner, Edmund G. *Dukes and Poets in Ferrara* [1904]. Reprint New York, 1968.

Gaye, Giovanni. *Carteggio inedito d'artisti dei secoli XIV, XV, XVI.* 3 vols. Florence, 1839–40.

Geisberg, M. *The German Single-Leaf Woodcut 1550–1650.* Revised and edited by W. L. Strauss II. New York, 1974.

Geissler, Heinrich. *Zeichnung in Deutschland.* Vol. 1, *Deutsche Zeichner 1540–1640.* Catalogue, Staatsgalerie Stuttgart. Stuttgart, 1980.

Génard, P. "Inventaire des biens saisis dans la maison du bourgmestre Antoine van Stralen, 1567." *Antwerpsch Archievenblad* 2 (1865): 266.

———. "Actes concernant le bourgmestre Antoine van Stralen." *Antwerpsch Archievenblad* 7 (1871): 1–321.

Gerlo, A. "Erasmus en Quentin Metsys." *Revue belge d'Archéologie et d'Histoire de l'Art* 14 (1944): 33–45.

———. *Erasme et ses portraitistes. Metsys, Dürer, Holbein.* Brussels, 1950.

Gersdorf, Ernst Gotthelf. "Zur Medaillenkunde. Der Meister H. R. 1535–1547." *Blätter für Münzfreunde* 8 (1872), columns 221–23.

Gessert, Oskar. "Augustin Adelmann und andere Heidelberger Meister." *Archiv für Medaillen- und Plakettenkunde* 3 (1921–22): 53–62.

———. "Johann Philipp von der Pütt." *Archiv für Medaillen- und Plakettenkunde* 4 (1923–24): 127–28.

Giehlow, Karl. "Beiträge zur Entstehungsgeschichte des Gebetbuches Kaiser Maximilians I." *Jahrbuch der kunsthistorischen Sammlungen des allerhöchsten Kaiserhauses* 20 (1988): 30–112.

Gierach, Erich. "Stefan Schlick." *Sudetendeutsche Lebensbilder* 1 (1926): 80–86.

Gilbert, Creighton. *Italian Art 1400–1500. Sources and Documents.* Englewood Cliffs, 1980.

Gill, Joseph. *The Council of Florence.* Cambridge University Press, 1959.

Gimeno, Javier. "Thèmes Américains de la médaille espagnole." *Médailles* (1987): 35–40.

Gimeno Rua, Ferando. "Los Artistas italianos y los comienzos de la medaglia en España." In *L'influenza della medaglia italiana nell'Europa dei sec. XV e XVI, Atti del IIº Convegno internazionale di Studio, Udine, 1973.* Udine, 1976.

Giovannoni, G., and Giovetti, P. *Medaglisti nell' eta di Mantegna e il trionfo de Cesare.* Mantua, 1992.

Gli Uffizi. Catalogo Generale. Florence, 1979.

Goffen, R. *Giovanni Bellini.* London, 1989.

Goldberg, B. *The Mirror and the Man.* Charlottesville, Virginia, 1985.

Goldschneider, L. *Unknown Renaissance Portraits.* New York, 1952.

Gomes Ferreira, Maria Teresa, and Pereira Coutinho, Maria Isabel. *Medalhas do Renascimento.* Catalogue of the Colecçao Calouste Gulbenkian. Lisbon, 1979.

Gonzalez-Palacios, Alvar. *Objects for a "Wunderkammer."* Exhibition catalogue, P. D. Colnaghi and Co., Ltd. London, 1981.

Gorini, Giovanni. "Appunti su Giovanni da Cavino." In *La medaglia d'arte: atti del primo convegno internazionale di studio, Udine 10–12 ottobre 1970.* Udine, 1973.

———. "New Studies on Giovanni da Cavino." In *Italian Medals.* Studies in the History of Art, vol. 21. Washington, 1987, pp. 45–54.

Gray, B. "Two Portraits of Mehmed II." *The Burlington Magazine* 61 (1932): 4–6.

Grayson, Cecil. "Alberti's Work in Painting and Sculpture: Appendix." In *Leon Battista Alberti: On Painting and On Sculpture.* London, 1972.

Greene, T. Whitcombe. "The Medallion of Philibert the Fair of Savoy and Margaret of Austria." *Numismatic Chronicle,* 3rd series 3 (1883): 288–96.

———. "Medals of the Hanna Family," *Numismatic Chronicle,* 3rd series 5 (1885): 148–52.

———. "Notes on Some Italian Medals." *Numismatic Chronicle,* 4th series 13 (1913): 413–21.

Grendler, Paul F. *Schooling in Renaissance Italy. Literacy and Learning 1300–1600.* Baltimore and London, 1989.

Grierson, E. *The Fatal Inheritance. Philip II and the Spanish Netherlands.* New York, 1969.

Grodecki, Catherine. "Les marchés de Germain Pilon pour la chapelle funéraire et les tombeaux des Birague en l'église Sainte-Catherine du Val des écoliers." *Revue de l'Art* 54 (1981): 61–78.

Groen van Prinsterer, G. *Archives ou Correspondance inédite de la maison d'Orange-Nassau.* First series, vol. 6 (1577–79). Leiden, 1839.

Grössing, Helmut. "Johannes Stabius. Ein Oberösterreicher im Kreis der Humanisten um Kaiser Maximilian I." *Mitteilungen des Oberösterreichischen Landesarchivs* 9 (1968): 239–64.

Grotemeyer, Paul. "Führer durch die Staatliche Münzsammlung in München, Teil 2." *Mitteilungen der Bayerischen Numismatischen Gesellschaft* 55 (1937): 1–40.

———. "Gussformen deutscher Medaillen des 16. Jahrhunderts." *Neue Beiträge zur süddeutschen Münzgeschichte* (1953): pp. 103–16.

———. "Da ich het die gestalt." *Deutsche Bildnismedaillen des 16. Jahrhunderts.* Munich, [1957].

———. "Eine Medaille des Andrea Doria von Christoph Weiditz." In *Centennial Publication of the American Numismatic Society.* New York, 1958, pp. 317–27.

———. "Die Statthaltermedaillen des Kurfürsten Friedrich des Weisen von Sachsen." *Münchner Jahrbuch der bildenden Kunst,* 3rd series 21 (1970): 143–66.

Grueber, H. A. "On a unique and unpublished medal of Anthony Browne, first Viscount Montagu." *Numismatic Chronicle,* 3rd series 6 (1886): 204–11.

———. *Catalogue of the Coins of the Roman Republic in the British Museum* [1910]. 3 vols. Reprint London, 1970.

Grüll, Georg. *Burgen und Schlösser im Salzkammergut und Alpenland.* Oberösterreichs Burgen und Schlösser, vol. 3. Vienna, 1963.

Grunebaum-Ballin, Paul. *Joseph Naci, duc de Naxos.* Etudes Juives, vol. 13. Paris, 1968.

Grunthal, H. "A Contemporary Gold Medal of Martin Luther." *American Numismatic Society Museum Notes* 6 (1954): 201–3.

Gruyer, Gustave. *L'Art Ferrarais à l'Epoque des Princes d'Este.* 2 vols. Paris, 1897.

Guenée, B., and Lehoux, F. *Les entrées royales françaises de 1328 à 1515.* Sources d'histoire médiévale, vol. 5. Paris, 1968.

Guerrino da Gubbio, Ser. *Cronaca.* Rerum italicarum scriptores, vol. 21, part 4. Edited by G. Mazzatinti. Bologna, 1902.

Guichenon, Samuel. *Histoire de Bresse et de Bugey.* Lyon, 1650.

Guido storico-artistica del duomo di Siena. Edited by E. M. Siena, 1908.

Guiffrey, J. J. "Guillaume Dupré, Sculpteur et Médalliste." *Nouvelles Archives de l'art français,* 1876, pp. 172–224.

———. *Inventaires de Jean, duc de Berry (1401–1416).* 2 vols. Paris, 1894–96.

Gundersheimer, Werner L. *Ferrara: The Style of a Renaissance Despotism.* Princeton, 1973.

Habich, Georg. "Hans Kels als Konterfetter." *Monatsberichte über Kunst und Kunstwissenschaft* 3, no. 1 (1903): 9–19.

———. "Beiträge zu Hans Daucher." *Monatsberichte über Kunst und Kunstwissenschaft* 3 (1903): 53–76.

———. "Studien zur deutschen Renaissancemedaille II: Hans Schwarz." *Jahrbuch der Kgl. Preussischen Kunstsammlungen* 27 (1906): 13–69.

———. "Studien zur deutschen Renaissancemedaille III: Friedrich Hagenauer." *Jahrbuch der Kgl. Preussischen Kunstsammlungen* 28 (1907): 181–98, 230–72.

———. "Hans Schwarz in Frankreich." *Mitteilungen der Bayerischen Numismatischen Gesellschaft* 29 (1911): 52–57.

———. "Studien zur deutschen Renaissancemedaille IV: Christoph Weiditz." *Jahrbuch der Kgl. Preussischen Kunstsammlungen* 34 (1913): 1–35.

———. "Über zwei Bildnisse Ottheinrichs von Hans Daucher." *Münchner Jahrbuch der bildenden Kunst,* 2nd series 9 (1914–15): 70f. and 212.

———. "Der Meister der Beltzinger (Martin Schaffner?)." *Jahrbuch der Kgl. Preussischen Kunstsammlungen* 36 (1915): 153–61.

———. *Die deutschen Medailleure des XVI. Jahrhunderts.* Halle, 1916.

———. "Dietrich Schro, der Monogrammist D S." *Archiv für Medaillen- und Plakettenkunde* 2 (1920–21): 29–33.

———. Review of Bange 1922. In *Archiv für Medaillen- und Plakettenkunde* 4 (1923–24): 178.

———. "Die Erasmus-Medaille." *Archiv für Medaillen- und Plakettenkunde* 6 (1923–24): 119–22.

———. *Die Medaillen der Italienischen Renaissance.* Stuttgart and Berlin, [1924].

———. "Peter Flötner oder Hieronymus Magdeburger." *Archiv für Medaillen- und Plakettenkunde* 5 (1925–26): 26–45.

———. "Jan de Vos oder Paulus von Vianen." *Das schwäbische Museum* (1927): 124–35.

———. *Der heimliche Flötner. Sendschreiben an Dr. J. L. Sponsel.* Munich, 1929.

———. *Die deutschen Schaumünzen des XVI. Jahrhunderts.* 5 vols. Munich, 1929–34.

Hall, James. *Dictionary of Subjects and Symbols in Art.* London, 1974. Revised ed. London, 1979.

Halm, Philipp Maria. "Studien zur Augsburger Bildnerei der Frührenaissance II: Hans Daucher." *Jahrbuch der Kgl. Preussischen Kunstsammlungen* 41 (1920): 283–343.

[Hamburger sale, 1924] *Kunstmedaillen.* Auction catalogue, Leo Hamburger, Frankfurt am Main, November 4, 1924.

Hampe, Theodor. *Matthes Gebel.* Nuremberg, 1902.

———. *Nürnberger Ratsverlässe.* Vienna and Leipzig, 1904.

———. "Allgäuer Studien zur Kunst und Kultur der Renaissance I. Der Kaufbeurer Patrizier Jörg Hörmann und seine Beziehungen zu Kunst und Künstlern." In *Festschrift Gustav von Bezold. Mitteilungen aus dem Germanischen Nationalmuseum Nürnberg.* Nuremberg, 1918–19, pp. 9–85.

———. "Allgäuer Studien zur Kunst und Kultur der Renaissance II. Zur Geneologie der Künstlerfamilie Kels." *Mitteilungen aus dem Germanischen Nationalmuseum Nürnberg,* 1918–19, pp. 42–49.

———, ed. *Das Trachtenbuch des Christoph Weiditz.* Berlin, 1927.

Haskell, Francis, and Penny, Nicholas. *Taste and the Antique.* New Haven and London, 1981.

Haupt, Albrecht. "Peter Flettners Herkommen und Jugendarbeit." *Jahrbuch der Kgl. Preussischen Kunstsammlungen* 26 (1905): 116–35, 148–68.

Hawkins, E. *Medallic Illustrations of the History of Great Britain and Ireland.* Edited by A. W. Franks and H. A. Grueber. London, 1885.

Head, Constance. *Imperial Twilight, The Paliologos Dynasty and the Decline of Byzantium.* Chicago, 1977.

Heiss, Aloiss. *Les Médailleurs de la Renaissance.* 9 vols. Paris, 1881–92.

———. "Jean de Candida, médailleur et diplomate sous Louis XI, Charles VIII et Louis XII." *Revue Numismatique,* 3rd series 8 (1890): 453–79.

Henkel, F. A., and Schöne, H. *Emblemata. Handbuch zur Sinnbildkunst des XVI. und XVII. Jahrhunderts.* Stuttgart, 1978.

Herald, Jacqueline. *Renaissance Dress in Italy 1400–1500.* London, 1981.

Hermania, F. *L'appartamento Borgia in Vaticano.* Rome, 1934.

Hermann, Hermann Julius. "Pier Jacopo Alari-Bonacolsi, genannt Antico." *Jahrbuch der Kunsthistorischen Sammlungen des Allerhöchsten Kaiserhauses* 28 (1910): 202–30.

Herrera, Adolfo. "Medallas del Principe don Felipe y de Juanelo Turriano." *Revista de Archivos, Bibliotecas y Museos* 9, no. 12 (1905): 266–70.

Herrgott, Marquard. *Nummotheca Principium Austriae.* 2 vols. Freiburg im Breisgau, 1752–53.

Hersey, G. L. *Alfonso II and the Artistic Renewal of Naples 1485–1495.* London and New York, 1969.

Heyken, Enno. *Chroniken der Bischöfe von Verden aus dem 16. Jahrhundert.* Veröffentlichungen des Instituts für historische Landesforschung der Universität Göttingen, vol. 20. Hildesheim, 1983.

Hill, George Francis. *Pisanello.* London, 1905.

———. "Notes on Italian Medals I: Some medals by Pastorino da Siena." *The Burlington Magazine* 9 (1906): 408–12.

———. "Notes on Italian Medals II: Some Italian medals in the British Museum." *The Burlington Magazine* 10 (1906–7): 384–87.

———. "Stephen H., Medallist and Painter." *The Burlington Magazine* 12 (1907–8): 355–63.

———. "The Medallist Lysippus." *The Burlington Magazine* 13 (1908): 274–86.

———. "Notes on Italian Medals VI: Three Wax Models." *The Burlington Magazine* 15 (1909): 31–35.

———. "Three pen-studies by Sperandio of Mantua." *The Burlington Magazine* 16 (1909–10): 24–25.

———. "Note on the mediaeval medals of Constantine and Heraclius," *Numismatic Chronicle,* 1910, pp. 110–16.

———. "Notes on Italian Medals X." *The Burlington Magazine* 18 (1911): 13–21.

———. *Portrait Medals of Italian Artists of the Renaissance.* London, 1912.

———. "Notes on Italian Medals XIII: Some Florentine Medals." *The Burlington Magazine* 22 (1912): 131–38.

———. "Notes on Italian medals XIV." *The Burlington Magazine* 23 (1913): 17–22.

———. "Notes on Italian Medals XVI: Two Wax Models for Medals." *The Burlington Magazine* 24 (1914): 211–17.

———. "Notes on Italian Medals XXI." *The Burlington Magazine* 29 (1916): 56–59.

———. "On the Technique of the Renaissance Medal." *The Burlington Magazine* 31 (November–December 1917): 178–83.

———. "Recent Acquisitions for public collections IV, Steven H. – The British Museum." *The Burlington Magazine* 185, vol. 33 (1918): 58.

———. *Medals of the Renaissance.* Oxford, 1920.

———. *The Medallic Portraits of Christ.* Oxford, 1920.

———. "Not in Armand." *Archiv für Medaillen- und Plakettenkunde* 2 (1920–21): 10–28, 45–53.

———. Review of Bernhart 1919. In *Numismatic Chronicle,* 5th series 1 (1921): 159–60.

———. *A Guide to the Department of Coins and Medals in the British Museum.* London, 1922.

———. *A Guide to the Exhibition of Medals of the Renaissance in the British Museum.* London, 1923.

———. "L'école des medailleurs de Mantoue à la fin du XVᵉ siècle." *Aréthuse* 1 (October 1923): 1–20.

———. "Die Erasmus-Medaille." *Archiv für Medaillen- und Plakettenkunde* VI (1923–24):119–22.

———. "Medals of Turkish Sultans." *Numismatic Chronicle* 6 (1926): 287–98.

———. "Gold Medal of Queen Mary Tudor." *British Museum Quarterly* 2 (1927): 37–38.

———. "Some Italian Medals of the Renaissance." In *Georg Habich zum 60. Geburtstag.* Munich, 1928, pp. 11–12.

———. "Andrea and Gianettino Doria." *Pantheon* 4 (1929): 500–501.

———. *A Corpus of the Italian Medals of the Renaissance before Cellini.* 2 vols. London, 1930.

———. "A Lost Medal by Pisanello." *Pantheon* 8 (1931): 487–88.

———. *The Gustave Dreyfus Collection of Renaissance Medals.* Oxford, 1931.

———. "Frate Antonio da Brescia." In *Miscellanea di Storia dell'Arte in onore di Igino Benvenuto Supino.* Florence, 1933.

Hill, G. F., and Brooke, G. C. *A Guide to the Exhibition of Historical Medals in the British Museum.* London, 1924.

Hill, G. F., and Pollard, Graham. *Renaissance Medals from the Samuel H. Kress Collection at the National Gallery of Art.* London and New York, 1967.

———. *Medals of the Renaissance.* London, 1978.

Hill, G. F., and Rosenheim, Max. "Notes on Some Italian Medals." *The Burlington Magazine* 12 (1907): 141–54.

Himmelmann, Nikolaus. "Ideale Nacktheit." *Zeitschrift für Kunstgeschichte* 48 (1985): 1–28.

Hind, Arthur M. *Engraving in England in the Sixteenth and Seventeenth Centuries.* Cambridge, 1955.

[Hirsch sale, 1969]. Catalogue No. 63, Gerhard Hirsch, Munich, July 1–4, 1969.

[His de la Salle sale, 1880] Auction catalogue, Sotheby's, London, November 22, 1880.

Hispania-Austria: i Re Cattolici Massimiliano I e gli inizi della casa d'Austria in Spagna. Exhibition catalogue. Museo de Santa Cruz, Toledo, and Castello di Ambras, Innsbruck. Innsbruck, 1992.

Hofman, H. A. *Constantijn Huygens (1596–1687).* Utrecht, 1983.

Hofmann, B. *Barbara von Hohenzollern, Markgräfin von Mantua.* Ansbach, 1881.

Hoheneck, Johann Georg Adam Baron, von. *Die löblichen Herren Herren Stände, von Herren- und Ritterstand, in dem Ertz-Herzogthum Oesterreich ob der Enns. . . .* Passau, 1747.

da Hollanda, F. *Da Pintura Antigua.* Porto, 1918.

Hollstein, F. W. H. *German Engravings, Etchings, and Woodcuts ca. 1400–1700.* 28 vols. Amsterdam, 1954–80. Reprint n.d.

Holzmair, Eduard. *Katalog der Sammlung Dr. Josef Brettauer. Medicina in nummis.* Vienna, 1937.

Hommel, L. *Marie de Bourgogne ou le Grand Heritage.* Brussels, 1951.

Hook, Judith. *Lorenzo de' Medici.* London, 1984.

Horne, Herbert P. *Botticelli, Painter of Florence.* Princeton, 1980.

Hume, M. *Two English queens and Philip.* London, 1908.

[Humphris sale, 1990] Sale catalogue, Cyril Humphris Gallery, London, July 1990.

Ilg, Albert. "Das Spielbrett von Hans Kels." *Jahrbuch der Kunsthistorischen Sammlungen des Allerhöchsten Kaiserhauses* 3 (1885): 53–78.

———. "Die Werke Leone Leoni's in den Kaiserlichen Kunstsammlungen." *Jahrbuch der Kunsthistorischen Sammlungen des Allerhöchsten Kaiserhauses* 5 (1887): 65–88.

Imhof, Christoph Andreas. *Sammlung eines Nürnbergischen Münz-Cabinets. . . .* Nuremberg, 1780–82.

Inventaire des médailles des rois de France, pour le Cabinet du roi [c. 1685] Unpublished, MS 59, Paris, Bibliothèque Nationale, Cabinet des Médailles.

Italian Renaissance Sculpture in the Time of Donatello.

Exhibition catalogue. Detroit Institute of Arts. Detroit, 1985.

Jacobs, Emil. "Die Mehemmed-Medaille von Bertoldo." *Jahrbuch der Kgl. Preussischen Sammlungen* 48 (1927): 1–17.

Jacobus de Voragine. *The Golden Legend of Jacobus de Voragine.* Edited and translated by Granger Ryan and Helmut Ripperger. New York, 1941.

Jacquart, Jean. "Le Marquis d'Effiat." *XVII Siécle*, 1959, pp. 298–313.

Jacquiot, F. J. *La Médaille au temps de Louis XIV.* Paris, 1970.

———. "Virgile dans les devises de médailles et de jetons de la Renaissance au XVIIIᵉ siècle." *Revue belge de Numismatique* 135 (1989): 97–109.

Janson, Horst W. "The Putto with the Death's Head." *Art Bulletin* 19 (1937): 423–49.

———. *The Sculpture of Donatello.* 2 vols. Princeton, 1957.

Jestaz, Bertrand. "De nouveaux bronzes italiens." *Revue du Louvre* 24, no. 2 (1974): 91–100.

Johnson, Cesare. "Cosimo I de' Medici e la sua 'Storia Metallica' nelle medaglie di Pietro Paolo Galeotti." *La Medaglia* 12 (1976): 14–46.

———. *Collezione Johnson.* 3 vols. Milan, 1990.

Johnson, Cesare, and Martini, Rodolfo. *Catalogo delle Medaglie I, Secolo XV.* Civiche raccolte numismatiche, comune di Milano. Milan, 1986.

———. *Catalogo delle Medaglie, II, Secolo XVI, Cavino.* Milan, 1989.

Johnson, Velia. "La nascità della medaglia italiana." *La Medaglia* 5 (1974): 7–25.

———. "La medaglia italiana in Europa durante i secoli XV e XVI." *La Medaglia* 8 (1975): 7–22.

———. "La medaglia barocca in Toscana." *La Medaglia* 10 (1975): 11–74.

Jones, J. R. "Cavino's Imitations of Roman Coins." *Spink Numismatic Circular* 73, no. 11 (November 1965): 232–33.

Jones, Mark. *Medals of the French Revolution.* London, 1977.

———. "The First Cast Medals and the Limbourgs. The Iconography and Attribution of the Constantine and Heraclius Medals." *Art History* 2 (1979): 35–44.

———. *The Art of the Medal.* London, 1979.

———. *Medals of the Sun King.* London, 1979.

———. *A Catalogue of the French Medals in the British Museum.* 2 vols. London, 1982–88.

———. "Guillaume Dupré." *The Medal* 9 (special issue 1986): 23–47.

———. "Medal-Making in France 1400–1650: The Italian Dimension." In *Italian Medals.* Studies in the History of Art, vol. 21. Washington, 1987.

Jones, Philip J. *The Malatesta of Rimini and the Papal State.* London, 1974.

Joost-Gaugier, Christiane L. "The casa degli specchi at Padua, its architect Annibale da Bassano, Tito Livio, and a peculiar historical connection." *Bollettino del Museo Civico di Padova* 72 (1983): 113–24.

José, Marie. *La Maison de Savoie, Les Origines.* Preface by Benedetto Croce. Paris, 1952.

Josephi, Walter. *Die Werke plastischer Kunst.* Kataloge des Germanischen Nationalmuseums. Nuremberg, 1910.

Jourda, Pierre. *Marguerite d'Angoulême, Duchesse d'Alençon, Reine de Navarre (1492–1549): Etude biographique et littéraire.* 2 vols. Bibliothèque littéraire de la Renaissance, new series 19. Paris, 1930.

Juncker, C. *Das goldene und silberne Ehrengedächtnis D. Martini Lutheri.* Frankfurt am Main, 1706.

Junius, Wilhelm. "Meister des thüringisch-sächsischen Cranach-Kreises." *Zeitschrift des Vereins für Thüringische Geschichte und Altertumskunde*, new series 31 (1935): 64–112.

Jürgensmeier, Friedhelm, ed. *Erzbischof Albrecht von Brandenburg (1490–1545). Ein Kirchen- und Reichsfürst der frühen Neuzeit.* Beiträge zur Mainzer Kirchengeschichte, vol. 3. Frankfurt, 1991.

Karabacek, J. von. *Abendländische Künstler zu Konstantinopel im XV. und XVI. Jahrh. I, Italienische Künstler am Hofe Muhammeds II. des Eroberers 1451–1481.* Vienna, 1918.

Katz, Victor. *Die erzgebirgische Prägemedaille des 16. Jahrhunderts.* Prague, 1932.

Kauffmann, Georg, ed. *Die Kunst des 16. Jahrhunderts.* Exhibition catalogue. Berlin, 1970.

Keary, C. F. *A Guide to the Italian Medals Exhibited in the King's Library.* London, 1881 (2nd ed. 1893).

Kemmerich, Max. *Die deutschen Kaiser und Könige im Bild.* Leipzig, 1910.

Kenner, Friedrich. "Bildnismedaillen der Spätrenaissance: Pastorino." *Jahrbuch der Kunsthistorischen Sammlungen des Allerhöchsten Kaiserhauses* 12 (1891): 84–164.

———. "Leone Leoni's Medaillen für den Kaiserlichen Hof." *Jahrbuch der Kunsthistorischen Sammlungen des Allerhöchsten Kaiserhauses* 13 (1892): 55–93.

———. "Die Bildnissammlung des Erzherzogs Ferdinands von Tirol." *Jahrbuch des K. K. Kaiserhauses Wien* 19 (1898).

King, C. W. *Antique Gems and Rings.* 2 vols. London, 1872.

King, Margaret L. "Book-lined Cells: Women and Humanism in the Early Italian Renaissance." In *Renaissance Humanism: Foundations, Forms, and Legacy.* Vol. 1, *Humanism in Italy.* Edited by Albert Rabil, Jr. Philadelphia, 1988, pp. 434–53.

[King sale, 1992] *The Elizabeth Washburn King Collection of Antique Greek Coins.* Christie's, New York, December 11, 1992.

Kirchner, W. *Alba.* Translated by W. Jappe Alberts. The Hague, 1968.

Klawans, Zander H. *Imitations and Inventions of Roman Coins.* Santa Monica, 1977.

Klinger, Linda, and Raby, Julian. "Barbarossa and Sinan: A portrait of two Ottoman corsairs from the collection of Paolo Giovio." In *Venezia e l'Oriente Vicino. Arte Veneziana e Arte Islamica.* Atti del primo simposio internazionale sull'arte veneziana e l'arte Islamica. Venice, 1987, pp. 47–59.

Kloos, Rudolf M. *Die Inschriften der Stadt und des Landkreises München.* Die deutschen Inschriften 5. Stuttgart, 1958.

Knecht, R. J. *Francis I.* Cambridge, 1982.

[Knoedler sale, 1968] *The French Bronzes 1500–1800.* Sale catalogue, M. Knoedler & Co., New York, 1968.

Knyphausen, K., Graf zu Inn. *Münz- und Medaillen-Kabinett.* Hannover, 1872–77.

Kobler, Friedrich. "Augsburg, Strassburg, Täuferbewegung: über den Goldschmied Laux Kreler." *Jahrbuch des Zentralinstituts für Kunstgeschichte* 1 (1985): 409–12.

Kohl, Benjamin G. "Humanism and Education." In *Renaissance Humanism: Foundations, Forms, and Legacy. Vol. 3, Humanism and the Disciplines.* Edited by Albert Rabil, Jr. Philadelphia, 1988.

Köhler, Johann David. *Historische Münzbelustigung. . . .* 22 parts. Nuremberg, 1729–50.

Kohlhaussen, Heinrich. *Nürnberger Goldschmiedekunst des Mittelalters und der Dürerzeit 1240 bis 1540.* Berlin, 1968.

Konigson, E. "La cité et le prince: premières entrées de Charles VIII (1484–1486)." In *Quinzième colloque international d'études humanistes. Tours, 10–22 juillet 1972. Les Fêtes de la Renaissance.* Paris, 1975.

Kowalski, Heinrich. *Die Augustalen Kaiser Friedrichs II. von Hohenstaufen.* Offprint from the *Schweizerische Numismatische Rundschau* 55 (1976).

Kratzsch, Klaus. *Bergstädte des Erzgebirges. Städtebau und Kunst zur Zeit der Reformation.* Munich, 1972.

Krautheimer, Richard. *Lorenzo Ghiberti.* 2 vols. 2nd ed. Princeton, 1970.

Kress, Johann Wilhelm. *Geschlechterbuch, begonnen 1640. Die Kressen samt derselben verschwägerte adelige Stammlinien Beschreibung.* Manuscript in the archives of the Germanisches Nationalmuseum, Nuremberg. Kress Archive, signature FA Kress no. 140.

Kress von Kressenstein, Baron Hans Karl. *Die Kressen, eine Familiengeschichte.* 2 vols. Aalen, 1985.

Kris, Ernst. *Meister und Meisterwerke der Steinscheidekunst.* Vienna, 1929.

———. "Zum Werk Peter Flötners und zur Geschichte der Nürnberger Goldschmiedekunst I, Ein Kokosnussbecher." *Pantheon* 8 (1931): 496–99.

Kubler, George. "A Medal by G. P. Poggini depicting Peru

and predicting Australia." *Mitteilungen des Kunsthistorischen Institutes in Florenz* 5 (1964): 149–52.

Kuhn, Charles Louis. "An Unknown Relief by Peter Flötner." *The Art Quarterly* 17 (1954): 109–15.

Kuhn, Hermann. "Hans Reinhart, ein Meister der mitteldeutschen Renaissance-Medaille." *Blätter für Münzfreunde* 76 (1941): 169–84.

Kunst der Reformationszeit. Exhibition catalogue. Berlin, 1983.

Kunsthandwerk der Dürerzeit. Exhibition catalogue. Berlin, 1971.

Kunst voor de beeldenstorm. Noordnederlandse kunst 1525–1580. Exhibition catalogue, Rijksmuseum. Amsterdam, 1986.

La Bretagne au temps des Ducs. Exhibition catalogue, Abbaye de Doulas and Musée Dobrée. Nantes, 1991–92.

Labus, Giovanni. *Museo della Reale Accademia di Mantova.* Mantua, 1837.

La Collection Frédéric Spitzer. Paris, 1890.

Lafaurie, Jean, and Prieur, Pierre. *Les monnaies des rois de France.* 2 vols. Paris, 1951–56.

Land im Mittelpunkt der Mächte. Die Herzogtümer Jülich-Kleve-Berg. Exhibition catalogue, Städtisches Museum Hans Koekkoek Kleve and Stadtmuseum Düsseldorf. Düsseldorf, 1984–85.

Lang, Andrew. *Portraits and Jewels of Mary Stuart.* Glasgow, 1906.

Lang, Karl Heinrich von, ed. *Regesta sive Rerum Boicarum autographa.* Vol. 3. Munich, 1825.

Lange, Konrad. *Peter Flötner als Bahnbrecher der deutschen Renaissance.* Berlin, 1897.

Langedijk, Karla. *The Portraits of the Medici. 15th to 18th Century.* 3 vols. Florence, 1981–87.

[Lanna sale, 1911] *Die Sammlung des Freiherrn Adalbert von Lanna.* Edited by H. Carl Krüger. Rudolph Lepke, Berlin, March 21–28, 1911.

[Lanz sale, 1985] *Auktion 33. Mittelalter und Neuzeit.* Dr. Hubert Lanz, Munich, April 30, 1985.

Lanzoni, G. *Sulle nozze di Federigo I Gonzaga con Margherita di Wittelsbach (1463).* Milan, 1898.

de Laprade, Jacques. "Note sur quelques portraits d'Henri IV gravés d'après François II Bunel." *La Revue des Arts* 3 (1953): 89–92.

Lavin, Irving. "On the Sources and Meaning of the Renaissance Portrait Bust." *Art Quarterly* 33, no. 3 (1970): 207–26.

Lavin, Marilyn Aronsberg. "Notes on the Iconography of Piero della Francesca's Fresco of Sigismondo Pandolfo Malatesta before St. Sigismond." *Art Bulletin* 56 (September 1974): 345–74.

Lawe, Kari. "La medaglia dell'Amorino bendato." In *The Court of Ferrara and its Patronage, 1441–1598.* Edited by Marianne Pade, Lene Waage Petersen, and Daniela Quarta. Copenhagen and Modena, 1990, p. 233–45.

Lawrence, Richard Hoe. *Medals by Giovanni Cavino, the "Paduan."* New York, 1883.

Lecoq, A.-M. *François Ier imaginaire. Symbolique et politique à l'aube de la Renaissance française.* Paris, 1987.

Lefevre, R. *"Madama" Margarita d'Austria (1522–1586).* Rome, 1986.

Leithe-Jasper, Manfred. *Renaissance Master Bronzes from the Collection of the Kunsthistorisches Museum, Vienna.* Exhibition catalogue, National Gallery of Art. Washington, 1986.

Leitschuh, Franz Friedrich. *Flötner-Studien.* Strassburg, 1904.

———. "Der Augsburger Medailleur Hans Schwarz in seinen Beziehungen zu Johannes Secundus." In *Studien und Quellen zur deutschen Kunstgeschichte des XV.-XVI. Jahrhunderts.* Freiburg (Switzerland), 1912.

Lelio Orsi. Exhibition catalogue, Teatro Valli. Edited by Giuliano Briganti and Jadranka Bentini. Reggio Emilia, 1987.

Lemaire, C. *Paris Ancien et Nouveau.* Paris, 1685.

Lembright, Robert L. *Louise of Savoy and Marguerite d'Angoulême: Renaissance Patronage and Religious Reform.* Dissertation, Ohio State University, 1974.

Le Muse e il Principe. Arte di Corte nel Rinascimento padano. Exhibition catalogue, Museo Poldi Pezzoli, Milan. 2 vols. Modena and Milan, 1991.

Lenger, Eike Eberhard. *Die Fugger in Hall i. T.* Tübingen, 1967.

Lepage, H. *Notes et documents sur les graveurs de monnaies et médailles et la fabrication des monnaies des ducs de Lorraine depuis la fin du XVe siècle.* Nancy, 1875.

Les Clouet et la cour des Rois de France. Exhibition catalogue, Bibliothèque Nationale. Paris, 1970.

Levin, William R. *Images of Love and Death in Late Medieval and Renaissance Art.* Exhibition catalogue, University of Michigan Museum of Art. Ann Arbor, 1975.

Levy Pisetzky, Rosita. *Storia del Costume in Italia.* 5 vols. Milan, 1964–69.

Lewis, Douglas. "Sculpture." In *National Gallery of Art, Washington.* Edited by John Walker. New York, 1975.

———. "The Washington Relief of *Peace* and its Pendant." In *Collaboration in Italian Renaissance Art.* New Haven and London, 1978, pp. 233–44.

———. "The Medallic Œuvre of 'Moderno'." In *Italian Medals.* Studies in the History of Art, vol. 21. Edited by J. Graham Pollard. Washington, 1987, pp. 77–97.

———. "The Plaquettes of 'Moderno' and His Followers." In *Italian Plaquettes.* Studies in the History of Art, vol. 22. Edited by Alison Luchs. Washington, 1989, pp. 105–41.

Lexikon für Theologie und Kirche. Edited by K. Hofmann. 2nd ed. Freiburg im Breisgau, n.d.

Lieb, Norbert. "Ottobeurer Bildhauer- und Kunstschreinerarbeiten des 16. Jahrhunderts. Beiträge zu Hans Kels d. J. und Thomas Heidelberger." *Münchner Jahrbuch der bildenden Kunst* 12 (1937–38): 50–64.

———. *Die Fugger und die Kunst im Zeitalter der Spätgotik und frühen Renaissance.* Vol. 1. Munich 1952.

———. *Die Fugger und die Kunst im Zeitalter der Hohen Renaissance.* Munich, 1958.

Lietzmann, Hilda. "Unbekannte Nachrichten zur Biographie von Antonio Abondio und Carlo Pallago." *Jahrbuch des Zentralinstituts für Kunstgeschichte* 5/6 (1989–90): 327–49.

Lingua, Paolo. *Andrea Doria.* Istituto Geografico de Agostini, 1984.

Lipschultz, Sandra LaWall. *Selected Works: The Minneapolis Institute of Arts.* Minneapolis, 1988.

Litta, Count Pompeo, et al. *Famiglie Celebri Italiane.* Milan, 1819–83.

Lloyd, C. "Reconsidering Sperandio." In *Italian Medals.* Studies in the History of Art, vol. 21. Edited by J. G. Pollard. Washington, 1987, pp. 99–113.

[Löbbecke sale, 1908] *Kunstmedaillen und Plaketten des XV. bis XVII. Jahrhunderts.* Auction catalogue of the Arthur Löbbecke Collection, Braunschweig. Jacob Hirsch, Munich, November 26, 1908.

[Löbbecke sale, 1929] *Médailles et Plaquettes Artistiques.* Sale catalogue of the Arthur Löbbecke Collection. J. Schulman, Amsterdam, June 17, 1929.

Löcher, Kurt. "Bildnismalerei des späten Mittelalters und der Renaissance in Deutschland." In *Altdeutsche Bilder der Sammlung Georg Schäfer Schweinfurt.* Exhibition catalogue. Schweinfurt, 1985, pp. 40–41.

Lochner, Johann Hieronymus. *Sammlung Merkwürdiger Medaillen.* 8 vols. Nuremberg, 1737–44.

Lomazzo, Giovanni Paolo. *Trattato dell'arte della pittura, scultura ed architettura.* Rome, 1844.

de Longpérier, Adrien. "Médaillon médit de Grazia Nasi." *Revue Numismatique,* new series 3 (1858): 89–104.

di Lorenzi, Giovanna. *Medaglie di Pisanello e della sua cercia.* Exhibition catalogue, Bargello. Florence, 1983.

Lorenzo de' Medici. *Lettere.* Edited by Nicolai Rubenstein. Florence, 1977.

Lo specchio e il doppio: dallo stagno di Narciso allo schermo televiso. Exhibition catalogue. Edited by G. Macchi and M. Vitale. Genoa, 1987.

Loubet, C. *Savonarole prophète assassiné?* Paris, 1967.

Louise de Savoie. "Journal." In *Nouvelle collection des memoires pour servir à l'histoire de France,* first series 5. Lyon and Paris, 1851, pp. 83–93.

Luckius, Johann Jakob. *Sylloge numismatum elegantiorum. . . .* Strassburg, 1620.

Lugli, A. "Le 'Symbolicae Quaestiones' di Achille Bocchi e la cultura dell'emblema in Emilia." In *Le Arti a Bologna e in Emilia dal XVI al XVII secolo.* Atti del XXIV Congresso internazionale di storia dell'Arte, Bologna 1979. Bologna, 1982.

Lühmann-Schmid, Irnfriede. "Peter Schro. Ein Mainzer Bildhauer und Backoffenschüler. 2." *Mainzer Zeitschrift* 71/72 (1976–77): 65–68.

Lustenberger, S. *Martin Schaffner. Maler zu Ulm.* Exhibition catalogue. Ulm, 1959.

Luzzati, Ivo. *Andrea Doria.* Milan, 1943.

Lynch, Michael, ed. *Mary Stewart: Queen in Three Kingdoms.* Oxford, 1988.

McCrory, M. "Domenico Compagni: Roman Medalist and Antiquities Dealer of the Cinquecento." In *Italian Medals.* Studies in the History of Art, vol. 21. Washington, 1987.

McFarlane, K. M. *Hans Memling.* Oxford, 1971.

Mackowsky, H. "Sperandio Mantovano." *Jahrbuch der Kgl. Preussischen Kunstsammlungen* 19 (1898): 178.

Madai, D. S. *Vollständiges Thaler-Cabinet . . . Erster Theil.* Königsberg, 1765.

Madden, F. "Portrait Painters of Queen Elizabeth." *Notes and Queries* 4 (1852): 238.

Maffei, Scipione. *Verona Illustrata.* 4 vols. Verona, 1731–32.

Magagnato, T., ed. *Da Altichiero a Pisanello.* Exhibition catalogue. Verona, 1958.

Magnaguti, Alessandro. "L'Eveneto del seicento." *Rivista Italiana di Numismatica,* 2nd series 31, no. 1 (1918): 101–6.

———. *Le medaglie mantovane.* Mantua, 1921.

———. *Ex nummis historia.* Vol. 9, *Le medaglie dei Gonzaga.* Rome, 1965.

Mai, G. *Medaillen und Plaketten.* Bildhefte des Kunstmuseums Düsseldorf, vol. 7. Düsseldorf, 1970.

Maijer, B. *Parma e Bruxelles. Committenza e collezionismo farnesiani alle due Corte.* Parma, 1988.

Majkowski, E. "Steven van Herwijck's serie der Jagellonenmedaillons en zijn vermeend verblijf in Polen, 1561–1562." *Jaarboek voor Munt- en Penningkunde* 24 (1937): 1–37.

Malagola, C. *Di Sperindio e delle cartiere, dei carrozzieri, armaioli, librai fabbricatori e pittori di vetri in Faenza sotto Carlo e Galeotto Manfredi.* Modena, 1888.

Malaguzzi Valeri, F. "La Chiesa 'della Santa' a Bologna." *Archivio Storico dell'Arte* 2 (1896): 84–86.

———. "L'oreficeria reggiana, 2." *Rassegna d'Arte* 10 (1910): 186.

Male, Emile. *Religious Art in France. The Thirteenth Century: A Study of Medieval Iconography and Its Sources.* Edited by Harry Bober. Princeton, 1984

Mallett, Michael. *Mercenaries and Their Masters: Warfare in Renaissance Italy.* Totowa, New Jersey, 1974.

Maltby, W. S. *Alba. A Biography of Fernando Alvarez de Toledo, Third Duke of Alba, 1507–1582.* Berkeley and London, 1983.

Malvezzi, N. *Giacomo Grati diplomatico bolognese del secolo XV.* Modena, 1879.

Mann, J. G. *Wallace Collection Catalogues. Sculpture: Marbles, Terra-Cottas and Bronzes. . . .* London, 1931.

Manteuffel, K. Zoege von. *Die Gemälde und Zeichnungen des Antonio Pisano aus Verona.* Halle, 1909.

Marchal, E. *La sculpture et les chefs-d'oeuvre de l'orfèvrerie belges.* Brussels, 1895.

Maresti, A. *Teatro Geneologico et istorico dell'antiche et illustri famiglie di Ferrara.* Ferrara, 1681.

Markova, Vittoria. "Un 'Baccanale' ritrovato di Giorgio Vasari. . . . " In *Kunst des Cinquecento in der Toskana.* Edited by Monika Cämmerer. Florence, 1992.

Marot, P. "L'édition des *Icones XXXV ad Sacrae historiae fidem compositae* de Pierre Woeiriot." *Gutenberg Jahrbuch* (1952): 136–45.

Marrow, D. *The Art Patronage of Maria de Medici.* Ann Arbor, 1982.

Martin, C., and Parker, G. *The Spanish Armada.* London, 1988.

Martin, F. R. "New Originals and Oriental Copies of Gentile Bellini found in the East." *The Burlington Magazine* 27 (1910): 5–6.

Martin Luther und die Reformation in Deutschland. Exhibition catalogue, Germanisches Nationalmuseum, Nuremberg. Frankfurt am Main, 1983.

Martinori, Edoardo. *Catalogo delle Monete di Zecche Italiane.* Perugia, 1913. Reprint Bologna, 1969.

———. *Annali della zecca di roma; Alessandro VI, Pio III, Giulio II*. Rome, 1918.

Maskell, A. *Wood Sculpture*. London, 1911.

Mattingly, H., et al. *A Catalogue of the Coins of the Roman Empire in the British Museum*. London, 1923–62.

Maué, Hermann. "Nürnberger Medaillen 1500–1700." In *Wenzel Jamnitzer und die Nürnberger Goldschmiedekunst 1500–1700*. Exhibition catalogue, Germanisches Nationalmuseum, Nuremberg. Munich, 1985, 151–59.

———. "Die Dedikationsmedaille der Stadt Nürnberg für Kaiser Karl V. von 1521." *Anzeiger des Germanischen Nationalmuseums* (1987): pp. 227–44.

———. "Hans Schwarz in Nürnberg 1519–1520." *The Medal* 13 (Autumn 1988): 12–17.

———. "Nürnberger Medaillenkunst zur Zeit Albrecht Dürers." In *Trésors Monétaires*. Supplement 2, *Medailles & Antiques*. Vol. 1. Bibliothèque Nationale, Paris, 1989, pp. 23–29.

———. Review of Trusted 1990. *The Medal* 18 (Spring 1991), p. 108.

———. "Die Medaille des Matthes Gebel auf den Tod des Georg Ploed aus dem Jahre 1532. Antikenrezeption oder Übernahme eines Motivs der italienischen Renaissance?" In *ΜΟΥΣΙΚΟΣ ΑΝΗΡ. Festschrift für Max Wegner zum 90. Geburtstag*. Antiquitas series 3, vol. 32. Bonn, 1992 (in press).

Maulde la Clavière, R. *Louise de Savoie et François Ier: Trente Ans de Jeunesse (1485–1515)*. Paris, 1895.

Maumené, C. "Le visage royale d'Henri IV, des médailles de Guillaume Dupré aux peintures de Rubens." *Demareteion* (1935): pp. 28–39.

Maumené, C., and d'Harcourt, L. *Iconographie des Rois de France*. Archives de l'art français, Nouvelle période, vol. 15, no. 1. Paris, 1929.

Mauritshuis, The Royal Cabinet of Paintings. Catalogue. The Hague, 1977.

Maximilian I. Exhibition catalogue. Innsbrucker Zeughaus. Innsbruck, 1969.

Maximilian I. 1459–1519. Exhibition catalogue. Nationalbibliothek, Vienna. Vienna, 1959.

Maxwell-Scott, Mary M. *Tragedy of Fotheringhay: Founded on the Journal of D. Bourgoing, Physician to Mary Queen of Scots, and on Unpublished Manuscript Documents*. London, 1912.

Mayer, Anton. *Die Domkirche zu Unser Lieben Frau in München*. Munich, 1868.

Mayer, Dorothy Moulton. *The Great Regent: Louise of Savoy, 1476–1531*. London, 1966.

Mazerolle, F. *Les médailleurs français du XVe siècle au mileau du XVIIe*. 3 vols. Paris, 1902–4.

———. "Coins de médailles de Conrad Bloc." *Revue belge de Numismatique* 79 (1927): 95–98.

———. *Jean Warin*. Paris, 1932.

Medaglie del Rinascimento. Catalogue of the Museo Civico. Bologna, 1960.

Médailles des anciens Pays-Bas. Contribution numismatique à l'histoire du protestantisme. Exhibition catalogue, Hôtel des Monnaies. Paris, 1956.

Medaljen genom tiderna. Exhibition catalogue. Stockholm, 1942.

Meijer, B. W. "The re-emergence of a sculptor: eight lifesize bronzes by Jacques Jonghelinck." *Oud-Holland* 93 (1979): 116–35.

Meiss, Millard. "Contributions to Two Elusive Masters." *The Burlington Magazine* 103 (1961): 65–66.

Mende, Matthias. *Dürer-Medaillen. Münzen, Medaillen, Plaketten von Dürer, auf Dürer, nach Dürer*. Nuremberg, 1983.

Menestrier, C. F. *Histoire du roy Louis le Grand*. Paris, 1691.

Mengden, Veronika von. *Das Ambraser Spielbrett von 1537. Hauptwerk des Hans Kels d. J.* Dissertation, Munich, 1972. Munich 1973.

Menz, H. *The Dresden Gallery*. London, 1962.

Merzbacher, Eugen. "Beiträge zur Kritik der deutschen Kunstmedaillen. I. Peter Flötner." *Mitteilungen der Bayerischen Numismatischen Gesellschaft* 18 (1899): 29–41.

[Merzbacher sale, 1900] *Kunst-Medaillen—Katalog hauptsächlich aus den Sammlungen zweier süddeutscher Kunstfreunde*. Auction catalogue, Eugen Merzbacher, Munich, May 1–2, 1900.

Metman, Yves. "Sceau de Charles le Téméraire duc de Bourgogne, 1433–1467–1477." *Le Club Français de la Médaille, Bulletin* 55/56 (1977): 172–75.

[Metzler sale, 1898] *Medaillen und Plaketten der Kunstsammlung W. P. Metzler in Frankfurt am Main*. Frankfurt, 1898.

Meyer zur Capellen, J. *Gentile Bellini*. Stuttgart, 1985.

Michaelson, H. "Cranachs des Älteren Beziehungen zur Plastik." *Jahrbuch der Kgl. Preussischen Kunstsammlungen* 21 (1900): pp. 271ff.

Michel, André. Review of Müntz 1887. *Gazette des Beaux-Arts* 38 (1888): 510–13.

Middeldorf, Ulrich. "Portraits by Francesco da Sangallo." *The Art Quarterly* 1 (1938): 109–38.

———. "On the Dilettante Sculptor." *Apollo* 107 (April 1978): 310–22. Reprinted in Ulrich Middeldorf. *Raccolta di Scritti, that is Collected Writings*. Florence, 1979–81, vol. 3, pp. 173–202.

———. "Medals in clay and other odd materials." *Faenza* 65 (1979): 270.

Middeldorf, Ulrich, and Goetz, Oswald. *Medals and Plaquettes from the Sigmund Morgenroth Collection*. Chicago, 1944.

Middeldorf, Ulrich, and Kriegbaum, Friedrich. "Forgotten Sculpture by Domenico Poggini." *The Burlington Magazine* 53 (July-December 1928): 9–17.

Middeldorf, Ulrich, and Stiebral, Dagmar. *Renaissance Medals and Plaquettes*. Florence, 1983.

Migeon, Gaston. "La collection de M. Gustave Dreyfus. IV. Les médailles." *Les Arts* 7 (August 1908): 1–32.

———. *Musée National du Louvre. Catalogue des Bronzes & Cuivres*. Paris, 1904.

Mitchell, Charles. "Il Tempio Malatestiano." In *Studi Malatestiani*. Istituto Storico Italiano per il Medio Evo. Studi Storici. Edited by P. J. Jones. Rome, 1978, fasc. 110–11.

Modern, Heinrich. "Paulus von Vianen." *Jahrbuch der kunsthistorischen Sammlungen des allerhöchsten Kaiserhauses* 15 (1894): 60–102.

Molinier, Émile. *Les bronzes de la Renaissance. Les plaquettes. Catalogue raisonné*. 2 vols. Paris, 1886.

de Montigny, C. "Des Faussaires. Jean Cavino et Alex. Bassiano, Padouans." In *Le Cabinet de l'Amateur et de l'Antiquité*. 2 vols. Paris, 1842–46.

[Morbio sale, 1882] *Catalog einer Sammlung italienischer Münzen aller Zeiten aus dem Nachlasse des Cavaliere Carlo Morbio in Mailand*. F. J. Wesener, Munich, October 16. 1882.

Moreau-Nélaton, Etienne. *Les Clouet, peintres officiels des Rois de France*. Paris, 1908.

———. *Les Clouets et leurs émulés*. 3 vols. Paris, 1924.

Morscheck, Charles R. Jr. *Relief Sculpture for the Façade of the Certosa da Pavia, 1473–1499*. London and New York, 1978.

Motta, E "Giacomo Jonghelinck e Leone Leoni in Milano (nuovi documenti)." *Rivista italiana di numismatica* 21 (1908): 75–76.

de la Moureyre-Gavoty, F. *Musée Jacquemart-André: sculpture italienne*. Paris, 1975.

Mousnier, Roland. *L'assassinat d'Henri IV, 14 mai 1610*. Paris, 1964.

Müller, Hannelore. "Die Künstlerfamilie Daucher." In *Lebensbilder aus dem Bayerischen Schwaben*. Vol. 6. Edited by Götz Baron von Pölnitz. Munich, 1958, pp. 131–65.

Muller, S. "De medailleur Ste. H. te Utrecht." *Tijdschrift voor Munt- en Penningkunde* 19 (1911): 175–80.

———. "De medailleur Steven van Herwijck te Utrecht." *Oud Holland* 40 (1922): 24–31.

———. "De penningen der Utrechtsche bisschoppen." *Oud Holland* 40 (1922): 86–91.

Müller, Theodor. "Hans Schwarz als Bildhauer." *Phoebus* 3 (1950–51): 25–30.

———. *Die Bildwerke in Holz, Ton und Stein von der Mitte des XV. bis gegen Mitte des XVI. Jahrhunderts*. Kataloge des Bayerischen Nationalmuseums München, vol. 13, part 2. Munich, 1959.

de Munter, M. V. "Jacques Zagar et ses médailles au buste de Frédéric Perrenot." *Revue belge de Numismatique* 70 (1914): 173–80.

Müntz, Eugene. "L'Atelier monetaire de Rome." *Revue Numismatique*, 3rd series 2 (1884): 220–332.

———. *Histoire de l'art pendant la Renaissance*. Paris, 1887.

Muratore, Dino. "Les origines de l'Ordre du collier de Savoie dit l'Annonciade." *Schweizer Archiv für Heraldik*, 1909–10.

Muratore, L. A., ed. *Cronaca Gestorum ac factorum memorabilium civitatis edita a Frate Hyeronimo de Bursellis*. Rerum italicarum scriptores 23, no. 2. Bologna (?), n.d.

Murray, P. "Bramante Paleocristiano." In *Studi Bramanteschi, Atti del Congresso internazionale: Milano-Urbino-Roma, 1970*. Rome, 1974, pp. 27–34.

Nahuys, M. "Letter de M. le comte M. Nahuys à M. R. Chalon, président de la Société royale de numismatique." *Revue belge de Numismatique*, 4th series 5 (1867): 506–10.

Natur und Antike in der Renaissance. Exhibition catalogue, Liebieghaus Museum, Frankfurt am Main. Frankfurt, 1985–86.

Négotiations Diplomatiques et Politiques du Président Jeannin, Ambassadeur et Ministre de France. 2nd ed. Paris, 1819.

[Neuburg sale, 1938] *Catalogue d'un cabinet renommée de médailles artistiques des XVe et XVIe siècles* [Neuburg Collection]. Auction catalogue, J. Schulman, Amsterdam, December 19, 1938.

Neudörfer, J. *Nachrichten von Künstlern und Werkleuten daselbst* [in Nuremberg] *aus dem Jahre 1547*. Edited by G. W. K. Lochner. Vienna, 1875.

Neue deutsche Biographie. Berlin.

Neues Allgemeines Künstler-Lexikon. Linz, 1909.

Neugebauer, S. *Selectorum Symbolum Heroicorum*. Frankfurt am Main, 1619.

New Catholic Encyclopedia. Washington, 1967.

Newton, S. *The Dress of the Venetians 1495–1525*. Aldershot, 1988.

Nickel, Helmut. "Two Falcon Devices of the Strozzi: an Attempt at Interpretation." *Metropolitan Museum Journal* 9 (1974): 229–32.

Nicolini, F. *L'Arte Napoletana del Rinascimento*. Naples, 1925.

Nohejlová, Emanuela. "Ceské medaile Severina Brachmanna." *Sborník Náradního Musea v Praze* 1 (1938–39): 61–119.

Norris, Andrea S., and Weber, Ingrid. *Medals and Plaquettes from the Molinari Collection at Bowdoin College*. Brunswick, Maine, 1976.

Nürnberg 1300–1550. Kunst der Gotik und Renaissance. Exhibition catalogue, Germanisches Nationalmuseum, Nuremberg, and The Metropolitan Museum of Art, New York. Munich, 1986.

[Oppenheimer sale, 1936] *Catalogue of the Important Collection of Medals . . . Henry Oppenheimer*. Christie's, London, July 27, 1936.

Ortmann, Wolf Dieter. *Historisches Ortsnamenbuch von Bayern. Landkreis Scheinfeld*. Munich, 1967.

Ossorio, A. *Ferdinandi Toletani Albae Ducis vita et res gestae*. 2 vols. Salamanca, 1669.

Ostermann, V. "Le medaglie friulane del secolo XV e XVI." *Rivista italiana di Numismatica* 1 (1888): 195–210.

Ovid [Publius Ovidius Naso]. *Metamorphoses*. Translated by Rolphe Humphries. Bloomington, Indiana, 1955.

———. *Metamorphoses*. Translated by Mary M. Innes. Penguin Books, London, 1975.

Paccagnini, G. *Pisanello alla corte dei Gonzaga*. Exhibition catalogue. Venice and Milan, 1972.

———. *Pisanello*. London, 1973.

Palacky, Franz. *Geschichte von Böhmen*. 5 vols. Prague, 1865.

Paltroni, P. *Commentari della vita et gesti dell'illustrissimo Federico Duca d'Urbino*. Edited by W. Tommasoli. Urbino, 1966.

Panofsky, Erwin. *Studies in Iconology*. New York and Evanston, 1962.

Panvini Rosati, Franco. *Medaglie e placchette italiane dal Rinascimento al XVIII secolo*. Exhibition catalogue. Rome, 1968.

Paolucci, Antonio. *I Gonzaga e L'Antico Percorso di Palazzo Ducale a Mantova*. Rome, 1988.

Papaleoni, G. *Le chiese di Condino.* Rovereto, 1913.

Pardi, G., ed. *Diario Ferrarese dall'anno 1409 sino al 1502 di autori incerti.* Rerum italicarum scriptores, vol. 26, no. 7. Bologna (?), n.d.

Parker, G. *The Dutch Revolt.* London and New York, 1977.

Pasini, Pier Giorgio. *I Malatesta e l'arte.* Bologna, 1983.

————. "Matteo de' Pasti, Problems of Style and Chronology." In *Italian Medals.* Studies in the History of Art, vol. 21. Edited by J. Graham Pollard. Washington, 1987.

————. *Cortesia e Geometria. Arte malatestiana fra Pisanello e Piero della Francesca.* Exhibition catalogue, Museo della città. Rimini, 1992.

Passamani, B. "Schede di scultura trentina dei secoli XV e XVI." *Studi trentini di scienze storiche* 46 (1967): 127.

Pastor, L. von. *Storia dei Papi.* Revised edition, Rome, 1959.

Pastoureau, Michel. "La naissance de la médaille: le problème emblématique." *Revue numismatique,* 6th series 24 (1982): 205–21.

————. "Une image nouvelle: La médaille du XVe siècle." *The Medal* 9 (1986): 5–8.

————. *Couleurs, images, symboles: Etudes d'histoire et d'anthropologie.* Paris, 1990.

Paulys Realencyclopädie der classischen Altertumswissenschaft. Stuttgart, 1901.

Pearce, Mary. "Costumi tedeschi e borgognoni in Italia nel 1452." *Commentari* 8 (1957): 244–47.

Pechstein, Klaus. *Goldschmiedewerke der Renaissance.* Kataloge des Kunstgewerbemuseums Berlin 5. Berlin, 1971.

————. "Peter Flötner (um 1495–1546)." In *Fränkische Lebensbilder.* Series VII A, vol. 11. Neustadt/Aisch, 1984, pp. 91–100.

Pény, F. *Jean Varin de Liège.* Liège, 1947.

Peroni, A. "L'Architettura e la scultura nei secoli XV e XVI." In *Storia di Brescia,* vol. 2. Brescia, 1963.

Perrault, C. *Les hommes illustres.* Paris, 1700.

"Per Sperandio da Mantova." *Rivista italiana di Numismatica* 24 (1911): 143–44.

Peter Flötner und die Renaissance in Deutschland. Exhibition catalogue. Nuremberg, 1946–47.

Petz, Hans. "Urkunden und Regesten aus dem königlichen Kreisarchiv zu Nürnberg." *Jahrbuch der kunsthistorischen Sammlungen des allerhöchsten Kaiserhauses* 10 (1889): 44–45.

[Peus sale, 1975] *Katalog 286. Schaumünzen der Renaissance.* Dr. Busso Peus Nachfolger, Frankfurt am Main, March 17, 1975.

[Peus sale, 1989] *Katalog 326.* Dr. Busso Peus Nachfolger, Frankfurt am Main, November 1–3, 1989.

Pfeiffer, Wolfgang. "Eine Bronzestatuette von Peter Flötner." *Zeitschrift für Kunstwissenschaft* 10 (1956): 53–56.

Philippe, A. "Un portrait sculpté du duc Antoine à l'église de Charmes-sur-Moselle." *Bulletin mensuel de la Société d'archéologie lorraine et du Musée historique lorrain.* March-April, 1928.

Pialorsi, Vincenzo. "Le Medaglie dei musei civici di Brescia." *La Medaglia* 17 (1982): 6–30.

————. "Medaglie relative a personaggi, avvenimenti e istituzioni di Brescia provincia (parte I, sec. XV–XVI)." *Medaglia* 17, no. 24 (1989): 7–34.

————. "Le medaglie per Altobello Averoldo." In *Il polittico Averoldi di Tiziano restaurato.* Exhibition catalogue, Monastero di Santa Giulia. Edited by E. Lucchesi Ragni and G. Agosti. Brescia, 1991.

del Piazzo, Marcello. *Protocolli del carteggio di Lorenzo il Magnifico per gli anni 1473–1474, 1477–1492.* Florence, 1956.

Pick, Behrend. "Die Medaillen." In *Meisterwerke der Kunst aus Sachsen und Thüringen.* Edited by Oscar Doering and Georg Voss. Magdeburg, n.d. [1905].

————. In *Festschrift Karl Koetschau.* 1928.

Picqué, C. "Médaillons et médailles des anciennes provinces belges." In *L'art ancien à l'exposition nationale belge.* Brussels and Paris, 1882, pp. 107–8.

————. "Iconographie de la Furie Espagnole." *Revue belge de Numismatique* 35 (1879): 292–93, 302–3.

Pietrangeli, Carlo. "Il Palazzo Astalli." *Capitolium* 43 (1968): 6-13.

Pinard. *Chronologie Historique-Militaire.* Paris, 1760–78.

Pinchart, Alexandre. "Jacques Jonghelinck." *Revue belge de*

Numismatique 2, no. 4 (1854): 209–39. Reprinted in *Recherches sur la vie et les travaux des graveurs de médailles, de sceaux et de monnaies des Pays-Bas.* Vol. 1. Brussels, 1858, pp. 312–42.

————. *Histoire de la gravure des médailles en Belgique depuis le XVIe siècle jusqu'en 1794.* Mémoires de l'Académie royale de Belgique. Classe des Beaux-Arts 34. Brussels, 1868.

————. *Histoire de la gravure des medailles en Belgique depuis le XVe siecle jusqu'en 1794.* Brussels, 1870.

————. "Médailles relatives à l'histoire des Pays-Bas." *Revue belge de Numismatique,* 5th series 3 (1871): 75.

Pini, Carlo, ed. *La Scrittura di Artisti Italiani.* Florence, 1869.

Piromalli, A. *La cultura a Ferrara al tempo di Ludovico Ariosto.* Rome, 1975.

Planiscig, Leo. *Andrea Riccio.* Vienna, 1927.

————. "Bronzi minori di Leone Leoni." *Dedalo* 7 (1927): 544–67.

————. "Maffeo Olivieri." *Dedalo* 12 (1932): 34–55.

Pliny [Gaius Plinius Secundus]. *The Natural History of Pliny.* Translated and edited by J. Bostock and H. T. Riley. London, 1857.

————. *Natural History.* Translated by H. Rackham. Loeb Classical Library, vol. 3. London, 1940.

Plon, Eugène. *Benvenuto Cellini, orfevre, médailleur, sculpteur.* Paris, 1883.

————. *Benvenuto Cellini: Nouvel appendice aux recherches sur son œuvre.* Paris, 1884.

————. *Les Maîtres Italiens au service de la Maison d'Autriche, Leone Leoni et Pompeo Leoni.* Paris, 1887.

Poilleux, Antony. *Le Duché de Valois pendant les quinzième et seizième siècles.* Paris, 1842.

Poliziano, Angelo. *Della congiura dei Pazzi (coniurationis commentarium).* Edited by Alessandro Perosa. Padua, 1958.

Pollard, J. Graham. "The medal of Jan van Gorp by Steven van Herwijck." In *Mints, Dies and Currency.* Essays dedicated to the memory of Albert Baldwin. Edited by R. A. C. Carson. London, 1971, pp. 325–29.

————. *Medaglie italiani del Rinascimento nel Museo Nazionale del Bargello.* 3 vols. Florence, 1984–85.

————. "England and the Italian medal." In *England and the Continental Renaissance. Essays in honour of J. B. Trapp.* Edited by Edward Chaney and Peter Mack. Woodbridge, 1990.

Pontieri, E. *Per la storia del regno di Ferrante I d'Aragona re di Napoli: Studi e ricerche.* 2nd ed. Naples, 1969.

Pope-Hennessy, John. *The Portrait in the Renaissance.* London and New York, 1963.

————. "The Italian Plaquette." *Proceedings of the British Academy* 50 (1964):63–85.

————. *Renaissance Bronzes from the Samuel H. Kress Collection. Reliefs. Plaquettes. Statuettes. Utensils and Mortars.* London, 1965.

————. *The Portrait in the Renaissance.* Washington, 1966.

————. *Italian Renaissance Sculpture.* 3rd ed. New York, 1985.

————. *Italian High Renaissance and Baroque Sculpture.* New York, 1985.

————. Review of the 1984 reprint of Hill 1930 edited by Pollard. *The Medal* 7 (winter 1985): 55.

————. *Cellini.* London and Basingstoke, 1985.

Pope-Hennessy, John, and Hodgkinson, T. *The Frick Collection. IV, German, Netherlandish, French and British Sculpture.* New York, 1970.

Porcher, J. "Jean de Candida et le Cardinal de Saint-Denis." *Mélanges d'Archéologie et d'Histoire* 39 (1921–22): 319–26.

Prag um 1600. Kunst und Kultur am Hofe Kaiser Rudolfs II. Exhibition catalogue. 2 vols. Vienna, 1988.

Probszt, Günter. *Ludwig Neufahrer, ein Linzer Medailleur des 16. Jahrhunderts.* Vienna, 1960.

Proske, Beatrice Gilman. "Leone Leoni's medallic types." *Notes Hispanic* 3 (1943): 48–57.

Puaux, A. *Madama, fille de Charles Quint.* Paris, 1987.

Pyke, Edward J. *A Biographical Dictionary of Wax Modellers.* Oxford, 1973. Supplements London, 1981, 1983, and 1986.

Raby, Julian. *El Gran Turco. Mehmed the Conqueror as a*

Patron of the Arts of Christendom. Unpublished dissertation. Oxford, 1980.

————. "Pride and Prejudice: Mehmed the Conqueror and the Italian Portrait Medal." In *Italian Medals.* Studies in the History of Art, vol. 21. Edited by J. Graham Pollard. Washington, 1987, pp. 171–94.

————. "Picturing the Levant." In *Circa 1492. Art in the Age of Exploration.* Exhibition catalogue, National Gallery of Art. Edited by Jay A. Levenson. Washington, New Haven, and London, 1991.

Rachfahl, F. *Margaretha von Parma, Statthalterin der Niederlande (1559–1567).* Munich and Leipzig, 1898.

Rady, Martyn. *The Emperor Charles V.* London and New York, 1988.

Rapp, J. "Das Tizian-Porträt in Kopenhagen: ein Bildnis des Giovanni Bellini." *Zeitschrift für Kunstgeschichte* 50 (1987): 365–68.

Rasmussen, Jörg. *Deutsche Kleinplastik der Renaissance und des Barock.* Bildhefte des Museums für Kunst und Gewerbe Hamburg, vol. 12. Hamburg, 1975.

————. "Untersuchungen zum Halleschen Heiltum des Kardinals Albrecht von Brandenburg. I." *Münchner Jahrbuch der bildenden Kunst,* 3rd series 27 (1976): 96–98.

————. "Kleinplastik unter Dürers Namen: Das New Yorker Rückenakt-Relief." *Städel-Jahrbuch,* new series 9 (1983): 131–44.

Rastrelli. *Notizie storiche italiana della famiglia Avalos.* Rome, 1896.

Raulich, I. *Storia di Carlo Emanuele I, duca di Savoia.* 2 vols. Milan, 1896–1902.

Rausch, K. *Der Burgundische Heirat Maximilians I.* Vienna, 1880.

Ravegnani Morosini, Mario. *Signorie e Principati: monete italiane con ritratto, 1450–1796.* N.p. [San Marino], 1984.

Reallexikon zur Deutschen Kunstgeschichte. Munich, 1973.

Reber, Horst. *Albrecht von Brandenburg. Kurfürst. Erzkanzler. Kardinal 1490–1545.* Exhibition catalogue, Landesmuseum Mainz. Mainz, 1990.

Recent Acquisitions and Promised Gifts, Sculpture, Drawings, Prints. Exhibition catalogue, National Gallery of Art. Washington, 1974.

Receuil des médailles. Manuscripts of the Royal Collection, Cabinet des Médailles. Paris, c. 1685.

Redona, P. Gebni. *Maffeo Olivieri e il crocifisso di Sarezzo.* Brescia, 1985.

Regesta sive Rerum Boicarum autographa. Edited by Karl Heinrich von Lang. 3 vols. Munich, 1825.

Regling, Kurt. "Medaillenstudien II. Eine Fürstensuite von Valentin Maler, 1575." *Jahrbuch der Preussischen Kunstsammlungen* 49 (1928): 93–101.

[Reichmann sale, 1921] *Kunstmedaillen.* Auction catalogue, A. Reichmann & Co., Halle, July 6, 1921.

Reilly, D. R. *Portrait Waxes.* London, 1953.

Reinach, Salomon. *Répertoire de la statuaire grecque et romaine.* Vol. 1. Paris, 1906.

"A Renaissance Bronze Portrait." *Bulletin of the Minneapolis Institute of Arts* 22, no. 18 (1933), pp. 86–87.

Renaissance in Österreich. Exhibition catalogue, Niederösterreichishe Landesausstellung auf Schloss Schallaburg. Vienna, 1974.

Reposati, R. *Della zecca di Gubbio e delle geste de'Conti e Duchi di Urbino.* Bologna, 1772.

Reusner, Nicholas. *Emblemata.* Frankfurt am Main, 1581.

Reymond, M. *La Sculpture Florentine.* Vol. 4. Florence, 1900.

Reynolds, G. "Portraits by Nicholas Hilliard and his assistants of King James I and his family." *The Walpole Society* 34 (1952–54): 14.

Ricci, Corrado. *Il Tempio Malatestiano* [1924]. Reprint, with appendix by Pier Giorgio Pasini, Rimini, 1974.

de Ricci, Seymour. *The Gustave Dreyfus Collection. Reliefs and Plaquettes.* Oxford, 1931.

Richelieu, Cardinal. *Lettres.* Paris, 1853–77.

Richter, Gisela M. A. *Engraved Gems of the Romans.* London, 1971.

Richter, Jean Paul, ed. *The literary works of Leonardo da Vinci.* 3rd ed. London, 1970.

Rietstap, J. B. *Armorial Général* [1887]. 2 vols. Reprint London, 1968.

Rigoni, Erice. *L'arte rinascimentale in Padova: Studi e Documenti.* Padua, 1970.

de Rinaldis, Aldo. *Medaglie dei Secoli XV e XVI nel Museo Nazionale di Napoli.* Naples, 1913.

Ripa, Cesare. *Iconologia* [1618]. Edited by Piero Buscaroli. Milan, 1992.

Rizzini, P. *Illustrazione dei Civici Musei di Brescia.* Part 2, *Medaglie, Serie italiana Secoli XV a XVIII.* Brescia, 1892.

Rizzoli, Luigi. "Due bassorilievi in bronzo di Giovanni da Cavino," *Bollettino del Museo Civico di Padova* 5 (1902): 69–76.

———. "Una medaglia del Bembo che non e opera di Benvenuto Cellini," *L'Arte* 4 (1905): 276–80.

Robertson, G. *Giovanni Bellini.* Oxford, 1968.

Robertson, William. *The History of the Reign of the Emperor Charles V.* 3 vols. Boston, 1857.

Robinson, J. C. *Catalogue of the Soulages Collection.* London, 1856.

Roggiero, Orazio. *La zecca dei Marchesi di Saluzzo.* Pinerolo, 1901.

Rognini, Luciano. "Galeazzo e Girolamo Mondella, artisti del Rinascimento veronese." *Atti e Memorie della Accademia di Agricultura, Scienze e Lettere di Verona,* series 6, vol. 25 (1975): 95–119.

Ronchini, A. "Leone Leoni d'Arezzo." *Atti e Memorie delle RR. Deputazioni di Storia Patria per le provincie modenesi e parmensi* 3 (1865): 9–41.

———. "Il Pastorino da Siena." *Atti e Memorie delle RR Deputazioni di Storia Patria per le provincie modenesi e parmensi* 5 (1870): 39-44.

Rondot, N. *Jean Marende et la médaille de Philibert le Beau et de Marguerite d'Autriche.* Lyon, 1883.

———. *Les sculpteurs de Lyon, du quatorzième au dix-huitième siècle.* Lyon and Paris, 1884.

———. *La médaille d'Anne de Bretagne et ses auteurs, Louis Lepère, Nicolas de Florence et Jean Lepère, 1494.* Lyon and Paris, 1885.

———. *Jacob Richier, sculpteur et médailleur.* Lyon, 1885.

———. *Jacques Gauvain, orfèvre, graveur et médailleur à Lyon au seizième siècle.* Lyon, 1887.

———. "Pierre Woeiriot (1532–1587)." In *L'art et les artistes à Lyon du XIVe au XVIIIe siècle. Etudes posthumes. . . .* Edited by A. Cartier and L. Galle. Lyon, 1902.

———. *Les médailleurs et les graveurs de monnaies, jetons et médailles en France.* Paris, 1904.

Roobaert, E. "Jan Walravens alias Oomken, schilder en rederijker te Brussel." *Bulletin des Musées royaux des Beaux-Arts de Belgique* 10, nos. 3–4 (1961): 83–100.

[Rosenheim sale, 1923] *Catalogue of the Collection of Medals, Plaquettes & Coins . . . Max Rosenheim and Maurice Rosenheim.* Sotheby, Wilkinson & Hodge, London, March 4, 1923.

Rosenthal, Earl. "Plus ultra, Non plus ultra, and the Columnar Device of Emperor Charles V." *Journal of the Warburg and Courtauld Institutes* 34 (1971): 204–28.

Rosenthal, L. *Manuels d'histoire de l'art. La gravure.* Paris, 1909.

Ross, M. C. "An Iron Plaque of Filippo Strozzi." *Art in America* 31, no. 3 (1943): 151–53.

Rossi, Francesco. "Maffeo Olivieri e la bronzistica bresciana del '500." *Arte Lombarda* 47/48 (1977): 122–23.

———. "Le Gemme Antiche e le Origini della Placchetta." In *Renaissance Plaquettes.* Studies in the History of Art, vol. 22. Edited by Alison Luchs. Washington, 1989.

Rossi, Umberto. "La Patria di Sperandio." *Gazzetta Numismatica* 6 (1886–87): 89–90.

———. "Francesco Marchi e le medaglie di Marguerita d'Austria." *Rivista italiana di Numismatica* 1 (1888): 333–350.

———. "I medaglisti del Rinascimento alla corte di Mantova. II, Pier Jacopo Alari-Bonacolsi, detto l'Antico." *Rivista italiana di Numismatica* 2 (1888): 161–94 and 433–38.

———. "Nuovi documenti: Pastorino a Reggio d'Emilia." *Archivio Storico dell'Arte* 1 (1888): 229–30.

———. "La collezione Carrand nel Museo Nazionale di Firenze. II." *Archivio Storico dell'Arte* 3 (1890): 30-31.

Rossmann, Kurt. "Der Ottheinrichsbau." In *Ottheinrich. Gedenkschrift zur vierhundertjährigen Wiederkehr seiner Kurfürstenzeit in der Pfalz (1556–1559).* Edited by Georg Poensgen. Heidelberg, 1956, pp. 261–73.

Rott, E. *Histoire de la représentation diplomatique de la France auprès des Cantons Suisses.* 4 vols. Paris, 1902–9.

Rott, Hans. *Ottheinrich und die Kunst.* Heidelberg, 1905.

———. *Quellen und Forschungen zur südwestdeutschen und schweizerischen Kunstgeschichte im XV. und XVI. Jahrhundert.* Vol. 3, *Der Oberrhein.* Stuttgart, 1936.

Rott, Hans, ed. "Die Schriften des Pfalzgrafen Ott Heinrich." *Mitteilungen zur Geschichte des Heidelberger Schlosses* 6 (1912): 21–191.

Roversi, G. *Inscrizioni Medievali Bolognesi.* Bologna, 1982.

Rowlands, J. *Holbein: the Paintings of Hans Holbein the Younger.* Oxford, 1985.

Rua, P. *Per la libertà d'Italia, pagine di letteratura politica del '600.* Turin, 1905.

Ruhmer, E. "Reliefs des Sperandio." *Pantheon* 18 (1960): 20–21.

Ruschi, Pietro. "I campanili di Santa Croce." In *Santa Croce nell'800.* Florence, 1986, pp. 18–38.

Ryder, Alan. *The Kingdom of Naples under Alfonso the Magnanimous.* Oxford, 1976.

———. *Alfonso the Magnanimous, King of Aragon, Naples, and Sicily, 1396–1458.* Oxford, 1990.

Sabbadini, Remigio. *La scuola e gli studi di Guarino Guarini Veronese.* Catania, 1896. Summarized in *Enciclopedia Italiana.* Milan, 1933, vol. 18, pp. 27–28.

———, ed. *Epistolario di Guarino Veronese.* 3 vols. Venice, 1919.

Sakisian, A. "The Portraits of Mehmed II." *The Burlington Magazine* 74 (1939): 172–81.

Sallet, Alfred von. "Medaillen Albrecht Dürers." *Zeitschrift für Numismatik* 2 (1875): 362–67.

———. "Deutsche Gussmedaillen aus dem 16. und dem Beginn des 17. Jahrhunderts." *Zeitschrift für Numismatik* 11 (1884): pp. 123–51.

Salmi, M. "Riflessioni sul Pisanello medaglista." *Annali dell'Istituto Italiano di Numismatica* (1957): pp. 13–23.

Salton, M. L. *The Salton Collection. Renaissance and Baroque Medals and Plaquettes.* Exhibition catalogue, Bowdoin College Museum of Art. 2nd ed. Brunswick, Maine, 1969.

Salvini, R., and Chiodi, A. M. *Mostra di Lelio Orsi.* Exhibition catalogue. Reggio Emilia, 1950.

Samaran, C. "Un Exemplaire de luxe de l' 'Histoire de France abrégée' de Jean de Candida." *Bibliothèque de l'Ecole des Chartes* 105 (1944): 185–89.

[Sambon sale, 1914] *Medaillen und Plaketten der Renaissance.* Auction catalogue, J. Hirsch, Munich, May 9, 1914.

Sanuto, M. *Diarii.* Venice, 1879–1903.

Sarre, F. "Ein Miniatur Gentile Bellinis gemalt 1479–80 in Konstantinopel." *Jahrbuch der Kgl. Preussischen Kunstsammlungen* 27 (1906): 302–6.

———. "Ein Miniatur Gentile Bellinis, Nachtrag." *Jahrbuch der Kgl. Preussischen Kunstsammlungen* 28 (1907): 51–52.

Sartori, Antonio. *Documenti per la storia dell'arte a Padova.* Vicenza, 1976.

de Saulcy, F. *Recherches sur les monnaies des ducs héréditaires de Lorraine.* Metz, 1841.

Saumaise, Pierre. *Eloge sur la vie de Pierre Janin.* Dijon, 1623.

Saur, Allgemeines Künstler-Lexikon, Die bildenden Künstler aller Zeiten und Völker. Munich, 1992.

Scardeone, Bernardino. *De antiquitate urbis Patavii et claris civibus Patavinis libri tres.* Basel, 1560.

Schadendorf, Wulf. "Peter Flötners Spielkarten für Francesco d'Este." *Anzeiger des Germanischen Nationalmuseums,* 1954–59, pp. 143–69.

Schädler, A. "Zur Kleinplastik von Christoph Weiditz." *Münchner Jahrbuch der bildenden Kunst,* 3rd series 38 (1987): 161–84.

Schärli, Beatrice. *Erasmus von Rotterdam.* Exhibition catalogue, Historisches Museum, Basel. Basel, 1986.

Schatzhaus Kärntens. Landesausstellung St. Paul 1991, 900 Jahre Benediktinerstift. Exhibition catalogue. Klagenfurt, 1991.

Schaumünzen des Hauses Hohenzollern. Exhibition catalogue. Berlin, 1901.

Scher, Stephen K. *The Medals in the Collection of the Duke of Berry.* Master's thesis, New York University, Institute of Fine Arts. New York, 1961.

———. "Doppeltaler [sic] of Johann Friedrich I, Elector of Saxony." *The Coat of Arms* 6, no. 48 (October 1961): 332–34.

———. "A Sixteenth-Century Wax Model." *The Medal* 9 (special issue, 1986): 15–21.

———. "Immortalitas in nummis: the Origins of the Italian Renaissance Medal." In *Trésors Monétaires,* supplement 2. Paris, 1989, pp. 1–19 and pls. I–IX.

———. "Veritas Odium Parit. Comments on a medal of Pietro Aretino." *The Medal* 14 (1989): 4–11.

Scher, Stephen K.; Marincola, Michele D.; and Poulet, Anne L. "Gothic, Renaissance, and Baroque Medals from the Museum of Fine Arts, Boston." *The Medal* 9 (special issue, 1986): 79–105.

Schindler, Herbert. *Augsburger Renaissance. Hans Daucher und die Bildhauer der Fuggerkapelle bei Sankt Anna.* Munich, 1985.

Schivenoglia, A. "Cronaca di Mantova dal 1445 al 1484." In *Raccolta di Cronisti e Documenti storici lombardi inediti.* Edited by Carlo d'Arco. Milan, 1857.

Schlosser, Julius von. *Werke der Kleinplastik in der Skulpturensammlung des A. H. Kaiserhauses.* Vol. 2. Vienna, 1911.

———. "Geschichte der Porträtbildnerei in Wachs." *Jahrbuch der Kunstsammlungen des Allerhöchsten Kaiserhauses* 19, no. 3 (1911).

Schmidt, Justus. *Die Linzer Kirchen.* Österreichische Kunsttopographie, vol. 36. Vienna, 1964.

Schneider, Laurie. "Leon Battista Alberti: Some Biographical Implications of the Winged Eye." *Art Bulletin* 72 (June 1990): 61–70.

Schnell, H. *Martin Luther und die Reformation auf Münzen und Medaillen.* Munich, 1983.

Schornbaum, Karl. *Das älteste Ehebuch der Pfarrei St. Sebald in Nürnberg 1524–1543.* Nuremberg, 1949.

[Schulman sale, 1956] Auction catalogue 226, J. Schulman, Amsterdam, January 30, 1956.

Schulz, Karl. *Antonio Abondio und seine Zeit.* Exhibition catalogue, Münzkabinett, Kunsthistorisches Museum. Vienna, 1988.

———. "Bemerkungen zu Antonio Abondio." *Jahrbuch der kunsthistorischen Sammlungen in Wien* 85/86 (1989–90): 155–61.

Schwarzwälder, Herbert. *Geschichte der freien Hansestadt Bremen.* Bremen, 1975.

Schweikhart, Gunter. "Bernardino India und die Idee des Künstlermuseums im 16. Jahrhundert." *Wallraf-Richartz-Jahrbuch* 51 (1990): 123–30.

Schweizerisches Künstler-Lexikon. Edited by Carl Brun. Frauenfeld, 1908.

Sculpture from the David Daniels Collection. Exhibition catalogue, Minneapolis Institute of Arts. Edited by Louise Lincoln. Minneapolis, 1979.

Sear, David. *Greek Coins and Their Values.* London, 1978.

Selbstbildnisse und Künstlerporträts von Lucas van Leyden bis Anton Raphael Mengs. Exhibition catalogue, Herzog Anton Ulrich-Museum, Braunschweig. Edited by Bodo Hedergott. Braunschweig, 1980.

Select Italian Medals. Exhibition catalogue, British Museum. London, 1920.

Serrure, C.-A. "Deux médailles de Stephanus Hollander." *Bulletin mensuel de numismatique et d'archéologie* 1, no. 12 (1882), 3–6.

Serrure, C. P. "Michel Mercator, de Venloo, Ciseleur de Médailles du Seizième Siècle." *Revue belge de Numismatique* 5 (1850): 113–21.

Settis, Salvatore. "Danae verso il 1495." *I Tatti Studies. Essays in the Renaissance* 1 (1985): 207–37.

Seward, Desmond. *Prince of the Renaissance: The Life of François I.* London, 1973.

Seymour, Charles, Jr. *Masterpieces of Sculpture from the National Gallery of Art.* New York, 1949.

———. *Art Treasures for America.* London, 1961.

Seznec, Jean. "Youth, Innocence and Death." *Journal of the Warburg Institute* 1 (1937–38): 298–303.

Sheard, Wendy Stedman. *Antiquity in the Renaissance.* Exhibition catalogue, Smith College Museum of Art. Northampton, Mass. Northampton, 1978.

Shearman, John. "Il 'Tiburio' di Bramante." In *Studi Bramanteschi, Atti del Congresso internazionale: Milano-Urbino-Roma, 1970.* Rome, 1974, pp. 567–73.

———. "The Fresco Decoration of Sixtus IV." In *The Sis-*

tine Chapel. *Michelangelo Rediscovered*. Edited by Carlo Pietrangeli. London, 1986.

Siebmacher, J. *Grosses und Allgemeines Wappenbuch*. Nuremberg, 1885–1904.

Sigismondo Pandolfo Malatesta e il suo tempo. Exhibition catalogue. Vicenza, 1974.

Silver, Larry. "Shining Armor: Maximilian I as Holy Roman Emperor." *The Art Institute of Chicago Museum Studies* 12 (1985): 9–29.

Simon, Kate. *A Renaissance Tapestry: The Gonzaga of Mantua*. New York, 1988.

Simonis, Julien. *L'Art du médailleur en Belgique. Contributions à l'étude de son histoire*. Brussels, 1900.

———. *L'Art du médailleur en Belgique. Nouvelles contributions à l'étude de son histoire*. Jemeppe-sur-Meuse, 1904.

Simons, Patricia. "Women in Frames: the Gaze, the Eye, the Profile in Renaissance Portraiture." *History Workshop* 25 (1988): 8.

Sindona, E. *Pisanello*. Milan, 1961.

Smailes, Helen, and Tompson, Duncan. *A Celebration of Mary, Queen of Scots: The Queen's Image*. Exhibition catalogue. Scottish National Portrait Gallery. Edinburgh, 1987.

Smith, Jeffrey Chipps. *Nuremberg, a Renaissance City, 1500–1518*. Exhibition catalogue. Austin, 1983.

Smith, P. "Mansart Studies II: The Val-de-Grâce." *The Burlington Magazine* 106 (1964): 115.

Smolderen, Luc. "Quentin Metsys, médailleur d'Erasme." *Scrinium Erasmianum* 2 (1969): 513–25.

———. "Jacques Jonghelinck, waradin de la Monnaie d'Anvers de 1572 à 1606." *Revue belge de Numismatique* 115 (1969): 83–147.

———. *La statue du duc d'Albe à Anvers par Jacques Jonghelinck, 1571*. Mémoires de l'Académie royale de Belgique. Classe des Beaux-Arts. 2nd series 14, no. 1. Brussels, 1972.

———. "Bacchus et les sept Planètes par Jacques Jonghelinck." *Revue des archéologues et historiens d'Art de Louvain* 10 (1977): 102–43.

———. "Le tombeau de Charles le Téméraire." *Revue belge d'Archéologie et d'Histoire de l'Art* 44–50 (1980–81): 21–53.

———. "Jonghelinck en Italie." *Revue belge de Numismatique* 130 (1984): 119–39.

———. "Jean Second médailleur." *Handelingen van de Koninklijke Kring voor Oudheidkunden, Letteren en Kunst van Mechelen* 90 (1986): 61–86.

———. "A Propos de Guillaume Dupré." *Revue Numismatique* 32 (1990): 246.

———. "Le séjour à Vienne de Conrad Bloc." *Revue belge de Numismatique* 137 (1991): 159–64.

Solms, Ernstotto, Count zu. *Solmser Medaillen des 16. Jahrhunderts*. Solms-Laubach, 1956.

[Sotheby Parke Bernet sale, 1980] Auction catalogue, Sotheby Parke Bernet, Monaco, May 26–27, 1980.

[Sotheby's sale, London, 1988] *Renaissance Medals, Coins and Paper Money*. Auction catalogue, Sotheby's, London, May 23–24, 1988.

[Sotheby's sale, New York, 1988] Auction catalogue, Sotheby's, New York, November 22–23, 1988.

Spätgotik am Oberrhein. Meisterwerke der Plastik und des Kunsthandwerks 1450–1530. Exhibition catalogue, Badisches Landesmuseum Karlsruhe. Karlsruhe, 1970.

Spencer, John R. "Speculations on the Origins of the Italian Renaissance Medal." In *Italian Medals*. Studies in the History of Art, vol. 21. Washington, 1987, pp. 202–3.

Sperling, Christine M. "Leon Battista Alberti's Inscriptions on the Holy Sepulchre in the Cappella Rucellai, San Pancrazio, Florence." *Journal of the Warburg and Courtauld Institutes* 16 (1989): 221–28.

Spink & Son's Numismatic Circular. Vol. 85, no. 1. London, 1977.

[Spitzer sale, 1893] Auction Catalogue, Frédéric Spitzer Collection. London, 1893.

Splendours of the Gonzaga. Exhibition catalogue, Victoria & Albert Museum, London. Edited by David Chambers and Jane Martineau. London, 1981.

Sponsel, Jean Louis. "Flötner-Studien." *Jahrbuch der Preussischen Kunstsammlungen* 45 (1924): 121–84, 214–76; and 46 (1925): 38–90.

———. "Peter Flötner, nicht Hieronymus Magdeburger."

Zeitschrift für Numismatik 37, nos. 1–4 (1927): 139–83.

Stafski, Heinz. *Der jüngere Peter Vischer*. Nuremberg, 1962.

Starkey, D., ed. *Henry VIII: A European Court in England*. Exhibition catalogue, London Maritime Museum. London, 1991.

Stein, Henri. "Nouveaux documents sur Jean de Candida diplomate." *Bibliothèque de l'Ecole des Chartres* 89 (1928): 235–39.

Steinmann, Ernst. *Die Porträtdarstellungen des Michelangelo*. Leipzig, 1913.

Sterling, Charles. "Une peinture certaine de Perréal enfin retrouvée." *L'Œil* 103–4 (1963): 5.

Stetten, Paul von. *Kunst-, Gewerb-, und Handwerks-Geschichte der Reichs-Stadt Augsburg*. Augsburg, 1779.

Stevenson, Seth William, et al. *Dictionary of Roman Coins, Republican and Imperial* [1889]. Reprint London, 1982.

Storia di Milano. Published by the Fondazione Trecani degli Alfieri per la Storia di Milano. Milan, 1953–66.

Strauss, Walter L., ed. *Hendrik Goltzius, 1558–1617. The Complete Engravings*. New York, 1977.

[Stroehlin sale, 1910] *Catalogue of the Stroehlin Collection of Coins and Medals. . . .* Sotheby, Wilkinson & Hodge, London, May 30–June 8, 1910.

Strong, Roy. *Portraits of Queen Elizabeth I*. Oxford, 1963.

———. *National Portrait Gallery: Tudor and Jacobean Portraits*. London 1969.

———. *Gloriana: the portraits of Elizabeth I*. London, 1987.

Strong, Roy, and Murrell, V. *Artists of the Tudor Court. The portrait miniature rediscovered*. Exhibition catalogue, Victoria & Albert Museum. London, 1983.

Strong, Roy, and Oman, Julia T. *Mary Queen of Scots, Evocation and Spectacle*. New York, 1972.

Suetonius [Caius Suetonius Tranquillus]. *The Lives of the Twelve Caesars*. Edited by E. S. Shuckburgh. London, 1903.

Suhle, Arthur. *Die deutsche Renaissance-Medaille*. Leipzig, 1950 (2nd ed. 1952).

Suida, W. *Bramante pittore e il Bramantino*. Milan, 1954.

Supino, B. *Il medagliere Mediceo nel R. Museo Nazionale di Firenze*. Florence, 1899.

Sütterlin, Berthold. *Geschichte Badens*. Vol. 1, *Frühzeit und Mittelalter*. Karlsruhe, 1965.

Symonds, John Addington. *The Renaissance in Italy*. 2 vols. New York, Modern Library edition, 1935.

Tacchi-Venturi, Pietro. "Note storiche e topografiche di Roma nel secolo XVI. . . . " *Studi e documenti di storia e diretto* 20 (1899): 308–10.

Tagliati, G. "Relazione fra la famiglia Romei e la corte estense nel secolo XV." In *Il Rinascimento nelle corti Paduana: Societa e cultura*. Edited by P. Rossi. Bari, 1977.

Tallement des Réaux, G. *Historiettes de Tallement des Réaux*. Paris, 1862.

———. *Historiettes*. Edited by Antoine Adam. Paris, 1960.

Tannenbaum, Samuel A., and Tannenbaum, Dorothy R. *Marie Stuart, Queen of Scots (A Concise bibliography)*. 3 vols. New York, 1944–46.

Taylor, Lou. *Mourning Dress: A Costume and Social History*. London, 1983.

Tentzel, Wilhlem Ernst. *Saxonia Numismatica Lineae Albertinae*. Dresden, 1705.

ter Molen, Johannes Rein. *Von Vianen, Een Utrechtse familie van zilversmeden met een internationale faam*. 2 vols. Leiden, 1984.

Terrasse, Charles. *Germain Pilon*. Paris, 1930.

———. *François I: Le Roi et le règne*. 3 vols. Paris, 1943–70.

de Tervarent, Guy. *Attributs et symboles dans l'art profane 1450–1600. Dictionnaire d'un langage perdu*. Geneva, 1958–64.

Teulet, Alexandre. *Liste chronologique et alphabétique des chevaliers et des officiers de l'Ordre du Saint-Esprit*. Paris, 1864.

The Medal—Mirror of History. Exhibition catalogue, British Museum. London, 1979.

The Picture Gallery Dresden: Old masters. Dresden, 1962.

Thesaurus antiquitatem et historiarum Italiae. Vol. 9. 1723.

Theseus Ambrosius. *Introductio in chaldaicam lingua. . . .* Rome, 1539.

Theuerkauff, Christian. *Der Mensch um 1500*. Exhibition catalogue, Staatliche Museen Preussischer Kulturbesitz, Skulpturengalerie. Berlin, 1977.

[Thieme-Becker] Ulrich Thieme and Felix Becker, eds. *Allgemeines Lexikon der Bildenden Künstler*. 37 vols. Leipzig, 1907–50.

Thode, Heinrich. *Mantegna*. Leipzig, 1897.

[Tietjen sale, 1991] 63. *Auktion*. Tietjen + Co., Hamburg, 1991.

[Tietjen sale, 1992] 65. *Auktion. Münzen und Medaillen*. Tietjen + Co., Hamburg, May 11, 1992.

Tilley, Arthur. "The Literary Circle of Margaret of Navarre." In *A Miscellany of Studies of Romance languages and Literatures presented to Leon E. Kastner*. Edited by Mary Williams and James A. de Rothschild. Cambridge, 1932, pp. 519–31.

Timann, Ursula. "Zum Lebenslauf von Georg Pencz," *Anzeiger des Germanischen Nationalmuseums*, 1990, pp. 97–112.

Tommasoli, W. *La Vita di Federico da Montefeltro (1422–1482)*. Urbino, 1978.

Tourneur, V. "Jehan de Candida: Diplomate et médailleur au service de la Maison de Bourgogne, 1472–1480." *Revue belge de Numismatique* 70 (1914): 381–411.

———. "Jehan de Candida: Diplomate et médailleur au service de la Maison de Bourgogne, 1472–1480 (suite)." *Revue belge de Numismatique* 71 (1919): 7–48.

———. "Jehan de Candida: diplomate et médailleur au service de la Maison de Bourgogne, 1472–1480 (suite et fin)." *Revue belge de Numismatique* 71 (1919): 251–300.

———. "Société Royale de Numismatique. Extraits des Procès Verbaux." *Revue belge de numismatique* 71 (1919): 355–72.

———. "Quentin Matsys médailleur." *Revue belge de Numismatique* 72 (1920): 139–60.

———. "La maison de Jacques Jongheling à Bruxelles." *Annales de la Société royale d'Archéologie de Bruxelles* 29 (1920): 209–13.

———. "Le médailleur anversois Steven van Herwijck (1557–1565)." *Revue belge de Numismatique* 73 (1921): 27–55.

———. "Steven van Herwijck, Médailleur anversois (1557–1565)." *Numismatic Chronicle* (1922): 91–132.

———. "Le médailleur Steven van Herwijck." *Revue belge de Numismatique* 74 (1922): 209–11.

———. "Simon Costière et Pierre Woeiriot." *Aréthuse* (1925): 85–88.

———. "Jan Symons, médailleur anversois." *Revue belge de Numismatique* 77 (1925): 45–55.

———. "Conrad Bloc, Médailleur anversois." *Revue belge de Numismatique* 77 (1925): 199–211.

———. "Le médailleur Jacques Jongheling et le Cardinal Granvelle, 1564–1578." *Revue belge de Numismatique* 79 (1927): 79–93.

———. "Steven van Herwijck et les baillis de l'Ordre de Malte à Utrecht." *Revue belge de Numismatique* 93 (1947): 59–66.

Toussaint, J. "Quentin Matsys, médailleur." *La vie numismatique* 36, no. 4 (1986): 120–30.

Toynbee, Jocelyn M. C. *Roman Medallions*. Reprinted with introduction by William E. Metcalf. New York, 1986.

Trapp, J. B. "The Owl's Ivy and the Poet's Bays, an Enquiry into Poetic Garlands." *Journal of the Warburg and Courtauld Institutes* 21 (1958): 227–55.

[Trau sale, 1904] *Münzen und Medaillen aller Länder aus dem Besitz des Herrn Franz Trau in Wien*. Brüder Egger, Vienna, January 11, 1904.

Trautmann, F. *Kunst und Kunstgewerbe vom frühesten Mittelalter bis Ende des achtzehnten Jahrhunderts*. Nördlingen, 1869.

Trease, Geoffrey. *The Condottieri*. New York, 1971.

Trento, Dario. *Benvenuto Cellini: opere non esposte e documenti notarili*. Florence, 1984.

Trésor de Numismatique et de Glyptique. . . . Paris, 1834–41. For convenience, citations in the notes are to the Italian section of this compendium (2 vols.), the French section (3 vols.), or the German section (1 vol.).

Treu, E. *Die Bildnisse des Erasmus von Rotterdam*. Basel, 1959.

Trevor-Roper, Hugh. *Princes and Artists: Patronage and*

Ideology at Four Hapsburg Courts, 1517–1633. London, 1976.

Tribolati, Pietro. "Due grandi incisori di conii della zecca 'cesarea' Milanese: Leone Leoni da Arezzo, Iacopo da Trezzo." *Rivista italiana di Numismatica* 57 (1955): 94–102.

Tricou, J. "Quelques médailles rares du Musée de Lyon, XVI–XVIIIᵉ s." In *Exposition internationale de numismatique.* Exhibition catalogue, Monnaie de Paris. Paris, 1953.

———. *Médailles lyonnaise du XVᵉ au XVIIIᵉ siècle.* Paris, 1958.

Troche, Ernst Günter. "Peter Flötner." *Die Besinnung* 2 (1947): 123–33.

Trusted, Marjorie. *German Renaissance Medals. A Catalogue of the Collection in the Victoria & Albert Museum.* London, 1990.

Tuttle, Patricia. "An Investigation of the Renaissance Casting Techniques of Incuse-Reverse and Double-Sided Medals." In *Italian Medals.* Studies in the History of Art, vol. 21. Edited by J. Graham Pollard. Washington, 1987, pp. 205–12.

Typotius, Jacob. *Symbola divina et humana.* 2 vols. Prague, 1601–3.

U. di S. [Umberto of Savoy]. *Le medaglie della Casa di Savoia.* Rome, 1980.

van Broeck, R. *The Myth of the Phoenix According to Classical and Early Christian Traditions.* Leiden, 1972.

van der Heijden, M. J. M. "Het godsdienstig element in de iconographie van de Nederlandsche Historiepenningen uit den Tachtigjarigen oorlog." *Jaarboek voor Munt- en Penningkunde* 35 (1948): 1–15.

van der Meer, G. "Herinnering aan een vastberaden uitgevoerde opdracht." *Jaarboek Oranje-Nassau Museum* (1983): 5–14.

van der Osten, Gert, and Vey, Horst. *Painting and Sculpture in Germany and the Netherlands, 1500–1600.* Penguin Books, Middlesex and Baltimore, 1969.

van de Ven, A. J. "De zestien kwartieren van George van Egmond, bisschop van Utrecht." *Jaarboekje van Oud-Utrecht* (1959): 87–99.

van Dorsten, J. "Steven van Herwyck's Elizabeth (1565). A Franco-Flemish political medal." *The Burlington Magazine* 111 (1969): 143–47.

van Durme, M. "Antoon Perrenot van Granvelle en Leone Leoni." *Revue belge de Philologie et d'Histoire* 27 (1949): 653–78.

———. *Antoon Perrenot, bisschop van Utrecht, cardinaal van Granvelle, minister van Karel V en van Filips II, 1517–1587.* Verhandeling van de Koninklijke Vlaamse Academie van België, Klasse der Letteren, vol. 15, no. 18. Brussels, 1953.

van Eeghem, W. "Rhetores Bruxellenses (16ᵈᵉ eeuw)." *Revue belge de Philologie et d'Histoire* 15 (1936): 75–78.

van Even, E. *Het Landjuweel van Antwerpen in 1561.* Louvain, 1861.

van Kerkwijk, A. O. *Jaarverslag van het Koninklijk Kabinet van Muntzen, Penningen en Gesneden Steenen te 's-Gravenhage.* The Hague, 1919.

———. "Portretpenningen van Prins Willem van Oranje en Charlotte de Bourbon." *Jaarboek voor Munt- en Penningkunde* 16 (1929): 103–14.

van Loon, G. *Beschryving der Nederlandsche Historipenningen.* 4 vols. The Hague, 1723.

———. *Histoire métallique des XVII Provinces des Pays-Bas.* 5 vols. [1732–37]. Reprint Leipzig, 1969.

van Luttervelt. "Bij een penning van Jacques Jonghelinck." *Jaarboek voor Munt- en Penningkunde* 42 (1955): 100–101.

van Mieris, Frans. *Historie der Nederlandsche Vorsten. . . .* 3 vols. The Hague, 1732–35.

van Thiel, Pieter J. J., et al. *All the Paintings of the Rijksmuseum in Amsterdam.* Translated and edited by Marianne Buikstra-de Boer et al. Amsterdam, 1976.

van Zuiden, D. S. "Testament van Frederick Alewijn." *Tijdschrift voor Munt- en Penningkunde* 21 (1913): 160.

Varchi, Benedetto. *I Sonetti.* Venice, 1555.

Vasari, Giorgio. *Le vite de' più eccellenti pittori, scultori ed architettori.* Edited by Gaetano Milanese. 8 vols. Florence, 1878–85 (2nd ed. 1906).

———. *Vasari on Technique.* Translated by Louisa S. Maclehose. New York, 1960.

———. *La Vita di Michelangelo.* Edited by Paolo Barocchi. 5 vols. Milan and Naples, 1962.

Vaudoyer, Jean-Louis. "La collection Gustave Dreyfus." In *L'amour de l'art* (1925): 245–64.

Veit, Ludwig. "Der Einfluss der italienischen Renaissance-Medaille auf die deutsche Renaissance-Medaille." In *L'Influenza della medaglia italiana nell'Europa dei sec. XV e XVI.* Atti del IIᵒ Convegno internazionale di studio Udine 6/9 ottobre 1973. Udine, 1976.

Venturi, Adolfo. "Ein Brief des Sperandio." *Der Kunstfreund* 1 (1885): 278–79.

———. "Leone Leoni incisore della zecca del duca di Ferrara." *Archivio Storico dell'Arte* 1 (1888): 327–28.

———. "Sperandio da Mantova." *Archivio Storico dell'Arte* 1 (1888): 385–439.

———. "Sperandio da Mantova (Appendice)." *Archivio Storico dell'Arte* 2 (1889): 229.

———. "Costanzo medaglista e pittore." *Archivio Storico dell'Arte* 4 (1891): 374–75.

———. *Le Vite dei Piu Eccellenti Pittori, Scultori e Architettori scritte da M. Giorgio Vasari pittore et architetto Aretino. I. Gentile da Fabriano e il Pisanello.* Florence, 1896.

———. *Storia dell'arte italiana.* Vol. 10, *La scultura del Cinquecento.* Part 1. Milan, 1935.

———. "Su alcune medaglie di Pisanello." *L'Arte* 38, no. 6 (1935): 30–38.

———. *Pisanello.* Rome, 1939.

Verlet, Pierre. *Les Bronzes Dorés Français du XVIIIᵉ siècle.* Paris, 1987.

Vermeule, Cornelius C. III. "Graeco-Roman Asia Minor to Renaissance Italy: Medallic and Related Arts." In *Italian Medals.* Studies in the History of Art, vol. 21. Edited by J. Graham Pollard. Washington, 1987, pp. 263–81.

Vespasiano da Bisticci. *Vite di Uomini illustri del secolo XV.* Edited by P. d'Ancona and E. Aeschlimann. Milan, 1951.

———. *Renaissance Princes, Popes & Prelates.* Introduction by Myron P. Gilmore. New York, 1963.

Vickers, Michael. "Some Preparatory Drawings for Pisanello's Medallion of John VIII Paleologus." *Art Bulletin* 60, no. 3 (September 1978): 417–24.

Vico, Anea. *Discorsi sopra le Medaglie degli Antichi.* Venice, 1555.

[Vidal Quadras y Ramón sale, 1892] *Catalogo de la coleccion de monedas de Manuel Vidal Quadras y Ramón de Barcelona.* 4 vols. Barcelona, 1892. Reprint Barcelona, 1975.

Villari, P. *The Life and Times of Girolamo Savonarola.* London, 1888.

Virgil [Publius Vergilius Maro]. *Georgics.* Translated by H. Rushton Fairclough. Cambridge, Massachusetts, 1942.

Visschers, P. *Iets over Jacob Jonghelinck, metaelgieter en penningsnijder, Octavio van Veen . . . en de gebroeders Collyns de Nole.* Antwerp, 1853.

Vitry, Paul, and Brière, Gaston. *L'Eglise abbatiale de Saint-Denis et ses Tombeaux.* Paris, 1925.

Vöge, Wilhelm. *Die deutschen Bildwerke und die der anderen cisalpinen Länder.* Königliche Museen zu Berlin. Beschreibung der Bildwerke der Christlichen Epochen, vol. 4. 2nd ed. Berlin, 1910.

Vollenweider, Marie-Louise. *Die Steinschneidekunst.* Stuttgart, 1966.

Volz, Peter. *Conrad Peutinger und das Entstehen der deutschen Medaillensitte zu Augsburg 1518.* Dissertation, Heidelberg, 1972.

———. "Unbekannte deutsche Schaumünzen des 16. Jahrhunderts." *Jahrbuch für Numismatik und Geldgeschichte* 31/32 (1981–82): 141–47.

Vom Taler zum Dollar, 1486–1986. Exhibition catalogue. Munich, 1986.

de Voogt, W. J. "Deux médailles du graveur Etienne de Hollande. Cesilia Veeselar – Floris Allewijn." *Revue belge de Numismatique,* 4th series 5 (1867): 347–49.

de Vos, P. D. *De vroedschap van Zierikzee van de tweede helft der zestiende eeuw tot 1795.* Middelburg, 1931.

Vroom, N. R. A. "Een raadselachtige ontwerpteekening voor een gebrandschilderd glas in de St. Lieven monsterkerk te Zierikzee." *Oud Holland* 59 (1942): 171–78.

Waddington, Raymond B. "Before Arcimboldo: Composite Portraits on Italian Medals." *The Medal* 14 (Spring 1989): 13–23.

Walker, John. *Portraits: 5000 Years.* New York, 1983.

Walther, Hans. *Carmina Medii Aevi posterioris Latina.* Vol. II/8, *Lateinische Sprichwörter und Sentenzen des Mittelalters und der frühen Neuzeit in alphabetischer Reihenfolge.* Göttingen, 1983.

Watkins, Renée. "L. B. Alberti's Emblem, the Winged Eye, and his name, Leo." *Mitteilungen des Kunsthistorischen Institutes in Florenz* 9 (November 1960): 256–58.

Weber, F. Parkes. *Aspects of Death in Art.* London, 1910.

Weber, Ingrid. "Bemerkungen zum Plakettenwerk von Peter Flötner." *Pantheon* 28 (1970): 521–25.

———. *Deutsche, Niederländische und Französische Renaissanceplaketten 1500–1650.* 2 vols. Munich, 1975.

———. "Venus Kallipygos, der 'Weibliche Rückenakt' nach Dürer." *Städel-Jahrbuch,* new series 9 (1983): 145–50.

Weech, Friedrich von. *Badische Geschichte.* Karlsruhe, 1890.

Weihrauch, Hans Robert. *Europäische Bronzestatuetten 15.-18. Jahrhundert.* Braunschweig, 1967.

Weiller, R. *Les médailles dans l'histoire du pays de Luxembourg.* Exhibition catalogue, Institut supérieur d'Archéologie et d'Histoire de l'Art de l'Université Catholique de Louvain. Louvain-la-Neuve, 1979.

Weinberger, M. "Sperandio und die Frage der Francia Skulpturen." *Münchner Jahrbuch der bildenden Kunst,* new series 7 (1930): 293–318.

Weinstein, D. *Savonarola and Florence.* Princeton, 1971.

Weiss, Dieter J. "Melchior Pfinzing (1481–1535)." In *Fränkische Lebensbilder* 14. Neustadt/Aisch, 1991, pp. 14–29.

Weiss, Roberto. "Une medaille a demi connue de Lysippus la Jeune." *Schweizer Münzblätter* 10 (1960): 7–10.

———. "The Medals of Pope Julius II (1503–1513)." *Journal of the Warburg and Courtauld Institutes* 28 (1965): 163–82.

———. *Pisanello's Medallion of the Emperor John VIII Paleologus.* London, 1966.

———. *The Renaissance Discovery of Classical Antiquity.* Oxford, 1969.

Wellens-de Donder, L. *Médailleurs et numismates de la Renaissance aux Pays-Bas.* Exhibition catalogue, Bibliothèque Royale. Brussels, 1959.

———. "La médaille 'Venus et l'Amour' de Steven van Herwijck." *Revue belge de Numismatique* 105 (1959): 165–70.

———. "Documents inédits relatifs à Jacques Jonghelinck." *Revue belge de Numismatique* 106 (1960): 295–305.

Welt im Umbruch. Augsburg zwischen Renaissance und Barock. Exhibition catalogue. 2 vols. Augsburg, 1980.

Wenzel Jamnitzer und die Nürnberger Goldschmiedekunst 1500–1700. Exhibition catalogue, Germanisches Nationalmuseum, Nuremberg. Munich, 1985.

de Werd, G. "Porträts des Herzogs Johann Wilhelm von Kleve." *Kalender für das Kleverland* (1977): 49–51.

Wethey, Harold E. *The Paintings of Titian.* 3 vols. London, 1971.

White, Lynn, Jr. "Indic Elements in the Iconography of Petrarch's 'Trionfo della morte'." *Speculum* 49, no. 2 (1974): 209.

Wied, Alexander. *Die Profanen Bau- und Kunstdenkmäler der Stadt Linz. Die Altstadt.* Österreichische Kunsttopographie, vol. 42. Vienna, 1977.

Wielandt, Friedrich. *Medaillen der Renaissance und des Barock.* Karlsruhe, n.d.

Wielandt, Friedrich, and Zeitz, Joachim. *Die Medaillen des Hauses Baden.* Karlsruhe, 1980.

Wiesflecker, Hermann. *Kaiser Maximilian I.* Vol 5, *Der Kaiser und seine Umwelt. Hof, Staat, Wirtschaft, Gesellschaft und Kultur.* Munich, 1986.

———. *Maximilian I. Die Fundamente des habsburgischen Weltreiches.* Vienna, 1991.

Wilde, J. *Venetian Art from Bellini to Titian.* London, 1974.

Wilhelm, Johannes. *Augsburger Wandmalerei 1368–1530. Künstler, Handwerker und Zunft.* Augsburg, 1983.

Will, Georg Andreas. *Der Nürnbergischen Münz-Belustigungen.* 4 vols. Altdorf, 1764–67.

Willem van Oranje, om vrijheid van geweten. Exhibition catalogue, Rijksmuseum. Amsterdam, 1984.

Williamson, G. C. "Mr. Francis Wellesley's Collection of Miniatures and Drawings, Part II." *The Connoisseur* 15 (1918): 64–66.

Wilson, Carolyn C. *Renaissance Small Bronze Sculpture and Associated Decorative Arts at the National Gallery of Art.* Washington, 1983.

Wind, Edgar. "Aenigma Termini." *Warburg Journal* 1 (1937–38): 66–69.

———. *Pagan Mysteries in the Renaissance.* New Haven, 1958 (2nd ed., New York and London, 1968.)

Wissgrill, Franz Karl. *Schauplatz des landsässigen Nieder-Österreichischen Adels.* Vienna, 1797.

Wittkower, Rudolf. *Allegory and the Migration of Symbols.* London, 1977.

Wixom, William D. *Renaissance Bronzes from Ohio Collections.* Exhibition catalogue. Cleveland, 1975.

Wölcker, Karl Wilhelm. *Nürnberger Geschlechterbücher.* Vol. 3, *1500–1600.* Manuscript in the library of the Germanisches Nationalmuseum, Nuremberg. Signature 2° Hs. 94402.

Wolff-Metternich, F. Graf. *Bramante und St. Peter, Collectanea Artis Historiae II.* Munich, 1975.

Wolff-Metternich, F. Graf, and Thoenes, C. *Die Frühen St.-Peter-Entwürfe, 1505–1514.* Veröffentlichungen der Bibliotheca Hertziana (Max Planck-Institut) 25. Tübingen, 1987.

Woods-Marsden, Joanna. *The Gonzaga of Mantua and Pisanello's Arthurian Frescoes.* Princeton, 1988.

———. "How Quattrocento Princes used Art: Sigismondo Pandolfo Malatesta of Rimini and *cose militari*." *Renaissance Studies* 3, no. 4 (December 1989): 387–414.

Woodward, W. H. *Vittorino da Feltre and other Humanist Educators* [1897]. Reprint Columbia, Missouri, 1963.

Wormald, Jenny. *Mary Queen of Scots. A Study in Failure.* London, 1991.

Yatsevich, A. G. *Antichniye motiviy u italyanskikh medalyerov Bozrozhdeniya.* New York, 1925.

Yriarte, Charles. *Un condottiere au XVᵉ siècle. Rimini, études sur les lettres et les arts à la cour des Malatesta.* Paris, 1882.

Zahn, Peter. *Die Inschriften der Friedhöfe St. Johannis, St. Rochus und Wöhrd zu Nürnberg.* Munich, 1972.

Zanoli, Anna. "Sugli affreschi di Pisanello nel Palazzo Ducale di Mantova." *Paragone* 24 (1973): 23–44.

Zeitler, Rudolf. "Frühe deutsche Medaillen 1518–1527. 1, Studien zur Entstehung des Stiles der Medaillenmeister Hans Schwarz, Christoph Weiditz und Friedrich Hagenauer." *Figura* (Uppsala) 1 (1951): 77–119.

Zeumer, Karl. *Die Goldene Bulle Kaiser Karls IV.* Quellen und Studien zur Verfassungsgeschichte des Deutschen Reiches in Mittelalter und Neuzeit, vol. 2. Weimar, 1908.

Zimermann, Heinrich, ed. *Urkunden und Regesten aus dem k. u. k. Haus-, Hof-, und Staats-Archiv in Wien* (= *Jahrbuch der Kunsthistorischen Sammlungen des Allerhöchsten Kaiserhauses* 1 (1883). Part 2, *Quellen zur Geschichte der kaiserlichen Haussammlungen*, pp. 1–78). Vienna, 1883.

Zimmermann, Heinrich. "Eine Nürnberger Silberkassette der Renaissance (1545)." *Berliner Museen. Berichte aus den ehem. Preussischen Kunstsammlungen*, new series 5 (1955): 15–19.

Zograf, A. N. *Stroganovskiyi dvoretz-muzei. Italyanskiye medali.* Petersburg, 1923.

Zorzi, Elda. "Un antiquario padovano del secolo XVI. Alessandro Maggi da Bassano." *Bollettino del museo civico di Padova* 51 (1962): 41–98.

475 Jahre Fürstentum Pfalz-Neuburg. Exhibition catalogue. Munich, 1980.

Index

Names in CAPITAL LETTERS refer to artists or schools whose medals are discussed and illustrated in this volume.
Page numbers in *italics* refer to illustrations.

A

Abel brothers, 278

Abondio, Alessandro, 395

ABONDIO, ANTONIO, 23, 158, 163, 169–73, 191, 292, 296, 384, 385, 395; *170–72, 196*

Accolti, Bernardo, 19

Achilles, 58, 176

Adam, 103

Adelmann (Heidelberg seal-maker), 278

Adrian VI, Pope, 148

Aeneas, 352

Aeneid, 352

Aeolus, 352

Affo, 155

Agnes, Saint, 396

Agrippa, Marcus Vipsanius, 395

Aich, Johann von, 237

Aich, Sibylla von, 237, 390; *236–37*

Alain, Marguerite, 397

Alard, Colonel, 337

Alari Bonacolsi, Antonio, 77

Alari Bonacolsi, Pier Jacopo di Antonio. *See* ANTICO.

Alba, Ferdinand, Duke of, 162, 346, 350, 351, 356, 357–58, 359, 398–99; *357*

ALBERTI, LEON BATTISTA, 18, 41–43, 46, 59, 60, 64, 73, 129, 375–76; *42, 66*

degli Albizzi, Albiera, 379

Albizzi, Giovanna, 135–36, 382; *136, 140–41*

Albrecht VII, Archduke, 173, 385; *172*

Albrecht of Brandenburg, Cardinal, 253–54, 392, 398; *253*

d'Albret, Henry II, King of Navarre, 306, 307

d'Albret, Jeanne, Queen of Navarre, 331

Albuquerque, Eleonore, 119

Alexander V, Pope, 40

Alexander VI, Pope, 40, 97, 110, 112, 126

Alexander VII, Pope, 385

Alexander Severus, 131

Alexander the Great, 43, 296, 375

Alfonso of Aragon, King of Naples, 40, 44, 50, 55, 58, 119–20, 128, 376, 381; *118–19*

Allewijn, Floris, 371, 399

Amedeo V, Count of Savoy, 385

Amedeo VI, Count of Savoy, 385

Amazons, 79, 80

Ambrosius, Theseus, 381

Amerbach, Basilius, 187

Amor, 44, 47. *See also* cupid; Eros; Love.

Andromeda, 169

Anna, Empress, 299

Anna of Bohemia and Hungary, 241, 245

Anna of Saxony, 373

Anne of Austria (wife of Louis XIII), 341, 342–43, 397; *342*

Anne of Austria (wife of Philip II), 166

Anne of Brittany, 27, 310–11, 312, 313, 396; *311, 321*

Anne of Denmark, 359

Anne of France, 307

Annunciation fresco, 43

Antaeus, 157

Anthony, Derick, 359

ANTICO (PIER JACOPO DI ANTONIO ALARI BONACOLSI), 18, 77–80, 81, 84–85, 87, 378; *78–79*

Antiquities of the Jews, 314, 396

Antoine, Duke of Lorraine and Bar, 313, 396; *313*

Antoine de Bourbon, Duke of Vendôme, 331

Antoninus Pius, 384

Apollo, 62, 102, 375

Apollonia, 395

Apparition of the Virgin with Saints Anthony and George, 43

d'Aquino, Antonella, 55

d'Aquino, Francesco, 55, 377

Architecture, personification of, 114, 115

Ardenti, Agostino, 186, 187

Ardenti, Alessandro, 186, 189

Areas of England and Wales, 359

Aretino, Pietro, 151, 154, 181–82, 383, 386; *181*

Aretino, Spinello, 132

Ariosto, Lodovico, 181

Arothschiez, Christof, 283

Arschot, Duke of (Philip of Croy), 356–57, 398; *356, 364–65*

Asia, 127, 128

dell'Assassino, Stella, 50

Astalli, Giulia, 379

Astallia, Giulia, 84–85, 379; *72, 83–84*

de Astallis, Iuliana, 379

de Astallis, Iulio, 379

Athanasius, 394

Atlas, 339

Attemstett (Adamstetter), Andreas, 299

degli Atti, Isotta, 59, 62–64, 73, 76, 377; *38, 61–63, 70–71*

Attila, 382

Attilius Regulus, 55

attributes. *See listings under specific objects.*

AUGSBURG SCHOOL, 218–19, 389; *218*

August of Brunswick, 395

August of Saxony, 393

Augustus (Octavian), 32, 41, 165, 301, 395

Augustus I, Elector of Saxony, 202, 287, 291, 295, 394, 395; *290–91*

d'Avalos, Tommaso, 58

de Avalos, Alfonso, 377

de Avalos, Don Iñigo, 44, 55, 58, 377; *55–56, 70*

de Avalos, Iñigo the Younger, 377

de Avalos, Rodrigo, 377

Avalus, Marcus, 377

Averoldo, Altobello, 108, 109–10, 380; *109*

B

Bacchus, 350

Badile, Giovanni, 58

Balde, Melchior, 371

Baldini, Bernardo, 164, 384

Baldovinetti, 379

del Balzo, Antonia, 78, 79, 81, 379

Bandello, Matteo, 84

delle Bande Nere, Giovanni, 174

Barbara Bo . . ., 163, 384

Barbara of Austria, 180

Barbara of Brandenburg, 54, 77, 91, 119, 378

Barbarigo, Doge Agostino, 94, 104

Barbaro, Marco, 380

del Barbigia, Bernardo, 382

Barbo, Pietro. *See* Paul II, Pope.

Baron, Eguinaire, 359

de' Baroncelli, Bernardo Bandini, 128, 131

Bartolommeo di Francesca, 112

Bartolommeo di Giovanni (father of Cavino), 182

Bassiano, Alessandro, 182, 183, 185, 386–87; *183*

baton, 96, 97, 171, 347

Battle of Nude Men, The, 131

Beauty, 135. *See also* Graces.

bees, 356

Begarelli, Antonio, 189

Bellano, Bartolommeo, 127

Bellerophon Taming Pegasus, 90

Belles Heures, 32

Bellini, Gentile, 18, 87, 88, 89, 104, 127

Bellini, Giovanni, 104, 380; *104–5*

Bellini, Jacopo, 43, 106

Belliniano, Vittore, 106

Bellona, 119, 120

Beltzinger, Amalie, 392

Beltzinger, Apollonia, 252, 392

Beltzinger, Christina, 249, 392; *249–50*

Beltzinger, Erasmus the Elder, 252

Beltzinger, Erasmus the Younger, 249, 392; *249, 251, 266*

BELTZINGER GROUP, MASTER OF THE, 249, 252, 392; *249–51, 266*

Beltzinger, Heinrich, 249

Beltzinger, Johannes, 392

Bembo, Cardinal Pietro, 21, 149, 173–74, 385; *174*

Benavides, Marco Mantova, 183, 185, 386

Bendidio, Battista, 87

Bentivoglio, Alessandro, 102

Bentivoglio, Annibale, 96–97

Bentivoglio, Giovanni, 96–97, 101, 102, 379, 380; *96, 98*

Bentivoglio, Sante, 97

Bérenger, Claudine, 337

Bernard, Saint, 59

Bernardonaccio. *See* Baldini, Bernardo.

Bernini, Giovanni Lorenzo, 385

BERTOLDO DI GIOVANNI, 21, 90, 126–29, 382; *127–30, 137*

de Bethune, Maximilien. *See* Sully, Duc de.

Bey, Pierre, 187

de Birague, René, 27, 315–17, 318, 319, 335, 396–97; *316–17, 322*

BLOC, COENRAAD, 372–73, 399; *368, 373–74*

Block, Anthonis, 360

Bloxsen, Lieven, 359–60, 399; *360*

boar, 185

Bocchi, Achille, 190, 387

Bohier, Thomas, 396

Boiano, Eustachio di Francesco, 111–12, 380; *111*

BOLDÙ, GIOVANNI, 19, 102–3, 106, 115, 260, 263, 380; *103*

Boleyn, Anne, 359

BOLSTERER, HANS, 24, 255, 278, 280, 282, 292, 393–94; *269, 280–82*

BOMBARDA, 23, 186, 189–91, 387; *190*

Bona of Savoy, 77

de Bonne, François. *See* Lesdiguières, Duc de.

Bono, Pietro, 102, 380

Bonus Eventus, 128

Bonzagno, Ippolita, 185–86

book, 58, 181, 185

Book of Common Prayer, 394

Book of Concord, 291

Bora, Katharina, 240

Borgia, Cesare, 90, 91, 97, 378

Borgia, Lucrezia, 87

Bothwell, Earl of (James Hepburn), 192

Botteus, Henry, 349

Botticelli, Sandro, 18, 84, 131, 135, 379, 382

"Boudoir-Medallistik," 191

de Bouzey, Urbaine, 314

Boy with a Thorn, 273

BRACHMANN, SEVERIN, 300, 395; *300*

Brahe, Tycho, 303, 395

BRAMANTE, DONATO, 14, 112, 114–15, 149, 381; *113–14, 139*

Brancaleoni, Gentile, 100

Brandon, Robert, 358

Brantôme, 121

Brasavola, Antonio Musa, 387

Brasavola, Girolamo, 387

Brenzoni, Niccolò, 43

DA BRESCIA, FRA ANTONIO, 19, 106, 108, 380; *107–8*

da Brescia, Giovanni Antonio, 80

Briçonnet, Pierre, 396

Briçonnet, Robert, 122, 126

da Briosco, Benedetto, 116

Brunelleschi, Filippo, 41, 73

Bruni, Enrico, 115

Bruyn, Bartholomäus (Bartel), 228, 237, 391

Budé, Guillaume, 309

Burgkmair, Hans, 208, 388

Butzer, Martin, 239, 391

C

Calixtus III, Pope, 21, 40

Calliope, 391

Cambi, Belisario, 190

Cambi family, 189–90, 387

Cambi, Leonora, 189, 190–91, 387; *190*

CANDIDA, GIOVANNI FILANGIERI, 18, 27, 28, 120, 121–23, 134, 307, 309, 381–82, 396; *123–25, 140*

Candida, Niccolò, 381

Candida, Salvatore Filangieri, 381

"Candida school," 309, 396

candle, 357

Capricorn, 165, 301, 384, 385, 395

Capua, Isabella, 158

Caracalla (Marcus Aurelius Antoninus), 103, 128, 330

Caradosso (Cristoforo Caradosso Foppa), 112, 114–15, 149, 381, 383

Caraffa, Antonio, 154

Carbone, Ludovico, 95

Carchesius, 391

Cardano, Girolamo, 158, 383

Cardinal Virtues, 149

Carluccio da Padova, 87

Carme, Guillaume, 313

da Carrara, Francesco I, 16, 21, 377

da Carrara, Francesco II, 16, 21

Cassola, Hieronymus, 208

Castaglione da Ancona, Giuseppi, 58, 377

da Castelbolognese, Giovanni Bernardi, 21

di Castello, Pierantonio, 112

Castel Sigismondo, 18, 63, 64, 73

Castiglione, Baldassare, 180, 379

Castiglione, Camillo, 180, 386; *180, 196*

da Castiglione, Saba, 114, 121

Catherine, Infanta of Spain, 177

Catherine of Aragon, 160

Cato, 378

Cattaneo, Danese, 174, 356

Cavino, Battista, 182

Cavino, Camillo, 182, 386

Cavino, Giandomenico, 182, 386

CAVINO, GIOVANNI, 21–22, 182–83, 386–87; *183–85, 196*

Cavitelli, Giustiniano, 91

Cellini, Benvenuto, 14, 21, 22, 27, 149, 164, 165, 166, 173–74, 183, 309, 375, 384, 385, 395

Celtis, Konrad, 23, 214, 219, 260

centaur, 176, 177

Cerberus, 154, 155

Ceres, 185, 386, 387

Cesati, Alessandro, 21

Charles, Archduke, 171

Charles, Duke of Alençon, 307

Charles the Bold, Duke of Burgundy, 18, 122, 123, 132, 381

Charles III, Duke of Lorraine, 333

Charles II, Duke of Savoy, 385

Charles I, King of England, 306, 339

Charles V, Emperor, 24, 148, 151, 158, 160, 161, 162, 163, 165, 166, 171, 180, 202, 203–4, 205, 219, 220, 224, 237, 241, 245, 275, 280, 283–84, 284–85, 287, 301, 307, 309, 313, 316, 319, 346, 347–48, 350, 351, 357, 370, 373, 384, 394, 398; *197, 203, 283, 285, 346*

Charles V, King of France, 306, 311

Charles VI, King of France, 40, 306, 375

Charles VII, King of France, 40, 306

Charles VIII, King of France, 18, 40, 77, 97, 116, 122, 123, 126, 134, 145, 202, 228, 306, 307, 311

Charles IX, King of France, 27, 148, 306, 314, 316, 317, 331, 397

Charles Emanuel I, Duke of Savoy, 148, 176–77, 385, 387; *176*

Charles of Lorraine, Cardinal, 319

Charles of the Palatinate, 295

Charlotte de Bourbon, 372–73, 399; *368, 373*

Chastity, 81, 135. *See also* Graces.

Chaucer, Geoffrey, 27

Chiron, 176

Chosroës II, King of Persia, 36, 37

Christ, 34, 53, 54, 145, 169, 182, 240–41, 312; *241*

Christ at the Column, 112

Christ's Farewell from Mary, 392

Christian I of Saxony, 202

Christian II of Saxony, 393

Christine of Lorraine, 330, 333, 397; *324, 333*

Christoph of Braunschweig, 212, 214, 389; *212–13*

Chronicle of the Kings of Sicily, 122

Chronos, 176

Cicero, Marcus Tullius, 15, 54, 108, 185, 378

Clara Maria of Brunswick, 395

Claude de France, 309

Clement VII, Pope, 148, 166, 348

da Clivate family, 116

Clot, Ianuae Iohannes, 116

Clouet, François, 273, 309, 319

Codex Vallardi, 53, 120, 376, 381

Coeffier, Antoine. *See* Ruzé, Antoine.

Colbert, Jean Baptiste, 337, 339

Colet, John, 27

Colin, Alexander, 278, 393

Colonna, Fabrizio, 154

Colonna, Livia, 385

Colonna, Marzio, 385

Colonna, Vespasiano, 79

Colyns, Jan, 354

Commentarii Urbani, 120, 381

Commodus, 386

compass, compasses, 114, 115, 149, 151, 161, 170

Compatre, Pietro, 90

Concini, Concino, Marquis d'Ancre, 341

Conference of Cologne, 357

Confessio Augustana, 255

connoisseurship, 28, 375

Constantine the Great, 16, 32–34, 36, 41, 53, 119, 375; *30, 33*

Constantine XI, Emperor, 40, 45

Contarini, Alidea, 108

Contarini, Dea, 106, 108, 380; *108*

Contarini, Marco Antonio, 182

Contarini, Pietro, 110

de' Conti Guidi, Giovanni Antonio, 382

Copernicus, 177, 385

Coradino, 59

coral, 168, 169

Cornaro, Girolamo, 182

Cornflower, The, 352

cornucopia, 79, 127, 183, 185

da Coreggio, Niccolò, 19

Correggia, Jacoba, 85, 87, 379; *72, 85–86*

Cortés, Hernán, 220, 224, 227, 390; *226–27*

Costa, Lorenzo, 97

Costabili, Margherita, 95

COSTANZO DA FERRARA, 21, 87–89, 127, 379; *88–89*

Costière, Simon, 314, 396; *314, 323*

Council of Trent, 169, 348

Cranach, Lucas, 233, 240, 254, 284, 285, 287, 295, 391, 394

cranes, 357

Cristoforo of Mantua, 120

Crivelli, Giovanni, 375

Cross, 33, 34, 35, 36, 45, 51. *See also* crucifix.

Croy, Philip of. *See* Arschot, Duke of.

crucifix, 51, 101, 136, 145, 288. *See also* Cross.

Cujas, Jacques, 333

Cumano, Belloto, 44, 376

Cupid, 350

Cyrus, 145

D

damascening, 176, 283, 291

Danae, 91

Dancing Maidens, 151

Daniel, Samuel, 359

Dantiscus, Bishop Johannes, 220, 224

Darnley, Lord (Henry Stewart), 192

Daucher, Adolf, 204

DAUCHER, HANS, 24, 204–5, 208–9, 218, 280, 388–89; *197, 205–10*

David, 62

David and a Companion with the Slain Goliath, 80

"Day of Dupes," 341

Death, 102, 103, 258, 260

Death of Orpheus, The, 81, 87

Decembrio, Pier Candida, 44, 376

Decker, Hans, 278

Dei, Bartolommeo, 126

Delatas, Elia, 178

Delatas, Rica, 178

dell'Abbate, Niccolò, 191

Della pittura, 41, 376

della Robbia, Andrea, 136, 145

della Robbia, Francesco Iacopo, 145

della Rovere, Clemente, 122, 125–26, 382; *125*

della Rovere, Francesco. *See* Sixtus IV, Pope.

della Rovere, Francesco Maria, 40, 90–91, 110, 148, 180

della Rovere, Giovanni, 100

della Rovere, Giuliano. *See* Julius II, Pope.

della Stufa, Sigismondo, 379

della Torre, Gianello, 160–61, 384; *161*

della Torre, Giulio, 19, 122

de l'Orme, Philibert, 314

Demosthenes, 108

De re aedificatoria, 41

De Re Militari, 59

Deschler, Joachim, 24, 255, 275–78, 300, 393; 276–77

Desjours, Jeanne, 337

devices, 15, 18, 47, 64, 78, 79, 112, 128, 275, 375, 393. *See also* emblems; *imprese.*

de Vos, Jan, 291, 299–300, 394, 395; 272, 298

de Vriendt, Cornelis (Floris), 350

Diana, 53, 154, 155, 161

Diane de Poitiers, 319

Diem, Magdalena, 393

Diet of Worms, 203, 255, 388

Diocletian, 386

Diomedes, 95

Diva Giulia, 79–80, 81, 378; 79

Doarte, Francesco, 154

dog, 35, 155. *See also* greyhound.

dolphin, 79, 152, 154, 157, 183, 227, 228, 330, 386

Domitian, 384

Donatello, 18, 21, 41, 62, 78, 126, 131, 174, 377

Doria, Andrea, 22, 151, 152, 224, 383, 389; 152

Dorothea of Saxony, 292, 395; 294–95

Double Portrait, 186

dove, 115, 116, 136, 240, 241, 288

Drentwett, Balduin, 292

di Duccio, Agostino, 59

du Plessis, François, 341

de Dupleto, Johann. *See* Thewen, Johann.

Duprat, Antoine, 313

Dupré, Guillaume, 27, 176, 191, 319–20, 329–31, 337, 343, 397; 320, 323–25, 327, 329, 331–35

Durand, Germaine, 397

Duranti, Durante, 385

Dürer, Albrecht, 23, 24, 80, 106, 203, 204, 205, 208, 212, 215, 218, 219, 253, 254, 349, 389, 392; 198, 203, 215–16

Duret de Chevry, Charles, 335–36, 397; 327, 335

Dürr, Ursula, 282, 393–94; 269, 282

Dürr, Wolfgang, 282

E

eagle, 47, 50, 134, 135, 171, 203, 301, 330, 386

Ebner, Hans, 275

Edict of Nantes, 331

Edward IV, King of England, 100

Edward VI, King of England, 148, 160, 306, 346

Eglestone, Dorcas, 371–72, 399; 368, 372

Egmond, Count Jan, 369

Egmont, Count Lamoral of, 352, 358

d'Egremont, Floris, 238

Eleanora of Austria (sister of Charles V), 309, 313

Eleanora of Austria (daughter of Ferdinand I), 180, 386

elephant, 18, 62, 64, 378

Elisabeth of Bavaria-Landshut, 278

Elisabeth of Denmark, 303

Elisabeth of the Palatinate, 260

Elizabeth I, Queen of England, 28, 148, 191, 192, 306, 346, 358–59, 360, 372, 399; 358, 366–67

Elisabeth, Duchess of Braunschweig-Calenberg, 303, 395; 303

Elizabeth de Valois, 166, 319

Elizabeth of Austria, 317, 397

Emanuel Philibert, Duke of Savoy, 148, 177, 319

emblems, 15, 54, 223. *See also* devices; *imprese.*

Enzola, Gianfrancesco, 112, 375

Enzola of Parma, 132

Erasmus, Desiderius, 27, 28, 244, 348, 349–50, 398; 29, 349, 361

Erhart, Gregor, 204, 208

Erich the Elder, Duke of Braunschweig-Calenberg, 303

Erich the Younger, Duke of Braunschweig-Calenberg, 303

ermine, 310, 396

Ermine, Collar of, 100

Ernst, Archduke, 173

Eros, 102, 103. *See also* Amor.

d'Este, Alfonso I, 40, 132

d'Este, Alfonso II, 148, 180, 190, 386, 387

d'Este, Baldassare, 59

d'Este, Beatrice, 19

d'Este, Borso, 40, 91, 95

d'Este, Eleonora, 180

d'Este, Ercole I, 40, 77, 91, 94

d'Este, Ercole II, 148, 177, 180, 181, 186, 189, 190, 387

d'Este, Ferrante, 87

d'Este, Francesco, 180

d'Este, Ginevra, 43, 73, 376

d'Este, Ippolito, 180

d'Este, Isabella, 19, 77, 78, 90, 114, 378

d'Este, Leonello, 18, 40, 43, 44, 46, 47–50, 51, 53, 58, 59, 60, 91, 95, 376; 47–48, 66

d'Este, Lucrezia, 180

d'Este, Luigi, 180

d'Este, Niccolò III, 40, 50, 91, 376

Euclid, 115

Eugenius IV, Pope, 40, 41, 43, 46, 51, 73

F

da Fabriano, Gentile, 43

Faella, Giacomo, 19

Faith, 103. *See also* Virtues.

falcon, falconry, 35, 125

Falkenberg, Ludwig, 239

Fame, 341, 342

da Fano, Pietro, 103

Farnese, Cardinal Alessandro, 351

Farnese, Duke Alessandro, 148, 346, 351, 357

Farnese, Ottavio, 148, 164, 177, 351

Farnese, Pier Luigi, 148, 151

Faustina, Empress, 387

Faustina Romana, 163

Feckeman, Abel, 399

fence, 312

Ferdinand, Archduke, 171

Ferdinand I, Emperor, 148, 151, 171, 180, 202, 241, 244, 245, 257, 258, 263, 275, 283–84, 346, 393, 394; 283

Ferdinand II, Emperor, 148, 173

Ferdinand I, King of Aragon, 119

Ferdinand II, King of Aragon, 348

Ferdinand of Toledo, 357

Fernberger, Johann, 257–58, 392; 258–59, 266

Fernberger, Ulrich the Elder, 392

Fernberger, Ulrich the Younger, 257–58, 392; 258–59, 266

Ferrante I, King of Naples, 40, 78, 87, 97, 100, 120

Ferrante II, King of Naples, 40, 90

Ferry II of Lorraine, 381

Fer vom Berge, Balthasar, 392

"Festival of Fools," 352

Ficino, Marsilio, 382

da Fiesole, Mino, 132

Filarete, 165

Fiorentino, Adriano, 90–91, 379; 90, 92, 138

Fiorentino, Niccolò, 21, 28, 85, 87, 132, 134–36, 145, 152, 356, 382; 2, 132–36, 140–42

Firmian zu Kronmetz, Baron Georg von, 234

Fischer, Peter the Younger, 24

fleur-de-lis, 310, 396

Flicker, Barbara, 241

Flicker, Hans, 241

Florence, personification of, 132

Flötner, Kaspar, 282

Flötner, Peter, 241, 282–84, 292, 392, 394; 283

de Foix, Marguerite, 115–16, 381, 396; *116–17*

Foppa, Cristoforo Caradosso. *See* Caradosso.

Fortitude, 64. *See also* Virtues.

Fortune, 78, 79, 90, 157, 158, 228, 341, 356

fountain, 33, 34, 53, 60, 62, 160, 161

Fountain of Life, 34, 53

Four Books on Human Proportions, 218

France, personification of, 341

Francesco of Saluzzo, 116

Francia, Francesco, 18, 94, 114

Francinae, F., 81

Francis, Dauphin of France, 313, 319

Francis II, Duke of Brittany, 311

Francis I, King of France, 27, 148, 151, 174, 202, 205, 228, 273, 275, 306, 307, 309, 313, 316, 319, 346, 348, 385, 393, 396, 398; *273–74, 309*

Francis II, King of France, 148, 166, 192, 306, 319

Frauenberger family, 300

Frederick I Barbarossa, 95

Frederick of Brandenburg, 394

Frederick II, Count Palatine, 205, 393

Frederick III, Count Palatine, 373

Frederick II, Emperor, 375

Frederick III, Emperor, 23, 40, 78, 95, 104, 122, 123, 128–29, 382; *128*

Frederick II, King of Denmark, 348

Frederick III of Saxony, 90, 202, 203, 204, 287

FRENCH SCHOOL, 307, 309; *307, 308, 309*

Frundsberg, Kaspar von, 234

Frundsberg, Margarete von, 233–34, 237, 390; *25, 200, 234*

Fugger, Anton, 228

Fugger, Georg, 241, 391

Fugger, Hans, 278

Fugger, Hester, 278

Fugger, Jakob, 245, 278

Fugger, Veronica, 278

Furtenagel, Jörg, 233

Furtenagel, Lukas, 233, 390; *200, 232–33*

G

Gabriele of Saluzzo, 116

Galeotti, Pietro di Francesco, 164

GALEOTTI, PIETRO PAOLO, 22, 149, 157, 163, 164–65, 169, 384; *164*

Galerius Maximianus, 386

Gambello, Antonio, 104

GAMBELLO, VETTOR DI ANTONIO, 19, 103–4, 106, 380; *104–5*

Garter, Order of the, 100

GAUVAIN, JACQUES, 27, 313, 396; *313*

GEBEL, MATTHES, 24, 103, 204, 215, 219, 244, 252, 254–55, 257–58, 263, 276, 280, 284, 388, 392, 393; *255–62, 266–68*

Gebhart, Utz, 393

Geminianus, Saint, 382

Gemma Augustea, 165

Gendorf, Christoph, 393

Genius, 183

Geometry, 115

Georg, Count of Württemberg, 248

Georg Johann of the Palatinate, 395

DI GEREMIA, CRISTOFORO, 18, 21, 119–20, 381; *118–19*

Gerhard, Hubert, 299

Geta, Pulius Septimius, 128

Geuder von Heroldsberg, Hans, 299

Geuder von Heroldsberg, Julius, 297, 299, 395; *297*

Geuder von Heroldsberg, Maria Magdalena, 395

Ghiberti, Lorenzo, 62, 377

Ghirlandaio, 84, 135–36, 379

Ghisulfo, Bernardo, 76

Giacondo, Fra, 114

Giambologna, 176

Gianlodovico of Saluzzo, 116

del Gilio, Giacomo, 94

Gillis, Peter, 349

di Giorgio, Francesco, 18

Giovanna of Austria, 177

Giovio, Paolo, 89, 379

Girolamo, Giovanni, 181

Giulia of Gazzuolo, 379

globe, 55, 58, 60, 166, 168, 301, 356

Glueknecht, Eva, 300, 395; *300*

Glueknecht, Michael, 300

Golden Fleece, Order of the, 152, 154, 171, 203, 209, 211, 370, 388, 389, 394; *283, 285, 301, 347, 356*

Golden Legend, 36, 37

Goltzius, Hendrik, 343

Goltzius, Hubert, 314

Gonzaga, Alessandro, 54

Gonzaga, Alfonso, 177, 189

Gonzaga, Camillo, 177

Gonzaga, Carlo, 54, 378

Gonzaga, Cecilia, 44, 52–53, 54, 85, 377; *12, 52, 57, 69*

Gonzaga, Cesare, 151

Gonzaga, Elisabetta, 19, 51, 73, 90–91, 379; *90, 92, 138*

Gonzaga, Evangelisto, 378

Gonzaga, Federigo I, 40, 76–77, 378; *77*

Gonzaga, Federigo II, 40, 76, 148, 180

Gonzaga, Ferrante, 148, 151, 154

Gonzaga, Ferdinando II, 148, 176

Gonzaga, Cardinal Francesco, 76, 94, 378

Gonzaga, Francesco II, 19, 40, 77, 91, 378

Gonzaga, Francesco III, 148

Gonzaga, Francesco IV, 330, 331

Gonzaga, Gianfrancesco, 40, 44, 52, 78, 96, 376, 378

Gonzaga, Gianlucido, 54

Gonzaga, Guglielmo, 148, 180

Gonzaga, Ippolita, 22, 23, 154–55, 158, 161, 383; *143, 153–55*

Gonzaga, Bishop Lodovico, 78, 84, 94

Gonzaga, Lodovico II, 40, 43, 44, 54, 77, 78, 103, 119, 376, 378

Gonzaga, Magdalena, de', 378

Gonzaga, Margherita, 50, 54

Gonzaga, Rodolfo, 378

Gonzaga, Vicenzo, 148

Gonzaga Colonna, Giulia, 79

Gonzaga di Rodigo, Gianfrancesco, 78–79, 91, 94, 378; *78*

Gonzalo de Córdoba, 116, 384

Gorgons, 168, 169, 348. *See also* Medusa.

Gossembrot, Ulrich, 23, 62

Gower, George, 358

Graces, Three, 21, 135, 136, 314

Gramaye, Thomas, 350

Grandi, Vincenzo, 181

de Granvelle, Antoine Perrenot, 151, 177, 350, 351–52, 383, 398; *352–53*

Grati, Andrea di Giacomo, 102, 380

Grati, Carlo, 101–2, 380; *99, 101, 138*

Grati, Giacomo di Peregrino d'Antonio, 101–2, 380

Gratiadei, Antonio, 122, 127, 382

Greece, personification of, 127, 128

Gregory XIII, Pope, 148, 158, 317

greyhound, 111, 112, 165, 380

Grien, Hans Baldung, 228

Grimani, Antonio, 108

Grimani, Cardinal Domenico, 80

Grünewald, Matthias, 254

de la Gruthuse, Jean, 122, 381

Guacialoti, Andrea. *See* Guazzaloti, Andrea.

Guarino da Verona, 43, 47, 54, 59–60, 62, 377; *60*

Guazzalotti, Andrea, 21, 122, 131

Guerrino da Gubbio, 380

de Guise, Charles. *See* Charles of Lorraine, Cardinal.

de Guise, Duke Francis, 319

de Guise, John. See John of Lorraine, Cardinal.

Guttenberg, Johann von, 392

H

Hadrian, 128, 384, 386, 387

HAGENAUER, FRIEDRICH, 24, 219, 220, 228, 230–31, 233–34, 237–40, 245, 252, 273, 284, 388, 390–91; *25, 200, 228–39*

Hagenauer, Nikolaus, 228

Hainhofer, Philipp, 299

Hallerin von Hallerstein, Maria, 299

Hamer, Leonhart, 233

de Hanna, Daniel, 152

de Hanna, Martin, 22, 151–52, 383; *152*

Hartman, Sigmund, 282

Hecate, 155

Hedio, Kaspar, 239, 391

Heinrich VIII, Duke of Braunschweig-Wolfenbüttel, 212

Heinrich Julius, Duke of Braunschweig-Wolfenbüttel, 295

Helena, Saint, 34, 35, 36

Helmschmid, Kolman, 391

Hengel, Christoph, 249, 392

Henneberg, Count Poppo of, 303

Henrietta Maria of France, 339

Henry VIII, King of England, 27, 148, 160, 192, 202, 205, 208, 227, 228, 306, 346, 359

Henry II, King of France, 27, 148, 180, 192, 202, 228, 306, 314, 317–19, 397; *318*

Henry III, King of France, 148, 306, 315, 317, 318, 331, 397

Henry IV, King of France, 148, 176–77, 306, 320, 329, 330–31, 333, 334, 336, 343, 397–98; *320, 328–29, 343*

Hepburn, James. See Bothwell, Earl of.

Heraclius, 16, 32, 35–37, 375; *34–35, 65*

Hercules, 34, 157, 181, 339, 388

Hermann, Georg, 244, 257, 392, 393; *256–57, 266*

Héroard, Jean, 337

de Héry, Claude, 397

HILLIARD, NICHOLAS, 28, 358–59, 399; *358, 366–67*

Hippocrene, 173

Hirschvogelin, Brigitta, 299

hive, 356

Hofmann, Jakob, 255, 292, 392, 395

Hogenberg, Remigius, 359

Holbein, Hans the Younger, 80, 227–28, 238, 349, 390

Holdermann, Georg, 296, 297, 395

Holy Annunziata, Order of the, 176, 385

Holy Ghost, Order of the, 317, 330, 336, 339, 343

Homer, 377

Honolt vom Luchs, Hans, 223

Honorius of Autun, 54, 377

Hoorn, Count of (Philip de Montmorency), 352, 358

Hope, 152, 214. *See also* Virtues.

Horace, 158

I

Idea del Tempio della Pittura, 112

Iliad, 58

Imhoff, Ludwig, 215

imprese, 42, 79, 81, 85, 359, 375, 378. *See also* devices; emblems.

India, Bernardino, 181

Innocent VIII, Pope, 40, 126, 132, 134

Isabella, Infanta of Spain, 173

Isabella of Portugal, 151, 241, 245

Isabella, Queen of Castile, 348

Isabelle de Bourbon, 123

Isabetta di Nocolo, 43

Isenburg-Grenzau, Count Johann von, 239, 391

Iustitia, personification of, 181

J

Jacoba, Duchess in Bavaria, 260, 392–93; *260–61, 268*

Jacobus de Voragine, 36, 37

Jacquet, Germain, 397

Jacquet, Mathieu, 319, 397

Jacquet, Nicolas-Gabriel, 343

James I, King of England, 306, 346, 358, 372

James IV, King of Scotland, 192

James V, King of Scotland, 192

Jamnitzer, Wenzel, 280, 291, 292, 395; *272, 292–93*

Janus, 166

Janus Secundus, 359

Jean de France, Duke of Berry, 16, 32, 37, 53, 375

Jeannin, Pierre, 333–35, 397; *325, 334*

Joachim I of Brandenburg, 254, 303

Joachim II of Brandenburg, 394

Joanna of Portugal, 158

Joanna II, Queen of Naples, 40, 119–20

Joham, Heinrich, 391

Johann of Saxony, 202, 287

Johann Friedrich of Saxony, 202, 285, 287, 394; *270, 286–87*

Johann Georg of Brandenburg, 291, 394; *290–91*

Johann Georg of Saxony, 393

John, Duke of Calabria, 122, 128, 381

John of Austria (Don John), 346, 357

John of Lorraine, Cardinal, 149, 163, 384

John VIII Paleologus, 40, 43, 44–46, 376; *45*

JONGHELINCK, JACQUES, 28, 169, 350–52, 359, 372, 398–99; *344, 351–57, 362–65*

Jonghelinck, Jan, 350

Jonghelinck, Nicolas, 350

Jonghelinck, Peter, 350

Jonghelinck, Thomas, 350

Josephus, Flavius, 314, 396

Juan II, King of Navarre, 120

Juana the Mad, 348

Julius Caesar, 32, 131

Julius II, Pope, 40, 97, 104, 110, 112, 114, 115, 125–26, 134, 148, 382; *125*

Julius III, Pope, 148, 182

Juno, 352

Jupiter, 42, 91

K

Kasimir of Brandenburg-Ansbach, 280

Kavadh-Siroe, King of Persia, 36

Kels, Georg, 391

KELS, HANS (Elder and Younger), 24, 241, 244, 245, 248, 388, 391; *243–44, 248*

Kels, Veit, 391

Kepler, Johannes, 303, 395

Ketzel, Barbara, 252–53, 392; *252*

Ketzel, Wolf, 253

Key, Adriaan, 373

Khelner, Maria, 300

Khevenhüller, Johann von, 170, 385

Kirchberger family, 392

Kolb (die-engraver), 176

Kolnpock, Nikolaus, 273, 393; *264, 269, 273*

KRAFFT, HANS, 203–4, 388; *197*

Kreler, Elisabeth, 245, 248, 391; *247, 266*

Kreler, Laux, 244–45, 248, 391; *246, 266*

Kress, Christoph, 255, 392; *255*

L

Ladislav, King of Hungary, 95

Laocoön, 174

Last Judgment, 80, 155

Laurana, Francesco, 18, 27, 122, 381

laurel, laurel wreath, 43, 60, 62, 76, 79, 85, 87, 112, 132, 161, 203, 219, 255, 257, 263, 273, 278, 282, 300, 301, 309, 341, 343, 347, 351, 359

LECLERC, NICOLAS, 310–11; *310–11, 321*

Lemercier, Jacques, 343

Lenoir, Alexandre, 397

Leo X, Pope, 40, 114, 148, 151, 173, 181

Leone, Ambrogio, 114

LEONI, LEONE, 22, 23, 149, 151–52, 154–55, 161, 163, 166, 177, 182, 183, 191, 348, 350, 352, 360, 383, 387; *143, 152–56*

Leoni, Pompeo, 28, 151, 158, 191, 360

Leopold Wilhelm, Archduke, 280

Lepère, Colin, 310

Lepère, Jean, 310, 313

Lepère, Louis, 310

Le Pois, Antoine, 314

Lercari, Franco, 157

Lesdiguières, Duc de (François de Bonne), 337

Leslie, John, 192, 388

di Leuti, Pellegrino, 154

Leyenberger, Fräulein (mistress of Maximilian I), 123

Lhuillier, Nicolas, 336

Liberal Arts, the, 135

Ligsalz, Sebastian, 230–31, 390; *200, 229–30*

Ligsalz, Ursula, 231, 390; *200, 231*

lily, 85, 134, 203

Limbourg brothers, 32, 37

lion, 33, 34, 44, 127, 168, 187, 310, 330, 339, 357

Lippi, Fra Filippo, 186

Livy, 111

Lixignolo, 59

llama, 166

Lockey, Rowland, 399

Lodovico II, Marquess of Saluzzo, 116

Loesch von Hilgertshausen, Augustin, 228, 230, 390, 392; *228*

Löffelholz (?). *See* Unknown youth.

Löffelholz family, 218

Löffelholz, Wilhelm, 389

Loffredo, Ferrante, 161–63, 384; *162–63, 193*

Lomazzo, Giampaolo, 112, 114, 164, 381

Lopez de Avalos, Ruy, 55

Lorch, Melchior, 218

Loredano, Jacopo, 109, 110–11, 380; *111*

Louis III, Duke of Anjou, 120

Louis XI, King of France, 40, 123, 306, 307

Louis XII, King of France, 27, 40, 116, 148, 151, 158, 202, 306, 307, 309, 310–11, 312, 313, 396; *310, 321*

Louis XIII, King of France, 306, 329, 330, 331, 334, 339, 341, 342, 343; *329*

Louis XIV, King of France, 27, 306, 337, 339, 342–43, 397; *342*

Louise of Savoy, 307, 309, 395–96; *307–8, 321*

Love, 81, 85, 86, 135. *See also* Amor; Graces.

love-knots, 177. *See also* Savoy knots.

Ludwig II, King of Hungary and Bohemia, 209, 211, 284, 389, 390; *197, 209–10*

Ludwig X of Bavaria, 228, 390

Luther, Martin, 233, 239, 240–41, 255, 287, 391; *240–41, 242, 265*

LYSIPPUS THE YOUNGER, 18–19, 21, 120–21, 122, 134, 381; *121*

M

Machiavelli, Pietro, 382

Madalene Mantuana, 81, 87

Maddalena Rossi, 87

Madruzzo, Cardinal Cristoforo, 384

Maenads, 87, 379

Magdalena Mantuana, 80–81, 84, 87, 378–79; *72, 81–82*

Magna Graecia, 127, 128, 162, 384

da Maiano, Benedetto, 135

Maier, Konrad, 255, 257, 392; *256–57, 266*

Malatesta, Carlo, 40, 51, 73

Malatesta, Domenico, 18, 40, 44, 50–52, 73, 102, 376; *17, 49–50, 67–68*

Malatesta, Galeotto Roberto, 40, 51, 73

Malatesta, Giovanni, 377

Malatesta, Guidobaldo, 40, 148, 180

Malatesta, Pandolfo III, 16, 40, 51, 73

Malatesta, Paola, 52

Malatesta, Sallustio, 63

Malatesta, Sigismondo Pandolfo, 18, 40, 44, 47, 50, 51, 59, 63, 64, 73, 76, 376, 378; *64, 70, 74–75*

Maler, Christian, 292, 394

Maler, Hans, 223–24

MALER, VALENTIN, 24, 169, 263, 291–92, 394–95; *272, 292–95*

Malipieri, Francesco, 110

Malipieri, Vincenzo, 110

Malpaghino da Ravenna, Giovanni, 54

Mancini, Antonio, 32

Manfredi, Carlo, 91, 94

Manfredi, Galeotto, 94

Mansart, François, 343

Mantegna, Andrea, 18, 76, 77, 78, 80, 119

MANTUAN SCHOOL, 84, 85, 87, 379; *72, 83, 84, 85, 86*

Manuel II Paleologus, 36, 40, 45

Marasca, Giulio, 120, 121

Marcello, Fra Antonio, 106

Marcellus II, Pope, 148

Marchi, Francesco, 351

de Marcillat, Guglielmo di Pietro, 177

Marcus Aurelius, 119

Marcus Aurelius, Column of, 129

Marcus Curtius, 76

de la Mare, Guillaume, 122

MARENDE, JEAN, 311–13, 396; *312*

Marescotti, Antonio, 59

Margaret of Austria (wife of Ottavio Farnese), 164

Margaret of Austria (wife of Philibert II), 311–13, 348, 351, 396; *312*

Margaret of Bavaria, 77

Margaret of France, 177

Margaret of Parma, 350, 398; *344, 362*

Margaret of Valois, 331

Margaret Tudor, 192

Margaretha of Baden-Spanheim, 263

Margarita (wife of Federigo Gonzaga), 180

Marguerite de Bourbon, 307

Marguerite of Angoulême, 307, 395–96; *307, 321*

marguerites, 312

de' Mari, Ascanio, 164

Maria, Empress, 171, 385; *171*

Maria, Infanta of Spain, 301

Maria Maddalena of Austria, 176

Maria of Aragon, 44, 50

Maria of Austria, 158, 383

Maria of Hungary, 151, 283–84, 351, 394; *283*

Marie of Castile, 120

de Marillac, Michel, 341

Marine Venus, 356

Marinoni, Cassandra, 157

Marot, Clément, 309

Mars, 79, 81, 119, 128, 330, 378

Mars and Victory, 81, 378

Marsuppini, Christofano, 175

Marsuppini, Elena, 175–76, 385; *175*

Martelli, Camilla, 177

Martin V, Pope, 40, 50, 51, 73

Martin, Richard, 371–72, 399; *368, 372*

Martin, Richard the Younger, 372

Martinengo, Camillo, 110

Martinengo, Marc Antonio, 103, 108

Martinengo da Barco family 110

Martinioni, Gianfrancesco, 149, 163

Mary Magdalene, 81

Mary of Burgundy, 122, 123, 311, 313, 347–48, 381; *123, 140*

Mary of Guise, 192

Mary Queen of Scots, 191–92, 388; *192,*

Mary Tudor, Queen of England, 28, 148, 158, 160, 166, 306, 346, 357, 359, 383; *20, 144, 159–60*

Marzano, Marino, 87

Masaccio, 41

Maserano, Filippo, 102, 380

Maslitzer, Hans, 282

Masolino da Panicale, 129

"Master of the Cardinal Albrecht," 220, 389

"Master of the Cardinal Bembo," 149, 383

"Master of the Simon Pistorius," 220, 389

Matsys, Christina, 349

Matsys, Cornelis, 348

Matsys, Jan, 348

MATSYS, QUENTIN, 28, 348–50, 398; *29, 349, 361*

Matthias, Emperor, 148, 172–73, 202, 299, 301, 303, 385; *172*

Maurice of Saxony, 202, 287, 289, 394

Maximianus, 386

Maximilian III, Archduke, 172–73, 299, 385; *172*

Maximilian I, Emperor, 18, 23–24, 40, 97, 102, 122, 123, 202, 203, 204, 208, 214–15, 218, 219, 230, 241, 278, 311, 312, 313, 347, 381, 388; *123–24, 140, 207–8*

Maximilian II, Emperor, 148, 151, 169, 171–72, 173, 202, 275, 301, 303, 385; *171–72, 196*

Mazzafirri, Michele, 176

Mechthilde of Bavaria, 260

"Medalist of 1523," the, 106, 109, 112

medallic techniques, 13–14, 21, 27, 32, 104, 166, 170, 174, 176, 204, 233, 263, 284, 303, 315, 337, 339, 348, 375. *See also* stone models; wax, wax models; wood models.

de' Medici, Alessandro, 148, 164

de' Medici, Carlo, 376

de' Medici, Catherine, 192, 314, 316, 317, 318, 319, 331, 333, 397

de' Medici, Cosimo ("the Elder"), 18, 40, 134, 382

de' Medici, Cosimo I, 148, 158, 164, 165, 166, 175, 180, 384

de' Medici, Cosimo II, 148, 176, 306, 330

de' Medici, Ferdinando I, 148, 176, 306, 330, 333

de' Medici, Filippo, 127, 129

de' Medici, Francesco I, 148, 166, 177

de' Medici, Francesco II, 330

de' Medici, Gian Giacomo, 151, 157

de' Medici, Giovanni, 376

de' Medici, Giuliano, 131, 134; *129*

de' Medici, Lorenzo, 40, 62, 126, 127, 128, 129, 132, 134, 135, 359, 382; *129–30, 132–33*

de' Medici, Lucrezia, 178, 180, 190, 191, 386, 387; *178–79*

de' Medici, Marie, 330–31, 333, 334, 385, 397; *320, 329*

de' Medici, Piero, 40, 59, 64

Medusa, 62, 119, 169

Mehmed II, Sultan, 21, 40, 59, 87, 88–89, 127–28, 379, 382; *88–89, 127, 137*

Meitting, Wilhelm, 233

Melanchthon, Philipp, 228, 237, 238–39, 240, 244, 280, 391; *238*

Melioli, Bartolommeo, 18, 87, 378, 379

Melsi, Giovanni, 185

Memling, Hans, 348

Memmo, Doge Marcantonio, 330, 331, 397; *323, 331–32*

Mengozzi, Lodovico, 63

Mercator, Elizabeth, 238, 391

Mercator, Michael, 237–38, 391; *238*

Meringer, Katharina, 220

Meringer, Lienhard (Lux), 218, 220; *220–21*

Michelangelo, 18, 21, 22, 80, 126, 151, 155, 383; *155–56*

Michelantonio, Marquess of Saluzzo, 116

Michiel, Marcantonio, 87–88

Michiel, Niccolò, 106, 108, 110, 380; *107–8*

Michiel, Simone, 106, 110, 380

Miette, Jean, 122, 381

Might, 357

"MILANESE SCHOOL," 149, 168–69, 383, 385; *149, 150, 168, 194*

da Milano, Laurana, 122, 381

da Milano, Pietro, 122, 381

Milicz, Nickel, 289

Minerva, 62, 79, 106, 170, 330, 378, 386

mirror, 121, 149

mirror-medals, 121

Miseroni, 387

MODERNO (GALEAZZO MONDELLA), 80–81, 87; *72, 81–82*

MOLA, GASPARE, 176–77, 385; *176*

Molinet, Jean, 123

Mondella, Galeazzo. *See* MODERNO.

Mondella, Giambattista, 80

Mondella, Girolamo, 80

da Montefeltro, Antonio, 91

da Montefeltro, Emilia Pia, 91

da Montefeltro, Federigo, 40, 54, 73, 90, 91, 97, 100–101, 380; *100*

da Montefeltro, Giovanna, 100

da Montefeltro, Guid'Antonio, 40, 51, 100

da Montefeltro, Guidobaldo, 90

da Montefeltro, Oddantonio, 40, 52, 100

da Montefeltro, Violante, 51

Montfort, Count Hugo of, 282

de Montmorency, Anne, 319

de Montmorency, Philip. *See* Hoorn, Count.

moon, 36, 37, 53, 127, 154

Mor, Anthonis, 28, 160, 360

More, Sir Thomas, 27, 348, 349

Morillon, Antoine, 359

mottoes, 15, 43, 64, 166, 169, 176, 177, 203, 258, 275, 285, 349, 351, 352, 354, 357, 359

de Mucini, Maria, 382

Mülich, Christoph, 220

Müller, Anna, 241

Müllner, Euphrosina, 263

Müllner, Dr. Johann, 263

Muses, 60, 62, 134, 173

myrtle, 123, 125, 174

N

Nasi, Grazia, 178, 386; *178*

Nasi, Grazia (aunt), 178

Nasi, Joseph, 178

Nasi, Samuel, 178

Necklace, Order of the, 385

Neefe, Johann and Kaspar, 299, 395

Nellenburg and Thüngen, Count Cristoph von, 234, 237, 390; *200, 234–35*

Neptune, 154, 350, 352

Nereids, 119, 381

Nero, 183, 382, 384

Neroni family, 382

Nessus, 81

Neudörfer, Johann, 275

NEUFAHRER, LUDWIG, 24, 263, 273, 275, 280, 393; *264, 269, 273–74*

Neumann, Katharina, 393

Nicholas V, Pope, 21, 40

Nicolaus (Ferrarese master), 59

Nicoletto da Modena, 80

Niger, Gaius Pescennius, 185

de Nores, Giovanni, 112

Norsa, Abramo Emanuele, 178

da Novara, Bartolino, 378

nudity, 33, 44, 53, 60, 78, 79, 90, 94, 102, 103, 109, 114, 377

Nuremberg castle, 284

Nuremberg patrician, 296–97, 395; *272, 296*

NUREMBERG SCHOOL, 219–20, 389; *219*

"NUREMBERG 1525–1527" workshop, 24, 228, 252–54, 255, 392; *252–53*

O

oak, 85, 134, 135, 287

Occasion, 378

Octavian. *See* Augustus.

Oefner, Adam, 248

olive, olive branch, 55, 351, 354

Olivier, René, 337

OLIVIERI, MAFFEO, 19, 103, 108–11, 380; *109, 111*

Opportunity, 81, 378

Orlando Furioso, 181

d'Orléans, Charles, 311

d'Orléans, Charles, Count of Angoulême, 307

Orsi, Lelio, 186, 189, 387

Orsini, Virginio, 90

Ottheinrich, Count of the Rhenish Palatinate, 204, 205, 278, 280, 388, 393; *269, 278–79*

OTTHEINRICH OF THE PALATINATE GROUP, MASTER OF THE, 278, 280, 393; *269, 278–79*

Ovid, 169, 185, 387

Ovid moralisé, 91

owl, 104

P

palisade. *See* fence.

Palissy, Bernard, 190, 387

palm, palm branch, 119, 341, 343, 351

Paltroni, P., 380

de' Paolo, Alessandra di Lionardo, 132

Paolo di Ragusa, 120

Papafava, Albertino, 106, 380

Parmigianino, 191

DE' PASTI, MATTEO, 18, 41, 42, 59–64, 377–78; *38, 60–64, 70–71, 74–75*

PASTORINO DE' PASTORINI, 22, 27, 169, 177–78, 190, 191, 385–86; *178–80, 196*

Patanella, Antonio, 383

Paul II, Pope, 40, 41, 95, 119, 129, 376, 377

Paul III, Pope, 148, 151, 154, 173

Paul IV, Pope, 148, 162

Paumgartner, Balthasar, 395

Paumgartner, Hieronymus, 276–77, 393; *277*

Pausanias, 386

Pavoni, Vittorio, 382

de Paxi, Michiel, 32

Pazzi Conspiracy, the, 129, 131–32, 134, 382; *129–30*

de' Pazzi, Francesco, 131

Peace, 158, 160

Peace of Augsburg, 348

Peck, Hans Peter, 275; *275*

PECK, KUNZ, 275, 393; *275*

Peck, Linhard, 275; *275*

Peck, Sebald, 275, 393; *275*

Pegasus, 134, 173, 174

Peisser, Hans, 275

pelican, 53, 54, 377

"Pelican in her Piety," 54

Pendaglia, Bartolommeo, 91, 94–96, 379; *93–95, 138*

Pendaglia, Gabriele, 95

Penitence, 103

Pérez, Gonzalo, 166, 168, 384

Perréal, Jean, 396

Perrenot, Frédéric, 359

Perseus, 91, 169

Perseus, 164

Peruzzi, Baldassare, 14

Peterle, Michael, 170

Petrarch, Francesco, 15, 16, 23, 27, 54, 64

Petzold, Hans, 218, 389, 395

Pfinzing brothers, 275, 389, 393

Pfinzing, Melchior, 211, 214–15, 389; *214*

Pfinzing, Paul, 389

Pfinzing, Seifried, 214

Pfinzing von Heuchling, Seifried, 395

Philethicus, Martinus, 120

Philibert II, Duke of Savoy, 306, 311–13, 396; *312*

Philibert of Baden, 260

Philip II, King of Spain, 22, 151, 152, 158, 160, 161, 165, 166, 168, 169, 177, 180, 301, 319, 346, 347–48, 350, 351, 352, 356, 357, 358, 359, 373, 384, 398; *166–67, 195, 347*

Philip of Bresse, Duke of Savoy, 306, 307

Philipp, Count of the Rhenish Palatinate, 204, 205, 280, 388, 389; *205–6*

Philipp I of Baden, 260

Philipp II of Baden, 260

Philippe de Gueldre, 313

phoenix, 81, 84, 85, 377

Piantanida, Pietro, 149, 163

Piccinino, Niccolò, 44, 100

Piccolomini, Aeneas Sylvius. *See* Pius II, Pope.

Pico della Mirandola, 136, 382

Piero di Cosimo, 84, 379

Pigna, Giambattista, 190, 387

Pigna, Violante Brasavola, 190, 387

Pillars of Hercules, 203, 285, 388, 394

Pilon, Claude, 397

PILON, GERMAIN, 27, 314–19, 320, 330, 335, 358, 396–97; *316–18, 322*

Pilon, Jean, 330

Pilon, Raphael, 397

Pinturicchio, 88, 115

Pio di Savoia family, 385

Pirckheimer, Willibald, 23, 349

da Pisa, Bartolommeo, 43

PISANELLO (PISANO), ANTONIO, 15–16, 18, 41, 43–59, 89, 96, 102, 120, 375, 376–77, 382; *12, 17, 45, 47–50, 52, 53, 55–57, 58, 66–70*

Pistorius, Johannes, 239, 391

Pius II, Pope, 21, 23, 40, 52, 73, 101

Pius III, Pope, 40

Pius IV, Pope, 148, 151, 169

Pius V, Pope, 148

planets, allegories of, 350

Plautilla, Empress, 330

Pliny, 121, 183, 384, 386

Ploed, Brigitha, 392

Ploed, Georg, 103, 258, 392; *258, 267*

Ploed, Hans, 392

Ploed, Susanna, 260

Pluto, 154, 155

Poggini, Domenico, 22, 164, 165

POGGINI, GIANPAOLO, 22, 28, 165–66, 384, 398; *166–67, 195*

Poggini, Michele, 165

Poliziano, Angelo, 131

Pollaiuolo, Antonio, 131, 379

Pompey the Great, 154

Pontano, Giovanni, 90

da Pordenone, Giovanni Antonio, 152

Porsena, Lars, 111

Portigiani, 176

Postumus, 386

presentation pieces, 19, 203–4, 311, 312, 315, 331, 333

Prevedari, Bernardo, 115

Prieur, Barthelémy, 320

Prieur, Madeleine, 320

PRIMAVERA, JACOPO, 191–92, 387–88; *192*

Principles of Measurement, The, 218

Prometheus, 176, 385

Prose della volgar lingua, 173

Proserpina, 154, 155

Prudence, 149. *See also* Virtues.

Pütt, Johann Philipp von der. *See* VON DER PÜTT, JOHANN PHILIPP.

putto, 103, 110, 258, 260

Pygmalion, 186

Q

Quartararo, Riccardo, 87

R

Raab, reconquest of, 395

Raiboldini, Francesco. *See* Francia, Francesco.

Raising of Drusiana, 131

Ramelli, Benedetto, 273

Raphael, 80, 115

Regiomontanus, 219

Regnier, Pierre, 337

Rehle, Joachim, 218, 223–24, 390; *224–25*

Rehlinger, Elisabeth, 223

Reichlinger von Horgau, Anna, 228

Reihing, Barbara, 244; *243, 244*

Reihing, Ludwig, 244

Reineck, Count Thomas von, 239, 391

REINHART, HANS THE ELDER, 24, 254, 284–85, 394; *270, 271, 285–89*

Reinhart, Hans the Younger, 284, 394

René, Duke of Anjou, 120, 122

René, Duke of Lorraine, 313

Renée de Bourbon, 313, 396; *313*

de Requesens, Luis, 346, 350

Resurrection, 189

Reusner, Nicholas, 330

Rhode, Johann, 212

Ribisch, Heinrich, 255, 257, 392; *256–57, 266*

Riccio, Andrea, 182, 183, 185, 386

Riccio, Battista, 386

Richard III, King of England, 73

Richelieu, Cardinal, 330, 331, 337, 339, 397; *26, 328*

RICHIER, JACOB, 336–37, 397; *304, 326, 336*

Ridolfi, Girolamo, 134, 382; *134*

Ridolfi, Lodovico, 134

Ripa, Cesare, 121, 183

Roberti della Grana, Gianfrancesco, 77

Rocca Malatestiana, 73

Rochefort, Count, 337

Romano, Giancristoforo, 19, 81, 114, 115, 378

Romano, Giulio, 80, 181, 309

Romei, Giovanni, 95

Rosen, Magdalena von, 233

Rosina (mistress of Maximilian I), 125

Rosseli, Cosimo, 84–85

Rossi, Gianantonio, 21

Rotengater, Anna, 249, 392

Rotengater, Hieronymus, 390

Rucellai, Costanza, 135

Rudolf II, Emperor, 148, 169, 170, 172, 173, 202, 299, 300–301, 303, 395; *301–2*

Rudolff, Anton, 223

Rudolff, Magdalene, 223, 244, 390; *222–23*

Ruggeri, Camilla, 189

Ruprecht, Count Palatine, 278

RUSPAGIARI, ALFONSO, 23, 180, 185–87, 190, 387; *146, 186–88, 196*

Rutlinger, Jan, 358

Ruzé, Antoine, 339, 397; *326–27, 338–40*

Ruzé, Martin, 339

S

Sabatini, Bernardo, 384

Sacrifice of Isaac, 189

Sagittarius, 176, 385

sail, 47, 50, 356

St. George and the Princess of Trebizond, 43

St. George, Order of the Knights of, 208, 388

St. John, Order of, 173

St. Michael, Order of, 310, 343

DE SAINT-PRIEST, JEAN, 310–11; *310–11, 321*

Saint-Simon, Duc de, 343

salamander, 273, 275, 396

Salvator medal, 282, 394

Salvioni, Luca, 185, 387; *184–85, 196*

Sänftl, Ursula, 233

San Francesco. *See* Tempio Malatestiano

da Sangallo, Clement, 175

DA SANGALLO, FRANCESCO, 174–76, 385; *175*

da Sangallo, Giuliano, 112, 114, 174

Sannazaro, Jacopo, 90

San Sebastiano, 41

Sansoni, Raffaello, 131

Sansovino, Jacopo, 151, 181

Sant' Andrea, 41

Sanuto, Leticia, 127, 128, 382

Sanuto, Marino, 106, 108, 110, 380

da Sarziano, Alberto, 62

Saulmon, Michelet, 32

Savelli, Bartolommeo di Sperandio, 91

Savonarola, Francesco, 183, 386

Savonarola, Girolamo, 136, 145, 382; *142, 145*

Savoy knots, 177, 312, 396. *See also* love-knots.

Sayn, Countess Maria of, 282

Scaevola, Caius Mucius, 110–11

scales, 160

Scapti, Cosimo, 386

Scarampi, Lodovico, 41, 119

Schaffner, Martin. *See* Beltzinger Group, Master of the.

Schall, Martin, 392

Schenck, Hans, 394

Scheubel, Johann, 248, 391; *248*

Schilherr, Anna, 295, 395; *295*

Schilherr, Matthias, 295, 395; *295*

Schlick, Count Stephan, 209, 211, 284, 389; *209*

Schlifer, Nicolaus, 102, 380

School of Athens, 115

Schro, Dietrich, 278

Schwarz, Hans, 24, 204, 205, 211–12, 214–15, 218, 220, 252, 257, 275, 280, 389; *198, 212–16*

Schwarz, Stephan, 211

Schwarz, Ulrich, 211

Scipio Africanus, 378

Scylla, 352

sea-centaurs, 119, 381

sea-dogs, 352

seahorses, 352

Seated Scribe, 88

Secco, Francesco, 378

Septimius Severus, 128, 129

Serbaldi da Pescia, Pier Maria, 381

serpent, 33, 34, 151, 299

Sesto family, 16, 375

Sforza, Francesco, 40, 44, 51, 58, 73, 91, 100, 112

Sforza, Francesco Maria, 148, 151, 165

Sforza, Galeazzo Maria, 40, 77, 114

Sforza, Giangaleazzo Maria, 40, 77, 97, 101, 114

Sforza, Ginevra, 59, 97

Sforza, Giovanni, 378

Sforza, Lodovico (brother of Galeazzo Maria), 114

Sforza, Lodovico ("il Moro"), 40, 180

Sforza, Massimiliano, 148

Sforza, Polissena, 63, 73, 377

Siege Perilous, 128

Sigismund, Emperor, 40, 46, 51, 73, 78

Sigismund, King of Sweden, 173

Sigismund of Brandenburg, 394

Signoretti, Gian Antonio, 23, 186, 189, 190–91

Sitzinger, Lukas (the Elder), 277–78, 393; *277*

Sitzinger, Lukas the Younger, 278

Sixtus IV, Pope, 21, 40, 77, 100, 104, 120, 122, 126, 134

skull, 102, 103, 258, 260, 263, 299

snake. *See* serpent.

Solari, Cristoforo, 103

Solario, Antonio ("lo Zingaro"), 87

de Solier, Charles, 227–28, 389, 390, 391; *199, 227*

Solms, Countess Ursula of, 280, 282, 393; *280–81*

Solms, Count Otto of, 278

Solms-Laubach, Friedrich Magnus of, 282

Solms-Lich, Count Reinhard I of, 282

Speculum ecclesiae, 54, 377

Spengler, Lazarus, 218

Sperandio of Mantua, 19, 91, 94–97, 100–102, 379–80; *93–96, 98–101, 138*

Stabius, Johannes, 203, 219–20, 389; *219*

Starck, Katharina, 215, 389; *198, 215*

Starck, Ulrich, 215, 389

Steffli, Matthias, 391

Stengel, Hans, 282

Stengl, Anna, 393

Stengl, Marx, 393

Stewart, Henry. *See* Darnley, Lord.

stone models, 13, 24, 209, 211, 219, 254, 257, 263, 276, 278, 280, 282, 291, 348, 349

Strozzi, Filippo, 134–35, 382; *135*

Strozzi, Nonina, 382

Strozzi, Tito, 121

studia humanitatis, 23, 60

Sturm, Johannes, 239, 391

Suetonius, 301, 395

Suleiman II, Sultan, 211

Summonte, 87–88

Susanne of Bavaria, 280

Symons, Jan, 350, 360

sword, 58, 96, 97, 101, 119, 136, 145, 161, 285, 287, 341, 351

syrinx, 189

T

Talpa, Bartolo, 76–77, 84, 378; *77*

Tancredi, Onorata, 154

Taverna, Chiara, 158

Tazza Farnese, 128

Taverna, Francesco, 157, 164–65, 384; *164*

Tempio Malatestiano, 41

temple, 160, 166

Terminus, 349, 350

Tetzel, Georg the Elder, 276, 393; *276*

Tetzel, Georg the Younger, 276

Thann, Anna von, 230

Thenn, Wolfgang, 393

Theogenes, 395

Theory of Fortification, The, 218

Thetys Festival, 359

Thevenot, François, 393

Thewen (Zhewen?), Johann, 239–40, 391; *239*

thunderbolt, 42, 78, 79, 343, 358

Tiber, allegory of the, 348

Tiberius, 32, 115

Time, 81, 378

Titans, 301

Titian, 110, 151, 152, 174, 385

Titus, Emperor, 384

toad, 299, 300

Tols, Engelken, 370, 371, 399; *370*

Tols, Johan, 370

Torelli, Ippolita, 180

Tornabuoni, Giovanna. *See* Albizzi, Giovanna.

Tortorino, Francesco, 169

Toscani, Alvise, 381

Trachtenbuch, 220

Trajan, Column of, 129

Treaty of Cateau-Cambrésis, 116, 319

Treaty of Lyon, 176

Trebizond, 127, 128

Tree of Life, 34

Tremblay, Barthélémy, 329

da Trento, Bernardino, 182

Très Riches Heures, 32

Treutler, Georg, 284

da Trezzo, Jacopo, 22, 23, 27, 28, 158, 160–61, 163, 166, 169, 170, 177, 191, 360, 383–84, 385; *20, 144, 159–61, 170*

Trinity medal, 284, 287–88, 394; *271, 288–89*

Triumph of Fame, 59

Triumphal Arch, 219

Trivulzio, Gianfermo, 149, 151

Trivulzio, Gianfrancesco, 149, 157–58, 383; *143, 157,*

Trivulzio, Giangiacomo, 114, 151, 158

Trivulzio, Scaramuccia, 149, 151, 158, 384; *142, 149–50*

Truth, 161, 162, 163

Tucherin von Simmelsdorf, Ursula, 299

Typotius, Jacob, 301, 395

U

Ulrich, Duke of Württemberg, 204
unicorn, 52, 53, 312
Unknown youth, 218–19; *198, 217, 218*
uomo universale, 59
da Urbino, Clemente, 120

V

de' Vadi, Filippo, 102, 380
Val-de-Grâce, 342–43
Valdes, Alfonso, 350
Valois series, 315, 317–19
Valturio, Roberto, 59
van de Kerck, Lysbeth, 370
van der Weyden, Rogier, 348
van Diemen, Adam, 370
van Diemen, Engelberta, 370
van Egmond, Bishop Joris, 360, 399; *369*
van Eyck, Jan, 348
van Herwijck, Cornelis, 360
VAN HERWIJCK, STEVEN, 28, 360, 369–72, 399; *368–72*
Vanitas, allegory of, 299–300, 395; *272, 298–99*
Vanity, 186, 387
van Scorel, Jan, 370
van Stralen, Anthony, 354, 356, 398; *354–55, 363*
van Vianen, Paulus, 299, 395
van Zuichem, Viglius, 350
Varchi, Benedetto, 164, 174

Vasari, Giorgio, 114–15, 126, 131, 136, 145, 149, 157, 164, 375, 381
Vechietti, Alessandro di Gino, 356
Veeselar, Cecilia, 370, 371, 399; *371*
Veeselar, Joris, 371
Venetia, personification of, 181
Venus, 34, 121, 135, 136, 387
Venus Marina, 91
Verzi, Niccolò, 185
Vespasian, 384
Vico, Enea, 104, 182, 314
Victor Amadeus I, Duke of Savoy, 148, 177
Victory, 78, 79, 81, 128, 341
Vigilance, 357
de Vignon, Marie, 336–37, 397; *304, 326, 336*
da Vinci, Leonardo, 18, 131, 132, 309, 311
Virgil, 76, 135, 387
Virgin and Child with St. Anne, 174
Virgin Mary, the, 32, 91, 135, 136, 312, 375
Virgo, 301
de Virieu, François, 373
Virtues, the, 58
Vischer, Hans, 254
Vischer, Peter the Younger, 254
Visconti, Carlo, 168–69, 385; *168, 194*
Visconti, Filippo Maria, 40, 43, 44, 96, 376
Vision of St. Eustace, 43
Vitelli, Niccolò, 100
Vitellius, Emperor, 386
VITTORIA, ALESSANDRO, 21, 181–82, 386; *181*
Vittorino da Feltre, 44, 47, 50, 52, 53–54, 60, 100, 120, 377; *53, 69*
da Volterra, Raphael Maffei, 120
von der Pütt, Hans, 297
VON DER PÜTT, JOHANN PHILIPP, 297, 299, 395; *297*
Vonica, Niccolò, 106
Vulcan, 170

W

Wahl, Hieronymus, 263, 393; *263, 268*
Walravens, Jan, 352, 354, 398; *354, 362*
WARIN, JEAN, 27, 337, 339, 341–43, 397; *26, 326–28, 338–42*
wax, wax models, 13, 14, 27, 135, 155, 161–63, 170, 171–72, 176, 177, 219, 220, 254, 292, 296–97, 299, 315, 348, 384, 389, 395, 396
weasel, 35
WEIDITZ, CHRISTOPH, 24, 205, 218, 219, 220, 223–24, 227–28, 244, 284, 388, 389–90; *199, 220–27*
Weiditz, Hans (the medalist's father), 220
Weiditz, Hans (the medalist's son), 224
Weller, Alexander, 260
Wenzel, Archduke, 173, 385; *172*
Wettenhaus Altar, 392
whistle, 237
Wied, Hermann von, 228, 237, 239
Wilhelm IV, Duke of Bavaria, 228, 230, 260, 390
William of Orange, Prince, 352, 356, 357, 358, 372–73, 399; *368, 373–74*
winged eye, 41–42, 375
Witten, Hans, 289
WOEIRIOT, PIERRE II, 314, 396; *314, 323*
WOLFF, TOBIAS, 289, 292, 295, 299, 393, 394; *290–91*
Wolsey, Cardinal, 391
wood models, 13, 24, 211, 215, 218–19, 220, 223, 227–28, 230–31, 233, 234, 237, 238, 239–40, 241, 244–45, 248, 249, 252, 263, 280, 284, 287, 348, 349

Z

ZAGAR, JACOB, 359–60, 399; *360*
Zaisinger, Matthias, 228
Zeus, 176, 301, 376
Zollern, Countess Helene von, 237
de' Zuhari, Luca, 81